The Fourth Genre

The Fourth Genre

Contemporary Writers of/on Creative Nonfiction

Robert L. Root, Jr.

Central Michigan University

Michael Steinberg

Michigan State University

Allyn and Bacon

Boston • London • Toronto • Sydney • Tokyo • Singapore

Vice President: *Eben W. Ludlow*
Series Editorial Assistant: *Linda D'Angelo*
Marketing Manager: *Lisa Kimball*
Sr. Editorial Production Administrator: *Susan McIntyre*
Editorial Production Service: *Ruttle, Shaw & Wetherill, Inc.*
Composition Buyer: *Linda Cox*
Manufacturing Buyer: *Suzanne Lareau*
Cover Administrator: *Jenny Hart*
Electronic Composition: *Omegatype Typography, Inc.*

Library of Congress Cataloging-in-Publication Data

Root, Robert L.
    The fourth genre : contemporary writers of/on creative nonfiction
/ Robert L. Root, Jr.
        p. cm.
    Includes bibliographical references.
    ISBN 0-205-27595-8 (alk. paper)
        1. Literature—Collections   2. Reportage literature.
    3. Reporters and reporting.   I. Steinberg, Michael, 1940–
    II. Title.
    PN6014.R65   1999
    808.88'8—dc21   98-23267
                                                                    CIP

Printed in the United States of America

10 9 8 7 6 5 4   04 03 02 01 00

The essay is a notoriously flexible and adaptable form. It possesses the freedom to move anywhere, in all directions. It acts as if all objects were equally near the center and as if "all subjects are linked to one another" (Montaigne) by free association. This freedom can be daunting, not only for the novice essayist confronting such latitude but for the critic attempting to pin down its formal properties.

—Phillip Lopate

Admirers of nailed-down definitions and tidy categories may not like to hear it, but all writers and readers are full-time imaginers, all prose is imaginative, and fiction and nonfiction are just two anarchic shades of ink swirling around the same mysterious well. Those of us who would tell a story can only dip in our pens. We can never claim full certainty as to which shade of ink we're using.

—David James Duncan

The boundaries of creative nonfiction will always be as fluid as water.

—Mary Clearman Blew

Don't spread it around, but it's a sweet time to be an essayist.

—Joseph Epstein

Contents

PART TWO • *Talking about Creative Nonfiction*   243

PART THREE • *Composing Creative Nonfiction*   *401*

**Alternative Contents: Approaches to Writing
and Discussing Creative Nonfiction: 459**

Index   463

Alternative Contents

Subgenres of Creative Nonfiction

PARTS ONE AND THREE • *Forms of Creative Nonfiction*

Memoir

Nature Essay

Personal Essay

Segmented Essay

Critical Essay

Literary Journalism

PARTS TWO AND THREE • *Processes and Criticism of Creative Nonfiction*

Memoir

Writing

Essay

Genre Issues

Academic Writing

Preface

Beginning the Conversation

Rationale and Overview

The Fourth Genre is an anthology devoted to contemporary works of creative nonfiction. The readings in all three sections encompass the genre's full spectrum: personal essays and memoirs, literary journalism, and academic/cultural criticism. Creative nonfiction is the kind of literary writing that regularly appears in small magazines, reviews, and journals, such as *The Georgia Review, Grand Tour,* and *The American Voice;* in trade magazines, such as *Harper's, Doubletake,* and *The New Yorker;* and in book-length essay and memoir collections. One of the hallmarks of this form is that the boundaries between subgenres are quite expansive. That's because its writers often braid narrative telling with fictional and poetic techniques and combine portraiture and self-reflection with reportage and critical analysis. In that regard *The Fourth Genre* highlights the elasticity and versatility of this still-evolving genre.

We also see creative nonfiction as the subject that binds together the three disparate strands in most English departments: literature, creative writing, and composition. Traditionally, the study of literature has been centered on analysis and interpretation in three genres—poetry, fiction, and drama; the study of creative writing has also focused on those genres; and composition has become the domain of nonfiction. We believe that this unnatural separation can be bridged by acknowledging creative nonfiction as the fourth genre. That is, we think of creative nonfiction simultaneously as a form of literature, as a goal of creative writing, and as the aesthetic impulse in composition.

This book, then, attempts to present creative nonfiction in a framework that emphasizes its keystone status:

- It is a reader for writers of creative nonfiction, providing a range of samples of the forms and strategies practiced by many contemporary writers.
- It is an anthology for students of nonfiction literature, providing not only examples of its variety but also theoretical and critical responses to the form by critics, teachers, and the writers themselves.
- It is a collection for students of composing practices, providing reflections on the forms and strategies by the essayists, memoirists, literary journalists, cultural critics, poets, and novelists who write creative nonfiction.

These specifications make *The Fourth Genre* most suitable for courses in composition, creative writing, and genre literature. And not coincidentally, these are the courses in which we used the book in its classroom testing stages.

The fact that each of us was simultaneously asked to develop courses in creative nonfiction at different universities also says something about the fourth genre's emergence in the past decade or so. Anthologies and collections of personal essays, nature writing, literary journalism, cultural criticism, travel writing, and memoirs have proliferated in recent years, and literary magazines have begun to include creative nonfiction and the essay among the forms they regularly publish. Workshops in creative nonfiction have also been featured at writers' conferences and writers' workshops, and individual conferences have been organized solely around "writing the self," "environmental writing," and "travel writing." *The Fourth Genre* therefore represents our attempt to compile a contemporary anthology that approaches creative nonfiction from a number of perspectives, trying not to let our efforts prescribe its boundaries or place limits on its possibilities.

Creative nonfiction encompasses a variety of styles, sensibilities, and forms. Its writers share a common desire to speak in a singular voice as active participants in their own experience. This impulse often overlaps the writer's need to mediate that experience by serving as a witness/correspondent, thus creating a unique synergy. As a result, creative nonfictionists may write to establish or define an identity, to explore and chronicle personal discoveries and changes, to examine personal conflicts, to interrogate their opinions, or to connect themselves to a larger heritage and community. Given this context, the style, focus, and structure of each work may vary. Any given piece can be lyrical, expository, meditative, informational, reflective, self-interrogative, exploratory, analytical, and/or whimsical. Moreover, a work's structure might be a traditional "linear" narrative or it may create its own disjunctive and segmented form.

To take advantage of the genre's flexibility and emphasis on the writer's presence and voice, we have chosen readings that are representative, accessible, and challenging to students in advanced composition and creative writing workshops, as well as to those in genre-specific literature courses. We assume that student readers will be asked to write their own creative nonfiction and that, at the same time, they will be developing a personal/critical theory that reflects the genre's possibilities.

Perhaps our most vital concern is to initiate a writer-to-reader conversation on and about creative nonfiction. Therefore, we've designed the book to be interactive by dividing it into three separate yet interconnected sections: a representative anthology of personal essays, memoirs, works of literary journalism, and personal cultural criticism as currently practiced by recognized and emerging writers; a gathering of essays and articles that centers on more general matters of craft, definition, and theory; and a section in which four emergent writers discuss how their accompanying works of creative nonfiction were composed.

This organization encourages student writers to learn their craft the way most successful writers have learned theirs: by reading what other writers have written, by picking up tips and ideas from writers about the way they write, and by applying specific strategies culled from the readings to their own writing.

Selections and Organization

The Fourth Genre's most distinctive features are the range and scope of the readings and the interconnectedness of the three sections. In selecting these particular works, we have tried to maintain a balance between writing that is serious and informal, rigorous and pleasurable. In all instances, our criteria were that the writings be stimulating and that they have literary worth; that they be wide-ranging in subject and form, familiar at times and challenging at others; and that they be strong examples of the kind of thought-provoking and authentic writing that is being done in the genre today.

In addition, several other considerations guided our choices, perhaps the most compelling of which was our desire to counterbalance the recent creative nonfiction anthologies and manuals that identify the genre as equivalent to literary journalism. Such books tend to place little emphasis on the personal, autobiographical, and "literary" impulses (discovery, exploration, reflection) that generate much of the writing that we call creative nonfiction. While we think of this genre as broad and inclusive, we feel that creative nonfiction's identity is more closely connected to the spirit of Montaigne's work than it is to matters of subject, reportage, and research. That is to say, Montaigne's essays were first and foremost intimate and *personal*, and he actively cultivated self-exploration and self-discovery. As such, his writings express the digressions, meanderings, meditations, ruminations, and speculations that characterize a singular, idiosyncratic mind at work. As Montaigne himself says, "It is myself I portray."

This point of view is not meant to duck the issue of self-examination as it extends to larger connections and broader subjects. Quite the contrary. In fact, we believe along with cultural critic Marianna Torgovnick that "All writing about self and culture is personal in that writers and critics find some of their richest material in experience.... Often our search for personal meaning is precisely what generates our passion and curiosity for the subjects we research and write about." It is this kind of curiosity and self-exploration that mark the majority of selections in this book—be they personal essays, memoirs, reportage, academic criticism, or a commingling of more than one of these subgenres.

Other concerns that guided our choices are:

- to interest aspiring writers and curious readers who come to this genre from an assortment of academic disciplines;
- to spotlight representative, accessible writers from a variety of fields—literature, science, nature writing, women's studies, journalism, rhetoric and composition, and cultural studies among them; and
- to offer readings that remind us of the breadth and possibilities of this continually evolving genre.

To these ends, we present the reader with a broad range of published samples. In addition, we provide essays and articles by writers and teachers about the forms in which they work. Along with pieces by established writers, we've tried to select works that are less frequently taught and anthologized—provocative writing that we think will stimulate fresh and enthusiastic responses from students and teachers. In choosing these particular readings, we're hoping that *The Fourth Genre* will generate numerous alternatives for using creative nonfiction in the classroom.

Part One, Writing Creative Nonfiction, is an anthology/sampler of contemporary creative nonfiction. It is intended to showcase the variety of voices and personas, the flexibility and expansiveness, and the range of subject matter and structures that creative nonfiction is able to embrace. Part One is also a representative mix of thematic explorations, self-portraitures, investigations into subject matter and ideas, and personal discoveries and disclosures. Not only do the specific subjects change as they are taken up by different writers, but also the techniques each writer uses to explore his or her subject can vary widely. Some writers use straightforward narrative and reportage; others blend narrative telling with fictional techniques such as scenes, characters, and dialogue; and still others explore their subjects in more lyrical, discursive, or poetic ways.

However diverse these approaches might be, the individual pieces are marked by the distinctiveness of the author's presence, no matter whether he or she is the center of the piece or an observer-reporter. Therefore, in all the writings in this section we witness the mind of the writer as he or she attempts to examine what Marianna Torgovnick describes as "some strongly felt experience, deeply held conviction, long-term interest, or problem that has irritated the mind."

In Part Two, Talking about Creative Nonfiction, we have chosen essays by working writers and teachers who are as passionate about discussing matters of craft as they are articulate in explaining their theories about the nature of creative nonfiction. Because several of these authors have also written pieces that appear in Part One, we invite the reader to pair selections to see what strategies, theories, and perspectives the writers have developed. In addition, we suggest that teachers and students explore how the essays in Part One serve as examples of the kinds of theoretical stances that the writers and teachers in Part Two advocate.

Another way to approach the writing in Part Two is to view it as a writer's conversation about the possibilities and boundaries of the genre. Consider, for example, the differing views on literal and invented truth in memoir as proposed by Mary Clearman Blew, Patricia Hampl, Fern Kupfer, and Annie Dillard; compare Phillip Lopate's idea of the personal essay as a "self-interrogative form" with Scott Russell Sander's notion of the essayist as "the singular first-person"; or examine passionate yet differing approaches by Marianna Torgovnick, Jane Tompkins, and Peter Elbow to using the personal voice in academic writing.

You can also use this section of the book to probe more deeply into the assortment of composing strategies—that is, the use of differing narrative stances and personas; the employment of disjunctive and segmented mosaics; and the pointedly fictional and poetical techniques that memoirists, personal essayists, literary journalists, and cultural critics adopt in their writings.

All of these perspectives, then, anchor the genre in the notions, theories, and designs of working writers, many of whom are also writing teachers. As such, they give the reader an "inside" and personal look at the various ways the genre is evolving, and at the same time they provide a broader, more inclusive view of how contemporary creative nonfiction is being written and defined.

In Part Three, Composing Creative Nonfiction, four writers add their voices to the conversation in an attempt to help the student (and teacher) bridge the gap between experienced and emergent writers. In addition to the pieces themselves, Maureen Stanton, Simone Poirier-Bures, Mary Elizabeth Pope, and Emily Chase discuss their composing processes, sharing decisions on the drafts and revisions that their works-in-progress have undergone. In so doing, they focus our attention on the writing process itself.

We created this section not only to give aspiring student writers an inside look at how these pieces evolved, but also to demonstrate the many possibilities that characterize this genre. We also think that student writers will benefit greatly from paying attention to the disclosures from emerging writers, especially as these writers supplement and reinforce the readings in Parts One and Two. In addition, the cross references between all three sections open up the conversation further by revealing additional aspects of its texts and authors. And finally, by pairing the emerging writers' works with their own comments about their work, we are encouraging and reinforcing the kind of dialogue established in Parts One and Two.

Essentially then, Part One is an anthology *of* creative nonfiction, Part Two is an anthology *on* creative nonfiction, and Part Three is a shorter collection *of and about* the writing of creative nonfiction.

The readings in all three sections and the book's interactive organization, therefore, express why we think that creative nonfiction is the most accessible and personal of all four literary genres, as well as why we believe that the time is ripe for extending this dialogue to curious and interested students.

Apparatus

In keeping with the spirit of the genre's flexibility, we have provided a minimum of editorial apparatus. We assume that teachers will mix and match whichever readings suit their inclinations and teaching designs. And rather than impose a thematic, historical, or subgeneric interpretation on its users, or lock the book into a pattern based on our course designs, we prefer to emphasize the genre's multiple dimensions and possibilities. Moreover, in keeping with our intent to acquaint students (and teachers) with the rich body of work that's being produced in creative nonfiction today, we've tried to make this anthology as flexible and user-friendly as possible. We want to give students permission to think of themselves as apprentice/fellow writers, to urge them to experience their writing as an inside out activity, and finally to guide them in learning to read in more "writerly" ways.

That said, along with this preface we have provided guidelines and rationales for using this book. The introduction, for example, offers an expanded discussion of why creative nonfiction is the fourth genre. It also contains a detailed explanation of what we think are the five main elements of creative nonfiction. In the section on Writers, Readers, and the Fourth Genre, we talk about the personal connections between writer and reader, while offering specific examples of why we think of creative nonfiction as both a literary and transactional genre. Here we also discuss creative nonfiction as a genre that pushes at boundaries, as well as a genre whose practitioners write primarily to connect themselves in more intimate, expressive, and personal ways with their readers. In the section entitled Joining the Conversation, we expand on the notion of why we designed *The Fourth Genre* as an inclusive, ongoing conversation about the art and craft of writing creative nonfiction. Moreover, in the introductions to all three sections—Part One's anthology, Part Two's readings about the genre, and Part Three's dialogue on composing processes—we offer overviews of each section, as well as suggestions for using the book interactively.

Another apparatus is contained in the book's three tables of contents, all of which suggest alternative ways to read and teach *The Fourth Genre*. The table of contents at the front of the book is organized alphabetically to give teachers and students the option of deciding which readings they will match up or pair with one another. Subgenres of Creative Nonfiction, the first alternative table of contents, cross references the readings from Parts One and Three according to Forms of Creative Nonfiction, and categorizes the Part Two and Part Three readings under the heading Processes and Criticism of Creative Nonfiction. Approaches to Writing and Discussing Creative Nonfiction, the second alternative table of contents, also categorizes the readings according to subgenres. Under each subgenre (memoir, personal essay, etc.), we offer readers three approaches for examining creative nonfiction: Writers on Their Work, Further Examples of the Form, and Further Discussion of the Form. All of these, of course, are meant to be suggestive rather than prescriptive.

In addition to the guidelines within the text, we have written a comprehensive and detailed instructor's manual. It gives specific teaching suggestions and explanations for using the text in three different classroom settings. More specifically, it provides an assortment of options for organizing the materials in composition, creative writing, and literary genre courses. In all instances we've included brief discussions of the readings as creative nonfiction, as well as suggestions for pairing or clustering selections according to subgenres, compatible themes, and issues of craft. We've also designed questions that offer different perspectives on the readings and address matters of composing. Finally, we have provided a variety of writing prompts and suggestions for dealing with students' writing in all three classroom settings.

Acknowledgments

The paths by which the two of us have come to creative nonfiction are familiar to many writers and teachers. Writing has played an important role in both of our lives. It has been the subject of college courses and postcollege workshops in poetry, fiction, drama, essay, environmental writing, film writing, and professional writing. It has been the preoccupation that has produced both published and unpublished work in a variety of forms—creative nonfiction, of course, but also poetry, fiction, drama, sports journalism, and radio commentary. As it does for so many other writers, the habit of writing colors the way we approach almost everything we do in life.

We also have been teachers for most of our adult lives, particularly of writing courses and courses on the teaching of composition. Happily, the center of our teaching and our scholarship alike has been the study of and immersion in the activity that energizes our nonacademic lives.

In recent years, we have initiated courses in creative nonfiction in Western Michigan University's MFA/Ph.D. program, in Michigan State University's American Studies graduate program, and in Central Michigan University's Composition and Communication master's program. As we designed these courses and consulted with one another, we agreed to encourage our students to write essays that covered a range of contemporary creative nonfiction and to give them a range of strategies through which to do that. Moreover, we invited them into the genre by asking them to consider not only what contemporary writers were publishing but also what those same writers were saying about the kind of work they do. As an ongoing activity, we continued to share our own work-in-progress with our students and to "publish" anthologies of student writing within the classes.

And so we have come to this book attempting to center creative nonfiction, to keep centered on it as writers and teachers and students of the fourth genre ourselves, and to invite further speculation about it by readers, writers, and teachers interested in how we write, think about, and teach creative nonfiction now.

Along the way we have been aided in our growth as writers and development as teachers of creative nonfiction by an array of colleagues, students, and teachers, as well by both our partners. In particular, we want to acknowledge the following:

From Michael Steinberg: The students in English 631 at Western Michigan University and Shirley Clay Scott, former English chair at Western, who gave me the opportunity to develop the MFA/Ph.D. program's first creative nonfiction workshop; the students in American Studies 891 at Michigan State University, and Peter Levine, the program's director, and David Cooper, the current acting director, for allowing me free rein in designing my course; Donald Murray, whose writing and teaching has continued to inspire me; Skip Renker, who provided valuable input and advice when I needed it; Doug Noverr, my department chair, and Pat McConeghy, associate dean of Arts and Letters, both of whom granted me release time from teaching to complete this book; Barbara Hope, the Director of the Stonecoast Writer's Conference, who over the course of three summers gave me the opportunity to develop a creative non-fiction workshop in conjunction with five wonderful colleagues: Phyllis Barber, David Bradley, Stephen Dunn, David Huddle, and Syd Lea. My special thanks to them for showing me how it's done. Thanks as well to Dr. Sam Plyler, who kept the faith throughout this project. And finally to Carole Berk Steinberg, my gratitude, as always, for her unconditional support and unflagging encouragement.

From Robert Root: The students in English 601 and English 593 at Central Michigan University, who first responded to these readings and wrote so many memorable essays themselves, in particular Carol Sanford, Mary Beth Pope, Sandra Smith, Emily Chase, and Amy Hough; the clerical staff in the Department of English at CMU, headed by Carol Swan and Carole Pasche, particularly the student assistants who worked on this manuscript, Jennifer Baars, Kelli S. Fedewa, Star Ittu, and Gretchen M. Morley; Becky Wildfong, Tom Root, and Caroline Root, good writers all; and Susan Root, whose understanding and support make all burdens lighter.

We are grateful for the recommendations and advice of the reviewers of the anthology, including Charles Anderson, University of Arkansas at Little Rock, and Doug Hesse, Illinois State University, the assistance of Linda D'Angelo, and the expert guidance of Eben Ludlow.

Robert L. Root, Jr. and Michael Steinberg

Introduction

Creative Nonfiction, the Fourth Genre

Creative nonfiction is the fourth genre. This assumption, declared in the title of this book, needs a little explaining. Usually literature has been divided into three major genres or types: poetry, drama, and fiction. Poets, dramatists, and novelists might arrange this trio in a different order, but the idea of three literary genres has, until very recently, dominated introductory courses in literature, generic divisions in literature textbooks, and categories of literature in bookstores. Everything that couldn't be classified in one of these genres or some subgenre belonging to them (epic poetry, horror novels) was classified as "nonfiction," even though, as Jocelyn Bartkevicius points out elsewhere in this collection, they could be classified as "nonpoetry" just as well. Unfortunately, this classification system suggests that everything that is nonfiction should also be considered nonliterature, a suggestion that is, well, nonsense.

We refer to creative or literary nonfiction as the fourth genre as a way of reminding readers that literary genres are not limited to three; we certainly do not intend the term to indicate ranking of the genres but rather to indicate their equality. It would be better to have a more succinct, exclusive term for the genre. Writers have been composing literary forms of nonfiction for centuries, even if only recently have they begun to use the terms *creative nonfiction* or *literary nonfiction* to separate it from the nonliterary forms of nonfiction. And, after all, although it is creative or imaginative or literary, its being nonfiction is still what distinguishes it from the other literary genres.

The shape of creative nonfiction is, in Robert Atwan's phrase, "malleable" and, in O. B. Hardison's, "Protean." Perhaps we can picture its throbbing, pulsing, mercurial existence as locations on a series of intersecting lines connecting the poles of the personal and the public, the diary and the report, the informal and the formal, the marginalia and the academic article, the imaginative and the expository. Creative nonfiction essays would be located on these lines somewhere within the boundaries set by neighboring genres, not only "the three creative genres" of fiction, poetry, and drama but also the "expressive" genres of diary, journal, and autobiography and the "objective" genres of traditional (as opposed to literary) journalism, criticism, and polemic and technical writing. It may be fair to say that creative nonfiction centers in the essay but continually strains against the boundaries of other genres, endeavoring to push them back and to expand its own space without altering its own identity.

The Elements of Creative Nonfiction

Yet despite all the elusiveness and malleability of the genre and the variety of its shapes, structures, and attitudes, works of creative nonfiction share a number of common elements, although they may not all be present all the time in uniform proportions. The most pronounced common elements of creative nonfiction are *personal presence, self-discovery and self-exploration, veracity, flexibility of form*, and *literary approaches to nonfiction*.

Personal Presence

Writers of creative nonfiction tend to make their personal presence felt in the writing. Whatever the subject matter may be—and it can be almost anything—most creative nonfiction writing, as Rosellen Brown says of the essay, "presents itself, if not as precisely true, then as an emanation of an identifiable speaking voice making statements for which it takes responsibility" (5). In such writing the reader encounters "a persona through whose unique vision experience or information will be filtered, perhaps distorted, perhaps questioned"; the writer's voice creates an identity that "will cast a shadow as dense and ambiguous as that of an imaginary protagonist. The self is surely a created character" (5).

Throughout the various forms of creative nonfiction, whether the subject is the writer's self (as perhaps in personal essays and memoirs) or an objective, observed reality outside the self (as perhaps in nature essays and personal cultural criticism), the reader is taken on a journey into the mind and personality of the writer. Some writers directly engage in interrogations of the self by unequivocally examining and confronting their own memories, prejudices, fears, even weaknesses. Others are more meditative and speculative, using the occasion of remembered or observed experience to connect to issues that extend beyond the self and to celebrate or question those connections. Still others establish greater distance from their subjects, taking more of an observer's role than a participant's role. Yet even as they stand along the sidelines we are aware of their presence, because their voice is personal, individual, not omniscient.

This sense of the author's presence is a familiar element of essays and memoirs, of course. These center on the author's private reflections and experiences. As essayist Phillip Lopate writes,

> The hallmark of the personal essay is its intimacy. The writer seems to be speaking directly into your ear, confiding everything from gossip to wisdom. Through sharing thoughts, memories, desires, complaints, and whimsies, the personal essayist sets up a relationship with the reader, a dialogue—a friendship, if you will, based on identification, understanding, testiness, and companionship. (xxiii)

But personal presence can also pull subject-oriented writing (principally journalistic and academic writing) into the realm of creative nonfiction. Arguing a need for "writerly models for writing about culture," Marianna Torgovnick insists, "Writing about culture is personal. Writers find their material in experience as well as books, and they leave a personal imprint on their subjects. They must feel free to explore the autobiographical motivation for their work, for often this motivation is precisely what generates writers' interests in their topics." (3). Including this personal voice in cultural criticism surrenders some of the authority—or the pretense of authority—generally found in academic writing, but substitutes for it the authority of apparent candor or personal honesty. What Rosellen Brown writes of the personal essayist is applicable to all creative nonfiction writers: "the complex delight of the essayist's voice is that it can admit to bewilderment without losing its authority" (7). This sense of personal presence is one of the most forceful elements of creative nonfiction.

Self-Discovery and Self-Exploration

As many writers in this book suggest—either directly or indirectly—this genre encourages self-discovery, self-exploration, and surprise. Often, the writer "is on a journey of discovery, often unasked for and unplanned," Rosellen Brown writes. "The essayist is an explorer, whereas the fiction writer is a landed inhabitant" (7). Phillip Lopate speaks of self-discovery that takes place in essays as writing that "not only monitors the self but helps it gel. The essay is an enactment of the creation of the self" (xliv). This genre grants writers permission to explore without knowing where they will end up, to be tentative, speculative, reflective. Because writing creative nonfiction so often reveals and expresses the writer's mind at work and play, the genre permits us to chart the more whimsical, nonrational twists and turns of our own imaginations and psyches. More frequently than not, the subject matter becomes the catalyst or trigger for some personal journey or inquiry or self-interrogation. Writers who seem most at home with this genre are those who like to delve and to inquire, to question, to explore, probe, meditate, analyze, turn things over, brood, worry—all of which creative nonfiction allows, even encourages.

Such interests may seem at first glance appropriate only to a narrow range of "confessional writing," but in much of the best creative nonfiction, writers use self-disclosure as a way of opening their writing to a more expansive exploration. This genre, then, is a good choice for writers who like to reach for connections that extend beyond the purely personal. As W. Scott Olson writes, "As the world becomes more problematic, it is in the little excursions and small observations that we can discover ourselves, that we can make an honest connection with others, that we can remind each other of what it means to belong to one another" (viii).

Flexibility of Form

One of the most exciting elements of creative nonfiction is the way in which contemporary writers "stretch the limits of the form" and "are developing a [nonfiction] prose that lives along the borders of fiction and poetry" (Atwan x). Contemporary creative nonfiction uses the full range of style and structure available to other literary and non-literary forms. Most often, readers have noticed the use of fictional devices in creative nonfiction, particularly in what is termed *the nonfiction novel* or in certain examples of literary journalism, which Mark Kramer has defined as "extended digressive narrative nonfiction" (21). Rosellen Brown, who refers to the personal essay as a "nonfiction narrative," believes it is "every bit as much an imaginative construction as a short story" and that "it must use some, if not all, of the techniques of fiction: plot, characterization, physical atmosphere, thematic complexity, stylistic appropriateness, psychological open-endedness" (5).

And yet, while narrative elements may frequently play a part in creative nonfiction, the genre often works with lyrical, dramatic, meditative, expository, and argumentative elements as well. As Annie Dillard says, "The essay can do everything a poem can do, and everything a short story can do—everything but fake it" (xvii). It can also do every thing a diary, a journal, a critical article, an editorial, a feature, and a report can do.

Moreover, perhaps more frequently than in other genres, creative nonfiction writers are likely to innovate and experiment with structure. They draw not only on narrative chronology and linear presentation but also on nonlinear, "disjunctive," or associative strategies. They use different angles and perspectives to illuminate a point or explore an idea, drawing on visual and cinematic techniques such as collages, mosaics, montages, and jump cuts. They can leap backward and forward in time, ignoring chronology of event to emphasize nonsequential connections and parallels; they can structure the essay around rooms in a house or cards in a tarot deck; they can interrupt exposition or narrative with passages from journals and letters or scenes from home movies. Part of the excitement of the genre is its openness to creative forms as well as to creative contents, its invitation to experiment and push at boundaries between genres, and its ability to draw on an unlimited range of literary techniques.

Veracity

Because it sometimes draws on the material of autobiography, history, journalism, biology, ecology, travel writing, medicine, and any number of other subjects, creative nonfiction is reliably factual, firmly anchored in real experience, whether the author has lived it or observed and recorded it. As essayist and memoirist Annie Dillard writes, "The elements in any nonfiction should be true not only artistically—the connects must hold at base and must be veracious, for that is the convention and the covenant between the nonfiction writer and his reader" ("Introduction" xvii). Like the rest of us, the nonfiction writer, she says, "thinks about actual things. He can make sense of them analytically or artistically. In either case he renders the real world coherent and meaningful, even if only bits of it, and even if that coherence and meaning reside only inside small texts" (xvii). For critic Barbara Lounsbery, who is principally speaking of literary journalism, factuality is central, by which she means: "Documentable subject matter chosen from the real world as opposed to 'invented' from the writer's mind"; she adds that "anything in the natural world is game for the nonfiction artist's attention" (xiii).

But factuality or veracity is a trickier element than it seems. As David James Duncan observes,

> We see into our memories in much the way that we see across the floor of a sunbaked desert: everything we conjure, every object, creature, or event we perceive in there, is

distorted, before it reaches us, by mirages created by subjectivity, time, and distance.... The best that a would-be nonfiction writer can do is use imperfect language to invoke imperfectly remembered events based on imperfect perceptions. (55)

Artistry needs some latitude; self-disclosure may be too risky to be total, particularly when it involves disclosure of others. Just as Thoreau compressed two years at Walden Pond into one to get the focus he needed for his great book, creative nonfiction writers sometimes alter the accuracy of events in order to achieve the accuracy of interpretation. Some of this is inadvertent—the great challenge of memoir writing is knowing how much we remember is reliable and accepting the likelihood that we are "inventing the truth." "You can't put together a memoir without cannibalizing your own life for parts," Annie Dillard writes in "To Fashion a Text." "The work battens on your memories. And it replaces them" (70). Memories blur over time and edit themselves into different forms that others who had the same experience might not recognize. Finding the language to describe experience sometimes alters it, and your description of the experience becomes the memory, the way a photograph does. At the least we may feel a need to omit the irrelevant detail or protect the privacy of others not as committed to our self-disclosure as we are. The truth may not necessarily be veracious enough to take into court or into a laboratory; it need only be veracious enough to satisfy the writer's purpose and the art of the writing.

Literary Approaches to Language

The language of creative nonfiction is as literary, as imaginative, as that of other literary genres and is similarly used for lyrical, narrative, and dramatic effects. What separates creative nonfiction from "noncreative nonfiction" (if we can be forgiven the use of that term for a moment to categorize all nonfiction outside this genre) is not only "the unique and subjective focus, concept, context and point of view in which the information is presented and defined" (Gutkind v–vi) but also the ways in which language serves the subject. This is partly what Chris Anderson is alluding to when he writes that certain essays and journalism are not literary (x), and what Barbara Lounsbery means by claiming that, no matter how well the other elements of a nonfiction work are achieved, "it may still fail the standards of literary nonfiction if its language is dull or diffuse" (xv). When Annie Dillard turned from writing poetry to writing literary nonfiction, she

> was delighted to find that nonfiction prose can also carry meaning in its structures and, like poetry, can tolerate all sorts of figurative language, as well as alliteration and even rhyme. The range of rhythms in prose is larger and grander than it is in poetry, and it can handle discursive ideas and plain information as well as character and story. It can do everything. I felt as though I had switched from a single reed instrument to a full orchestra. ("To Fashion" 74–75)

When writers of poetry or fiction turn to creative nonfiction, as poet Mary Karr does in her memoir, *The Liar's Club*, or poet Garrett Hongo does in his memoir, *Volcano*, they bring with them the literary language possible in those other genres and are able to use it.

Poets and novelists aren't the only ones drawing on literary techniques in nonfiction. Some journalists have taken so literary an approach to their reportage that they have created a writing form that straddles literature and journalism, and often can be identified as a form of creative nonfiction. In addition, a number of primarily academic writers have sought a more personal perspective in the cultural criticism they write. They have made the language of their academic discourse more expansive, more intimate, more literary, allowing the reader to share their subjective reactions to the ideas and experiences they discuss. Like Thoreau, they retain rather than omit "the *I*, or first person," acknowledging, as he did, that we "commonly do not remember that it is, after all, always the first person that is speaking" (3). By doing so they do not simply present their information or opinions but also extend *themselves* toward the reader and draw the reader closer. In essence, they move the written work beyond presentation into conversation.

The writer in creative nonfiction is often the reader's guide, pointing out the sights along the way, the places of interest where special attention is required. In such writing the reader is treated like a spectator or an audience. But often the writer is the reader's surrogate, inviting her to share the author's space in imagination and to respond to the experience as if she is living it. In such writing the reader is treated like a participant. In creative nonfiction, then, in addition to exploring the information being presented—the ways in which various ideas, events, or scenes connect to one another and relate to some overarching theme or concept or premise—the reader also has to examine the role the writer takes in the work. The writer's role and the structure of the writing are not as predictable in creative nonfiction as they are in other forms, such as the news article or the academic research paper, the sermon or the lecture. The structure of the essay or article may be experimental or unexpected, an attempt to generate literary form out of subject matter instead of trying to wedge subject matter into an all-purpose literary form. When it departs from linear, tightly unified forms to achieve its purpose, contemporary creative nonfiction does not simply meander or ramble like the traditional essay ("My Style and my mind alike go roaming," Montaigne said [761]); instead, it moves in jumpcuts, flashbacks, flashforwards, concentric or parallel or tangential strands. Readers sometimes have to let the works themselves tell them how they should be read.

Writers, Readers, and the Fourth Genre

The interaction between the writer and the genre in which the writer works influences the outcome of the work. Writers of other nonfiction forms such as criticism, journalism, scholarship, or technical and professional writing tend to leave themselves out of the work and to view the work as a means to an end; they want to explain, report, inform, or propose. For them the text they produce is a vehicle, a container or package, to transport information and ideas to someone else, the intended readers. Some people have referred to these forms as *transactional writing*. Writers of other literary forms such as poetry, fiction, and drama tend to put themselves in the work and to view the work as an end in itself; they want to reflect, explore, speculate, imagine, and discover, and the text they create is a structure, an anchored shape like a sculpture or a monument or a building, to which interested readers are drawn. The result is often called *poetic* or *creative writing*. Writers of creative nonfiction by definition share the qualities of both groups of writers, and the work they create reflects varying measures of both kinds of writing.

Many creative nonfiction writers whose works are found in this book joined this conversation from the direction of their writing in other literary genres. Experienced poets or fictionists, they came to the fourth genre by way of personal essays and memoirs, nonfiction forms compatible with the desire for lyric and narrative expression, the desire to give voice to memory and meditation and acts of emotional and intellectual discovery. They came to it not only because of a need to write nonfiction but also because of a desire for creative expression. Similarly, creative nonfiction is also written by critics, journalists, and scholars who approach their writing in the way that essayists and memoirists do—that is, by inhabiting the work and by approaching it from a literary perspective more than (or as much as) from a critical, reportorial, or scholarly perspective.

We do not necessarily see sharply definable boundaries here, whose coordinates we can map precisely—neighboring nonfiction forms often share the same terrain for a long distance on either side of their common border. Yet, just as when you are traveling you don't need precise knowledge of geography or topography to sense that you're not in Kansas (or Vermont or California) anymore, so in reading you can also sense when a text is a work of "literary" nonfiction and not the "transactional" forms usual to journalism, scholarship, or criticism.

Because nonfiction in general has sometimes, mistakenly, been regarded as if it were an arid, barren wasteland of nonliterature surrounding lush, fertile oases of literature, it is important to make this clear: a great deal of nonfiction has always been literary, and it is the contemporary writers of literary or creative forms of nonfiction who are the focus of this book. The nonliterary forms of nonfiction are not our focus, but in some of those forms it is frequently difficult to notice when a writer slips over the border into the literary form. To make it easier to talk about creative nonfiction, then, we urge you to see it centered in the approaches taken by the essayist and memoirist and spiraling outward toward aesthetically oriented critics and literary journalists.

Readers come to creative nonfiction with different expectations from those they bring to the other genres. At the core of those expectations may be, in a sense, the hope of becoming engaged in a conversation. Much fiction, drama, poetry, and film is presented as performance, as entertainment essentially enclosed within itself—we are usually expected to appreciate or admire its creators' artistry whether we are encouraged to acknowledge their intensity or insight. Much nonliterary nonfiction (various forms of journalism and academic writing, for example) is presented as a transaction delivering information, sometimes objective, sometimes argumentative—we are usually expected to receive or accept their creators' knowledge or data the way we would a lecture or a news broadcast. Creative nonfiction, which is simultaneously literary and transactional, integrates these discourse aims: it brings artistry to information and actuality to imagination, and it draws on the expressive aim that lies below the surface in all writing. Expressive writing breaks the surface most notably in personal writing such as journals, diaries, and letters, but it has connected with the reader most prominently in the personal or familiar essay. Other forms of writing have at center the personal impulse, the need for expression, but the essay has traditionally been the outlet by which that impulse finds public voice.

Readers turn to creative nonfiction to find a place to connect to the personal voice, to connect not to art or knowledge alone but to another mind. This means that writers too have a place to connect, a genre that gives them permission to speak in the first person singular, not only about their knowledge and their beliefs but also about their uncertainties and their passions, not only about where they stand but also about the ways they arrived there, not only about the worlds they have either imagined or documented but also about the worlds they have experienced or inhabit now. Creative nonfiction may be the genre in which both reader and writer feel most connected to one another.

Joining the Conversation

We think of *The Fourth Genre* as an inclusive, ongoing conversation about the art and craft of writing creative nonfiction. We want to exemplify and describe this evolving genre, allow it to define itself and preserve its vital elasticity, and avoid arbitrary and imprecise subcategorizing and classifying. Unlike conversations in real life, a conversation in an anthology allows only one speaker at a time to speak and no one is interrupted by anyone else. The reader is the one who has to make the individual speakers connect. We've tried to make the conversation a little easier to follow by putting the speakers in different rooms. The people who simply share their own examples of creative nonfiction have the largest room, at the front of the anthology, where the writing more or less speaks for itself. The people who have ideas and opinions about the nature of this genre, the kinds of writing it contains and the kinds of writers who produce it, have another room, where both those who write creative nonfiction and those who study or examine it have their opportunities to speak. In the final room are those who attempt to explain how they wrote their own specific examples of creative nonfiction—the circumstances of composition and the tribulations of drafting and revising—where the conversation focuses on the composing processes of working writers.

In real life you would not be able to hear all the speakers in this conversation, but in an anthology you can, because the speakers wait until you get to them before they speak. In spite of the layout of the place, you should feel free to wander back and forth among the rooms, following someone else's recommendations or your own inclinations and intuitions. Naturally, we encourage you to join the conversation, provide your own examples, discuss your own ideas of genre, theory, and technique, share your own composing processes.

Read selections in Part One, Writing Creative Nonfiction, to get a sense of the range of contemporary creative nonfiction. The writers here reveal the variety of voices and personas, the flexibility and expansiveness, and the breadth of subject matter and structures creative nonfiction may adopt. It is a representative blend. It includes examples of the personal essay, the memoir, the travel essay, the nature essay, literary journalism, and personal cultural criticism. (See the Alternative Contents: Subgenres of Creative

Nonfiction for further subdivisions and categories.) These selections also present a range of forms and structures, from the narrative and the lyrical to the discursive and the reportorial, from the traditional (chronology or argument) to the individual and unconventional (unique arrangements of segments or organization around a pattern of tarot cards).

Many of these works demonstrate the futility of labels, qualifying easily under the genre heading of creative nonfiction for personal presence, literary language, and other defining elements but straddling the boundaries of two or more subgenres, perhaps simultaneously literary journalism and personal essay, travel narrative and environmental reporting, or memoir and cultural criticism. Instead they model the intimate relationship between form and content in creative nonfiction. Perhaps they will also suggest to you ways to invent forms that serve your own ends as a writer.

Read selections in Part Two, Talking about Creative Nonfiction, to get a sense of what writers, critics, and scholars have to say about the nature of creative nonfiction and its various subgenres. Many of the authors in this section have also written selections in Part One. They take the form personally, sometimes discussing their own personal motives and composing strategies, sometimes the elements of the form in which they work. As some of them point out, the tradition of essayist goes back centuries, to the work of Montaigne, Addison and Steele, Lamb and Hazlitt, and as this genre reemerges, it is contemporary practitioners, for the most part—the people who write and teach creative nonfiction—who are setting the terms of this conversation. This section mixes thoughts, opinions, speculations, critiques, theories, and assertions by working writers about the art and craft of their genre.

Many of the Part Two pieces can be paired with essays in Part One. Writing in Part One often serves as examples of the more theoretical positions in Part Two; writing in Part Two often gives new perspective on writing in Part One. So you can compare memoirs with the memoirists' discussion of the form, essays with the essayists' reflections on being essayists, cultural criticism with the critics' justifications for personal academic writing.

Other authors also give us insight into the forms and issues of creative nonfiction—the art of the memoir or of literary journalism, the elements of the disjunctive form or the question of truthfulness in nonfiction texts. Such essays attempt to give a personal perspective to a critical speculation on the forms in which the writers are working. They ground the genre in the behaviors and motives of working writers rather than in disembodied theories of literature or composing. They give the reader the opportunity to step back from the individual readings and take a longer view of process and text.

Read selections in Part Three, Composing Creative Nonfiction, for a sense of the work habits, craft techniques, and serendipity used to create a work of creative nonfiction. Here a group of writers discuss their composing processes for specific works, also reproduced in this section. They share drafts, explain revisions, and map the motives for changes in their works-in-progress. They focus our attention in this conversation on the most fundamental aspect of the work, the composing itself, and bring us to the place where the reader can continue the conversation as a writer. If Part One gives us examples of the variety of creative nonfiction and Part Two gives us a lively discussion of the practices and products of the genre, Part Three gives us a chance to sit at the shoulder of the writer herself and follow her through the twists and turns of creation. These writers reflect in their practices the ways writers in other parts of the book created their own selections. By example they suggest ideas and strategies that we can use in our own composing processes.

We think the fourth genre is the most accessible and urgent genre. It may not be necessary to read all three parts of this book or to read all selections in the parts you do read to get a sense of what creative nonfiction is about. We hope the book is flexible enough that readers can get what they want from it by coming at it from a number of different directions. Yet readers who do read in all three parts will get a fuller understanding of the breadth and power of this genre. And because the time is particularly right for other writers to join this conversation, we hope that wide reading in this book will help spur your writing of creative nonfiction and give you a writer's perspective on the art and craft of the fourth genre.

Robert L. Root, Jr. and Michael Steinberg

Works Cited

Anderson, Chris. "Introduction: Literary Nonfiction and Composition." *Literary Nonfiction: Theory, Criticism, Pedagogy*. Ed. Chris Anderson. Carbondale: Southern Illinois University Press, 1989. ix–xxvi.

Atwan, Robert. "Foreword." *The Best American Essays 1988*. Boston: Ticknor and Fields, 1988. ix–xi.

Brown, Rosellen. "Introduction." *Ploughshares* 20:2/3 (Fall 1994): 5–8.

Dillard, Annie. "Introduction." *The Best American Essays 1988*. Boston: Ticknor and Fields, 1988. xiii–xxii.

———. "To Fashion a Text." *Inventing the Truth: The Art and Craft of Memoir*. Ed. William Zinsser. Boston: Houghton-Mifflin, 1987. 53–76.

Duncan, David James. "Nonfiction = Fiction." *Orion* 15:3 (Summer 1996): 55–57.

Gutkind, Lee. "From the Editor." *Creative Nonfiction* 1:1 (1993): v–vi.

Hongo, Garrett. *Volcano: A Memoir of Hawai'i*. New York: Knopf, 1995.

Karr, Mary. *The Liar's Club: A Memoir*. New York: Viking Penguin, 1995.

Kramer, Mark. "Breakable Rules for Literary Journalists." *Literary Journalism*. Ed. Norman Sims and Mark Kramer. New York: Ballantine, 1995. 21–34.

Lopate, Phillip. "Introduction." *The Art of the Personal Essay: An Anthology from the Classical Era to the Present*. New York: Anchor/Doubleday, 1994. xxiii–liv.

Lounsbery, Barbara. *The Art of Fact: Contemporary Artists of Nonfiction*. Contributions to the Study of World Literature, No. 35. New York: Greenwood Press, 1990.

Montaigne, Michel de. *The Complete Works*. Trans. Donald M. Frame. Stanford: Stanford University Press, 1957. 761.

Olson, W. Scott. "Introduction." *Old Friends, New Neighbors: A Celebration of the American Essay*. Ed. W. Scott Olson. *American Literary Review* 5:2 (Fall 1994): v–viii.

Thoreau, Henry. *Walden*. Ed. J. Lyndon Shanley. Princeton: Princeton University Press, 1973. 3.

Torgovnick, Marianna. "Introduction." *Eloquent Obsessions: Writing Cultural Criticism*. Ed. Marianna Torgovnick. Durham: Duke University Press, 1994.

The Fourth Genre

Part I

Writing Creative Nonfiction

Contemporary creative nonfiction, like any other literary genre, offers a great deal of latitude to writers in terms of what they are able to do in the form. "There are as many kinds of essays as there are human attitudes or poses," the great American essayist E. B. White once observed. "The essayist rises in the morning and, if he has work to do, selects his garb from an unusually extensive wardrobe: he can pull on any sort of shirt, be any sort of person, according to his mood or his subject matter—philosopher, scold, jester, raconteur, confidant, devil's advocate, enthusiast." (vii) In general the observation is appropriate for the whole range of creative nonfiction.

This section of the book samples widely from the range of contemporary creative nonfiction. Its selections reveal the variety of voices and personas, the flexibility and expansiveness, and the range of subject matter and structures creative nonfiction may adopt. It is a representative blend, demonstrating the malleability of the genre. Some pieces are fairly straightforward examples of the traditional personal essay, such as Kathleen Norris exploring the paradoxical theme of celibate passions and Phillip Lopate rambling discursively over the subject of his own body. Others center on nature or environmental or ecological topics but vary their approaches; William DeBuys uses an investigative approach to water use in the West, Annie Dillard makes an intimate experience of an encounter with a weasel, and Gretel Ehrlich gives us a journal-like essay on sheepherding. Some examples of literary journalism center on different approaches to examining place, as Pico Iyer does with Los Angeles International Airport, John McPhee with Scotland, and Jeffrey Tayler with the Congo River. The personal approach to cultural criticism allows Vicki Hearne to explore the intelligence of primates and Jane Tompkins to ponder the significance of a museum commemorating Buffalo Bill Cody.

The range of approaches within a subgrouping suggests the flexibility of the form, the ways writers use creative nonfiction not as a vessel to be filled with meaning but rather as a way of constructing a shape appropriate to the meaning they create by writing. The ways that Mary Clearman Blew, Judith Ortiz Cofer, and Patricia Hampl present their remembrances of parents and of childhood vary as much as did their experiences growing up. The techniques with which other memoirists present the past vary as well. For example, Phyllis Barber uses a highly fictional technique of development for her childhood visit to the atomic bomb site, Frank Conroy presents his memoir of shooting pool almost as an instruction manual, and Sydney Lea conducts his piece as a lyrical essay rather than a personal narrative. These readings suggest that the writer's feeling about the subject has more to do with the way the final version reads than any arbitrary set of generic guidelines. Even as we hint at the variety of pieces in this part of the book, we have to acknowledge the futility of labels. Most of the selections can be classified in a number of ways. For example, Brenda Peterson's "Animal Allies" can be treated as an example of American nature writing and set beside the other writing on that subject, but it is set in a classroom with such detail that it simultaneously can be regarded as a personal essay on child psychology and as an article on teaching. Here, as in so many of these readings, we discover again that it is not a uniform structure or organization that links these selections but the common thread of the writer's personal presence, sometimes at considerable remove in essays not obviously about personal experience yet nevertheless there, examining subject matter in the light of personal inquiry.

A number of these pieces are what we term *segmented essays*, selections that try out nonlinear patterns or structures. Mary Clearman Blew's essay weaves among different family members and different times and events to piece together elements of family history; Nancy Willard builds her essay about friendship around an arrangement of tarot cards; Naomi Shihab Nye collects three miniature memoirs under one collective heading. Such structures let us see how intimately form and content are connected in creative nonfiction and how they can be invented to serve the ends of the author. Moreover, they help extend our understanding of the range of writing creative nonfictionists do.

"What happened to the writer is not what matters; what matters is the large sense that the writer is able to *make* of what happened," Vivian Gornick once observed, writing about the author's presence in memoirs. "The narrator in a memoir is an instrument of illumination, but it's the writing itself that provides revelation." (5) These selections suggest to us the possibilities of form, structure, voice, persona, approach, presentation, ways of describing what happened, and ways of making sense of what happened. Reading widely in Part One will not only give you a solid sense of what we write when we write creative nonfiction but will also open up your own possibilities for subject matter and design. Reading other writers triggers our own memories and our own speculations. We do not so much imitate others' subjects and structures as use them as a bridge to our resources and inventions.

Part One, Writing Creative Nonfiction, is in effect a minianthology of contemporary writing. As such it is complemented by the other two parts of the book, and we invite you to explore those other sections in connection with your reading in this part. For example, when reading the memoirs by Mary Clearman Blew and Patricia Hampl in Part One, you may want to read their essays about the memoir in Part Two, a section in which writers talk about creative nonfiction, and Simone Poirier-Bures's selections about memoir in Part Three, which pairs writers' essays with articles explaining how they wrote them. Or you might follow up Jane Tompkins's essay on the Buffalo Bill museum in Part One with readings by Tompkins, Peter Elbow, and Marianna Torgovnick about personal academic writing in Part Two and Emily Chase's pair of readings in Part Three, a literary essay and an account of writing the literary essay. Because Chase's selections are about Michel de Montaigne and Richard Rodriguez, they can also be read along with Rodriguez's essay, "Late Victorians," in Part One. There are many possibilities for interaction among these three sections of the book.

Writers always find it helpful to see what other writers are doing, to hear them talk about how they are doing it, and to free associate with their own memories and reflections from the ideas and stories that others share. Those who read these selections with a writer's eye will discover insights and perspectives that will serve their own writing well.

Works Cited

Gornick, Vivian. "The Memoir Boom." *Women's Review of Books* 13:10–11 (July 1996):5
White, E. B. "Foreword." *Essays of E. B. White.* New York: Harper and Row, 1997. vii.

Oh, Say Can You See?

Phyllis Barber

Over a radio microphone, into the nation's and FDR's ears, Grandma sang "The Star-Spangled Banner." "Oh, say can you see," she sang, my grandma who ironed for nickels and scrubbed for dimes, "by the dawn's early light, what so proudly we hailed?" Everybody in Boulder City recommended her for the program because they'd heard her at lots of funerals.

A big black open car full of VIPs delivered her home from the dedication ceremony. She waved good-bye. That's what my daddy told me.

I think she sang by the memorial, in between the statues—broad-chested men flanked by tall stiff wings pointing skyward. I hope those ninety-six men who died building the dam got fluffier wings, or else they probably never will fly out of their graves.

More than anything, I remember the dam and that story about Grandma. But there was an atom bomb test too—a rip in the sky, a gash that showed the sky's insides for a minute. I remember thinking about my Band-Aid box. I never could have unwrapped enough Band-Aids even if I had pulled the red string exactly down the side crease without tearing into the flat side of the paper where the red letters are printed. After that minute passed, the sky's blood and the earth's dust made a big cloud, a busy one. It drifts over my mind sometimes.

I got my first chance at swearing because of Hoover Dam—"I went to the dam to get some dam water. I asked the dam man for some of his dam water and the dam man said no."

Damns were frowned on at my house. So I chanted the forbidden whenever I could, with a flourish, making sure Mama and Daddy heard.

Actually, we called it Boulder Dam. At one time or another, everybody talked about jumping off or sliding down the curving concrete, but nobody did it except one time a man from New York did. His note said he lost his money gambling in Las Vegas and that nothing mattered anyway.

"He looked like a mass of jelly," said Uncle Tommy, an electrician at the dam.

"Could you see his face at all?" I asked.

5

"It was like a leaky puzzle, liquid in the cracks."

I wanted to ask more, but my Aunt Grace changed the subject.

Whenever anybody came to visit we always took them to see the dam. Down to Black Canyon, down to 120 degrees in the shade where heat ricocheted off sizzling boulders.

Every time, even now, I stop at the memorial on the Nevada side. The two bronzed angels stand guard over a message: "It is fitting that the flag of our country should fly in honor of those men…inspired by a vision of lonely lands made fruitful." My sister Elaine used to say that some of them fell off scaffolds into wet, pouring cement. Concrete soup. I always looked to see if a hand or a foot stuck out anywhere in the dam and checked for bumps on the surface.

The cloud had bumps, swollen and bulging. I've seen many shapes of clouds in my life—lambs, potatoes, even alligators, but I saw only one like that lumpy mushroom. Its cap reminded me of the North Wind, the puffy-cheeked one who bets with the Sun and blows fiercely to get coats off people's backs. Instead of sky and trees, it blew into the earth and got everything back in its face—sand, splintered tumbleweeds, thousands of years of rocks battering their own kind, crashing, colliding against each other, the dry desert silt, jaggedly rising from ribboned gullies and rain patterns on the sand, rising into a cloud that looked like a mushroom capped by the swollen-cheeked North Wind.

My father was proud of Hoover Dam. He helped build it, drove trucks hauling fill. He also loved the desert. Mama never thought much of it, not much at all.

"Herman, it's so hot here, so dusty. No creeks, no greenery. It's not human to live here."

My daddy always smiled when she started in. I liked his smile when she seemed unhappy.

"Herman, can't we move before it's too late?"

Daddy never argued this subject. He just reminded Mama of his mother, the grandma who sang, and how she saved her family with a letter to her relative: "Can't find work. We've tried everything in the Great Basin—farming in Idaho, mining in Nevada, selling shoes in Utah. Thought you might have a place for my husband and sons helping on that big new dam."

"It seemed like we were heading for Mecca, it did," he used to say. "All those mirages on the highway and our tires never getting wet. Sunshine, wide open-armed skies, and promises."

"Promises? Of what?" Mama asked. "How can you cultivate rocks in Black Canyon, Hoover Dam cement, the sand, the sage, the yucca?"

"I have a job, a wife, three children, and an address," he said.

"God bless the government."

The one time Mama did leave the desert and the dam, the time when my father put on his navy uniform with the brass buttons to go sailing in the Pacific, she wasn't treated as she should have been. Daddy always reminded her. Mother thought her relatives would help out with me and Elaine when she moved to Idaho Falls, Idaho, but all extra hands were needed for milking, haying, harvesting potatoes.

"I'm sorry, but—" they all said.

Mama taught school—six grades in one room. She was tired at night when she picked me up from the scratch-and-bite nursery school for war orphans. She didn't talk much then, so I looked for Daddy under the covers, under the bed, and in the bathtub.

"Why did Daddy go away? Is he coming back?"

Mama read letters to us, words like China, Okinawa, kamikaze, Battleship *Missouri*, destroyers, phrases like "I miss you," "When the war is over," and "When we get back home to Boulder City, I'll roll down Administration Hill with Elaine and Phyllis."

Rolling. Me rolling, repeating my face to the green grass. The cloud rolling, repeating itself to the open sky. And deep inside the busy cloud topped by the North Wind puffing in the wrong direction, a fire burned. Not a bonfire, but a tall fire hedged by a column of jumbled whites, browns, and grays. A thick fire mostly hidden but not quite. Black smoke twisted away from the red fire, sometimes losing itself in the confusion, sometimes slithering out into the blue. The cloud burned, scarring its belly, melting its insides with red and yellow while it rolled over and over in the same place.

We still pass Administration Hill every time we drive to the dam to go on the world's longest elevator ride, dropping down deep into the stomach, the belly of Hoover, to the hum of big red generators with white round lights on top.

The guide always talks about kilowatts, power to southern California, and spill-over precautions. I used to watch the ant tractors and drivers circling the generators stories below while he explained.

"Now if you'll follow me, we'll go directly into the Nevada diversion tunnel," a voice from a bullhorn said. Our feet echoed through a dripping cave, man-blasted, the voice said.

Water roared through a giant gray penstock (the guide called it) under the square observation room. I barely heard his speech. He pointed to yellow, red, blue, and green lines on a painted chart under a green metal lampshade. Outside the glassed, chicken-wired window, a man balanced on a catwalk to check bolts twice his size. The room trembled. The water rushed. I was glad I didn't have to tightrope catwalks and check pipes as big as the world.

"If you'll step this way, I'll lead you now to the base of the dam. Watch your step, ladies and gentlemen."

Outside, we looked up, up, everywhere up. Big cables stretched across, miles overhead—cables that lowered tons of railroad cars onto the tracks where we stood. I moved my toe quickly at the thought. Over the edge of the wall, the Colorado whirled green pools into white foam.

One time I told my mother the river must be mad.

"Rivers don't get angry, Phyllis," she said.

"This one does. It doesn't like going through all those tunnels and generators. It would suck me down forever if I fell in."

"You won't fall in. Mother's here to protect you."

Reassured, I ran from the wall to the center point where I could spread-eagle across two states.

"Ma'am," blared the bullhorn, "will you kindly keep your child with the tour group?"

My mother jerked me back into Arizona, told me to stop wandering off, to stay with the group.

Once when I was about six, Uncle Tommy scooped me into his arms. The temperature must have been 128 degrees that day.

"See, Phyllis honey. See the steepest, longest slide on earth." He not only held me up, but leaned me over the edge to see better.

"Uncle Tommy. Put me down." I kicked and squirmed.

"Not yet, honey. Look at the big river down there. We stopped that river. We did it. Look. We harnessed it. That's where you were a few minutes ago on the tour. See the railroad tracks?" He held me with only one arm as he pointed.

"Uncle Tommy. Put me down. Please. I don't like to look there." My head buried into his gray uniform but got stopped at the metal numbers on his badge.

"Ah, come on honey. Uncle Tommy wouldn't let anything happen to you." He still held me so I could see over the edge.

"Let me down. Let me down."

"Gee, why are you so upset. I wouldn't—"

I ran away from his words, away to the car that boiled the closest two feet of air around its metal surface. The door handle was untouchable, unopenable. I couldn't hide away to cry. I had to do it in the air, on top of that dam, in front of people from Manila, Cheyenne, and Pittsburgh.

I used to wonder if there had been devils in that redfire cloud. My mother always talked about how devils like fire and red and gambling, even how the world would end by fire because of them. I imagined horns balancing on top of their red caps that buttoned tight, holding all that cunning close between their ears while they rolled and tumbled in the churning clouds, while the fire burned yellow and red at the center and in my eyes when I think about it.

One night after Uncle Tommy leaned me out over the edge of the dam, he and my mother balanced a bed on the overhead cables, thousands of feet above concrete and water.

"You have disobeyed again," Mama said. "Always running off."

"I'm sorry."

"You'll have to sleep out there tonight, Phyllis. Maybe you'll learn to listen."

"Please, Mother, not at the dam. I'll be good. I'll listen. I won't go away without telling you ever again."

"Just climb up the ladder, honey," said Uncle Tommy. "Nothing to worry about."

"Please no," I said as I climbed the ladder, up, up, high above the scenic viewpoint where tourists said "ooh" and "aahhh." The wind blew, the cables rose and fell and twirled jump rope. I wore my blue furry Donald Duck slippers and my rosy chenille bathrobe, and I put one and then another foot ahead, in front. For a minute I walked on the wind and wasn't afraid. Then I got to the creaking bed, leaning downside at every shift in weight.

"Rock-a-bye baby," Mama sang from the cliff's edge. "Hush-a-bye." Uncle Tommy accompanied her on his trumpet.

The bed started to slip. The bedsprings scraped over the cables, fingernails on a blackboard, slipping one by one.

"Mama," I screamed.

Mama leaned as far out over the edge as she could while Uncle Tommy held her knees. We stretched for each other. Like long, rubbery, airless balloons we stretched and stretched, arching, reaching, trying to connect.

"Hold me, Mama."

Our fingertips only pointed at each other as I passed.

I tried to make a sail out of the quilt. I stood up to catch the wind with it but couldn't keep my balance. One Donald Duck slipper, followed by the other, followed by me in rosy chenille, sailed through the night toward the dam to get some dam water from the dam man.

After it mushroomed, the cloud started to break apart and dot the sky, and I thought of the time I climbed a leafless tree. Instead of watching where I was going, I talked to Rocky, my dog, who jumped and yelped at the bottom. Someone else had broken the twig that raked my cheek, that beaded the slash with red. A necklace of red pearls, almost. Dot dash dot. A design that stared at me in the mirror until it got better and faded away just like the cloud did.

Everybody wants to see the dam. It's famous. One day when I was about ten, another big black car, open and full of important men, drove through Boulder City. Flags stuck out on both sides of the windshield, rippling. I tried every possible angle to see Ike, running around legs, pushing through to openings but finding none. I was missing everything. Everybody who had closed shop and home for the afternoon was crowding to see Ike, too.

"Daddy, hold me up so I can see."

His dark blue uniformed arms full of baby brother, he pointed to the sill of Central Market's picture window. Stacks of returnable glass bottles towered behind the pane and wiggled every time a reflected parade watcher moved.

I climbed to the ledge as the fire engine and two police cars sirened past. Even standing there, I could see only flashing red lights, the backs of heads, and an occasional helium balloon drifting, ownerless.

"Daddy, I can't see."

Somehow he managed to pick me up in time. Ike, his uniform dotted with brass and ribbons, looked just like the *Newsreel* pictures at the Boulder Theatre. He smiled and waved just like on *Newsreel*, too. I didn't need to see him after all. I already knew.

I liked the high school band best. The flags and the band.

"Children," my daddy said at the dinner table that night, "you are lucky to live in America." His blue eyes moistened as they always did when he talked about God and country. We all knelt by our chairs, and Daddy said, "We thank thee for such men as General Eisenhower to lead our great country. Bless our friends and relatives. Help us to live in peace. In the name of Jesus Christ, amen."

I saw Ike again on *Newsreel* several weeks later. He was still waving and smiling, framed by the granite-like building blocks of the dam. He didn't look too big next to the dam. Neither did his friends.

One morning, about five o'clock, our gray Plymouth drove in the opposite direction from the dam, toward Las Vegas, out by Railroad Pass where Uncle Tommy played trumpet on Saturday night. Elaine and I kept warm under a friendship quilt and read the embroidered names of Mama's old friends, waiting.

"It's time," Daddy said. "Watch. Don't miss this. We should be able to see everything, even if it is seventy-five miles away."

We waited some more, eating apples and crackers.

"It's got to be time," he said.

My neck cramped. I looked at the sunrise.

"There it is, there it is," he yelled.

I saw the flash, but mostly my father's face and his brass buttons that seemed to glow red for one instant.

"That's how I came home to you, everybody. Just look at that power."

The cloud flowered, mushroomed, turned itself inside out, and poured into the sky. Red fire burned in the middle of browns and grays, colors that hid the red almost. But it was there—the fire burning at the center, the red fire that charred the North Wind's puffed cheeks and squeezed eyes until it blew itself away, trailing black smoke and its pride. It was there in the middle of the rising columns of earth and clouds boiling over, clouds bursting into clouds, whipping themselves inside out, changing colors over and over. Red, yellow, and black, colors from the fire. Gray, brown, and beige, sand from the desert floor, Daddy said.

And then the picture blurred at its edges, unfocused itself into other shapes—smoke arches, long floating strings, dots and dashes. In no time at all, everything floated away, on the jet stream, Daddy told us.

"I thought it would last longer," I said. "Won't they do it again?"

Daddy laughed, "It's time to go home now and get some hot breakfast. Wasn't that amazing, kids?"

Everyone who had gotten up to watch the blast talked about it in school that day. "Did you see it?" Our desert land had been chosen once again for an important government project.

The front page of that night's newspaper had pictures of the before and after—frame houses before, no frame houses after; dummied soldiers before, no recognizable dummies after. Surprised cattle lay flat out in the dead grass on their sides, their hair singed white on the up side. Yucca Flats. Frenchman Flats. Mercury Test Site. Household words.

"Nobody can get us now," my daddy said.

I don't think about it much, but sometimes when I punch my pillow for more fluff, ready to settle into sleep, the cloud mists into long red airy fingers over everything, reaching across the stark blue.

The Unwanted Child

Mary Clearman Blew

December 1958. I lie on my back on an examination table in a Missoula clinic while the middle-aged doctor whose name I found in the Yellow Pages inserts his speculum and takes a look. He turns to the sink and washes his hands.

"Yes, you're pregnant," he says. "Congratulations, Mommy."

His confirmation settles over me like a fog that won't lift. Myself I can manage for, but for myself and *it?*

After I get dressed, he says, "I'll want to see you again in a month, Mommy."

If he calls me Mommy again, I will break his glasses and grind them in his face, grind them until he has no face. I will kick him right in his obscene fat paunch. I will bury my foot in his disgusting flesh.

I walk through the glass doors and between the shoveled banks of snow to the parking lot where my young husband waits in the car.

"You're not, are you?" he says.

"Yes."

"Yes, you're not?"

"Yes, I am! Jeez!"

His feelings are hurt. But he persists: "I just don't think you are. I just don't see how you could be."

He has a theory on the correct use of condoms, a theory considerably more flexible than the one outlined by the doctor I visited just before our marriage three months ago, and which he has been arguing with increasing anxiety ever since I missed my second period. I stare out the car window at the back of the clinic while he expounds on his theory for the zillionth time. What difference does it make now? Why can't he shut up? If I have to listen to him much longer, I will kill him, too.

At last, even his arguments wear thin against the irrefutable fact. As he turns the key in the ignition his eyes are deep with fear.

"But I'll stand by you," he promises.

Why get married at eighteen?

When you get married, you can move into married student housing. It's a shambles, it's a complex of converted World War II barracks known as the Strips, it's so sorry the wind blows through the cracks around the windows and it lacks hot-water heaters and electric stoves, but at least it's not the dormitory, which is otherwise the required residence of all women at the University of Montana. Although no such regulations apply to male students, single women must be signed in and ready for bed check by ten o'clock on weeknights and one on weekends. No alcohol, no phones in rooms. Women must not be reported on campus in slacks or shorts (unless they can prove they are on their way to a physical education class), and on Sundays they may not appear except in heels, hose, and hat. A curious side effect of marriage, however, is that the responsibility for one's virtue is automatically transferred from the dean of women to one's husband. Miss Maurine Clow never does bed checks or beer checks in the Strips.

When you get married, you can quit making out in the back seat of a parked car and go to bed in a bed. All young women in 1958 like sex. Maybe their mothers had headaches or hang-ups, but *they* are normal, healthy women with normal, healthy desires, and they know the joy they will find in their husbands' arms will—well, be better than making out, which, though none of us will admit it, is getting to be boring. We spend hours shivering with our clothes off in cars parked in Pattee Canyon in subzero weather, groping and being groped and feeling embarrassed when other cars crunch by in the snow, full of onlookers with craning necks, and worrying about the classes we're not attending because making out takes so much time. We are normal, healthy women with normal, healthy desires if we have to die to prove it. Nobody has ever said out loud that she would like to go to bed and *get it over with* and get on with something else.

There's another reason for getting married at eighteen, but it's more complicated.

By getting married I have eluded Dean Maurine Clow only to fall into the hands of in-laws.

"We have to tell the folks," my husband insists. "They'll want to know."

His letter elicits the predictable long-distance phone call from them. I make him answer it. While he talks to them I rattle dishes in the kitchen, knowing exactly how they look, his momma and his daddy in their suffocating Helena living room hung with mounted elk antlers and religious calendars, their heads together over the phone, their faces wreathed in big grins at his news.

"They want to talk to you," he says finally. Then, "Come on!"

I take the phone with fear and hatred. "Hello?"

"Well!!!" My mother-in-law's voice carols over the miles. "I guess this is finally the end of college for you!"

A week after Christmas I lean against the sink in my mother's kitchen at the ranch and watch her wash clothes.

She uses a Maytag washing machine with a wringer and a monotonous, daylong chugging motor which, she often says, is a damn sight better than a washboard. She starts by filling the tub with boiling water and soap flakes. Then she agitates her whites for twenty minutes, fishes them out with her big fork, and feeds them sheet by sheet into the wringer. After she rinses them by hand, she reverses the wringer, and feeds them back through, creased and steaming hot, and carries them out to the clothesline to freeze dry. By this time the water in the tub has cooled off enough for the coloreds. She'll keep running through her loads until she's down to the blue jeans and the water is thick and greasy. My mother has spent twenty-five years of Mondays on the washing.

I know I have to tell her I'm pregnant.

She's talking about college, she's quoting my grandmother, who believes that every woman should be self-sufficient. Even though I'm married now, even though I had finished only one year at the University of Montana before I got married, my grandmother has agreed to go on lending me what I need for tuition and books. Unlike my in-laws, who have not hesitated to tell me I should go to work as a typist or a waitress to support my husband through college (after all, he will be supporting me for the rest of my life), my grandmother believes I should get my own credentials.

My mother and grandmother talk about a teaching certificate as if it were a gold ring which, if I could just grab it, would entitle the two of them to draw a long breath of relief. Normally I hate to listen to their talk. They don't even know you can't get a two-year teaching certificate now, you have to go the full four years.

But beyond the certificate question, college has become something that I never expected and cannot explain: not something to grab and have done with but a door opening, a glimpse of an endless passage and professors who occasionally beckon from far ahead—like lovely, elderly Marguerite Ephron, who lately has been leading four or five of us through the *Aeneid*. Latin class has been my sanctuary for the past few months; Latin has been my solace from conflict that otherwise has left me as steamed and agitated as my mother's whites, now churning away in the Maytag; Latin in part because it is taught by Mrs. Ephron, always serene, endlessly patient, mercilessly thorough, who teaches at the university while Mr. Ephron works at home, in a basement full of typewriters with special keyboards, on the translations of obscure clay tablets.

So I've been accepting my grandmother's money under false pretenses. I'm not going to spend my life teaching around Fergus County the way she did, the way my mother would have if she hadn't married my father. I've married my husband under false pretenses, too; he's a good fly-fishing Helena boy who has no idea in the world of becoming a Mr. Ephron. But, subversive as a foundling in a fairy tale, I have tried to explain none of my new aspirations to my mother or grandmother or, least of all, my husband and his parents, who are mightily distressed as it is by my borrowing money for my own education.

"—and it's all got to be paid back, you'll be starting your lives in *debt!*"

"—the important thing is to get *him* through, *he's* the one who's got to go out and face the world!"

"—what on earth do you think you'll do with your education?"

And now all the argument is pointless, the question of teaching certificate over quest for identity, the importance of my husband's future over mine, the relentless struggle with the in-laws over what is most mine, my self. I'm done for, knocked out of the running by the application of a faulty condom theory.

"Mom," I blurt, "I'm pregnant."

She gasps. And before she can let out that breath, a frame of memory freezes with her in it, poised over her rinse tub, looking at me through the rising steam and the grinding wringer. Right now I'm much too miserable to wonder what she sees when she looks at me: her oldest daughter, her bookish child, the daydreamer, the one she usually can't stand, the one who takes everything too seriously, who will never learn to take no for an answer. Thin and strong and blue-jeaned, bespectacled and crop-haired, this girl could pass for fifteen right now and won't be able to buy beer in grocery stores for years without showing her driver's license. This girl who is too miserable to look her mother in the face, who otherwise might see in her mother's eyes the years of blight and disappointment. She does hear what her mother says:

"Oh, Mary, no!"

My mother was an unwanted child. The fourth daughter of a homesteading family racked by drought and debt, she was only a year old when the sister nearest her in age died of a cancerous tumor. She was only two years old when the fifth and last child, the cherished boy, was born. She was never studious like her older sisters nor, of course, was she a boy, and she was never able to find her own ground to stand on until she married.

Growing up, I heard her version often, for my mother was given to a kind of continuous oral interpretation of herself and her situation. Standing over the sink or stove, hoeing the garden, running her sewing machine with the permanent angry line deepening between her eyes, she talked. Unlike the stories our grandmothers told, which, like fairy tales, narrated the events of the past but avoided psychological speculation ("Great-great-aunt Somebody-or-other was home alone making soap when the Indians came, so she waited until they got close enough, and then she, threw a ladle of lye on them…"), my mother's dwelt on the motives behind the darkest family impulses.

"Ma never should have had me. It was her own fault. She never should have had me if she didn't want me."

"But then you wouldn't have been born!" I interrupted, horrified at the thought of not being.

"Wouldn't have mattered to me," she said. "I'd never have known the difference."

What I cannot remember today is whom my mother was telling her story to. Our grandmothers told their stories to my little sisters and me, to entertain us, but my mother's bitter words flowed past us like a river current past small, ignored onlookers who eavesdropped from its shores. I remember her words, compulsive, repetitious, spilling out over her work—for she was always working—and I was awed by her courage. What could be less comprehensible than not wanting to be? More fearsome than annihilation?

Nor can I remember enough about the circumstances of my mother's life during the late 1940s and the early 1950s to know why she was so angry, why she was so compelled to deconstruct her childhood. Her lot was not easy. She had married into a close-knit family that kept to itself. She had her husband's mother on her hands all her life, and on top of the normal isolation and hard work of a ranch wife of those years, she had to provide home schooling for her children.

And my father's health was precarious, and the ranch was failing. The reality of that closed life along the river bottom became more and more attenuated by the outward reality of banks and interest rates and the shifting course of agribusiness. She was touchy with money worries. She saw the circumstances of her sisters' lives grow easier as her own grew harder. Perhaps these were reasons enough for rage.

I recall my mother in her middle thirties through the telescoped eye of the child which distorts the intentions of parents and enlarges them to giants. Of course she was larger than life. Unlike my father, with his spectrum of ailments, she was never sick. She was never hospitalized in her life for any reason but childbirth, never came down with anything worse than a cold. She lugged the armloads of wood and buckets of water and slops and ashes that came with cooking and washing and ironing in a kitchen with a wood range and no plumbing; she provided the endless starchy meals of roast meat and potatoes and gravy; she kept salads on her table and fresh or home-canned vegetables at a time when iceberg lettuce was a town affectation.

She was clear-skinned, with large gray eyes that often seemed fixed on some point far beyond our familiar slopes and cutbanks. And even allowing for the child's telescoped eye, she was a tall woman who thought of herself as oversized. She was the tallest of her sisters. "*As big as Doris* is what they used to say about me!"

Bigness to her was a curse. "You big ox!" she would fling at me over some altercation with my little sister. True to the imperative that is handed down through the generations, I in turn bought my clothes two sizes too large for years.

All adult ranch women were fat. I remember hardly a woman out of her teens in those years who was not fat. The few exceptions were the women who had, virtually, become a third sex by taking on men's work in the fields and corrals; they might stay as skinny and tough in their Levi's as hired hands.

But women who remained women baked cakes and cream pies and breads and sweet rolls with the eggs from their own chickens and the milk and butter and cream from the cows they milked, and they ate heavily from appetite and from fatigue and from the monotony of their isolation. They wore starched cotton print dresses and starched aprons and walked ponderously beside their whiplash husbands. My mother, unless she was going to be riding or helping in the hayfields, always wore those shapeless, starched dresses she sewed herself, always cut from the same pattern, always layered over with an apron.

What was she so angry about? Why was her forehead kneaded permanently into a frown? It was a revelation for me one afternoon when she answered a knock at the screen door, and she smiled, and her voice lifted to greet an old friend of hers and my father's from their single days. Color rose in her face, and she looked pretty as she told him where he could find my father. Was that how outsiders always saw her?

Other ranch women seemed cheerful enough on the rare occasions when they came in out of the gumbo. Spying on them as they sat on benches in the shade outside the horticulture house at the county fair or visited in the cabs of trucks at rodeos, I wondered if these women, too, were angry when they were alone with only their children to observe them. What secrets lay behind those vast placid, smiling faces, and what stories could their children tell?

My mother believed that her mother had loved her brother best and her older sisters next best. "He was always The Boy and they were The Girls, and Ma was proud of how well they did in school," she explained again and again to the walls, the stove, the floor she was mopping, "and I was just Doris. I was average."

Knowing how my grandmother had misjudged my mother, I felt guilty about how much I longed for her visits. I loved my grandmother and her fresh supply of stories about the children who went to the schools she taught, the games they played, and the books they read. School for me was an emblem of the world outside our creek-bottom meadows and fenced mountain slopes. At eight, I was still being taught at home; our gumbo road was impassable for most of the school months, and my father preferred that we be kept safe from contact with "them damn town kids," as he called them. Subversively I begged my grandmother to repeat her stories again and again, and I tried to imagine what it must be like to see other children every day and to have a real desk and real lessons. Other than my little sister, my playmates were mostly cats. But my grandmother brought with her the breath of elsewhere.

My mother's resentment whitened in intensity during the weeks before a visit from my grandmother, smoldered during the visit itself, and flared up again as soon as my grandmother was safely down the road to her next school. "I wonder if she ever realizes she wouldn't even have any grandchildren if I hadn't got married and had some kids! *The Girls* never had any kids! Some people should never have kids! Some people should never get married!"

With a child's logic, I thought she was talking about me. I thought I was responsible for her anger. I was preoccupied for a long time with a story I had read about a fisherman who was granted three wishes; he had used his wishes badly, but I was sure I could do better, given the chance. I thought a lot about how I would use three wishes, how I would use their potential for lifting me out of the present.

"What would you wish for, if you had three wishes?" I prodded my mother.

She turned her faraway gray eyes on me, as though she had not been ranting about The Girls the moment before. "I'd wish you'd be good," she said.

That was what she always said, no matter how often I asked her. With everything under the sun to wish for, that unfailing answer was a perplexity and a worry.

I was my grandmother's namesake, and I was a bookworm like my mother's older sisters. Nobody could pry my nose out of a book to do my chores, even though I was marked to be the outdoor-working child, even though I was supposed to be my father's boy.

Other signs that I was not a boy arose to trouble us both and account, I thought, for my mother's one wish.

"Mary's getting a butt on her just like a girl," she remarked one night as I climbed out of the tub. Alarmed, I craned my neck to see what had changed about my eight-year-old buttocks.

"Next thing, you'll be mooning in the mirror and wanting to pluck your eyebrows like the rest of 'em," she said.

"I will not," I said doubtfully.

I could find no way through the contradiction. On the one hand, I was a boy (except that I also was a bookworm), and my chores were always in the barns and corrals, never the kitchen. *You don't know how to cook on a wood stove?* my mother-in-law was to cry in disbelief. *And you grew up on a ranch?*

To act like a boy was approved; to cry or show fear was to invite ridicule. *Sissy! Big bellercalf!* On the other hand, I was scolded for hanging around the men, the way ranch boys did. I was not a boy (my buttocks, my vanity). What was I?

"Your dad's boy," my mother answered comfortingly when I asked her. She named a woman I knew. "Just like Hazel. Her dad can't get along without her."

Hazel was a tough, shy woman who rode fences and pulled calves and took no interest in the country dances or the "running around" her sisters did on weekends. Hazel never used lipstick or permed her hair; she wore it cut almost like a man's. Seen at the occasional rodeo or bull sale in her decently pressed pearl-button shirt and new Levi's, she stuck close to her dad. Like me, Hazel apparently was not permitted to hang around the men.

What Hazel did not seem interested in was any kind of fun, and a great resolve arose in me that, whatever I was, I was going to have…whatever it was. I would get married, even if I wasn't supposed to.

But my mother had another, darker reason to be angry with me, and I knew it. The reason had broken over me suddenly the summer I was seven and had been playing, on warm afternoons, in a rain barrel full of water. Splashing around, elbows and knees knocking against the side of the barrel, I enjoyed the rare sensation of being wet all over. My little sister, four, came and stood on tiptoe to watch. It occurred to me to boost her into the barrel with me.

My mother burst out of the kitchen door and snatched her back.

"What are you trying to do, kill her?" she shouted.

I stared back at her, wet, dumbfounded.

Her eyes blazed over me, her brows knotted at their worst. "And after you'd drowned her, I suppose you'd have slunk off to hide somewhere until it was all over!"

It had never crossed my mind to kill my sister, or that my mother might think I wanted to. (Although I had, once, drowned a setting of baby chicks in a rain barrel.) But that afternoon, dripping in my underpants, goose-bumped and ashamed, I watched her carry my sister into the house and then I did go off to hide until it was, somehow, all over, for she never mentioned it at dinner.

The chicks had been balls of yellow fuzz, and I had been three. I wanted them to swim. I can just remember catching a chick and holding it in the water until it stopped squirming and then laying it down to catch a fresh one. I didn't stop until I had drowned the whole dozen and laid them out in a sodden yellow row.

What the mind refuses to allow to surface is characterized by a suspicious absence. Of detail, of associations. Memories skirt the edge of nothing. There is for me about this incident that suspicious absence. What is being withheld?

Had I, for instance, given my mother cause to believe I might harm my sister? Children have done such harm, and worse. What can be submerged deeper, denied more vehemently, than the murderous impulse? At four, my sister was a tender, trusting little girl with my mother's wide gray eyes and brows. A younger sister of an older sister. A good girl. Mommy's girl.

What do I really know about my mother's feelings toward her own dead sister? Kathryn's dolls had been put away; my mother was never allowed to touch them.

"I'll never, never love one of my kids more than another!" she screamed at my father in one of her afternoons of white rage. The context is missing.

During the good years, when cattle prices were high enough to pay the year's bills and a little extra, my mother bought wallpaper out of a catalog and stuck it to her lumpy walls. She enameled her kitchen white, and she sewed narrow strips of cloth she called "drapes" to hang at the sides of her windows. She bought a stiff tight cylinder of linoleum at Sears, Roebuck in town and hauled it home in the back of the pickup and unrolled it in a shiny flowered oblong in the middle of her splintery front room floor.

Occasionally I would find her sitting in her front room on her "davenport," which she had saved for and bought used, her lap full of sewing and her forehead relaxed out of its knot. For a moment there was her room around her as she wanted it to look: the clutter subdued, the new linoleum mopped and quivering under the chair legs that held down its corners, the tension of the opposing floral patterns of wallpaper, drapes, and slipcovers held in brief, illusory harmony by the force of her vision.

How hard she tried for her daughters! Over the slow thirty miles of gumbo and gravel we drove to town every summer for dentist appointments at a time when pulling teeth was still a more common remedy than filling them, when our own father and his mother wore false teeth before they were forty.

During the good years, we drove the thirty miles for piano lessons. An upright Kimball was purchased and hauled home in the back of the pickup. Its carved oak leaves and ivories dominated the front room, where she found time to "sit with us" every day as we practiced. With a pencil she pointed out the notes she had learned to read during her five scant quarters in normal school, and made us read them aloud. "F sharp!" she would scream over the throb of the Maytag in the kitchen as one of us pounded away.

She carped about bookworms, but she located the dim old Carnegie library in town and got library cards for us even though, as country kids, we weren't strictly entitled to them. After that, trips home from town with sacks of groceries included armloads of library books. Against certain strictures, she could be counted on. When, in my teens, I came home with my account of the new book the librarian kept in her desk drawer and refused to check out to me, my mother straightened her back as I knew she would. "She thinks she can tell one of my kids what she can read and what she can't read?"

On our next visit to the library, she marched up the stone steps and into the mote-filled sanctum with me.

The white-haired librarian glanced up inquiringly.

"You got *From Here to Eternity?*"

The librarian looked at me, then at my mother. Without a word she reached into her drawer and took out a heavy volume. She stamped it and handed it to my mother, who handed it to me.

How did she determine that books and dentistry and piano lessons were necessities for her daughters, and what battles did she fight for them as slipping cattle prices put even a gallon of white enamel paint or a sheet of new linoleum beyond her reach?

Disaster followed disaster on the ranch. An entire season's hay crop lost to a combination of ancient machinery that would not hold together and heavy rains that would not let up. A whole year's calf crop lost because the cows had been pastured in timber that had been logged, and when they ate the pine needles from the downed tops, they spontaneously aborted. As my father grew less and less able to face the reality of the downward spiral, what could she hope to hold together with her pathetic floral drapes and floral slipcovers?

Bundled in coats and overshoes in the premature February dark, our white breaths as one, my mother and I huddle in the shadow of the chicken house. By moonlight we watch the white-tailed deer that have slipped down out of the timber to feed from the haystack a scant fifty yards away. Cautiously I raise my father's rifle to my shoulder. I'm not all that good a marksman, I hate the inevitable explosive crack, but I brace myself on the corner of the chicken house and sight carefully and remember to squeeze. Ka-crack!

Eight taupe shapes shoot up their heads and spring for cover. A single mound remains in the snow near the haystack. By the time my mother and I have climbed through the fence and trudged up to the haystack, all movement from the doe is reflexive. "Nice and fat," says my mother.

Working together with our butcher knives, we lop off her scent glands and slit her and gut her and save the heart and liver in a bucket for breakfast. Then, each taking a leg, we drag her down the field, under the fence, around the chicken house and into the kitchen, where we will skin her out and butcher her.

We are two mid-twentieth-century women putting meat on the table for the next few weeks. Neither of us has ever had a hunting license, and if we did, hunting season is long closed, but we're serene about what we're doing. "Eating our hay, aren't they?" says my mother. "We're entitled to a little venison. The main thing is not to tell anybody what we're doing."

And the pregnant eighteen-year-old? What about her?

In June of 1959 she sits up in the hospital bed, holding in her arms a small warm scrap whose temples are deeply dented from the forceps. She cannot remember birthing him, only the long hours alone before the anesthetic took over. She feels little this morning, only a dull worry about the money, money, money for college in the fall.

The in-laws are a steady, insistent, increasingly frantic chorus of disapproval over her plans. *But, Mary! Tiny babies have to be kept warm!* her mother-in-law keeps repeating, pathetically, ever since she was told about Mary's plans for fall quarter.

But, Mary! How can you expect to go to college and take good care of a husband and a baby?

Finally, *We're going to put our foot down!*

She knows that somehow she has got to extricate herself from these sappy folks. About the baby, she feels only a mild curiosity. Life where there was none before. The rise and fall of his tiny chest. She has him on her hands now. She must take care of him.

Why not an abortion?

Because the thought never crossed her mind. Another suspicious absence, another void for memory to skirt. What she knew about abortion was passed around the midnight parties in the girls' dormitory: *You drink one part turpentine with two parts sugar.* Or was it the other way around?...*two parts turpentine to one part sugar. You drink gin in a hot bath...*

She has always hated the smell of gin. It reminds her of the pine needles her father's cattle ate, and how their calves were born shallow-breathed and shriveled, and how they died. She knows a young married woman who begged her husband to hit her in the stomach and abort their fourth child.

Once, in her eighth month, the doctor had shot her a look across his table. "If you don't want this baby," he said, "I know plenty of people who do."

"I want it," she lied.

No, but really. What is to become of this eighteen-year-old and her baby?

Well, she's read all the sentimental literature they shove on the high school girls. She knows how the plot is supposed to turn out.

Basically, she has two choices.

One, she can invest all her hopes for her own future in this sleeping scrap. *Son, it was always my dream to climb to the stars. Now the tears of joy spring at the sight of you with your college diploma...*

Even at eighteen, this lilylicking is enough to make her sick.

Or two, she can abandon the baby and the husband and become really successful and really evil. This is the more attractive version of the plot, but she doesn't really believe in it. Nobody she knows has tried it. It seems as out of reach from ordinary daylight Montana as Joan Crawford or the Duchess of Windsor or the moon. As she lies propped up in bed with the sleeping scrap in her arms, looking out over the dusty downtown rooftops settling into noon in the waning Eisenhower years, she knows very well that Joan Crawford will never play the story of her life.

What, then? What choice is left to her?

What outcome could possibly be worth all this uproar? Her husband is on the verge of tears these days; he's only twenty himself, and he had no idea what trouble he was marrying into, his parents pleading and arguing and threatening, even his brothers and their wives chiming in with their opinions, even the minister getting into it, even the neighbors; and meanwhile his wife's grandmother firing off red-hot letters from her side, meanwhile his wife's mother refusing to budge an inch—united, those two women are as formidable as a pair of rhinoceroses, though of course he has no idea in the world what it took to unite them.

All this widening emotional vortex over whether or not one Montana girl will finish college. What kind of genius would she have to be to justify it all? Will it be enough that, thirty years later, she will have read approximately 16,250 freshman English essays out of an estimated lifetime total of 32,000?

Will it be enough, over the years, that she remembers the frozen frame of her mother's face over the rinse tub that day after Christmas in 1958 and wonders whether she can do as much for her son as was done for her? Or that she often wonders whether she really lied when she said, *I want it?*

Will it be enough? What else is there?

Silent Dancing

Judith Ortiz Cofer

We have a home movie of this party. Several times my mother and I have watched it together, and I have asked questions about the silent revelers coming in and out of focus. It is grainy and of short duration, but it's a great visual aid to my memory of life at that time. And it is in color—the only complete scene in color I can recall from those years.

We lived in Puerto Rico until my brother was born in 1954. Soon after, because of economic pressures on our growing family, my father joined the United States Navy. He was assigned to duty on a ship in Brooklyn Yard—a place of cement and steel that was to be his home base in the States until his retirement more than twenty years later. He left the Island first, alone, going to New York City and tracking down his uncle who lived with his family across the Hudson River in Paterson, New Jersey. There my father found a tiny apartment in a huge tenement that had once housed Jewish families but was just being taken over and transformed by Puerto Ricans, overflowing from New York City. In 1955 he sent for us. My mother was only twenty years old, I was not quite three, and my brother was a toddler when we arrived at El Building, as the place had been christened by its newest residents.

My memories of life in Paterson during those first few years are all in shades of gray. Maybe I was too young to absorb vivid colors and details, or to discriminate between the slate blue of the winter sky and the darker hues of the snow-bearing clouds, but that single color washes over the whole period. The building we lived in was gray, as were the streets, filled with slush the first few months of my life there. The coat my father had bought for me was similar in color and too big; it sat heavily on my thin frame.

I do remember the way the heater pipes banged and rattled, startling all of us out of sleep until we got so used to the sound that we automatically shut it out or raised our voices above the racket. The hiss from the valve punctuated my sleep (which has always been fitful) like a nonhuman presence in the room—a dragon sleeping at the entrance of my childhood. But the pipes were also a connection to all the other lives being lived around us. Having come from a house designed for a single family back in Puerto Rico—my mother's extended-family home—it was curious to know that strangers lived under our floor and above our heads, and that the heater pipe went through everyone's apartment. (My first spanking in Paterson came as a result of playing tunes on the pipes in my room to see if there would be an answer.) My mother was as new to this concept of beehive life as I was, but she had been given strict orders by my father to keep the doors locked, the noise down, ourselves to ourselves.

It seems that Father had learned some painful lessons about prejudice while searching for an apartment in Paterson. Not until years later did I hear how much resistance he had encountered with landlords who were panicking at the influx of Latinos into a neighborhood that had been Jewish for a couple of generations. It made no difference that it was the American phenomenon of ethnic turnover which was changing the urban core of Paterson, and that the human flood could not be held back with an accusing finger.

"You Cuban?" one man had asked my father, pointing at his name tag on the navy uniform—even though my father had the fair skin and light brown hair of his northern Spanish background, and the name Ortiz is as common in Puerto Rico as Johnson is in the United States.

"No," my father had answered, looking past the finger into his adversary's angry eyes. "I'm Puerto Rican."

"Same shit." And the door closed.

My father could have passed as European, but we couldn't. My brother and I both have our mother's black hair and olive skin, and so we lived in El Building and visited our great-uncle and his fair children on the next block. It was their private joke that they were the German branch of the family. Not many years later that area too would be mainly Puerto Rican. It was as if the heart of the city map were being gradually colored brown—*café con leche* brown. Our color.

The movie opens with a sweep of the living room. It is "typical" immigrant Puerto Rican decor for the time: the sofa and chairs are square and hard-looking, upholstered in bright colors (blue and yellow in this instance) and covered with the transparent plastic that furniture salesmen then were so adept at convincing women to buy. The linoleum on the floor is light blue; where it had been subjected to spike heels, as it was in most places, there were dime-size indentations all over it that cannot be seen in this movie. The room is full of people dressed up: dark suits for the men, red dresses for the women. When I have asked my mother why most of the women are in red that night, she has shrugged and said, "I don't remember. Just a coincidence." She doesn't have my obsession for assigning symbolism to everything.

The three women in red sitting on the couch are my mother, my eighteen-year-old cousin, and her brother's girlfriend. The novia *is just up from the Island, which is apparent in her body language. She sits up formally, her dress pulled over her knees. She is a pretty girl, but her posture makes her look insecure, lost in her full-skirted dress, which she has carefully tucked around her to make room for my gorgeous cousin, her future sister-in-law. My cousin has grown up in Paterson and is in her last year of high school. She doesn't have a trace of what Puerto Ricans call* la mancha *(literally, the stain: the mark of the new immigrant—something about the posture, the voice, or the humble demeanor that makes it obvious to everyone the person has just arrived on the mainland). My cousin is wearing a light, sequined, cocktail dress. Her brown hair has been lightened with peroxide around the bangs, and she is holding a cigarette expertly between her fingers, bringing it up to her mouth in a sensuous arc of her arm as she talks animatedly. My mother, who has come up to sit between the two women, both only a few years younger than herself, is somewhere between the poles they represent in our culture.*

It became my father's obsession to get out of the barrio, and thus we were never permitted to form bonds with the place or with the people who lived there. Yet El Building was a comfort to my mother, who never got over yearning for *la isla*. She felt surrounded by her language: the walls were thin, and voices speaking and arguing in Spanish could be heard all day. *Salsas* blasted out of radios, turned on early in the morning and left on for company. Women seemed to cook rice and beans perpetually—the strong aroma of boiling red kidney beans permeated the hallways.

Though Father preferred that we do our grocery shopping at the supermarket when he came home on weekend leaves, my mother insisted that she could cook only with products whose labels she could read. Consequently, during the week I accompanied her and my little brother to La Bodega—a hole-in-the-wall grocery store across the street from El Building. There we squeezed down three narrow aisles jammed with various products. Goya and Libby's—those were the trademarks that were trusted by her *mamá*, so my mother bought many cans of Goya beans, soups, and condiments, as well as little cans of Libby's fruit juices for us. And she also bought Colgate toothpaste and Palmolive soap. (The final *e* is pronounced in both these products in Spanish, so for many years I believed that they were manufactured on the Island. I remember my surprise at first hearing a commercial on television in which "Colgate" rhymed with "ate.") We always lingered at La Bodega, for it was there that Mother breathed best, taking in the familiar aromas of the foods she knew from Mamá's kitchen. It was also there that she got to speak to the other women of El Building without violating outright Father's dictates against fraternizing with our neighbors.

Yet Father did his best to make our "assimilation" painless. I can still see him carrying a real Christmas tree up several flights of stairs to our apartment, leaving a trail of aromatic pine. He carried it formally, as if it were a flag in a parade. We were the only ones in El Building that I knew of who got presents on both Christmas and *día de Reyes*, the day when the Three Kings brought gifts to Christ and to Hispanic children.

Our supreme luxury in El Building was having our own television set. It must have been a result of Father's guilt feelings over the isolation he had imposed on us, but we were among the first in the barrio to have one. My brother quickly became an avid watcher of Captain Kangaroo and Jungle Jim, while I loved all the series showing families. By the time I started first grade, I could have drawn a map of Middle America as exemplified by the lives of characters in *Father Knows Best, The Donna Reed Show, Leave It to Beaver, My Three Sons,* and (my favorite) *Bachelor Father,* where John Forsythe treated his adopted teenage daughter like a princess because he was rich and had a Chinese houseboy to do everything for him. In truth, compared to our neighbors in El Building, we were rich. My father's navy check provided us with financial security and a standard of living that the factory workers envied. The only thing his money could not buy us was a place to live away from the barrio—his greatest wish, Mother's greatest fear.

In the home movie the men are shown next, sitting around a card table set up in one corner of the living room, playing dominoes. The clack of the ivory pieces was a familiar sound. I heard it in many houses on the Island and in many apartments in Paterson. In Leave It to Beaver, *the Cleavers played bridge in every other episode; in my childhood, the men started every social occasion with a hotly debated round of dominoes. The women would sit around and watch, but they never participated in the games.*

 Here and there you can see a small child. Children were always brought to parties and, whenever they got sleepy, were put to bed in the host's bedroom. Babysitting was a concept unrecognized by the Puerto Rican women I knew: a responsible mother did not leave her children with any stranger. And in a culture where children are not considered intrusive, there was no need to leave the children at home. We went where our mother went.

Of my preschool years I have only impressions: the sharp bite of the wind in December as we walked with our parents toward the brightly lit stores downtown; how I felt like a stuffed doll in my heavy coat, boots, and mittens; how good it was to walk into the five-and-dime and sit at the counter drinking hot chocolate. On Saturdays our whole family would walk downtown to shop at the big department stores on Broadway. Mother bought all our clothes at Penney's and Sears, and she liked to buy her dresses at the women's specialty shops like Lerner's and Diana's. At some point we'd go into Woolworth's and sit at the soda fountain to eat.

 We never ran into other Latinos at these stores or when eating out, and it became clear to me only years later that the women from El Building shopped mainly in other places—stores owned by other Puerto Ricans or by Jewish merchants who had philosophically accepted our presence in the city and decided to make us their good customers, if not real neighbors and friends. These establishments were located not downtown but in the blocks around our street, and they were referred to generically as La Tienda, El Bazar, La Bodega, La Botánica. Everyone knew what was meant. These were the stores where your face did not turn a clerk to stone, where your money was as green as anyone else's.

One New Year's Eve we were dressed up like child models in the Sears catalogue: my brother in a miniature man's suit and bow tie, and I in black patent-leather shoes and a frilly dress with several layers of crinoline underneath. My mother wore a bright red dress that night, I remember, and spike heels; her long black hair hung to her waist. Father, who usually wore his navy uniform during his short visits home, had put on a dark civilian suit for the occasion: we had been invited to his uncle's house for a big celebration. Everyone was excited because my mother's brother Hernan—a bachelor who could indulge himself with luxuries—had bought a home movie camera, which he would be trying out that night.

 Even the home movie cannot fill in the sensory details such a gathering left imprinted in a child's brain. The thick sweetness of women's perfumes mixing with the ever-present smells of food cooking in the kitchen: meat and plantain *pasteles,* as well as the ubiquitous rice dish made special with pigeon peas—*gandules*—and seasoned with precious *sofrito* sent up from the Island by somebody's mother or smuggled in by a recent traveler. *Sofrito* was one of the items that women hoarded, since it was hardly ever in stock at La Bodega. It was the flavor of Puerto Rico.

The men drank Palo Viejo rum, and some of the younger ones got weepy. The first time I saw a grown man cry was at a New Year's Eve party: he had been reminded of his mother by the smells in the kitchen. But what I remember most were the boiled *pasteles*, plantain or yucca rectangles stuffed with corned beef or other meats, olives, and many other savory ingredients, all wrapped in banana leaves. Everybody had to fish one out with a fork. There was always a "trick" *pastel*—one without stuffing—and whoever got that one was the "New Year's Fool."

There was also the music. Long-playing albums were treated like precious china in these homes. Mexican recordings were popular, but the songs that brought tears to my mother's eyes were sung by the melancholy Daniel Santos, whose life as a drug addict was the stuff of legend. Felipe Rodríguez was a particular favorite of couples, since he sang about faithless women and brokenhearted men. There is a snatch of one lyric that has stuck in my mind like a needle on a worn groove: *De piedra ha de ser mi cama, de piedra la cabezera…la mujer que a mi me quiera…ha de quererme de veras. Ay, Ay, Ay, corazón, porque no amas…*I must have heard it a thousand times since the idea of a bed made of stone, and its connection to love, first troubled me with its disturbing images.

The five-minute home movie ends with people dancing in a circle—the creative filmmaker must have set it up, so that all of them could file past him. It is both comical and sad to watch silent dancing. Since there is no justification for the absurd movements that music provides for some of us, people appear frantic, their faces embarrassingly intense. It's as if you were watching sex. Yet for years, I've had dreams in the form of this home movie. In a recurring scene, familiar faces push themselves forward into my mind's eye, plastering their features into distorted close-ups. And I'm asking them: "Who is *she?* Who is the old woman I don't recognize? Is she an aunt? Somebody's wife? Tell me who she is."

"See the beauty mark on her cheek as big as a hill on the lunar landscape of her face—well, that runs in the family. The women on your father's side of the family wrinkle early; it's the price they pay for that fair skin. The young girl with the green stain on her wedding dress is *la novia*—just up from the Island. See, she lowers her eyes when she approaches the camera, as she's supposed to. Decent girls never look at you directly in the face. *Humilde*, humble, a girl should express humility in all her actions. She will make a good wife for your cousin. He should consider himself lucky to have met her only weeks after she arrived here. If he marries her quickly, she will make him a good Puerto Rican-style wife; but if he waits too long, she will be corrupted by the city, just like your cousin there."

"She means me. I do what I want. This is not some primitive island I live on. Do they expect me to wear a black mantilla on my head and go to mass every day? Not me. I'm an American woman, and I will do as I please. I can type faster than anyone in my senior class at Central High, and I'm going to be a secretary to a lawyer when I graduate. I can pass for an American girl anywhere—I've tried it. At least for Italian, anyway—I never speak Spanish in public. I hate these parties, but I wanted the dress. I look better than any of these *humildes* here. *My* life is going to be different. I have an American boyfriend. He is older and has a car. My parents don't know it, but I sneak out of the house late at night sometimes to be with him. If I marry him, even my name will be American. I hate rice and beans—that's what makes these women fat."

"Your *prima* is pregnant by that man she's been sneaking around with. Would I lie to you? I'm your *tía política*, your great-uncle's common-law wife—the one he abandoned on the Island to go marry your cousin's mother. *I* was not invited to this party, of course, but I came anyway. I came to tell you that story about your cousin that you've always wanted to hear. Do you remember the comment your mother made to a neighbor that has always haunted you? The only thing you heard was your cousin's name, and then you saw your mother pick up your doll from the couch and say: 'It was as big as this doll when they flushed it down the toilet.' This image has bothered you for years, hasn't it? You had nightmares about babies being flushed down the toilet, and you wondered why anyone would do such a horrible thing. You didn't dare ask your mother about it. She would only tell you that you had not heard her right, and yell at you for listening to adult conversations. But later, when you were old enough to know about abortions, you suspected.

"I am here to tell you that you were right. Your cousin was growing an *americanito* in her belly when this movie was made. Soon after, she put something long and pointy into her pretty self, thinking maybe she could get rid of the problem before breakfast and still make it to her first class at the high school. Well, *niña*, her screams could be heard downtown. Your aunt, her *mamá*, who had been a midwife on the Island, managed to pull the little thing out. Yes, they probably flushed it down the toilet. What else could they do with it—give it a Christian burial in a little white casket with blue bows and ribbons? Nobody wanted that baby—least of all the father, a teacher at her school with a house in West Paterson that he was filling with real children, and a wife who was a natural blonde.

"Girl, the scandal sent your uncle back to the bottle. And guess where your cousin ended up? Irony of ironies. She was sent to a village in Puerto Rico to live with a relative on her mother's side: a place so far away from civilization that you have to ride a mule to reach it. A real change in scenery. She found a man there—women like that cannot live without male company—but believe me, the men in Puerto Rico know how to put a saddle on a woman like her. *La gringa*, they call her. Ha, ha, ha. *La gringa* is what she always wanted to be...."

The old woman's mouth becomes a cavernous black hole I fall into. And as I fall, I can feel the reverberations of her laughter. I hear the echoes of her last mocking words: *la gringa, la gringa!* And the conga line keeps moving silently past me. There is no music in my dream for the dancers.

When Odysseus visits Hades to see the spirit of his mother, he makes an offering of sacrificial blood, but since all the souls crave an audience with the living, he has to listen to many of them before he can ask questions. I, too, have to hear the dead and the forgotten speak in my dream. Those who are still part of my life remain silent, going around and around in their dance. The others keep pressing their faces forward to say things about the past.

My father's uncle is last in line. He is dying of alcoholism, shrunken and shriveled like a monkey, his face a mass of wrinkles and broken arteries. As he comes closer I realize that in his features I can see my whole family. If you were to stretch that rubbery flesh, you could find my father's face, and deep within *that* face—my own. I don't want to look into those eyes ringed in purple. In a few years he will retreat into silence, and take a long, long time to die. *Move back, Tío,* I tell him. *I don't want to hear what you have to say. Give the dancers room to move. Soon it will be midnight. Who is the New Year's Fool this time?*

Running the Table

Frank Conroy

When I was fifteen and living in New York City, I was supposed to be going to Stuyvesant High School and in fact I did actually show up three or four times a week, full of gloom, anger and adolescent narcissism. The world was a dark place for me in those days. I lived in a kind of tunnel of melancholy, constantly in trouble at home, in school and occasionally with the police. (Pitching pennies, sneaking into movies, jumping the turnstile in the subway, stealing paperback books—fairly serious stuff in that earlier, more innocent time.) I was haunted by a sense of chaos, chaos within and chaos without. Which is perhaps why the orderliness of pool, the Euclidean cleanness of it, so appealed to me. The formality of pool struck me as soothing and reassuring, a sort of oasis of coolness, utterly rational and yet not without its elegant little mysteries. But I'm getting ahead of myself.

One day, meandering around 14th Street, I stepped through the open doors on an impulse and mounted the long, broad stairway. Halfway up I heard the click of the balls. What a marvelous sound! Precise, sharp, crisp, and yet somehow mellow. There was an intimacy to the sound that thrilled me. At the top of the stairs I pushed through saloon-style swinging doors and entered a vast, hushed, dim hall. Rows of pool tables stretched away in every direction, almost all of them empty at this early hour, but here and there in the distance, a pool of light, figures in silhouette circling, bending, taking shots. Nearby, two old men were playing a game I would later learn to be billiards on a large table without pockets. The click of the three balls, two white, one red, was what I had heard on the stairs. The men played unhurriedly, pausing now and then with their cues held like walking sticks to stare down at the street below. Cigar smoke swirled in the air.

I had walked into Julian's, little knowing that it was one of the most important pool halls on the East Coast. I was impressed by the stark functionality of the place—the absence of decoration of any kind. It seemed almost institutional in its atmosphere, right down to the large poster hung on the cashier's cage setting out the rules and regulations. No drinking, no eating, no sitting on the edges of the tables, no spitting except in the cuspidors, no massé shots, etc. Tables were twenty-five cents an hour. Cue sticks were to be found on racks against the walls. Balls available from the cashier as he clocked you in.

"How do you play?" I asked.

The cashier was bald and overweight. He wore, for some reason, a green eye-shade. "You from Stuyvesant?"

I nodded, and he grunted, reached down to some hidden shelf and gave me a small paper pamphlet, pushing it forward across the worn wooden counter. I scanned it quickly. Basic information about straight pool, eight ball, nine ball, billiards, snooker and a few other games. "Start with straight pool," he said. "Go over there and watch those guys on twenty-two for a while. Sit still, don't talk, and don't move around."

I did as I was told, sitting on a kind of mini-bleachers against the wall, my chin in my hands. The two men playing were in their twenties, an Abbott-and-Costello duo, thin Bud wearing a vest and smoking constantly, pudgy Lou moving delicately around the table, using the bridge now and then because of his short arms. They paid no attention to me and played with concentration, silent except for calling combinations.

"Six off the thirteen," Lou said.

Bud nodded. They only called combinations. All straight shots, no matter how difficult, were presumably obvious. After a while, with a few discreet glances at my pamphlet, I began to get the hang of it. All the balls, striped and solid, were fair game. You simply kept shooting until you missed, and then it was the other guy's turn. After each run, you moved some beads on a wire overhead with the tip of your cue, marking up the number of balls you'd sunk. So much for the rules. What was amazing was the shooting.

Object balls clipped so fine they moved sideways. Bank shots off the cushion into a pocket. Long combinations. Breakout shots in which a whole cluster of balls would explode in all directions while one from the middle would limp into a nearby pocket. And it didn't take long to realize that making a given shot was only part of what was going on. Controlling the position of the cue ball after the shot was equally important, so as to have a makable next shot. I could see that strategy was involved, although how they made the cue ball behave so differently in similar situations seemed nothing short of magical. Lou completed a run of nine or ten balls and reached fifty on the wire overhead. He had won, apparently.

"Double or nothing?"

Bud shook his head. Money changed hands. Lou put the balls in a tray, turned out the light over the table, and both men checked out at the cashier's. I sat for a while, thinking over what I had seen, reading the pamphlet again. I didn't have enough money to play that day, but I knew I was coming back.

Sometime in the late sixties, as an adult, I went to the Botanic Garden in Brooklyn to visit the recently completed Zen rock garden. It was a meticulous re-creation of a particular installation from a particular Japanese monastery. No one else was there. I sat on the bench gazing at the spiral patterns in the sand, looking at the black rocks set like volcanic islands in a white sea. Peace. Tranquility. As absurd as it may sound, I was reminded of my childhood experience of Julian's on a quiet afternoon—a sense of harmony, of an entirely disinterested material world entirely unaffected by one's perception of it.

For me, at fifteen, Julian's was a sort of retreat, a withdrawal from the world. I would shoot for hours at a time, racking up, breaking, shooting, racking up, breaking, shooting, in a solitary trance. Or I would surrender to the ritual of practice—setting up long shots over the length of the table again and again, trying to sink a shot with the same configuration ten times in a row, and then twenty, and then a more difficult configuration to a different pocket three times in a row, and then five, etc. I did not get bored with the repetition. Every time a ball went in the pocket I felt satisfaction. When I missed I simply ignored the fact, reset the shot and tried again. This went on for several weeks at a remote table in a far corner of the hall—table nineteen—which nobody else ever seemed to want. Once in a while I'd play with another kid, usually also from Stuyvesant, and split the time. After a couple of months I would sometimes play for the time—loser pays—against opponents who looked even weaker than myself. But most of the time I played alone.

Late one afternoon, racking up on table nineteen for perhaps the tenth time, I noticed a man sitting in the gloom up against the wall. He was extremely thin, with a narrow face and a protruding brow. He wore a double-breasted suit and two-tone shoes, one leg dangling languidly over the other. He gave me an almost imperceptible nod. I chalked the tip of my cue, went to the head of the table and stroked a clean break. Aware that I was being watched, I studied the lie of the balls for a moment and proceeded to sink seven in a row, everything going according to plan, until I scratched. I pulled up the cue ball and the object ball, recreated the shot and scratched again.

"Why don't you use English?" he asked quietly.

I stared at the table. "What's English?"

A moment's pause. "Set it up again," he said.

I did so.

"Aim, but don't hit. Pretend you're going to shoot."

I made a bridge with my left hand, aimed at the object ball and held the tip of my stick right behind the center of the cue ball.

"All right. All lined up?"

"Yes," I said, almost flat on the table.

"Do not change the line. Are you aiming at the center of the cue ball?"

"Yes."

"Aim a quarter of an inch higher."

"You mean I should. . . ." For some reason what he was suggesting seemed almost sacrilegious.

"Yes, yes. Don't hit the cue ball in the center. Strike a quarter of an inch above. Now go ahead. Shoot."

I made my stroke, watched the object ball go in, and watched the cue ball take a different path after impact than it had before. It didn't scratch this time, but missed the pocket, bounced smartly off the cushion and rolled to a stop near the center of the table for an easy next shot.

"Hey. That's terrific!" I said.

"That's English." He unfolded his legs and stood up. He came over and took the pool cue from my hands. "If a person pays attention," he said, "a person can learn about ninety-five percent of what he needs to know in about ten minutes. Ten minutes for the principles, then who knows how many years for the practice." His dark, deep-set eyes gave his face a vaguely ominous cast. "You want to learn?"

"Absolutely," I said without hesitation. "Yes."

As it turned out, it took about half an hour. The man teaching me was called Smilin' Jack, after the comic-strip character and presumably because of his glum demeanor. He was a Julian's regular, and it was my good luck to have caught him when somebody had stood him up for what was to have been a money game. I could sense that he enjoyed going through the drill—articulate, methodical, explicating on cause and effect with quiet relish, moving the balls around the table with no wasted motion whatsoever, executing the demo shots with a stroke as smooth as powdered silk—it was an elegant dance, with commentary. A sort of offering to the gods of pool.

I cannot possibly recount here what I learned. Follow, draw, left and right English and how they affect the movement of the cue ball after impact. The object ball picking up opposite English from the cue ball. The effectiveness of different kinds of English as a function of distance (between cue ball and object ball) and of speed. *Sliding* the cue ball. Playing the diamond points. Shooting a ball frozen on the cushion. How to read combinations, and on and on. I paid very close attention and jotted down what notes I could. (*Over*shoot bank shots to the side pockets. *Under*shoot bank shots to the corner pockets.) At the end of the half hour my head ached. In addition to trying to grasp the principles, I'd been trying to film the whole thing, to superimpose an eidetic memory on the cells of my brain, so I could retrieve what I'd seen at will. I was exhausted.

He handed me the stick, shot his cuffs and adjusted the front of his jacket with a slight forward movement of his shoulders. "That should keep you busy for a while." Then he simply walked away.

"Thanks," I called after him.

Without looking back, he raised his hand and gave a laconic little wave.

Practice, practice. Months of practice. It was a delicate business, English, affected by things like the relative roughness of the cue tip and its ability to hold chalk, or the condition of the felt, or infinitesimal degrees of table lean. But it worked. There was no doubt about it, when you got the feel of it you greatly increased your power over the all-important position of the cue ball. There was a word for it—the "leave," as in "good shot, but a tough leave." And of course the more you could control the leave, the more deeply involved was the strategy—planning out how to sink twelve balls in a row, rather than just five or six. Progress was slow, but it was tangible, and very, very satisfying. I began to beat people. I moved off table nineteen up toward the middle of the hall and began to beat almost everybody from Stuyvesant.

The most important hurdle for a straight-pool player involves being able to run into the second rack. You have to sink fourteen balls and leave the fifteenth ball and the cue ball positioned in such a way as to be able to sink the last ball (breaking open the new rack at the same time) and have a good enough leave to start all over again. I achieved this shortly before my sixteenth birthday, with a run of twenty-three.

The owners of Julian's recognized the accomplishment as a significant rite of passage and awarded certain privileges to those who had achieved it. During my last year of high school a cue of my own selection, with my name taped to the handle, was kept in a special rack behind the cashier's cage. No one else could use that particular cue stick. It was reserved, along with thirty or forty others for young players who had distinguished themselves.

I was a nonentity at school, but I could walk up to the cage at Julian's and the cashier would reach back for my stick and say, "Hey, Frank. How's it going?"

What a splendid place it was.

There's a lot to feel in pool, a physical aspect to the game, which means you have to play all the time to stay good. I've lost most of my chops (to borrow a word from jazz), but I still drop down to my local bar, the Foxhead, every now and then to play on the undersize table. It's a challenge arrangement. Put your name on the chalkboard, slip two quarters in the slot when it's your turn, and try to win.

There's a good deal more chance in eight ball, your basic bar game, than in straight pool, but it's fun. We've got some regulars. Jerry, a middle-aged man with a gorgeous stroke (a nationally ranked player in his youth), can beat anybody who walks into the place if he isn't furious at having to play doubles, at kids slopping beer onto the felt, or some other infraction of civilized behavior. There's Doug, a graduate student who always looks as if he'd spent the previous night in a cardboard box in an alley and who hits every shot as hard as he can, leaving the question of where the cue ball is going to end up more or less to the gods, in the hope that they will thus tangibly express the favor in which they hold him. (He is a poet.) We have George, an engineer, who exhausts our patience by approaching each situation with extreme care, circling the table several times, leaning over to stare down at a cluster of balls in what appears to be a hypnotic trance, chalking up with the care of Vermeer at the easel and running through a complicated series of various facial and physical tics before committing himself. There's Henry, who programs the jukebox to play "Brown Sugar" ten times in a row before he racks up. We've got students, working people, teachers, nurses (Yes. Women! Smilin' Jack would be scandalized) and barflies. We've got everybody at the Foxhead.

There are nights when I can hold the table for a couple of hours, but not very often. My touch is mostly gone, and bifocals make things difficult. Still, a bit of Julian's is still with me and, at the very least, I talk a good game.

Aerial Reconnaissance

William DeBuys

I sit near the back of the southwest-bound flight, beside a window. A burly Indian slides in next to me, barely squeezing between the armrests. He wears shades and a black T-shirt with the image of a silicone-chested bar dancer splayed across the front.

"Where you headed?" I ask him.

"Vegas," he says. "To catch the Dead. You?"

"San Diego," I say, leaving it at that, my purpose being still new and not easily explained.

An artificially tanned Anglo with rings on each hand the size of lug nuts takes the aisle seat. For all his bronzing he looks dangerously gray. "I hate takeoffs," he says, fastening his belt, and the gold chain around his neck flashes as he swallows.

"Yah, me, too," says the Indian amiably. He proceeds to describe how he just got out of the service and, taking off from London on the last leg home, the engine outside his window blew up. "Whoa man, good thing they have long runways in England 'cause we used every inch. I was thinking I was gonna die."

His story fails to relax Jewelry-Man, now the color of cement.

The plane fills quickly. Sombreroed tourists disentangle from their bags. A troupe of tall, black athletes in identical earphones and leather jackets fold themselves like mantises into their seats. A baby screams two rows ahead on the right. There is commotion in the back as a clot of polyestered real estate types claims a block of rows, guffawing loudly and fratlike: "Manny, gimme that mag. Looks like it's got dirty pictures." "Shut up, Ferdie, you're bothering the lady in front." "Really, lady, I'm just trying to keep these guys under control. If you don't amuse 'em, they tear up the seats."

A young couple sits in front of me. His eyes are only slightly less doelike than hers. A prim little man in a cheap suit fills out their row. He chatters at the seeming bride even before he settles. "It's just a really great day, isn't it?" he foams, and I think I hear in his smarmy greeting the lulling, sick cadence of an evangelist. I can see the side and back of his head, which is all but hairless, not from baldness but from an excess of barbering. Already he is telling the polite, compliant bride his six reasons why the new year we've just begun is the best in the history of mankind to be alive. One of the six reasons is the miracle of "instant travel," which only twelve people in the world really understand. He's one of them.

We taxi for miles, and the concertgoing Dead Head Puebloan next to me, who introduced himself as Lawrence, says, "Maybe we are driving to Arizona." Jewelry-Man, his face in a migraine wince, never opens his eyes, and the shorn evangelist prattles on: "Know why our opportunities are superior to any others in the history of the world? Because America...." Then the roar, acceleration, and up.

Pretty soon Jewelry-Man is feeling better. He gets the flight attendant to bring him a Bloody Mary and asks Lawrence what he plans to do now that he's out of the military. Lawrence says he gave it a lot of thought. When he got home from Europe, he worked on his old V-8, dual-carb Toronado until he got it to crank. Then he rolled on down to Coronado Auto Salvage in Albuquerque. He traded the clunker for $250 and spent the bundle on a set of golf clubs at the Pueblo's pro shop. Golf is pretty much where it's at at the Pueblo, he explains, because tribal members play free on the new course.

Jewelry-Man bypasses the subject of golf nirvana but allows as how he knows something about salvage yards, since he owns three and is on his way to buy a fourth. "Keep your eye on scrap," he says. "It's goin' through the roof." He takes a pull on his swizzle straw. "Scrap is gold."

We descend through smog to Phoenix, over houses in tight rows, over the ruined desert pitted with swimming pools, over gangrenous golf courses sucking their millions of gallons a day, over the blue junkie veins of aqueducts stretching to the horizon.

We land and Lawrence leaves to catch his connection to Vegas. A tall dyed blonde with a silken voice and no wedding ring takes his place. She wears a pink V-necked sweater, soft as peach fuzz, and no one can mistake that the only thing underneath is her own abundant self. As she shrugs and twists to settle in her seat, Jewelry-Man takes heart. By the time we are airborne, he has conquered his nausea and learned that she is a housecleaner from Palm Springs who takes off six weeks at this time every year just to travel. He travels a great deal too, he tells her. He is in the recycling business, a helluva growth industry. "The first million was easier than I thought it would be. The second was easier than that...."

West from Phoenix the desert simplifies and, at this early hour, wears the colors and patterns that mapmakers use for its portrait. Rand McNally tan paints the unclothed plains, and *Geographic* green stipples the woodlands. Each bare mountain and range of hills casts its shadow in relief-map indigo, and lava flows reveal the same disordered swirls, sand dunes the same puffy circles, as one finds on an atlas plate. A sudden intense rectangle, green as rain forest and miles long on the side, betrays the alfalfa farm and well field of some lesser water duke. A full-scale replication of Timbuktu would have contrasted less with the vast enfolding desert, but as feats of transforming the earth go, this exclamatory island of verdure is mere foretaste. On the horizon not far ahead stretches the blue ribbon of the Colorado River and, beyond it, California, land of water kings and emperors.

The color of the formerly great Colorado must not slip by unnoticed: It is a *blue* ribbon, the same baby jumpsuit blue beloved by cartographers for rivers and creeks of all kinds. Its presence here is no less than an epitaph for the natural West. We look down from above and see a river no longer brown, as would befit a stream formerly as silt-laden as any on earth, nor still less red, which is what Juan de Oñate had in mind in 1604 when he called a side stem *Colorado.*

Today, assuredly, the river is blue, and so are the sprawling tepid lakes behind the monumental dams that block its canyons. The water mirrors the cloudless Southwestern sky while houseboaters putt-putt up the side canyons to drink and belch and jet skiers roar across its domesticated surface. Beneath them the earthen harvest of the immense eroding intermountain West settles invisibly, whole deltas in suspended transit behind the great white emboli of the dams, a series of geologic Ellis Islands, where immigrant grains of soil arrive and arrive and arrive, never departing.

The plane now crosses above the Colorado where the river exits its final canyon and pools behind the gleaming colonnaded works of Imperial Dam. Beside it, the self-proclaimed "resort" of Imperial Oasis shines with Airstream aluminum and RV sheet metal of every conceivable color.

Here at Imperial Dam is the end of a river and the beginning of a story.

When I first visited Imperial Dam, I drove up from the south across the Gila River and Yuma Proving Ground. It did not surprise me, crossing a low bridge, that the Gila, a lesser river, had no water. In the Southwest, a river—to be a river—need not carry water, only provide it for irrigation, which the Gila does generously to the ultimate drop. What surprised me was that the Gila had been plowed, a phenomenon that approached Homeric strangeness—like the sea shining red as wine or the great sailor Odysseus marching inland with an oar on his shoulder until he should come to a place where no one knew the oar's purpose. Here, the plowed river, as puzzling to me as an oar to an inland bedouin, may have had more to do in an immediate sense with floodway maintenance than with expiating sin or placating gods, but the sight of it still did not prepare me for misplacing the Colorado.

I knew I was close to the mighty Colorado, after crossing the bestirred desert of the proving ground, when I came to a series of green-water ditches in a marsh where blackbirds trilled. I drove along a short causeway and up a low ridge of sand expecting any second to see the great river of Wyoming, Colorado, and Utah, of the Grand Canyon itself, diminished but vibrant, spread across its plain. But at the top of the sand ridge the road turned south, and I marveled that even here, downstream of so much monumental plumbing, the muscular Colorado still forced highways and human plans to bend. On I drove several miles, ever southward, and saw no river nor any chance to turn west, where the river ought to be. Only slowly did I begin to suspect that the river had not forced the road from its logical path so much as, somehow, it had evaded me. I was traveling alone, a condition in which one entertains thoughts that do not occur in company. Had I crossed the river and missed it? Had I blacked out? Was I even now in a twilight of consciousness? Worse had happened in other times and places, and I had been on the road without rest since Show Low, nearly four hundred miles away.

Anxious to get my bearings, I pulled over where a dirt road met the highway, and there encountered a barrier and a sign proclaiming, "All American Canal, Property of Imperial Irrigation District." I got out of the car and heard the whispering suck of great waters moving fast. A hundred steps forward and I stood at the canal's concrete bank. At my feet ran the brawny, unimpeded flush of the mighty, canyon-carving River of the West.

Centuries of miles since sunrise to reach it, and now I realized that the stagnant marsh where blackbirds trembled with desire was the old main channel of the Colorado—and a mapmaker's lie. Atlases innumerable notwithstanding, the blue line of the Colorado reaches no saltwater outlet in the Gulf of California, nor has it done so meaningfully for decades except during rare periods of "natural disaster" when the raging Gila plays havoc with southern Arizona and spews its floodwaters past the reach of engineers. The base flow of the tamed Colorado flows by way of one aqueduct to Los Angeles and San Diego, by way of another to Phoenix and Tucson. It flows to the farms of greater Yuma by various siphons and canals. And most decisively and definitively it flows westward across the driest, hottest desert in the United States to the Imperial Valley and Salton Sink of southeastern California. It accomplishes this unlikely journey by way of its current main channel, the All American Canal, whose name provides full answer to anyone south of the border naive enough to wonder where the river went.

From the air there is no mystery. The green-water ditch, crowded on either side by a gauze of tamarisk, trickles down toward Yuma and the Mexican line. Terraces of cotton fields and mesquite woodlands shield it on either side from the great dun vastness of the desert. But what draws the eye is the perfect and unnatural geometry, delivered whole from the draftsman's triangle and S-curve, of the blue All American Canal branching gracefully from its lesser parent and arcing sinuously through gravel hills toward unseen destinations.

Our 737 follows. The canal snakes into a wilderness of sand—the Algodones Dunes, once a menace to travelers but today a noisy and ever-ravaged playground for the ORV and dirt bike tribe. The canal contours the shifting slopes under plumes of sand, twisting in long parabolic curves, blue on buff. For a time the waterway roughly parallels Interstate 5, the main highway from Yuma to San Diego, whose engineers— or their lunatic successors—conquered the capriciousness of the landscape by paving a great swath of the dune crest with asphalt, creating a parking lot large enough to be seen from space.

Past this congealed petrochemical rug, the dunes again swirl, and in their midst the canal divides, its smaller portion angling northward toward purple-black mountains, the larger sidling to the border, where it soon runs laser-straight as far as the eye can see. Now a haze lies on the land, a thickening murk of moisture, smoke, and dust, and through it, there emerges an apparition of monumental cultivation, checkerboard lines and quilted greens and yellows on a scale as large as the Texas plains, waist high in cotton, or endless Iowa, buried in corn. It is an agricultural sea capacious enough for as many amber waves of grain as would inundate half of Kansas or the Ukraine, field after field, square and rectangle, fallow and full, Nile green and bile green, ground glass and jade. The twill of crop rows runs here with the sun, there athwart, everywhere at different angles, each a new weave of shadow, dirt, and leaf.

This is the Imperial Valley, where the last waters of the Colorado River feed half a million acres of cropland and, by extension, the people of the United States. In its fields grow dozens of varieties of head lettuce, leaf lettuce, iceberg and romaine, carrots, artichokes, asparagus, beans, beets, broccoli, celery, cilantro, cucumbers, bok choy, eggplants, peppers, cabbages, and kale, collards, and cauliflower. But that's just a start. One must not omit the onions, garlic, parsnips and squash, potatoes and tomatoes, watermelons, muskmelons, honeydews, and cantaloupes, not to mention wheat, barley, sorghum, oil seeds, alfalfa, sweet corn and feed corn, sugar beets, nuts, dates, lemons, oranges, tangerines, and grapefruit, Sudan, Bermuda, and rye grasses, cotton and other fibers, nearly the entire complex of cultigens supporting North American civilization, as well as its animals, who are here represented by roughly a million sheep and feedlot cattle, plus dairy cows, swine, farmed catfish, and enough commercially tended bees to keep the organs of the plants and the air humming. Here, beyond the reach of frost and chill, the growing season is in a state of perpetual motion: disking, planting, irrigating, harvesting, disking, planting, and on again, restlessly and efficiently, thanks to armies of work-starved, brown-skinned pickers and packers, thanks to endless boxcars and truck caravans of fertilizer, pesticide, herbicide, and machinery. And water, *gracias a Dios*, that without which nothing can be, a great continental river delivering the equivalent of lakes, bays, and inland seas, all of it originating in distant lands with different climates, all making possible in this place the environmental semblance—from a seedling's point of view—of forty inches of annual rainfall, where less than five actually come from the sky. (And the farmer hardly welcomes those few natural inches, for they muddy roads, cause ditch banks to slough, and mar the perfection of his absolute control.) The result is the apotheosis of industrial agriculture: Here food is not grown so much as manufactured.

And farther to the north, shining placidly like an oval mirror to the sky, a mirror large enough to reflect the vanity of a powerful and prosperous nation, lies Salton Sea, the vast inland lake that receives the leachate and dross of those fields, just as the fields first receive in the Colorado's water the leachate and dross of countless other fields elsewhere in the quarter-billion-acre watershed. Selenium salts washed from Wyoming end their poisonous travels here, as do the progressively richer effluents of fields and towns in Colorado, Utah, New Mexico, Arizona, and Nevada, to say nothing of the raw sewage that flows north across the international boundary from Mexicali along the misnamed New River—such a spumy, fetid, viral broth as to disable an onlooker's appetite for weeks.

The desert basin beneath this droning jet, half food factory, half sump, is what the intermountain West boils down to—or leaches or evaporates or otherwise reduces to, the verb being variable though the process has never been, the process being as immutable as the law of gravity, which is in fact the only law its acolytes have not refashioned to their purpose.

Gravity decrees that in low places consequences collect, and here is the lowest of the low: poor Salton Sea, foul and maligned, its sometimes wildly fluctuating surface lying over two hundred feet below the level of the nearby Gulf of California and its unseen, toxic, and nacreous bottom still sixty feet deeper than that. This is the place, below in hazy view yet many hours and miles away by rental car and highway, that I have boarded this plane to explore.

I blame the trip on a photograph. The image, black and white, shows an empty, altogether abandoned swimming pool yawning like a gutted melon beneath its useless diving board. A solitary, drought-murdered palm stands guard in the minimal back-ground, and the entire tableau is duplicated by reflection in the accumulated liquid filth at the bottom of the pool. This ruin, I learned, was part of the once-vaunted Salton Bay Yacht Club, chief jewel of a sprawling real estate promotion staged in vacant desert beside the Salton Sea. Its brochures, film clips, and other come-ons, replete with leggy, sun-bronzed models lounging beside this very pool, promised a Palm Springs lifestyle for people of ordinary means. It was to be the land of Summum Bonum—step right up and take a look:

Here's life without work, and golf forever! Year-round sunshine! Fishing, sailing, no urban congestion! Affordable greens fees, plus bingo, drinks, and dancing after dark! Never mind the goosefart stench of the water's edge or an entire river of Mexi-can sewage flowing up from the south. Never mind that lots were sold from airplanes and tents in a rush to grab the dollars of the guileless. Never mind that the money boys in this and every other development up and down the sea were ready at any second to turn off the irrigation of their make-believe and pull out, leaving yacht clubs, golf courses, and palm trees by the thousands to wither and die in the solar wind. Never mind that they did exactly that, as any fool with half an eye could have seen they would. Never mind, never mind. The train, my friend, is leaving the station. I've got another call. Do you want to get in on the ground floor or not? Buy one homesite for investment and another for yourself! The first will pay for the second. Just get out of the way and watch your money double, triple, quadruple! The future won't wait—I know you and the missus would like to be part of it.

The photograph completes the tale. There in the putrescent liquid at the bottom of the pool you can see what happened when the adman's dreamy appeals to ordinary greed and indolence turned belly-up. Suffice to say that the image of the pool—the sump within the sump at the end of the West—suggested that more rivers than one ended in the Salton Sink. Clearly, the Colorado subsided into nothingness there, but possibly another river did as well, a river of the spirit and of dreams, which are no less a part of the American West. This other river, I thought, might rise from notions, born centuries ago, of free land and westward migration; it might, flowing through time, change character as long rivers do, reflecting not the country from which it departed but the country in which endlessly it arrives and shedding along the way all connection to hoary ideas about labor and fair reward, about building things to last. Perhaps along the way its current might gradually metamorphose into something unknown and unforeseen at the headwaters, an honest-to-god New River, changed by Gold Rush, Hollywood, and postwar defense bonanzas, flowing onward through and past the frozen, face-lift smiles of Palm Springs, where kisses taste like margaritas and golf clubs rattle timelessly, past the diamonds and concha belts and the country clubs that smell faintly of disinfectant, and flowing ever onward down the eastward slope of San Gorgonio Pass, descending past the shacks of migrant crop pickers and unemployed Indians, down to the loneliest of deserts, pressing ever toward the mirage, barely out of reach, of the pool in the sun and the girl by the pool, her beckoning smile as bright as the white linen suit of the master of ceremonies, whose voice in your ear reminds you over and over that this deal, played right, is the only real estate jackpot you'll ever need; and his mesmeric chant sings you onward, palm trees swaying, toward the smiling, long-legged girl, toward the bar at the country club, where faces turn in welcome, toward the quiet house on the cul-de-sac with its wet bar, climate control, and carpets soft as beds, onward toward the promise—*deal again! fifty on black!*—of getting something for nothing, then doubling that.

All this, the photograph seemed to say, lay in the sump within a sump at the end of the West.

The plane has crossed the mountains and now descends toward San Diego. Joan Myers, a photographer I have known for years, will meet me at the airport. It was she who captured the image of the defunct and squalid pool, as well as scores of others no less expressive of corrosion, abuse, and abandonment.

By edict of the pilot, tray tables are put away and seatbacks returned to their full upright positions. Now I can see warships in the harbor. The plane lurches, buffeted by wind. Jewelry-Man now matches the putty color of the paneling of the aircraft. The glamorous housecleaner takes notice, and pity. She covers his white knuckles with elegant fingers and lavender false nails. The stricken junk dealer twitches with pain and pleasure.

In the row ahead the small, prim man still preaches to the seeming bride. I cannot make out his words, only the earnest and unctuous tone, the studied cadence of the televangelist, and I cannot help but picture him in the theater of a new and cavernous Baptist church, the nave not a nave but a soundstage equipped with spotlights, ceiling microphones, and camera boxes all set for Sunday broadcast.

We land and taxi. At last we stop. The prim man stands. "Now please tell me again," he smarms, "what was that pretty name of yours?"

"Joann," the bride replies.

"Now that's a real easy name for me to remember," he says, as though Joann's name were exotic like Svetlana or Clytemnestra.

"That's a real easy name for me to remember," he repeats, and now for the first time I can see his cocker spaniel eyes—earnest and guiltless and, ipso facto, depraved. "Joann is the name of the second girl I ever dated, and I only dated three." He leans forward and in a hushed voice confides, "I married the third."

Who now, that very third, appears smiling at his elbow amid the jostling, disembarking crowd, plump as a life jacket and her hair the same color. And the man goes on, "You know I really enjoyed talking to you and I dearly want to thank you for listening."

"My pleasure," the bride lies hopelessly.

"Well, and you understand these things," the small man says. "Not many do. You say to most people, 'Which will you take, $500,000 cash right here, right now, or a penny a day, doubled at the end, each day for a month?' And nine out of ten will take the cash up front. But how wrong, how shortsighted they are, because—and now you understand this as few people do—because that penny a day, doubled at the end, would be twenty-one million four hundred seventy-four thousand eight hundred thirty-six dollars and forty-six cents by the end of the month, I kid you not. That, Joann, is the power of compounding. Very few people understand it, but let it be your guide and your happiness will grow like the penny."

The small man jerks to attention and nods his head at Joann in a nearly Prussian salute, which he finishes with an actual wink. Then he strains to reach the overhead bin and hauls down a giant leather briefcase that shines like mahogany.

I realize I misjudged him from the start. He's not a huckster for salvation. What this man sells surpasses even that. His product is not mere afterlife but paradise, now, right here—start today, take the pledge, join the program. Give compounding a chance to work its magic, and with the right guide and these easily affordable materials, you too can enter the ranks of the elect.

The line of passengers is moving. Orange-headed wife before him, the too-shorn, hope-spewing, dollar-down-and-forever-to-pay, all-American dream merchant sallies to the teeming city.

We're in southern California.

Living Like Weasels

Annie Dillard

A weasel is wild. Who knows what he thinks? He sleeps in his underground den, his tail draped over his nose. Sometimes he lives in his den for two days without leaving. Outside, he stalks rabbits, mice, muskrats, and birds, killing more bodies than he can eat warm, and often dragging the carcasses home. Obedient to instinct, he bites his prey at the neck, either splitting the jugular vein at the throat or crunching the brain at the base of the skull, and he does not let go. One naturalist refused to kill a weasel who was socketed into his hand deeply as a rattlesnake. The man could in no way pry the tiny weasel off, and he had to walk half a mile to water, the weasel dangling from his palm, and soak him off like a stubborn label.

And once, says Ernest Thompson Seton—once, a man shot an eagle out of the sky. He examined the eagle and found the dry skull of a weasel fixed by the jaws to his throat. The supposition is that the eagle had pounced on the weasel and the weasel swiveled and bit as instinct taught him, tooth to neck, and nearly won. I would like to have seen that eagle from the air a few weeks or months before he was shot: was, the whole weasel still attached to his feathered throat, a fur pendant? Or did the eagle eat what he could reach, gutting the living weasel with his talons before his breast, bending his beak, cleaning the beautiful airborne bones?

I have been reading about weasels because I saw one last week. I startled a weasel who startled me, and we exchanged a long glance.

Twenty minutes from my house, through the woods by the quarry and across the highway, is Hollins Pond, a remarkable piece of shallowness, where I like to go at sunset and sit on a tree trunk. Hollins Pond is also called Murray's Pond; it covers two acres of bottomland near Tinker Creek with six inches of water and six thousand lily pads. In winter, brown-and-white steers stand in the middle of it, merely dampening their hooves; from the distant shore they look like miracle itself, complete with miracle's nonchalance. Now, in summer, the steers are gone. The water lilies have blossomed and spread to a green horizontal plane that is terra firma to plodding blackbirds, and tremulous ceiling to black leeches, crayfish, and carp.

This is, mind you, suburbia. It is a five-minute walk in three directions to rows of houses, though none is visible here. There's a 55 mph highway at one end of the pond, and a nesting pair of wood ducks at the other. Under every bush is a muskrat hole or a beer can. The far end is an alternating series of fields and woods, fields and woods, threaded everywhere with motorcycle tracks—in whose bare clay wild turtles lay eggs.

So. I had crossed the highway, stepped over two low barbed-wire fences, and traced the motorcycle path in all gratitude through the wild rose and poison ivy of the pond's shoreline up into high grassy fields. Then I cut down through the woods to the mossy fallen tree where I sit. This tree is excellent. It makes a dry, upholstered bench at the upper, marshy end of the pond, a plush jetty raised from the thorny shore between a shallow blue body of water and a deep blue body of sky. The sun had just set. I was relaxed on the tree trunk, ensconced in the lap of lichen, watching the lily pads at my feet tremble and part dreamily over the thrusting path of a carp. A yellow bird appeared to my right and flew behind me. It caught my eye; I swiveled around—and the next instant, inexplicably, I was looking down at a weasel, who was looking up at me.

Weasel! I'd never seen one wild before. He was ten inches long, thin as a curve, a mus-cled ribbon, brown as fruitwood, soft-furred, alert. His face was fierce, small and pointed as a lizard's; he would have made a good arrowhead. There was just a dot of chin, maybe two brown hairs' worth, and then the pure white fur began that spread down his underside. He had two black eyes I didn't see, any more than you see a window.

The weasel was stunned into stillness as he was emerging from beneath an enor-mous shaggy wild rose bush four feet away. I was stunned into stillness twisted back-ward on the tree trunk. Our eyes locked, and someone threw away the key.

Our look was as if two lovers, or deadly enemies, met unexpectedly on an over-grown path when each had been thinking of something else: a clearing blow to the gut. It was also a bright blow to the brain, or a sudden beating of brains, with all the charge and intimate grate of rubbed balloons. It emptied our lungs. It felled the forest, moved the fields, and drained the pond; the world dismantled and tumbled into that black hole of eyes. If you and I looked at each other that way, our skulls would split and drop to our shoulders. But we don't. We keep our skulls. So.

He disappeared. This was only last week, and already I don't remember what shattered the enchantment. I think I blinked, I think I retrieved my brain from the weasel's brain, and tried to memorize what I was seeing, and the weasel felt the yank of separation, the careening splashdown into real life and the urgent current of instinct. He vanished under the wild rose. I waited motionless, my mind suddenly full of data and my spirit with pleadings, but he didn't return.

Please do not tell me about "approach-avoidance conflicts." I tell you I've been in that weasel's brain for sixty seconds, and he was in mine. Brains are private places, mut-tering through unique and secret tapes—but the weasel and I both plugged into another tape simultaneously, for a sweet and shocking time. Can I help it if it was a blank?

What goes on in his brain the rest of the time? What does a weasel think about? He won't say. His journal is tracks in clay, a spray of feathers, mouse blood and bone: uncollected, unconnected, loose-leaf, and blown.

I would like to learn, or remember, how to live. I come to Hollins Pond not so much to learn how to live as, frankly, to forget about it. That is, I don't think I can learn from a wild animal how to live in particular—shall I suck warm blood, hold my tail high, walk with my footprints precisely over the prints of my hands?—but I might learn something of mindlessness, something of the purity of living in the physical senses and the dignity of living without bias or motive. The weasel lives in necessity and we live in choice, hating necessity and dying at the last ignobly in its talons. I would like to live as I should, as the weasel lives as he should. And I suspect that for me the way is like the weasel's: open to time and death painlessly, noticing everything, remembering nothing, choosing the given with a fierce and pointed will.

I missed my chance. I should have gone for the throat. I should have lunged for that streak of white under the weasel's chin and held on, held on through mud and into the wild rose, held on for a dearer life. We could live under the wild rose wild as weasels, mute and uncomprehending. I could very calmly go wild. I could live two days in the den, curled, leaning on mouse fur, sniffing bird bones, blinking, licking, breathing musk, my hair tangled in the roots of grasses. Down is a good place to go, where the mind is single. Down is out, out of your ever-loving mind and back to your careless senses. I remember muteness as a prolonged and giddy fast, where every moment is a feast of utterance received. Time and events are merely poured, unremarked, and ingested directly, like blood pulsed into my gut through a jugular vein. Could two live that way? Could two live under the wild rose, and explore by the pond, so that the smooth mind of each is as everywhere present to the other, and as received and as unchallenged, as falling snow?

We could, you know. We can live any way we want. People take vows of poverty, chastity, and obedience—even of silence—by choice. The thing is to stalk your calling in a certain skilled and supple way, to locate the most tender and live spot and plug into that pulse. This is yielding, not fighting. A weasel doesn't "attack" anything; a weasel lives as he's meant to, yielding at every moment to the perfect freedom of single necessity.

I think it would be well, and proper, and obedient, and pure, to grasp your one necessity and not let it go, to dangle from it limp wherever it takes you. Then even death, where you're going no matter how you live, cannot you part. Seize it and let it seize you up aloft even, till your eyes burn out and drop; let your musky flesh fall off in shreds, and let your very bones unhinge and scatter, loosened over fields, over fields and woods, lightly, thoughtless, from any height at all, from as high as eagles.

From a Sheepherder's Notebook: Three Days

Gretel Ehrlich

When the phone rang, it was John: "Maurice just upped and quit and there ain't nobody else around, so you better get packed. I'm taking you out to herd sheep." I walked to his trailerhouse. He smoked impatiently while I gathered my belongings. "Do you know *anything* about herding sheep after all this time?" he asked playfully. "No, not really." I was serious. "Well, it's too late now. You'll just have to figure it out. And there ain't no phones up there either!"

He left me off on a ridge at five in the morning with a mare and a border collie. "Last I saw the sheep, they was headed for them hills," he said, pointing up toward a dry ruffle of badlands. "I'll pull your wagon up ahead about two miles. You'll see it. Just go up that ridge, turn left at the pink rock, then keep agoing. And don't forget to bring the damned sheep."

Morning. Sagesmell, sunsquint, birdsong, cool wind. I have no idea where I am, how to get to the nearest paved road, or how to find the sheep. There are tracks going everywhere so I follow what appear to be the most definite ones. The horse picks a path through sagebrush. I watch the dog. We walk for several miles. Nothing. Then both sets of ears prick up. The dog looks at me imploringly. The sheep are in the draw ahead.

Move them slow or fast? Which crossing at the river? Which pink rock? It's like being a first-time mother, but mother now to two thousand sheep who give me the kind of disdainful look a teenager would his parent and, with my back turned, can get into as much trouble. I control the urge to keep them neatly arranged, bunched up by the dog, and, instead, let them spread out and fill up. Grass being scarce on spring range, they scatter.

Up the valley, I encounter a slalom course of oil rigs and fenced spills I hadn't been warned about. The lambs, predictably mischievous, emerge dripping black. Freed from those obstacles, I ride ahead to find the wagon which, I admit, I'm afraid I'll never see, leaving the sheep on the good faith that they'll stay on their uphill drift toward me.

"Where are my boundaries?" I'd asked John.

"Boundaries?" He looked puzzled for a minute. "Hell, Gretel, it's all the outfit's land, thirty or forty miles in any direction. Take them anywhere they want to go."

On the next ridge I find my wagon. It's a traditional sheepherder's wagon, rounded top, tiny wood cookstove, bed across the back, built-in benches and drawers. The rubber wheels and long tongue make it portable. The camp tender pulls it (now with a pickup, earlier with teams) from camp to camp as the feed is consumed, every two weeks or so. Sheep begin appearing and graze toward me. I picket my horse. The dog runs for shade to lick his sore feet. The view from the dutch doors of the wagon is to the southeast, down the long slit of a valley. If I rode north, I'd be in Montana within the day, and next week I'll begin the fifty-mile trail east to the Big Horns.

Three days before summer solstice; except to cook and sleep I spend every waking hour outside. Tides of weather bring the days and take them away. Every night a bobcat visits, perched at a discreet distance on a rock, facing me. A full moon, helium-filled, cruises through clouds and is lost behind rimrock. No paper cutout, this moon, but ripe and splendid. Then Venus, then the North Star. Time for bed. Are the sheep bedded down? Should I ride back to check them?

Morning. Blue air comes ringed with coyotes. The ewes wake clearing their communal throats like old men. Lambs shake their flop-eared heads at leaves of grass, negotiating the blade. People have asked in the past, "What do you do out there? Don't you get bored?" The problem seems to be something else. There's too much of everything here. I can't pace myself to it.

Down the valley the sheep move in a frontline phalanx, then turn suddenly in a card-stacked sequential falling, as though they had turned themselves inside out, and resume feeding again in whimsical processions. I think of town, of John's trailer-house, the clean-bitten lawn, his fanatical obsession with neatness and work, his small talk with hired hands, my eyesore stacks of books and notes covering an empty bed, John smoking in the dark of early morning, drinking coffee, waiting for daylight to stream in.

After eating I return to the sheep, full of queasy fears that they will have vanished and I'll be pulled off the range to face those firing-squad looks of John's as he says, "I knew you'd screw up. Just like you screw up everything." But the sheep are there. I can't stop looking at them. They're there, paralyzing the hillside with thousands of mincing feet, their bodies pressed together as they move, saucerlike, scanning the earth for a landing.

Thunderstorm. Sheep feed far up a ridge I don't want them to go over, so the dog, horse, and I hotfoot it to the top and ambush them, yelling and hooting them back down. Cleverly, the horse uses me as a windbreak when the front moves in. Lightning fades and blooms. As we descend quickly, my rein-holding arm looks to me like a blank stick. I feel numb. Numb in all this vividness. I don't seem to occupy my life fully.

Down in the valley again I send the dog "way around" to turn the sheep, but he takes the law into his own hands and chases a lamb off a cliff. She's wedged upside down in a draw on the other side of the creek. It will take twenty minutes to reach her, and the rest of the sheep have already trailed ahead. This numbness is a wrist twisting inside my throat. A lone pine tree whistles, its needles are novocaine. "In nature there are neither rewards nor punishments; there are only consequences." I can't remember who said that. I ride on.

One dead. Will she be reborn? And as what? The dog that nips lambs' heels into butchering chutes? I look back. The "dead" lamb convulses into action and scrambles up the ledge to find his mother.

Twin terrors: to be awake; to be asleep.

All day clouds hang over the Beartooth Mountains. Looking for a place out of the wind, I follow a dry streambed to a sheltered inlet. In front of me, there's something sticking straight up. It's the shell of a dead frog propped up against a rock with its legs crossed at the ankles. A cartoonist's idea of a frog relaxing, but this one's skin is paper-thin, mouth opened as if to scream. I lean close. "It's too late, you're already dead!"

Because I forgot to bring hand cream or a hat, sun targets in on me like frostbite. The dog, horse, and I move through sagebrush in unison, a fortress against wind. Sheep ticks ride my peeling skin. The dog pees, then baptizes himself at the water hole—full immersion—lapping at spitting rain. Afterward, he rolls in dust and reappears with sage twigs and rabbit brush strung up in his coat, as though in disguise—a Shakespearian dog. Above me, oil wells are ridge-top jewelry adorning the skyline with ludicrous sexual pumps. Hump, hump go the wells. Hump, hump go the drones who gather that black soup, insatiable.

We walk the fuselage of the valley. A rattlesnake passes going the other way; plenty of warning but so close to my feet I hop the rest of the day. I come upon the tin-bright litter of a former sheep camp: Spam cans flattened to the ground, their keys sticking up as if ready to open my grave.

Sun is in and out after the storm. In a long gully, the lambs gambol, charging in small brigades up one side, then the other. Ewes look on bored. When the lamb-fun peters out, the whole band comes apart in a generous spread the way sheep ranchers like them. Here and there lambs, almost as big as their mothers, kneel with a contagiously enthusiastic wiggle, bumping the bag with a goatlike butt to take a long draw of milk.

Night. Nighthawks whir. Meadowlarks throw their heads back in one ecstatic song after another. In the wagon I find a piece of broken mirror big enough to see my face: blood drizzles from cracked lips, gnats have eaten away at my ears.

To herd sheep is to discover a new human gear somewhere between second and reverse—a slow, steady trot of keenness with no speed. There is no flab in these days. But the constant movement of sheep from water hole to water hole, from camp to camp, becomes a form of longing. But for what?

The ten other herders who work for this ranch begin to trail their sheep toward summer range in the Big Horns. They're ahead of me, though I can't see them for the curve of the earth. One-armed Red, Grady, and Ed; Bob, who always bakes a pie when he sees me riding toward his camp; Fred, wearer of rags; "Amorous Albert"; Rudy, Bertha, and Ed; and, finally, Doug, who travels circuslike with a menagerie of goats, roosters, colts, and dogs and keeps warm in the winter by sleeping with one of the nannies. A peaceful army, of which I am the tail end, moving in ragtag unison across the prairie.

A day goes by. Every shiver of grass counts. The shallows and dapples in air that give grass life are like water. The bobcat returns nightly. During easy jags of sleep the dog's dreampaws chase coyotes. I ride to the sheep. Empty sky, an absolute blue. Empty heart. Sunburned face blotches brown. Another layer of skin to peel, to meet myself again in the mirror. A plane passes overhead—probably the government trapper. I'm waving hello, but he speeds away.

Now it's tomorrow. I can hear John's truck, the stock racks speak before I can actually see him, and it's a long time shortening the distance between us.

"Hello."

"Hello."

He turns away because something tender he doesn't want me to see registers in his face.

"I'm moving you up on the bench. Take the sheep right out the tail end of this valley, then take them to water. It's where the tree is. I'll set your wagon by that road."

"What road?" I ask timidly.

Then he does look at me. He's trying to suppress a smile but speaks impatiently.

"You can see to hell and back up there, Gretel."

I ride to the sheep, but the heat of the day has already come on sizzling. It's too late to get them moving; they shade up defiantly, their heads knitted together into a wool umbrella. From the ridge there's whooping and yelling and rocks being thrown. It's John trying to get the sheep moving again. In a dust blizzard we squeeze them up the road, over a sharp lip onto the bench.

Here, there's wide-open country. A view. Sheep string out excitedly. I can see a hundred miles in every direction. When I catch up with John I get off my horse. We stand facing each other, then embrace quickly. He holds me close, then pulls away briskly and scuffles the sandy dirt with his boot.

"I've got to get back to town. Need anything?"

"Naw…I'm fine. Maybe a hat.…"

He turns and walks his long-legged walk across the benchland. In the distance, at the pickup, an empty beer can falls on the ground when he gets in. I can hear his radio as he bumps toward town. Dust rises like an evening gown behind his truck. It flies free for a moment, then returns, leisurely, to the habitual road—that bruised string which leads to and from my heart.

Parish Streets

Patricia Hampl

Lexington, Oxford, Chatsworth, continuing down Grand Avenue to Milton and Avon, as far as St. Albans—the streets of our neighborhood had an English, even an Anglican, ring to them. But we were Catholic, and the parishes of the diocese, unmarked and ghostly as they were, posted borders more decisive than the street signs we passed on our way to St. Luke's grade school or, later, walking in the other direction to Visitation Convent for high school.

We were like people with dual citizenship. I *lived* on Linwood Avenue, but I *belonged* to St. Luke's. That was the lingo. Mothers spoke of daughters who were going to the junior-senior prom with boys "from Nativity" or "from St. Mark's," as if from fiefdoms across the sea.

"Where you from?" a boy livid with acne asked when we startled each other lurking behind a pillar in the St. Thomas Academy gym at a Friday night freshman mixer.

"Ladies' choice!" one of the mothers cried from a dim corner where a portable hi-fi was set up. She rasped the needle over the vinyl, and Fats Domino came on, insinuating a heavier pleasure than I yet knew: *I found my thrill…on Blueberry Hill.*

"I'm from Holy Spirit," the boy said, as if he'd been beamed in to stand by the tepid Cokes and tuna sandwiches and the bowls of sweating potato chips on the refreshments table.

Parish members did not blush to describe themselves as being "from Immaculate Conception." Somewhere north, near the city line, there was even a parish frankly named Maternity of Mary. But then, in those years, the 1950s and early 1960s, breeding was a low-grade fever pulsing amongst us unmentioned, like a buzz or hum you get used to and cease to hear. The white noise of matrimonial sex.

On Sundays the gray stone nave of St. Luke's church, big as a warehouse, was packed with families of eight or ten sitting in the honey-colored pews. The fathers wore brown suits. In memory they appear spectrally thin, wraithlike and spent, like trees hollowed of their pulp. The wives were petite and cheerful with helmet-like haircuts. Perkiness was their main trait. But what did they say, these small women, how did they talk? Mrs. Healy, mother of fourteen ("They can afford them," my mother said, as if to excuse her paltry two. "He's a doctor."), never uttered a word, as far as I remember. Even pregnant, she was somehow wiry, as if poised for a tennis match. Maybe these women only wore a *look* of perkiness, and like their lean husbands, they were sapped of personal strength. Maybe they were simply tense.

Not everyone around us was Catholic. Mr. Kirby, a widower who was our next door neighbor, was Methodist—whatever that was. The Nugents across the street behind their cement retaining wall and double row of giant salvia, were Lutheran, more or less. The Williams family, who subscribed to the *New Yorker* and had a living room outfitted with spare Danish furniture, were Episcopalian. They referred to their minister as a priest—a plagiarism that embarrassed me for them because I liked them and their light, airy ways.

As for the Bertrams, our nearest neighbors to the west, it could only be said that Mrs. Bertram, dressed in a narrow suit with a peplum jacket and a hat made of the same heathery wool, went *somewhere* via taxi on Sunday mornings. Mr. Bertram went nowhere—on Sunday or on any other day. He was understood, during my entire girlhood, to be indoors, resting.

Weekdays, Mrs. Bertram took the bus to her job downtown. Mr. Bertram stayed home behind their birchwood Venetian blinds in an aquarium half-light, not an invalid (we never thought of him that way), but a man whose occupation it was to rest. Sometimes in the summer he ventured forth with a large wrench-like gadget to root out the masses of dandelions that gave the Bertram lawn a temporary brilliance in June.

I associated him with the Wizard of Oz. He was small and mild-looking, going bald. He gave the impression of extreme pallor except for small, very dark eyes.

It was a firm neighborhood rumor that Mr. Bertram had been a screenwriter in Hollywood. Yes, that pallor was a writer's pallor; those small dark eyes were a writer's eyes. They saw, they noted.

He allowed me to assist him in the rooting-out of his dandelions. I wanted to ask him about Hollywood—had he met Audrey Hepburn? I couldn't bring myself to manœuvre for information on such an important subject. But I did feel something serious was called for here. I introduced religion while he plunged the dandelion gadget deep into the lawn.

No, he said, he did not go to church. "But you do believe in God?" I asked, hardly daring to hope he did not. I longed for novelty.

He paused for a moment and looked up at the sky where big, spreading clouds streamed by. "God isn't the problem," he said.

Some ancient fissure split open, a fine crack in reality: so there *was* a problem. Just as I'd always felt. Beneath the family solidity, the claustrophobia of mother-father-brother-me, past the emphatic certainties of St. Luke's catechism class, there was a problem that would never go away. Mr. Bertram stood amid his dandelions, resigned as a Buddha, looking up at the sky which gave back nothing but drifting white shapes on the blue.

What alarmed me was my feeling of recognition. Of course there was a problem. It wasn't God. Life itself was a problem. Something was not right, would never be right. I'd sensed it all along, some kind of fishy vestigial quiver in the spine. It was bred in the bone, way past thought. Life, deep down, lacked the substantiality that it *seemed* to display. The physical world, full of detail and interest, was a parched topsoil that could be blown away.

This lack, this blankness akin to chronic disappointment, was everywhere, under the perkiness, lurking even within my own happiness. "What are you going to do today?" my father said when he saw me digging in the backyard on his way to work at the greenhouse.

"I'm digging to China," I said.

"Well, I'll see you at lunch," he said, "if you're still here."

I wouldn't bite. I frowned and went back to work with the bent tablespoon my mother had given me. It wasn't a game. I wanted out. I was on a desperate journey that only looked like play. I couldn't explain.

The blank disappointment, masked as weariness, played on the faces of people on the St. Clair bus. They looked out the windows, coming home from downtown, unseeing: clearly nothing interested them. What were they thinking of? The passing scene was not beautiful enough—was that it?—to catch their eye. Like the empty clouds Mr. Bertram turned to, their blank looks gave back nothing. There was an unshivered shiver in each of us, a shudder we managed to hold back.

We got off the bus at Oxford where, one spring, in the lime green house behind the catalpa tree on the corner, Mr. Lenart (whom we didn't know well) had slung a pair of tire chains over a rafter in the basement and hanged himself. Such things happened. Only the tight clutch of family life ("The family that prays together stays together.") could keep things rolling along. Step out of the tight, bright circle, and you might find yourself dragging your chains down to the basement.

The perverse insubstantiality of the material world was the problem: reality refused to be real enough. Nothing could keep you steadfastly happy. That was clear. Some people blamed God. But I sensed that Mr. Bertram was right not to take that tack. *God is not the problem.* The clouds passing in the big sky kept dissipating, changing form. That was the problem—but so what? Such worries resolved nothing, and were best left unworried—the unshivered shiver.

There was no one to blame. You could only retire, like Mr. Bertram, stay indoors behind your birchwood blinds, and contemplate the impossibility of things, allowing the Hollywood glitter of reality to fade away and become a vague local rumor.

There were other ways of coping. Mrs. Krueger, several houses down with a big garden rolling with hydrangea bushes, held as her faith a passionate belief in knowledge. She sold *World Book* encyclopedias. After trying Christian Science and a stint with the Unitarians, she had settled down as an agnostic. There seemed to be a lot of reading involved with being an agnostic, pamphlets and books, long citations on cultural anthropology in the *World Book*. It was an abstruse religion, and Mrs. Krueger seemed to belong to some ladies' auxiliary of disbelief.

But it didn't really matter what Mrs. Krueger decided about "the deity-idea," as she called God. No matter what they believed, our neighbors lived not just on Linwood Avenue; they were in St. Luke's parish too, whether they knew it or not. We claimed the territory. And we claimed them—even as we dismissed them. They were all non-Catholics, the term that disposed nicely of all spiritual otherness.

Let the Protestants go their schismatic ways; the Lutherans could splice themselves into synods any which way. Believers, non-believers, even Jews (the Kroners on
the corner) or a breed as rare as the Greek Orthodox whose church was across the
street from St. Luke's—they were all non-Catholics, just so much extraneous spiritual
matter orbiting the nethersphere.

Or maybe it was more intimate than that, and we dismissed the rest of the world
as we would our own serfs. We saw the Lutherans and Presbyterians, even those snob-
bish Episcopalians, as rude colonials, non-Catholics all, doing the best they could out
there in the bush to imitate the ways of the homeland. *We* were the homeland.

Jimmy Guiliani was a bully. He pulled my hair when he ran by me on Oxford as
we all walked home from St. Luke's, the girls like a midget army in navy jumpers and
white blouses, the boys with the greater authority of free civilians without uniforms.
They all wore pretty much the same thing anyway: corduroy pants worn smooth at the
knees and flannel shirts, usually plaid.

I wasn't the only one Jimmy picked on. He pulled Moira Murphy's hair, he
punched Tommy Hague. He struck without reason, indiscriminately, so full of violence it may have been pent-up enthusiasm released at random after the long day
leashed in school. Catholic kids were alleged, by public school kids, to be mean fighters, dirty fighters.

Jimmy Guiliani was the worst, a terror, hated and feared by Sister Julia's entire
third grade class.

So, it came as a surprise when, after many weeks of his tyranny, I managed to
land a sure kick to his groin and he collapsed in a heap and cried real tears. "You
shouldn't *do* that to a boy," he said, whimpering. He was almost primly admonishing.
"Do you know how that feels?"

It's not correct to say that it was a sure kick. I just kicked. I took no aim and had
no idea I'd hit paydirt—or why. Even when the tears started to his eyes and he doubled
over clutching himself, I didn't understand.

But I liked it when he asked if I knew how it felt. For a brief, hopeful moment I
thought he would tell me, that he would explain. Yes, tell me: how *does* it feel? And
what's *there*, anyway? It was the first time the male body imposed itself.

I felt an odd satisfaction. I'd made contact. I wasn't glad I had hurt him, I wasn't
even pleased to have taken the group's revenge on the class bully. I hadn't planned to
kick him. It all just *happened*—as most physical encounters do. I was more astonished
than he that I had succeeded in wounding him, I think. In a simple way, I wanted to
say I was sorry. But I liked being taken seriously, and could not forfeit that rare pleasure by making an apology.

For a few weeks after I kicked him, I had a crush on Jimmy Guiliani. Not because I'd hurt him. But because he had paused, looked right at me, and implored me
to see things from his point of view. *Do you know how it feels?*

I didn't know—and yet I did. As soon as he asked, I realized obscurely that I did
know how it felt. I knew what was there between his legs where he hurt. I ceased to be
ignorant at that moment. And sex began—with a blow.

The surprise of knowing what I hadn't realized I knew seemed beautifully private, but also illicit. That was a problem. I had no desire to be an outlaw. The way I
saw it, you were supposed to know what you had been *taught*. This involved being

given segments of knowledge by someone (usually a nun) designated to dole out information in measured drams, like strong medicine.

Children were clean slates others were meant to write on.

But here was evidence I was not a blank slate at all. I was scribbled all over with intuitions, premonitions, vague resonances clamoring to give their signals. I had caught Mr. Bertram's skyward look and its implicit promise: life will be tough. There was no point in blaming God—the Catholic habit. Or even more Catholic, blaming the nuns, which allowed you to blame Mother and God all in one package.

And here was Jimmy Guiliani drawing out of me this other knowledge, bred of empathy and a swift kick to his privates. *Yes, I know how it feels.*

The hierarchy we lived in, a great linked chain of religious being, seemed set to control every entrance and exit to and from the mind and heart. The buff-colored *Baltimore Catechism*, small and square, read like an owner's manual for a very complicated vehicle. There was something pleasant, lulling and rhythmic, like heavily rhymed poetry, about the sing-song Q-and-A format. Who would not give over heart, if not mind, to the brisk nannyish assurance of the Baltimore prose:

> Who made you?
> *God made me.*
>
> Why did God make you?
> *God made me to know, love and serve Him in this world, in order to*
> *be happy with Him forever in the next.*

What pleasant lines to commit to memory. And how harmless our Jesuitical discussions about what, exactly, constituted a meatless spaghetti sauce on Friday. Strict constructionists said no meat of any kind should ever, at any time, have made its way into the tomato sauce; easy liberals held with the notion that meatballs could be lurking around in the sauce, as long as you didn't eat them. My brother lobbied valiantly for the meatball *intactus* but present. My mother said nothing doing. They raged for years.

Father Flannery, who owned his own airplane and drove a sports car, had given Peter some ammunition when he'd been asked to rule on the meatball question in the confessional. My mother would hear none of it. "I don't want to know what goes on between you and your confessor," she said, taking the high road.

"A priest, Ma, a *priest*," my brother cried. "This is an ordained priest saying right there in the sanctity of the confessional that meatballs are OK."

But we were going to heaven my mother's way.

Life was like that—crazy. Full of hair-splitting, and odd rituals. We got our throats blessed on St. Blaise day in February, with the priest holding oversized beeswax candles in an X around our necks, to ward off death by choking on fishbones. There were smudged foreheads on Ash Wednesday, and home May altars with plaster statuettes of the Virgin festooned with lilacs. Advent wreaths and nightly family rosary vigils during October (Rosary Month), the entire family on their knees in the living room.

There were snatches of stories about nuns who beat kids with rulers in the coat room; the priest who had a twenty-year affair with a member of the Altar and Rosary Society; the other priest in love with an altar boy—they'd had to send him away. Not St. Luke's stories—oh no, certainly not—but stories, floating, as stories do, from inner ear to inner ear, respecting no parish boundaries. Part of the ether.

And with it all, a relentless xenophobia about other religions. "It's going to be a mixed marriage, I understand," one of my aunts murmured about a friend's daughter who was marrying an Episcopalian. So what if he called himself High Church? What did that change? He was a non-Catholic.

And now, educated out of it all, well climbed into the professions, the Catholics find each other at cocktail parties and get going. The nun stories, the first confession traumas—and a tone of rage and dismay that seems to bewilder even the tellers of these tales.

Nobody says, when asked, "I'm Catholic." It's always, "Yes, I was brought up Catholic." Anything to put it at a distance, to diminish the presence of that grabby heritage that is not racial but acts as if it were. "You never get over it, you know," a fortyish lawyer told me a while ago at a party where we found ourselves huddled by the chips and dip, as if we were at a St. Thomas mixer once again.

He seemed to feel he was speaking to someone with the same hopeless congenital condition. "It's different now, of course," he said. "But when we were growing up back there...." Ah yes, the past isn't a time. It's a place. And it's always there.

He had a very Jimmy Guiliani look to him. A chastened rascal. "I'm divorced," he said. We both smiled: there's no going to hell anymore. "Do they still have mortal sin?" he asked wistfully.

The love-hate lurch of a Catholic upbringing, like having an extra set of parents to contend with. Or an added national allegiance—not to the Vatican, as we were warned that the Baptists thought during John Kennedy's campaign for president. The allegiance was to a different realm. It was the implacable loyalty of faith, that flawless relation between self and existence which we were born into. A strange country where people prayed and believed impossible things.

The nuns who taught us, rigged up in their bold black habits with the big round wimples stiff as frisbees, walked our parish streets; they moved from convent to church in twos or threes, dipping in the side door of the huge church "for a little adoration," as they would say. The roly-poly Irish-born monsignor told us to stand straight and proud when he met us slouching along Summit toward class. And fashionable Father Flannery who, every night, took a gentle, companionable walk with the old Irish pastor, the two of them taking out white handkerchiefs, waving them for safety, as they crossed the busy avenue on the way home in the dark, swallowed in their black suits and cassocks, invisible in the gloom.

But the one I would like to summon up most and to have pass me on Oxford as I head off to St. Luke's in the early morning mist, one of those mid-May weekdays, the lilacs just starting to spill, that one I want most to materialize from "back there"—I don't know her name, where, exactly, she lived, or who she was. We never spoke, in fact. We just passed each other, she coming home from six o'clock daily Mass, I going early to school to practice the piano for an hour before class began.

She was a "parish lady," part of the anonymous population that thickened our world, people who were always there, who were solidly part of us, part of what we were, but who never emerged beyond the bounds of being parishioners to become persons.

We met every morning, just past the Healy's low brick wall. She wore a librarian's cardigan sweater. She must have been about forty-five, and I sensed she was not married. Unlike Dr. and Mrs. Harrigan who walked smartly along Summit holding hands, their bright Irish setter accompanying them as far as the church door where he waited till Mass was over, the lady in the cardigan was always alone.

I saw her coming all the way from Grand where she had to pause for the traffic. She never rushed across the street, zipping past a truck, but waited until the coast was completely clear, and passed across keeping her slow, almost floating pace. A lovely, peaceful gait, no rush to it.

When finally we were close enough to make eye contact, she looked up, straight into my face, and smiled. It was such a *complete* smile, so entire, that it startled me every time, as if I'd heard my name called out on the street of a foreign city.

She was a homely woman, plain and pale, unnoticeable. But I felt—how to put it—that she shed light. The mornings were often frail with mist, the light uncertain and tender. The smile was a brief flood of light. She loved me, I felt.

I knew what it was about. She was praying. Her hand, stuck in her cardigan pocket, held one of the crystal beads of her rosary. I knew this. I'd once seen her take it out of the left pocket and quickly replace it after she had found the handkerchief she needed.

If I had seen a nun mumbling the rosary along Summit (and that did happen), it would not have meant much to me. But here on Oxford, the side street we used as a sleepy corridor to St. Luke's, it was a different thing. The parish lady was not a nun. She was a person who prayed, who prayed alone, for no reason that I understood. But there was no question that she prayed without ceasing, as the strange scriptural line instructed.

She didn't look up to the blank clouds for a response, as Mr. Bertram did in his stoic way. Her head was bowed, quite unconsciously. And when she raised it, keeping her hand in her pocket where the clear beads were, she looked straight into the eyes of the person passing by. It was not an invasive look, but one brimming with a secret which, if only she had words, it was clear she would like to tell.

Can an Ape Tell a Joke?

Vicki Hearne

W. H. Auden wrote that poetry survives in those places where "executives would never want to tamper." Similarly, the knowledge of animals survives in places where academics would never want to tamper, even now that many of them have added their voices to the babble that presently obscures the reality of animals. It survives in the circus, eerily revealed by Mark Twain as a place where truth is guarded by scams—by what most would consider tawdry but which Huckleberry Finn embraced as "gaudy." It lives in the shabbier parts of public parks where dog obedience classes are conducted. And it lives at the racetrack, where the beauty of the horses, glowing as though each were the darling of the infinite god of detail, stands in sharp contrast to the gray faces of the gamblers.

But perhaps the least likely place one would expect to find deep knowledge about animals is in a trained-orangutan act on a Las Vegas stage—specifically, in the act performed for many years by Bobby Berosini and his five orangutans at the Stardust Hotel and Casino. I first saw Bobby Berosini's Vegas act three years ago, shortly after he received an unwelcome dose of national celebrity. Now that I've spent a week with him and his orangutans, and watched a dozen of his performances, I'm convinced that he deserves his celebrity, though not for the reasons he has come by it.

I would not ordinarily have ventured to Las Vegas to watch a trained-orangutan show, but Bobby Berosini, who immigrated to the United States from his native Czechoslovakia in 1964, is no ordinary animal trainer. I had heard he'd won numerous comedy awards for his act, and that he had probably done more with orangutans—famously difficult animals to train—than any trainer ever has. But this was not the reason for his sudden notoriety. He had been accused in 1989 of abusing his orangutans by, among others, People for the Ethical Treatment of Animals. This in itself was not unusual: these days animal trainers are regularly attacked by animal-rights activists. What was unusual in this case was that the trainer had fought back, suing PETA for defamation and invasion of privacy. And, most unusual of all, he had won his case: after a five-week trial in which Berosini brought his orangutans into court, a jury found

PETA, along with several individual activists, guilty of "reckless disregard of the truth" and awarded Berosini $3.1 million in damages. (The judgment is currently on appeal.)

Berosini did not sue for harassment, but while I was in Las Vegas his Australian-born wife, Joan, described to me the harrowing experience of receiving repeated death threats against themselves and their animals in the middle of the night; of spending six months living with armed security guards twenty-four hours a day; and of being forced to shop at a different supermarket each day, since some of the threats had detailed plans to poison the orangs' food. (Many animal-rights activists believe that wild animals are better off dead than confined in any way by humans.) Even today, the harassment continues: when Berosini recently moved his act to the Five Star Theatre in Branson, Missouri, the PETA picketers followed.

Mad as some of these tactics were, the charges against Bobby Berosini were not ones that could be summarily dismissed. PETA had circulated a videotape, made surreptitiously backstage by a Stardust dancer, that purported to document the abuse. The tape, which was broadcast on *Entertainment Tonight*, is of extremely poor quality, but it appears to show Berosini and his assistants on about a half-dozen occasions preparing the animals to go onstage. In each instance one of the orangutans—it's hard to tell, but it looks like the same orang each time—seems to act up and is then threatened, shaken, or struck by Berosini with a wand or baton of some kind.

Jeanne Roush, then PETA's director of research and investigations, and one of the losing defendants, charged that the orangs were routinely beaten into submission right before going onstage. Berosini said that, on each of the occasions videotaped, he had had to correct the orangutan backstage because a dancer was making sounds of distressed animals to rile the orangutans. Before I got to Las Vegas, it was impossible to sort out who was telling the truth, so I decided not to pay too much attention to what was being said on either side.

What I would pay attention to, I decided, was what I saw myself—and what, as an animal trainer, I know about animals. I know, for example, that the "correction" of an animal in training is an intricate and poorly understood subject. Properly applied at the right moment, a correction will cause the animal to stop aggressive behavior and perform happily and well. But a correction that expresses the trainer's anger, impatience, or fear, or that is applied when the animal is honestly confused rather than disobedient, will leave the animal unable to perform. Since no one had said that the orangs muffed their performances after the corrections we see on the tape, I can only assume that Berosini was using good judgment.

I assume this also from the uncontested fact that the animals were performing live, twice a night, six nights a week, at liberty—that is, without any physical restraint on an unguarded stage. Roger Fouts, a primatologist who testified in another performing-ape case, said that "you can get anyone to do anything if you beat them," but, in fact, this is not so. You can perhaps accomplish a fair amount by beating an animal or person who cannot escape (though you can't thereby engage the victim's higher faculties), but not if you beat an animal or person you then leave at liberty.

These thoughts occurred to me before I had had a chance to watch Berosini work, so I came to Las Vegas prepared to doubt PETA's charges. And after spending a week with Berosini, watching twelve performances and joining him backstage before several of them, I saw nothing to make me think he was a cruel or phony trainer—no thumps, no fists. (Could Berosini have acted differently while I was around? Possibly, but any trainer who behaves differently in public than in private will soon lose the respect of his animals.)

What I did see, there amid the Vegas glitz and against the ugly backdrop of this furious animal-rights battle, was mastery, and even a kind of miracle. Berosini and his orangs are, to be sure, masters of much that is gaudy—his act is a half hour of animal slapstick and off-color skits sandwiched between the usual Vegas dancing girls and boys; the orangs wear shorts and funny hats and make obscene gestures to the audience. But Bobby Berosini and his orangs are masters of something else as well—of the miracle that was unavailable to Job, who, as the voice in the whirlwind thunderously reminded him, could not engage the wild animals in any fruitful, cooperative enterprise. Bobby Berosini can.

As well as being a gifted trainer, Berosini is a gifted comedian, though by his reckoning he is not the only comedian on the Stardust stage. When I asked him, between shows in the Stardust's coffee shop, what motivates his orangs to work, he said to me, passionately, "We are comedians. *We* are comedians. Do you understand me?"

Comedians? Orangutans? This is not a reasonable remark, from the point of view of either popular or institutionally sanctioned knowledge about animals. If, as many human-rights activists and academics believe, animals are capable of feeling and suffering but not of elaborate intentions and creative thought, then Berosini's orangs *must* be beaten into submission, since food rewards would not be powerful enough to motivate their complex actions. Besides, animals could not possibly know the mood or muse of comedy. They lack the conceptual apparatus to handle the mischievous shifts in meaning required for jokes.

When Berosini told me that his orangutans are comedians, I nodded my head vigorously; the enchantment of the act had not worn off. But what does it mean to say of an animal that he or she is a comedian? This question leads back onstage, to the act itself, and to the sorts of questions Berosini and his orangs toss about, invert, capsize, and rescue, only to turn them on their head, time and time again.

The running theme of the act is "How I Train Them." Berosini keeps saying to the audience, "People ask me how I get them to do things," or "People ask me how I train them," and then he supplies different "answers." At one point the answer is, "You have to show them who is boss." He brings Rusty out to show him who is boss, and Rusty not only refuses to jump onto the stool provided for the purpose but tricks his trainer into doing so by pretending incomprehension until Berosini finally demonstrates, jumping onto the stool himself. Once Berosini has dutifully jumped, Rusty invites the audience to applaud.

Berosini goes on to mock much scientific and popular wisdom about operant conditioning—training that relies more on the carrot than on the stick—by demonstrating how he doesn't need to train the orangutans at all because "I have magic orang cookies." A fast and lively slapstick round results from his failed attempts to get Bo to eat a cookie; the cookie is juggled, spit into the audience, hidden, fed to Berosini, but never eaten by the orangutan.

Then there is yet another variation on the theme: "People ask me how I train them. The truth is, I do not have to train them, because I just mesmerize them." Bo is then asked to come forward and be a hypnotic subject. There is much crooning of "You are getting very, very sleepy." Bo drops her shoulders, stands more and more still, and—wonder of wonders—closes her eyes. Pleased with the trance, the "trainer" whispers, "Are you asleep?" All of a sudden Bo grins outrageously, nods her head vigorously, and then immediately droops back into her "mesmerized" posture. The joke, again, is on Berosini—or, rather, on the Berosini character, who, of course, stands for the audience and for our overblown ideas about our superior intelligence and ability to control the world.

As Berosini explains when he is offstage, the way he trains is not "traditional," in that he does not teach his animals "tricks" but rather teaches them through the flow of their intelligence interacting with his. He explains that whereas a suggestion for a move or gesture or gag often originates with him, it is just as likely to come from the orangutan; the trainer must be as adept at picking up cues from the animals as they are at picking up cues from him. And orangutans demand this kind of handling. "I do not train them to do what I know how to do," he told me, "because you just cannot do that. It doesn't work!" According to Berosini, orangutans are the hardest of all the apes to teach a trick to because they are so self-contained, so mentally poised. The same idea is expressed in scholarly literature on orangs with reference to their marked lack of social interaction in the wild. Unlike most other apes, they are not dependent on social support and approval, which vastly complicates the training relationship. An orangutan is irredeemably his or her own person—"the most poetic of the apes," as primate researcher Lyn Miles once told me.

Miles had in mind the difference between orangutans and chimps. Chimps are much admired for their use of tools and their problem-solving relationship with things as they find them. A chimp looks inferential, ingenious, and ever so active while taking the various IQ tests that science presents him with—a hexagonal peg, say, and several holes of different shapes, only one of them hexagonal. Here, the chimp shows his tremendous initiative right away, holding the peg this way and that, trying out this, that, and the other hole; this, that, and the other angle. He *experiments*, he is filled with the inventor's work ethic; he tries, essays, tests, probes, he is full of the integrity of logic, or if not logic then at least something very American: he is so enterprising, so resourceful.

Give your orangutan the hexagonal peg and the several different holes, hide behind the two-way mirror, and watch how he engages the problem. And watch and watch and watch—because he will not engage the problem. He uses the peg to scratch his back, has a look-see at his right wrist, makes a halfhearted and soon abandoned attempt to use his fur for a macramé project, stares dreamily out the window if there is one and at nothing in particular if there is not, and the sun begins to set. (The sun will also set if you are observing a chimp, but the chimp is a lot busier, so you are less likely to mark the moment in your notes. An orangutan observer has plenty of time to be a student of the varieties of sunset.) You watch, and the orang dreams, and your notes perhaps consist of nothing more than memoranda on the behavior of the clock, when casually, and as if thinking of something else, the orangutan slips the hexagonal peg into the hexagonal hole. And continues staring off dreamily.

Professor Miles says that this sort of behavior contradicts the traditional finding that orangs are dumber than chimps. It is rather, she says, that chimps are problem-oriented whereas orangs are insight-oriented, the dreamers and visionaries of the world of the great apes. Which is all well and good, but how do you entertain five hundred people for half an hour twice a night, every night, six nights a week, for seven years, with animals whose forte is meditation, animals who do not do tricks? It's like trying to entertain a Las Vegas audience with five performing poets.

In the wild, too, orangs have not provided ethologists with the glamorous behaviors that, say, Jane Goodall's chimps have given her. I found no reports of orangs doing anything like the equivalent of fashioning special sticks to fish for termites, for instance. Orang observers instead report such exciting phenomena as the "fruit stare," which some people say is a function of the difficulty orangutans have foraging for food in the wild. Orangutans need to develop the fruit stare because trees can be coy about when, where, and how much they fruit, and the fruit is often hidden in the canopy of leaves. The fruit stare is an expression of reverie, but it is a reverie directed outward rather than inward—"like thinking with your eyes," naturalist Sy Montgomery has said. "That's why they are so spaced out."

But all this only explains why there are not many orangutan acts in the world and not how Bobby Berosini manages to put on an orangutan act night after night.

What Berosini says, again and again, is, "We are comedians. Do you understand me? Do you realize what I am telling you? We are comedians, my orangs and I." His voice is urgent now, but not frantic the way it is when PETA and the charges of abuse and the harassment are the topic. The act, he explains, is a collaboration: "Rusty will have an idea for a gag, and maybe I don't like his idea, but often I do, so I leave my gag aside and accept his idea, or maybe I sometimes insist that we still do it the other way. Or maybe Tiga insists that the old way was funnier, and then I have to laugh at myself and accept what she says. She has as many ideas as I do. She is an old campaigner, Tiga, she knows what she is doing."

I find the act screamingly funny, not only because the timing is so good but because the content is so intelligent, even if the orang humor can be a bit coarse. There are, for instance, the many sardonic jokes about "monkeys" and "monkey business." These are jokes about the audience, about humanity's ignorance about its fellow primates, because, of course, orangs are not monkeys—they are, along with chimps, gorillas, and humans, great apes. But this is the sort of detail people consistently get wrong. One witness in another performing-ape controversy told me a story about a zookeeper and an animal he referred to as "some sort of monkey." I pressed to discover what sort, and he said, "It doesn't matter. They're all monkeys, aren't they?"

Well, no, they are not, and it does matter, especially when you are claiming to speak with authority about the animals in question. I've listened to anthropologist Daniel Povinelli hold forth passionately about the importance of understanding the differences not only between monkeys and apes but also between different species of

ape and different species of monkey. He says that there are pronounced morphological differences between monkeys and apes, and also pronounced psychological differences: "The apes are doing something different." For Povinelli, it is almost as radical
a mistake to confuse monkeys with apes as it would be to confuse elephants with pigs
or wolves with golden retrievers. "Evolution would be impossible without difference,"
Povinelli points out. "There can hardly be anything more fundamental than recognizing, studying, and appreciating the enormous differences, especially the psychological
differences, among different animals."

Povinelli and Berosini are very different people, with very different relationships
to animals, but they have in common a passionate belief that the details about an animal, whether psychological or morphological, are not merely pedantic decorations
but should compel our respect. Berosini is a performer and Povinelli is a scientist, so
they would probably disagree about what counts as a violation of this code, but they
meet in insisting that there is such a code and that it matters. Indeed, when I told
Povinelli that in his act Berosini calls his animals "monkeys" and makes no attempt to
correct himself, he was somewhat shocked and not entirely reassured by my explanation of the dark comic irony of the usage.

Berosini, however, is nothing if not canny; it means something when he monkeys around. When Bo nods her head vigorously or applauds his "wit" when he makes
a "monkey" joke, there is a sophisticated edge here, as if a physicist were joking
around by blurring the difference between an atom and a molecule.

You have to know a great deal more than the bulk of the audience knows, or
cares to know, about animals and the politics of animals in order to hear the sardonic
implications in the reiteration of the "just monkeys" bit. These darker jibes ride on the
back of traditional slapstick, but the jokes are, as perhaps true slapstick always is, constructed both from and about our intellectual ineptitude and hubris; every time one of
the orangs makes a "monkey" out of Berosini, the joke is on us. Our brutishness and
our intellectual incompetence are one.

But the act is comedy, true comedy, and not merely a collection of dark and sardonic jokes. The orangs and the audience and humanity itself, as represented by the
character Berosini portrays, are redeemed in the end, in part by the sheer quicksilver
beauty of the timing. When the audience laughs, at times with true joy, a joy free of
malice, it is, after all, humanity that is being celebrated, since the ability to laugh
without malice at one's own failings—and to see in those failings one's connection
with everyone else in the room, a connection made through laughter—is no mean ethical feat.

If Berosini's act can be said to have one overriding theme, it is training—
obedience—itself. "Obedience" comes from an old French word that means "to hear"
or "to heed," "to pay attention to." The great trainers of every kind of animal, from
parakeet to dog to elephant, have said for millennia that you cannot get an animal to
heed you unless you heed the animal; obedience in this sense is a symmetrical relationship. In a given instance it may start with the human, who perhaps says to the dog,
"Joe, sit!" Soon, however, the dog will take the command and turn it, use it to respond,
to say something back. The dog might, for example, take to sitting in a sprightly fashion when one gets out a dumbbell, as if to say: "Yes, that's it, let's go!" It is at this

moment that true training with any species, including humans, either begins or fails. If the human obeys, hears, heeds, responds to what the animal is now saying, then training begins. If the human "drops" the animal at this point, not realizing that the task has only begun, then the dog or orangutan will disobey.

Animals, like people, are motivated in many ways. Berosini's orangs are motivated offstage in the same way they appear to be motivated onstage: when they make a gesture, they get a response. Their trainer obeys them, unless they are committing mayhem. The intelligent responsiveness of animals is for us one of the most deeply attractive things about them, not only because we are a lonesome and threatened tribe but because intelligent responsiveness is a central, abiding good. The intelligent responsiveness of trainers, which some of them call respect, is what makes trainers attractive to animals, and may be the whole of the secret of "having a way with animals."

In the comic mismatch between the Berosini character's ideas about the orangs and the nature of the orangs themselves as they triumph continually over the would-be lordly "trainer," our fond hopes are mocked, but not cruelly. The world, which is to say the human project, is in trouble, but within the tiny world of Berosini's act a way is found, even if it is a stumbling, awkward way, to true responsiveness between ourselves and animals. Even the audience gets a response, as when Rusty invites us to applaud Berosini or when Tiga gives an audience member one of her "magic orang cookies," and does so gently, though without a hint of subservience.

Berosini also gets laughs by mocking the character of the orangs—Tiga's onstage character has a drinking problem and loose morals—but the "How I Train Them" series of gags is the most intellectually satisfying part of the act. Interestingly, Bo's simulation of the hypnotic trance is a play on the sort of spacy consciousness ethologists have observed in orangutans. There is the same dreaminess, the trance that frames the unpredictable moment of alert intelligence. Bo's eyes are closed, but otherwise she seems to be imitating the fruit stare in much the same way that a dressage horse—one so highly educated that we say he or she "dances"—imitates, with some variations, the postures and gestures of a horse in "nature."

The radical claim being made here is that the animals are "referring to," or at least imitating, these gestures deliberately, with some sense—if not precisely our sense—of the meaning of what they are doing. Berosini says that Bo is in on the joke, or at least on *some* joke, and that it is her interest and pleasure in such monkeying around that make it possible for him to work with her as he does. This is speculative, of course, but it could be argued that Berosini's is a more parsimonious explanation than an explanation based on conditioning would be. Indeed, it's questionable whether any model of conditioning, however elaborate, can explain behavior this complex, particularly since every performance the act changes, with both Berosini and the orangs offering improvisations. Talk of conditioned responses may be helpful in understanding part of a trained animal's development (or, for that matter, a dancer's or a poet's or an actor's or a philosopher's), but animal performance at this level makes more sense when viewed as rudimentary expressions of at least one primeval artistic impulse—the impulse to play with meaning.

Bo's trance-breaking grin is wonderfully timed, a case of high slapstick, if there can be such a thing; it is also, for me at least, an eerie instant of revelation in which I see something fairly exact in Berosini's claim that his orangs are comedians. But how might such an animal joke come about? Let's say that you are teaching the animal to be "mesmerized," and the animal spontaneously adds the mischievous nodding grin. This is a joke about who's in control, though not necessarily a joke about hypnosis. You accept the move and ask for it on purpose next time, and it becomes part of the routine. The animal offers it spontaneously at first, and then continues with it, perhaps for the same reason we repeat a phrase or a joke—because it felt so delicious the first time.

Berosini's act gives the orangs a point of view, one that I find credible as an animal point of view, and it gives their intelligence pride of place, as do other clever disobedience acts in the tradition—an ancient tradition going back to the Greeks, in which the *eiron*, or apparently lowly character, triumphs over the apparently noble character through wit, awareness, quickness of perception. (The word *eiron* gives us our word "irony.") In circus and movie tradition, the most familiar form of such comedy is the disobedient-dog act, in which the trainer character attempts to induce the dogs to display loyalty, nobility, and willing service; instead, they trip the trainer, disgrace the legacy of Rin Tin Tin by stealing a purse from an audience member, "bite" the trainer, and so on.

It is not Lassie and Rin Tin Tin themselves who are mocked by the disobedient-dog act but rather our own self-serving ideas of the selflessness of dogs, such as the pious notion that dogs "want to please" and work "for love of the handler." Berosini's orangs work with this sort of material wonderfully, displaying their intelligence against the backdrop of our ideas of their debasement.

If Berosini's comedy is somewhat dark and sharp-edged when you take a close look at it, that may be in part because of the tradition of comedy he inherits as a Czech, a tradition that has had to learn, over and over again, how to ensure the survival of intelligence in forms that escape the more violent scrutiny of various regimes. At any rate, the act I saw is one kind of shield for the mind, one kind of comic courage by means of which sanity survives amid social and political darkness.

One of Berosini's most famous monkey jokes occurred in court. During my stay in Las Vegas shortly after the 1990 trial, I heard it at least two dozen times. At one point during Berosini's testimony, PETA's lawyer asked him to tell the audience how he taught Bo to give the finger. He replied, "I'll give you a demonstration of how to give the finger if you want." This is just the way his orangs perform in his act, ragging him, continually foiling him with impudence, back talk, irreverence, impiety. And they give him the finger. In one way or another, most animals do give their trainers the finger—a great deal of animal humor is coarse, to put it mildly. I have long suspected that the real reason it was for so long heresy, an excommunicable offense, to say that animals have souls is that if you say they have souls, then their jokes and comments have meaning, and no bureaucratic or ecclesiastical or philanthropic dignity can survive animal vaudeville.

Joan Berosini told me that one juror, who asked to remain anonymous, said after the case was over, "It would be abuse to take the orangs away from Bobby." Is there anything to this, anything that can be understood without elevating Berosini to Patron

Saint of Apes—a position that would destroy his comic art and that is, in any case, already held by Jane Goodall? Or, to turn the question around, what is the source of the improbable idea that the act's flow and liveliness and energy could possibly be achieved by beatings?

I do not think that the orangs mean their antics the way the audience interprets them. But I do think they mean *something* by them, and that they are motivated to stay onstage, rather than run loose in the audience, not by terror—which is a poor motivator—but by an interest in what they are doing.

So what *do* they mean, what are they doing? I am convinced that some animals—quite a few Airedales, for example, and also Border collies—are interested, and take pleasure, in something like the grammar of gesture itself, much as a dancer does. A bird dog in the field intends to retrieve the bird; the same dog cantering gaily after a dumbbell in an obedience ring "means" only that movement—not the retrieving of a bird, but the glorious gestures of retrieving. A Lippizaner means not to display himself before mares (which is what his movements would mean in "nature") but to call attention to the grandeur and intricacy of the display. These gestures are all metaphors, second inheritances of nature, in the same way poetry is a second inheritance of language. To call any of this—or poetry or dance, for that matter—"play," as some are wont to do, misses the point; it is work that is as serious as play, to borrow a phrase from the poet John Hollander. Such work is the highest use and pleasure of the mind, and orangutans plainly do have minds. The mind may remain satisfied in the wild, where the primitive problems of survival overwhelm other impulses, but if the other great apes are as close to us psychologically as some people claim and have minds, then it is good for those minds to develop.

And yet training in and of itself, apart from questions of abuse, makes people uneasy. In medieval times ecclesiasts believed that trained animals had devils in them—that dancing dogs were dancing satanically. In our time the idea of the "unnatural" has replaced the idea of the demonic, and for some it does not matter whether or not animals are abused, since keeping and training them is itself "unnatural" or "ethologically inappropriate," as though it were unnatural to develop the mind. These days the contemporary horror of the "unnatural" infects visions of life with domestic animals as well, but the possibility of the hearth—by which I mean a place where the human and animal may sit side by side—is much more likely to be denied when wild animals are in question.

Certainly you cannot have the same relationship with a wolf as with a dog, yet it does not follow from this that there can be *no* relationship. Today, at a time when the habitats of wild animals are rapidly disappearing, the terms of this relationship need to be reinvented, not abjured. We need to learn what we can from Berosini and other trainers—but particularly the wild-animal trainers—about how this might be done. A dog and her trainer, or a horse and his trainer, do not have to "meet each other halfway," because they already share the same social space. An orangutan and his trainer, however, must travel some conceptual distance to meet each other and work together. That this is possible, what it means that it is possible, what implications it has for the possibilities of mutual respect between wild animals and humans—this strikes me as a matter of urgent importance.

That is, I believe not only that the training of wild animals is acceptable but that the knowledge trainers have, which has been eschewed by science and philosophy and the church for millennia, may contain clues to imaginative and enlightened ways we might escape our age's violence and sentimentality toward the nonhuman world, and thereby genuinely take up the burden of our responsibility toward animals. In the Book of Job, the voice in the whirlwind points out that the wild goat and the unicorn and the ostrich and the warhorse are beyond Job. But the orangutan is not beyond Bobby Berosini, and it behooves us to understand why, to know that there is something to understand, and that the prurient contemplation of abuse, so popular in a self-servingly sentimental climate, will not open understanding here. Furthermore, the mongering of irresponsible images of abuse only obscures our views of the real cruelties that do exist.

James Thurber, who defended the intelligence of animals and animal wit as vigorously as anyone ever has, once wrote this about human wit: "The perfect tribute to perfection in comedy is not immediate laughter, but a curious and instantaneous tendency of the eyes to fill." This, I keep thinking, and not weepy displays of ignorant outrage and pity, is the tribute owed to Berosini's orangs. But be careful your vision does not mist too much. Bo and Rusty and Tiga and Niki and Benny are quite clear-eyed. Trainers speak often of how uncannily good animals are at "reading" people, and of training as a humbling activity. That's because when you train an animal you teach yourself and the animal a "language" by means of which the animal can tell you more than you may have wanted to know about what he or she sees in looking at you. If there is a moral to the act that the orangs are in on, it is this: be sure that when Tiga looks into your eyes she finds a clarity and amused intelligence fit to answer her own, lest she turn from you, leaving you in the foolish darkness yet again.

Fraternity

Garrett Hongo

It was high school in Gardena. I was in classes mostly with Japanese American kids—*kotonks*, Mainland Japanese, their ethnic pet name originated, during the war, with derisive Hawaiian GIs who thought of the sound of a coconut being hit with a hammer. Sansei *kotonks* were sons and daughters of the Nisei *kotonks* who had been sent off to the concentration camps during World War II. School was tepid, boring. We wanted cars, we wanted clothes, we wanted everything whites and blacks wanted to know about sex but were afraid to tell us. We "bee-essed" with the black kids in the school parking lot full of coastal fog before classes. We beat the white kids in math, in science, in typing. We ran track and elected cheerleaders. We *ruled*, we said. We were dumb, teeming with attitude and prejudice.

Bored, I took a creative writing class with an "academically mixed" bunch of students. There were Chicanos, whites, a black woman, and a troika of Japanese women who sat together on the other side of the room from me. They said nothing—*ever*—and wrote naturalistically correct *haiku*. Suddenly among boisterous non-Japanese, I enjoyed the gabbing, the bright foam of free talk that the teacher encouraged. An aging man in baggy pants that he wore with suspenders, he announced he was retiring at the end of the year and that he wanted no trouble, that he was going to read "Eee-bee White" during our hour of class every day, that we were welcome to read whatever we wanted so long as we gave him a list ahead of time, and that we could talk as much as we wanted so long as we left him alone. We could read, we could write, we could jive each other all class long. It was freedom. And I took advantage.

I sat next to a Chicano my age named Pacheco and behind a white girl a class younger than me named Regina. Behind us was a curly-headed white guy who played saxophone in the marching band. He'd been in academic classes with me, the only Caucasian among Japanese, a Korean, and a few Chinese. He was a joker, and I liked him, but usually stayed away—we didn't fraternize much across the races, though our school was supposed to be an experiment in integration.

Gardena H.S. wasn't so much a mix or blend as a mosaic. Along with a few whites and blacks, Japanese were in the tough, college-prep, "advanced placement" scholastic track. Most whites and blacks were in the regular curriculum of shop, business skills, and a minimum of academic courses. The "dumb Japs" were in there with them. And the Chicanos filled up what were called the *remedial* classes, all taught imperiously only in English, with no provision for language acquisition. We were a student body of about three thousand, and we walked edgily around each other, swaggering when we could, sliding the steel taps on our big black shoes along the concrete outdoor walkways when we wanted to attract a little attention, making a jest of our strut, a music in the rhythm of our walking. Blacks were bused in from Compton; the whites, Japanese, and Chicanos came from around the town. Girls seemed to me an ethnic group of their own too, giggling and forming social clubs, sponsoring dances, teaching some of us the steps.

Crazes of dress moved through our populations—for Chicanos: woolen Pendletons over thin undershirts and a crucifix; big low-top oxfords; khaki work trousers, starched and pressed; for the *bloods:* rayon and satin shirts in metallic "fly-ass" colors; pegged gabardine slacks; cheap moccasin-toed shoes from downtown shops in L.A.; and for us *Buddhas:* high-collar Kensingtons of pastel cloths, Aī tapered "Racer" slacks, and the same moccasin shoes as the bloods, who were our brothers. It was crazy. And *inviolable.* Dress and social behavior were a code one did not break for fear of ostracism and reprisal. Bad dressers were ridiculed. Offending speakers were beaten, tripped walking into the john, and set upon by gangs. They *wailed* on you if you fucked up. A girl was nothing except pride, an ornament of some guy's crude power and expertise in negotiating the intricacies of this inner-city semiotic of cultural display and hidden violence. I did not know girls.

I talked to Regina, saying "white girl" one time. She told me not to call her that, that she was *Portuguese* if anything, that I better *know* that white people were *always* something too. From vague memories of Hawai'i, I reached for the few words in *Portuguese* that I knew. I asked her about the sweet bread her mother baked, about heavy donuts fried in oil and rolled in sugar. I said *bon dea* for "good day" to her. I read the books she talked about—Steinbeck, Kesey, Salinger, and Baldwin. Her mother brought paperbacks home from the salon she worked in, putting up other women's hair—*rich* women's. We made up our reading list from books her mother knew. I wanted desperately to impress her, so I began to write poetry too, imitating some melancholy rock and country-and-western lyrics. She invited me to her house after school. It was on the way, so I walked her home. It became a practice.

Her father was a big, diabetic man from Texas. With his shirt off, he showed me how he shot himself with insulin, poking the needle under the hairy red skin on his stomach, working it over the bulge of fat around his belly. He laughed a lot and shared his beer. There were other guys over too—white guys from the football team, a Filipino, and one other Japanese guy who played left tackle. They were tough, raucous, and talked easily, excitedly. I stood alone in the front yard one day, holding a soft drink in my hand, the barbecue party going on around me. Regina and her mother were baking bread inside. No one knew exactly what was going on, and I was still trying to pretend all was casual.

I took photographs of her. We had a picnic on the coast by the lighthouse near Marineland, on the bluffs over the Pacific. It was foggy, mist upon us and the tall, droopy grasses in the field we walked through, but we made do. She wrapped herself in the blanket she'd brought for us to sit on. We were in the tall grasses of the headlands far from the coast road. She posed. I changed lenses, dropping film canisters, other things. She waved to me, unbuttoning the blouse she was wearing, her body full of a fragrance. The warm, yeasty scent of her skin smelled like bread under bronze silk.

We couldn't be seen together—not at the private, car-club-sponsored Japanese dances out in the Crenshaw District, not at the whites-dominated dances after school in the high school gym. Whites did not see Buddhas, and Buddhas did not see bloods. We were to stay with our own—*that* was the code—though we mixed some in the lunch line, in a few classes, on the football field, and in gym. We segregated ourselves.

Regina and I went to the Chicano dances in El Monte. Pacheco introduced us to them. Regina, tanned Portuguese, passed for Chicana, so long as she kept her mouth shut and her lashes long. Pacheco showed her what skirts to wear, his quick hands fluttering through the crinolines and taffetas in her closet at home. He advised me to grow a mustache and let my black hair go long in the back, to slick it down with pomade and to fluff it up in front, then seal it all in hair spray. I bought brown Pendletons and blue navy-surplus bell-bottoms. I bought hard, steel-toed shoes. We learned trots and tangos. We learned *cuecas* and polkas. We *passed, ese,* and had a good time for a couple of months.

One day, Regina got hurt. She was stopped by one of the football players at the beach. She was stepping onto a bus when he came up behind her and grabbed her arm. She tried to twist away, and the arm snapped. She crumpled. Everyone ran. She rode in a friend's car to the hospital that day and had the arm set. She didn't call me.

I heard about it after school the next day, crossing the street against the light. It was summer, and I was taking classes while Regina spent her days at the beach. I'd see her weekdays, stopping at her house on the way home. I was going to her when, just outside the gates of our school, a guy I knew taunted me with the news. He was Japanese, and it was strange to hear him say anything about Regina. I hadn't realized anyone from my crowd knew about us.

I wanted to run the rest of the way to her house. I crossed over a rise of bare earth, then down to a bedded railway—a strip line so that scrap steel and aluminum could be shipped from the switching stations and railyards downtown to steel and aeronautical factories near our school. Brown hummocks rose above eye level and masked the track of crossties, steel rails, and the long bed of gravel. I was set upon there by a troop of Japanese boys. A crowd of them encircled me, taunting, then a single gangly fellow I recognized from gym class executed most of the blows. They beat me, grinding my face in the gravel, shouting epithets like *inu* ("dog"), *cow-fucker,* and *paddy-lover.*

I've seen hand-sized reef fish, in a ritual of spawning, leave their singular lairs, gathering in smallish, excitable schools—a critical mass—and, electrified by their circling assembly, suddenly burst the cluster apart with sequences of soloing, males alternating, pouncing above the finning group, clouding the crystalline waters above the circle with a roll of milt.

All spring and summer, I'd been immune, unaware of the enmity of the crowd. I hadn't realized that, in society, humiliation is a force more powerful than love. Love does not exist in society, but only between two, or among a family. A kid from Hawai'i, I'd undergone no real initiation in shame or social victimization yet and maintained an arrogant season out of bounds, imagining I was exempt. It was humiliating to have been sent to Camp. The Japanese American community understood their public disgrace and lived modestly, with deep prohibitions. I was acting outside of this history. I could cross boundaries, I thought. But I was not yet initiated into the knowledge that we Japanese were *not* like anyone else, that we lived in a community of violent shame. I paid for my naïveté with a bashing I still feel today, with cuts that healed with scars I can still run my fingers along. I can still taste the blood, remember the split skin under the mustache on my upper lip, and feel the depth of an anger that must have been *historical, tribal,* arising from fears of dissolution and diaspora.

Separated societies police their own separations. I was hated one day, and with an intensity I could not have foreseen. I was lifted by my clothes, the hands of my schoolmates at the nape of my shirt collar and the back of the waistband of my trousers, and I was hurled against the scrawny trunk of a little jacaranda tree and beaten there, fists cracking against my arms as I tried to cover my face, thumping along my sides and back, booted feet flailing at my legs. I squirmed, crawled, cried out. And I wept. Out of fear and humiliation and a psychic wounding I understand only now. I was *hated.* I was high and needed lowering. My acts were canceled. Regina was canceled. Both by our own peoples, enacting parallel vengeances of their own, taking our bodies from us.

Our trystings were over, and, later that summer, Regina simply moved away. Her father was retiring, she said, and had found a nice trailer park up by Morro Bay. She wouldn't see me before she left. I had to surprise her at a Laundromat one Saturday. She gave me a paperback book. She laughed, made light of everything, but there was a complete *fear* of me that I felt from her, deeply, one I had not felt before—at least, it had never registered. *Race.* It is an exclusion, a punishment, imposed by the group. I've felt it often since. It is a fear of *fraternity.* A fraternity that is forbidden. I wept, but let her go.

Where Worlds Collide

Pico Iyer

They come out, blinking, into the bleached, forgetful sunshine, in Dodgers caps and Rodeo Drive T-shirts, with the maps their cousins have drawn for them and the images they've brought over from *Cops* and *Terminator 2;* they come out, dazed, disoriented, heads still partly in the clouds, bodies still several time zones—or centuries— away, and they step into the Promised Land.

In front of them is a Van Stop, a Bus Stop, a Courtesy Tram Stop, and a Shuttle Bus Stop (the shuttles themselves tracing circuits A, B, and C). At the Shuttle Bus Stop, they see the All American Shuttle, the Apollo Shuttle, Celebrity Airport Livery, the Great American Stageline, the Movie Shuttle, the Transport, Ride-4-You, and forty-two other magic buses waiting to whisk them everywhere from Bakersfield to Disneyland. They see Koreans piling into the Taeguk Airport Shuttle and the Seoul Shuttle, which will take them to Koreatown without their ever feeling they've left home; they see newcomers from the Middle East disappearing under the Arabic script of the Sahara Shuttle. They see fast-talking, finger-snapping, palm-slapping jive artists straight from their TV screens shouting incomprehensible slogans about deals, destinations, and drugs. Over there is a block-long white limo, a Lincoln Continental, and, over there, a black Chevy Blazer with Mexican stickers all over its windows, being towed. They have arrived in the Land of Opportunity, and the opportunities are swirling dizzily, promiscuously, around them.

They have already braved the ranks of Asian officials, the criminal-looking security men in jackets that say "Elsinore Airport Services," the men shaking tins that say "Helping America's Hopeless." They have already seen the tilting mugs that say "California: a new slant on life" and the portable fruit machines in the gift shop. They have already, perhaps, visited the rest room where someone has written, "Yes on Proposition 187. Mexicans go home," the snack bar where a slice of pizza costs $3.19 (18 quetzals, they think in horror, or 35,000 dong), and the sign that urges them to try the Cockatoo Inn Grand Hotel. The latest arrivals at Los Angeles International Airport are ready now to claim their new lives.

Above them in the terminal, voices are repeating, over and over, in Japanese, Spanish, and unintelligible English, "Maintain visual contact with your personal property at all times." Out on the sidewalk, a man's voice and a woman's voice are alternating an unending refrain: "The white zone is for loading and unloading of passengers only. No parking." There are "Do Not Cross" yellow lines cordoning off parts of the sidewalk and "Wells Fargo Alarm Services" stickers on the windows; there are "Aviation Safeguard" signs on the baggage carts and "Beware of Solicitors" signs on the columns; there are even special phones "To Report Trouble." More male and female voices are intoning, continuously, "Do not leave your car unattended" and "Unattended cars are subject to immediate tow-away." There are no military planes on the tarmac here, the newcomers notice, no khaki soldiers in fatigues, no instructions not to take photographs, as at home; but there are civilian restrictions every bit as strict as in many a police state.

"This Terminal Is in a Medfly Quarantine Area," says the sign between the terminals. "Stop the Spread of Medfly!" If, by chance, the new Americans have to enter a parking lot on their way out, they will be faced with "Cars left over 30 days may be impounded at Owner's Expense" and "Do not enter without a ticket." It will cost them $16 if they lose their parking ticket, they read, and $56 if they park in the wrong zone. Around them is an unending cacophony of antitheft devices, sirens, beepers, and car-door openers; lights are flashing everywhere, and the man who fines them $16 for losing their parking ticket has the tribal scars of Tigre across his forehead.

The blue skies and palm trees they saw on TV are scarcely visible from here: just an undifferentiated smoggy haze, billboards advertising Nissan and Panasonic and Canon, and beyond those an endlessly receding mess of gray streets. Overhead, they can see the all-too-familiar signs of Hilton and Hyatt and Holiday Inn; in the distance, a sea of tract houses, mini-malls, and high-rises. The City of Angels awaits them.

It is a commonplace nowadays to say that cities look more and more like airports, cross-cultural spaces that are a gathering of tribes and races and variegated tongues; and it has always been true that airports are in many ways like miniature cities, whole, self-sufficient communities, with their own chapels and museums and gymnasiums. Not only have airports colored our speech (teaching us about being upgraded, bumped, and put on standby, coaching us in the ways of fly-by-night operations, holding patterns, and the Mile High Club); they have also taught us their own rules, their own codes, their own customs. We eat and sleep and shower in airports; we pray and weep and kiss there. Some people stay for days at a time in these perfectly convenient, hermetically sealed, climate-controlled duty-free zones, which offer a kind of caesura from the obligations of daily life.

Airports are also, of course, the new epicenters and paradigms of our dawning post-national age—not just the bus terminals of the global village but the prototypes, in some sense, for our polyglot, multicolored, user-friendly future. And in their very universality—like the mall, the motel, or the McDonald's outlet—they advance the notion of a future in which all the world's a multiculture. If you believe that more and more of the world is a kind of mongrel hybrid in which many cities (Sydney, Toronto, Singapore) are simply suburbs of a single universal order, then Los Angeles's LAX,

London's Heathrow, and Hong Kong's Kai Tak are merely stages on some great global Circle Line, shuttling variations on a common global theme. Mass travel has made L.A. contiguous to Seoul and adjacent to São Paulo, and has made all of them now feel a little like bedroom communities for Tokyo.

And as with most social trends, especially the ones involving tomorrow, what is true of the world is doubly true of America, and what is doubly true of America is quadruply true of Los Angeles. L.A., legendarily, has more Thais than any city but Bangkok, more Koreans than any city but Seoul, more El Salvadorans than any city outside of San Salvador, more Druze than anywhere but Beirut; it is, at the very least, the easternmost outpost of Asia and the northernmost province of Mexico. When I stopped at a Traveler's Aid desk at LAX recently, I was told I could request help in Khamu, Mien, Tigrinya, Tajiki, Pashto, Dari, Pangasinan, Pampangan, Waray-Waray, Bambara, Twi, and Bicolano (as well, of course, as French, German, and eleven languages from India). LAX is as clear an image as exists today of the world we are about to enter, and of the world that's entering us.

For me, though, LAX has always had a more personal resonance: it was in LAX that I arrived myself as a new immigrant, in 1966; and from the time I was in the fourth grade, it was to LAX that I would go three times a year, as an "unaccompanied minor," to fly to school in London—and to LAX that I returned three times a year for my holidays. Sometimes it seems as if I have spent half my life in LAX. For me, it is the site of my liberation (from school, from the Old World, from home) and the place where I came to design my own new future.

Often when I have set off from L.A. to some distant place—Havana, say, or Hanoi, or Pyongyang—I have felt that the multicultural drama on display in LAX, the interaction of exoticism and familiarity, was just as bizarre as anything I would find when I arrived at my foreign destination. The airport is an Amy Tan novel, a short story by Bharati Mukherjee, a Henry James sketch set to an MTV beat; it is a cross-generational saga about Chang Hsieng meeting his daughter Cindy and finding that she's wearing a nose ring now and is shacked up with a surfer from Berlin. The very best kind of airport reading to be found in LAX these days is the triple-decker melodrama being played out all around one—a complex tragicomedy of love and war and exile, about people fleeing centuries-old rivalries and thirteenth-century mullahs and stepping out into a fresh, forgetful, born-again city that is rewriting its script every moment.

Not long ago I went to spend a week in LAX. I haunted the airport by day and by night, I joined the gloomy drinkers listening to air-control-tower instructions on earphones at the Proud Bird bar. I listened each morning to Airport Radio (530 AM), and I slept each night at the Airport Sheraton or the Airport Hilton. I lived off cellophaned crackers and Styrofoam cups of tea, browsed for hours among Best Actor statuettes and Beverly Hills magnets, and tried to see what kinds of America the city presents to the new Americans, who are remaking America each day.

It is almost too easy to say that LAX is a perfect metaphor for L.A., a flat, spaced-out desert kind of place, highly automotive, not deeply hospitable, with little reading matter and no organizing principle. (There are eight satellites without a center here, many international arrivals are shunted out into the bleak basement of Terminal 2, and there is no airline that serves to dominate LAX as Pan Am once did JFK.) Whereas "SIN" is a famously ironical airline code for Singapore, cathedral of puritanical rectitude, "LAX" has always seemed perilously well chosen for a city whose main industries were traditionally thought to be laxity and relaxation. LAX is at once a vacuum waiting to be colonized and a joyless theme park—Tomorrowland, Adventureland, and Fantasyland all at once.

The postcards on sale here (made in Korea) dutifully call the airport "one of the busiest and most beautiful air facilities in the world," and it is certainly true that LAX, with thirty thousand international arrivals each day—roughly the same number of tourists that have visited the Himalayan country of Bhutan in its entire history—is not uncrowded. But bigger is less and less related to better: in a recent survey of travel facilities, *Business Traveller* placed LAX among the five worst airports in the world for customs, luggage retrieval, and passport processing.

LAX is, in fact, a surprisingly shabby and hollowed-out kind of place, certainly not adorned with the amenities one might expect of the world's strongest and richest power. When you come out into the Arrivals area in the International Terminal, you will find exactly one tiny snack bar, which serves nine items; of them, five are identified as Cheese Dog, Chili Dog, Chili Cheese Dog, Nachos with Cheese, and Chili Cheese Nachos. There is a large panel on the wall offering rental-car services and hotels, and the newly deplaned American dreamer can choose between the Cadillac Hotel, the Banana Bungalow (which offers a Basketball Court, "Free Toast," "Free Bed Sheets," and "Free Movies and Parties"), and the Backpacker's Paradise (with "Free Afternoon Tea and Crumpets" and "Free Evening Party Including Food and Champagne").

Around one in the terminal is a swirl of priests rattling cans, Iranians in suits brandishing pictures of torture victims, and Japanese girls in Goofy hats. "I'm looking for something called Clearasil," a distinguished-looking Indian man diffidently tells a cashier. "Clearasil?" shouts the girl. "For your face?"

Upstairs, in the Terrace Restaurant, passengers are gulping down "Dutch Chocolate" and "Japanese Coffee" while students translate back and forth between English and American, explaining that "soliciting" loses something of its cachet when you go across the Atlantic. A fat man is nuzzling the neck of his outrageously pretty Filipina companion, and a few Brits are staring doubtfully at the sign that assures them that seafood is "cheerfully served at your table!" Only in America, they are doubtless thinking. A man goes from table to table, plunking down on each one a key chain attached to a globe. As soon as an unsuspecting customer picks one up, touched by the largesse of the New World and convinced now that there is such a thing as a free lunch in America, the man appears again, flashes a sign that says "I Am a Deaf," and requests a dollar for the gift.

At a bank of phones, a saffron-robed monk gingerly inserts a credit card, while schoolkids page Jesse Jackson at the nearest "white courtesy telephone." One notable feature of the modern airport is that it is wired, with a vengeance: even in a tiny, two-urinal men's room, I found two telephones on offer; LAX bars rent out cellular phones; and in the Arrivals area, as you come out into the land of plenty, you face a bank of forty-six phones of every kind, with screens and buttons and translations, from which newcomers are calling direct to Bangalore or Baghdad. Airports are places for connections of all kinds and *loci classici*, perhaps, for a world ruled by IDD and MCI, DOS and JAL.

Yet for all these grounding reminders of the world outside, everywhere I went in the airport I felt myself in an odd kind of twilight zone of consciousness, that weight-less limbo of a world in which people are between lives and between selves, almost sleepwalking, not really sure of who or where they are. Light-headed from the trips they've taken, ears popping and eyes about to do so, under a potent foreign influence, people are at the far edge of themselves in airports, ready to break down or through. You see strangers pouring out their life stories to strangers here, or making new life stories with other strangers. Everything is at once intensified and slightly unreal. One L.A. psychiatrist advises shy women to practice their flirting here, and religious groups circle in the hope of catching unattached souls.

Airports, which often have a kind of perpetual morning-after feeling (the end of the holiday, the end of the affair), are places where everyone is ruled by the clock, but all the clocks show different times. These days, after all, we fly not only into yesterday or this morning when we go across the world but into different decades, often, of the world's life and our own: in ten or fifteen hours, we are taken back into the twelfth century or into worlds we haven't seen since childhood. And in the process we are sub-jected to transitions more jolting than any imagined by Oscar Wilde or Sigmund Freud: if the average individual today sees as many images in a day as a Victorian saw in a lifetime, the average person today also has to negotiate switches between conti-nents inconceivable only fifty years ago. Frequent fliers like Ted Turner have actually become ill from touching down and taking off so often; but, in less diagnosable ways, all of us are being asked to handle difficult suspensions of the laws of Nature and Soci-ety when moving between competing worlds.

This helps to compound the strange statelessness of airports, where all bets are off and all laws are annulled—modern equivalents, perhaps, to the hundred yards of no-man's-land between two frontier crossings. In airports we are often in dreamy, floating, out-of-body states, as ready to be claimed as that suitcase on Carousel C. Even I, not traveling, didn't know sometimes if I was awake or asleep in LAX, as I heard an announcer intone, "John Cheever, John Cheever, please contact a Northwest representative in the Baggage Claim area. John Cheever, please contact a service rep-resentative at the Northwest Baggage Claim area."

As I started to sink into this odd, amphibious, bipolar state, I could begin to see why a place like LAX is a particular zone of fear, more terrifying to many people than anywhere but the dentist's office. Though dying in a plane is, notoriously, twenty times less likely than dying in a car, every single airline crash is front-page news and so dramatic—not a single death but three hundred—that airports are for many people kill-ing grounds. Their runways are associated in the mind's (televisual) eye with hostages and hijackings; with bodies on the tarmac or antiterrorist squads storming the plane.

That general sense of unsettledness is doubtless intensified by all the people in uniform in LAX. There are ten different security agencies working the Tom Bradley

Terminal alone, and the streets outside are jam-packed with Airport Police cars, FBI men, and black-clad airport policemen on bicycles. All of them do as much, I suspect, to instill fear as to still it. "People are scared here," a gloomy Pakistani security guard told me, "because undercover are working. Police are working. You could be undercover, I could be undercover. Who knows?"

And just as L.A. is a province of the future in part because so many people take it to be the future, so it is a danger zone precisely because it is imagined to be dangerous. In Osaka's new $16 billion airport recently, I cross-examined the Skynet computer (in the Departures area) about what to expect when arriving at LAX or any other foreign airport. "Guard against theft in the arrival hall," it told me (and, presumably, even warier Japanese). "A thief is waiting for a chance to take advantage of you." Elsewhere it added, "Do not dress too touristy," and, "Be on your guard when approached by a group of suspicious-looking children, such as girls wearing bright-colored shirts and scarves." True to such dark prognostications, the side doors of the Airport Sheraton at LAX are locked every day from 8:00 P.M. to 6:00 A.M., and you cannot even activate the elevators without a room key. "Be extra careful in parking garages and stairwells," the hotel advises visitors. "Always try to use the main entrance to your hotel, particularly late in the evening. Never answer your hotel room door without verifying who is there."

One reason airports enjoy such central status in our imaginations is that they play such a large part in forming our first (which is sometimes our last) impression of a place; this is the reason that poor countries often throw all their resources into making their airports sleek, with beautifully landscaped roads leading out of them into town. L.A., by contrast, has the bareness of arrogance, or simple inhospitality. Usually what you see as you approach the city is a grim penitential haze through which is visible nothing but rows of gray buildings, a few dun-hued warehouses, and ribbons of dirty freeway: a no-colored blur without even the comforting lapis ornaments of the swimming pools that dot New York or Johannesburg. (Ideally, in fact, one should enter L.A. by night, when the whole city pulses like an electric grid of lights—or the back of a transistor radio, in Thomas Pynchon's inspired metaphor. While I was staying in LAX, Jackie Collins actually told *Los Angeles* magazine that "Flying in [to LAX] at night is just an orgasmic thrill.") You land, with a bump, on a mess of gray runways with no signs of welcome, a hangar that says "Tans W rld Airlines," another broken sign that announces "Tom Bradl y International Ai port," and an air-control tower under scaffolding.

The first thing that greeted me on a recent arrival was a row of Asians sitting on the floor of the terminal, under a sign that told them of a $25,000 fine for bringing in the wrong kinds of food. As I passed through endless corridors, I was faced with almost nothing except long escalators (a surprisingly high percentage of the accidents recorded at airports comes from escalators, bewildering to newcomers) and bare hallways. The other surprise, for many of my fellow travelers, no doubt, was that almost no one we saw looked like Robert Redford or Julia Roberts or, indeed, like anyone belonging to the race we'd been celebrating in our in-flight movies. As we passed into the huge, bare assembly hall that is the Customs and Immigration Center here, I was directed into one of the chaotic lines by a Noriko and formally admitted to the country by a C. Chen. The man waiting to transfer my baggage (as a beagle sniffed around us in a coat that said "Agriculture's Beagle Brigade" on one side and "Protecting American Agriculture" on the other) was named Yoji Yosaka. And the first sign I saw, when I stepped into America, was a big board being waved by the "Executive Sedan Service" for one "Mr. T. Ego."

For many immigrants, in fact, LAX is quietly offering them a view of their own near futures: the woman at the Host Coffee Shop is themselves, in a sense, two years from now, and the man sweeping up the refuse is the American dream in practice. The staff at the airport seems to be made up almost entirely of recent immigrants: on my very first afternoon there, I was served by a Hoa, an Ephraim, and a Glinda; the wait-people at a coffee shop in Terminal 5 were called Ignacio, Ever, Aura, and Erick. Even at the Airport Sheraton (where the employees all wear nameplates), I was checked in by Viera (from "Bratislavia") and ran into Hasmik and Yovik (from Ethiopia), Faye (from Vietnam), Ingrid (from Guatemala City), Khrystyne (from Long Beach, by way of Phnom Penh, I think), and Moe (from West L.A., she said). Many of the bright-eyed dreamers who arrive at LAX so full of hope never actually leave the place.

The deeper drama of any airport is that it features a kind of interaction almost unique in our lives, wherein many of us do not know whom we are going to meet or whom others are going to meet in us. You see people standing at the barriers outside the Customs area looking into their pasts, while wide-open newcomers drift out, searching for their futures. Lovers do not know if they will see the same person who kissed them good-bye a month ago; grandparents wonder what the baby they last saw twenty years ago will look like now.

In L.A. all of this has an added charge, because unlike many cities, it is not a hub but a terminus: a place where people come to arrive. Thus many of the meetings you witness are between the haves and the hope-to-haves, between those who are affecting a new ease in their new home and those who are here in search of that ease. Both parties, especially if they are un-American by birth, are eager to stress their Americanness or their fitness for America; and both, as they look at each other's made-up self, see themselves either before or after a stay in L.A.'s theater of transformation. And so they stream in, wearing running shoes or cowboy hats or 49ers jackets, anxious to make a good first impression; and the people who wait for them, under a halfhearted mural of Desertland, are often American enough not to try to look the part. Juan and Esperanza both have ponytails now, and Kimmie is wearing a Harley-Davidson cap backwards and necking with a Japanese guy; the uncle from Delhi arrives to find that Rajiv not only has grown darker but has lost weight, so that he looks more like a peasant from back home than ever.

And the newcomers pour in in astonishing numbers. A typical Sunday evening, in a single hour, sees flights arriving from England, Taiwan, the Philippines, Indonesia, Mexico, Austria, Germany, Spain, Costa Rica, and Guatemala; and each new group colors and transforms the airport: an explosion of tropical shades from Hawaiian Air, a rash of blue blazers and white shirts around the early flight from Tokyo. Red-haired Thais bearing pirated Schwarzenegger videos, lonely Africans in Aerial Assault sneakers, farmers from changeless Confucian cultures peering into the smiles of a Prozac city, children whose parents can't pronounce their names. Many of them are returning, like Odysseus, with the spoils of war: young brides from Luzon, business cards from Shanghai, boxes of macadamia nuts from Oahu. And for many of them the whole wild carnival will feature sights they have never seen before: Japanese look anxiously at the first El Salvadorans they've ever seen, and El Salvadorans ogle sleek girls from Bangkok in thigh-high boots. All of them, moreover, may not be pleased to realize that the America they've dreamed of is, in fact, a land of tacos and pita and pad thai—full, indeed, of the very Third World cultures that other Third Worlders look down upon.

One day over lunch I asked my Ethiopian waitress about her life here. She liked it well enough, she said, but still she missed her home. And yet, she added, she couldn't go back. "Why not?" I asked, still smiling. "Because they killed my family," she said. "Two years back. They killed my father. They killed my brother." "They," I realized, referred to the Tigreans—many of them working just down the corridor in other parts of the hotel. So, too, Tibetans who have finally managed to flee their Chinese-occupied homeland arrive at LAX to find Chinese faces everywhere; those who fled the Sandinistas find themselves standing next to Sandinistas fleeing their successors. And all these people from ancient cultures find themselves in a country as amnesiac as the morning, where World War II is just a rumor and the Gulf War a distant memory. Their pasts are escaped, yes, but by the same token they are unlikely to be honored.

It is dangerously tempting to start formulating socioeconomic principles in the midst of LAX: people from rich countries (Germany and Japan, say) travel light, if only because they are sure that they can return any time; those from poor countries come with their whole lives in cardboard boxes imperfectly tied with string. People from poor countries are often met by huge crowds—for them each arrival is a special occasion—and stagger through customs with string bags and Gold Digger apple crates, their addresses handwritten on them in pencil; the Okinawan honeymooners, by contrast, in the color-coordinated outfits they will change every day, somehow have packed all their needs into a tiny case.

If airports have some of the excitement of bars, because so many people are composing (and decomposing) selves there, they also have some of the sadness of bars, the poignancy of people sitting unclaimed while everyone around them has paired off. A pretty girl dressed in next to nothing sits alone in an empty Baggage Claim area, waiting for a date who never comes; a Vietnamese man, lost, tells an official that he has friends in Orange County who can help him, but when the friends are contacted, they say they know no one from Vietnam. I hear of a woman who got off and asked for "San Mateo," only to learn that she was meant to disembark in San Francisco; and a woman from Nigeria who came out expecting to see her husband in Monroe, Louisiana, only to learn that someone in Lagos had mistaken "La." on her itinerary for "L.A."

The greetings I saw in the Arrivals area were much more tentative than I had expected, less passionate—as ritualized in their way as the kisses placed on Bob Barker's cheek—and much of that may be because so many people are meeting strangers, even if they are meeting people they once knew. Places like LAX—places like L.A.—perpetuate the sense that everyone is a stranger in our new floating world. I spent one afternoon in the airport with a Californian blonde, and I saw her complimented on her English by a sweet Korean woman and asked by an Iranian if she was Indian. Airports have some of the unsteady brashness of singles bars, where no one knows quite what is expected of them. "Mike, is that you?" "Oh, I didn't recognize you." "I'd have known you anywhere." "It's so kind of you to come and pick me up." And already at a loss, a young Japanese girl and a broad, lonely-looking man head off toward the parking lot, not knowing, in any sense, who is going to be in the driver's seat.

The driving takes place, of course, in what many of the newcomers, primed by video screenings of *L.A. Law* and *Speed*, regard as the ultimate heart of darkness, a place at least as forbidding and dangerous as Africa must have seemed to the Victorians. They have heard about how America is the murder capital of the world; they have seen Rodney King get pummeled by L.A.'s finest; they know of the city as the site of drive-by shootings and freeway snipers, of riots and celebrity murders. The "homeless" and the "tempest-tost" that the Statue of Liberty invites are arriving, increasingly, in a city that is itself famous for its homeless population and its fires, floods, and earthquakes.

In that context, the ideal symbol of LAX is, perhaps, the great object that for thirty years has been the distinctive image of the place: the ugly white quadruped that sits in the middle of the airport like a beached white whale or a jet-age beetle, featuring a 360-degree circular restaurant that does not revolve and an observation deck from which the main view is of twenty-three thousand parking places. The Theme Building, at 201 World Way, is a sad image of a future that never arrived, a monument to Kennedy-era idealism and the thrusting modernity of the American empire when it was in its prime; it now has the poignancy of an abandoned present with its price tag stuck to it. When you go there (and almost nobody does) you are greeted by photos of Saturn's rings and Jupiter and its moons, by a plaque laid down by L.B.J. and a whole set of symbols from the time when NASA was shooting for the heavens. Now the "landmark" building, with its "gourmet-type restaurant," looks like a relic from a time long past, when it must have looked like the face of the future.

Upstairs, a few desperately merry waiters are serving nonalcoholic drinks and cheeseburgers to sallow diners who look as if they've arrived at the end of the world; on the tarmac outside, speedbirds inch ahead like cars in a traffic jam. "Hello All the New People of LAX—Welcome," says the graffiti on the elevator.

The Theme Restaurant comes to us from an era when L.A. was leading the world. Nowadays, of course, L.A. is being formed and reformed and led by the world around it. And as I got ready to leave LAX, I could not help but feel that the Theme Building stands, more and more, for a city left behind by our accelerating planet. LAX, I was coming to realize, was a good deal scruffier than the airports even of Bangkok or Jakarta, more chaotic, more suggestive of Third World lawlessness. And the city around it is no more golden than Seoul, no more sunny than Taipei, and no more laid-back than Moscow. Beverly Hills, after all, is largely speaking Farsi now. Hollywood Boulevard is sleazier than 42nd Street. And Malibu is falling into the sea.

Yet just as I was about to give up on L.A. as yesterday's piece of modernity, I got on the shuttle bus that moves between the terminals in a never-ending loop. The seats next to me were taken by two tough-looking dudes from nearby South Central, who were riding the free buses and helping people on and off with their cases (acting, I presumed, on the safe assumption that the Japanese, say, new to the country and bewildered, had been warned beforehand to tip often and handsomely for every service they received). In between terminals, as a terrified-looking Miss Kudo and her friend guarded their luggage, en route from Nagoya to Las Vegas, the two gold-plated sharks talked about the Raiders' last game and the Lakers' next season. Then one of them, without warning, announced, "The bottom line is the spirit is with you. When you work out, you chill out and, like, you meditate in your spirit. You know what I mean? Meditation is recreation. Learn math, follow your path. That's all I do, man, that's all I live for: learnin' about God, learnin' about Jesus. I am *possessed* by that spirit. You know, I used to have all these problems, with the flute and all, but when I heard about God, I learned about the body, the mind, and the flesh. People forget, they don't know, that the Bible isn't talkin' about the flesh, it's talkin' about the spirit. And I was reborn again in the spirit."

His friend nodded. "When you recreate, you meditate. Recreation is a spiritually uplifting experience."

"Yeah. When you do that, you allow the spirit to breathe."

"Because you're gettin' into the physical world. You're lettin' the spirit flow. You're helpin' the secretion of the endorphins in the brain."

Nearby, the Soldiers of the Cross of Christ Church stood by the escalators, taking donations, and a man in a dog collar approached another stranger.

I watched the hustlers allowing the spirit to breathe, I heard the Hare Krishna devotees plying their wares, I spotted some Farrakhan flunkies collecting a dollar for a copy of their newspaper, *The Final Call*—redemption and corruption all around us in the air—and I thought: welcome to America, Miss Kudo, welcome to L.A.

On the Bubble

Sydney Lea

Early June of 1992, below Stonehouse Mountain, Grafton County, New Hampshire—a place and time in which snowsqualls, routine enough just weeks ago, will at last deserve the name freakish. In freshet beds where waters flared and vanished, frail shoots of jewelweed declare themselves; grass bursts the voles' winter tunnels; geese trail the Connecticut northward; the buck deer's antlers are in velvet; the woodchuck's busy to double in weight; trout sip the ponds' ephemerids; everywhere, the lovesick insistence of birds.

Our family has lived ten years on this foothill's flank, but soon after dawn this morning—beckoned by the full day ahead—I hiked down from its mild summit for perhaps the last time. The ramble, especially under such circumstances, brought back the many I'd made there, in company or alone, one recollection summoning another, and that one still another, till outward prospects opened onto vaster, more labyrinthine inward views.

I suddenly found myself at the June of 1989, three years gone. Unseasonable as any late spring's for a hunt, that forenoon had still invited my scout's eye; for companions therefore I had my gun dogs, two of them dead since. And because I'm also forever scouting more than game—no easy name for it—I'd also brought along my thirdborn, Jordan. He'd turned five less than a month before; I would manage to haul him in his riding pack through one more year.

As soon as we struck height-of-land, my boy reached into his jacket and fetched out paraphernalia for blowing bubbles. What few he managed were pea-sized and, hustled by a hard wind, quickly burst against the granite moraine where we stood. Jordan, however, is more stubborn a soul than I will ever quite understand, no matter that, despite its costs, I share the quality myself, in spades. For all my untypically rationalistic discouragement, he persisted until in a momentary lull he somehow produced one outsized sphere. Perhaps six inches around, it lifted off his dipper, fighting like a hot-air balloon for altitude—which it couldn't sustain. As my son watched in an agony between rage and sorrow, the great thing sank slowly toward stone. On lighting, though, it remained miraculously intact—tenuous, quivering. I could actually hear the catch in Jordan's breath as he beheld in its film the reflections of a whole domain: high blue crossed by thunderheads, skinny black upland spruces, weathered crags and windfalls, glyphs of animal trails.

He and I would miss all this directly.

Then the bubble vanished. No obvious pop, only evanescence. And in the aftermoment, by quenchless habit I began to conjure metaphors. The perdurability of the mountain, the transience of human constructs, the rest. But all sorts of things—inner and outer, gross and subtle—blocked my scheme, and I gave it up. If I've discovered nothing else, I know that one can't simply will his figures.

Besides, there seemed enough in the plain spectacle of the child, dazed by these quicksilver splendors and their disappearance, to cause a familiar commotion. I was moved by more than his mere smallness, the puff of his bewildered lips, the way his pale, forgotten hand spilled the bubble-jar's contents. I felt, almost physically, the curse fallen on his parents' wish for him and his sisters and brothers: that we might leave these young spirits among the apparent unchangeables that had nourished our own— this wish in fact had moved us all to Stonehouse Mountain, whose very name seemed auspicious. Between eternities of stone and mountain, a house might nestle for good.

Not that I'd left my former town, some miles to the south, altogether cheerfully, having cherished it so for the preceding decade and a half. Yet after that time, I watched the village and its surroundings transform themselves, overnight it seemed, into a sprawl of bedrooms for the burgeoning college-and-commercial cluster downriver. The jobs—far scarcer in actuality than in developers' fabulations—had arrived and departed so quickly that, on looking one day, I found native families gone, their farms become "grounds."

Eighty-year-old Harry Franklin, among the few who stayed, put matters succinctly: "We're just like anyplace else now."

This morning's reverie on my son's bright bubble must have established a motif of fragile glories, that motif in turn leading to further recollections, which otherwise seem willy-nilly, or at least nonchronological. I shortly found myself leaping to the autumn of 1991. That was a fall like many another in obvious respects: fragile, yes— flares of maple racing into the umbers and beiges of oak or beech; short summer shadows stretched suddenly long after noontime; big-fingered ferns gone arthritic as the swamps showed the first pale ice at their margins. But even more than usual, I'd been out and busy. From the final weekend of September till the middle one in November, I chased birds pretty much every day. Nasty work, of course, but necessary: my two youngest pointers were just at field training age. If, as usual, I lamented the headlong rush of those weeks, it was as much because the pups deserved more exposure than I could cram into a season as because of my ineradicable elegiac streak.

Therefore, when it came to deer season (which, precisely for being dogless, shakes less passion from me anyhow than the grouse months), I hunted too rarely and casually. But this was of necessity, too. A part of me would choose to spend as much time year-round in the wild as it had done all fall with the pointers, yet I must now and then come indoors, there to ponder other things: my children growing up; my wife ageing into a greater and greater handsomeness, in every sense of that word; reflections like these passing—so far as possible—into articulation.

In short, as the eleventh month of '91 advanced on the twelfth, I spared only an hour here and another there to follow the whitetail, preoccupied as I was with separate pursuits. Such an approach may reap results in places like Pennsylvania or Texas, but in my edge of New England—herd thinner, woods thicker—it's apt, barring dumb luck, to end in failure.

It did. It didn't.

My first morning out was all Indian summer crackle underfoot, but by the second, several days later, conditions had turned ideal: a light snow fallen on unfrozen ground, sign would be clear, the going quiet. Moreover, though as always I'd cherished October's game more than the bigger game of the moment, there was and is something about November that exerts a stronger *aesthetic* appeal. I know that to say so puts me in a distinct minority, but the austerity of that period just before real snow—of sharply contoured branch and trunk, granite and cloud—oddly braces my soul.

I recall setting off in that second dawn at a brisk clip, which I meant to keep till I came on something interesting. This didn't take long: less than a mile from home, on a brushed-over twitch road at the north end of Stonehouse, I fairly struck a turnpike, deer tracks everywhere. Mostly skippers and does, of course, but one heel-heavy trail, too, fresh as paint, every third print ruddy with rut. I wondered for the hundredth time how a buck can manage to produce so much of that dribble—as if this were the chief internal mystery in such a creature.

There's a certain special outcropping on Stonehouse Mountain that, though short of the summit, provides as bold a view: the loftier Whites to northeastward in the distance, and—closer below—that bijou, Mason Pond. Flush with first settlement here, my wife and I happened onto this ledge in one of our early, desultory explorations. No sign of human presence around us or in the vista, we found it hard to suppose that a lone soul knew or remembered this corner of forest, which then belonged, technically, to an unknown out-of-stater. We spoke of rigging a sledge some winter, dragging materials to the site for a shack, even installing our extra woodstove. Then we'd make occasional getaways. If our cabin were found and dismantled, what harm? We'd have had it for a spell anyway.

These musings preceded our small children. And someone else soon bought that flank of mountain anyhow, for which he now plans fifteen "luxury estates." Thus our musings turned to idle dreams before we owned a prayer of making them otherwise, but neither dream nor prayer will utterly die; we still name that spot "The Shack." It stays on, somehow, as a place in mind. Yet how can we pass such inner property down to those same children?

I'd been saying something else, however, before sorrow and anger broke in. Taking the buck's track last fall, I shortly found myself exactly at The Shack. Perhaps that very sorrow and anger distracted me; in any case, I relaxed concentration as one so easily does, and I missed my deer until too late. A good buck, right enough. Although I couldn't count horns, of course, there looked like a thicket of them as he bolted into softwood cover: I could see that much, and the bulk of him, and the almost black color which typifies our trophy ridge-runners. I could have shot—and would have, in my youth—yet I knew that it would be no more than luck if my slug hit, that it would go in from behind. It would ruin a share of venison, and might do far worse: I'll haltingly acknowledge some atavistic excitement in following a blood trail—but not a long one.

I performed an old charade of rage, complete with misdirected oaths at the vanished prey: "Why, you son of a *bitch!* I'll fix *you!*" But in truth I remained happy at my own calm and resignation; I'd rest the fellow a spell and then pick him up again. Brushing the scarf of snow from a blowdown, I sat and lit a pipe. When I checked my watch, though, it astonished me as ever: two full hours gone, all I'd allotted for this morning's chase. No, I wouldn't fix that buck, not today. Instead I'd follow an arc down to our house, semi-alert, just in case I jumped something else on the way. But that would be accident, too, and in any case my thoughts had already gone elsewhere.

The younger children must be getting up about now; it pleased me to imagine them at a front window, frowzy, curious, and then the sleep on their necks a warmth against my cold face. They'd grow up so soon. The thought of my firstborn Creston, off at college just now, was bittersweet; how thoughtful and decent and *interesting* a man he'd become; yet how wouldn't I miss the vanished little boy in him? And the next child, Erika, was already fourteen, bright and beautiful.

I'd have stopped the whole lot in their tracks if I could, or maybe even moved them backwards in time—back to Jordan's age, or three-year-old Catherine's, or even to the age of the next tiny mystery, who'd arrive in his or her splendor a month from that deer-hunting day. I'd load each one by turns in the battered old pack, heft them, march them with me into the wonderful highlands. We'd see things together again.

By a cellar hole in a certain burntland, an abandoned Model A lay for decades: we named the place Henry's Clearing, after the car's inventor. I have a picture of my oldest son astride the wreck's springless seat. He's ten. Beside him, a popple sapling has grown through the floorboards; it rests a feathery branch on the rust-orange dashboard, as a slim, slightly apprehensive adolescent girl might rest her fingertips. The skins of child and tree seemed translucent that morning and—far more than in the photograph—they remain that way to my interior eye.

Six months ago my big boy turned twenty. His companion popple is dead, scalped by the local developer when his crew removed the jalopy as an eyesore. One of his intended access roads will pass through the old burn. As I approached Henry's Clearing, I imagined gleaming foreign sedans, run hub-deep into March goo and left to replace the Model A. Such a fantasy made me grin—but only momentarily. Pavement would follow, sure as death.

Just east of Henry's, I froze—my impulse strange but familiar to anyone who's hunted long enough. I felt sure a deer stood somewhere near. Don't ask how. It couldn't have been my hearing, which is not worth much (and which forty years of shooting haven't improved). In my time, if children contracted ear infections, they went to a doctor and got them lanced. That fact is worth remembering, perhaps, while I rhapsodize on bygone days: I seem to have had those infections every other week, so my aural channels are a maze of scar tissue. Even though my sons and daughters appear equally susceptible to their father's old malady, they will never, like him, confuse some inward clatter of the eardrum with duck flight, some high whine through it with a building wind, some uncertainly located pop with the far report of a firearm. None will wonder, as I soon did near that burn, whether an actual or illusory squelch sounded in dampening snow.

I chose, at least for the moment, to believe in the sound's reality, and I felt gratified once again that a belief could still make my heart rap. I smelled an odor like the ozone warning of electrical storm. My mouth went cotton. Slowly I settled my backside onto a boulder, watching until my eyes teared and I had no choice but to blink. Then I watched some more, shivering, willing the deer of my intuitions around the shoulder of the knoll and into Henry's Clearing—broadside, big. My younger son, seven by now, could eat four chops at a go.

A different man would have waited even longer. I, however, began in due course to doubt my own instincts, even if I'd had reason to curse such reckless doubt in the past. But as I say, I had home on the brain by now, and was unsure anyhow that I wanted a buck I'd done so little to deserve, supposing he *were* on hand. As the game thins out, its supporting habitat savaged by conspirators in greed, a hunter should place demands on himself; he should do things right or not at all.

In 1991, that ravenous seven-year-old fairly wriggled with enthusiasm for the woods and the quarry. Stuck unmoving to my perch, I remembered the same fever from my childhood. With him, flesh of my flesh, I could somehow chafe again for a first armed trip to the field. I too could hang on a porch door, awaiting a parent's return from his hunt. Then I could smell the cold dirt on his dogs, the humid stench of birdfeathers in the gamebag. My father would suffer my slow services: I could kneel and undo his bootlaces, the aroma of man falling all over me.

It had only been four short decades before, after all, that I'd done and felt these things. But when four more had passed, when the boy had reached my age, when it was 2031, what of this sort would thrill him, in fact or imagination or memory? What would keep him watching as I watched, even as a chilly dampness climbed through pantswool into my bones? *Where* would he sit, and what would he pass on to his own children? What could I myself pass on—from here, from there?

I needed to disrupt my own mood, and so—the wind northwest, straight in my face—I decided to sneak over for a look through the burn, a mere twenty yards from my stand. I took most of that distance easy, a little at a time, eyeing the spot where I'd have to scooch to keep my profile under the slope's, injuries to each knee speaking more sternly now than in the sports-crazy boyhood that produced them.

Step, stop, wait. Step, stop, wait.

I flinched as a raven *whoof-whoof-whoofed* low overhead, across the fire-cleared ground and gone. The bird left a deeper quiet than the one it had broken, and I lingered within it till by God I did hear something! A small racket in brush around the corner. I sucked my teeth, trying to swallow but trying also to reason: if I'd heard a deer at all, odds favored a doe; or it might as easily turn out to be a plain old red squirrel, famous for disproportionate ruckus in a calm woods.

Five squatting steps further on, inch by inch I straightened. Over the knoll's rim, some forty yards down the former tote road, sure enough I detected fur and motion. A flag? No. Though I couldn't yet tell to what else, it belonged to no deer. Wrong color for a start: chocolate brown, highlit by cinnamon.

At length the animal slipped from brush and showed its shape entire. Still unable to identify it, I could see it was large. I stood fixed as a pillar while it made its unmistakable way toward me. The wind had picked up some, but kept moving toward me too. Better and better.

Then, something familiar but inexplicable: rather than growing bigger, my creature began to shrink as it came on. Noting the fussy lope of the weasel family, I thought: Well, I'll be damned, an otter! I'd happened on such apparent strays before, especially in the cold months, far from any watershed worth the name. Better and better.

Then I noticed the too-prominent ears, and I briefly imagined: *marten!* But this fellow, even as he got smaller, looked heavier than martens, which in any case, alas, had vanished from virtually all of New Hampshire some time ago. And yet since he is to the more common black as one to five, the pure-brown fisher—as he eventually became—proved no disappointment...especially as he kept up his nosey progress. The wind from behind him blew more insistently now: I could see backhairs ruffle like a field of late hay, and vague cloud-shadows skidding past on the coarse wet turf.

A good hound couldn't have smelled me from that animal's quarter; but just as the human, without any sensory clue, may occasionally surmise the nearness of the nonhuman, so now my fisher *felt* something out of the ordinary, stopped in his tracks, raised his head, sniffed the useless air.

We were in full sight of each other, but my eyes were the better. How many minutes, then, did we stand like that? One? Four? Ten? We stayed equally motionless, but my mind continued to run anyhow. And the fisher's? Were there images in his brain too, and if so, how did they look? How had it happened that a man could see his boy blow soap bubbles in another season and another niche of this very mountain, and still somehow be here this morning? Was my wife happy enough with our life together? Did the fisher believe he'd find hare in Henry's Clearing? Had he found them before? Did he store that experience? How? Was he in fact a she? Who had owned the Model A? Would anyone store memories of me? Did God really count each bird that fell and, having counted, what did He conclude? Why does blue show up under scarred paper birchbark like that tree's five yards to the animal's right? What made this particular scar? Did you feel the cold in Idaho, say, as you did in New England? Could a person go on fathering children and still complain about his world's crowding?

Perhaps I didn't think these exact thoughts just then. I mean to present less my mind's *content* than the way it kept filling with things apparently random and unaccountable. What had any to do with an outsized weasel, to whom I was about to wave or speak, excited as always to witness a wild thing's most frantic flight? No time to say. Suddenly, the big wind blew a gap in the overcast, and a filament of sun struck the fisher. The guard hairs of his coat became a numinous, gilded aura, I gasped, the cloud cover seated itself again, the creature bounded into near woods, took to the treetops, leaping from one to another out of sight.

I stayed on for a spell, some bloodheat distracting me from weather's authority. But the wind soon gathered a few horizontal rainsplots, and I came to: my knuckles ached on the rifle, my wet bottom burned with the cold, and a gloom descended, which was instantaneous as the clouds' return and sadly common in my middle life. In what direction would my fisher's children fly, and my own, once the 'dozers had coughed and quit, the backhoes dug and gone?

Oh, I'd seen something that morning. I'd see it till my own dark hole got dug. And after that?

The adored father who was my first guide died in the February of my twenty-third year. I married the following June, though my better soul found something wrong in taking such an important step while still gripped by a mourning so heavy and confusing. I'd never been a deliberate boy, never would be; but even I had enough sense to know I was acting unsensibly.

Why, then, did I let things proceed? Well, however much I'd played the hell-raiser from earliest schooldays, I'd often likewise shown counterinstincts toward politeness. To this day I retain both these sides of my character, neither a pure virtue nor a pure vice, and each still in periodic, painful contest with the other. In 1966, wedding day approaching, I felt compelling reasons to stop the whole business, even if that meant sabotaging everybody else's plans. But my mannerly disinclination to rock boats prevailed: I stayed the good boy. How, after all, could I break off an arrangement that appeared to gratify my mother so? Hadn't she suffered enough for a spell? Wouldn't I likewise insult the memory of her husband, who'd been similarly fond of my bride-to-be? ("I've known you all your life," he joked to me when I announced our engagement, "and this is the first really *bright* decision I've caught you at.")

Monkeysuits and gowns—all fitted. Preacher, organist, orchestra—all hired. On and on, and no decent way out, I imagined; no time even to decide whether I really wanted a way. And thus, in the confidence of my sublime ignorance, I concluded that I could always divorce if married life didn't work out.

Sixteen years and two children later, my wife and I did part company. Because of that son and that daughter, I will never seriously unwish those years; but they were undeniably hard for me in many respects, and surely more so for my spouse. At length I believed, and still do, that no solution other than divorce would leave us both sane; yet the pain of it overwhelmed me. What hurt, above all, might I bestow as inheritance? The agony of that time lives on in me, though I soon remarried (more happily than anyone deserves), and have remained in a contact with those first children as close and loving as with the three who have followed.

These are thoughts, however odd, that I *do* know I had as I lingered on Stonehouse Mountain this morning, recalling a bubble and a brown fisher. And I thought of how, from an astonishingly young age, I'd vowed to find a region—some beautiful and intriguing country, home to fleet, wild things—and marry it. Thought how I'd courted the wilder parts of Maine, New Hampshire, and Vermont all through my adolescence and then, in my twenties, tied the knot with upper New England.

And I thought, as the poet wrote, of "fallings from us, vanishings."

For a long stretch, I'd remained so in love with this Grafton County that even on the worst day of mudtime my heart would stutter at the simple sight of a certain slope or tree or stream. The stubborn green of an October sidehill surrounded by darkening woods seemed a marvel that all by itself proved life worthwhile. I remember a July moon over Kenyon Hill so apparently near that my first little girl, not yet two at the time, made clutching gestures toward it, imagining candy. I remember my oldest son's wide-eyed, slack-jawed stare at the bank of Trout Brook, from which a January mink had just scampered into nearby jackfirs. I remember the scarlet tanager that came daily out of yellow May woods to a maple by the bedroom where my wife nursed another baby son. I remember that son's little sister, giggling as we cracked the skim-ice on a late March pool with pointy sticks. And now the newest baby goes cross-eyed and furrow-browed as a sulphur butterfly lights on her carriage. In mind it's as if in all seasons the wide, good universe were there for the sake of each child alone.

In recent years, though, my love affair has found itself in trouble. I can no longer take its passions straight, because for every moment of the old exaltation—for every field or moon or mink, every bird or puddle, every blue butterfly or sun-dazed fisher—there comes a grimly compensating recognition. All these glories are under attack as never before.

But have I another divorce in me? And if so, on what grounds? Does one abandon the love of one's life because she's been assaulted? Doesn't one defend her to the death? Here, while so accurate in other respects, the marriage analogy fails. Though I can cherish the lands and waters and animals of a place with a human affection, none will ever *become* human: indeed, that their inner lives remain so irretrievably otherwise is the greater part of their seductiveness to imagination.

But let my puny allegories stand or fall as they will. How little they matter anyhow. I *have* fought as hard as was in me against those luxury "estates" I mentioned earlier, to the extent that on several occasions I've scarcely restrained myself (or been restrained by others) from physical violence. In company with my wife and friends and neighbors, I have poured cash, time, and fervor into the battle, and as I write our side has happily prevailed. Yet I have also read my *mene, mene, tekel, upharsin.* The town planning board's rejection of a swinish proposal takes note of the dirt-road intersection below us, which the members consider too tricky for such sudden increase in traffic. Nothing noted of the greater, the more obscene peril: that in future deliberations an unencumbered mountainside will be considered not a wondrous treasure but a chunk of real estate.

When things have reached such a turn, "conservation"—however ardently I practice and support it—looks depressingly irrelevant to a stubborn fool like me, because by then something is already past conserving, irretrievably lost. Something spiritual: once banished, no *genius loci* accepts reinvitation; we're mucking around with eternals here.

For all of that, there will doubtless soon be talk of compromise. (One vociferous—and almost marvelously feather-headed—townsman who spoke all along in the project's favor has lately been elected as a "planner.") Perhaps the developer will settle for seven luxury homes on the wild side of Stonehouse, not fifteen; perhaps he'll put aside a larger segment of his property for conservancy, the one that from the start he has called a park (the very word suggesting the awful diminishment I speak of). Not that my mind will disapprove these enforced concessions, which will be better than nothing. It's only that my heart is an absolutist: mere terms having changed, this stretch of woods and hillside will never again suffice for me and my family.

It's time to go.

For a long while, I pledged I'd never inhabit ground I couldn't pee on in broad daylight without worry over observation. Whatever burdens it imposes on her for reasons of gender, my wife has joined in the oath. The day the developer filed his plan with the town, we vowed we'd resist it to the end; but we also put our Stonehouse home on the market and went looking for a bigger spread somewhere else, outside the gentrifying web, affordable. The spot we found sits a good way upriver, and in one respect I should be satisfied for good: with nearly three hundred acres of scrub and ledge to choose from, I'll relieve myself where I damned well please.

Yet my old stipulation, which I once considered a telling metaphor, seems the palest of whimsies now. Even after we discovered the new site—full of game and cedar swamp, bordered by granite palisade, barely dotted by a bungalow and workshop—I recognized for my own part that our move could at best be a holding action. One can piss his bladder out on the earth and still be shriven of all that really matters. The breadth and situation of the place will ensure privacy, but this isn't what we're after. It is not only that both my wife and I relish the human connectedness of a true community, the kind of community that so-called development does much to sunder; it's also that if we reach the point of valuing privacy over other qualities, we will have admitted defeat, will have bought a mere illusion. If ours becomes the last domain of apparent wildness in the country or state, then we'll live in a park ourselves, as artificial as some millionaire's fenced-in preserve or that biospheric bubble one lately reads of. We may not see another soul from where we live, but as I say, the very air will have changed.

What on earth can I want, then? I ask the same of myself, to the point of hysteria; and in answering I sometimes recall the title of a poem by an unlikely hero, insurance executive Wallace Stevens: "The Pleasures of Merely circulating." Or I summon the closing passage of yet another of his poems, "Esthétique du mal":

> *And out of what one sees and hears and out*
> *Of what one feels, who could have thought to make*
> *So many selves, so many sensuous worlds,*
> *As if the air, the midday air, was swarming*
> *With the metaphysical changes that occur,*
> *Merely in living as and where we live.*

I want to live where a meeting with a brown-phase fisher is never a commonplace, but always a *possibility*. I would a hundred times prefer to encounter that creature on home ground than travel to Kenya or wherever to behold a basking leopard. Tourism won't do: to thrill at that leopard, I'd have to inhabit his landscape. I'd rather wander a path across the very landscape I dwell in, certain that by such mere circulation, however stealthily undertaken, I might slip among its secretive, metaphysical wonders, as I've done for so much of my life.

Where on the planet can such country lie anymore? That, of course, is the rub. The leopard's every move has been charted by the organizers of the photographic safari; the guests will not fail to snap him from their Land Rovers. Amazing, then, that I recall dim markings on maps of Africa, representing—we were told—places untrod by human feet. Though our teachers betrayed, needless to say, their Eurocentric notions of humanity, notions whose political implications still prove enormous, I—as a child of European extraction myself—must admit my childhood enchantment with these obtuse descriptions. As a grownup I wince to know that someone may have fitted the big cat with a radio transmitter, kin to the cassette players in the native villages where young men pass in knock-off Michael Jordan basketball shoes. So much for what we called darkest Africa, whose very undarkening, whose whitening, fits my mood of disaster.

More locally, how staggering to read New Englander Ralph Waldo Emerson's claim of a bare hundred and sixty years ago—less than twice the span of his own rich lifetime—that "*Nature*, in the common sense, refers to essences unchanged by man; space, the air, the river, the leaf."

Fifteen luxury estates on Stonehouse Mountain.

From the White Mountains to the Black Forest, foliage shriveling in its acid bath.

The "blue Danube," so thick you can almost walk across it.

The crew of the spaceship Atlantis—one member no doubt on watch for orbiting junk—beams congratulations to *Star Wars* producer George Lucas at the goddamned Academy Award ceremonies.

For me such bad news underlies even a fair amount of good news: for example, that the frightening hole our ingenuity has rent in the ozone layer can perhaps be patched up by the same ingenuity. Logic requires me to rejoice at such a prospect, but I claim no logic for my feelings: should human nature repair what it has wrought in nonhuman, there will no longer *be* such a thing as the nonhuman. The heavens themselves are park enough as it is. That moon's no magical candy for a daughter, even in my fancy. And though she and her sisters and brothers have all been keen for evening hikes to high prominences, they've never looked on stars that kindled in a truly unknown realm. I feel almost cursed to have been so blessed myself as a child.

And yes, how stubborn old blessing has made me! On the day that a rocket flew up to probe Venus, two grouse flew up ahead of my great bitch Bessie. Don't ask me to name that rocket nor say what of use its crew brought home; but until I die I'll remember each inch of the joyously arduous trek up the maple-crazy slope above Pony Hill, and Bessie's point on that double.

"Does No One at All Ever Feel This Way in the Least?" asked Robert Frost in a poem so entitled, one already quaint by 1952. And quainter still, I answer him yes:

> *And now, O sea, you're lost by aeroplane.*
> *Our sailors ride a bullet for a boat.*
> *Our coverage of distance is so facile*
> *It makes us to have had a sea in vain.*
> *Our moat around us is no more a moat,*
> *Our continent no more a moated castle.*

I know the argument—to which, again, I can offer no logical counter—that it's as much a "natural" thing for human speculation and endeavor to keep broadening themselves as it is for my fisher to root a hare from under some fallen hemlock, or for me to fire on a pair of game birds; and that the 747 has its roots in the warrior's chariot—not to mention that my precision-made Winchester looks back on his pike. Perhaps some son or daughter will delight, as many people obviously must, in a naturalism so conceived. I recognize here that I speak, as one tends to do, of things that have charged my *own* imaginative life, things whose alteration feels like painful, personal attack, and whose disappearance bodes a death.

So mortally wounded, I come back and back to the same painful stand: What father am I? What vision do I leave behind?

It may sound as though my restlessness were new, and my younger love for this north country the emotion of a naive boy. But my only genuine naïveté lay in a radical underestimation of the *speed* with which today's remote New England corner—let alone those dark African map-splotches—would become tomorrow's suburb or resort. Although I began to dream of Idaho when the very first fern bar opened in the nearest town of size, it was a bit as I'd dreamed of divorce even as I married for the first time: my innocence, as I say, was to feel no immediate urgency in either speculation.

I had spent a good deal of time in the west, and had loved every minute; yet there existed something deep within me that clove to the density, the greenery, the variety of the woods and even of the much maligned weather in the upper Northeast. What could be more beautiful than the Yellowstone reaches of Montana, the Green River valley in Utah, the Wind River Mountains in Wyoming, the Sangre de Cristos in New Mexico, the Maroon Bells of Colorado? But I remained no more than a rapt visitor among these intoxications, and while I got a kick out of cowboys, I identified, however presumptuously, with backland Yankees.

I did recognize, for all of this, one powerful advantage the Western mountain states held over my beloved trio of Maine, New Hampshire, and Vermont. They were, so to say, a little closer to dark old Africa. That is, even if they were equally prey to the international conspiracy against beauty and wonder (indeed, perhaps more so: once, seeing a Wyoming strip mine, I imagined my damnation in advance), those states beyond the Mississippi had *size*. If a pustule like Aspen popped up and festered, that still left a hell of a lot of Colorado; so did Rocky Flats. For every Jackson Hole and every wretched mineral operation, there existed a hundred barely populated hamlets to east or south or north. Once the cake got frosted near Santa Fe, you could trek back into mountains that made our own look like loaves on a shelf.

And since I'd for some reason never been to Idaho, nor ever heard it much spoken of by exactly the wrong people, it became a new place in mind. Vague, latent. That Idaho.

I finally visited the state late last summer, and at least where I roamed, it looked all the Idaho it ever could. I found things that have long bound me to the East—forests, chiefly, and none restricted like many Western stands to single species—combined with a superb, non-Eastern vastness. I even came on a stretch of river that would serve: not blue-ribbon stuff, but its trout being wild it was good enough, in part precisely for being yet undiscovered by the blue-ribbon crowd in their spanking Orvis duds. Though all my reserves had been poured into the new property back home, I did discover a modest riverside farm for sale at a beggar's price. Someday, maybe, I thought—before it's too late.

It was too late already. Not long after getting home, my brain crowded with fantasies which I believed I'd sobered out of, I read the inevitable, crushing article in one of my conservation magazines. There was furor in good quarters over a proposed development (what a word! as if God had left the job undone) on the fabulous Snake River. The golf course; the jetboat marina; the complex of condominiums with 24-hour security. This horror will quite likely fail to go through, but there will be another compromise, and, for all its hard effects on my soul, something in my blood—the very blood I've passed on to five children—will not be compromised.

And yet it must.

I look out the window of a house laid bare: high on Stonehouse Mountain, where the foliage comes late, the scrawny hardwoods have just started to show their meek pastels, which they seem to pull back into themselves whenever a cloud sails over. In our driveway my truck cringes under its burden of furniture, books, dog crates, crockery, firearms. Orts and fragments.

Suddenly I recall one more walk, with my fourth child Catherine in the venerable riding pack. It was the sort of languid August midday when the woods go silent as a cave, so that the little girl's voice seemed to fill the countryside. *Yesterday*, she sang, *all my troubles seemed so far away./Now it looks as though they're here to stay./Oh, I believe in yesterday.* She was three years old, and the song but a song; yet I needed to labor some against my own tears, her tune ringing truer than she could yet know.

Within my lifetime no jetboat will roil the waters beside the farm I found in Idaho. But once my children live there, they'll hear such a snarl in their own—the *tock* of the clubbed ball, the growl of the patrolling Rottweiler. I whistle for the blonde son and daughter who want to ride north with me in the truck; I sigh and try to feel practical, since I know what I know: as well to move our paltry twenty-five New England miles as to wrench up stakes more radically.

There seems wrench enough, after all, in leaving one more local town where once we dreamed of permanence, where a handful of friends and a handful of wilds will remain. The prospect of hunting up their replacements elsewhere seems sufficiently daunting too. Inner lives, both human and natural, will reveal themselves at a slow pace; that's the rural New England manner. Yet the greater ache is that those lives, like the ones we abandon today, may prove as fragile as our boy's one bold and bright expression, a few short hours past, up there at height-of-land.

Portrait of My Body

Phillip Lopate

I am a man who tilts. When I am sitting, my head slants to the right; when walking, the upper part of my body reaches forward to catch a sneak preview of the street. One way or another, I seem to be off-center—or "uncentered," to use the jargon of holism. My lousy posture, a tendency to slump or put myself into lazy, contorted misalignments, undoubtedly contributes to lower back pain. For a while I correct my bad habits, do morning exercises, sit straight, breathe deeply, but always an inner demon that insists on approaching the world askew resists perpendicularity.

I think if I had broader shoulders I would be more squarely anchored. But my shoulders are narrow, barely wider than my hips. This has always made shopping for suits an embarrassing business. (Françoise Gilot's *Life with Picasso* tells how Picasso was so touchy about his disproportionate body—in his case all shoulders, no legs— that he insisted the tailor fit him at home.)

When I was growing up in Brooklyn, my hero was Sandy Koufax, the Dodgers' Jewish pitcher. In the doldrums of Hebrew choir practice at Feigenbaum's Mansion & Catering Hall, I would fantasize striking out the side, even whiffing twenty-seven batters in a row. Lack of shoulder development put an end to this identification; I became a writer instead of a Koufax.

It occurs to me that the restless angling of my head is an attempt to distract viewers' attention from its paltry base. I want people to look at my head, partly because I live in my head most of the time. My sister, a trained masseuse, often warns me of the penalties, like neck tension, that may arise from failing to integrate body and mind. Once, about ten years ago, she and I were at the beach and she was scrutinizing my body with a sister's critical eye. "You're getting flabby," she said. "You should exercise every day. I do—look at me, not an ounce of fat." She pulled at her midriff, celebrating (as is her wont) her physical attributes with the third-person enthusiasm of a carnival barker.

"But"—she threw me a bone—"you do have a powerful head. There's an intensity...." A graduate student of mine (who was slightly loony) told someone that she regularly saw an aura around my head in class. One reason I like to teach is that it focuses fifteen or so dependent gazes on me with such paranoiac intensity as cannot help but generate an aura in my behalf.

I also have a commanding stare, large sad brown eyes that can be read as either gentle or severe. Once I watched several hours of myself on videotape. I discovered to my horror that my face moved at different rates: sometimes my mouth would be laughing, eyebrows circumflexed in mirth, while my eyes coolly gauged the interviewer to see what effect I was making. I am something of an actor. And, as with many performers, the mood I sense most in myself is that of energy-conserving watchfulness; but this expression is often mistaken (perhaps because of the way brown eyes are read in our culture) for sympathy. I see myself as determined to the point of stubbornness, selfish, even a bit cruel—in any case, I am all too aware of the limits of my compassion, so that it puzzles me when people report a first impression of me as gentle, kind, solicitous. In my youth I felt obliged to come across as dynamic, arrogant, intimidating, the life of the party; now, surer of myself, I hold back some energy, thereby winning time to gather information and make better judgments. This results sometimes in a misimpression of my being mildly depressed. Of course, the simple truth is that I have less energy than I once did, and that accumulated experiences have made me, almost against my will, kinder and sadder.

Sometimes I can feel my mouth arching downward in an ironic smile, which, at its best, reassures others that we need not take everything so seriously—because we are all in the same comedy together—and, at its worst, expresses a superior skepticism. This smile, which can be charming when not supercilious, has elements of the bashful that mesh with the worldly—the shyness, let us say, of a cultivated man who is often embarrassed for others by their willful shallowness or self-deception. Many times, however, my ironic smile is nothing more than a neutral stall among people who do not seem to appreciate my "contribution." I hate that pain-in-the-ass half-smile of mine; I want to jump in, participate, be loud, thoughtless, vulgar.

Often I give off a sort of psychic stench to myself, I do not like myself at all, but out of stubborn pride I act like a man who does. I appear for all the world poised, contented, sanguine when inside I may be feeling self-revulsion bordering on the suicidal. What a wonder to be so misread! Of course, if in the beginning I had thought I was coming across accurately, I never would have bothered to become a writer. And the truth is I am not misread, because another part of me is never less than fully contented with myself.

I am vain about these parts of my body: my eyes, my fingers, my legs. It is true that my legs are long and not unshapely, but my vanity about them has less to do with their comeliness than with their contribution to my height. Montaigne, a man who was himself on the short side, wrote that "the beauty of stature is the only beauty of men." But even if Montaigne had never said it, I would continue to attribute a good deal of my self-worth and benevolent liberalism to being tall. When I go out into the street, I feel well-disposed toward the (mostly shorter) swarms of humanity; crowds not only do not dismay, they enliven me; and I am tempted to think that my passion for urbanism is linked to my height. By no means am I suggesting that only tall people love cities; merely that, in my case, part of the pleasure I derive from walking in crowded streets issues from a confidence that I can see above the heads of others, and cut a fairly impressive, elevated figure as I saunter along the sidewalk.

Some of my best friends have been—short. Brilliant men, brimming with poetic and worldly ideas, they deserved all of my and the world's respect. Yet at times I have had to master an impulse to rumple their heads; and I suspect they have developed manners of a more formal, *noli me tangere* nature, largely in response to this petting impulse of taller others.

The accident of my tallness has inclined me to both a seemingly egalitarian informality and a desire to lead. Had I not been a writer, I would surely have become a politician; I was even headed in that direction in my teens. Ever since I shot up to a little over six feet, I have had at my command what feels like a natural, Gregory Peck authority when addressing an audience. Far from experiencing stage fright, I have actually sought out situations in which I could make speeches, give readings, sit on panel discussions, and generally tower over everyone else onstage. To be tall is to look down on the world and meet its eyes on your terms. But this topic, the noblesse oblige of tall men, is a dangerously provoking one, and so let us say no more about it.

The mental image of one's body changes slower than one's body. Mine was for a long while arrested in my early twenties, when I was tall and thin (165 pounds) and gobbled down whatever I felt like. I ate food that was cheap and filling, cheeseburgers, pizza, without any thought to putting on weight. But a young person's metabolism is more dietetically forgiving. To compound the problem, the older you get, the more cultivated your palate grows—and the more life's setbacks make you inclined to fill the hollowness of disappointment with the pleasures of the table.

Between the age of thirty and forty I put on ten pounds, mostly around the midsection. Since then my gut has suffered another expansion, and I tip the scales at over 180. That I took a while to notice the change may be shown by my continuing to purchase clothes at my primordial adult size (33 waist, 15½ collar), until a girlfriend started pointing out that all my clothes were too tight. I rationalized this circumstance as the result of changing fashions (thinking myself still subconsciously loyal to the sixties' penchant for skintight fits) and laundry shrinkage rather than anything to do with my own body. She began buying me larger replacements for birthdays or holidays, and I found I enjoyed this "baggier" style, which allowed me to button my trousers comfortably, or to wear a tie and, for the first time in years, close my top shirt button. But it took even longer before I was able to enter a clothing store myself and give the salesman realistically enlarged size numbers.

Clothes can disguise the defects of one's body, up to a point. I get dressed with great optimism, adding one color to another, mixing my favorite Japanese and Italian designers, matching the patterns and textures, selecting ties, then proceed to the bathroom mirror to judge the result. There is an ideal in my mind of the effect I am essaying by wearing a particular choice of garments, based, no doubt, on male models in fashion ads—and I fall so far short of this insouciant gigolo handsomeness that I cannot help but be a little disappointed when I turn up so depressingly myself, narrow-shouldered, Talmudic, that grim, set mouth, that long, narrow face, those appraising eyes, the Semitic hooked nose, all of which express both the strain of intellectual overachieving and the tabula rasa of immaturity…for it is still, underneath, a boy in the mirror. A boy with a rapidly receding hairline.

How is it that I've remained a boy all this time, into my late forties? I remember, at seventeen, drawing a self-portrait of myself as I looked in the mirror. I was so appalled at the weak chin and pleading eyes that I ended up focusing on the neckline of the cotton T-shirt. Ever since then I have tried to toughen myself up, but I still encounter in the glass that haunted uncertainty—shielded by a bluffing shell of cynicism, perhaps, but untouched by wisdom. So I approach the mirror warily, without lighting up as much as I would for the least of my acquaintances; I go one-on-one with that frowning schmuck.

And yet, it would be insulting to those who labor under the burden of true ugliness to palm myself off as an unattractive man. I'm at times almost handsome, if you squinted your eyes and rounded me off to the nearest *beau idéal*. I lack even a shred of cowboy virility, true, but I believe I fall into a category of adorable nerd or absentminded professor that awakens the amorous curiosity of some women. "Cute" is a word often applied to me by those I've been fortunate enough to attract. Then again, I attract only women of a certain lopsided prettiness: the head-turning, professional beauties never fall for me. They seem to look right through me, in fact. Their utter lack of interest in my appeal has always fascinated me. Can it be so simple an explanation as that beauty calls to beauty, as wealth to wealth?

I think of poor (though not in his writing gifts) Cesare Pavese, who kept chasing after starlets, models, and ballerinas—exquisite lovelies who couldn't appreciate his morose coffeehouse charm. Before he killed himself, he wrote a poem addressed to one of them, "Death Will Come Bearing Your Eyes"—thereby unfairly promoting her from rejecting lover to unwitting executioner. Perhaps he believed that only beautiful women (not literary critics, who kept awarding him prestigious prizes) saw him clearly, with twenty-twenty vision, and had the right to judge him. Had I been more headstrong, if masochistic, I might have followed his path and chased some beauty until she was forced to tell me, like an oracle, what it was about me, physically, that so failed to excite her. Then I might know something crucial about my body, before I passed into my next reincarnation.

Jung says somewhere that we pay dearly over many years to learn about ourselves what a stranger can see at a glance. This is the way I feel about my back. Fitting rooms aside, we none of us know what we look like from the back. It is the area of ourselves whose presentation we can least control, and which therefore may be the most honest part of us.

I divide backs into two kinds: my own and everyone else's. The others' backs are often mysterious, exquisite, and uncannily sympathetic. I have always loved backs. To walk behind a pretty woman in a backless dress and savor how a good pair of shoulder blades, heightened by shadow, has the same power to pierce the heart as chiseled cheekbones!…I wonder what it says about me that I worship a part of the body that signals a turning away. Does it mean I'm a glutton for being abandoned, or a timid voyeur who prefers a surreptitious gaze that will not be met and challenged? I only know I have often felt the deepest love at just that moment when the beloved turns her back to me to get some sleep.

I have no autoerotic feelings about my own back. I cannot even picture it; visually it is a stranger to me. I know it only as an annoyance, which came into my consciousness twenty years ago, when I started getting lower back pain. Yes, we all know that homo sapiens is constructed incorrectly; our erect posture puts too much pressure on the base of the spine; more workdays are lost because of lower back pain than any other cause. Being a writer, I sit all day, compounding the problem. My back is the enemy of my writing life: if I don't do exercises daily, I immediately ache; and if I do, I am still not spared. I could say more, but there is nothing duller than lower back pain. So common, mundane an ailment brings no credit to the sufferer. One has to dramatize it somehow, as in the phrase "I threw my back out."

Here is a gossip column about my body: My eyebrows grow quite bushy across my forehead, and whenever I get my hair cut, the barber asks me diplomatically if I want them trimmed or not. (I generally say no, associating bushy eyebrows with Balzackian virility, *élan vital*; but sometimes I acquiesce, to soothe his fastidiousness).... My belly button is a modest, embedded slit, not a jaunty swirl like my father's. Still, I like to sniff the odor that comes from jabbing my finger in it: a very ripe, underground smell, impossible to describe, but let us say a combination of old gym socks and stuffed derma (the Yiddish word for this oniony dish of ground intestines is, fittingly, *kishkas*).... I have a scar on my tongue from childhood, which I can only surmise I received by landing it on a sharp object, somehow. Or perhaps I bit it hard. I have the habit of sticking my tongue out like a dog when exerting myself physically, as though to urge my muscles on; and maybe I accidentally chomped into it at such a moment.... I gnash my teeth, sleeping or waking. Awake, the sensation makes me feel alert and in contact with the world when I start to drift off in a daydream. Another way of grounding myself is to pinch my cheek—drawing a pocket of flesh downward and squeezing it— as I once saw JFK do in a filmed motorcade. I do this cheek-pinching especially when I am trying to keep mentally focused during teaching or other public situations. I also scratch the nape of my neck under public stress, so much so that I raise welts or sores which then eventually grow scabs; and I take great delight in secretly picking the scabs off.... My nose itches whenever I think about it, and I scratch it often, especially lying in bed trying to fall asleep (maybe because I am conscious of my breathing then). I also pick my nose with formidable thoroughness when no one, I hope, is looking.... There is a white scar about the size of a quarter on the juicy part of my knee; I got it as a boy running into a car fender, and I can still remember staring with detached calm at the blood that gushed from it like a pretty, half-eaten peach. Otherwise, the sight of my own blood makes me awfully nervous. I used to faint dead away when a blood sample was taken, and now I can control the impulse to do so only by biting the insides of my cheeks while steadfastly looking away from the needle's action.... I like to clean out my ear wax as often as possible (the smell is curiously sulfurous; I associate it with the bodies of dead insects). I refuse to listen to warnings that it is dangerous to stick cleaning objects into your ears. I love Q-Tips immoderately; I buy them in huge quantities and store them the way a former refugee will stock canned foodstuffs.... My toes are long and apelike; I have very little fellow feeling for them; they are so far away, they may as well belong to someone else.... My flattish buttocks are not offensively large, but neither do they have the "dream" configuration one sees in jeans ads. Perhaps for this reason, it disturbed me puritanically when asses started to be treated by Madison Avenue, around the seventies, as crucial sexual equipment, and I began to receive compositions from teenage girl students declaring that they liked some boy because he had "a cute butt." It confused me; I had thought the action was elsewhere.

About my penis there is nothing, I think, unusual. It has a brown stem, and a pink mushroom head where the foreskin is pulled back. Like most heterosexual males, I have little comparative knowledge to go by, so that I always feel like an outsider when I am around women or gay men who talk zestfully about differences in penises. I am afraid that they might judge me harshly, ridicule me like the boys who stripped me of my bathing suit in summer camp when I was ten. But perhaps they would simply declare it an ordinary penis, which changes size with the stimulus or weather or time of day. Actually, my penis does have a peculiarity: it has two peeing holes. They are very close to each other, so that usually only one stream of urine issues, but sometimes a hair gets caught across them, or some such contretemps, and they squirt out in two directions at once.

This part of me, which is so synecdochically identified with the male body (as the term "male member" indicates), has given me both too little, and too much, information about what it means to be a man. It has a personality like a cat's. I have prayed to it to behave better, to be less frisky, or more; I have followed its nose in matters of love, ignoring good sense, and paid the price; but I have also come to appreciate that it has its own specialized form of intelligence which must be listened to, or another price will be extracted.

Even to say the word "impotence" aloud makes me nervous. I used to tremble when I saw it in print, and its close relation, "importance," if hastily scanned, had the same effect, as if they were publishing a secret about me. But why should it be *my* secret, when my penis has regularly given me erections lo these many years—except for about a dozen times, mostly when I was younger? Because, even if it has not been that big a problem for me, it has dominated my thinking as an adult male. I've no sooner to go to bed with a woman than I'm in suspense. The power of the flaccid penis's statement, "I don't want you," is so stark, so cruelly direct, that it continues to exert a fascination out of all proportion to its actual incidence. Those few times when I was unable to function were like a wall forcing me to take another path—just as, after I tried to kill myself at seventeen, I was obliged to give up pessimism for a time. Each had instructed me by its too painful manner that I could not handle the world as I had previously construed it, that my confusion and rage were being found out. I would have to get more wily or else grow up.

Yet for the very reason that I was compelled to leave them behind, these two options of my youth, impotence and suicide, continue to command an underground loyalty, as though they were more "honest" than the devious strategies of potency and survival which I adopted. Put it this way: sometimes we encounter a person who has had a nervous breakdown years before and who seems cemented over sloppily, his vulnerability ruthlessly guarded against as dangerous; we sense he left a crucial part of himself back in the chaos of breakdown, and has since grown rigidly jovial. So suicide and impotence became for me "the roads not taken," the paths I had repressed.

Whenever I hear an anecdote about impotence—a woman who successfully coaxed an ex-priest who had been celibate and unable to make love, first by lying next to him for six months without any touching, then by cuddling for six more months, then by easing him slowly into a sexual embrace—I think they are talking about me. I identify completely: this, in spite of the fact, which I promise not to repeat again, that I have generally been able to do it whenever called upon. Believe it or not, I am not boasting when I say that: a part of me is contemptuous of this virility, as though it were merely a mechanical trick that violated my true nature, that of an impotent man absolutely frightened of women, absolutely secluded, cut off.

I now see the way I have idealized impotence: I've connected it with pushing the world away, as a kind of integrity, as in Molière's *The Misanthrope*—connected it with that part of me which, gregarious socializer that I am, continues to insist that I am a recluse, too good for this life. Of course, it is not true that I am terrified of women. I exaggerate my terror of them for dramatic effect, or for the purposes of a good scare.

My final word about impotence: Once, in a period when I was going out with many women, as though purposely trying to ignore my hypersensitive side and force it to grow callous by thrusting myself into foreign situations (not only sexual) and seeing if I was able to "rise to the occasion," I dated a woman who was attractive, tall and blond, named Susan. She had something to do with the pop music business, was a follower of the visionary religious futurist Teilhard de Chardin, and considered herself a religious pacifist. In fact, she told me her telephone number in the form of the anagram, N-O-T-O-W-A-R. I thought she was joking and laughed aloud, but she gave me a solemn look. In passing, I should say that all the women with whom I was impotent or close to it had solemn natures. The sex act has always seemed to me in many ways ridiculous, and I am most comfortable when a woman who enters the sheets with me shares that sense of the comic pomposity behind such a grandiloquently rhetorical use of the flesh. It is as though the prose of the body were being drastically squeezed into metrical verse. I would not have known how to stop guffawing had I been D. H. Lawrence's lover, and I am sure he would have been pretty annoyed at me. But a smile saying "All this will pass" has an erotic effect on me like nothing else.

They claim that men who have long, long fingers also have lengthy penises. I can tell you with a surety that my fingers are long and sensitive, the most perfect, elegant, handsome part of my anatomy. They are not entirely perfect—the last knuckle of my right middle finger is twisted permanently, broken in a softball game when I was trying to block the plate—but even this slight disfigurement, harbinger of mortality, adds to the pleasure I take in my hands' rugged beauty. My penis does not excite in me nearly the same contemplative delight when I look at it as do my fingers. Pianists' hands, I have been told often; and though I do not play the piano, I derive an aesthetic satisfaction from them that is as pure and Apollonian as any I am capable of. I can stare at my fingers for hours. No wonder I have them so often in my mouth, biting my fingernails to bring them closer. When I write, I almost feel that they, and not my intellect, are the clever progenitors of the text. Whatever narcissism, fetishism, and proud sense of masculinity I possess about my body must begin and end with my fingers.

Carnal Acts

Nancy Mairs

Inviting me to speak at her small liberal-arts college during Women's Week, a young woman set me a task: "We would be pleased," she wrote, "if you could talk on how you cope with your MS disability, and also how you discovered your voice as a writer." Oh, Lord, I thought in dismay, how am I going to pull this one off? How can I yoke two such disparate subjects into a coherent presentation, without doing violence to one, or the other, or both, or myself? This is going to take some fancy footwork, and my feet scarcely carry out the basic steps, let alone anything elaborate.

To make matters worse, the assumption underlying each of her questions struck me as suspect. To ask *how* I cope with multiple sclerosis suggests that I *do* cope. Now, "to cope," *Webster's Third* tells me, is "to face or encounter and to find necessary expedients to overcome problems and difficulties." In these terms, I have to confess, I don't feel like much of a coper. I'm likely to deal with my problems and difficulties by squawking and flapping around like that hysterical chicken who was convinced the sky was falling. Never mind that in my case the sky really *is* falling. In response to a clonk on the head, regardless of its origin, one might comport oneself with a grace and courtesy I generally lack.

As for "finding" my voice, the implication is that it was at one time lost or missing. But I don't think it ever was. Ask my mother, who will tell you a little wearily that I was speaking full sentences by the time I was a year old and could never be silenced again. As for its being a writer's voice, it seems to have become one early on. Ask Mother again. At the age of eight I rewrote the Trojan War, she will say, and what Nestor was about to do to Helen at the end doesn't bear discussion in polite company.

Faced with these uncertainties, I took my own teacherly advice, something, I must confess, I don't always do. "If an idea is giving you trouble," I tell my writing students, "put it on the back burner and let it simmer while you do something else. Go to the movies. Reread a stack of old love letters. Sit in your history class and take detailed notes on the Teapot Dome scandal. If you've got your idea in mind, it will go on cooking at some level no matter what else you're doing." "I've had an idea for my documented essay on the back burner," one of my students once scribbled in her journal, "and I think it's just boiled over!"

I can't claim to have reached such a flash point. But in the weeks I've had the themes "disability" and "voice" sitting around in my head, they seem to have converged on their own, without my having to wrench them together and bind them with hoops of tough rhetoric. They *are* related, indeed interdependent, with an intimacy that has for some reason remained, until now, submerged below the surface of my attention. Forced to juxtapose them, I yank them out of the depths, a little startled to discover how they were intertwined down there out of sight. This kind of discovery can unnerve you at first. You feel like a giant hand that, pulling two swimmers out of the water, two separate heads bobbling on the iridescent swells, finds the two bodies below, legs coiled around each other, in an ecstasy of copulation. You don't quite know where to turn your eyes.

Perhaps the place to start illuminating this erotic connection between who I am and how I speak lies in history. I have known that I have multiple sclerosis for about seventeen years now, though the disease probably started long before. The hypothesis is that the disease process, in which the protective covering of the nerves in the brain and spinal cord is eaten away and replaced by scar tissue, "hard patches," is caused by an autoimmune reaction to a slow-acting virus. Research suggests that I was infected by this virus, which no one has ever seen and which therefore, technically, doesn't even "exist," between the ages of four and fifteen. In effect, living with this mysterious mechanism feels like having your present self, and the past selves it embodies, haunted by a capricious and meanspirited ghost, unseen except for its footprints, which trips you even when you're watching where you're going, knocks glassware out of your hand, squeezes the urine out of your bladder before you reach the bathroom, and weights your whole body with a weariness no amount of rest can relieve. An alien invader must be at work. But of course it's not. It's your own body. That is, it's you.

This, for me, has been the most difficult aspect of adjusting to a chronic incurable degenerative disease: the fact that it has rammed my "self" straight back into the body I had been trained to believe it could, through highminded acts and aspirations, rise above. The Western tradition of distinguishing the body from the mind and/or the soul is so ancient as to have become part of our collective unconscious, if one is inclined to believe in such a noumenon, or at least to have become an unquestioned element in the social instruction we impose upon infants from birth, in much the same way we inculcate, without reflection, the gender distinctions "female" and "male." I *have* a body, you are likely to say if you talk about embodiment at all; you don't say, I *am* a body. A body is a separate entity possessable by the "I"; the "I" and the body aren't, as the copula would make them, grammatically indistinguishable.

To widen the rift between the self and the body, we treat our bodies as subordinates, inferior in moral status. Open association with them shames us. In fact, we treat our bodies with very much the same distance and ambivalence women have traditionally received from men in our culture. Sometimes this treatment is benevolent, even respectful, but all too often it is tainted by outright sadism. I think of the body-building regimens that have become popular in the last decade or so, with the complicated vacillations they reflect between self-worship and self-degradation: joggers and aerobic dancers and weightlifters all beating their bodies into shape. "No pain, no gain," the saying goes. "Feel the burn." Bodies get treated like wayward women who have to be shown who's boss, even if it means slapping them around a little. I'm not for a moment opposing rugged exercise here. I'm simply questioning the spirit in which it is often undertaken.

Since, as Hélène Cixous points out in her essay on women and writing, "Sorties,"* thought has always worked "through dual, hierarchical oppositions" (p. 64), the mind/body split cannot possibly be innocent. The utterance of an "I" immediately calls into being its opposite, the "not-I," Western discourse being unequipped to conceive "that which is neither 'I' nor 'not-I,'" "that which is both 'I' and 'not-I,'" or some other permutation which language doesn't permit me to speak. The "not-I" is, by definition, other. And we've never been too fond of the other. We prefer the same. We tend to ascribe to the other those qualities we prefer not to associate with our selves: it is the hidden, the dark, the secret, the shameful. Thus, when the "I" takes possession of the body, it makes the body into an other, direct object of a transitive verb, with all the other's repudiated and potentially dangerous qualities.

At the least, then, the body had best be viewed with suspicion. And a woman's body is particularly suspect, since so much of it is in fact hidden, dark, secret, carried about on the inside where, even with the aid of a speculum, one can never perceive all of it in the plain light of day, a graspable whole. I, for one, have never understood why anyone would want to carry all that delicate stuff around on the outside. It would make you awfully anxious, I should think, put you constantly on the defensive, create a kind of siege mentality that viewed all other beings, even your own kind, as threats to be warded off with spears and guns and atomic missiles. And you'd never get to experience that inward dreaming that comes when your flesh surrounds all your treasures, holding them close, like a sturdy shuttered house. Be my personal skepticism as it may, however, as a cultural woman I bear just as much shame as any woman for my dark, enfolded secrets. Let the word for my external genitals tell the tale: my pudendum, from the Latin infinitive meaning "to be ashamed."

It's bad enough to carry your genitals like a sealed envelope bearing the cipher that, once unlocked, might loose the chaotic flood of female pleasure—*jouissance*, the French call it—upon the world-of-the-same. But I have an additional reason to feel shame for my body, less explicitly connected with its sexuality: it is a crippled body. Thus it is doubly other, not merely by the homo-sexual standards of patriarchal culture but by the standards of physical desirability erected for every body in our world. Men, who are by definition exonerated from shame in sexual terms (this doesn't mean that an individual man might not experience sexual shame, of course; remember that I'm talking in general about discourse, not folks), may—more likely must—experience bodily shame if they are crippled. I won't presume to speak about the details of their experience, however. I don't know enough. I'll just go on telling what it's like to be a crippled woman, trusting that, since we're fellow creatures who've been living together for some thousands of years now, much of my experience will resonate with theirs.

*In *The Newly Born Woman*, translated by Betsy Wing (Minneapolis: University of Minnesota Press, 1986).

I was never a beautiful woman, and for that reason I've spent most of my life (together with probably at least 95 percent of the female population of the United States) suffering from the shame of falling short of an unattainable standard. The ideal woman of my generation was…perky, I think you'd say, rather than gorgeous. Blond hair pulled into a bouncing ponytail. Wide blue eyes, a turned-up nose with maybe a scattering of golden freckles across it, a small mouth with full lips over straight white teeth. Her breasts were large but well harnessed high on her chest; her tiny waist flared to hips just wide enough to give the crinolines under her circle skirt a starting outward push. In terms of personality, she was outgoing, even bubbly, not pensive or mysterious. Her milieu was the front fender of a white Corvette convertible, surrounded by teasing crewcuts, dressed in black flats, a sissy blouse, and the letter sweater of the Corvette owner. Needless to say, she never missed a prom.

Ten years or so later, when I first noticed the symptoms that would be diagnosed as MS, I was probably looking my best. Not beautiful still, but the ideal had shifted enough so that my flat chest and narrow hips gave me an elegantly attenuated shape, set off by a thick mass of long, straight, shining hair. I had terrific legs, long and shapely, revealed nearly to the pudendum by the fashionable miniskirts and hot pants I adopted with more enthusiasm than delicacy of taste. Not surprisingly, I suppose, during this time I involved myself in several pretty torrid love affairs.

The beginning of MS wasn't too bad. The first symptom, besides the pernicious fatigue that had begun to devour me, was "foot drop," the inability to raise my left foot at the ankle. As a consequence, I'd started to limp, but I could still wear high heels, and a bit of a limp might seem more intriguing than repulsive. After a few months, when the doctor suggested a cane, a crippled friend gave me quite an elegant wood-and-silver one, which I carried with a fair amount of panache. The real blow to my self-image came when I had to get a brace. As braces go, it's not bad: lightweight plastic molded to my foot and leg, fitting down into an ordinary shoe and secured around my calf by a Velcro strap. It reduces my limp and, more important, the danger of tripping and falling. But it meant the end of high heels. And it's ugly. Not as ugly as I think it is, I gather, but still pretty ugly. It signified for me, and perhaps still does, the permanence and irreversibility of my condition. The brace makes my MS concrete and forces me to wear it on the outside. As soon as I strapped the brace on, I climbed into trousers and stayed there (though not in the same trousers, of course). The idea of going around with my bare brace hanging out seemed almost as indecent as exposing my breasts. Not until 1984, soon after I won the Western States Book Award for poetry, did I put on a skirt short enough to reveal my plasticized leg. The connection between winning a writing award and baring my brace is not merely fortuitous; being affirmed as a writer really did embolden me. Since then, I've grown so accustomed to wearing skirts that I don't think about my brace any more than I think about my cane. I've incorporated them, I suppose: made them, in their necessity, insensate but fundamental parts of my body.

Meanwhile, I had to adjust to the most outward and visible sign of all, a three-wheeled electric scooter called an Amigo. This lessens my fatigue and increases my range terrifically, but it also shouts out to the world, "Here is a woman who can't stand on her own two feet." At the same time, paradoxically, it renders me invisible, reducing me to the height of a seven-year-old, with a child's attendant low status. "Would she like smoking or nonsmoking?" the gate agent assigning me a seat asks the friend traveling with me. In crowds I see nothing but buttocks. I can tell you the name of every type of designer jeans ever sold. The wearers, eyes front, trip over me and fall across my handlebars into my lap. "Hey!" I want to shout to the lofty world. "Down here! There's a person down here!" But I'm not, by their standards, quite a person anymore.

My self-esteem diminishes further as age and illness strip from me the features that made me, for a brief while anyway, a good-looking, even sexy, young woman. No more long, bounding strides: I shuffle along with the timid gait I remember observing, with pity and impatience, in the little old ladies at Boston's Symphony Hall on Friday afternoons. No more lithe, girlish figure: my belly sags from the loss of muscle tone, which also creates all kinds of intestinal disruptions, hopelessly humiliating in a society in which excretory functions remain strictly unspeakable. No more sex, either, if society had its way. The sexuality of the disabled so repulses most people that you can hardly get a doctor, let alone a member of the general population, to consider the issues it raises. Cripples simply aren't supposed to Want It, much less Do It. Fortunately, I've got a husband with a strong libido and a weak sense of social propriety, or else I'd find myself perforce practicing a vow of chastity I never cared to take.

Afflicted by the general shame of having a body at all, and the specific shame of having one weakened and misshapen by disease, I ought not to be able to hold my head up in public. And yet I've gotten into the habit of holding my head up in public, sometimes under excruciating circumstances. Recently, for instance, I had to give a reading at the University of Arizona. Having smashed three of my front teeth in a fall onto the concrete floor of my screened porch, I was in the process of getting them crowned, and the temporary crowns flew out during dinner right before the reading. What to do? I wanted, of course, to rush home and hide till the dental office opened the next morning. But I couldn't very well break my word at this last moment. So, looking like Hansel and Gretel's witch, and lisping worse than the Wife of Bath, I got up on stage and read. Somehow, over the years, I've learned how to set shame aside and do what I have to do.

Here, I think, is where my "voice" comes in. Because, in spite of my demurral at the beginning, I do in fact cope with my disability at least some of the time. And I do so, I think, by speaking about it, and about the whole experience of being a body, specifically a female body, out loud, in a clear, level tone that drowns out the frantic whispers of my mother, my grandmothers, all the other trainers of wayward childish tongues: "Sssh! Sssh! Nice girls don't talk like that. Don't mention sweat. Don't mention menstrual blood. Don't ask what your grandfather does on his business trips. Don't laugh so loud. You sound like a loon. Keep your voice down. Don't tell. Don't tell. Don't tell." Speaking out loud is an antidote to shame. I want to distinguish clearly here between "shame," as I'm using the word, and "guilt" and "embarrassment," which, though equally painful, are not similarly poisonous. Guilt arises from performing a forbidden act or failing to perform a required one. In either case, the guilty person can, through reparation, erase the offense and start fresh. Embarrassment, less opprobrious though not necessarily less distressing, is generally caused by acting in a socially stupid or awkward way. When I trip and sprawl in public, when I wet myself, when my front teeth fly out, I feel horribly embarrassed, but, like the pain of childbirth, the sensation blurs and dissolves in time. If it didn't, every child would be an only child, and no one would set foot in public after the onset of puberty, when embarrassment erupts like a geyser and bathes one's whole life in its bitter stream. Shame may attach itself to guilt or embarrassment, complicating their resolution, but it is not the same emotion. I feel guilt or embarrassment for something I've done; shame, for who I am. I may stop doing bad or stupid things, but I can't stop being. How then can I help but be ashamed? Of the three conditions, this is the one that cracks and stifles my voice.

I can subvert its power, I've found, by acknowledging who I am, shame and all, and, in doing so, raising what was hidden, dark, secret about my life into the plain light of shared human experience. What we aren't permitted to utter holds us, each isolated from every other, in a kind of solipsistic thrall. Without any way to check our reality against anyone else's, we assume that our fears and shortcomings are ours alone. One of the strangest consequences of publishing a collection of personal essays called *Plaintext* has been the steady trickle of letters and telephone calls saying essentially, in a tone of unmistakable relief, "Oh, me too! Me too!" It's as though the part I thought was solo has turned out to be a chorus. But none of us was singing loud enough for the others to hear.

Singing loud enough demands a particular kind of voice, I think. And I was wrong to suggest, at the beginning, that I've always had my voice. I have indeed always had *a* voice, but it wasn't *this* voice, the one with which I could call up and transform my hidden self from a naughty girl into a woman talking directly to others like herself. Recently, in the process of writing a new book, a memoir entitled *Remembering the Bone House*, I've had occasion to read some of my early writing, from college, high school, even junior high. It's not an experience I recommend to anyone susceptible to shame. Not that the writing was all that bad. I was surprised at how competent a lot of it was. Here was a writer who already knew precisely how the language worked. But the voice…oh, the voice was all wrong: maudlin, rhapsodic, breaking here and there into little shrieks, almost, you might say, hysterical. It was a voice that had shucked off its own body, its own homely life of Cheerios for breakfast and seventy pages of Chaucer to read before the exam on Tuesday and a planter's wart growing painfully on the ball of its foot, and reeled now wraithlike through the air, seeking incarnation only as the heroine who enacts her doomed love for the tall, dark, mysterious stranger. If it didn't get that part, it wouldn't play at all.

Among all these overheated and vaporous imaginings, I must have retained some shred of sense, because I stopped writing prose entirely, except for scholarly papers, for nearly twenty years. I even forgot, not exactly that I had written prose, but at least what kind of prose it was. So when I needed to take up the process again, I could start almost fresh, using the vocal range I'd gotten used to in years of asking the waiter in the Greek restaurant for an extra anchovy on my salad, congratulating the puppy on making a puddle outside rather than inside the patio door, pondering with my daughter the vagaries of female orgasm, saying goodbye to my husband, and hello, and goodbye, and hello. This new voice—thoughtful, affectionate, often amused—

was essential because what I needed to write about when I returned to prose was an attempt I'd made not long before to kill myself, and suicide simply refuses to be spoken of authentically in highflown romantic language. It's too ugly. Too shameful. Too strictly a bodily event. And, yes, too funny as well, though people are sometimes shocked to find humor shoved up against suicide. They don't like the incongruity. But let's face it, life (real life, I mean, not the edited-for-television version) is a cacophonous affair from start to finish. I might have wanted to portray my suicidal self as a languishing maiden, too exquisitely sensitive to sustain life's wounding pressures on her soul. (I didn't want to, as a matter of fact, but I might have.) The truth remained, regardless of my desires, that when my husband lugged me into the emergency room, my hair matted, my face swollen and gray, my nightgown streaked with blood and urine, I was no frail and tender spirit. I was a body, and one in a hell of a mess.

I "should" have kept quiet about that experience. I know the rules of polite discourse. I should have kept my shame, and the nearly lethal sense of isolation and alienation it brought, to myself. And I might have, except for something the psychiatrist in the emergency room had told my husband. "You might as well take her home," he said. "If she wants to kill herself, she'll do it no matter how many precautions we take. They always do." *They* always do. I was one of "them," whoever they were. I was, in this context anyway, not singular, not aberrant, but typical. I think it was this sense of commonality with others I didn't even know, a sense of being returned somehow, in spite of my appalling act, to the human family, that urged me to write that first essay, not merely speaking out but calling out, perhaps. "Here's the way I am," it said. "How about you?" And the answer came, as I've said: "Me too! Me too!"

This has been the kind of work I've continued to do: to scrutinize the details of my own experience and to report what I see, and what I think about what I see, as lucidly and accurately as possible. But because feminine experience has been immemorially devalued and repressed, I continue to find this task terrifying. "Every woman has known the torture of beginning to speak aloud," Cixous writes, "heart beating as if to break, occasionally falling into loss of language, ground and language slipping out from under her, because for woman speaking—even just opening her mouth—in public is something rash, a transgression" (p. 92).

The voice I summon up wants to crack, to whisper, to trail back into silence. "I'm sorry to have nothing more than this to say," it wants to apologize. "I shouldn't be taking up your time. I've never fought in a war, or even in a schoolyard free-for-all. I've never tried to see who could piss farthest up the barn wall. I've never even been to a whorehouse. All the important formative experiences have passed me by. I was raped once. I've borne two children. Milk trickling out of my breasts, blood trickling from between my legs. You don't want to hear about it. Sometimes I'm too scared to leave my house. Not scared *of* anything, just scared: mouth dry, bowels writhing. When the fear got really bad, they locked me up for six months, but that was years ago. I'm getting old now. Misshapen, too. I don't blame you if you can't get it up. No one could possibly desire a body like this. It's not your fault. It's mine. Forgive me. I didn't mean to start crying. I'm sorry…sorry…sorry…."

An easy solace to the anxiety of speaking aloud: this slow subsidence beneath the waves of shame, back into what Cixous calls "this body that has been worse than confiscated, a body replaced with a disturbing stranger, sick or dead, who so often is a bad influence, the cause and place of inhibitions. By censuring the body," she goes on, "breath and speech are censored at the same time" (p. 97). But I am not going back, not going under one more time. To do so would demonstrate a failure of nerve far worse than the depredations of MS have caused. Paradoxically, losing one sort of nerve has given me another. No one is going to take my breath away. No one is going to leave me speechless. To be silent is to comply with the standard of feminine grace. But my crippled body already violates all notions of feminine grace. What more have I got to lose? I've gone beyond shame. I'm shameless, you might say. You know, as in "shameless hussy"? A woman with her bare brace and her tongue hanging out.

I've "found" my voice, then, just where it ought to have been, in the body-warmed breath escaping my lungs and throat. Forced by the exigencies of physical disease to embrace my self in the flesh, I couldn't write bodiless prose. The voice is the creature of the body that produces it. I speak as a crippled woman. At the same time, in the utterance I redeem both "cripple" and "woman" from the shameful silences by which I have often felt surrounded, contained, set apart; I give myself permission to live openly among others, to reach out for them, stroke them with fingers and sighs. No body, no voice; no voice, no body. That's what I know in my bones.

From Birnam Wood to Dunsinane

John McPhee

In most families, a generation or two is time enough to erase even a major infamy, but centuries upon centuries have not in this respect been kind to the Macbeths, as anyone knows who knows one. I've known several Macbeths, and I particularly remember the moments in which I met them, because in most instances a faint shadow seemed to cross their faces when their surname was exposed to yet another stranger. The latest of these is R. C. Macbeth, of Scarsdale. We were introduced—as travellers, as strangers, in a small town in New England—by a motelkeeper who was serving our breakfast, and who in her friendly way seemed to think that we would have much to say to each other simply because our names were derivationally Scottish. This Macbeth was a big, broad-shouldered man with bright eyes and an engagingly unprepossessing manner. As it happened, he did have a lot to say. He had scarcely sat down before he was well into a mild harangue about the injuries that had been done to his family through poetic license and dramatic journalism—manipulations of the pen. He said that his collateral ancestor Macbeth, King of Scotland, was a good king and is buried with other Scottish kings on the island Iona in a sanctuary where only authentic and duly entitled kings are at rest; that no one who had poached the throne of Scotland would ever have been buried, or at least would have long remained buried, on Iona; that Macbeth, in 1040, killed King Duncan not in bed but in battle; that Macbeth's claim to rule the Scots was as legitimate as Duncan's, each, through his mother, being a great-grandson of King Kenneth I; and that Macbeth settled the claim, as was the custom in his time, with his sword in fair and open fight. His reign lasted seventeen years. I could be well assured that something quite different from tyranny or depravity was the atmosphere that generally emanated from his fortress on the summit of Dunsinane Hill.

I said to Mr. Macbeth, "I'm sorry you have this cross to bear."

Macbeth lifted his coffee cup, indicating that he would drink to that. He drank. Then he said, "I've never been to Scotland. In a year or two, though, I'm going to go."

I said, "Let me give you a name and address. Donald Sinclair, Balbeggie, Perthshire. I'll write it down. He's a farmer. He's the cousin of a friend of mine. I don't know Sinclair very well, but I don't think he would mind if you were to seek him out, which is what I did once. I was in Scotland with my family, and one day—just for the experience—we went by the most direct way we could find from Birnam Wood to Dunsinane. It's a ten-mile trip. Sinclair calls himself a tenant farmer. Technically, that's what he is, but his father-in-law happens to be his landlord, and the family owns a very handsome piece of Perthshire—five thousand acres. Their estate is called Dunsinnan, and more or less in the middle of it is Dunsinane Hill."

Macbeth slowly set down his plastic coffee cup on the Formica surface of the table. I told him the details of the pilgrimage as I had made it.

Birnam Wood, on the edge of the Craigvinean Forest, stands across the River Tay from a medieval town, Dunkeld, and has been replaced to some extent by Birnam, a village that developed in the late nineteenth century. Birnam Wood now is deep and thick, dark green, with an understory of gorse and bracken, and white slashes of birch angling upward among larches and pines. In all likelihood, the boughs of such trees could not have been the boughs that went to Dunsinane. Apparently the forest was once predominantly oak. The present Birnam Wood, cut who knows how many times, seems to be merely a collateral descendant of the forest that once was there, for the presence of a number of slim oaks among the pines suggests what must have been, in the virgin stand, the climax tree. The army assembled by Siward, Malcolm, and Macduff would have marched under oak leaves. By the river is one immensely impressive piece of evidence suggesting that this was so. One tree, an oak, remains from—according to local testimony—the time of Macbeth. It stands in a riparian grove of grasses, weeds, and rusting junk. Nothing much is made of it. I used up half a morning finding it. A postman on the principal street of Birnam had told me about it. "The old trees are away now, unfortunately. But there is still one left. It is propped up." We picked our way downhill—my four small daughters, my wife, and I—along dirt pathways strewn with discarded plastic bottles and fragments of broken glass. The groundscape was somewhat cleaner and more inviting closer to the river, where another path ran along parallel to the current and passed under the high canopies of trees at least a century old. These were whips, seedlings, saplings by comparison with the tree we finally found. There it was, standing without fence or fanfare, its trunk outmassing the Heidelberg tun, its roemerian canopy all but stopping the sunlight: the last tree of Birnam Wood, a living monument to the value of staying put.

My wife and children and I joined hands, and we wrapped ourselves to the tree with arms extended. The six of us reached less than halfway around. The big oak was so gnarled that it appeared to be covered with highly magnified warts. Each of ten principal limbs had the diameter of a major oak in itself, and the lower ones, jutting out almost horizontally, were supported in six places by columns set in the ground. One great limb was dead. In the base of the trunk were cavelike holes. Lichen grew on the bark as if the tree were already down and moldering. But despite all that, the tree was green throughout its canopy—leafy and alive. This big oak alone could have camouflaged an army.

We sat down on the riverbank and had lunch. The Tay was fast, clear, and shallow, and about two hundred yards downstream was a small rip, a touch of white water. The flow was southerly, in the general direction of Dunsinane, so the army would have moved for some distance along the river on its way to the hill. We ate cold roast beef, white chocolate, and Islay Mini-Dunlop cheese. I reached up and took a leaf from the great oak, and we began the journey.

First, we stopped in at the Esso Autodiesel & Petrol Agency in Birnam and had the tank of our car filled, for five shillings sixpence halfpenny the gallon. The attendant gave the children Esso tiger tails. Below Birnam the riverine countryside was lush with wheat fields, haycocks, oats, barley. Multicolored lupines and wild foxgloves grew in meadows where herds of Aberdeen Angus were sleeping, all draped together with their necks across the necks of the cows beside them. It was a clear day, warm but not hot. A tractor plowing a field was followed by flights of seagulls. The gulls were eating the worms that the tractor turned up. We moved through a grove of seventy-foot cedars, copper beeches, and hemlocks on a dark lane running among standing stones, through weirdly overgrown formal gardens, and past an Italianate castle no more than a century old, now boarded shut and falling to ruin. We later found in a book on Dunkeld and Birnam that this (Murthly Castle) had been the home of an exotic peer who had once ornamented the grounds with herds of buffalo from Wyoming. In his milieu, he may not have been eccentric. Even today, we know someone in the same part of Perthshire who keeps a considerable herd of pet red deer, and when he goes off in summer to the far north—to Caithness—he takes his red deer with him in chartered freight cars.

Murthly Hospital, for mental patients, came soon after Murthly Castle and was about a third of the way from Birnam Wood to Dunsinane. Like the decaying structure upriver, the main buildings of the hospital, amorphous and ugly, must have been about a century old, and in their setting among woods and fields by the Tay they did not seem as forbidding in the sunlight as they must in the gloom of rain. The place belied itself, if it ever could, this day. Women sat on benches in brightly colored straw hats. Men in coveralls bowled on a lawn. Others gardened. Distress was invisible, but nonetheless my children were unnaturally quiet. Doctors crossed the grounds in white jackets. A big nurse, whose size was a kind of manifesto of control, carried a fragile and extremely old woman in her arms. Rows of stone cottages had names over their doors like Tuke, Robertson, Bruce. Among them, a giant and rusting television aerial was planted in the earth like a tree. One of the men on the bowling court left the game and ran toward us, smiling and waving his arms. I did not for a moment know what I wanted to do. He was running hard. Was I going to avoid him and renew, in one more way, his hurt; or was I going to become enskeined in a dialogue that could, in the end, be even less successful in the breaking? I left him behind, standing by the road, without expression, watching us go.

The country opened out again beyond the hospital, and the river made an erratic series of turns to the north, the east, the southeast, and, finally, the southwest, forming an irregular loop about two miles broad. Anybody moving overland from

Birnam Wood to Dunsinane would cross this loop, and so did we, first going through the Haugh of Kercock, a low-lying meadow by the river. In a fank in the meadow, men were shearing sheep. Lambs were bleating wildly. Shorn ewes stood around looking silly and naked. One man had the head of a ewe in his arms, and was wrestling with her desperately, rolling on the ground. Moving on, we skirted a marshland called the Bloody Inches. Beautiful farm country followed toward Kinclaven, a village by the Tay, on the far side of the loop. In the fields, huge strawstacks had been constructed like houses—rectangular, with vertical walls, and tops sloping up to ridgelines. Moving along an unpaved lane, we came to a church that was black with age, and among the tombstones beside it a man was digging a grave. We stopped to ask him the way to Dunsinane. He said he had been digging graves there forty-four years and had been born and raised in Kinclaven but had no idea how to get to Dunsinane. He said, "It's not far. It's a small place, I can tell you that." His shovel struck something in the ground. He explained that when he digs graves he often encounters the foundations of churches that, one after another, had been on the site before this one. A church must have been there when Macbeth's castle stood on Dunsinane Hill. According to the Scottish historian R. L. Mackie, Macbeth was so religious that he once made a pilgrimage to Rome. All the way to the Vatican and back, he flung money at the poor. Since he lived less than five miles away from Kinclaven, he and Lady Macbeth must have gone to church here from time to time.

We crossed the river, made a right, went through a railway embankment, made a left at Cargill Smithy, and began a long upgrade toward Gallowhill, Wolfhill, and Dunsinnan, through villages of strawstacks, and more wheat, oats, and barley in dark-red earth. We found Donald Sinclair among his steadings, some two miles from Dunsinane Hill.

Sinclair seemed amused that we wanted to climb his hill, and not at all put out. I had thought that people must come in battalions to Dunsinane, and that Sinclair probably spent a lot of his time protecting his land. He said that was not the case. A busload of Boy Scouts from Perth might turn up once in a rare while, but that was about all. Few people seem to realize that there really is a Dunsinane Hill. Shakespeare, he said, took an "n" out of Dunsinnan and added an "e," but did not create the hill. "The name in Gaelic means 'hill of the ants.' Streams of little men went up and down the hill when the castle was being built. Shall we go?"

We drove with him through fields and in woodland, made a few turns, and all at once saw a high green hill fringed with rowan trees and mountain ash in blossom. Dunsinane is at the southwestern end of the serrated line of the Sidlaw Hills. The other Sidlaws, reaching away to the northeast, were all mauve-brown with heather, and Dunsinane stood out among them because it was bright green. Heather apparently will not grow where man has ever performed his constructions. Even from the foot of Dunsinane, we could see that its summit was flat—absolutely truncated, as if it had been sliced level with a knife. We started up its grassy, southern slope. Sinclair's Herefords were grazing there. 'I raise beef cattle,' he said. "They summer on the hill. When a busload of Boy Scouts comes, it is much to my horror, because I've got a bull amongst the cows here." Sinclair was wearing wide-wale corduroy trousers, a threadbare baggy sweater, a shirt, a wool tie. Still in his forties, a tall man, he looked weathered, as if he had always been there. He seemed to be at one with his land and his hill, and nothing about his loose-postured walk suggested that he was a graduate of Sandhurst, which he was—a career military man, born off a wheat farm in Manitoba, raised in England, an Army officer from the Second World War until the early nineteen-sixties, when he became the tenant farmer of Dunsinane Hill. We went around a shoulder of the terrain. "There he is," Sinclair said. We passed close by a congenial-looking Hereford bull. He was rust-red, almost top-heavy, the kind of animal that appears to consist of about nine tons of solid steak, and, with his white-rug face, to be as fierce as Ferdinand. "We call him Old Joe."

The slopes of the hill rose and converged with an almost volcanic symmetry, so the climb became quite steep. We passed a spring. "This is where Macbeth got his water," Sinclair said. "The sort of outer fortifications must have reached this far." We kept moving up, breathing hard and not talking for a while, until Sinclair paused for a moment, tilted his head back, looked up at the summit, and said, "It's pretty impregnable, I should think. I shouldn't like to climb up here and have people pouring boiling oil on me."

The summit was flat and oval, and Macbeth's floor plan was evident there, for the foundation protruded in lumpy ridges under the turf. The castle was no cramped little broch. It was a hundred and twenty feet wide and two hundred and twenty-five feet long—just slightly larger than the Parthenon. Hill of the ants, indeed: Macbeth apparently did not do things by halves. The view from the summit over the patchwork Scottish countryside was extraordinary. It is a virtual certainty that Shakespeare never set eyes on Dunsinane. If he had, he would have described it. In fact, his entire description of Dunsinane Hill comes in two words, "high" and "great."

> *Macbeth shall never vanquished be until*
> *Great Birnam Wood to high Dunsinane Hill*
> *Shall come against him.*

> *Great Dunsinane he strongly fortifies:*
> *Some say he's mad.*

Curlews and oyster catchers cried overhead. This was June, and we could see the Grampians, far in the distance, with snow still on them. We could see, three hundred and sixty degrees around us, a fifth of Scotland—to Fife, to Dundee—and out over the North Sea. It would be hard to imagine a more apt or beautiful setting for a fortress home. Sinclair said that the Picts had chosen the spot centuries before Macbeth, and that Dunsinane had been only one of a whole line of Pictish forts in the Sidlaws—"a sort of defense effort against the Vikings."

We sat down on the base of a rampart. A cool, erratic wind was blowing. Sinclair told us, offhandedly, that the supposed Stone of Scone now in Westminster Abbey is actually a worthless rock from Dunsinane Hill. He said that the real Stone of Scone had been buried in Dunsinane Hill long ago, when the substitute was chosen, and that the real one had been dug up in the nineteenth century only to be reburied after a short time, and that despite all the more recent flurries about the (fake) Stone of Scone in Westminster Abbey, the real one was still there in the hill. Sinclair pointed out Scone, over toward Perth, and added that that was the dullest direction to look in, for, with the dubious exceptions of Scone and Perth, "you can't see anything madly exciting." Closer in and on a more northerly line, he called attention to a small stone house trimmed in red, and he said, "That is where Macbeth settled his three wise women." Moving his hand, pointing, he said, "That farm down there is called Balmalcolm. The next one is Fairy Green, where they found a Pictish stone called the Spunky Dell. The trees down here on the north slope were planted by my father-in-law. He's reforesting. They are five-year-old Scotch pines and some larch."

Macbeth did not die at Dunsinane. Birnam Wood moved, and so forth, according to Holinshed's questionable *Chronicles*, but Macbeth was ignominiously driven away, a fugitive king humbled before his people, and he lived three more years before he was killed, by Malcolm Canmore (Big-Headed Malcolm), on some undramatic moor in Aberdeen. I had been reading W. C. Mackenzie's history of the Highlands only a few days before this, and there on the summit of Dunsinane I found that I could almost remember verbatim Mackenzie's summary line: "By the irony of circumstances, Macbeth, branded as long as literature lasts with the stain of blood, was the friend of the poor, the protector of the monks, and the first Scottish king whose name appears in ecclesiastical records as the benefactor of the Church." It simply was not in him to shout at an enemy here on these ramparts in the hour of his death:

> *I will not yield,*
> *To kiss the ground before young Malcolm's feet*
> *And to be baited with the rabble's curse.*
> *Though Birnam Wood be come to Dunsinane,*
> *And thou oppos'd, being of no woman born,*
> *Yet I will try the last. Before my body*
> *I throw my warlike shield. Lay on, Macduff,*
> *And damn'd be him that first cries "Hold, enough!"*

The race being what it is, we prefer him the second way, and Shakespeare knew what we wanted. I had been twirling by its stem the leaf from the Birnam oak, and I dropped it on the top of the hill. We went down to Sinclair's farmhouse for tea, and tea included, among other things, banana sandwiches and Nesquik chocolate milk shakes.

Mr. Macbeth, after a struggle over the check, paid for my breakfast. As we parted, he told me that he had once been a salesman of advertising space for a magazine, and that he had spent half his days in reception foyers waiting to get in to see various kinds of executives. On arrival, he would give his name routinely to the receptionist, then sit down, pick up a magazine, and wait. During this interval, slow, obscure, primordial stirrings would apparently go on in the receptionist's mind, for time and again—and never, he thought, with conscious intent—the receptionist would eventually say to him, "You may go in now, Mr. Macduff."

From Outside, In

Barbara Mellix

Two years ago, when I started writing this paper, trying to bring order out of chaos, my ten-year-old daughter was suffering from an acute attack of boredom. She drifted in and out of the room complaining that she had nothing to do, no one to "be with" because none of her friends were at home. Patiently I explained that I was working on something special and needed peace and quiet, and I suggested that she paint, read, or work with her computer. None of these interested her. Finally, she pulled up a chair to my desk and watched me, now and then heaving long, loud sighs. After two or three minutes (nine or ten sighs), I lost my patience. "Looka here, Allie," I said, "you too old for this kinda carryin' on. I done told you this is important. You wronger than dirt to be in here haggin' me like this and you know it. Now git on outta here and leave me off before I put my foot all the way down."

I was at home, alone with my family, and my daughter understood that this way of speaking was appropriate in that context. She knew, as a matter of fact, that it was almost inevitable; when I get angry at home, I speak some of my finest, most cherished black English. Had I been speaking to my daughter in this manner in certain other environments, she would have been shocked and probably worried that I had taken leave of my sense of propriety.

Like my children, I grew up speaking what I considered two distinctly different languages—black English and standard English (or as I thought of them then, the ordinary everyday speech of "country" coloreds and "proper" English—and in the process of acquiring these languages, I developed an understanding of when, where, and how to use them. But unlike my children, I grew up in a world that was primarily black. My friends, neighbors, minister, teachers—almost everybody I associated with every day—were black. And we spoke to one another in our own special language: *That sho is a pretty dress you got on. If she don' soon leave me off I'm gon tell her head a mess. I was so mad I could'a pissed a blue nail. He all the time trying to low-rate somebody. Ain't that just about the nastiest thing you ever set ears on?*

Then there were the "others," the "proper" blacks, transplanted relatives and one-time friends who came home from the city for weddings, funerals, and vacations.

112

And the whites. To these we spoke standard English. "Ain't?" my mother would yell at me when I used the term in the presence of "others." "You *know* better than that." And I would hang my head in shame and say the "proper" word.

I remember one summer sitting in my grandmother's house in Greeleyville, South Carolina, when it was full of the chatter of city relatives who were home on vacation. My parents sat quietly, only now and then volunteering a comment or answering a question. My mother's face took on a strained expression when she spoke. I could see that she was being careful to say just the right words in just the right way. Her voice sounded thick, muffled. And when she finished speaking, she would lapse into silence, her proper smile on her face. My father was more articulate, more aggressive. He spoke quickly, his words sharp and clear. But he held his proud head higher, a signal that he, too, was uncomfortable. My sisters and brothers and I stared at our aunts, uncles, and cousins, speaking only when prompted. Even then, we hesitated, formed our sentences in our minds, then spoke softly, shyly.

My parents looked small and anxious during those occasions, and I waited impatiently for our leave-taking when we would mock our relatives the moment we were out of their hearing. "Reeely," we would say to one another, flexing our wrists and rolling our eyes, "how dooo you stan' this heat? Chile, it just too hy*ooo*-mid for words." Our relatives had made us feel "country," and this was our way of regaining pride in ourselves while getting a little revenge in the bargain. The words bubbled in our throats and rolled across our tongues, a balming.

As a child I felt this same doubleness in uptown Greeleyville where the whites lived. "Ain't that a pretty dress you're wearing!" Toby, the town policeman, said to me one day when I was fifteen. "Thank you very much," I replied, my voice barely audible in my own ears. The words felt wrong in my mouth, rigid, foreign. It was not that I had never spoken that phrase before—it was common in black English, too—but I was extremely conscious that this was an occasion for proper English. I had taken out my English and put it on as I did my church clothes, and I felt as if I were wearing my Sunday best in the middle of the week. It did not matter that Toby had not spoken grammatically correct English. He was white and could speak as he wished. I had something to prove. Toby did not.

Speaking standard English to whites was our way of demonstrating that we knew their language and could use it. Speaking it to standard-English-speaking blacks was our way of showing them that we, as well as they, could "put on airs." But when we spoke standard English, we acknowledged (to ourselves and to others—but primarily to ourselves) that our customary way of speaking was inferior. We felt foolish, embarrassed, somehow diminished because we were ashamed to be our real selves. We were reserved, shy in the presence of those who owned and/or spoke *the* language.

My parents never set aside time to drill us in standard English. Their forms of instruction were less formal. When my father was feeling particularly expansive, he would regale us with tales of his exploits in the outside world. In almost flawless English, complete with dialogue and flavored with gestures and embellishment, he told us about his attempt to get a haircut at a white barbershop; his refusal to acknowledge one of the town merchants until the man addressed him as "Mister"; the time he refused to step off the sidewalk uptown to let some whites pass; his airplane trip to

New York City (to visit a sick relative) during which the stewardesses and porters—recognizing that he was a "gentleman"—addressed him as "Sir." I did not realize then—nor, I think, did my father—that he was teaching us, among other things, standard English and the relationship between language and power.

My mother's approach was different. Often, when one of us said, "I'm gon wash off my feet," she would say, "And what will you walk on if you wash them off?" Everyone would laugh at the victim of my mother's "proper" mood. But it was different when one of us children was in a proper mood. "You think you are so superior," I said to my oldest sister one day when we were arguing and she was winning. "Superior!" my sister mocked. "You mean I'm acting 'biggidy'?" My sisters and brothers sniggered, then joined in teasing me. Finally, my mother said, "Leave your sister alone. There's nothing wrong with using proper English." There was a half-smile on her face. I had gotten "uppity," had "put on airs" for no good reason. I was at home, alone with the family, and I hadn't been prompted by one of my mother's proper moods. But there was also a proud light in my mother's eyes; her children were learning English very well.

Not until years later, as a college student, did I begin to understand our ambivalence toward English, our scorn of it, our need to master it, to own and be owned by it—an ambivalence that extended to the public-school classroom. In our school, where there were no whites, my teachers taught standard English but used black English to do it. When my grammar school teachers wanted us to write, for example, they usually said something like, "I want y'all to write five sentences that make a statement. Anybody git done before the rest can color." It was probably almost those exact words that led me to write these sentences in 1953 when I was in the second grade:

> The white clouds are pretty.
> There are only 15 people in our room.
> We will go to gym.
> We have a new poster.
> We may go out doors.

Second grade came after "Little First" and "Big First," so by then I knew the implied rules that accompanied all writing assignments. Writing was an occasion for proper English. I was not to write in the way we spoke to one another: The white clouds pretty; There ain't but 15 people in our room; We going to gym; We got a new poster; We can go out in the yard. Rather I was to use the language of "other": clouds *are*, there *are*, we *will*, we *have*, we *may*.

My sentences were short, rigid, perfunctory, like the letters my mother wrote to relatives:

> Dear Papa,
>
> How are you? How is Mattie? Fine I hope. We are fine. We will come to see you Sunday. Cousin Ned will give us a ride.
>
> Love,
> Daughter

The language was not ours. It was something from outside us, something we used for special occasions.

But my coloring on the other side of that second-grade paper is different. I drew three hearts and a sun. The sun has a smiling face that radiates and envelops everything it touches. And although the sun and its world are enclosed in a circle, the colors I used—red, blue, green, purple, orange, yellow, black—indicate that I was less restricted with drawing and coloring than I was with writing standard English. My valentines were not just red. My sun was not just a yellow ball in the sky.

By the time I reached the twelfth grade, speaking and writing standard English had taken on new importance. Each year, about half of the newly graduated seniors of our school moved to large cities—particularly in the North—to live with relatives and find work. Our English teacher constantly corrected our grammar: "Not 'ain't,' but 'isn't.'" We seldom wrote papers, and even those few were usually plot summaries of short stories. When our teacher returned the papers, she usually lectured on the importance of using standard English: "I *am*; you *are*; he, she, or it *is*," she would say, writing on the chalkboard as she spoke. "How you gon git a job talking about 'I is,' or 'I isn't' or 'I ain't'?"

In Pittsburgh, where I moved after graduation, I watched my aunt and uncle—who had always spoken standard English when in Greeleyville—switch from black English to standard English to a mixture of the two, according to where they were or who they were with. At home and with certain close relatives, friends, and neighbors, they spoke black English. With those less close, they spoke a mixture. In public and with strangers, they generally spoke standard English.

In time, I learned to speak standard English with ease and to switch smoothly from black to standard or a mixture, and back again. But no matter where I was, no matter what the situation or occasion, I continued to write as I had in school:

> Dear Mommie,
>
> How are you? How is everybody else? Fine I hope. I am fine. So are Aunt and Uncle. Tell everyone I said hello. I will write again soon.
>
> Love,
> Barbara

At work, at a health insurance company, I learned to write letters to customers. I studied form letters and letters written by co-workers, memorizing the phrases and the ways in which they were used. I dictated:

> Thank you for your letter of January 5. We have made the changes in your coverage you requested. Your new premium will be $150 every three months. We are pleased to have been of service to you.

In a sense, I was proud of the letters I wrote for the company: they were proof of my ability to survive in the city, the outside world—an indication of my growing mastery of English. But they also indicate that writing was still mechanical for me, something that didn't require much thought.

Reading also became a more significant part of my life during those early years in Pittsburgh. I had always liked reading, but now I devoted more and more of my spare time to it. I read romances, mysteries, popular novels. Looking back, I realize that the books I liked best were simple, unambiguous: good versus bad and right versus wrong with right rewarded and wrong punished, mysteries unraveled and all set right in the end. It was how I remembered life in Greeleyville.

Of course I was romanticizing. Life in Greeleyville had not been so very uncomplicated. Back there I had been—first as a child, then as a young woman with limited experience in the outside world—living in a relatively closed-in society. But there were implicit and explicit principles that guided our way of life and shaped our relationships with one another and the people outside—principles that a newcomer would find elusive and baffling. In Pittsburgh, I had matured, become more experienced: I had worked at three different jobs, associated with a wider range of people, married, had children. This new environment with different prescripts for living required that I speak standard English much of the time, and slowly, imperceptibly, I had ceased seeing a sharp distinction between myself and "others." Reading romances and mysteries, characterized by dichotomy, was a way of shying away from change, from the person I was becoming.

But that other part of me—that part which took great pride in my ability to hold a job writing business letters—was increasingly drawn to the new developments in my life and the attending possibilities, opportunities for even greater change. If I could write letters for a nationally known business, could I not also do something better, more challenging, more important? Could I not, perhaps, go to college and become a school teacher? For years, afraid and a little embarrassed, I did no more than imagine this different me, this possible me. But sixteen years after coming north, when my youngest daughter entered kindergarten, I found myself unable—or unwilling—to resist the lure of possibility. I enrolled in my first college course: Basic Writing, at the University of Pittsburgh.

For the first time in my life, I was required to write extensively about myself. Using the most formal English at my command, I wrote these sentences near the beginning of the term:

> One of my duties as a homemaker is simply picking up after others. A day seldom passes that I don't search for a mislaid toy, book, or gym shoe, etc. I change the Ty-D-Bol, fight "ring around the collar," and keep our laundry smelling "April fresh." Occasionally, I settle arguments between my children and suggest things to do when they're bored. Taking telephone messages for my oldest daughter is my newest (and sometimes most aggravating) chore. Hanging the toilet paper roll is my most insignificant.

My concern was to use "appropriate" language, to sound as if I belonged in a college classroom. But I felt separate from the language—as if it did not and could not belong to me. I couldn't think and feel genuinely in that language, couldn't make it express what I thought and felt about being a housewife. A part of me resented, among other things, being judged by such things as the appearance of my family's laundry and toilet bowl, but in that language I could only imagine and write about a conventional housewife.

For the most part, the remainder of the term was a period of adjustment, a time of trying to find my bearings as a student in a college composition class, to learn to shut out my black English whenever I composed, and to prevent it from creeping into my formulations; a time for trying to grasp the language of the classroom and reproduce it in my prose; for trying to talk about myself in that language, reach others through it. Each experience of writing was like standing naked and revealing my imperfection, my "otherness." And each new assignment was another chance to make myself over in language, reshape myself, make myself "better" in my rapidly changing image of a student in a college composition class.

But writing became increasingly unmanageable as the term progressed, and by the end of the semester, my sentences sounded like this:

> My excitement was soon dampened, however, by what seemed like a small voice in the back of my head saying that I should be careful with my long awaited opportunity. I felt frustrated and this seemed to make it difficult to concentrate.

There is a poverty of language in these sentences. By this point, I knew that the clichéd language of my Housewife essay was unacceptable, and I generally recognized trite expressions. At the same time, I hadn't yet mastered the language of the classroom, hadn't yet come to see it as belonging to me. Most notable is the lifelessness of the prose, the apparent absence of a person behind the words. I wanted those sentences—and the rest of the essay—to convey the anguish of yearning to, at once, become something more and yet remain the same. I had the sensation of being split in two, part of me going into a future the other part didn't believe possible. As that person, the student writer at that moment, I was essentially mute. I could not—in the process of composing—use the language of the old me, yet I couldn't imagine myself in the language of "others."

I found this particularly discouraging because at midsemester I had been writing in a much different way. Note the language of this introduction to an essay I had written then, near the middle of the term:

> Pain is a constant companion to the people in "Footwork." Their jobs are physically damaging. Employers are insensitive to their feelings and in many cases add to their problems. The general public wounds them further by treating them with disgrace because of what they do for a living. Although the workers are as diverse as they are similar, there is a definite link between them. They suffer a great deal of abuse.

The voice here is stronger, more confident, appropriating terms like "physically damaging," "wounds them further," "insensitive," "diverse"—terms I couldn't have imagined using when writing about my own experience—and shaping them into sentences like, "Although the workers are as diverse as they are similar, there is a definite link between them." And there is the sense of a personality behind the prose, someone who sympathizes with the workers: "The general public wounds them further by treating them with disgrace because of what they do for a living."

What caused these differences? I was, I believed, explaining other people's thoughts and feelings, and I was free to move about in the language of "others" so long as I was speaking *of* others. I was unaware that I was transforming into my best classroom language my own thoughts and feelings about people whose experiences and ways of speaking were in many ways similar to mine.

The following year, unable to turn back or to let go of what had become something of an obsession with language (and hoping to catch and hold the sense of control that had eluded me in Basic Writing), I enrolled in a research writing course. I spent most of the term learning how to prepare for and write a research paper. I chose sex education as my subject and spent hours in libraries, searching for information, reading, taking notes. Then (not without messiness and often-demoralizing frustration) I organized my information into categories, wrote a thesis statement, and composed my paper—a series of paraphrases and quotations spaced between carefully constructed transitions. The process and results felt artificial, but as I would later come to realize I was passing through a necessary stage. My sentences sounded like this:

> This reserve becomes understandable with examination of who the abusers are. In an overwhelming number of cases, they are people the victims know and trust. Family members, relatives, neighbors and close family friends commit seventy-five percent of all reported sex crimes against children, and parents, parent substitutes and relatives are the offenders in thirty to eighty percent of all reported cases.[12] While assault by strangers does occur, it is less common, and is usually a single episode.[13] But abuse by family members, relatives and acquaintances may continue for an extended period of time. In cases of incest, for example, children are abused repeatedly for an average of eight years.[14] In such cases, "the use of physical force is rarely necessary because of the child's trusting, dependent relationship with the offender. The child's cooperation is often facilitated by the adult's position of dominance, an offer of material goods, a threat of physical violence, or a misrepresentation of moral standards."[15]

The completed paper gave me a sense of profound satisfaction, and I read it often after my professor returned it. I know now that what I was pleased with was the language I used and the professional voice it helped me maintain. "Use better words," my teacher had snapped at me one day after reading the notes I'd begun accumulating from my research, and slowly I began taking on the language of my sources. In my next set of notes, I used the word "vacillating"; my professor applauded. And by the time I composed the final draft, I felt at ease with terms like "overwhelming number of cases," "single episode," and "reserve," and I shaped them into sentences similar to those of my "expert" sources.

If I were writing the paper today, I would of course do some things differently. Rather than open with an anecdote—as my teacher suggested—I would begin simply with a quotation that caught my interest as I was researching my paper (and which I scribbled, without its source, in the margin of my notebook): "Truth does not do so much good in the world as the semblance of truth does evil." The quotation felt right because it captured what was for me the central idea of my essay—an idea that emerged gradually during the making of my paper—and expressed it in a way I would like to have said it. The anecdote, a hypothetical situation I invented to conform to the information in the paper, felt forced and insincere because it represented—to a great degree—my teacher's understanding of the essay, *her* idea of what in it was most significant. Improving upon my previous experiences with writing, I was beginning to think and feel in the language I used, to find my own voices in it, to sense that how one speaks influences how one means. But I was not yet secure enough, comfortable enough with the language to trust my intuition.

Now that I know that to seek knowledge, freedom, and autonomy means always to be in the concentrated process of becoming—always to be venturing into new territory, feeling one's way at first, then getting one's balance, negotiating, accommodating, discovering one's self in ways that previously defined "others"—I sometimes get tired. And I ask myself why I keep on participating in this highbrow form of violence, this slamming against perplexity. But there is no real futility in the question, no hint of that part of the old me who stood outside standard English, hugging to herself a disabling mistrust of a language she thought could not represent a person with her history and experience. Rather, the question represents a person who feels the consequence of her education, the weight of her possibilities as a teacher and writer and human being, a voice in society. And I would not change that person, would not give back the good burden that accompanies my growing expertise, my increasing power to shape myself in language and share that self with "others."

"To speak," says Frantz Fanon, "means to be in a position to use a certain syntax, to grasp the morphology of this or that language, but it means above all to assume a culture, to support the weight of a civilization."[*] To write means to do the same, but in a more profound sense. However, Fanon also says that to achieve mastery means to "get" in a position of power, to "grasp," to "assume." This, I have learned—both as a student and subsequently as a teacher—can involve tremendous emotional and psychological conflict for those attempting to master academic discourse. Although as a beginning student writer I had a fairly good grasp of ordinary spoken English and was proficient at what Labov calls "code-switching" (and what John Baugh in *Black Street Speech* terms "style shifting"), when I came face to face with the demands of academic writing, I grew increasingly self-conscious, constantly aware of my status as a black and a speaker of one of the many black English vernaculars—a traditional outsider. For the first time, I experienced my sense of doubleness as something menacing, a built-in enemy. Whenever I turned inward for salvation, the balm so available during my childhood, I found instead this new fragmentation which spoke to me in many voices. It was the voice of my desire to prosper, but at the same time it spoke of what I had relinquished and could not regain: a safe way of being, a state of powerlessness which exempted me from responsibility for who I was and might be. And it accused me of betrayal, of turning away from blackness. To recover balance, I had to take on the language of the academy, the language of "others." And to do that, I had to learn

[*]*Black Skin, White Masks* (1952; rpt. New York: Grove Press, 1967), pp. 17–18.

to imagine myself a part of the culture of that language, and therefore someone free to manage that language, to take liberties with it. Writing and rewriting, practicing, experimenting, I came to comprehend more fully the generative power of language. I discovered—with the help of some especially sensitive teachers—that through writing one can continually bring new selves into being, each with new responsibilities and difficulties, but also with new possibilities. Remarkable power, indeed. I write and continually give birth to myself.

Amid Onions and Oranges, a Boy Becomes a Man

Donald M. Murray

Recently I reread John Updike's classic short story, "A & P," in which a teenage clerk makes a decision that will change his life, and as I enter Updike's small grocery in the 1960s I am transported to Miller's Market in Wollaston, where I worked almost 60 years ago.

I am stunned by the immediacy of my crash-landing into the past. I am 14 and my hands are learning to take two tucks in the grocery apron, and twice wrap the ties around my waist. I am skinny again.

I smell the earthy odor of root crops, the sawdust on the floor, the blood dripping from a fresh-cut chicken, the Pall Mall cigarette that hangs from my lip, the mark of my passage—I then think—from boy to man.

My hands can tip the boxes on the sidewalk just right to display the oranges, potatoes, carrots, onions, apples I stack in rising rows. I know how to take a cleaver and split a great green Hubbard squash so Mrs. Deming will have 7 pounds in one piece, no more.

My legs know how to bend to lug a 100-pound bag of potatoes in from the shed or get my shoulder under a side of beef from the truck so I can stagger-carry it into the refrigerator and hang it on a hook.

Updike's prose has taken me not into his life but into my own. I again know how to mix meat, filler, spices for Scottish beef sausages and the tricks of this trade as I grind the sausage and feed it into the natural intestine casing, twisting off each sausage at just the right length.

How many trades I learned in that crowded little store with Mr. Miller, a giant who always wore rubber boots and a straw hat; tiny, bustling Mrs. Miller, who bossed the boss and us all; Marshall, their son; Mike, the butcher, who got so drunk every

Saturday I often had to hold him up but who never, ever nicked a finger as his cleaver crashed down or his trimming knife—more than razor sharp—zipped around a roast.

I could still prop the hearing unit of an old-fashioned tall telephone on my shoulder and write an order.

And Mr. Miller taught the retailer's trade. When Mrs. Temple asks about the cabbage, I'm to look at Mr. Miller, turn away and whisper, "Not today. Try the beets."

She'll always trust me, Mr. Miller, master of deception, assures me. And when Mrs. Wheeler comes in and asks about the beets, I look at Mr. Miller and whisper, "Not today. Try the cabbage."

In weeks I have housewives who will buy only from me, I am so honest, so innocent, so young, so very trustworthy.

I am even allowed, in an emergency, to drive the truck to Quincy Market in Boston or to make deliveries—two years before I have a license. My leg still stretches to reach the brake.

And I become a grown-up, not when I light up another Pall Mall, go over to the diner with Mike the butcher and drink a mug of coffee, or even when I drive the truck to market.

I come close to being a grown-up when I see the secret list of those who owe the store so much that they are not allowed to charge anything—not a bottle or milk, not a loaf of bread. Our name is high on the list.

I become a grown-up when I discover that my mother, despite the list, has talked Mr. Miller into allowing her to charge against my 50-cents-a-day pay before I earn it.

I tell Mr. Miller not to allow her to charge against my salary. It is a close neighborhood, and Mr. Miller must know that Father brings home more money than most. I have to explain that Mother spends it on gifts for her friends and does not pay our bills.

I feel again the hot flush of shame and then the necessary coldness that allowed me, even at 14, to distance myself from my family.

But not to escape. Past and present merge. I did graduate from Miller's Market, clambered firmly into the middle class, living in, even owning a single-family home, mortgage paid off.

Reliving that day in Miller's Market when I betrayed Mother, I feel the need to protect her and the contradictory need to protect myself.

I read about the boy in the A & P and the very different decision he makes, and, through the skillful magic of Updike's prose, I read my own story.

And although I am no Updike, the magic continues: As you read my story, many of you have heard your own.

Celibate Passion

Kathleen Norris

> *The Cherub was stationed at the gate of the earthly paradise with his flaming sword to teach us that no one will enter the heavenly paradise who is not pierced with the sword of love.*
>
> —St. Francis de Sales, *Treatise on the Love of God*

Celibacy is a field day for ideologues. Conservative Catholics, particularly those who were raised in the pre-Vatican II church, tend to speak of celibacy as if it were an idealized, angelic state, while feminist theologians such as Uta Ranke-Heinemann say, angrily, that "celibate hatred of sex is hatred of women." That celibacy constitutes the hatred of sex seems to be a given in the popular mythology of contemporary America, and we need only look at newspaper accounts of sex abuse by priests to see evidence of celibacy that isn't working. One could well assume that this is celibacy, impure and simple. And this is unfortunate, because celibacy practiced rightly is not at all a hatred of sex; in fact it has the potential to address the sexual idolatry of our culture in a most helpful way.

One benefit of the nearly ten years that I've been a Benedictine oblate has been the development of deep friendships with celibate men and women. This has led me to ponder celibacy that works, practiced by people who are fully aware of themselves as sexual beings but who express their sexuality in a celibate way. That is, they manage to sublimate their sexual energies toward another purpose than sexual intercourse and procreation. Are they perverse, their lives necessarily stunted? Cultural prejudice would say yes, but I have my doubts. I've seen too many wise old monks and nuns whose lengthy formation in celibate practice has allowed them to incarnate hospitality in the deepest sense. In them, the constraints of celibacy have somehow been transformed into an openness that attracts people of all ages, all social classes. They exude a sense of freedom. They also genderbend, at least in my dreams. Sister Jeremy will appear as a warrior on horseback, Father Robert as a wise old woman tending a fire.

The younger celibates of my acquaintance are more edgy. Still contending mightily with what one friend calls "the raging orchestra of my hormones," they are more obviously struggling to contain their desires for intimacy, for physical touch, within the bounds of celibacy. Often they find their loneliness intensified by the incomprehension of others. In a culture that denies the value of their striving, they are made to feel like fools, or worse.

Americans are remarkably tone-deaf when it comes to the expression of sexuality. The sexual formation that many of us receive is like the refrain of an old Fugs' song: "Why do ya like boobs a lot—ya gotta like boobs a lot." The jiggle of tits and ass, penis and pectorals, assault us everywhere—billboards, magazines, television, movies. Orgasm becomes just another goal; we undress for success. It's no wonder that in all this powerful noise, the quiet tones of celibacy are lost; that we have such trouble comprehending what it could mean to dedicate one's sexual drives in such a way that genital activity and procreation are precluded. But celibate people have taught me that celibacy, practiced rightly, does indeed have something valuable to say to the rest of us. Specifically, they have helped me better appreciate both the nature of friendship, and what it means to be married.

They have also helped me recognize that celibacy, like monogamy, is not a matter of the will disdaining and conquering the desires of the flesh but a discipline requiring what many people think of as undesirable, if not impossible—a conscious form of sublimation. Like many people who came into adulthood during the sexually permissive 1960s, I've tended to equate sublimation with repression. But my celibate friends have made me see the light; accepting sublimation as a normal part of adulthood makes me more realistic about human sexual capacities and expression. It helps me to respect the bonds and boundaries of marriage.

Any marriage has times of separation, ill-health, or just plain crankiness, in which sexual intercourse is ill-advised. And it is precisely the skills of celibate friendship—fostering intimacy through letters, conversation, performing mundane tasks together (thus rendering them pleasurable), savoring the holy simplicity of a shared meal, or a walk together at dusk—that can help a marriage survive the rough spots. When you can't make love physically, you figure out other ways to do it.

Monastic people are celibate for a very practical reason: the kind of community life to which they aspire can't be sustained if people are pairing off. Even in churches in which the clergy are often married—Episcopal and Russian Orthodox, for example—their monks and nuns are celibate. And while monastic novices may be carried along for a time on the swells of communal spirit, when that blissful period inevitably comes to an end, the loneliness is profound. One gregarious monk in his early thirties told me that just as he thought he'd settled into the monastery, he woke up in a panic one morning, wondering if he'd wake up lonely every morning for the rest of his life.

Another monk I know regards celibacy as an expression of the essential human loneliness, a perspective that helps him as a hospital chaplain, when he is called upon to minister to the dying. I knew him when he was still resisting his celibate call—it usually came out as anger directed toward his abbot and community, more rarely as misogyny—and I was fascinated to observe the process by which he came to accept the sacrifices that a celibate, monastic life requires. He's easier to be with now; he's a better friend.

This is not irony so much as grace, that in learning to be faithful to his vow of celibacy, the monk developed his talent for relationship. It's a common occurrence. I've seen the demands of Benedictine hospitality—that they receive all visitors as Christ—convert shy young men who fear women into monks who can enjoy their company. I've witnessed this process of transformation at work in older monks as well. One friend, who had entered the monastery very young, was, when I first met him, still suffering acutely from an inadequate and harmful sexual formation. Taught that as a monk he should avoid women, he faced a crisis when he encountered women as students and colleagues on a college faculty. Fear of his own sexual desires translated all too easily into misogyny. As a good Benedictine, however, he recognized, prayed over, and explored the possibilities for conversion in this situation. Simply put, he's over it now. I'm one of many women who count him as a dear friend, including several who became serious scholars because he urged them on.

One reason I enjoy celibates is that they tend to value friendship very highly. And my friendships with celibate men, both gay and straight, give me some hope that men and women don't live in alternate universes. In 1990s America, this sometimes feels like a countercultural perspective. Male celibacy, in particular, can become radically countercultural if it is perceived as a rejection of the consumerist model of sexuality, a model that reduces women to the sum of her parts. I have never had a monk friend make an insinuating remark along the lines of, "You have beautiful eyes" (or legs, breasts, knees, elbows, nostrils), the usual catalogue of remarks that women grow accustomed to deflecting. A monk is supposed to give up the idea of possessing anything and, in this culture, that includes women.

Ideally, in giving up the sexual pursuit of women (whether as demons or as idealized vessels of purity), the male celibate learns to relate to them as human beings. That many fail to do so, that the power structures of the Catholic church all but dictate failure in this regard, comes as no surprise. What is a surprise is what happens when it works. Once, after I'd spent a week in a monastery, I boarded a crowded Greyhound bus and took the first available seat. My seatmate, a man, soon engaged me in conversation, and it took me a while to realize that he wasn't simply being friendly, he was coming on to me. I remember feeling foolish for being so slow to catch on. I remember thinking, "No wonder this guy is acting so strange; he didn't take a vow of celibacy."

When it works, when men have truly given up the idea of possessing women, healing can occur. I once met a woman in a monastery guest house who had come there because she was pulling herself together after being raped, and said she needed to feel safe around men again. I've seen young monks astonish an obese and homely college student by listening to her with as much interest and respect as to her conventionally pretty roommate. On my fortieth birthday, as I happily blew out four candles on a cupcake ("one for each decade," a monk in his twenties cheerfully proclaimed), I realized that I could enjoy growing old with these guys. They were helping me to blow away my fears of middle age.

As celibacy takes hold in a person, over the years, as monastic values supersede the values of the culture outside the monastery, celibates become people who can radically affect those of us out "in the world," if only because they've learned how to listen without possessiveness, without imposing themselves. With someone who is practicing celibacy well, we may sense that we're being listened to in a refreshingly deep way. And this is the purpose of celibacy, not to attain some impossibly cerebral goal mistakenly conceived as "holiness" but to make oneself available to others, body *and* soul. Celibacy, simply put, is a form of ministry—not an achievement one can put on a résumé but a subtle form of service to others. In theological terms, one dedicates one's sexuality to God through Jesus Christ, a concept and a terminology I find extremely hard to grasp. All I can do is to catch a glimpse of people who are doing it, incarnating celibacy in a mysterious, pleasing, and gracious way.

The attractiveness of the celibate is that he or she can make us feel appreciated, enlarged, no matter who we are. I have two nun friends who invariably have that effect on me, whatever the circumstances of our lives on the infrequent occasions when we meet. The thoughtful way in which they converse, listening and responding with complete attention, seems always a marvel. And when I first met a man I'll call Tom, he had much the same effect on me. I wrote in my notebook, "such tenderness in a man…and a surprising, gentle, kindly grasp of who I am." (Poets aren't used to being listened to, let alone understood, by theologians.) As our friendship deepened, I found that even brief, casual conversations with him would often inspire me to dive into old, half-finished poems in an attempt to bring them to fruition.

I realized, of course, that I had found a remarkable friend, a Muse. I was also aware that Tom and I were fast approaching the rocky shoals of infatuation, a man and a woman, both decidedly heterosexual, responding to each other in unmistakably sexual ways. We laughed; we had playful conversations as well as serious ones; we took delight in each other. At times we were alarmingly responsive to one another, and it was all too easy to fantasize about expressing that responsiveness in physical ways.

The danger was real, but not insurmountable; I sensed that if our infatuation were to develop into love, that is, to ground itself in grace rather than utility, our respect for each other's commitments—his to celibacy, mine to monogamy—would make the boundaries of behavior very clear. We had few regrets, and yet for both of us there was an underlying sadness, the pain of something incomplete. Suddenly, the difference between celibate friendship and celibate passion had become all too clear to me; at times the pain was excruciating.

Tom and I each faced a crisis the year we met—his mother died, I suffered a disastrous betrayal—and it was the intensity of these unexpected, unwelcome experiences that helped me to understand that in the realm of the sacred, what seems incomplete or unattainable may be abundance, after all. Human relationships are by their nature incomplete—after twenty-one years, my husband remains a mystery to me, and I to him, and that is as it should be. Only hope allows us to know and enjoy the depth of our intimacy.

Appreciating Tom's presence in my life as a miraculous, unmerited gift helped me to place our relationship in its proper, religious context, and also to understand why it was that when I'd seek him out to pray with me, I'd always leave feeling so much better than when I came. This was celibacy at its best, a man's sexual energies so devoted to the care of others that a few words could lift me out of despair, give me the strength to reclaim my life. Abundance indeed. Celibate love was at the heart of it, although I can't fully comprehend the mystery of why this should be so. Celibate passion—elusive, tensile, holy.

Three Pokes of a Thistle

Naomi Shihab Nye

Hiding inside the Good Girl

"She has the devil inside her," said my first report card from first grade. I walked home slowly, holding it out from my body, a thistle, a thorn, to my mother, who read the inside, then the note on the back. She cried mightily, heaves of underground rivers, we stood looking deep into the earth as water rushed by.

I didn't know who he was.

One day I'd smashed John's nose on the pencil sharpener and broken it. Stood in the cloakroom smelling the rust of coats. I said No. No thank you. I already read that and it's not a very good story. Jane doesn't do much. I want the spider who talks. The family of little women and their thousand days. No. What I had for breakfast is a secret. I didn't want to tell them I ate dried apricots. I listened to their lineage of eggs. I listened to the bacon crackle in everyone else's pail. Thank you.

What shall we do, what shall we do? Please, I beg you. Our pajamas were flying from the line, waists pinned, their legs fat with fabulous air. My mother peeled beets, her fingers stained deep red. She was bleeding dinner for us. She was getting up and lying down.

Once I came home from school in the middle of the day in a taxi. School gave me a stomachache. I rode in the front passenger seat. It would be expensive. My mother stood at the screen door peering out, my baby brother perched on her hip. She wore an apron. The taxi pulled up in front of the blue mailbox I viewed as an animal across from our house—his opening mouth. Right before I climbed out, another car hit the taxi hard from behind so my mother saw me fly from the front seat to the back. Her mouth wide open, the baby dangling from her like fringe. She came toward us running. I climbed up onto the ledge inside the back window to examine the wreckage. The taxi driver's visored cap had blown out the window. He was shaking his head side to side as if he had water in his ears.

You, you, look what a stomachache gets you. Whiplash.

The doctor felt my neck.

Later I sat on the front steps staring at the spot where it had happened. What about that other driver? He cried when the policeman arrived. He was an old man coming to mail a letter. I was incidental to the scene, but it couldn't have happened without me. *If you had just stayed where you belonged....* My classmates sealed into their desks laboring over pages of subtraction, while out in the world, cars were banging together. Yellow roses opened slowly on a bush beside my step. I was thinking how everything looked from far away.

Then I was old. A hundred years before I found it, Mark Twain inscribed the front of his first-edition leatherbound book, "BE GOOD—AND YOU WILL BE LONESOME." In black ink, with a flourish. He signed his name. My friend had the book in a box in her attic and did not know. It was from her mother's collection. I carried it down the stairs, trembling. My friend said, "Do you think it is valuable?"

Language Barrier

Basically our father spoke English perfectly, though he still got his *b*s and *p*s mixed up. He had a gentle, deliberate way of choosing words. I could feel him reaching up into the air to find them. At night, he told us whimsical, curling "Joha" stories which hypnotized us to sleep. I especially liked the big cooking pan that gave birth to the little pan. My friend Marcia's father who grew up in the United States hardly talked. He built airplanes. I didn't think I would want to fly in anything he made. When Marcia asked him a question, he grunted a kind of pig sound. He sank his face into the paper. My father spilled out musical lines, a horizon of graceful buildings standing beside one another in a distant city. You could imagine people living inside one of my father's words.

He said a few things to us in Arabic—fragrant syllables after we ate, blessings when he hugged us. He hugged us all the time. He said, "I love you" all the time. But I didn't learn how to say "Thank you" in Arabic till I was fourteen, which struck me, even then, as a preposterous omission.

Marcia's father seemed tired. He had seven children because he was a Catholic, Marcia said. I didn't get it. Marcia's mother threw away the leftovers from their table after dinner. My mother carefully wrapped the last little mound of mashed potato inside waxed paper. We'd eat it later.

I felt comfortable in the world of so many different people. Their voices floated around the neighborhood like pollen. On the next block, French-Canadians made blueberry pie. I wanted a slice. It is true that a girl knocked on our door one day and asked to "see the Arab," but I was not insulted. I was mystified. Who?

Sometimes Marcia and I slept together on our screened-in back porch, or in a big green tent in her yard. She was easy to scare. I said the giant harvest moon was coming to eat her and she hid under her pillow. She told me spider stories. We had fun trading little terrors.

When I was almost ready to move away, Marcia and I stood in Dade Park together one last time. I said good-bye to the swings and benches and wooden seesaws with chipped red paint. Two bigger boys rode up on bicycles and circled us. We'd never seen them before. One of them asked if we knew how to do the F-word. I had no idea what they were talking about. Marcia said she knew, but wouldn't tell me. The boys circled the basketball courts, eyeing us strangely. Walking home with Marcia, I felt almost glad to be moving away from her. She stuck her chest out. She said, "Did you ever wish someone would touch you in a private place?"

I looked in the big dictionary at home. Hundreds of F-words I didn't know reached their hands out so it took a long time. And I asked my mother, whose face was so smooth and beautiful and filled with sadness because nothing was quite as good as it could be.

She didn't know either.

Bra Strap

It felt like a taunt, the elastic strap of Karen's bra visible beneath her white blouse in front of me in fifth grade. I saw it even before Douglas snapped it. Who did she think she was, growing older without me?

I spent the night with her one Saturday. In the bathtub together, we splashed and soaped, jingling our talk of teachers, boys, and holidays. But my eyes were on her chest, the great pale fruits growing there. Already they mounded toward stems.

She caught me looking and said, "So?" Sighing, as if she were already tired. Said, "In my family they grow early." Downstairs her bosomy mother stacked cups in a high old cabinet that smelled of grandmother's hair. I could hear her clinking. In my family they barely grew at all. I had been proud of my mother's boyishness, her lithe trunk and straight legs.

Now I couldn't stop thinking about it: what was there, what wasn't there. The mounds on the fronts of certain dolls with candy-coated names. One by one, watching the backs of my friends' blouses, I saw them all fall under the spell. I begged my mother, who said, "For what? Just to be like everybody else?"

Pausing near the underwear displays at Famous and Barr, I asked to be measured, sizing up boxes. "Training Bra"—what were we in training for?

When Louise fell off her front porch and a stake went all the way through her, I heard teachers whispering, "Hope this doesn't ruin her for the future." We discussed the word "impaled." What future? The mysteries of ovaries had not yet been explained. Little factories for eggs. Little secret nests. On the day we saw the film, I didn't like it. If that was what the future meant, I didn't want it anymore. As I was staring out the window afterwards, my mouth tasted like pennies, my throat closed up. The leaves on the trees blurred together so they could carry me.

I sat on a swivel chair practicing handwritings. The backwards slant, the loopy up-and-down. Who would I ever be? My mother was inside the lawyer's office signing papers about the business. That waiting room, with its dull wooden side tables and gloomy magazines, had absolutely nothing to do with me. Never for a second was I drawn toward the world of the dreary professional. I would be a violinist with the

Zurich symphony. I would play percussion in a traveling band. I would bake zucchini muffins in Yarmouth, Nova Scotia.

In the car traveling slowly home under a thick gray sky, I worked up courage. Rain, rain, the intimacy of cars. At a stoplight, staring hard at my mother, I asked, "What really happens between men and women to make babies?"

She jumped as if I'd thrown ice at her.

"Not *that!* Not *now!*" From red to green, the light, the light. "There is *oh so much you do not know.*"

It was all she ever told me. The weight of my ignorance pressed upon us both.

Later she slipped me a book, *Little Me, Big Me.* One of the more incomprehensible documents of any childhood: "When a man and a woman love one another enough, he puts his arms around her and part of him goes into part of her and the greatness of their love for one another causes this to feel pleasurable."

On my twelfth birthday, my father came home with our first tape recorder. My mother produced a bouquet of shiny boxes, including a long, slim one. My Lutheran grandparents sat neatly on the couch as the heavy reels wound up our words. "Do you like it? Is it just what you've been waiting for?"

They wanted me to hold it up to my body, the way I would when I put it on. My mother shushing, "Oh, I guess it's private!"

Later the tape would play someone's giggles in the background. My brother? Or the gangs of little girl angels that congregate around our heads, chanting, "Don't grow up, don't grow up!"

I never liked wearing it as much as I did thinking about it.

Animal Allies

Brenda Peterson

"My imaginary friend really lived once," the teenage girl began, head bent, her fingers twisting her long red hair. She stood in the circle of other adolescents gathered in my Seattle Arts and Lectures storytelling class at the summer Seattle Academy. Here were kids from all over the city—every color and class, all strangers one to another. Over the next two weeks we would become a fierce tribe, telling our own and our tribe's story. Our first assignment was to introduce our imaginary friends from childhood. This shy fourteen-year-old girl, Sarah, had struck me on the first day because she always sat next to me, as if under my wing, and though her freckles and stylish clothes suggested she was a popular girl, her demeanor showed the detachment of someone deeply preoccupied. She never met my eye, nor did she join in the first few days of storytelling when the ten boys and four girls were regaling one another with futuristic characters called Shiva and Darshon, Masters of the Universe. So far the story lines we'd imagined were more Pac-Man than drama. After the first two days I counted a legion of characters killed off in intergalactic battle. The settings for all these stories portrayed the earth as an environmental wasteland, a ruined shell hardly shelter to anything animal or human. One of the girls called herself Nero the White Wolf and wandered the blackened tundra howling her powerful despair; another girl was a unicorn whose horn always told the truth. All the stories were full of plagues and nuclear wars—even though this is the generation that has witnessed the fall of the Berlin Wall, the end of the Cold War. Their imaginations have been shaped by a childhood story line that anticipates the end of this world.

After three days of stories set on an earth besieged by disease and barren of nature, I made a rule: No more characters or animals could die this first week. I asked if someone might imagine a living world, one that survives even our species.

It was on this third day of group storytelling that Sarah jumped into the circle and told her story:

"My imaginary friend is called Angel now because she's in heaven, but her real name was Katie," Sarah began. "She was my best friend from fourth to tenth grade.

She had freckles like me and brown hair and more boyfriends—sometimes five at a time—because Katie said, 'I *like* to be confused!' She was a real sister too and we used to say we'd be friends for life...." Sarah stopped, gave me a furtive glance and then gulped in a great breath of air like someone drowning, about to go down. Her eyes fixed inward, her voice dropped to a monotone. "Then one day last year, Katie and I were walking home from school and a red sports car came up behind us. Someone yelled, 'Hey, Katie!' She turned...and he blew her head off. A bullet grazed my skull, too, and I blacked out. When I woke up, Katie was gone, dead forever." Sarah stopped, stared down at her feet and murmured in that same terrible monotone, "Cops never found her murderer, case is closed."

All the kids shifted and took a deep breath, although Sarah herself was barely breathing at all. "Let's take some time to write," I told the kids and put on a cello concerto for them to listen to while they wrote. As they did their assignment, the kids glanced over surreptitiously at Sarah, who sat staring at her hands in her lap.

I did not know what to do with her story; she had offered it to a group of kids she had known but three days. It explained her self-imposed exile during lunch hours and while waiting for the bus. All I knew was that she'd brought this most important story of her life into the circle of storytellers and it could not be ignored as if *she* were a case to be closed. This story lived in her, would define and shape her young life. Because she had given it to us, we needed to witness and receive—and perhaps tell it back to her in the ancient tradition of tribal call and response.

"Listen," I told the group as the cello faded and they looked up from their work. "We're going to talk story the way they used to long ago when people sat around at night in circles just like this one. That was a time when we still listened to animals and trees and didn't think ourselves so alone in this world. Now we're going to carry out jungle justice and find Katie's killer. We'll call him before our tribe. All right? Who wants to begin the story?"

All the Shivas and Darshons and Masters of the Universe volunteered to be heroes on this quest. Nero the White Wolf asked to be a scout. Unicorn, with her truth-saving horn, was declared judge. Another character joined the hunt: Fish, whose translucent belly was a shining "soul mirror" that could reveal one's true nature to anyone who looked into it.

A fierce commander of this hunt was Rat, whose army of computerized comrades could read brain waves and call down lightning lasers as weapons. Rat began the questioning and performed the early detective work. Katie, speaking from beyond the earth, as Sarah put it, gave us other facts. We learned that two weeks before Katie's murder, one of her boyfriends was shot outside a restaurant by a man in the same red car—another drive-by death. So Sarah had not only seen her best friend killed at her side, but she had also walked out into a parking lot to find Katie leaning over her boyfriend's body. For Sarah, it had been two murders by age thirteen.

With the help of our myriad computer-character legions we determined that the murderer was a man named Carlos, a drug lord who used local gangs to deal cocaine. At a party Carlos has misinterpreted Katie's videotaping her friends dancing as witnessing a big drug deal. For that, Rat said, "This dude decides Katie's got to go down. So yo, man, he offs her without a second thought."

Bad dude, indeed, this Carlos. And who was going to play Carlos now that all the tribe knew his crime? I took on the role, and as I told my story I felt my face hardening into a contempt that carried me far away from these young pursuers, deep into the Amazon jungle where Rat and his own computer armies couldn't follow, where all their space-age equipment had to be shed until there was only hand-to-hand simple fate.

In the Amazon, the kids changed without effort, in an easy shape-shifting to their animal selves. Suddenly there were no more Masters of the Universe with inter-galactic weapons—there was instead Jaguar and Snake, Fish and Pink Dolphin. There was powerful claw and all-knowing serpent, there was Fish who could grow big and small, and a dolphin whose sonar saw past the skin. We were now a tribe of animals, pawing, running, invisible in our jungle, eyes shining in the night, seeing Carlos as he canoed the mighty river, laughing because he did not know he had animals track-ing him.

All through the story I'd kept my eye on Sarah who played the role of her dead friend. The detachment I'd first seen in her was in fact the deadness Sarah carried, the violence that had hollowed her out inside, the friend who haunted her imagination. But now her face was alive, responding to each animal's report of tracking Carlos. She hung on the words, looking suddenly very young, like a small girl eagerly awaiting her turn to enter the circling jump rope.

"I'm getting away from you," I said, snarling as I'd imagined Carlos would. I paddled my canoe and gave a harsh laugh, "I'll escape, easy!"

"No!" Sarah shouted. "Let *me* tell it!"

"Tell it!" her tribe shouted.

"Well, Carlos only thinks he's escaping," Sarah smiled, waving her hands. "He's escaped from so many he's harmed before. But I call out 'FISH!' And Fish comes. He swims alongside the canoe and grows bigger, bigger until at last Carlos turns and sees this HUGE river monster swimming right alongside him and that man is afraid because suddenly Fish turns his belly up to Carlos's face. Fish forces him to look into that soul mirror. Carlos sees everyone he's ever killed and all the people who loved them and got left behind. And Carlos sees Katie and me and what he's done to us. He sees everything and he knows his soul is black. And he really doesn't want to die now because he knows then he'll stare into his soul mirror forever. But Fish makes him keep looking until Carlos starts screaming he's sorry, he's so sorry. Then…Fish *eats* him!"

The animals roared and cawed and congratulated Sarah for calling Fish to mirror a murderer's soul before taking jungle justice. Class had ended, but no one wanted to leave. We wanted to stay in our jungle, stay within our animals—and so we did. I asked them to close their eyes and call their animals to accompany them home. I told them that some South American tribes believe that when you are born, an animal is born with you. This animal protects and lives alongside you even if it's far away in an Amazon jungle—it came into the world at the same time you did. And, I told them, it dies with you to guide you back into the spirit world.

The kids decided to go home and make animal masks, returning the next day wearing the faces of their chosen animal. When they came into class the next day it was as if we never left the Amazon. Someone dimmed the lights, there were drawings everywhere of jaguars and chimps and snakes. Elaborate masks had replaced the Masters of the Universe who began this tribal journey. We sat behind our masks in a circle with the lights low and there was an acute, alert energy running between us, as eyes met behind animal faces.

I realize that I, who grew up in the forest wild, who first memorized the earth with my hands, have every reason to feel this familiar animal resonance. But many of these teenagers have barely been in the woods; in fact, many inner city kids are *afraid* of nature. They would not willingly sign up for an Outward Bound program or backpacking trek; they don't think about recycling in a world they believe already ruined and in their imaginations abandoned for intergalactic nomad futures. These kids are not environmentalists who worry about saving nature. And yet, when imagining an Amazon forest too thick for weapons to penetrate, too primitive for their futuristic Pac-Man battles, they return instinctively to their animal selves. These are animals they have only seen in zoos or on television, yet there is a profound identification, an ease of inhabiting another species that portends great hope for our own species's survival. Not because nature is "out there" to be saved or sanctioned, but because nature is *in* them. The ancient, green world has never left us though we have long ago left the forest.

What happens when we call upon our inner landscape to connect with the living rainforests still left in the natural world? I believe our imagination can be as mutually nurturing as an umbilical cord between our bodies and the planet. As we told our Amazon stories over the next week of class, gathered in a circle of animal masks, we could feel the rainforest growing in that sterile classroom. Lights low, surrounded by serpents, the jaguar clan, the elephants, I'd as often hear growls, hisses, and howls as words. Between this little classroom and the vast Amazon rainforest stretched a fine thread of story that grew thicker each day, capable of carrying our jungle meditations.

When Elephant stood in the circle and said simply, "My kind are dying out," there was outrage from the other animals.

"We'll stop those poachers!" cried Rat and Chimp. "We'll call Jaguar clan to protect you." And they did.

This protection is of a kind that reaches the other side of the world. Children's imagination is a primal force, just as strong as lobbying efforts and boycotts and endangered species acts. When children claim another species as not only their imaginary friend, but also as the animal within them—their ally—doesn't that change the outer world?

This class believes it to be so. They may be young, but their memories and alliances with the animals are very old. By telling their own animal stories they are practicing ecology at its most profound and healing level. Story as ecology—it's so simple, something we've forgotten. In our environmental wars the emphasis has been on saving species, not *becoming* them. We've fallen into an environmental fundamentalism that calls down hellfire and brimstone on the evil polluters and self-righteously struts about protecting other species as if we are gods who can save their souls.

But the animals' souls are not in our hands. Only our own souls are within our ken. It is our own spiritual relationship to animals that must evolve. Any change begins with imagining ourselves in a new way. And who has preserved their imaginations as a natural resource most deeply? Not adults, who so often have strip-mined their dreams and imagination for material dross. Those who sit behind the wheel of a Jaguar have probably forgotten the wild, black cat that first ran with them as children. Imagination is relegated to nighttime dreams, which are then dismissed in favor of "the real world." But children, like some adults, know that the real world stretches farther than what we can see—that's why they shift easily between visions of our tribal past and our future worlds. The limits of the adult world are there for these teenagers, but they still have a foot in the vast inner magic of childhood. It is this magical connection I called upon when I asked the kids to do the Dance of the Animals.

The day of the big dance I awoke with a sharp pain at my right eye. Seems my Siamese, who has always slept draped around my head, had stretched and his claw caught the corner of my eye. In the mirror I saw a two-inch scratch streaking from my eye like jungle make-up or a primitive face-painting. "The mark of the wildcat," the kids pronounced it when I walked into the dimly lit room to be met by a circle of familiar creatures. Never in ten years had my Siamese scratched my face. I took it as a sign that the dance began in his animal dream.

I put on my cobra mask and hissed a greeting to Chimp, Rat, Jaguar, and Unicorn. Keen eyes tracked me from behind colorful masks. I held up my rain stick which was also our talking stick and called the creatures one by one into the circle. "Sister Snake!" I called. "Begin the dance!"

Slowly, in rhythm to the deep, bell-like beat of my Northwest Native drum, each animal entered the circle and soon the dance sounded like this: Boom, step, twirl, and slither and stalk and snarl and chirp and caw, caw. Glide, glow, growl, and whistle and howl and shriek and trill and hiss, hiss. Each dance was distinct—from the undulating serpent on his belly, to the dainty high hoofing of Unicorn, from the syncopated stomps of Chimp on all-fours to Rat's covert jitterbug behind the stalking half-dark Jaguar. We danced, and the humid, lush jungle filled this room.

In that story line stretching between us and the Amazon, we connected with those animals and their spirits. And in return, we were complete—with animals as soul mirrors. We remembered who we were, by allowing the animals inside us to survive.

The dance is not over as long as we have our animal partners. When the kids left our last class, they still wore their masks fiercely. I was told that even on the bus they stayed deep in their animal character. I like to imagine those strong, young animals out there now in this wider jungle. I believe that Rat will survive the inner-city gangs; that Chimp will find his characteristic comedy even as his parents deal with divorce; I hope that Unicorn will always remember her mystical truth-telling horn. And as for Sarah who joined the Jaguar clan, elected as the first girl-leader over much mutinous boy-growling—Sarah knows the darkness she stalks and the nightmares that stalk her. She has animal eyes to see, to find even a murderer. Taking her catlike, graceful leave, she handed me a poem she'd written; it said "Now I can see in the dark" and was signed "Jaguar—Future Poet."

Late Victorians

Richard Rodriguez

Saint Augustine writes from his cope of dust that we are restless hearts, for earth is not our true home. Human unhappiness is evidence of our immortality. Intuition tells us we are meant for some other city.

Elizabeth Taylor, quoted in a magazine article of twenty years ago, spoke of cerulean Richard Burton days on her yacht, days that were nevertheless undermined by the elemental private reflection: This must end.

On a Sunday in summer, ten years ago, I was walking home from the Latin mass at Saint Patrick's, the old Irish parish downtown, when I saw thousands of people on Market Street. It was San Francisco's Gay Freedom Day parade—not the first, but the first I ever saw. Private lives were becoming public. There were marching bands. There were floats. Banners blocked single lives thematically into a processional mass, not unlike the consortiums of the blessed in Renaissance paintings, each saint cherishing the apparatus of his martyrdom: GAY DENTISTS. BLACK AND WHITE LOVERS. GAYS FROM BAKERSFIELD. LATINA LESBIANS. From the foot of Market Street they marched, east to west, following the mythic American path toward optimism.

I followed the parade to Civic Center Plaza, where flags of routine nations yielded sovereignty to a multitude. Pastel billows flowed over all.

Five years later, another parade. Politicians waved from white convertibles. Dykes on Bikes revved up, thumbs upped. But now banners bore the acronyms of death. AIDS. ARC. Drums were muffled as passing, plum-spotted young men slid by on motorized cable cars.

Though I am alive now, I do not believe that an old man's pessimism is truer than a young man's optimism simply because it comes after. There are things a young man knows that are true and are not yet in the old man's power to recollect. Spring has its sappy wisdom. Lonely teenagers still arrive in San Francisco aboard Greyhound buses. The city can still seem, I imagine, by comparison to where they came from, paradise.

Four years ago, on a Sunday in winter, a brilliant spring afternoon, I was jogging near Fort Point while overhead a young woman was, with difficulty, climbing over the railing of the Golden Gate Bridge. Holding down her skirt with one hand, with the other she waved to a startled spectator (the newspaper next day quoted a workman who was painting the bridge) before she stepped onto the sky.

To land like a spilled purse at my feet.

Serendipity has an eschatological tang here. Always has. Few American cities have had the experience, as we have had, of watching the civic body burn even as we stood, out of body, on a hillside, in a movie theater. Jeanette MacDonald's loony scatting of "San Francisco" has become our go-to-hell anthem. San Francisco has taken some heightened pleasure from the circus of final things. To Atlantis, to Pompeii, to the Pillar of Salt, we add the Golden Gate Bridge, not golden at all but rust red. San Francisco toys with the tragic conclusion.

For most of its brief life, San Francisco has entertained an idea of itself as heaven on earth, whether as Gold Town or City Beautiful or Treasure Island or Haight-Ashbury.

San Francisco can support both comic and tragic conclusions because the city is geographically *in extremis*, a metaphor for the farthest-flung possibility, a metaphor for the end of the line. Land's end.

To speak of San Francisco as land's end is to read the map from one direction only—as Europeans would read or as the East Coast has always read it. In my lifetime, San Francisco has become an Asian city. To speak, therefore, of San Francisco as land's end is to betray parochialism. Before my parents came to California from Mexico, they saw San Francisco as the North. The West was not west for them.

I cannot claim for myself the memory of a skyline such as the one César saw. César came to San Francisco in middle age; César came here as to some final place. He was born in South America; he had grown up in Paris; he had been everywhere, done everything; he assumed the world. Yet César was not condescending toward San Francisco, not at all. Here César saw revolution, and he embraced it.

Whereas I live here because I was born here. I grew up ninety miles away, in Sacramento. San Francisco was the nearest, the easiest, the inevitable city, since I needed a city. And yet I live here surrounded by people for whom San Francisco is a quest.

I have never looked for utopia on a map. Of course, I believe in human advancement. I believe in medicine, in astrophysics, in washing machines. But my compass takes its cardinal point from tragedy. If I respond to the metaphor of spring, I nevertheless learned, years ago, from my Mexican parents, from my Irish nuns, to count on winter. The point of Eden for me, for us, is not approach but expulsion.

After I met César in 1984, our friendly debate concerning the halcyon properties of San Francisco ranged from restaurant to restaurant. I spoke of limits. César boasted of freedoms.

It was César's conceit to add to the gates of Jerusalem, to add to the soccer fields of Tijuana, one other dreamscape hoped for the world over. It was the view from a hill, through a mesh of electrical tram wires, of an urban neighborhood in a valley. The vision took its name from the protruding wedge of a theater marquee. Here César raised his glass without discretion: To the Castro.

There were times, dear César, when you tried to switch sides if only to scorn American optimism, which, I remind you, had already become your own. At the high school where César taught, teachers and parents had organized a campaign to keep kids from driving themselves to the junior prom in an attempt to forestall liquor and death. Such a scheme momentarily reawakened César's Latin skepticism.

Didn't the Americans know? (His tone exaggerated incredulity.) Teenagers will crash into lampposts on their way home from proms, and there is nothing to be done about it. You cannot forbid tragedy.

By California standards I live in an old house. But not haunted. There are too many tall windows, there is too much salty light, especially in winter, though the windows rattle, rattle in summer when the fog lies overhead, and the house creaks and prowls at night. I feel myself immune to any confidence it seeks to tell.

To grow up homosexual is to live with secrets and within secrets. In no other place are those secrets more closely guarded than within the family home. The grammar of the gay city borrows metaphors from the nineteenth-century house. "Coming out of the closet" is predicated upon family laundry, dirty linen, skeletons.

I live in a tall Victorian house that has been converted to four apartments; four single men.

Neighborhood streets are named to honor nineteenth-century men of action, men of distant fame. Clay. Jackson. Scott. Pierce. Many Victorians in the neighborhood date from before the 1906 earthquake and fire.

Architectural historians credit the gay movement of the 1970s with the urban restoration of San Francisco. Twenty years ago this was a borderline neighborhood. This room, like all the rooms of the house, was painted headache green, apple green, boardinghouse green. In the 1970s homosexuals moved into black and working-class parts of the city, where they were perceived as pioneers or as blockbusters, depending.

Two decades ago some of the least expensive sections of San Francisco were wooden Victorian sections. It was thus a coincidence of the market that gay men found themselves living with the architectural metaphor for family. No other architecture in the American imagination is more evocative of family than the Victorian house. In those same years, the 1970s, and within those same Victorian houses, homosexuals were living rebellious lives to challenge the foundations of domesticity.

Was "queer bashing" as much a manifestation of homophobia as a reaction against gentrification? One heard the complaint often enough that gay men were as promiscuous with their capital as otherwise, buying, fixing up, then selling and moving on. Two incomes, no children, described an unfair advantage. No sooner would flower boxes begin to appear than an anonymous reply was smeared on the sidewalk out front: KILL FAGGOTS.

The three- or four-story Victorian house, like the Victorian novel, was built to contain several generations and several classes under one roof, behind a single oaken door. What strikes me is the confidence of Victorian architecture. Stairs, connecting one story with another, describe the confidence that bound generations together through time, confidence that the family would inherit the earth.

If Victorian houses exude a sturdy optimism by day, they are also associated in our imaginations with the Gothic—with shadows and cobwebby gimcrack, long corridors.

The nineteenth century was remarkable for escalating optimism even as it excavated the back stairs, the descending architecture of nightmare—Freud's labor and Engels's.

I live on the second story, in rooms that have been rendered as empty as Yorick's skull—gutted, unrattled, in various ways unlocked, added skylights and new windows, new doors. The hallway remains the darkest part of the house.

This winter the hallway and lobby are being repainted to resemble an eighteenth-century French foyer. Of late we had walls and carpet of Sienese red; a baroque mirror hung in an alcove by the stairwell. Now we are to have enlightened austerity of an expensive sort—black-and-white marble floors and faux masonry. A man comes in the afternoons to texture the walls with a sponge and a rag and to paint white mortar lines that create an illusion of permanence, of stone.

The renovation of Victorian San Francisco into dollhouses for libertines may have seemed, in the 1970s, an evasion of what the city was actually becoming. San Francisco's rows of storied houses proclaimed a multigenerational orthodoxy, all the while masking the city's unconventional soul. Elsewhere, meanwhile, domestic America was coming undone.

Suburban Los Angeles, the prototype for a new America, was characterized by a more apparently radical residential architecture. There was, for example, the work of Frank Gehry. In the 1970s Gehry exploded the nuclear-family house, turning it inside out intellectually and in fact. Though, in a way, Gehry merely completed the logic of the postwar suburban tract house with its one story, its sliding glass doors, Formica kitchen, two-car garage. The tract house exchanged privacy for mobility. Heterosexuals opted for the one-lifetime house, the freeway, the birth-control pill, minimalist fiction.

The age-old description of homosexuality is of a sin against nature. Moralistic society has always judged emotion literally. The homosexual was sinful because he had no kosher place to stick it. In attempting to drape the architecture of sodomy with art, homosexuals have lived for thousands of years against the expectations of nature. Barren as Shakers and, interestingly, as concerned with the small effect, homosexuals have made a covenant against nature. Homosexual survival lay in artifice, in plumage, in lampshades, sonnets, musical comedy, couture, syntax, religious ceremony, opera, lacquer, irony.

I once asked Enrique, an interior decorator, if he had many homosexual clients. *"Mais non,"* said he, flexing his eyelids. "Queers don't need decorators. They were born knowing how. All this A.S.I.D. stuff—tests and regulations—as if you can confer a homosexual diploma on a suburban housewife by granting her a discount card."

A knack? The genius, we are beginning to fear in an age of AIDS, is irreplaceable—but does it exist? The question is whether the darling affinities are innate to homosexuality or whether they are compensatory. Why have so many homosexuals retired into the small effect, the ineffectual career, the stereotype, the card shop, the florist? *Be gentle with me?* Or do homosexuals know things others do not?

This way power lay: Once upon a time the homosexual appropriated to himself a mystical province, that of taste. Taste, which is, after all, the insecurity of the middle class, became the homosexual's licentiate to challenge the rule of nature. (The fairy in his blood, he intimated.)

Deciding how best to stick it may be only an architectural problem or a question of physics or of engineering or of cabinetry. Nevertheless, society's condemnation forced the homosexual to find his redemption outside nature. *We'll put a little skirt here.* The impulse is not to create but to re-create, to sham, to convert, to sauce, to rouge, to fragrance, to prettify. No effect is too small or too ephemeral to be snatched away from nature, to be ushered toward the perfection of artificiality. *We'll bring out the highlights there.* The homosexual has marshaled the architecture of the straight world to the very gates of Versailles—that great Vatican of fairyland—beyond which power is converted to leisure. In San Francisco in the 1980s the highest form of art became interior decoration. The glory hole was thus converted to an eighteenth-century French foyer.

I live away from the street, in a back apartment, in two rooms. I use my bedroom as a visitor's room—the sleigh bed tricked up with shams into a sofa—whereas I rarely invite anyone into my library, the public room, where I write, the public gesture.

I read in my bedroom in the afternoon because the light is good there, especially now, in winter, when the sun recedes from the earth.

There is a door in the south wall that leads to a balcony. The door was once a window. Inside the door, inside my bedroom, are twin green shutters. They are false shutters, of no function beyond wit. The shutters open into the room; they have the effect of turning my apartment inside out.

A few months ago I hired a man to paint the shutters green. I wanted the green shutters of Manet—you know the ones I mean—I wanted a weathered look, as of verdigris. For several days the painter labored, rubbing his paints into the wood and then wiping them off again. In this way he rehearsed for me decades of the ravages of weather. Yellow enough? Black?

The painter left one afternoon, saying he would return the next day, leaving behind his tubes, his brushes, his sponges and rags. He never returned. Someone told me he has AIDS.

Repainted façades extend now from Jackson Street south into what was once the heart of the black "Mo"—black Fillmore Street. Today there are watercress sandwiches at three o'clock where recently there had been loudmouthed kids, hole-in-the-wall bars, pimps. Now there are tweeds and perambulators, matrons and nannies. Yuppies. And gays.

The gay male revolution had greater influence on San Francisco in the 1970s than did the feminist revolution. Feminists, with whom I include lesbians—such was the inclusiveness of the feminist movement—were preoccupied with career, with escape from the house in order to create a sexually democratic city. Homosexual men sought to reclaim the house, the house that traditionally had been the reward for heterosexuality, with all its selfless tasks and burdens.

Leisure defined the gay male revolution. The gay political movement began, by most accounts, in 1969, with the Stonewall riots in New York City, whereby gay men fought to defend the nonconformity of their leisure.

It was no coincidence that homosexuals migrated to San Francisco in the 1970s, for the city was famed as a playful place, more Catholic than Protestant in its eschatological intuition. In 1975 the state of California legalized consensual homosexuality, and about that same time Castro Street, southwest of downtown, began to eclipse Polk Street as the homosexual address in San Francisco. Polk Street was a string of bars. The Castro was an entire district. The Castro had Victorian houses and churches, bookstores and restaurants, gyms, dry cleaners, supermarkets, and an elected member of the Board of Supervisors. The Castro supported baths and bars, but there was nothing furtive about them. On Castro Street the light of day penetrated gay life through clear plate-glass windows. The light of day discovered a new confidence, a new politics, Also a new look—a noncosmopolitan, Burt Reynolds, butch-kid style: beer, ball games, Levi's, short hair, muscles.

Gay men who lived elsewhere in the city, in Pacific Heights or in the Richmond, often spoke with derision of "Castro Street clones," describing the look, or scorned what they called the ghettoization of homosexuality. To an older generation of homosexuals, the blatancy of sexuality on Castro Street threatened the discreet compromise they had negotiated with a tolerant city.

As the Castro district thrived, Folsom Street, south of Market, also began to thrive, as if in counterdistinction to the utopian Castro. The Folsom Street area was a warehouse district of puddled alleys and deserted streets. Folsom Street offered an assortment of leather bars, an evening's regress to the outlaw sexuality of the fifties, the forties, the nineteenth century, and so on—an eroticism of the dark of the Reeperbahn, or of the guardsman's barracks.

The Castro district implied that sexuality was more crucial, that homosexuality was the central fact of identity. The Castro district, with its ice cream parlors and hardware stores, was the revolutionary place.

Into which carloads of vacant-eyed teenagers from other districts or from middle-class suburbs would drive after dark, cruising the neighborhood for solitary victims.

The ultimate gay basher was a city supervisor named Dan White, ex-cop, ex-boxer, ex-fireman, ex-altar boy. Dan White had grown up in the Castro district; he recognized the Castro revolution for what it was. Gays had achieved power over him. He murdered the mayor and he murdered the homosexual member of the Board of Supervisors.

Katherine, a sophisticate if ever there was one, nevertheless dismisses the two men descending the aisle at the opera house: "All so sleek and smooth-jowled and silver-haired—they don't seem real, poor darlings. It must be because they don't have children."

Lodged within Katherine's complaint is the perennial heterosexual annoyance with the homosexual's freedom from child rearing, which places the homosexual not so much beyond the pale as it relegates the homosexual outside "responsible" life.

It was the glamour of gay life, after all, as much as it was the feminist call to career, that encouraged heterosexuals in the 1970s to excuse themselves from nature, to swallow the birth-control pill. Who needs children? The gay bar became the paradigm for the singles bar. The gay couple became the paradigm for the selfish couple—

all dressed up and everywhere to go. And there was the example of the gay house in illustrated life-style magazines. At the same time that suburban housewives were looking outside the home for fulfillment, gay men were reintroducing a new generation in the city—heterosexual men and women—to the complacencies of the barren house.

Puritanical America dismissed gay camp followers as yuppies; the term means to suggest infantility. Yuppies were obsessive and awkward in their materialism. Whereas gays arranged a decorative life against a barren state, yuppies sought early returns, lives that were not to be all toil and spin. Yuppies, trained to careerism from the cradle, wavered in their pursuit of the northern European ethic—indeed, we might now call it the pan-Pacific ethic—in favor of the Mediterranean, the Latin, the Catholic, the Castro, the Gay.

The international architectural idioms of Skidmore, Owings & Merrill, which defined the city's skyline in the 1970s, betrayed no awareness of any street-level debate concerning the primacy of play in San Francisco nor of any human dramas resulting from urban redevelopment. The repellent office tower was a fortress raised against the sky, against the street, against the idea of a city. Offices were hives where money was made, and damn all.

In the 1970s San Francisco was divided between the interests of downtown and the pleasures of the neighborhoods. Neighborhoods asserted idiosyncrasy, human scale, light. San Francisco neighborhoods perceived downtown as working against their influence in determining what the city should be. Thus neighborhoods seceded from the idea of a city.

The gay movement rejected downtown as representing "straight" conformity. But was it possible that heterosexual Union Street was related to Castro Street? Was it possible that either was related to the Latino Mission district? Or to the Sino-Russian Richmond? San Francisco, though complimented worldwide for holding its center, was in fact without a vision of itself entire.

In the 1980s, in deference to the neighborhoods, City Hall would attempt a counterreformation of downtown, forbidding "Manhattanization." Shadows were legislated away from parks and playgrounds. Height restrictions were lowered beneath an existing skyline. Design, too, fell under the retrojurisdiction of the city planner's office. The Victorian house was presented to architects as a model of what the city wanted to uphold and to become. In heterosexual neighborhoods, one saw newly built Victorians. Downtown, postmodernist prescriptions for playfulness advised skyscrapers to wear party hats, buttons, comic mustaches. Philip Johnson yielded to the dollhouse impulse to perch angels atop one of his skyscrapers.

In the 1970s, like a lot of men and women in this city, I joined a gym. My club, I've even caught myself calling it.

In the gay city of the 1970s, bodybuilding became an architectural preoccupation of the upper middle class. Bodybuilding is a parody of labor, a useless accumulation of the laborer's bulk and strength. No useful task is accomplished. And yet there is something businesslike about the habitués, and the gym is filled with the punch-clock logic of the workplace. Machines clank and hum. Needles on gauges toll spent calories.

The gym is at once a closet of privacy and an exhibition gallery. All four walls are mirrored.

I study my body in the mirror. Physical revelation—nakedness—is no longer possible, cannot be desired, for the body is shrouded in meat and wears itself.

The intent is some merciless press of body against a standard, perfect mold. Bodies are "cut" or "pumped" or "buffed" as on an assembly line in Turin. A body becomes so many extrovert parts. Delts, pecs, lats.

I harness myself in a Nautilus cage.

Lats become wings. For the gym is nothing if not the occasion for transcendence. From homosexual to autosexual…

I lift weights over my head, baring my teeth like an animal with the strain.

…to nonsexual. The effect of the overdeveloped body is the miniaturization of the sexual organs—of no function beyond wit. Behold the ape become Blakean angel, revolving in an empyrean of mirrors.

The nineteenth-century mirror over the fireplace in my bedroom was purchased by a decorator from the estate of a man who died last year of AIDS. It is a top-heavy piece, confusing styles. Two ebony-painted columns support a frieze of painted glass above the mirror. The frieze depicts three bourgeois Graces and a couple of free-range cherubs. The lake of the mirror has formed a cataract, and at its edges it is beginning to corrode.

Thus the mirror that now draws upon my room owns some bright curse, maybe—some memory not mine.

As I regard this mirror, I imagine Saint Augustine's meditation slowly hardening into syllogism, passing down through centuries to confound us: Evil is the absence of good.

We have become accustomed to figures disappearing from our landscape. Does this not lead us to interrogate the landscape?

With reason do we invest mirrors with the superstition of memory, for they, though glass, though liquid captured in a bay, are so often less fragile than we are. They—bright ovals or rectangles or rounds—bump down unscathed, unspilled through centuries, whereas we…

The man in the red baseball cap used to jog so religiously on Marina Green. By the time it occurs to me that I have not seen him for months, I realize he may be dead—not lapsed, not moved away. People come and go in the city, it's true. But in San Francisco in 1990, death has become as routine an explanation for disappearance as Allied Van Lines.

AIDS, it has been discovered, is a plague of absence. Absence opened in the blood. Absence condensed into the fluid of passing emotion. Absence shot through opalescent tugs of semen to deflower the city.

And then AIDS, it was discovered, is a nonmetaphorical disease, a disease like any other. Absence sprang from substance—a virus, a hairy bubble perched upon a needle, a platter of no intention served round: fever, blisters, a death sentence.

At first I heard only a few names, names connected, perhaps, with the right faces, perhaps not. People vaguely remembered, as through the cataract of this mirror, from dinner parties or from intermissions. A few articles in the press. The rumored celebrities. But within months the slow beating of the blood had found its bay.

One of San Francisco's gay newspapers, the *Bay Area Reporter*, began to accept advertisements from funeral parlors and casket makers, inserting them between the randy ads for leather bars and tanning salons. The *Reporter* invited homemade obituaries—lovers writing of lovers, friends remembering friends and the blessings of unexceptional life.

Peter. Carlos. Gary. Asel. Perry. Nikos.

Healthy snapshots accompany each annal. At the Russian River. By the Christmas tree. Lifting a beer. In uniform. A dinner jacket. A satin gown.

He was born in Puerto La Libertad, El Salvador.

He attended Apple Valley High School, where he was their first male cheerleader.

From El Paso. From Medford. From Germany. From Long Island.

I moved back to San Francisco in 1979. Oh, I had had some salad days elsewhere, but by 1979 I was a wintry man. I came here in order not to be distracted by the ambitions or, for that matter, the pleasures of others but to pursue my own ambition. Once here, though, I found the company of men who pursued an earthly paradise charming. Skepticism became my demeanor toward them—I was the dinner-party skeptic, a firm believer in Original Sin and in the limits of possibility.

Which charmed them.

He was a dancer.

He settled into the interior-design department of Gump's, where he worked until his illness.

He was a teacher.

César, for example.

César could shave the rind from any assertion to expose its pulp and jelly. But César was otherwise ruled by pulp. César loved everything that ripened in time. Freshmen. Bordeaux. César could fashion liturgy from an artichoke. Yesterday it was not ready (cocking his head, rotating the artichoke in his hand over a pot of cold water). Tomorrow will be too late (Yorick's skull). Today it is perfect (as he lit the fire beneath the pot). We will eat it now.

If he's lucky, he's got a year, a doctor told me. If not, he's got two.

The phone rang. AIDS had tagged a friend. And then the phone rang again. And then the phone rang again. Michael had tested positive. Adrian, well, what he had assumed were shingles…Paul was back in the hospital. And César, dammit, César, even César, especially César.

That winter before his death César traveled back to South America. On his return to San Francisco he described to me how he had walked with his mother in her garden—his mother chafing her hands as if she were cold. But it was not cold, he said. They moved slowly. Her summer garden was prolonging itself this year, she said. The cicadas will not stop singing.

When he lay on his deathbed, César said everyone else he knew might get AIDS and die. He said I would be the only one spared—"spared" was supposed to have been chased with irony, I knew, but his voice was too weak to do the job. "You are too circumspect," he said then, wagging his finger upon the coverlet.

So I was going to live to see that the garden of earthly delights was, after all, only wallpaper—was that it, César? Hadn't I always said so? It was then I saw that the greater sin against heaven was my unwillingness to embrace life.

It was not as in some Victorian novel—the curtains drawn, the pillows plumped, the streets strewn with sawdust. It was not to be a matter of custards in covered dishes, steaming possets, *Try a little of this, my dear.* Or gathering up the issues of *Architectural Digest* strewn about the bed. Closing the biography of Diana Cooper and marking its place. Or the unfolding of discretionary screens, morphine, parrots, pavilions.

César experienced agony.

Four of his high school students sawed through a Vivaldi quartet in the corridor outside his hospital room, prolonging the hideous garden.

In the presence of his lover Gregory and friends, Scott passed from this life…

He died peacefully at home in his lover Ron's arms.

Immediately after a friend led a prayer for him to be taken home and while his dear mother was reciting the Twenty-third Psalm, Bill peacefully took his last breath.

I stood aloof at César's memorial, the kind of party he would enjoy, everyone said. And so for a time César lay improperly buried, unconvincingly resurrected in the conditional: would enjoy. What else could they say? César had no religion beyond aesthetic bravery.

Sunlight remains. Traffic remains. Nocturnal chic attaches to some discovered restaurant. A new novel is reviewed in the *New York Times.* And the mirror rasps on its hook. The mirror is lifted down.

A priest friend, a good friend, who out of naïveté plays the cynic, tells me—this is on a bright, billowy day; we are standing outside—"It's not as sad as you may think. There is at least spectacle in the death of the young. Come to the funeral of an old lady sometime if you want to feel an empty church."

I will grant my priest friend this much: that it is easier, easier on me, to sit with gay men in hospitals than with the staring old. Young men talk as much as they are able.

But those who gather around the young man's bed do not see spectacle. This doll is Death. I have seen people caressing it, staring Death down. I have seen people wipe its tears, wipe its ass; I have seen people kiss Death on his lips, where once there were lips.

Chris was inspired after his own diagnosis in July 1987 with the truth and reality of how such a terrible disease could bring out the love, warmth, and support of so many friends and family.

Sometimes no family came. If there was family, it was usually mother. Mom. With her suitcase and with the torn flap of an envelope in her hand.

Brenda. Pat. Connie. Toni. Soledad.

Or parents came but then left without reconciliation, some preferring to say cancer.

But others came. Sissies were not, after all, afraid of Death. They walked his dog. They washed his dishes. They bought his groceries. They massaged his poor back. They changed his bandages. They emptied his bedpan.

Men who sought the aesthetic ordering of existence were recalled to nature. Men who aspired to the mock-angelic settled for the shirt of hair. The gay community of San Francisco, having found freedom, consented to necessity—to all that the proud world had for so long held up to them, withheld from them, as "real humanity."

And if gays took care of their own, they were not alone. AIDS was a disease of the entire city; its victims were as often black, Hispanic, straight. Neither were Charity and Mercy only white, only male, only gay. Others came. There were nurses and nuns and the couple from next door, co-workers, strangers, teenagers, corporations, pensioners. A community was forming over the city.

Cary and Rick's friends and family wish to thank the many people who provided both small and great kindnesses.

He was attended to and lovingly cared for by the staff at Coming Home Hospice.

And the saints of this city have names listed in the phone book, names I heard called through a microphone one cold Sunday in Advent as I sat in Most Holy Redeemer Church. It might have been any of the churches or community centers in the Castro district, but it happened at Most Holy Redeemer at a time in the history of the world when the Roman Catholic Church still pronounced the homosexual a sinner.

A woman at the microphone called upon volunteers from the AIDS Support Group to come forward. One by one, in twos and threes, throughout the church, people stood up, young men and women, and middle-aged and old, straight, gay, and all of them shy at being called. Yet they came forward and assembled in the sanctuary, facing the congregation, grinning self-consciously at one another, their hands hidden behind them.

I am preoccupied by the fussing of a man sitting in the pew directly in front of me—in his seventies, frail, his iodine-colored hair combed forward and pasted upon his forehead. Fingers of porcelain clutch the pearly beads of what must have been his mother's rosary. He is not the sort of man any gay man would have chosen to become in the 1970s. He is probably not what he himself expected to become. Something of the old dear about him, wizened butterfly, powdered old pouf. Certainly he is what I fear becoming. And then he rises, this old monkey, with the most beatific dignity, in answer to the microphone, and he strides into the sanctuary to take his place in the company of the Blessed.

So this is it—this, what looks like a Christmas party in an insurance office and not as in Renaissance paintings, and not as we had always thought, not some flower-strewn, some sequined curtain call of grease-painted heroes gesturing to the stalls. A lady with a plastic candy cane pinned to her lapel. A Castro clone with a red bandanna exploding from his hip pocket. A perfume-counter lady with an Hermès scarf mantled upon her left shoulder. A black man in a checkered sports coat. The pink-haired punkess with a jewel in her nose. Here, too, is the gay couple in middle age, wearing interchangeable plaid shirts and corduroy pants. Blood and shit and Mr. Happy Face. These know the weight of bodies.

Bill died.
…Passed on to heaven.
…Turning over in his bed one night and then gone.

These learned to love what is corruptible, while I, barren skeptic, reader of Saint Augustine, curator of the earthly paradise, inheritor of the empty mirror, I shift my tailbone upon the cold, hard pew.

Designs for Escape

Witold Rybczynski

Last summer, I was in Montreal on a brief visit from Philadelphia, where I now live. I had some small business to conduct there, but the visit was mainly an opportunity to look up old friends. I called Danièle, whom I hadn't seen in a couple of years, and we arranged to have dinner together that evening. She promised to take me to a new bistro, and I looked forward to it: Montreal is no longer the premier city of Canada—that role now belongs to Toronto—and it seemed a bit shabbier than I remembered, but it still has more than its share of exceptional restaurants.

"Shall we meet there?" I asked.

"No," she said, "you must come by the apartment first." She told me excitedly that she wanted to show me the plans of a weekend house that she and Luc were going to build. Danièle is not an architectural neophyte: she had been married to an architect for twenty years. True, the marriage had ended in divorce—Luc, her current beau, is in public relations—and I didn't remember her having expressed strong ideas about architecture in the past. But I knew her ex well; he had been a student of mine. You can't live with someone for twenty years and not be influenced by what that person does. At least, that's what my wife tells me. So I was curious to see what sort of house Danièle had come up with.

She and Luc and I sat around the kitchen table, and they showed me snapshots of the site, which was in the Laurentian Mountains, a popular recreation area north of Montreal. The Laurentians are an old volcanic range, and the worn, rounded mountains recall the Berkshires or the Catskills, but they're wilder, with fewer signs of human habitation. Though I prefer pastoral scenery—rolling fields and gentle hills—to mountains, I had to admit that Danièle and Luc's land was beautiful: a wooded hilltop with long views in several directions.

I sensed that Danièle was a bit nervous about showing me the drawings of the house. That was understandable. She knew that I taught architecture and wrote about domestic design. She and her husband had helped my wife and me when we built our own house in the country. Now it was her turn. Building a house for yourself is exciting, because of the feeling of possibility that a new house carries, and because creating

149

shelter is a basic human urge, whether or not you are an architect. It is the same urge that makes children erect playhouses out of blankets and cardboard boxes, and build sandcastles at the beach. But building a house—a real house—is also scary, and not just because of the money involved or the fear of making mistakes. A new house is revealing. It tells you—and everyone else—"This is how I live. This is what's important to me. This is what I dream about." I think that's why home magazines—from *Ladies' Home Journal* to *Architectural Digest*—have always been popular. It's not just a matter of looking for decorating hints. Rather, houses intrigue us because they tell us so much about their owners.

Danièle spread out the sketches, which had been prepared by a local architect. Siting is always a crucial decision for a country house. I could see that the house would stand almost at the top of the hill, and so would be approached from below, as, ideally, it should be; walking down to a house is always unpleasant. The hilltop had obviously been chosen for the views it offered, but it also meant that the house would be some distance from the road, and would require a short walk through the trees to arrive at the front door.

The floor layout of the house was simple enough. Because of the sloping ground, the lower level, containing two bedrooms and a bathroom, would be dug partly into the ground. The floor above, which could be entered directly from the upper part of the slope, would hold the living areas, and there would be a sleeping loft in a sort of tower. Danièle explained that they wanted to be able to rent a room to skiers during the winter season, which was why the lower level would have its own front door and could be separated from the rest of the house. The exterior would be mainly wood, with several sloping roofs. It was hard to put your finger on the architectural style of the house. It wasn't going to have the curved eaves and dormer windows of the traditional Breton style, which is still popular with many Québécois. Although the functional-looking window frames and rather spare exterior couldn't be called old-fashioned, neither did they seem aggressively modern. I suppose most people would use the term "contemporary."

The three of us got into a long discussion about how best to rearrange one of the bathrooms. I pointed out that if they moved the door to the other side and changed the site of the toilet, they could gain space and improve the circulation in the kitchen area as well. Not very inspirational stuff. I could see that Luc and Danièle expected something more. I had unconsciously fallen into a bad habit of architecture teachers: if you really don't know what to say about a project, focus on some practical improvement, no matter how small. How often had I sat on design juries at the university, taking part in interminable discussions about fire exits or corridor widths, when the real problem was something else entirely.

It wasn't that Danièle and Luc's house looked boring—quite the opposite. "The architect told us that she worked hard to make each side of the house different," Danièle explained. Differences there certainly were, and, I thought, that was part of the problem. The little house was trying too hard to be unusual and interesting. The perimeter was animated by indentations and protrusions—architectural bumps and grinds. Instead of a single sheltering gable, the roof was broken up into several slopes. This is a favorite device of commercial homebuilders and is obviously a crowd pleaser, though the roof has always seemed to me an odd thing to spend your money on. The complexity of the roof was mirrored by the intricacy of the fenestration: there were half a dozen different window shapes and sizes. The modest house was hardly in a league with Frank Gehry and Peter Eisenman, but it *was* busy.

I realized that I had to say something more substantive about the house, but I wasn't sure where to start. I think that small, inexpensive houses like Danièle and Luc's should be as simple as possible. This is partly a question of economics; complexity costs money, after all, and I would rather see a restricted budget devoted to better-quality materials than to architectural bravura. But it is also an aesthetic issue. I like plain farmhouses and straightforward country buildings. They usually look good in the landscape, and they have a kind of directness and honesty that appeals to me. True, they are often really just boxes, but boxes can be given charm through relatively inexpensive details of construction, such as bay windows, trellises, and even shutters.

A simple way to dress up a house is to add a porch. Porches, with their columns, balustrades, and ornamental fretwork, are pleasant to look at, and they are also pleasant places to sit. They are like rooms, but without walls, and they encourage the sort of lazy inactivity that has always seemed to me to be the essence of leisure. I noticed that Danièle's house didn't have any covered outdoor area, and I suggested that they might consider adding a screened porch. This would also be a useful feature, since the Laurentian summers are notorious for their mosquitoes and blackflies.

"No," Luc said. "A porch won't do at all. Porches and balconies are something for a city house. We want our house to look rustic."

That was interesting. I had always associated porches and verandas with country houses. Evidently, for Danièle and Luc they were an urban feature. (Indeed, Montreal row houses traditionally do have verandas.) A little later, they asked me what sort of material I thought should be used to finish the inside walls. I said that I liked plaster wallboard—that it was inexpensive, you could paint it whatever color you wanted, and, furthermore, it was fire-resistant—an important consideration when you're building miles from a fire station. They looked skeptical and said that they had been thinking, rather, of wood. "We want this to be a different sort of place, where we can get away from our city life," Luc said.

A lot of architecture has to do with images—and imaginings. For one person, getting away means a broad porch with a rocking chair and a slowly turning ceiling fan. The image may be the result of a remembered family photograph, or a painting, or even the experience of a real porch somewhere. That particular porch image has haunted me for years—I think I saw it first in a magazine ad for whiskey. And one of the side benefits of watching the film "Out of Africa" is the beautiful porch of Karen Blixen's plantation house in Kenya, with Mozart's Clarinet Concerto playing on a windup gramophone. Alas, for Luc a porch was just a utilitarian appendage. Moreover, the image it conjured up for him was not rural but urban. I also had the impression that he considered porches to be old-fashioned—or maybe just places for old people.

I have always liked farmhouse kitchens—large, comfortable rooms where you can cook and eat and socialize around the kitchen table. (That's probably a remembered image, too.) The plans of Danièle and Luc's house, on the other hand, showed a small efficiency kitchen, with a separate dining area. It was an arrangement that reminded me—but, obviously, not them—of a city apartment. I realized that their idea of getting away from it all was more dynamic than mine: not a cabin in the woods but a striking ski chalet on a hilltop, with different views from each room, beamed ceilings, knotty-pine walls, and a dramatic fireplace. I was starting to understand why the house looked the way it did. It was not a question of money—theirs was hardly an extravagant house. It reflected a different idea of rusticity.

Getting away from it all has a long history; almost as soon as people started living in towns, they felt the need to build country retreats. In ancient times, it was the common practice of wealthy Romans to decamp periodically to country estates. "You should take the first opportunity yourself to leave the din, the futile bustle, and the useless occupations of the city," Pliny the Younger wrote in a letter to a friend. Pliny owned two country retreats, one a large agricultural estate in present-day Umbria, the other his famous seaside villa in Latium, of which he wrote, "There I do most of my writing, and, instead of the land I lack, I work to cultivate myself." The sentiment—re-creation—is recognizably modern. Modern-sounding, too, is the Renaissance architect Leon Battista Alberti's advice that "if the villa is not distant, but close by a gate of the city, it will make it easier and more convenient to flit, with wife and children, between town and villa, whenever desirable."

In nineteenth-century America, such flitting usually meant taking a steamboat or a train. Summer houses sprang up along the Hudson River, in New York, and the Schuylkill, in Philadelphia, or in places like Newport, Rhode Island. In Newport you'll find many early examples of the Shingle Style, one of the high accomplishments of American architecture. The Watts Sherman house, designed by the great architect H. H. Richardson in 1874, is irregular in composition, and the granite, the half-timbering, and the wooden shingles on the exterior give it the picturesque appearance that is a trademark of the Shingle Style. Still, it is provided with a drawing room, a dining room, and a library, and so is not really a radical departure from a typical middle-class suburban or urban house of the period.

Although rich New Yorkers commuted to their villas in Newport, these were summer houses, not weekend houses. Indeed, the full weekend—a two-day holiday at the end of the workweek—didn't appear until the twentieth century. It arrived first in Britain, as a one-and-a-half-day holiday, and by the early nineteen-hundreds more and more Americans were also working "short Saturdays." Eventually, the five-day workweek became commonplace, and the combination of the two-day holiday and the automobile produced the vast proliferation of weekend retreats that we know today.

The weekend cottage continues the time-tested tradition of the summer getaway house, but with a crucial difference. Instead of being used for an entire season, it is chiefly a two-day retreat. Hence it is less a place of long and lazy summers than of sometimes frantic spurts of recreation. Perhaps that's why the architecture is often intentionally unusual, with dramatic fireplaces, tall spaces, and cantilevered decks. That was what Luc meant when he said he wanted "a different sort of place." It was probably the late architect Charles Moore who started the trend toward spatial excitement. In the mid-nineteen-sixties he designed a series of weekend houses, chiefly in

Northern California, with deceptively simple exteriors and with interiors that were a cross between barns and jungle gyms. Although designed with considerable sophistication, these houses could also be described as the architectural equivalent of the then popular leisure suit. That is, they were intended to put people instantaneously in a different mood and also to tell the world that here the owner was off duty. Moore's approach was influential, and versions of his houses sprang up in vacation spots from Colorado to Vermont.

Like many people, I spend my weekends in a worn pair of shorts and an old polo shirt. Perhaps that's why my ideal of a weekend house is more like a farmhouse—commodious rather than exciting, a place to kick your shoes off and relax, a place that can get scuffed up and still feel comfortable. Sculptural staircases and eye-popping fireplaces are not a priority. Now, I don't want to give the impression that I think weekend houses should be Thoreau-style shacks, without conveniences, or even without luxuries. I would have no objection to a Miele range and a Sub-Zero refrigerator in my country kitchen. After all, that has always been the paradoxical thing about second homes: we want to feel that we're roughing it, but we want our comforts, too. Pliny schlepped around his villa in an old tunic, but he had a proper warmed swimming bath as well as a banqueting hall. When Richardson designed the Watts Sherman house in Newport, he made it look rustic, but he also incorporated a novel amenity. Central heating. Even Thoreau, whose cabin at Walden Pond didn't have a kitchen (in warm weather, he cooked outside over an open fire), regularly walked to nearby Concord to have dinner at friends' houses.

I remember once visiting an Adirondack camp on Lower Saranac Lake. It was one of many in the area that had been built by rich New Yorkers during the Gilded Age. The house itself was typical—a charming, rough-hewn log building with a massive granite fireplace, columns made of peeled and polished tree trunks, and spartan Art-and-Crafts-style furniture. Here was rusticity laid on with a trowel. When this particular camp, Knollwood, was built, in 1899, it consisted of six cottages, a so-called casino (a social gathering place, not a gambling hall), and a boathouse, all designed by William Coulter, the architect of some of the buildings at Sagamore, the Vanderbilts' famous camp. Although the ample cottages contained several bedrooms, there were originally only small service kitchens. That was because the six families and their guests had their meals prepared and served to them in the casino, which did have a large kitchen. You went boating on the lake and hiking in the forest, but that was no reason you couldn't have a proper dinner, prepared by your New York cook. The Knollwood boathouse contains canoes and handmade Adirondack guide boats but also, on the upper floor, a huge billiard table. I don't think I would require a billiard table in my ideal weekend house, but, on the other hand, I wouldn't do without a compact-disk player. Getting away from it all has always involved compromise as well as a certain degree of make-believe.

It's hard to comment on—let alone judge—other people's fantasies. If Danièle and Luc wanted a house in the country, well, they would have to make their own compromises. I don't think I was really much help to my friends; our ideas of weekend houses were probably just too different. Anyway, we all went out to dinner, the atmosphere in the bistro was convivial, the food was excellent, and everyone had a good time. A week later, when I got home to Philadelphia, I just couldn't resist making some sketches of my own, trying to accommodate all their requirements. I drew a little cottage, twenty feet by thirty feet, clapboard above and with a stone base—for the two bedrooms—below. The house was sheltered by a broad gable roof (to accommodate the sleeping loft). The loft looked down on the main living space, a large family room with a kitchen at one end and a sitting area at the other. In the center of the room, a Franklin stove served for warming cold toes and cold plates. A pair of glazed doors opened onto a large screened porch. It was only a sketch, just to keep my hand in, I told myself. But if I shut my eyes I could almost hear the strains of the Clarinet Concerto in the woods.

Cloud Crossing

Scott Russell Sanders

Clouds are temporary creatures. So is the Milky Way, for that matter, if you take the long entropic view of things. I awake on a Saturday in mid-October with the ache of nightmares in my brain, as if I have strained a muscle in my head. Just a week before I turn thirty-three, just a month before my son turns one, I do not need physics or nightmares to remind me that we also are temporary creatures.

Baby Jesse is changing cloud-fast before my eyes. His perky voice begins pinning labels on dogs and bathtubs and sun. When I say, "Want to go for a walk?" on this morning that began with nightmares of entropy, he does not crawl towards me as he would have done only a few days ago. He tugs himself upright with the help of a chair, then staggers toward me like a refugee crossing the border, arms outstretched, crowing, "Wa! Wa!"

So I pack baby and water and graham crackers into the car, and drive thirty miles southeast of Eugene, Oregon, to a trailhead on Hardesty Mountain. There are several hiking paths to the top, ranging in length from one mile to six. I choose the shortest, because I will be carrying Jesse's twenty-two pounds on my back. I have not come here to labor, to be reminded of my hustling heart. I have come to watch clouds.

Markers on the logging road tell us when we drive up past 2,500 feet, then 2,750 and 3,000. Around 3,250 the Fiat noses through the first vapors, great wrinkled slabs of clouds that thicken on the windshield. In the back seat Jesse strains against his safety harness, his hands fisted on the window, hungry to get out there into that white stuff. I drive the last few hundred yards to the trailhead with lights on, in case we meet a car groping its way down the mountain.

Beside a wooden sign carved to announce HARDESTY MOUNTAIN TRAIL, I park the Fiat with its muzzle downhill, so we can coast back to the highway after our walk in case the weary machine refuses to start. I lean the backpack against the bumper and guide Jesse's excited feet through the leg-holes, one of his calves in each of my hands. "Wa! Wa!" he cries, and almost tips the pack over into the sorrel dust of the logging road. Shouldering the pack requires acrobatic balancing, to keep him from tumbling out while I snake my arms through the straps. Once safely aloft, assured of a ride, he jounces so hard in the seat that I stagger a few paces with the same drunken uncertainty he shows in his own walking.

Clouds embrace us. Far overhead, between the fretted crowns of the Douglas fir, I see hints of blue. Down here among the roots and matted needles, the air is mist. My beard soon grows damp; beads glisten on my eyelashes. A few yards along the trail a Forest Service board, with miniature roof to protect its messages, informs us we are at 3,600 feet and must hike to 4,237 in order to reach the top of Hardesty. Since I came to see the clouds, not to swim in them, I hope we are able to climb above them into that tantalizing blue.

On my back Jesse carries on a fierce indecipherable oration concerning the wonders of this ghostly forest. Giddy with being outside and aloft, he drums on my head, yanks fistfuls of my hair. Every trunk we pass tempts him more strongly than the apple tree could ever have tempted Eve and Adam. He lurches from side to side, outstretched fingers desperate to feel the bark. I pause at a mammoth stump to let him touch. Viewed up close, the bark looks like a contour map of the Badlands, an eroded landscape where you might expect to uncover fossils. While Jesse traces the awesome ridges and fissures, I squint to read another Forest Service sign. No motorized vehicles, it warns, and no pack animals.

I surely qualify as a pack animal. For long spells in my adult life, while moving house or humping rucksacks onto trains or hauling firewood, I have felt more like a donkey than anything else. I have felt most like a beast of burden when hauling my two children, first Eva and now Jesse. My neck and shoulders never forget their weight from one portage to another. And I realize that carrying Jesse up the mountain to see clouds is a penance as well as a pleasure—penance for the hours I have sat glaring at my typewriter while he scrabbled mewing outside my door, penance for the thousands of things my wife has not been able to do on account of my word mania, penance for all the countless times I have told daughter Eva "no, I can't; I am writing." I know the rangers did not have human beasts in mind when they posted their sign, yet I am content to be a pack animal, saddled with my crowing son.

As I resume walking, I feel a tug. Jesse snaps a chunk of bark from the stump and carries it with him, to examine at leisure. Beneath one of the rare cottonwoods I pick up a leathery golden leaf, which I hand over my shoulder to the baby, who clutches it by the stem and turns it slowly around, tickling his nose with the starpoints. The leaf is a wonder to him, and therefore also to me. Everything he notices, every pebble, every layered slab of bark, is renewed for me. Once I carried Eva outside, in the first spring of her life, and a gust of wind caught her full in the face. She blinked, and then gazed at the invisible breath as if it were a flight of angels streaming past. Holding her in the crook of my arm that day, I rediscovered wind.

Fascinated by his leaf, Jesse snuggles down in the pack and rides quietly. My heart begins to dance faster as the trail zigzags up the mountain through a series of switchbacks. Autumn has been dry in Oregon, so the dirt underfoot is powdery. Someone has been along here inspecting mushrooms. The discarded ones litter the trail like blackening pancakes. Except for the path, worn raw by deer and hikers, the floor of the woods is covered with moss. Fallen wood is soon hidden by the creeping emerald carpet, the land burying its own dead. Limegreen moss clings fuzzily to the upright trunks and dangles in fluffy hanks from limbs, like freshly dyed wool hung out to dry. A wad of it caught in the fist squeezes down to nothing.

A lurch from the backpack tells me that Jesse has spied some new temptation in the forest. Craning around, I see his spidery little hands reaching for the sky. Then I also look up, and notice the shafts of light slanting down through the treetops. The light seems substantial, as if made of glass, like the rays of searchlights that carve up the night sky to celebrate a store's opening or a war's end. "Light," I say to Jesse. "Sunlight. We're almost above the clouds." Wherever the beams strike, they turn cobwebs into jeweled diagrams, bracelet limbs with rhinestones of dew. Cloud vapors turn to smoke.

The blue glimpsed between trees gradually thickens, turns solid, and we emerge onto a treeless stony ridge. Clear sky above, flotillas of clouds below, mountains humping their dark green backs as far as I can see. The sight of so many slick backs arching above the clouds reminds me of watching porpoises from a ship in the Gulf of Mexico. Vapors spiral up and down between cloud layers as if on escalators. Entire continents and hemispheres and galaxies of mist drift by. I sit on the trail with backpack propped against a stone ledge, to watch this migration.

No peace for meditation with an eleven-month-old on your back. An ache in my shoulders signals that Jesse, so near the ground, is leaning out of the pack to capture something. A pebble or beetle to swallow? A stick to gnaw? Moss, it turns out, an emerald hunk of it ripped from the rockface. "Moss," I tell him, as he rotates this treasure about three inches in front of his eyes. "Here, feel," and I stroke one of his palms across the velvety clump. He tugs the hand free and resumes his private exploration. This independence grows on him these days faster than his hair.

"Clouds," I tell him, pointing out into the gulf of air. Jesse glances up, sees only vagueness where I see a ballet of shapes, and so he resumes his scrutiny of the moss. "Not to eat," I warn him. When I check on him again half a minute later, the moss is half its former size and his lips are powdered with green. Nothing to do but hoist him out of the pack, dig what I can from his mouth, then plop him back in, meanwhile risking spilling both of us down the mountainside. A glance down the dizzying slope reminds me of my wife's warning, that I have no business climbing this mountain alone with a baby. She's right, of course. But guilt, like the grace of God, works in strange ways, and guilt drives me up here among the skittery rocks to watch clouds with my son.

"Let Daddy have it," I say, teasing the hunk of moss from his hand. "Have a stick, pretty stick." While he imprints the stick with the marks of his teeth, four above and two below, I spit on the underside of the moss and glue it back down to the rock. Grow, I urge it, Looking more closely at the rockface, I see that it is crumbling beneath roots and weather, sloughing away like old skin. The entire mountain is migrating, not so swiftly as the clouds, but just as surely, heading grain by grain to the sea.

Jesse seems to have acquired some of the mountain's mass as I stand upright again and hoist his full weight. With the stick he idly swats me on the ear.

The trail carries us through woods again, then up along a ridge to the clearing at the top of Hardesty Mountain. There is no dramatic feeling of expansiveness, as there is on some peaks, because here the view is divvied up into modest sweeps by Douglas firs, cottonwoods, great gangling heaps of briars. The forest has laid siege to the rocky crest, and will abolish the view altogether before Jesse is old enough to carry his own baby up here. For now, by moving from spot to spot on the summit, I can see in all directions. What I see mostly are a few thousand square miles of humpbacked mountains looming through the clouds. Once in Ohio I lived in a valley which the Army Corps of Engineers thought would make a convenient bed for a reservoir. So the Mahoning River was dammed, and as the waters backed up in that valley, covering everything but the highest ridges, drowning my childhood, they looked very much like these clouds poured among the mountains.

"Ba! Ba!" Jesse suddenly bellows, leaping in his saddle like a bronco rider.

Bath, I wonder? Bed? Bottle? Ball? He has been prolific of B-words lately, and their tail-ends are hard to tell apart. Ball, I finally decide, for there at the end of the arrow made by his arm is the moon, a chalky peachpit hanging down near the horizon. "Moon," I say.

"Ba! Ba!" he insists.

Let it stay a ball for awhile, something to play catch with, roll across the linoleum. His sister's first sentence was, "There's the moon." Her second was, "Want it, Daddy." So began her astronomical yearnings, my astronomical failures. She has the itch for space flight in her, my daughter does. Jesse is still too much of a pup for me to say whether he has caught it.

We explore the mountaintop while the ocean of cloud gradually rises. There are charred rings from old campfires. In a sandy patch, red-painted bricks are laid in the shape of a letter A. Not large enough to be visible from airplanes. If Hardesty Mountain were in a story by Hawthorne, of course, I could use the scarlet A to accuse it of some vast geological harlotry. If this were a folklore mountain, I could explain the letter as an alphabetical inscription left by giants. But since this is no literary landscape, I decide that the bricks formed the foundation for some telescope or radio transmitter or other gizmo back in the days when this summit had a lookout tower.

Nearby is another remnant from those days, a square plank cover for a cistern. The boards are weathered to a silvery sheen, with rows of rustblackened nailheads marking the joints. Through a square opening at the center of the planks I catch a glint. Water? Still gathering here after all these years? Leaning over the hole, one boot on the brittle planks, I see that the glint is from a tin can. The cistern is choked with trash.

At the very peak, amid a jumble of rocks, we find nine concrete piers that once supported the fire tower. By squatting down beside one of those piers I can rest Jesse's weight on the concrete, and relieve the throb in my neck. I imagine the effort of hauling enough materials up this mountain to build a tower. Surely they used horses, or mules. Not men with backpacks. So what became of the tower when the Forest Service, graduated to spotter planes, no longer needed it? Did they pry out every nail and carry the boards back down again? A glance at the ground between my feet supplies the answer. Wedged among the rocks, where rains cannot wash them away, are chunks of glass, some of them an inch thick. I pick up one that resembles a tongue, about the size for a cocker spaniel. Another one, a wad of convolutions, might be a crystalline brain. Peering up through it at the sun, I see fracture lines and tiny bubbles. Frozen in the seams where one molten layer lapped onto another there are ashes. Of course they didn't dismantle the tower and lug its skeleton down the mountain. They waited for a windless day after a drenching rain and they burned it.

The spectacle fills me: the mountain peak like a great torch, a volcano, the tower heaving on its nine legs, the windows bursting from the heat, tumbling among the rocks, fusing into molten blobs, the glass taking on whatever shape it cooled against.

There should be nails. Looking closer I find them among the shards of glass, sixteen-penny nails mostly, what we called spikes when I was building houses. Each one is somber with rust, but perfectly straight, never having been pried from wood. I think of the men who drove those nails—the way sweat stung in their eyes, the way their forearms clenched with every stroke of the hammer—and I wonder if any of them were still around when the tower burned. The Geological Survey marker, a round lead disk driven into a rock beside one of the piers, is dated 1916. Most likely the tower already stood atop the mountain in that year. Most likely the builders are all dead by now.

So on its last day the Hardesty fire tower became a fire tower in earnest. Yesterday I read that two American physicists shared the Nobel Prize for discovering the background radiation left over from the Big Bang, which set our universe in motion some fifteen billion years ago. Some things last—not forever, of course, but for a long time—things like radiation, like bits of glass. I gather a few of the nails, some lumps of glass, a screw. Stuffing these shreds of evidence in my pocket, I discover the graham cracker in its wrapping of cellophane, and I realize I have not thought of Jesse for some minutes, have forgotten that he is riding me. That can mean only one thing. Sure enough, he is asleep, head scrunched down into the pack. Even while I peek at him over my shoulder he is changing, neurons hooking up secret connections in his brain, calcium swelling his bones as mud gathers in river deltas.

Smell warns me that the clouds have reached us. Looking out, the only peaks I can see are the Three Sisters, each of them a shade over 10,000 feet. Except for those peaks and the rocks where I stand, everything is cotton. There are no more clouds to watch, only Cloud, unanimous whiteness, an utter absence of shape. A panic seizes me—the same panic I used to feel as a child crossing the street when approaching cars seemed to have my name written on their grills. Suddenly the morning's nightmare comes back to me: everything I know is chalked upon a blackboard, and, while I watch, a hand erases every last mark.

Terror drives me down the Hardesty trail, down through vapors that leach color from the ferns, past trees that are dissolving. Stumps and downed logs lose their shape, merge into the clouds. The last hundred yards of the trail I jog. Yet Jesse never wakes until I haul him out of the pack and wrestle him into the car harness. His bellowing defies the clouds, the creeping emptiness. I bribe him with sips of water, a graham cracker, a song. But nothing comforts him, or comforts me, as we drive down the seven graveled miles of logging road to the highway. There we sink into open space again. The clouds are a featureless gray overhead.

As soon as the wheels are ringing beneath us on the blacktop, Jesse's internal weather shifts, and he begins one of his calm babbling orations, contentedly munching his cracker. The thread of his voice slowly draws me out of the annihilating ocean of whiteness. "Moon," he is piping from the back seat, "moon, moon!"

Pliny and the Mountain Mouse

Reg Saner

Dim though his brain may be, the marmot feels winter will come soon. And long. Longer than any of his previous twelve. From each of these, gaunt after seven or more months of hibernation in a rocky burrow, he has wakened; to at once waddle forth, to rummage spring snow for juicy alpine tundra plants, to mate, to sun, now and then to frolic with others in his chummy colony, and—properly fattened—to reenter the burrow: again to sleep away winter.

His "language" of gesture and squeaks is enormously older than words; but no European language names even the continent this particular marmot lives on. His region of high rocks hasn't yet been discovered by Old World tongues, though one day it will be called "colorado" by men speaking a version of Latin. That his home among granite chunks sits twelve thousand feet in the air, with superb mountain views on three sides, the marmot-brain translates to *always*, and *always* to *is*.

Even for this marmot, whose sense of history isn't wider than body fat and the sun's present height, today's rise and set of sky is numbered: August 24, A.D. 79.

You and I aren't here yet. At such altitude, nobody is. In A.D. 79, "nobody" is still only Indians. "Somebody" is only a marmot. Cool wind, blowing lightly out of late summer, licks his pelt. Opulent tufts of cinnamon fur lift along the plump back, slur a moment, subside. Because in the warmish afternoon, his ridgeline is only just dappled by the fast blue shadows of cloud-faces that mythologies copy, this marmot suns. He lies full-stretch on a rock slab. To stir himself overmuch would burn off precious fat his busy incisors have nibbled all the brief tundra summer to acquire, so he moves only his head, in those quick, darting glances small animals learn from their instructors the foxes, the coyotes, the eagles.

Close cousin to groundhogs and woodchucks, the high-country *Marmota flaviventris*, or yellow-bellied kind, often relies on talus-piles of granite to provide fortresslike burrows only a bear or wolverine could dilapidate. Such hideaways protect the numerous offspring, five or six to a litter, which by summer's end are full grown.

Does the marmot breed to defeat predators, or do they prey on his colony to defeat his fast breeding? The answer is part of that circle whose opposites create each other; the molecular keys in the blood, the living shapes taken by time. A ravenous hawk; a slightly ludicrous bag of fat fur. Appetites that have learned how to repeat themselves. To what end? None that any living creature—now or to come—ever will know. To be. Each to do its kind.

Seven thousand miles to the east, in the Roman resort town of Herculaneum, guests leaving a dinner party find their way home through moonlit, sultry, sea-level air; air that thickens to an indigo blur across the Neapolitan bay toward the naval base at Misenum. There, sweating out the dog days of August—even at night—sits Pliny the Elder, a science writer whose tireless goose quill nibbles away at the creamy blankness on a fresh vellum. Pliny is himself fat as butter, and sweats as if he were melting, but he is as usual hard at it well before dawn, an omnivore of other men's books, which—he frankly admits—his own writing feeds on, just as his compulsive quill-nib feeds on blank vellum like a tiny animal storing up fame.

Among stones of a continent Pliny never heard of, the marmot has eaten back his lost bulk hardly a day too soon, and has almost finished lining his burrow with tundra grasses gathered for stuffing into the sleeping chamber as insulation and nest. Food will be body fat, however much his summer's nibbling has managed to accrue. And high-country autumn comes early. He knows it not as a name but a time when his world begins entering more into shadow. *If the oncoming winter is neither too deep nor too long, his body fat will suffice.*

During hard winters, however, dormancy proves a risky survival device. One marmot in five either freezes outright or starves. Among the small mercies of nature, on this twenty-fourth day of Augustus, is this particular marmot's blindness to his future. Breeze tousling his glossy pelt doesn't tell what it hears: that the oncoming season is coming to kill him, turn him to stone. And to quench the others sharing the family burrow.

Heat haze of southern Italy, moon-silvered. Pliny sweats, dips his quill into an ink-horn, and shares the same ignorance.

Just now, however, his scientific compulsion spurs him to update earlier pages of his already voluminous *Natural History*. Pliny is inserting some new facts about marmots, which he calls Alpine mice; "Some people say they form a chain and let themselves down into their cave that way, male and female alternately holding the next creature's tail by the teeth. One, lying on its back, hugs a bundle of grass and is hauled in by the others. Consequently at this season their backs show marks of rubbing."

Pliny's view of human life is rather gloomy; mankind as he knows it staggers along from misery to fresh misery, ruin to ruin. But the natural world! As inexhaustible as fascinating. "Some people say" may sound, he is fully aware, hardly better than gossip; yet nature is so prodigal of oddities that one's wildest guess may prove too tame. Like the haymaking marmot his pen has just described, Pliny's habit of reaping truth from old books and storing it up in his own year-upon-year scribbling, book after book, rules his waking hours so compulsively he hardly spares time to bathe, much less to ask himself, "Why?" Nor will he ever.

He never will, because what neither Pliny-the-nature-writer nor his friends across the bay in Herculaneum and Stabiae foresee is, simply, "Nature": in a few hours the trim, vineyarded summit of Vesuvius will blow sky high. In a few hours, Pliny's concern for those friends and his scientific curiosity will combine to strangle him. Soon, on the undiscovered continent of which Pliny knows nothing, a particular "Alpine mouse" will waddle into his burrow, plug the entrance with small stones and hay, then begin a winter trance no summer can waken.

The same incurable yen that draws Pliny unaware toward his suffocation saves his nephew. Before setting sail across the Bay of Naples for his fatal lesson in volcanology, the uncle invites Pliny the Younger—an eighteen-year-old—to come along if he wants. In aftertimes, by then an author himself, the nephew will recall, "To this invitation I answered that I'd rather continue studying. Besides, as it happened, my uncle had assigned me an essay to write." Writer's itch runs in the family.

At twelve thousand feet along an unknown continental divide, the night of twenty-fourth Augustus opens with snow crystals flying past; ice migrations of white flies that sting like salt. Meanwhile, along the Vesuvian shores it is finally morning. All night a hailstorm of pumice has scorched the roofs of Stabiae, piling up, drifting. A cinder snow that smokes. Roof beams crack and collapse, house walls totter.

By the seashore Pliny the Elder gulps at the air, supported between two slaves who lay him down on a scrap of sailcloth. He calls for cold water, drinks it, flops back. By now volcanic ash has begun its steady, floating fall. It descends soundlessly. Panicked Romans scatter the stuff as they run, stumble, collapse. Lightly, the ash begins to clothe each fallen body. In a few days it will smother the town. Years hence, in a reminiscent mood Pliny the Younger will sit—obese as his uncle—pushing a quill across vellum: "Three mornings later his body was found on the spot, intact…more like a man asleep than dead."

Three mornings later it is evening in another country, whose mountain sun has just set. Lofty ridgelines looking down into their own lakes see that sunset dismantled. Summer-plump, backside ruddied by alpenglow, the marmot stands hindlegged atop his rock, forepaws snugged against chest-fur, nose whiskers twitching, brown eyes staring east. He gives a reedy squeak. Answered by another…then another. A marmot "harem" and colony, a dozen in all, talking to themselves. They've harvested tundra plants, almost enough. How hard they've worked their worn pelts show: the narrow squeeze to and fro since midsummer, carrying cut grasses past snug entrance rocks and deep into the burrow, has scraped their back-fur haggard.

A trained and patient ear, or a marmot's, could identify as many as six distinctive variants on the shrill calls that led ancient Alpine people to nickname these animals "whistlers": Calls of "Eaglehawk!" Calls of "My rock, not yours!" Calls of "Fox!" Calls of "Love *me*! Love *me*! Love *me*!" Calls of "Wingflown! Foxgone!" No wonder their silly, piping squeaks this evening are almost musical. After a gestation of about a month, the summer's young have reached full size of six to ten pounds in just weeks.

Only the last of the haymaking remains. Abruptly the east-squinting marmot, boss male of the harem, falls silent. Up out of the distant, alluvial, proto-Coloradan plain floats a great fullness, a moon pale as winter; pale as a sun made of snow.

We can be here now. It's our turn…to be, and be curious. We know all about Pompeii, Stabiae; know Herculaneum too was buried. Oh yes, volcanic detritus enclosed many of the dead so perfectly that—in modern times, once Pliny's contemporaries had, as it were, evaporated—plaster casts could be made of their living absences. Lime-white, like snowmen. Startlingly "us," therefore touching. Theoretically. Anyhow, we ourselves avoid erupting volcanoes.

And, yes, it is poignant—in theory—to think of a marmot family in its burrow, like a banked fire; each furry curl asleep, nose between hind paws, like so many embers ashed over. Winter sets in: the marmot body temperature dips to about ten degrees above freezing. From pulsing twice every second the hibernating heart slows to half that. Then slower. Finally, as much as a full quarter-minute or more goes by… between beats.

During hibernation marmots rouse, stir somewhat, then sleep again—unless their body fat runs out, or winter cold runs too long too deep, and the tiny heart ceases. As when a lit match, held upright, weakens till its shrunken flame seeps back into the matchhead; a glow, a red cinder—suddenly black.

But the small, distant deaths of animals common as wind don't sadden anyone. No more than we're saddened by all the once-upon-a-time crickets and dormice ashed over at Pompeii. Besides, those life-like but plaster agonies recovered from Pompeiian dailyness are of folks who would have died ages ago, even if Vesuvius's summit hadn't smithereened. Centuries *are* distance, aren't they?

Of his unswerving industry, how much did Pliny expect would survive? Apart from his considerable military service, he wrote a work twenty "books" long on Rome's wars with Germany, wrote an eight-book text on rhetoric, penned a lengthy chronicle of his own times in thirty-one books, and crowned his literary achievement with that eccentric museum, his *Natural History*, gleaned from authors and treatises innumerable. Time, which called Pliny out of the dust into sunlight, and which lent him his encyclopaedic curiosity, has ground nearly all that to powder. He knew well how "Nature" begets and devours us, just as Chronos ate his own children. Of Pliny's written mind, only the *Natural History* has made it all the way to now.

As for his year upon year of curious labor, might some lost remnants exist as an undetectable nuance in what the European mind has become? Surely so. However, such consolation feels cheerless as a cubic meter of interstellar medium: one or two floating atoms, the rest a black vacuum.

Which makes Pliny's compulsive curiosity, despite his patchwork and pack-rat science, all the more touching. Laborious days and nights belied his own glum estimate of the human situation. We survive by not believing what we know. Is that because our unconscious knows something truer than fact? Maybe it knows that what we most admire can't die, including the best of ourselves—which we don't invent, merely inherit or borrow. And which, like the world, is nobody's possession. Is wavelengths, passing through us.

And passing through those wilderness creatures that cold will freeze solid this winter? A gnat is the weight of astonishing centuries, surely as a finch wing has been shaped by however old the sky is. But our emotions require of objects a certain size to help bridge the gap between them and ourselves. Where's the line to be drawn? At bugs on a windshield? By no means even then. So says reason. Reason says the line must be a circle wide as our minds.

So when it comes to the spark in all animal hardihood—meaning ours—I often see an outcrop on Colorado's continental divide. To think mountains "majestic" we mustn't inhale overlong their bone-barren summits and crazed smash-ups of rock. A few hours, or days; then clear out. Nothing has been here since the beginning, but great crags pretend they have. They pretend we living things aren't here at all; or if so, mere passing fancies of the sun. Even in midsummer their petrified light can chill, so winter near their summits can be—in the root sense of the word—terrific. To look at ice cliffs long, and in storm, and alone…kills the heart. Nonetheless, atop one uppermost slab near the Corona trail suns a lone marmot; sluggish, dim-witted, inconsiderable, heroic.

Straight overhead the sky is an ultraviolet blue so intense it verges on purple. Late August sun drills down. Light breeze pours over the divide, ruffling the marmot's pelt, glossy as a chestnut. Moment to moment his head winks north, winks west in quick, circumspicuous caution. The sunning torso, plump as a loaf, doesn't stir. He sees me, and sees me keeping my distance. He has no idea.

He knows nothing, really, of the success of his own species, doesn't know that his ancestors reached North America from Asia, across the land bridge spanning what is now the Bering Strait, and were at home here, just like this, when Pliny the Elder wrote and Vesuvius erupted. Now found all over the globe, he has gone where not even the map can go, hearing rivers that had never been heard. He has been snared, trapped, poisoned, and shot: for his fur in Mongolia, for his oil in lands diverse as Switzerland and Siberia. Under the guise of woodchuck he is thought a mere varmint and thus—in much of the United States—an appropriate focus for gunsights. His avatars waddled about and snoozed beneath Pleistocene skies of the Ice Age. He is content to live where little else can. He endures.

How could he know that I, the biped who under a backpack leans slightly forward and stares, admire his stamina entirely? How could either of us foresee that his serio-comic, jawless profile, his buck teeth, twitchy nose whiskers and sluff of a tail, his wide-eyed blinkings and lookouts for predators will combine with the twelve thousand foot altitude to make his silly bump of a figure not only wholeheartedly dear to me but—long as I live—half immortal?

When did humans first find the marmot amusing? Pliny's account seems to have been written with a smile. Certainly the mountain mouse—as the French tongue still names him—once delighted Europeans visiting the fairs and markets where animal trainers entertained; among the camels and tame bears, spectators could see many a humble marmot "dancing" to flute notes played by its keeper, often a child from the Tyrol.

Amusement, however, did not prevent Alpine dwellers in modern times from hunting the slow creature almost to extinction, both for its fat—reputed to cure rheumatism, among other ills—and for its pelt. As late as 1944 an estimated sixteen thousand marmots were killed in Switzerland alone, till naturalists persuaded pharmaceutical dealers that marmot-annihilation would benefit no one. Though belief in the curative powers of marmot fat still persists among folk of the European Alps, the animals have dodged the threat of extinction. In contrast, Mongolia's Bobac marmot breeds so fast no such threat exists—despite the millions of furs annually harvested there, and the many hundreds of tons of marmot fat. And despite the fact that Mongolian marmots often carry plague.

As for me, before and since, I've seen marmots by the hundreds, seen their low profiles flow over or peer out of rock piles from here to the end of the world. In Alaska's Brooks Range I made my first acquaintance with his species by way of a raided food cache the critters gnawed into. In Switzerland's sole national park I've watched marmot youngsters wrestle each other repeatedly, as we did when kids, for the sheer fun of it, toppling, flopping, grappling each other and rolling together downhill. That Swiss pair didn't behave *like* human kids. Their play-wrestling seemed *identical.*

On a frosty mid-July night high in Colorado's Gore Range the weird roar that woke me was marmot incisors munching a hole in my empty Nalgene waterbottle. One twilight evening just below the 14,200-foot summit of Longs Peak, bright marmot-whistles seemed to match the first few stars like question and answer. A mile from the crest of Arapahoe Pass there's a particularly untimid marmot who, as I approach, rises hindlegged to his full height of some eighteen inches and, in exactly the same spot, tries to stare me down. Amid that shattered labyrinth of stone chaos, his world and home, what a bold fellow he is! Since marmots live but a dozen years or thereabouts, his annual defiance feels huge. We gaze at each other. In our silence much seems possible, though nothing much happens: two creatures, looking a little farther than themselves.

But that *other* marmot surviving miles away on the Corona Trail—why should he, a dozen years after my glimpse of him, continue to seem so special? There where the left hand slopes away as alpine tundra, half meadow, and the right hand is sheer fall, hundreds of feet down to rockscapes ugly as slag, down toward acres of grit-littered, permanent snow, my emblematic marmot at first seemed no different from hundreds. It's just that, to remember what sheer courage looks like, my mind's eye often invokes him.

There, under a sky barely fly-specked with ravens, and atop a jut of flat granite, he suns. Wind ruffles his fur. He blinks, peers around him at nothing. At what there is. His instincts and eyes, his nut-brown pelt, his nose and paws, all seem shapes taken by a design whose true name I don't know—any more than that dim creature knew his. Which I see, now, given his Old World origins, might as well have been Pliny.

The Masked Marvel's Last Toehold

Richard Selzer

MORNING ROUNDS.

On the fifth floor of the hospital, in the west wing, I know that a man is sitting up in his bed, waiting for me. Elihu Koontz is seventy-five, and he is diabetic. It is two weeks since I amputated his left leg just below the knee. I walk down the corridor, but I do not go straight into his room. Instead, I pause in the doorway. He is not yet aware of my presence, but gazes down at the place in the bed where his leg used to be, and where now there is the collapsed leg of his pajamas. He is totally absorbed, like an athlete appraising the details of his body. What is he thinking, I wonder. Is he dreaming the outline of his toes. Does he see there his foot's incandescent ghost? Could he be angry? Feel that I have taken from him something for which he yearns now with all his heart? Has he forgotten so soon the pain? It was a pain so great as to set him apart from all other men, in a red-hot place where he had no kith or kin. What of those black gorilla toes and the soupy mess that was his heel? I watch him from the doorway. It is a kind of spying, I know.

Save for a white fringe open at the front, Elihu Koontz is bald. The hair has grown too long and is wilted. He wears it as one would wear a day-old laurel wreath. He is naked to the waist, so that I can see his breasts. They are the breasts of Buddha, inverted triangles from which the nipples swing, dark as garnets.

I have seen enough. I step into the room, and he sees that I am there.

"How did the night go, Elihu?"

He looks at me for a long moment. "Shut the door," he says.

I do, and move to the side of the bed. He takes my left hand in both of his, gazes at it, turns it over, then back, fondling, at last holding it up to his cheek. I do not withdraw from this loving. After a while he relinquishes my hand, and looks up at me.

"How is the pain?" I ask.

He does not answer, but continues to look at me in silence. I know at once that he has made a decision.

"Ever hear of The Masked Marvel?" He says this in a low voice, almost a whisper.

"What?"

"The Masked Marvel," he says. "You never heard of him?"

"No."

He clucks his tongue. He is exasperated.

All at once there is a recollection. It is dim, distant, but coming near.

"Do you mean the wrestler?"

Eagerly, he nods, and the breasts bob. How gnomish he looks, oval as the huge helpless egg of some outlandish lizard. He has very long arms, which, now and then, he unfurls to reach for things—a carafe of water, a get-well card. He gazes up at me, urging. He *wants* me to remember.

"Well...yes," I say. I am straining backward in time.

"I saw him wrestle in Toronto long ago."

"Ha!" He smiles. "You saw *me*." And his index finger, held rigid and upright, bounces in the air.

The man has said something shocking, unacceptable. It must be challenged.

"You?" I am trying to smile.

Again that jab of the finger. "You saw *me*."

"No," I say. But even then, something about Elihu Koontz, those prolonged arms, the shape of his head, the sudden agility with which he leans from his bed to get a large brown envelope from his nightstand, something is forcing me toward a memory. He rummages through his papers, old newspaper clippings, photographs, and I remember....

It is almost forty years ago. I am ten years old. I have been sent to Toronto to spend the summer with relatives. Uncle Max has bought two tickets to the wrestling match. He is taking me that night.

"He isn't allowed," says Aunt Sarah to me. Uncle Max has angina.

"He gets too excited," she says.

"I wish you wouldn't go, Max," she says.

"You mind your own business," he says.

And we go. Out into the warm Canadian evening. I am not only abroad, I am abroad in the *evening!* I have never been taken out in the evening. I am terribly excited. The trolleys, the lights, the horns. It is a bazaar. At the Maple Leaf Gardens, we sit high and near the center. The vast arena is dark except for the brilliance of the ring at the bottom.

It begins.

The wrestlers circle. They grapple. They are all haunch and paunch. I am shocked by their ugliness, but I do not show it. Uncle Max is exhilarated. He leans forward, his eyes unblinking, on his face a look of enormous happiness. One after the other, a pair of wrestlers enter the ring. The two men join, twist, jerk, tug, bend, yank, and throw. Then they leave and are replaced by another pair. At last it is the main event. "The Angel vs. The Masked Marvel."

On the cover of the program notes, there is a picture of The Angel hanging from the limb of a tree, a noose of thick rope around his neck. The Angel hangs just so for an hour every day, it is explained, to strengthen his neck. The Masked Marvel's trademark is a black stocking cap with holes for the eyes and mouth. He is never seen without it, states the program. No one knows who The Masked Marvel really is!

"Good," says Uncle Max. "Now you'll see something." He is fidgeting, waiting for them to appear. They come down separate aisles, climb into the ring from opposite sides. I have never seen anything like them. It is The Angel's neck that first captures the eye. The shaved nape rises in twin columns to puff into the white hood of a sloped and bosselated skull that is too small. As though, strangled by the sinews of that neck, the skull had long since withered and shrunk. The thing about The Angel is the absence of any mystery in his body. It is simply *there*. A monosyllabic announcement. A grunt. One looks and knows everything at once, the fat thighs, the gigantic buttocks, the great spine from which hang knotted ropes and pale aprons of beef. And that prehistoric head. He is all of a single hideous piece, The Angel is. No detachables.

The Masked Marvel seems dwarfish. His fingers dangle kneeward. His short legs are slightly bowed as if under the weight of the cask they are forced to heft about. He has breasts that swing when he moves! I have never seen such breasts on a man before.

There is a sudden ungraceful movement, and they close upon one another. The Angel stoops and hugs The Marvel about the waist, locking his hands behind The Marvel's back. Now he straightens and lifts The Marvel as though he were uprooting a tree. Thus he holds him, then stoops again, thrusts one hand through The Marvel's crotch, and with the other grabs him by the neck. He rears and…The Marvel is aloft! For a long moment, The Angel stands as though deciding where to make the toss. Then throws. Was that board or bone that splintered there? Again and again, The Angel hurls himself upon the body of The Masked Marvel.

Now The Angel rises over the fallen Marvel, picks up one foot in both of his hands, and twists the toes downward. It is far beyond the tensile strength of mere ligament, mere cartilage. The Masked Marvel does not hide his agony, but pounds and slaps the floor with his hand, now and then reaching up toward The Angel in an attitude of supplication. I have never seen such suffering. And all the while his black mask rolls from side to side, the mouth pulled to a tight slit through which issues an endless hiss that I can hear from where I sit. All at once, I hear a shouting close by.

"Break it off! Tear off a leg and throw it up here!"

It is Uncle Max. Even in the darkness I can see that he is gray. A band of sweat stands upon his upper lip. He is on his feet now, panting, one fist pressed at his chest, the other raised warlike toward the ring. For the first time I begin to think that something terrible might happen here. Aunt Sarah was right.

"Sit down, Uncle Max," I say. "Take a pill, please."

He reaches for the pillbox, gropes, and swallows without taking his gaze from the wrestlers. I wait for him to sit down.

"That's not fair," I say, "twisting his toes like that."

"It's the toehold," he explains.

"But it's not *fair,*" I say again. The whole of the evil is laid open for me to perceive. I am trembling.

And now The Angel does something unspeakable. Holding the foot of The Marvel at full twist with one hand, he bends and grasps the mask where it clings to the back of The Marvel's head. And he pulls. He is going to strip it off! Lay bare an ultimate carnal mystery! Suddenly it is beyond mere physical violence. Now I am on my feet, shouting into the Maple Leaf Gardens.

"Watch out," I scream. "Stop him. Please, somebody, stop him."

Next to me, Uncle Max is chuckling.

Yet The Masked Marvel hears me, I know it. And rallies from his bed of pain. Thrusting with his free heel, he strikes The Angel at the back of the knee. The Angel falls. The Masked Marvel is on top of him, pinning his shoulders to the mat. One! Two! Three! And it is over. Uncle Max is strangely still. I am gasping for breath. All this I remember as I stand at the bedside of Elihu Koontz.

Once again, I am in the operating room. It is two years since I amputated the left leg of Elihu Koontz. Now it is his right leg which is gangrenous. I have already scrubbed. I stand to one side wearing my gown and gloves. And...*I am masked.* Upon the table lies Elihu Koontz, pinned in a fierce white light. Spinal anesthesia has been administered. One of his arms is taped to a board placed at a right angle to his body. Into this arm, a needle has been placed. Fluid drips here from a bottle overhead. With his other hand, Elihu Koontz beats feebly at the side of the operating table. His head rolls from side to side. His mouth is pulled into weeping. It seems to me that I have never seen such misery.

An orderly stands at the foot of the table, holding Elihu Koontz's leg aloft by the toes so that the intern can scrub the limb with antiseptic solutions. The intern paints the foot, ankle, leg, and thigh, both front and back, three times. From a corner of the room where I wait, I look down as from an amphitheater. Then I think of Uncle Max yelling, "Tear off a leg. Throw it up here." And I think that forty years later I am making the catch.

"It's not fair," I say aloud. But no one hears me. I step forward to break The Masked Marvel's last toehold.

In the Combat Zone

Leslie Marmon Silko

Women seldom discuss our wariness or the precautions we take after dark each time we leave the apartment, car, or office to go on the most brief errand. We take for granted that we are targeted as easy prey by muggers, rapists, and serial killers. This is our lot as women in the United States. We try to avoid going anywhere alone after dark, although economic necessity sends women out night after night. We do what must be done, but always we are alert, on guard and ready. We have to be aware of persons walking on the sidewalk behind us; we have to pay attention to others who board an elevator we're on. We try to avoid all staircases and deserted parking garages when we are alone. Constant vigilance requires considerable energy and concentration seldom required of men.

I used to assume that most men were aware of this fact of women's lives, but I was wrong. They may notice our reluctance to drive at night to the convenience store alone, but they don't know or don't want to know the experience of a woman out alone at night. Men who have been in combat know the feeling of being a predator's target, but it is difficult for men to admit that we women live our entire lives in a combat zone. Men have the power to end violence against women in the home, but they feel helpless to protect women from violent strangers. Because men feel guilt and anger at their inability to shoulder responsibility for the safety of their wives, sisters, and daughters, we don't often discuss random acts of violence against women.

When we were children, my sisters and I used to go to Albuquerque with my father. Sometimes strangers would tell my father it was too bad that he had three girls and no sons. My father, who has always preferred the company of women, used to reply that he was glad to have girls and not boys, because he might not get along as well with boys. Furthermore, he'd say, "My girls can do anything your boys can do, and my girls can do it better." He had in mind, of course, shooting and hunting.

When I was six years old, my father took me along as he hunted deer; he showed me how to walk quietly, to move along and then to stop and listen carefully before taking another step. A year later, he traded a pistol for a little single shot .22 rifle just my size.

He took me and my younger sisters down to the dump by the river and taught us how to shoot. We rummaged through the trash for bottles and glass jars; it was great fun to take aim at a pickle jar and watch it shatter. If the Rio San Jose had water running in it, we threw bottles for moving targets in the muddy current. My father told us that a .22 bullet can travel a mile, so we had to be careful where we aimed. The river was a good place because it was below the villages and away from the houses; the high clay riverbanks wouldn't let any bullets stray. Gun safety was drilled into us. We were cautioned about other children whose parents might not teach them properly; if we ever saw another child with a gun, we knew to get away. Guns were not toys. My father did not approve of BB guns because they were classified as toys. I had a .22 rifle when I was seven years old. If I felt like shooting, all I had to do was tell my parents where I was going, take my rifle and a box of 12 shells and go. I was never tempted to shoot at birds or animals because whatever was killed had to be eaten. Now, I realize how odd this must seem; a seven-year-old with a little .22 rifle and a box of ammunition, target shooting alone at the river. But that was how people lived at Laguna when I was growing up; children were given responsibility from an early age.

Laguna Pueblo people hunted deer for winter meat. When I was thirteen I carried George Pearl's saddle carbine, a .30-30, and hunted deer for the first time. When I was fourteen, I killed my first mule deer buck with one shot through the heart.

Guns were for target shooting and guns were for hunting, but also I knew that Grandma Lily carried a little purse gun with her whenever she drove alone to Albuquerque or Los Lunas. One night my mother and my grandmother were driving the fifty miles from Albuquerque to Laguna down Route 66 when three men in a car tried to force my grandmother's car off the highway. Route 66 was not so heavily traveled as Interstate 40 is now, and there were many long stretches of highway where no other car passed for minutes on end. Payrolls at the Jackpile Uranium Mine were large in the 1950s, and my mother or my grandmother had to bring home thousands from the bank in Albuquerque to cash the miners' checks on paydays.

After that night, my father bought my mother a pink nickel-plated snubnose .22 revolver with a white bone grip. Grandma Lily carried a tiny Beretta as black as her prayer book. As my sisters and I got older, my father taught us to handle and shoot handguns, revolvers mostly, because back then, semiautomatic pistols were not as reliable—they frequently jammed. I will never forget the day my father told us three girls that we never had to let a man hit us or terrorize us because no matter how big and strong the man was, a gun in our hand equalized all differences of size and strength.

Much has been written about violence in the home and spousal abuse. I wish to focus instead on violence from strangers toward women because this form of violence terrifies women more, despite the fact that most women are murdered by a spouse, relative, fellow employee, or next-door neighbor, not a stranger. Domestic violence kills many more women and children than strangers kill, but domestic violence also follows more predictable patterns and is more familiar—he comes home drunk and she knows what comes next. A good deal of the terror of a stranger's attack comes from its suddenness and unexpectedness. Attacks by strangers occur with enough frequency that battered women and children often cite their fears of such attacks as reasons for remaining in abusive domestic situations. They fear the violence they imagine strangers will inflict upon them more than they fear the abusive home. More than one feminist has pointed out that rapists and serial killers help keep the patriarchy in place.

An individual woman may be terrorized by her spouse, but women are not sufficiently terrorized that we avoid marriage. Yet many women I know, including myself, try to avoid going outside of their homes alone after dark. Big deal, you say; well yes, it is a big deal since most lectures, performances, and films are presented at night; so are dinners and other social events. Women out alone at night who are assaulted by strangers are put on trial by public opinion: Any woman out alone after dark is asking for trouble. Presently, for millions of women of all socioeconomic backgrounds, sundown is lockdown. We are prisoners of violent strangers.

Daylight doesn't neccessarily make the streets safe for women. In the early 1980s, a rapist operated in Tucson in the afternoon near the University of Arizona campus. He often accosted two women at once, forced them into residential alleys, then raped each one with a knife to her throat and forced the other to watch. Afterward the women said that part of the horror of their attack was that all around them, everything appeared normal. They could see people inside their houses and cars going down the street—all around them life was going on as usual while their lives were being changed forever.

The afternoon rapist was not the only rapist in Tucson at that time; there was the prime-time rapist, the potbellied rapist, and the apologetic rapist all operating in Tucson in the 1980s. The prime-time rapist was actually two men who invaded comfortable foothills homes during television prime time when residents were preoccupied with television and eating dinner. The prime-time rapists terrorized entire families; they raped the women and sometimes they raped the men. Family members were forced to go to automatic bank machines, to bring back cash to end the ordeal. Potbelly rapist and apologetic rapist need little comment, except to note that the apologetic rapist was good looking, well educated, and smart enough to break out of jail for one last rape followed by profuse apologies and his capture in the University of Arizona library. Local papers recounted details about Tucson's last notorious rapist, the red bandanna rapist. In the late 1970s this rapist attacked more than twenty women over a three-year period, and Tucson police were powerless to stop him. Then one night, the rapist broke into a midtown home where the lone resident, a woman, shot him four times in the chest with a .38 caliber revolver.

In midtown Tucson, on a weekday afternoon, I was driving down Campbell Avenue to the pet store. Suddenly the vehicle behind me began to weave into my lane, so I beeped the horn politely. The vehicle swerved back to its lane, but then in my rearview mirror I saw the small late-model truck change lanes and begin to follow my car very closely. I drove a few blocks without looking in the rearview mirror, but in my sideview mirror I saw the compact truck was right behind me. OK. Some motorists stay upset for two or three blocks, some require ten blocks or more to recover their senses. Stoplight after stoplight, when I glanced into the rearview mirror I saw the man—in his early thirties, tall, white, brown hair, and dark glasses. This guy must not have a job if he has the time to follow me for miles—oh, ohhh! No beast more danger-ous in the U.S.A. than an unemployed white man.

At this point I had to make a decision: do I forget about the trip to the pet store and head for the police station downtown, four miles away? Why should I have to let this stranger dictate my schedule for the afternoon? The man might dare to follow me to the police station, but by the time I reach the front door of the station, he'd be gone. No crime was committed; no Arizona law forbids tailgating someone for miles or for turning into a parking lot behind them. What could the police do? I had no license plate number to report because Arizona requires only one license plate, on the rear bumper of the vehicle. Anyway, I was within a block of the pet store where I knew I could get help from the pet store owners. I would feel better about this incident if it was not allowed to ruin my trip to the pet store.

The guy was right on my rear bumper; if I'd had to stop suddenly for any reason, there'd have been a collision. I decide I will not stop even if he does ram into the rear of my car. I study this guy's face in my rearview mirror, six feet two inches tall, 175 pounds, medium complexion, short hair, trimmed moustache. He thinks he can intim-idate me because I am a woman, five feet five inches tall, 140 pounds. But I am not afraid, I am furious. I refuse to be intimidated. I won't play his game. I can tell by the face I see in the mirror this guy has done this before; he enjoys using his truck to menace lone women.

I keep thinking he will quit, or he will figure that he's scared me enough; but he seems to sense that I am not afraid. It's true. I am not afraid because years ago my father taught my sisters and me that we did not have to be afraid. He'll give up when I turn into the parking lot outside the Pet Store, I think. But I watch in my rearview mirror; he's right on my rear bumper. As his truck turns into the parking lot behind my car, I reach over and open the glove compartment. I take out the holster with my .38 special and lay it on the car seat beside me.

I turned my car into a parking spot so quickly that I was facing my stalker who had momentarily stopped his truck and was watching me. I slid the .38 out of its hol-ster onto my lap, I watched the stranger's face, trying to determine whether he would jump out of his truck with a baseball bat or gun and come after me. I felt calm. No pounding heart or rapid breathing. My early experience deer hunting had prepared me well. I did not panic because I felt I could stop him if he tried to harm me. I was in no hurry. I sat in the car and waited to see what choice my stalker would make. I looked directly at him without fear because I had my .38 and I was ready to use it. The expression on my face must have been unfamiliar to him; he was used to seeing terror in the eyes of the women he followed. The expression on my face communicated a warning: if he approached the car window, I'd kill him.

He took a last look at me then sped away. I stayed in my car until his truck dis-appeared in the traffic of Campbell Avenue.

I walked into the pet store shaken. I had felt able to protect myself throughout the incident, but it left me emotionally drained and exhausted. The stranger had only pursued me—how much worse to be battered or raped.

Years before, I was unarmed the afternoon that two drunken deer hunters threatened to shoot me off my horse with razor-edged hunting crossbows. I was riding a colt on a national park trail near my home in the Tucson Mountains. These young white men in their late twenties were complete strangers who might have shot me if the colt had not galloped away erratically bucking and leaping—a moving target too difficult for the drunken bow hunters to aim at. The colt brought me to my ranch house where I called the county sheriff's office and the park ranger. I live in a sparsely populated area where my nearest neighbor is a quarter-mile away. I was afraid the men might have followed me back to my house so I took the .44 magnum out from under my pillow and strapped it around my waist until the sheriff or park ranger arrived. Forty-five minutes later, the park ranger arrived—the deputy sheriff arrived fifteen minutes after him. The drunken bow hunters were apprehended on the national park and arrested for illegally hunting; their bows and arrows were seized as evidence for the duration of bow hunting season. In southern Arizona that is enough punishment; I didn't want to take a chance of stirring up additional animosity with these men because I lived alone then; I chose not to make a complaint about their threatening words and gestures. I did not feel that I backed away by not pressing charges; I feared that if I pressed assault charges against these men, they would feel that I was challenging them to all-out war. I did not want to have to kill either of them if they came after me, as I thought they might. With my marksmanship and my .243 caliber hunting rifle from the old days, I am confident that I could stop idiots like these. But to have to take the life of another person is a terrible experience I will always try to avoid.

It isn't height or weight or strength that make women easy targets; from infancy women are taught to be self-sacrificing, passive victims. I was taught differently. Women have the right to protect themselves from death or bodily harm. By becoming strong and potentially lethal individuals, women destroy the fantasy that we are sitting ducks for predatory strangers.

In a great many cultures, women are taught to depend upon others, not themselves, for protection from bodily harm. Women are not taught to defend themselves from strangers because fathers and husbands fear the consequences themselves. In the United States, women depend upon the courts and the police; but as many women have learned the hard way, the police cannot be outside your house twenty-four hours a day. I don't want more police. More police on the street will not protect women. A few policemen are rapists and killers of women themselves; their uniforms and squad cars give them an advantage. No, I will be responsible for my own safety, thank you.

Women need to decide who has the primary responsibility for the health and safety of their bodies. We don't trust the State to manage our reproductive organs, yet most of us blindly trust that the State will protect us (and our reproductive organs) from predatory strangers. One look at the rape and murder statistics for women (excluding domestic incidents) and it is clear that the government FAILS to protect women from the violence of strangers. Some may cry out for a "stronger" State, more police, mandatory sentences, and swifter executions. Over the years we have seen the U.S. prison population become the largest in the world, executions take place every week now, inner-city communities are occupied by the National Guard, and people of color are harassed by police, but guess what? A woman out alone, night or day, is confronted with more danger of random violence from strangers than ever before. As the U.S. economy continues "to downsize," and the good jobs disappear forever, our urban and rural landscapes will include more desperate, angry men with nothing to lose.

Only women can put a stop to the "open season" on women by strangers. Women are TAUGHT to be easy targets by their mothers, aunts, and grandmothers who themselves were taught that "a women doesn't kill" or "a woman doesn't learn how to use a weapon." Women must learn how to take aggressive action individually, apart from the police and the courts.

Presently twenty-one states issue permits to carry concealed weapons; most states require lengthy gun safety courses and a police security check before issuing a permit. Inexpensive but excellent gun safety and self-defense courses designed for women are also available from every quality gun dealer who hopes to sell you a handgun at the end of the course. Those who object to firearms need trained companion dogs or collectives of six or more women to escort one another day and night. We must destroy the myth that women are born to be easy targets.

I Stand Here Writing

Nancy Sommers

I stand in my kitchen, wiping the cardamom, coriander, and cayenne off my fingers. My head is abuzz with words, with bits and pieces of conversation. I hear a phrase I have read recently, something about "a radical loss of certainty." But, I wonder, how did the sentence begin? I search the air for the rest of the sentence, can't find it, shake some more cardamom, and a bit of coriander. Then, by some play of mind, I am back home again in Indiana with my family, sitting around the kitchen table. Two people are talking, and there are three opinions; three people are talking, and there are six opinions. Opinions grow exponentially. I fight my way back to that sentence. Writing, that's how it begins: "Writing is a radical loss of certainty." (Or is it uncertainty?) It isn't so great for the chicken when all these voices start showing up, with all these sentences hanging in mid-air, but the voices keep me company. I am a writer, not a cook, and the truth is I don't care much about the chicken. Stories beget stories. Writing emerges from writing.

The truth. Has truth anything to do with the facts? All I know is that no matter how many facts I might clutter my life with, I am as bound to the primordial drama of my family as the earth is to the sun. This year my father, the son of a severe Prussian matriarch, watched me indulge my daughters, and announced to me that he wished I had been his mother. This year, my thirty-ninth, my last year to be thirty-something, my mother—who has a touch of magic, who can walk into the middle of a field of millions of clovers and find the *one* with four leaves—has begun to think I need help. She sends me cards monthly with four-leaf clovers taped inside. Two words neatly printed in capital letters—GOOD LUCK!! I look at these clovers and hear Reynolds Price's words: "Nobody under forty can believe how nearly everything's inherited." I wonder what my mother knows, what she is trying to tell me about the facts of my life.

When I was in high school studying French, laboring to conjugate verbs, the numerous four-leaf clovers my mother had carefully pressed inside her French dictionary made me imagine her in a field of clovers lyrically conjugating verbs of love. This is the only romantic image I have of my mother, a shy and conservative woman whose own mother died when she was five, whose grandparents were killed by the Nazis, who fled Germany at age thirteen with her father and sister. Despite the sheer facts of her life, despite the accumulation of grim knowable data, the truth is my mother is an optimistic person. She has the curious capacity always to be looking for luck, putting her faith in four-leaf clovers, ladybugs, pennies, and other amulets of fortune. She has a vision different from mine, one the facts alone can't explain. I, her daughter, was left, for a long time, seeing only the ironies; they were my defense against the facts of my life.

In this world of my inheritance in which daughters can become their fathers' mothers and mothers know their daughters are entering into a world where only sheer good luck will guide them, I hear from my own daughters that I am not in tune with their worlds, that I am just like a 50s mom, that they are 90s children, and I should stop acting so primitive. My children laugh uproariously at my autograph book, a 1959 artifact they unearthed in the basement of my parents' home. "Never kiss by the garden gate. Love is blind, but the neighbors ain't," wrote one friend. And my best friend, who introduced herself to me on the first day of first grade, looking me straight in the eye—and whispering through her crooked little teeth "the Jews killed Jesus"— wrote in this autograph book: "Mary had a little lamb. Her father shot it dead. Now she carries it to school between two slices of bread."

My ten-year-old daughter, Rachel, writes notes to me in hieroglyphics and tapes signs on the refrigerator in Urdu. "Salaarn Namma Man Rachaal Ast" reads one sign. Simply translated it means "Hello, my name is Rachel." Alex, my seven-year-old daughter, writes me lists, new lists each month, visibly reminding me of the many things I need to buy or do for her. This month's list includes a little refrigerator filled with Coke and candy; ears pierced; a new toilet; neon nail polish and *real* adult make-up.

How do I look at these facts? How do I embrace these experiences, these texts of my life, and translate them into ideas? How do I make sense of them and the conversations they engender in my head? I look at Alex's list and wonder what kind of feminist daughter I am raising whose deepest desires include neon nail polish and *real* adult make-up. Looking at her lists a different way, I wonder if this second child of mine is asking me for something larger, something more permanent and real than adult make-up. Maybe I got that sentence wrong. Maybe it is that "Love (as well as writing) involves a radical loss of certainty."

Love is blind, but the neighbors ain't. Mary's father shot her little lamb dead, and now she carries it to school between two slices of bread. I hear these rhymes today, and they don't say to me what they say to my daughters. They don't seem so innocent. I hear them and think about the ways in which my neighbors in Indiana could only see my family as Jews from Germany, exotic strangers who ate tongue, outsiders who didn't celebrate Christmas. I wonder if my daughter Rachel needs to tell me her name in Urdu because she thinks we don't share a common language. These sources change meaning when I ask the questions in a different way. They introduce new ironies, new questions.

I want to understand these living, breathing, primary sources all around me. I want to be, in Henry James's words, "a person upon whom nothing is lost." These sources speak to me of love and loss, of memory and desire, of the ways in which we come to understand something through difference and opposition. Two years ago I learned the word *segue* from one of my students. At first the word seemed peculiar. Segue sounded like something you did only on the Los Angeles freeway. Now I hear that word everywhere, and I have begun using it. I want to know how to segue from one idea to the next, from one thought to the fragment lying beside it. But the connections don't always come with four-leaf clovers and the words GOOD LUCK neatly printed beside them.

My academic need to find connections sends me to the library. There are eleven million books in my University's libraries. Certainly these sanctioned voices, these authorities, these published sources can help me find the connections. Someone, probably some three thousand someones, has studied what it is like to be the child of survivors. Someone has written a manual on how the granddaughter of a severe Prussian matriarch and the daughter of a collector of amulets ought to raise feminist daughters. I want to walk into the fields of writing, into those eleven million books, and find the one book that will explain it all. But I've learned to expect less from such sources. They seldom have the answers. And the answers they do have reveal themselves to me at the most unexpected times. I have been led astray more than once while searching books for the truth.

Once I learned a lesson about borrowing someone else's words and losing my own.

I was fourteen, light years away from thirty-something. High school debate teams across the nation were arguing the pros and cons of the United States Military Aid Policy. It all came back to me as I listened to the news of the Persian Gulf War, as I listened to Stormin' Norman giving his morning briefings, an eerie resonance, all our arguments, the millions of combative words—sorties—fired back and forth. In my first practice debate, not having had enough time to assemble my own sources, I borrowed quote cards from my teammates. I attempted to bolster my position that the U.S. should limit its military aid by reading a quote in my best debate style: "W. W. Rostow says: 'We should not give military aid to India because it will exacerbate endemic rivalries.'"

Under cross-examination, my nemesis, Bobby Rosenfeld, the neighbor kid, who always knew the right answers, began firing a series of questions at me without stopping to let me answer:

"Nancy, can you tell me who W. W. Rostow is? And can you tell me why he might say this? Nancy, can you tell me what 'exacerbate' means? Can you tell me what 'endemic rivalries' are? And exactly what does it mean to 'exacerbate endemic rivalries'?"

I didn't know. I simply did not know who W. W. Rostow was, why he might have said that, what "exacerbate" meant, or what an "endemic rivalry" was. Millions of four-leaf clovers couldn't have helped me. I might as well have been speaking Urdu. I didn't know who my source was, the context of the source, nor the literal meaning of the words I had read. Borrowing words from authorities had left me without any words of my own.

My debate partner and I went on that year to win the Indiana state championship and to place third in the nationals. Bobby Rosenfeld never cross-examined me again, but for twenty years he has appeared in my dreams. I am not certain why I would dream so frequently about this scrawny kid whom I despised. I think, though, that he became for me what the Sea Dyak tribe of Borneo calls a *ngarong*, a dream guide, someone guiding me to understanding. In this case, Bobby guided me to understand the endemic rivalries within myself. The last time Bobby appeared in a dream he had become a woman.

I learned a more valuable lesson about sources as a college senior. I was the kind of student who loved words, words out of context, words that swirled around inside my mouth, words like *exacerbate, undulating, lugubrious,* and *zeugma.* "She stained her honour or her new brocade," wrote Alexander Pope. I would try to write zeugmas whenever I could, exacerbating my already lugubrious prose. Within the English department, I was known more for my long hair, untamed and untranslatable, and for my long distance bicycle rides than for my scholarship.

For my senior thesis, I picked Emerson's essay "Eloquence." Harrison Hayford, my advisor, suggested that I might just get off my bicycle, get lost in the library, and read all of Emerson's essays, journals, letters. I had picked one of Emerson's least distinguished essays, an essay that the critics mentioned only in passing, and if I were not entirely on my own, I had at least carved out new territory for myself.

I spent weeks in the library reading Emerson's journals, reading newspaper accounts from Rockford and Peoria, Illinois, where he had first delivered "Eloquence" as a speech. Emerson stood at the podium, the wind blowing his papers hither and yon, calmly picking them up, and proceeding to read page 8 followed by page 3, followed by page 6, followed by page 2. No one seemed to know the difference. Emerson's Midwestern audience was overwhelmed by this strange man from Concord, Massachusetts, this eloquent stranger whose unit of expression was the sentence.

As I sat in the library, wearing my QUESTION AUTHORITY T-shirt, I could admire this man who delivered his Divinity School Address in 1838, speaking words so repugnant to the genteel people of Cambridge that it was almost thirty years before Harvard felt safe having him around again. I could understand the Midwestern audience's awe and adulation as they listened but didn't quite comprehend Emerson's stunning oratory. I had joined the debate team not to argue the U.S. Military Aid Policy, but to learn how to be an orator who could stun audiences, to learn a personal eloquence I could never learn at home. Perhaps only children of immigrant parents can understand the embarrassing moments of inarticulateness, the missed connections that come from learning to speak a language from parents who claim a different mother tongue.

As an undergraduate, I wanted to free myself from that mother tongue. Four-leaf clovers and amulets of oppression weighed heavy on my mind, and I could see no connection whatsoever between those facts of my life and the untranslatable side of myself that set me in opposition to authority. And then along came Emerson. Like his Midwest audience, I didn't care about having him whole. I liked the promise and the rhapsodic freedom I found in his sentences, in his invitation to seize life as our dictionary, to believe that "Life was not something to be learned but to be lived." I loved his insistence that "the one thing of value is the active soul." I read that "Books are for the scholar's idle time," and I knew that he had given me permission to explore the world.

Going into Emerson was like walking into a revelation; it was the first time I had gone into the texts not looking for a specific answer, and it was the first time the texts gave me the answers I needed. Never mind that I got only part of what Emerson was telling me. I got inspiration, I got insight, and I began to care deeply about my work.

Today I reread the man who set me off on a new road, and I find a different kind of wisdom. Today I reread "The American Scholar," and I don't underline the sentence "Books are for the scholar's idle time." I continue to the next paragraph, underlining the sentence "One must be an inventor to read well." The second sentence doesn't contradict the one I read twenty years ago, but it means more today. I bring more to it, and I know that I can walk into text after text, source after source, and they will give me insight, but not answers. I have learned too that my sources can surprise me. Like my mother, I find myself sometimes surrounded by a field of four-leaf clovers, there for the picking, waiting to see what I can make of them. But I must be an inventor if I am to read those sources well, if I am to imagine the connections.

As I stand in my kitchen, the voices that come to me come by way of a lifetime of reading, they come on the waves of life, and they seem to be helping me translate the untranslatable. They come, not at my bidding, but when I least expect them, when I am receptive enough to listen to their voices. They come when I am open.

If I could teach my students one lesson about writing it would be to see themselves as sources, as places from which ideas originate, to see themselves as Emerson's transparent eyeball, all that they have read and experienced—the dictionaries of their lives—circulating through them. I want them to learn how sources thicken, complicate, enlarge writing, but I want them to know too how it is always the writer's voice, vision, and argument that create the new source. I want my students to see that nothing reveals itself straight out, especially the sources all around them. But I know enough by now that this Emersonian ideal can't be passed on in one lesson or even a semester of lessons.

Many of the students who come to my classes have been trained to collect facts; they act as if their primary job is to accumulate enough authorities so that there is no doubt about the "truth" of their thesis. They most often disappear behind the weight and permanence of their borrowed words, moving their pens, mouthing the words of others, allowing sources to speak through them unquestioned, unexamined.

At the outset, many of my students think that personal writing is writing about the death of their grandmother. Academic writing is reporting what Elizabeth Kübler-Ross has written about death and dying. Being personal, I want to show my students, does not mean being autobiographical. Being academic does not mean being remote, distant, imponderable. Being personal means bringing their judgments and interpretation to bear on what they read and write, learning that they never leave themselves behind even when they write academic essays.

Last year, David Gray came into my essay class disappointed about everything. He didn't like the time of the class, didn't like the reading list, didn't seem to like me. Nothing pleased him. "If this is a class on the essay," he asked the first day, "why aren't we reading real essayists like Addison, Steele, and Lamb?" On the second day, after being asked to read Annie Dillard's "Living Like Weasels," David complained that a weasel wasn't a fit subject for an essay. "Writers need big subjects. Look at Melville. He needed a whale for *Moby-Dick*. A weasel—that's nothing but a rodent." And so it continued for a few weeks.

I kept my equanimity in class, but at home I'd tell my family about this kid who kept testing me, seizing me like Dillard's weasel, and not letting go. I secretly wanted him out of my class. But then again, I sensed in him a kindred spirit, someone else who needed to question authority

I wanted my students to write exploratory essays about education, so I asked them to think of a time when they had learned something, and then a time when they had tried to learn something but couldn't. I wanted them to see what ideas and connections they could find between these two very different experiences and the other essays they were reading for the class. I wanted the various sources to work as catalysts. I wanted my students to find a way to talk back to those other writers. The assigned texts were an odd assortment with few apparent connections. I hoped my students would find the common ground, but also the moments of tension, the contradictions, and the ambiguities in those sources.

David used the assigned texts as a catalyst for his thinking, but as was his way, he went beyond the texts I offered and chose his own. He begins his essay, "Dulcis Est Sapientia," with an account of his high school Latin class, suggesting that he once knew declensions, that he had a knack for conjugations, but has forgotten them. He tells us that if his teacher were to appear suddenly today and demand the perfect subjunctive of *venire*, he would stutter hopelessly.

About that Latin class, David asks, "What is going on here? Did I once know Latin and forget it through disuse? Perhaps I never learned Latin at all. What I learned was a bunch of words which, with the aid of various ending sounds, indicated that Gaius was either a good man delivering messages to the lieutenant or a general who struck camp at the seventh hour. I may have known it once, but I never learned it." The class never gave David the gift of language. There was something awry in the method.

What is learning? That's what David explores in his essay as he moves from his Latin lesson to thinking about surrealist paintings, to thinking about barriers we create, to Plato, to an airplane ride in which he observed a mother teaching her child concepts of color and number, all the time taking his readers along with him on his journey, questioning sources, reflecting, expanding, and enriching his growing sense that learning should stress ideas rather than merely accumulating facts and information.

David draws his essay to a close with an analysis of a joke: A man goes to a cocktail party and gets soused. He approaches his host and asks, "Pardon me, but do lemons whistle?"

The host looks at him oddly and answers, "No, lemons don't whistle."

"Oh dear," says the guest, "then I'm afraid I just squeezed your canary into my gin and tonic."

David reflects about the significance of this joke: "One need not be an ornithologist to get the joke, but one must know that canaries are yellow and that they whistle…. What constitutes the joke is a connection made between two things…

which have absolutely nothing in common except for their yellowness. It would never occur to us to make a comparison between the two, let alone to confuse one with the other. But this is the value of the joke, to force into our consciousness the ideas which we held but never actively considered.... This knocking down of barriers between ideas is parallel to the process that occurs in all learning. The barriers that we set...suddenly crumble; the boundaries...are extended to include other modes of thought." Learning, like joking, David argues, gives us pleasure by satisfying our innate capacity to recognize coherence, to discern patterns and connections.

David's essay, like any essay, does not intend to offer the last word on its subject. The civilizing influence of an essay is that it keeps the conversation going, chronicling an intellectual journey, reflecting conversations with sources. I am confident that when David writes for his philosophy course he won't tell a joke anywhere in his essay. But if the joke—if any of his sources—serves him as a catalyst for his thinking, if he makes connections among the sources that circulate within him, between Plato and surrealism, between Latin lessons and motherchild lessons—the dictionaries of *his* life—then he has learned something valuable about writing.

I say to myself that I don't believe in luck. And yet. Not too long ago Rachel came home speaking with some anxiety about an achievement test that she had to take at school. Wanting to comfort her, I urged her to take my rabbit's foot to school the next day. Always alert to life's ironies, Rachel said, "Sure, Mom, a rabbit's foot will really help me find the answers. And even if it did, how would I know the answer the next time when I didn't have that furry little claw?" The next day, proud of her ease in taking the test, she remained perplexed by the one question that seized her and wouldn't let go. She tried it on me: "Here's the question," she said. "Can you figure out which of these sentences cannot be true?"

a. We warmed our hands by the fire.
b. The rain poured in and around the windows.
c. The wind beckoned us to open the door.

Only in the mind of someone who writes achievement tests, and wants to close the door on the imagination, could the one false sentence be "The wind beckoned us to open the door." Probably to this kind of mind, Emerson's sentence "Life is our dictionary" is also not a true sentence.

But life *is* our dictionary, and that's how we know that the wind can beckon us to open the door. Like Emerson, we let the wind blow our pages hither and yon, forcing us to start in the middle, moving from page 8 to page 2, forward to page 7, moving back and forth in time, losing our certainty.

Like Emerson, I love basic units, the words themselves, words like cardamom, coriander, words that play around in my head, swirl around in my mouth. The challenge, of course, is not to be a ventriloquist—not to be a mouther of words—but to be open to other voices, untranslatable as they might be. Being open to the unexpected, we can embrace complexities: canaries and lemons, amulets and autograph books, fathers who want their daughters to be their mothers, and daughters who write notes in Urdu—all those odd, unusual conjunctions can come together and speak through us.

The other day, I called my mother and told her about this essay, told her that I had been thinking about the gold bracelet she took with her as one of her few possessions from Germany—a thin gold chain with three amulets: a mushroom, a lady bug, and, of course, a four-leaf clover. Two other charms fell off years ago—she lost one, I the other. I used to worry over the missing links, thinking only of the loss, of what we could never retrieve. When I look at the bracelet now, I think about the Prussian matriarch, my grandmother, and my whole primordial family drama. I think too of Emerson and the pages that blew in the wind and the gaps that seemed not to matter. The bracelet is but one of many sources that intrigues me. Considering them in whatever order they appear, with whatever gaps, I want to see where they will lead me, what they tell me.

With writing and with teaching, as well as with love, we don't know how the sentence will begin and, rarely ever, how it will end. Having the courage to live with uncertainty, ambiguity, even doubt, we can walk into all of those fields of writing, knowing that we will find volumes upon volumes bidding *us* enter. We need only be inventors, we need only give freely and abundantly to the texts, imagining even as we write that we too will be a source from which other readers can draw sustenance.

Trading Off: A Memoir

Michael Steinberg

"Only a child expects justice."
—Gore Vidal

Jack Kerchman, my old high school baseball coach, was a classic ball-buster, a lot like those Marine D.I.'s you see in old World War II movies. A Jew himself, "Mr. K" had a reputation for hazing the Jewish players that he thought were too soft. One of them was me.

I started hearing stories about Mr. K in the mid-fifties, when I was in junior high. In three years at the high school, his football teams won Queens (borough) championships, and the baseball team got as far as the city championship semi-finals. People in the Rockaways—neighborhood kids, parents, local merchants—began to take notice. Winning teams and wars have a way of galvanizing a neighborhood, especially in New York, where everything is measured and articulated in terms of "turf."

According to the buzz on the playgrounds Mr. K was an obsessed man. Max Weinstein, a tight end on the football team, told us about the impassioned locker room speeches. Before each new season, Kerchman would gather the team around him in the boys' shower and reminisce about his old college days at Syracuse, where he was a one-hundred-sixty-pound offensive guard and defensive nose tackle for coach Biggie Munn. He proudly revealed how after the war he'd had a tryout with the New York Giants and had made it to the last cut. He always finished up by saying that he did it all "on a little talent, a big heart, and a whole lot of guts."

A Jew from the roughest part of the lower East Side, Mr. K believed that young Jewish boys, especially those from my suburban neighborhood, were "candy-asses" and quitters. At football tryouts he talked about the time he liberated a concentration camp at the end of World War II, and of how important it was for the next generation of Jews to "toughen up." So at the first scrimmage of each new season, he made the

Jewish boys play without equipment. And if you were Jewish and you wanted to pitch for the baseball team, you had to show him you could brush hitters back by throwing at their heads.

The rumors were enough to convince Ritchie Zeitler and Bobby Brower, the two best athletes in our neighborhood, to transfer to a local prep school. The stories frightened and fascinated me. But I knew I'd be trying out for the high school baseball team next year and I wanted to see this Kerchman character in action, so in September of my last year in junior high, I collared Mike Rubin and Barry Aronowsky, two of my summer league baseball buddies, and off we went to the first Saturday home football game. Outside the high school field, the street hawkers sold hot dogs and popcorn, along with Rockaway High pennants, pom-poms, and trinkets. In the bleachers, students and parents chanted, "Let's go, Seahorses! Seahorses, let's go!" The cheerleaders bounced up and down in their red-and-blue sweaters and short, pleated skirts, as the football team ran out on the field. Most of the players were only a few years older than me, but in their scarlet helmets and full gear they looked like Roman gladiators.

As I scanned the field, I saw the pitcher's mound to the right of the south goalpost. For a long, slow moment, I floated free of the razzmatazz while I imagined myself standing on that mound in a Rockaway baseball uniform. My parents, kid brother, and friends were all in the stands, and the cheerleaders were chanting my name as I went into my wind-up and got ready to snap off a sharp, dipping curve ball.

Then I spotted Kerchman standing in front of the team bench. He was in his late thirties, maybe five eight, heavyset, wearing a chocolate-brown porkpie hat and rumpled tweed topcoat. You could hear him yelling above the crowd noise. Sometimes he'd hurl his hat to the ground and scream obscenities at a player who screwed up. He reacted to missed blocks, fumbles, broken plays—whatever derailed the game plan he'd engineered in his head. A couple of times I saw him hold offending players by the shoulder pads and shake them back and forth; and once when he was really angry, he grabbed Stuie Schneider, a Jewish kid from my neighborhood, by the jersey and tattooed him with vicious open-handed helmet slaps. His temper tantrums frightened and fascinated me; I wondered why anyone, Jewish or not, would want to play for such an animal. Then that image of me on the mound would kick back in.

My two friends had seen enough, so I went back alone to the rest of the football games that season. When I announced I was going to try out for baseball next year they told me I was crazy to even think about it.

They didn't understand. It wasn't a matter of merely wanting to play: I had to play. My dad, an old semi-pro infielder, had taught me how to play ball when I was eight. After dinner, out in the backyard, he'd hit me ground balls and pop flies until the sun dipped below the Union Carbide tank near the bay. On Sundays, he took me to Riss Park to watch him play fast-pitch softball double-headers with a bunch of other middle-aged jocks. By the time I turned nine, I wanted to be a ballplayer like him.

As soon as the weather turned mild, I'd scale the schoolyard fence, or be out on the street with my friends playing punchball or stickball. On weekends we'd trek twenty blocks up to Riis Park for marathon choose-up baseball games on the grass and dirt fields. Even when we went to the beach, the first thing we'd do was carve out a patch of sand near the water's edge and get up a diamond ball game.

After school, I'd grab a broomstick and run down to Casey's Lot, a weed-choked, rock-infested vacant field on the corner of 129th Street and Beach Channel Drive. There I'd pretend I was Duke Snider or Willie Mays or Mickey Mantle, and I'd swat stones across the road into Jamaica Bay until my palms sprouted blood blisters. At night, my brother and I would grab a pink "Spauldeen" high-bouncer and play stoop baseball till the streetlights flickered on.

As much as I loved to play, though, I knew I'd never be one of the top jocks. I was what coaches called a "shlepper," a slightly ungraceful athlete who somehow managed to get the job done. Whatever the sport, I would work hard at it, no matter what the cost—and there was always a cost. At thirteen, I was cut from the local Police Athletic League (P.A.L.) squad. Coach Bluetrich told me that I didn't have the quick reflexes needed to play shortstop. Not playing was unthinkable, so I made up a lie. I told Bluetrich I could pitch. There isn't a coach in his right mind who wouldn't take on an extra batting practice pitcher. The next day he gave me an old torn uniform two sizes too big, and told me to concentrate on throwing strikes to the hitters.

That summer I taught myself how to pitch. I cut a twelve-inch hole in a bedsheet, and at night in my backyard I threw hundreds of rubber-covered baseballs at the target. I got the balls by trading my Topp's bubble gum cards with a friend who worked at the local batting range. Under the pretense of teaching my kid brother how to bat, I pitched shaved tennis balls to him for hours. By shaving the fuzz, you could make the ball curve and dip crazily.

I didn't throw hard enough to have what coaches call a "live arm." In fact, my ex-teammate Andy Makrides still likes to remind me, "You had three speeds, Mike, slow, slower, slowest. And your sinker was just a dying quail. You were lucky that the pitcher's mound was sixty feet, six inches, because if someone ever moved it back a half a foot, all your pitches would bounce before they got to the plate."

But I worked at it. I read how-to books on pitching and studied the strengths and weaknesses of professional hitters on TV. All summer I taught myself how to throw curve balls, sliders, knuckle balls, and sinkers. I kept honing my control, and by mid-July, I could throw four out of every five pitches through the bedsheet hole.

My improvement took Bluetrich by surprise. By the end of the summer I was the team's second starter. In the borough championship game, Bluetrich started me ahead of Lee Adnepos. Lee was my best friend and team captain, and up until then, the team's ace pitcher. We lost the game 3–2, and Lee was so upset that he didn't speak to me for two months.

I was happy I got to pitch the big game, but I knew Lee had worked as hard as I did. So by age thirteen, I was already vaguely sensing where all this was headed. Character and hard work didn't have a whole lot to do with who played and who sat. It was a simple trade-off: coaches used you if they thought you could help them win games, and you put up with them because you wanted to play.

Knowing this gave me even more incentive. I improved so much that the next summer, I convinced myself that I had a chance to make the high school baseball team. A lot of others had the same illusion, though. Three hundred dreamers came out for football and another two hundred for baseball. With a student body of over three thousand, Far Rockaway was the only high school in the entire district and Mr. K had his pick of all the best jocks on the Rockaway peninsula.

As tryouts approached I knew I needed an "in." My dad, a traveling salesman, always preached to us, "It's not what you know, but who you know." Well, I knew Gail Sloane, my parents' friend from across the street. Gail was an attractive woman who worked in the central office at the junior high where Kerchman taught Hygiene and Guidance, of all things. The summer before I started high school, I asked Gail to put in a word for me.

It was early September, my first day of high school. Baseball tryouts were in February, so I figured I had plenty of time before I had to worry about Kerchman. In first period homeroom, though, the teacher handed me a note: "Be at my office 3 o'clock sharp." It was signed by Mr. K. By three, my stomach was in knots.

Kerchman's "office" was across from the boiler room, deep in the bowels of the ancient brick building. To get there, you had to walk past the showers and through the boys' locker room. Opening the stairwell door, I inhaled the steam from the shower, and above the hum and buzz of locker-room banter and casual small talk, I heard the clackety-clack-clack of aluminum cleats hitting the cement floor. An entire bank of lockers was reserved for Angelo Labrizzi, Mickey Imbrianni, and Leon Cholakis, the veterans I'd been watching for the past year. I'd seen them around school and at the State Diner jock table, but here in their domain they had the undeniable aura of a prestigious, exclusive club.

Though football would never be my sport, playing varsity baseball offered many of the same privileges. I'd already witnessed it for myself: Adults—your own parents—and your friends, actually paid money to watch *you* play; cheerleaders chanted your name ("Steinberg, Steinberg, he's our man. If he can't do it, no one can!"), and they kicked their bare legs so high you could see their red silk panties. After school, you sat at the jock table in the State Diner; you got to wear a tan leather jacket with a big blue-and-red "R" across the left breast, and your girlfriend wore your letter sweater to school. Maybe the biggest ego-trip of all was everybody watching with envy when you left sixth-period Econ to go on road trips.

I tried to push those thoughts out of my mind as I timidly knocked on Kerchman's door. "It's open," he rasped in a deep, gravelly voice. The room was a ten-foot-square box, a glorified cubbyhole smelling of wintergreen, Merthiolate, and stale sweat socks. The brown cement floor was coated with dust and rotted-out orange peels, and on all four sides were makeshift two-by-four equipment bays, overflowing with old scuffed helmets, broken shoulder pads, torn jerseys and pants, muddy cleats, and deflated footballs, all randomly piled on top of one another. Mr. K stood under a bare light bulb wearing a baseball hat, white socks, and a jockstrap. He was holding his sweatpants and chewing a plug of tobacco. "You're Steinberg, right?" He said my name, "Stein-berg," slowly, enunciating and stretching out both syllables.

"I don't beat around the bush, Stein-berg. You're here for one reason and one reason only. Because Gail Sloane told me you were a reliable kid. What I'm looking for, Stein-berg, is an assistant football manager. I'm willing to take a chance on you."

I wanted to run out of the room and find a place to cry. Assistant football managers were glorified water boys; they did all the "shitwork," everything from being stretcher bearers to toting the equipment. He sensed my disappointment and waited a beat while I composed myself.

"Gail also tells me you're a pitcher," he muttered, as he slipped into his sweatpants.

Another tense beat. Finally he said, "In February, you'll get your chance to show me what you've got." To make certain there was no misunderstanding between us, he added, "Just like everyone else."

Then he said, "So what's it going to be, Stein-berg?"

It had all happened too fast. I couldn't think straight. In a trembling, uncertain voice, I told him I'd think about it and let him know tomorrow.

My parents told me to make up my own mind. Anticipating his own embarrassment, my brother advised me to tell the coach to "shove it." That night I lay awake, endlessly debating: "Let's say I take the offer. Will it diminish me in Kerchman's eyes? Will he write me off as a pitcher? Suppose I take this job and don't complain? Will it give me an edge at baseball tryouts?"

The next day in sixth-period Math, I convinced myself I had to take it. Later, when I told Kerchman the news, his only comment was, "Good, we've got that settled. Report to Krause, the head manager, right away. Get some sweats and cleats, and as soon as practice ends, clean up this room. Get everything stacked up in the right bins, mop the floor, and get this place shaped up."

On his way out the door, he said, "And make sure we've got enough Merthiolate, cotton swabs, gauze and tape. First game's in a week and when we step out on that field, I want us looking sharp and ready. We set the example, Stein-berg. If we do our job, the players will do theirs. You understand me, son?"

Before I could open my mouth, he said "Let us hope, Stein-berg, that you're not one of those candy-ass Jewish quitters."

I wanted so badly to tell him to take the job and shove it. But I told myself, "He's testing you, trying to see how much you can take. Just hang in there."

Along with doing the coach's dirty work, I had to put up with a lot of crap from the other student managers and star players. Moose Imbrianni sent me on a fool's errand for a bucket of steam; I searched for a rabbit's foot for Leon Cholakis and came up with a pair of lucky dice for Angelo Labrizzi. Before games I taped ankles, treated minor injuries and sprains, and inflated the footballs. At half-time I cut the lemons and oranges. During games I'd scrape mud off cleats, carry the water buckets and equipment, and help injured players off the field. After the games ended, I had to stay and clean out the locker room.

The worst jobs, though, were water boy and stretcher bearer. It was bad enough that I had to run out there in front of thousands of people during the time-outs. But it was humiliating to have to listen to the taunts and jeers of my friends. Whenever I heard "Hey water boy, I'm thirsty, bring the bucket over here!" or "Man down on the fifty, medic; get the stretcher!" I wanted to run off the field and just keep going. Away from practice, I avoided my friends. As often as I could, I took the public bus to school, and I stayed away from dances and neighborhood parties. I thought constantly about quitting, but I was already in too deep. If I quit now, I could kiss my baseball dreams goodbye.

Much as I hated those menial jobs, watching Kerchman in action still intrigued me. In his pre-game pep-talks, he invoked the names of past Far Rockaway football heroes, and gave impassioned sermons on the value of courage, character, loyalty, and team play. His practice scrimmages were grueling tests of stamina and fortitude. If players didn't execute according to his expectations, he'd single them out for public ridicule. His favorite victim was poor Stuie Schneider.

One mid-season practice, it was getting late and everyone was whipped. On a drop-back pass play, Stuie gently brush-blocked Harold Zimmerman, the oncoming defensive tackle. Harold and Stuie were friends and neither one wanted to hurt the other, especially in a meaningless scrimmage. But as soon as Kerchman smelled it, he stopped the scrimmage and gave them the "Jews are chickenshits" routine. Then without warning, it turned into a scene right out of *High Noon*.

"Let's see what you're made of, Schneider," he said. Without pads or a helmet, the coach took a three-point stance on the defensive line and came charging right at Stuie. As scared as he was to hit the coach, Stuie knew what the stakes were, so he knocked Kerchman right on his butt. Everyone looked down at the ground and pawed the dirt with their cleats, waiting to see what the coach would do. Just as Harold shot Stuie an "Oh shit" look, Mr. K got up and brushed himself off. Then he clapped Stuie warmly on his shoulder pads, stuck out his jaw and spat out a wad of brown tobacco juice. "That's the right way to hit," he said to the rest of the squad. "You make the man pay."

It didn't take me long to understand what Kerchman was trying to teach the Jewish players. In an early season game against St. Francis Prep, Stevie Berman, our star quarterback, was picking the St. Francis secondary apart with his passing game. When we lined up offensively, their guys tried to unnerve Stevie, calling him "dirty Jew," and "kike," and yelling, "The Jews killed Christ." We'd heard it all before—at our own practices. All it did was make our linemen block harder. By the end of the first quarter, we were ahead by three touchdowns, and everyone could sense a fight coming. On the next offensive series, their nose tackle deliberately broke Stevie's leg as he lay pinned at the bottom of a pileup. It's an easy trick: you just grab a guy's leg and twist. As we carried Stevie off on a stretcher, Mr. K grabbed his hand and said, "Don't you worry pal, they'll pay for this."

Leon Cholakis, our 275-pound All-City tackle, lived for moments like this. All game, he'd been waiting for Coach K to turn him loose. Sure enough, on the next offensive series, Cholakis hurled himself full force on their prone quarterback and fractured the guy's collarbone. Even on the sidelines, you could hear the bone snap. It made me nauseous, yet a piece of me felt like cheering Kerchman for protecting his players.

At the season-ending awards banquet, Kerchman surprised me again by giving me a varsity letter. When I stepped up to the podium, he shook my hand and said, "Nice job, son, see you in the spring." It would have been a breach of decorum for a student manager to wear his letter; still, the gesture flattered me and my hopes shot up.

On February 15th, over two hundred jittery hopefuls gathered for baseball tryouts in the high school gym. Kerchman announced that he had only ten spots to fill and that four of them would be pitchers. Then he began the tryouts. Standing twenty yards away, he swatted rubber-covered baseballs at the would-be fielders. When he ripped a hard grounder at a player, the rubber ball would skip off the basketball court's wood surface and spin crazily across the floor. If the fielder missed the ball, it would rocket into the gymnasium's brick wall with a loud "thwack," then ricochet back. The terrified rookies watched from the oval running track above the gym while those veterans who'd already survived this ritual stood confidently behind the coach, horsing around and heckling the newcomers.

The last to try out were the new pitchers. To make this ordeal more unsettling, Kerchman placed seven or eight pitchers in a line across the width of the basketball floor. We each had our own catcher, and one hitter to pitch to. No nets or batting cages. Kerchman stood up on the running track, and when he blew his whistle all the pitchers threw to the hitters. It was rough enough trying to concentrate on throwing strikes to varsity hitters, but as soon as you let go with a pitch, line drives and ground balls went whizzing past you. It was a scene right out of a Keystone Kops movie.

We did this drill for three consecutive days before I was able to screen out all the distractions and dangers. By the last day, my arm ached every time I threw a pitch. I was sure I would never make the cut. Two days later, Kerchman posted the final squad list. One spot was sure to go to Mike Saperstein, a cocky, Jewish left-hander from my neighborhood. I disliked him, yet envied his arrogance. A rich kid with a chip on his shoulder, he was handsome, a good athlete, a ladies' man, and an honors student. Saperstein kissed no one's ass. Like Kerchman, you either came to him on his terms or Sap simply ignored you.

As I scanned the alphabetically listed names, right below "Saperstein" was "Steinberg." At first I thought there must be another Steinberg, but when I read my first name, I was so happy I wanted to phone everyone I knew. When I went to the equipment cage, though, the student manager informed me that "batting practice pitchers don't get uniforms." Nor, as I learned, did they travel to road games with the rest of the team. Then came the kicker. "At home games," he said, "your job is to stand at the home plate entrance and retrieve the foul balls that are hit out of the park."

My gut burned; I wanted to march right into Kerchman's office and ask him why. But I already knew what he'd say. He'd cut at least three or four pitchers who were far more talented than I was. When I calmed down, I reminded myself that at least I'd made the team. I remembered my P.A.L. days and how surprised Bluetrich was by my progress. Maybe if I worked hard enough and improved, Mr. K would give me a chance to pitch.

When I began throwing batting practice, Kerchman was observant enough to see that I could throw strikes. But I was cannon fodder, just what Mr. K and the hitters wanted. In the beginning, most of the veterans teased me because I couldn't throw very hard. "Hey water boy, toss that watermelon up here," Imbrianni kidded. This time the hazing didn't bother me. Two years of summer league had taught me that big, free-swinging sluggers like Imbrianni were usually too impatient. They wanted to crank everything out of the park. When I threw off-speed sliders and curves, most of the time the big hitters overswung and popped the ball up. I got a real kick out of that. I also enjoyed it when I got to pitch a few intrasquad game innings with the varsity fielders behind me. I had a good sinker and when it was working, the best a batter could do was to hit a hard grounder, a piece of cake for a good infielder.

I wasn't doing too badly for a flunky, but when I looked to Mr. K for some kind of acknowledgment, he'd say things to the hitters like, "What's with you guys? If you let a little piss-ant like Steinberg here make you look like a monkey, what's gonna happen when you face a really good pitcher?"

Then there were days when I'd have to stay late to pitch batting practice to the scrubs. The worst times were those Saturday mornings in March when the stiff ocean breezes blew winter's last snow flurries across the frozen diamond, and the rest of the team sat huddled in parkas while Henry Koslan, another scrubbie, and I threw batting practice. Another painful indignity was having to listen to the varsity players complain about how hard Mr. K was driving them. Those guys didn't know how good they had it.

By mid-season I was feeling so down that I had to do a psych job on myself just to get to practice. The team was good, I rationalized, on the way to winning the league championship. Imbrianni was leading the city in hitting. Stevie Berman and Jack Gartner, both still juniors, were two of the best pitchers in New York. Even Mr. K's protégé, Mike Saperstein, only got to pitch the last few innings of a blow-out. It was only my first year, I kept reminding myself. I just had to wait my turn. But chasing those damn foul balls while my friends in the stands ragged on me was too much like the humiliation I'd felt as a freshman football manager. By season's end I was just putting in time. We won our last five games and cruised into the playoffs. Just when it seemed that we might go all the way, Berman had his only off game of the season, and we were eliminated in the borough finals.

The long season ended, as always, with the traditional awards banquet. The local media, school bigwigs, and our families all attended. I got a minor letter and enviously watched each member of the "big team" receive his varsity letter. It came as no surprise that Imbrianni won the John Kelly Award, the gold medal that traditionally went to the team's inspirational leader and most valuable player. Next year it would be my turn: I'd prove to that S.O.B. I could pitch for him.

Over the summer, I grew a couple of inches and put on twenty pounds. I worked in a factory lifting heavy boxes, ran two miles a day, and worked out with weights. On those nights when we didn't play a summer league game, I went over to Al Seidman's to work on new pitches and strategies. Al was a friend of my dad's and a former minor-league pitcher. Three nights a week in his backyard, he made me concentrate on pitching to specific spots. Al also showed me how to throw the curve ball at three different speeds, and in post-workout conversations he doped out strategies for out-thinking hitters. When I went to the Dodger games on Saturday, I sat behind home plate and kept detailed notes; I charted the good hitters' tendencies, and scrutinized the best pitcher's mechanics.

That fall I wasn't planning on being an assistant football manager again. On the first day of practice, though, Mr. K cornered me in the boy's john, and told me this year I'd be the liaison between the football players and the head manager. "Look at this as a promotion, Stein-berg," he said, while I stood at the latrine fumbling with my zipper. It later occurred to me that this was the first time Kerchman had ever sought me out for anything. There was no way I could turn him down.

That season, I had a much easier time of it. Mostly I worked with Krause, delegating my old chores to the junior managers. On game days, I stood behind the bench, keeping the stats, and after the games I wrote up the results for the newspapers. At the banquet I got another varsity letter that I couldn't wear. The one I wanted I was determined to earn this spring. By early January, I'd already begun working on it, throwing indoors with Bob Milner, the team's second-string catcher.

This time at tryouts I practiced with the veterans, made the cut, and got a uniform. I knew I had to wait my turn behind Berman, Gartner, and Saperstein, but I hadn't counted on Andy Makrides and Steve Coan. Both were a year younger than me, and both were big and strong and threw hard. I sensed I was being passed over, but I pitched batting practice and took studious notes on opposing hitters. It was hard, but I kept my mouth shut and waited my turn. Just as I was ready to confront Kerchman, he gave me three innings in the last pre-season game. The man knew just how far he could go with me.

I knew if I didn't show him something special right then, I might never get another chance. I started out tight, my concentration was off. I walked the first man, got the next on a force play, then gave up a hard-hit double, and walked another man. I remembered Al Seidman's advice, "Keep the ball low and change your speeds," and I got through that inning and the next two without giving up a run. Even doing less than my best convinced me I could pitch at this level. What mattered was that Kerchman believed it; and I knew I'd have to wait to find that out.

I got my answer when the league season began. We had another strong team. Berman and Gartner pitched the important games, Saperstein got an occasional start, and was first man out of the bullpen. In the blowouts, Makrides and Coan always got to finish. I never even got a call to warm-up. During the bus trips home and in the locker room, everyone partied. I felt invisible. To avoid having to deal with teammates, I'd linger in the shower and wait for the cliques to leave. Then I'd dress alone, and take the bus home by myself. The few times I hung out at the State Diner with the rest of the team, I had to watch the guys preen for the cheerleaders and hold court for the crowd. And when I read the write-ups in the newspapers about our great team, I was sure I was missing out on something special, something that might never happen again. What if we won the city championship and I never got to play?

During the games I found myself silently rooting against my own team. I sat on the bench or in the bullpen and prayed that we'd get blown out, just so he'd give me a few innings. At night I dreamed up scenarios where Mr. K would be up at bat and I'd hit him in the head with a pitch. Or, I'd be at bat and I'd rip a line drive right at his nuts. There were so many days when I was mad enough to walk into his office and confront him, but I was sure that he'd order me to turn in my uniform. If I quit, I wanted it to be on my terms. With three games left, the team clinched the Queens championship. Everyone got crazy on the bus ride home, and when we arrived back at school, the cheerleaders and a crowd of screaming boosters greeted us. I slipped away as fast as I could.

Some guys can handle sitting on the bench, wearing a uniform and boasting to envious friends that they're on a winning team. Henry Koslan, the other batting-practice pitcher, had that kind of disposition. Henry went to practice every day, never got in a game, and never complained. The Koslans of the world are blessed: somehow they've learned to accept their destiny without questioning it.

Not me, though. Every time I sat and watched, I ached to participate, to contribute; I needed to be acknowledged, especially by this coach, this hard-nosed Jewish street-fighter, this man whose ethic puzzled and repulsed me. I wanted Kerchman's respect and naively I believed that if I did what Mr. K asked of me, and didn't complain or quit, eventually I'd earn his approval. Too absorbed in self-pity, I'd forgotten what I'd learned from Joe Bluetrich three years ago. Hard work didn't matter, character didn't matter, respect and approval didn't matter. In coaches' minds, the only thing that counts is winning games. But you couldn't win games if you didn't pitch. There was still enough time to earn the letter. Surely Kerchman owed me that much, didn't he?

The next game was at home and we were playing Richmond Hill, a weak team. It was a perfect opportunity for him to make it all up to me. But in front of the home crowd, in front of my friends and family, Kerchman started Henry Koslan. I was stunned, but I figured I'd get my innings later on. Before he even got an out, Koslan gave up six runs. I kept waiting for Kerchman to tell me to head for the bullpen and warm up. Instead he brought in Saperstein, then Coan, then Makrides. How could he pass me up? What was he thinking?

I sat on the bench and brooded, counting the put-outs until the game would end. In the last inning we were two runs down when he told me to warm up. I wanted to scream, "What took you so fucking long?" Instead, I threw listlessly, waiting for the end. But with two outs, we loaded the bases. A single would tie the game. Suddenly I saw myself out there pitching with the game on the line. That got my adrenaline going and I started throwing harder. I prayed for a banjo hit, a blooper, a dying quail, a nubber with eyes—anything to get me in there. But Hausig's fly ball ended the game and my dream. Next thing I knew I was standing in Kerchman's office, screaming wildly at him, tears running down my face.

He stood there in his jockstrap and undershirt and didn't say a word. When I wound down, he shook his head and said, "Not bad. I didn't think you had the balls for this." Then he let me have it.

He began to lecture me about the importance of momentum to a winning team, about morale and confidence, and how the team couldn't afford a losing streak right before the playoff. I wanted to say, "What about my goddamn morale, how about my confidence?" But in a voice I didn't recognize, I blurted out, "You don't even have to pitch me, coach. Put me in the outfield, let me bat just one time. I just want my letter."

As soon as I got the words out I knew I'd said the wrong thing. "I decide who plays and who doesn't," he snapped. And then, as if he knew he'd gone too far, he backed off. "Your day in the sun will come." His eyes narrowed and he spat out, "And you better be good and goddamn ready when it does."

I walked home in a daze, thinking about how life would be without Kerchman. No more five-hour practices and sitting on the bench, no more getting home at nine o'clock too tired to even do my homework or to hang-out at Irv's candy store with the guys. Now was the perfect time to tell him to take the uniform and stick it up his ass. But I waffled. There was only one more week to get through. Not wanting to give him the satisfaction, I told myself to stick it out until the end of the season, then put it all behind me.

I went to the last two games pretending not to care what happened. But Kerchman had one trick left. He called me in to pitch the last two innings of a tune-up game. We were winning by six runs, so there was nothing at stake. Too surprised to be nervous, I packed two seasons of frustration and rage into those innings. I bore down and concentrated like it was the last game of the World Series. I threw curve balls and sinkers, I changed speeds and mixed locations. I got all six hitters in a row, easy outs. It felt so exhilarating to be out there that I wanted those two innings to last forever. When they were over, I was so high I wanted the varsity letter more than ever. Once I got it, I could walk away from the whole thing. Clean break, nothing more to prove to him—or to myself.

As it turned out we were eliminated again in the borough finals, by the same team and same pitcher that had beat us last year. For the first time since I'd known him, Kerchman didn't yell on the trip home or make a locker-room speech. He just went into his office and shut the door. I was relieved and elated that this painful season was over; I couldn't wait to turn in my uniform and get the hell out of there. But when I passed by his office, Mr. K was still sitting in his uniform staring at the wall. I realized that it was more than just a play-off loss to him. He was losing two All-City pitchers and two All-Queens seniors from a squad that had won three straight borough championships. Next year, he'd be starting from scratch. My first impulse was to feel sorry for him.

At the banquet, the mood was subdued. Still, it was a prestigious event. Kerchman had invited the past years' Kelly Award winners to make the customary inspirational speeches. When I listened to them deliver the old rah-rah, I remembered how good it had felt to pitch those last few innings. Stevie Berman and Jack Gartner shared the Kelly Award, and Mike Hausig won *The Long Island Press* M.V.P. trophy. Next year, those guys would be gone. No matter, I'd made up my mind to pack it in.

Then Koslan received his varsity letter. That sealed it. I knew I had to be next. When Kerchman shook my hand and handed me a minor letter instead, my stomach turned over and I had to bite my lower lip hard. I don't recall a single detail from the rest of the evening. I didn't even wait for my dad or brother to take me home. For hours I wandered around the neighborhood, playing the same tape over and over in my head: "How could I have let him do this to me? Why didn't I quit when I had the chance? Why didn't I throw the letter back in his face?"

When I came out of it, I was wandering barefoot on the beach, my suit pants rolled up to my knees. I took the letter out of my jacket and scaled it like a seashell out to sea. I felt some relief when it disappeared into the black water, but that night and for three nights after that, I didn't sleep for more than a few hours at a time.

The last week of school I avoided my teammates and friends, and cut out as soon as the three o'clock bell rang. When school ended, there was no question that I was through with Kerchman.

With the pressure off, that summer I pitched better than ever. I even beat Makrides for the league championship and was a starter on an American Legion team that went all the way to the state finals. Yet every time I thought about Kerchman and the baseball banquet, the sting was still there.

The first week of the next school year I was chosen sports editor of the paper, and given my own monthly column—head-shot, byline, the whole works. When the *New York Times* and *Herald Tribune* sports desks assigned me to write up the high school football games for them, I said to myself, who needs baseball? Who needs to put up with Kerchman's horseshit?

A week after football practice started, I was working late at the paper when Kerchman phoned. "Where the goddamned hell have you been?" he rasped. "You're my head football manager. Get your ass down here!" What chutzpah the man had! I stammered that I'd made other commitments this year and I wouldn't be coming back; then I braced myself for the fall-out. All he said was, "I see," and hung up. Instead of feeling vindicated, relieved, I felt guilty, like somehow I'd undermined him. It was all I could do to fight off the impulse to call him back.

Two days later, Andy Makrides called and dropped the news on me that Henry Koslan had died of Leukemia. Kerchman had known about Koslan's condition for almost a year, but he'd promised the family he wouldn't tell anybody. Makrides said that the baseball team would be attending a memorial service the next day and Kerchman wanted me there.

Mr. K's backhanded gesture didn't compensate for what he'd done to me for two years, but it did explain a few things. After the service, I told him I'd take the job, but only if I got time off to write my column. I deliberately made no mention of baseball.

The next day Mr. K held a special squad meeting. "If any of you gives Steinberg any flak," he told the troops, "you'll answer to me." It was the first time he'd pronounced my name with the right emphasis. Momentarily I was flattered—he'd never said anything like that about Krause or any of the other student managers—but I decided to reserve my judgment.

As his second in command, I delegated all the menial jobs to the new assistants. During the season, I became a kind of silent confidant to this obsessed coach. When the other managers scurried around servicing the players, I stood next to him taking notes on a clipboard while he muttered complicated strategies to me. Though I felt a secret pride at being taken into his confidence, I was angry with myself for feeling so beholden to him.

In the early practice sessions, I noticed a change in Mr. K. He still threw temper tantrums when we lost games we should have won, and he still inflicted public punishments on players who screwed up, but I never heard him make one cruel or derogatory remark about Jews being quitters or "candy-asses." With so many of his veterans graduated, Kerchman had resigned himself to rebuilding the team. Several times that season in fact, he caught me off-guard by sending me to counsel some of the more troubled players. I wondered what he had up his sleeve.

At the banquet, he gave me the customary "See you in a few months" line, as he handed me my third useless letter. This time I wasn't going to get my hopes up. I wasn't even sure I'd try out for baseball.

Two weeks before tryouts, I was working late on my sports column when I came across an article in the *Long Island Press* sports section. It quoted Kerchman as saying, "The mainstays of my pitching staff in this rebuilding season will be my two seniors, Mike Saperstein and Mike Steinberg. Juniors Andy Makrides and Steve Coan will be the number-two and -three starters." About Mike Steinberg, he went on to say that "the right-hander will be the first man out of the bullpen, as well as an occasional starter. He has excellent control and an effective sinker, both important weapons for a relief pitcher." I read the interview over again before it finally sunk in. Two more articles spotlighting me and Saperstein soon appeared, one of them in the school paper, written by my own sports reporter. It was just too seductive. How could I pass it up? I had to at least call his hand on this one. Didn't I?

From minute one of the new season, practices were like a day at the beach. Because I was part of Kerchman's inner sanctum, all of the new players looked up to me, strangers in my classes—even some of my teachers—treated me with a respect I'd never experienced. When I sat at the State Diner jock table, girls fawned all over us. I loved it, yet part of me was waiting for the other shoe to drop.

In the pre-season games, Mr. K made sure I got to throw a few innings in every game. By the time we opened our league season, I couldn't wait to get out there and show him what I could do. In the first home game, against Wilson Vocational, Kerchman brought me in to relieve Saperstein. It was the last inning of a scoreless game, and Mike had pitched beautifully. Everyone on the bench saw he was getting tired, but when Mr. K came out to the mound, Sap did something I'd never seen before. In front of the team, fans, and school officials, he screamed, "I'm throwing a shutout here! The scouts came to see me pitch, not Steinberg!" Normally, Mr. K would can a player's ass for a lot less than that, but Sap was our best pitcher, and Kerchman needed him. Bringing me in was his only way of keeping his hot-headed ace in line.

Maybe it was because Sap's outburst had shaken me up, or because my parents, brother, and girlfriend were watching—maybe I was tight because this was my first league game. Whatever the reasons, I froze up. I threw my warm-ups in a daze. My first pitch to Fletcher Thompson, Wilson's best hitter, was a gut shot, a letter-high fast ball that he jacked out of the park. As I watched the ball disappear, I was sure Saperstein would come charging out to the mound and strangle me. That is, if Kerchman didn't beat him to it.

My cheeks burned and my shirt was soaked with flop sweat. How could I have thrown him a fast ball when I didn't even *have* a fast ball? Thinking about it tightened me up even more, and I walked the next two men on eight pitches. I looked to the bench, then to the bullpen for help. Nobody was throwing. Kerchman was going to leave me in to take a beating or to pitch my way through it. Just knowing that somehow settled me down, and I started concentrating on what I knew how to do best. Keeping the ball low and mixing my pitches, I got the next three outs. In the bottom half of the inning our first baseman, Dickie Webb, hit a home run off Thompson. The game ended in a tie, called on account of darkness. I should have been relieved at getting off the hook so easily, but it ate away at me that I'd almost blown the game. The hardest part was knowing that if I didn't get another chance to redeem myself, I'd carry my failure and shame for the rest of the season—and for who knows how much longer after that.

The next game was away, at Jamaica High. Right away, we got off to a five-run lead. But Makrides lasted only four innings before they tied it up. I looked over at Kerchman, but he'd already signaled for Coan to warm up. No surprise there; still, it felt like a razor nick. We went ahead again, but Coan couldn't hold the lead. It's a terrible thing to have to root against your own teammate, but I did, and when Jamaica got within a run of us, I began to feel a flicker of hope. In the Jamaica half of the fifth, with the score tied and the bases loaded, Kerchman motioned at me to warm up. Just before he put me in he said, "Show me you've got the guts I think you have." Then he handed me the ball. It was all I needed to hear.

Right from the start, I held my concentration and made sure I kept the ball down and away. By forcing the batters to hit ground balls, I got my three outs without giving up a run. We scored four more times and won the game, 10–6. When it was over, I'd pitched three scoreless, hitless innings. The full impact didn't register until the bus ride home, when for the first time, I joined in as we yelled and whistled and hooted out the window at the girls on the street. We loudly sang along as Dion and the Belmonts harmonized, "I Wonder Why" on the bus radio. Everyone on the team—except Saperstein—signed the winning game ball for me. That night as I walked home in the dark, it began to rain. I slid the baseball under my jacket pocket and clutched it to my chest. When I got to my block, I was soaking wet, crying hysterically, and singing "I Wonder Why" at the top of my voice.

Like most coaches who find a winning combination, Kerchman went with the same formula almost every game. He'd start Saperstein, Makrides or Coan, and in the fifth or sixth inning of close games, he'd come in with me. Usually, I got my outs, but the one time I blew a lead I couldn't study or sleep until I pitched again.

All spring it felt strange to read my name in the newspaper write-ups, sign autographs for neighborhood kids, and listen to the cheerleaders chant "Steinberg! Steinberg!" My new problem, of course, was Mike Saperstein. He hated sharing the limelight, especially with a former scrubbie. Every time I came in to relieve him, Sap took it as a personal insult. "You better not blow my game, peckerhead," he said one time. And on another occasion, "Keep it low, jerk-off. I don't want my E.R.A. getting screwed up because you can't keep the fuckin' ball in the park." But after two years of Mr. K's hazing, Mike couldn't rattle me. I was pitching well and I knew it.

With a week left, our rag-tag team was in a four-way tie for first place. The whole season came down to consecutive road games against the three other leaders. In the re-match against Wilson Vocational, Saperstein threw eleven innings of one-hit ball before he walked two men and gave up a sacrifice bunt. At that point, Kerchman brought me in. We had a 1–0 lead and they had the tying run on third, the winning run on second. With everything on the line, I had to pitch to Fletcher Thompson again. From the bench, Saperstein screamed, "Walk him, asshole!" This time, Sap was right—with first base open, it was the obvious strategy—but Mr. K didn't agree. He came out to the mound and ordered me to pitch to him.

I knew Thompson would be salivating to get another crack at me. Tease him, I told myself. Keep the ball low and away, out of his kitchen. Walk him if you have to, but don't give him anything fat to hit. On a two and one slider that was deliberately low and outside, he reached out and uppercut a soft fly ball to left field. Ira Heid dove and caught it on his shoe tops. When the runner at third tagged and headed home, Ira bounced up and threw him out at the plate. Bang-bang play. The game was over; we were still alive. When I got to the bench, Saperstein was livid, and to tell you the truth, I didn't blame him. He'd pitched an almost perfect game for twelve innings; I threw just four pitches and got the game ball—and the next day's headline.

Against Andrew Jackson High, Kerchman put me in again in the last inning of a 5–4 game. Coan was pitching with a one-run lead and they had the bases loaded and no outs. At bat was Otto Agostinelli, a six-four free-swinger who led the league in home runs and strikeouts. My favorite kind of hitter. For reasons I'll never understand, Kerchman waited until Coan went all the way down to 3–0 on Agostinelli before he yanked him and brought me in. It was an impossible situation.

"You've got a run to give, but that's all." He spat a plug of tobacco juice and slapped the ball into my glove. "Get me out of this with a tie. I just want one more at-bat."

I was sure that with a 3–0 count, even Otto would be under orders to take the first two pitches. So I threw him two strikes, both gut shots with nothing on them. I saw him grimace on the second one. He wanted that pitch back. With the count full, I had a chance. He'd seen my first two pitches and he'd be looking for another cripple right down the middle. On the 3–2 pitch, I gambled and jammed him with a sinker that should have been ball four. He swung, thank God, and tapped a weak ground ball to me. Easy force-play at home plate. One gone.

A kind of seesaw psych game goes on between a pitcher and opposing hitters. At first you've got to prove yourself to them; they're all over you, yelling stuff like "Come on, cream puff, show me what you got!" But once you get that first out, the pressure shifts, and the hitters start to tighten up. And that's just what happened. The last two outs were almost too easy. A soft line drive to second base, a grounder to third, and that was the game.

On the bus trip home I wanted to sink back in my seat and enjoy what I had just accomplished, but I didn't have that luxury. We still had to beat Van Buren. Their pitcher, Joe Sabbaritto, was the top prospect in the city, and their three and four hitters, Bill McNab and Al Schumacher, were leading the borough in hitting.

For the first three innings of the Van Buren game, Sabbaritto was throwing over ninety miles an hour. But he couldn't find the plate, and when he did, his catcher couldn't hold onto the ball. Kerchman knew that when this guy got his rhythm back, we'd never hit the ball in fair territory again. So we scratched out five runs on walks, passed balls, bunts, errors, and stolen bases. In the third inning, Sabbaritto found the groove and then he shut us down, striking out eight of the next nine hitters. He was throwing so hard his fast ball looked like an aspirin tablet as it buzzed past.

Meanwhile, Van Buren kept pecking away at the lead, and when I relieved Makrides in the sixth inning we were ahead 5–4. With two out and two men on, McNab hit a hard single to tie the score. I knew we were in trouble.

From the sixth inning on, there was a strange sense of inevitability about the game. We all felt it. There was no chatter on the bench. Even Mr. K was subdued, almost as if he, too, was hypnotized by what Sabbaritto was doing out there. We were in a tie game with the league title on the line, yet it felt like our team was ten runs down. It was weird going out there every inning and knowing that unless Sabbaritto had another sudden wild streak, we wouldn't score again. It didn't look like that was going to happen, so I decided to take it one batter at a time. I created my own private little game-within-a-game just to see how long I could make the real game last.

Mainly on adrenaline and fear, I got through six more scoreless innings. But in the bottom of the thirteenth McNab got to third on a misplayed fly ball, and on a 2–2 count, Schumacher punched a weak-ass sinker past the shortstop for the winning hit. For the last six innings I'd known it had to end this way—we all did. On the bus ride home no one said a word. One minute I was empty and sad because I'd lost the season's biggest game; the next minute I was elated because I'd pitched the seven best innings of my life.

A few days later I realized that we'd gone way beyond even Kerchman's expectations. He knew it too. So much so that at the banquet, he gave *everyone* a varsity letter. While I was chewing on that injustice, Mr. K began to recite the customary platitudes before giving out the Kelly Award. I'd heard the speech so many times that I tuned most of it out. Besides, Louie Stroller, the student manager, had leaked it to several of us that the Kelly already had Saperstein's name engraved on it.

Mike was a jerk, but he'd had a great season. We all knew he deserved the award. I looked over at him and I could read his mind: with one hand he was slipping the medal around some pretty cheerleader's neck; with his free hand he was reaching down her blouse to cop a feel. So when Kerchman announced my name and said to that roomful of people, "Mike Steinberg is a kid who's made the most out of a little bit of talent, a big heart, and a whole lot of guts," I was too stunned to move. Before I could even stand up, Sap yelled, "I don't fucking believe this!" and stormed out of the restaurant, kicking over tables and chairs as he went. I hated Sap for upstaging me again, but I admired his chutzpah. A year earlier in that same room, I'd wanted to stand up and tell Kerchman to stick it. Instead I let him sweet-talk me into playing. And now this.

I can't recall how I got to the dais, but I remember standing next to him—my thoughts scrambled, my throat so dry I couldn't swallow. Kerchman had his arm draped around my shoulder, flashbulbs were popping all around me, and everyone was standing and applauding. I squinted through tears, frantically searching the crowd for a glimpse of my dad and brother.

Last year while rummaging through an old trunk, I found the Kelly Award and a memoir my brother had written about his own high school baseball days. *In his locker room speeches,* Alan wrote, *Mr. K talked about this little Jewish relief pitcher whose uniform didn't fit and who didn't have a whole lot of talent. But the boy, he said, always seemed to be at his best under extreme pressure. In fact he'd bring this kid into impossible situations—tie game, bases loaded no outs, that kind of thing—and he'd say to him, "Son, I want you to get me two ground balls and a pop fly." And that pitcher, my brother Mike, would somehow figure out a way to get the other team to hit two ground balls and a pop fly.*

As I scanned the passage my first response was: "A typical Kerchman speech; the old psych job for the benefit of the rookies." But I was also moved by what I'd read. Some part of me knew that in his own perverse way Mr. K had given me what I had been asking for all along: a nod of acceptance from one kind of Jew to another.

Vessel of Last Resort

Jeffrey Tayler

Joseph Conrad traveled 1100 miles up the Congo River to find the heart of darkness; I was sure I had seen it at mile one. I stood on the rusty, urine-stained deck of a cargo barge watching Kinshasa, the capital of Zaire, recede into a humid gray haze. The city that from Brazzaville had looked so prosperous, with its skyscrapers and dock cranes, turned out up close to be a farrago of squalor and raucous mayhem: troops of beggars limping on pretzeled legs clogged the multilane Boulevard du 30 Juin; fires smoldered in refuse heaps alive with the ulcerous, emaciated bodies of those too weak to beg; silver Mercedes rocketed through the rubble, scattering crowds, carrying their owners to hush-hush diamond deals in posh Gombe. And outside the confines of the modern district, in the old Cité and beyond, gangs of youths armed with guns and knives patrolled slums four million strong. Someone must have gone mad here to let all this happen: if present-day Kinshasa wasn't Kurtz's "Inner Station," I didn't know what was. With our barge cabled to its bow, the white-and-blue *pousseur*, or pusher boat, headed out toward mid-river, and we were free of Kinshasa's stench. It was evening; the day's heat was abating. Ahead, toward the Equator, the sky and water dissolved into a mist of luminous azure.

Travel on the Congo, or Zaire, River has never been easy, and with the chaos prevailing in the country since 1990, when Mobutu Sese Seko, Zaire's President-for-life dictator, declared a transitional period to democracy, it has become more difficult than ever. The army, unpaid, has run amok several times, carrying out huge *pillages*; the economy has collapsed; and ONATRA, the national transportation company, has gone bankrupt, only rarely sending upriver its one functioning Congo barge—actually a floating slum of some half a dozen barges lashed to an ailing pusher boat. As a result, merchants have turned to private barges for transport and to conduct trade with the interior, where most of Zaire's 45 million people live, and where roads, if they exist at all, are truck-swallowing quagmires for most of the year. But the barges lack even the skeletal amenities (rat-infested cabins, clogged toilets, starchy food) that the ONATRA boats offered, and travel is brutally basic. For the equivalent of thirty dollars you get a space on a rusty steel deck and no more. That will have to suffice for two to six weeks of floating through some of the steamiest terrain on earth. Zairians wondered what misfortune could have driven me to take the barge, and every expatriate I met in Kinshasa said that such crafts were not for non-Zairians. "When cholera breaks out on board," an American missionary warned me, "people just die and they throw the bodies overboard." A British expat said that the last tourist to take a barge to Kisangani had arrived, but dead of malaria.

I was no old Africa hand when I arrived in Zaire, no seasoned veteran of tropical travel. In fact, I had spent the three previous years in Russia, and a desire to escape the cold and break out of the gray-bureaucracy syndrome I suffered from there had a lot to do with my thoughts' running Equatorward at every idle moment that winter. When, in February, I came upon the British explorer Henry Morton Stanley's account of his voyage down the Congo, I was mesmerized. The desire seized me, *possessed* me, to quit the northland and travel this greatest of all sub-Saharan Africa's rivers, no matter what the risks or discomforts. I was not a missionary or a naturalist, nor was I a vacationer expecting the civilized pleasures of an all-inclusive Kenyan gamepark safari; rather, I was a northerner gripped by a monomania for the primal truth of the Congo, and the only cure would be a crucible on its muddy waters.

The deck was empty save for a few crew members and a pimpled pastor from Lukolela engrossed in a Jimmy Swaggart tract. But our solitude was not to last: we were drawing toward the port at Selza, a suburb of Kinshasa, where a crowd was scrimmaging on the pier. Even before we docked, people started casting aboard foam mattresses and baskets and bales of cloth, leaping over the watery divide onto our deck. Gendarmes thrashed at the crowd with rope whips, but in vain: by the time we moored, every inch was occupied. Tinny Zairian pop blared forth from the barge's loudspeakers. The floating river fête had begun.

The owner, Nguma, had taken pity on me and assigned me a crew member's cabin; but with a loudspeaker over the door and no windows, it turned out to be a noisy oven. I gathered up my mosquito net and sheets and billeted myself in solitude above the bridge on the *pousseur*. Feeling nauseated with shock from the crowds, the heat, and the excitement of the trip, I lay down on my foam mattress and peered through the gauze at the stars, thinking back on the history of this enormous river, the second longest in Africa. Stanley had fought his way down it from Nyangwe in 1876 and 1877, losing many of the members of his expedition to disease, to drowning, and to battles with the tribes that live on the middle and upper banks even today. My trip, tame as it was by comparison, still seemed an impossible feat: this cramped floating crate of steel had to chug up 1100 miles of jungle river. If I got sick, if *anyone* got sick, if we broke down, there was nothing to be done about it but hope that Providence, so clearly unmoved by the tableau of mass suffering in Zaire, might decide to make a gesture of divine benevolence toward us. Many merchants, I was to learn, had had friends die on the river, from cholera or malaria or other, nameless fevers—a fate I hoped to avoid with half a dozen vaccines and a satchel stuffed full of Nivaquine and Paludrine pills, the malaria prophylaxes commonly prescribed in Zaire. The commencement of every voyage up the Congo was thus attended by fervent prayers for Godspeed, by whispered supplications to fetishes, by wailing farewells from relatives on shore. Our voyage was no exception. No one was certain who would arrive alive in Kisangani.

Dawn found us coursing past grassy flatland marked here and there by trees whose majestic canopies spread like giant green mushroom caps. I climbed down the ladder from the upper deck.

"Would you like to bathe?" asked Jean, the lean, neat, green-eyed chief accountant. "My room has the only bath on the barge."

He led me around the *pousseur* and through his quarters to the "bathroom"—a slimy metallic cubicle with a hole in the floor—and handed me a bucket filled with unctuous green water, bath-warm with a frothy head, drawn as it was straight from the Congo's hot currents. As I scrubbed and rinsed with it, I had the sensation that it was an organic fluid. It felt viscous, sebaceous; I seemed to be bathing in plasma. It stung my eyes, and I wondered how river blindness was transmitted (not like this, it turns out).

Everywhere on deck straw mats lay strewn with bolts of cloth, sacks of sugar and salt, malaria pills in white boxes, batteries, needles and thread and scissors, cookie tins, Bic pens, school notebooks with green covers. The merchants—who were the majority of the barge's passengers—laughed and bantered among themselves in Lingala, the language most widely spoken along the river, interrupting their discourse to shout, "*Ey, mondele* ["white man"]! *Bonjour!*" as I walked by. Mothers scrubbed down two-year-olds, skillets sizzled with onions and chunks of fish in palm oil, thump-thump-thumps resounded as women in rainbow robes pounded plantains into mash with carved mallets. A congregation led by the pastor from Lukolela chanted Lingala spirituals at the stern.

I chatted, in French, as I walked around. Among the merchants there were high hopes for the income this voyage might bring, as well as fear. A twenty-five-year-old man originally from Bandundu said to me, "I was a tailor in Kin, but when the *pillages* began, in 1991, I lost my business, so I took to the barges. I have a fiancée—she'll leave me if I can't buy her dresses and jewelry. So here I am, risking this voyage. People get diarrhea and dysentery on these trips, and sometimes the boats sink. Man proposes, but God disposes."

Those who have taken to the barges confront head-on the timeless, primal phenomena of sun, rain, wind, and heat, and engage in a pattern of trade millennia old. All day they sell their basically urban merchandise to villagers paddling up in dugout canoes, immediately using their profits to buy the manioc root, smoked fish, monkey, crocodile, and antelope offered by these same villagers. The merchants then hawk these foodstuffs in the huge markets of Kisangani after the ascent of the river or Kinshasa after the descent. Even crew members stockpile smoked fish or monkey for their families at home. Everyone aboard becomes a *débrouillard*—a master at getting by—or doesn't last.

Day three found us amid whitecapped waters and buffeting winds. We chugged ahead into rushing rafts of water hyacinth, through the part of the river known as le Chenal, a narrow strait paralleled by low mountains. The sky was lowering and iron-gray, with lightning flickering from the Equator ahead. No pirogues came out to meet us; villages were few. But the first signs of a great jungle were appearing: on ridges stood massive, broad-boughed trees, and the savanna's underbrush gathered into higher and denser clumps.

The next day began with a flurry of shouts in rainy fog. Loaded with pineapples and manioc tubers, pirogues in V-shaped formations of three and four were shooting toward us through the mizzle and docking at our sides. I stood at the railing composing shots on my Nikon.

"*Nina! Nina!*" someone shouted. "*Nina!*" An excited murmur arose on deck. A man with "*Nina*" on his lips forced his way through the crowd and hurled himself overboard, just missing a pirogue. Thirty feet from the barge floated a fish the size of an inner tube, dead and belly-up in the choppy gray waters.

"An electric catfish, a *nina!*" a boy next to me shouted. "What a prize! It will bring him ten dollars." But the man missed it, it floated past, and then the drama for those on deck became whether he could catch up with the barge again. He thrashed the water in a sloppy crawl, landing near the *pousseur* at the stern, and hoisted himself aboard. A hero for the entertainment he had provided, he raised his arms to general applause.

The heat in the Kinshasa region had been bearable, but my travel mates warned me that after Bolobo, which we had just passed, the climate would turn equatorial. The next dawn dragonflies and fat, sluggish moths covered my mosquito net. The river had become a sheet of glass spreading to infinity around us, overhung by a suffocating mist; the air had turned heavy, gone sour with tropical rot. No banks were visible, although the occasional island—a ragged outcropping of black tree silhouettes—drifted by in the steam. Noon brought white heat and steely white light; the Congo became a lifeless, utterly still lake of glare, ten miles wide, all colors reduced to black and gray against the white of water and sky. The barge's surfaces became untouchably hot, and shade diminished as the incandescent ball of the sun rose directly overhead. The merchants erected tarps up and down the deck and lay prostrate under them, torpid with the heat.

Dusk came. We were a spearhead slicing into an azure river-and-sky melange, seemingly released from the bounds of earth, floating in a blue domain. Astern, to the west, the river was bankless, tinctured lilac, bleeding red, running into cool purple with the sun's descent.

Recovered from the day's heat, I sat under the light behind the owner's cabin trying to read V. S. Naipaul, a futile endeavor given the moths and cicadas swirling around me. Then something golf-ball-sized slammed into my temple. I looked down and saw a huge armored beetle writhing at my feet. Djili, the freight manager, came over and picked it up. "We eat these beetles, you know. Come over and answer a few questions." He led me to a circle of palm-wine drinkers at the bow. Marijuana, called *bangi* in Lingala, was being smoked on the deck, and its pungently sweet aroma perfumed the air. The drinkers were chasing their wine with fat white fried palm grubs that they selected from a bowl at their feet.

"Your country is supposed to stand for human rights, but what about the rights of a man?" Djili asked, biting off the head of a grub and chewing it lustily a few inches from my face. "Have a grub. I hear that your government would forbid me to have more than one wife. I should be able to have as many wives as I choose—that's my right as a man. But your government would forbid it. *C'est pas juste.*"

Fearfully tasting my grub, and finding it chewy and squirting hot palm oil, I muttered something about polygamy being un-Christian, but this only provoked a tirade. *I am eating a larva,* I said to myself.

"Un-Christian? Polygamy goes back to Jesus' day! It's your government that's unchristian, allowing pornography in the streets and forbidding me my basic rights as a man! Here, try a caterpillar." Djili held out a bowl of the brown squirming things. Still inwardly reeling from the grub, I had to refuse, but a little girl, looking at me wide-eyed, took one of the living creatures and chomped it to pieces, swallowing it with a gulp. We talked, or I should say Djili raved, until night fell and the mosquitoes drove me off the bow.

The ninth day found us hugging the bank close to the great jungle, a tangled mass of green lucent in its nearest reaches with sunlight pouring in from above, but dark and gloomy farther in. Occasionally a monkey would scream and bound branch to branch back into the trees, or red-and-gray parrots would squawk and take flight. Huge, gangly birds that the locals call *kulokoko* screeched at the sight of us, like pterodactyls horrified to discover men trespassing in their prehistoric domain, and *wuff-wuffed* away in heavy-winged flight. Once, I caught sight of a cobra, some fifteen feet long and black, swimming along the hyacinth, its emblematic curved head and neck slicing the coffee-brown water. We were deep in the midst of an Africa many would have thought vanished centuries ago, an Africa as eternal as the dugout canoes and the blood-red sunsets.

One day a villager paddled up with a five-foot-long live crocodile, its jaws roped shut, in the bottom of his pirogue; it was bought by Maurice, a merchant from Kinshasa. "I'll smoke this and sell it," he said. "It'll pay for my return ticket." He and the villager struggled to get the thrashing black reptile out of the pirogue without receiving a blow from its tail or dropping it into the water; several bystanders helped, but the croc still whacked one boy in the face with its tail. When they had dragged it away from the edge of the deck, Maurice took to pounding in its skull with the handle of a machete until it ceased struggling, its emerald eyes slit with black and staring fiercely, even in death.

At night the specters of great trees loomed black against the Milky Way's lustrous wash of stardust. With our spotlight probing the waters in front of us, searching for shoals, illuminating swirling beetles and crow-sized bats, with mosquitoes showing like a fine mist in their millions, we threaded our way through a dark labyrinth of isles. Drumbeats announcing our arrival resounded from villages ahead; 700 miles into the jungle we were still beset by pirogues, many carrying stacks of monkey carcasses, blackened, their eyes and mouths wide open as if they had been smoked alive in stark terror. Some paddlers were bare-breasted women, others men in loincloths. Once we ran over a pirogue, occasioning loss of property but not of life: its occupants jumped free in time. All night there were shouts, drumbeats, armadas of canoes laden with bush meat streaming toward us.

Late the next evening I was watching a dispute between the barge's security chief, Augustin, and a couple of drunken fishermen when the barge lurched. I grabbed the rail; others fell flailing into their merchandise. The engine sputtered, and crew members raced toward the *pousseur*, jumping over cooking pots and sacks of salt. The engine roared, coughed. Behind the propellers the spotlight showed fulminating clouds of sand in the water. We had run aground so violently that one of our two rudders had been severed and an engine incapacitated.

I was exhausted. Almost three weeks of heat and crowd and hassle on the barge seemed to have drained the life out of me. Nze, the chief mechanic, said that this was a serious accident that could delay us by three days at least. We were already a week late. I wanted to scream. To the south, over the forest, lightning flared silently at first, and then with rumbles of thunder. We sat still, with the Congo's warm fluids rushing past our motionless bow in a rippling V.

In despair I retired to my spot above the bridge. A full moon hung over the silhouettes of trees on the distant bank and dappled the waters below with its orange glow. Nevertheless rain came that night, soft and slight in the beginning, and then hot, copious, and pummeling. I gathered up my net and retreated to the awning under the bridge. Until dawn I watched the lightning flare up and show the vast river around us. I shuddered at the crash of thunderbolts that seemed aimed at our craft on the open water.

After a long repair session on a sandbar the next morning, during which the mechanics detached the broken rudder and then placed the good rudder next to the engine that worked, we started up again and moved on toward the blackclouded horizon, past five-story-tall broad-canopied trees guarding the entrance to the jungle like jealous sentinels.

At noon we began drawing near a stretch of sandy shore. Villagers, mainly young men in rags, came whooping and hollering out of their huts. They leaped into their pirogues and paddled furiously toward us. Augustin whistled in alarm. The owner emerged onto the bridge platform bearing an automatic rifle. The villagers let loose what sounded like a war cry, and Augustin yelled to them not to dock, but some tried anyway. At this the owner brandished his rifle and began firing shots into the air, and the villagers abandoned the barge, with one pirogue capsizing in our violent, single-engine wake.

"It is dangerous here," the owner said. "These people are cannibals. They will see you and say, 'Ah, the flesh of the *mondele* is like sugar!" He laughed uproariously. "This is a dangerous area for robbers and murderers. The deep jungle is wild in people as well as beasts."

A boy on the bank made a motion with his arms as if machine-gunning me, and soon all his little pals imitated him. Desi, a merchant from Lokutu, turned to me. "You see, they fear you, the *mondele*," he said. "White people to them are murderers, villains. The children hear how the Belgians used to eat little boys and girls, and they think you, any white, is a Belgian. For them to kill you would be an act of self-defense."

Eleven hundred miles and twenty-one days after leaving Kinshasa we pulled into Kisangani, in the very heart of equatorial Africa. The merchants, though they complained that business had been bad on this run and that they would barely break even, laughed and shouted jokes to one another as they struggled to haul their smoked fish and bush meat to the huge market. Here Conrad's Marlow alighted to find a spiritually diseased and languishing Kurtz, but here I was to disembark into mainstream modern African life, with no ceremony, no commentary ready to deliver on the malaise of twentieth-century humanity's soul. Dazed with fatigue, disoriented, I followed the merchants off the barge and began making my way up toward the dusty main street, with its placarded hotels and diamond traders, with the bells of the city's broad white cathedral chiming over the din of the crowds.

Seven Wonders

Lewis Thomas

A while ago I received a letter from a magazine editor inviting me to join six other people at dinner to make a list of the Seven Wonders of the Modern World, to replace the seven old, out-of-date Wonders. I replied that I couldn't manage it, not on short order anyway, but still the question keeps hanging around in the lobby of my mind. I had to look up the old biodegradable Wonders, the Hanging Gardens of Babylon and all the rest, and then I had to look up that word "wonder" to make sure I understood what it meant. It occurred to me that if the magazine could get any seven people to agree on a list of any such seven things you'd have the modern Seven Wonders right there at the dinner table.

Wonder is a word to wonder about. It contains a mixture of messages: something marvelous and miraculous, surprising, raising unanswerable questions about itself, making the observer wonder, even raising skeptical questions like, "I *wonder* about that." Miraculous and marvelous are clues; both words come from an ancient Indo-European root meaning simply to smile or to laugh. Anything wonderful is something to smile in the presence of, in admiration (which, by the way, comes from the same root, along with, of all telling words, "mirror").

I decided to try making a list, not for the magazine's dinner party but for this occasion: seven things I wonder about the most.

I shall hold the first for the last, and move along.

My Number Two Wonder is a bacterial species never seen on the face of the earth until 1982, creatures never dreamed of before, living violation of what we used to regard as the laws of nature, things literally straight out of Hell. Or anyway what we used to think of as Hell, the hot unlivable interior of the earth. Such regions have recently come into scientific view from the research submarines designed to descend twenty-five hundred meters or more to the edge of deep holes in the sea bottom, where open vents spew superheated seawater in plumes from chimneys in the earth's crust, known to oceanographic scientists as "black smokers." This is not just hot water, or steam, or even steam under pressure as exists in a laboratory autoclave (which we have relied upon for decades as the surest way to destroy all microbial life). This is extremely hot water under extremely high pressure, with temperatures in excess of 300 degrees centigrade. At such heat, the existence of life as we know it would be simply inconceivable. Proteins and DNA would fall apart, enzymes would melt away, anything alive would die instantaneously. We have long since ruled out the possibility of life on Venus because of that planet's comparable temperature; we have ruled out the possibility of life in the earliest years of this planet, four billion or so years ago, on the same ground.

B. J. A. Baross and J. W. Deming have recently discovered the presence of thriving colonies of bacteria in water fished directly from these deep-sea vents. Moreover, when brought to the surface, encased in titanium syringes and seated in pressurized chambers heated to 250 degrees centigrade, the bacteria not only survive but reproduce themselves enthusiastically. They can be killed only by chilling them down in boiling water.

And yet they look just like ordinary bacteria. Under the electron microscope they have the same essential structure—cell walls, ribosomes, and all. If they were, as is now being suggested, the original archebacteria, ancestors of us all, how did they or their progeny ever learn to cool down? I cannot think of a more wonderful trick.

My Number Three Wonder is *oncideres*, a species of beetle encountered by a pathologist friend of mine who lives in Houston and has a lot of mimosa trees in his backyard. This beetle is not new, but it qualifies as a Modern Wonder because of the exceedingly modern questions raised for evolutionary biologists about the three consecutive things on the mind of the female of the species. Her first thought is for a mimosa tree, which she finds and climbs, ignoring all other kinds of trees in the vicinity. Her second thought is for the laying of eggs, which she does by crawling out on a limb, cutting a longitudinal slit with her mandible and depositing her eggs beneath the slit. Her third and last thought concerns the welfare of her offspring; beetle larvae cannot survive in live wood, so she backs up a foot or so and cuts a neat circular girdle all around the limb, through the bark and down into the cambium. It takes her eight hours to finish this cabinetwork. Then she leaves and where she goes I do not know. The limb dies from the girdling, falls to the ground in the next breeze, the larvae feed and grow into the next generation, and the questions lie there unanswered. How on earth did these three linked thoughts in her mind evolve together in evolution? How could any one of the three become fixed as beetle behavior by itself, without the other two? What are the odds favoring three totally separate bits of behavior—liking a particular tree, cutting a slit for eggs, and then girdling the limb—happening together by random chance among a beetle's genes? Does this smart beetle know what she is doing? And how did the mimosa tree enter the picture in its evolution? Left to themselves, unpruned, mimosa trees have a life expectancy of twenty-five to thirty years. Pruned each year, which is what the beetle's girdling labor accomplishes, the tree can flourish for a century. The mimosa-beetle relationship is an elegant example of symbiotic partnership, a phenomenon now recognized as pervasive in nature. It is good for us to have around on our intellectual mantelpiece such creatures as this insect and its friend the tree, for they keep reminding us how little we know about nature.

The Fourth Wonder on my list is an infectious agent known as the scrapie virus, which causes a fatal disease of the brain in sheep, goats, and several laboratory animals. A close cousin of scrapie is the C-J virus, the cause of some cases of senile dementia in human beings. These are called "slow viruses," for the excellent reason that an animal exposed to infection today will not become ill until a year and a half or two years from today. The agent, whatever it is, can propagate itself in abundance from a few infectious units today to more than a billion next year. I use the phrase "whatever it is" advisedly. Nobody has yet been able to find any DNA or RNA in the scrapie or C-J viruses. It may be there, but if so it exists in amounts too small to detect. Meanwhile, there is plenty of protein, leading to a serious proposal that the virus may indeed be *all* protein. But protein, so far as we know, does not replicate itself all by itself, not on this planet anyway. Looked at this way, the scrapie agent seems the strangest thing in all biology and, until someone in some laboratory figures out what it is, a candidate for Modern Wonder.

My Fifth Wonder is the olfactory receptor cell, located in the epithelial tissue high in the nose, sniffing the air for clues to the environment, the fragrance of friends, the smell of leaf smoke, breakfast, nighttime and bedtime, and a rose, even, it is said, the odor of sanctity. The cell that does all these things, firing off urgent messages into the deepest parts of the brain, switching on one strange unaccountable memory after another, is itself a proper brain cell, a certified neuron belonging to the brain but miles away out in the open air, nosing around the world. How it manages to make sense of what it senses, discriminating between jasmine and anything else non-jasmine with infallibility, is one of the deep secrets of neurobiology. This would be wonder enough, but there is more. This population of brain cells, unlike any other neurons of the vertebrate central nervous system, turns itself over every few weeks; cells wear out, die, and are replaced by brand-new cells rewired to the same deep centers miles back in the brain, sensing and remembering the same wonderful smells. If and when we reach an understanding of these cells and their functions, including the moods and whims under their governance, we will know a lot more about the mind than we do now, a world away.

Sixth on my list is, I hesitate to say, another insect, the termite. This time, though, it is not the single insect that is the Wonder, it is the collectivity. There is nothing at all wonderful about a single, solitary termite, indeed there is really no such creature, functionally speaking, as a lone termite, any more than we can imagine a genuinely solitary human being; no such thing. Two or three termites gathered together on a dish are not much better; they may move about and touch each other nervously, but nothing happens. But keep adding more termites until they reach a critical mass, and then the miracle begins. As though they had suddenly received a piece of extraordinary news, they organize in platoons and begin stacking up pellets to precisely the right height, then turning the arches to connect the columns, constructing the cathedral and its chambers in which the colony will live out its life for the decades ahead, air-conditioned and humidity-controlled, following the chemical blueprint coded in their genes, flawlessly, stoneblind. They are not the dense mass of individual insects they appear to be; they are an organism, a thoughtful, meditative brain on a legs. All we really know about this new thing is that it does its architecture and 'ring by a complex system of chemical signals.

ne Seventh Wonder of the modern world is a human child, any child. I used to wonder about childhood and the evolution of our species. It seemed to me unparsimonious to keep expending all that energy on such a long period of vulnerability and defenselessness, with nothing to show for it, in biological terms, beyond the feckless, irresponsible pleasure of childhood. After all, I used to think, it is one sixth of a whole human life span! Why didn't our evolution take care of that, allowing us to jump cat-like from our juvenile to our adult (and, as I thought) productive stage of life? I had forgotten about language, the single human trait that marks us out as specifically human, the property that enables our survival as the most compulsively, biologically, obsessively social of all creatures on earth, more interdependent and interconnected even than the famous social insects. I had forgotten that, and forgotten that children *do* that in childhood. Language is what childhood is for.

There is another related but different creature, nothing like so wonderful as a human child, nothing like so hopeful, something to worry about all day and all night. It is *us*, aggregated together in our collective, critical masses. So far, we have learned how to be useful to each other only when we collect in small groups—families, circles of friends, once in a while (although still rarely) committees. The drive to be useful is encoded in our genes. But when we gather in very large numbers, as in the modern nation-state, we seem capable of levels of folly and self-destruction to be found nowhere else in all of Nature.

As a species, taking all in all, we are still too young, too juvenile, to be trusted. We have spread across the face of the earth in just a few thousand years, no time at all as evolution clocks time, covering all livable parts of the planet, endangering other forms of life, and now threatening ourselves. As a species, we have everything in the world to learn about living, but we may be running out of time. Provisionally, but only provisionally, we are a Wonder.

And now the first on my list, the one I put off at the beginning of making a list, the first of all Wonders of the modern world. To name this one, you have to redefine the world as it has indeed been redefined in this most scientific of all centuries. We named the place we live in the *world* long ago, from the Indo-European root *wiros*, which meant man. We now live in the whole universe, that stupefying piece of expanding geometry. Our suburbs are the local solar system, into which, sooner or later, we will spread life, and then, likely, beyond into the galaxy. Of all celestial bodies within reach or view, as far as we can see, out to the edge, the most wonderful and marvelous and mysterious is turning out to be our own planet earth. There is nothing to match it anywhere, not yet anyway.

It is a living system, an immense organism, still developing, regulating itself, making its own oxygen, maintaining its own temperature, keeping all its infinite living parts connected and interdependent, including us. It is the strangest of all places, and there is everything in the world to learn about it. It can keep us awake and jubilant with questions for millennia ahead, if we can learn not to meddle and not to destroy. Our great hope is in being such a young species, thinking in language only a short while, still learning, still growing up.

We are not like the social insects. They have only the one way of doing things and they will do it forever, coded for that way. We are coded differently, not just for binary choices, *go* or *no-go*. We can go four ways at once, depending on how the air feels: *go, no-go,* but also *maybe,* plus *what the hell let's give it a try.* We are in for one surprise after another if we keep at it and keep alive. We can build structures for human society never seen before, thoughts never thought before, music never heard before.

Provided we do not kill ourselves off, and provided we can connect ourselves by the affection and respect for which I believe our genes are also coded, there is no end to what we might do on or off this planet.

At this early stage in our evolution, now through our infancy and into our childhood and then, with luck, our growing up, what our species needs most of all, right now, is simply a future.

At the Buffalo Bill Museum, June 1988

Jane Tompkins

The video at the entrance to the Buffalo Bill Historical Center says that Buffalo Bill was the most famous American of his time, that by 1900 more than a billion words had been written about him, and that he had a progressive vision of the West. Buffalo Bill had worked as a cattle driver, a wagoneer, a Pony Express rider, a buffalo hunter for the railroad, a hunting guide, an army scout and sometime Indian fighter; he wrote dime novels about himself and an autobiography by the age of thirty-four, by which time he was already famous; and then he began another set of careers, first as an actor, performing on the urban stage in wintertime melodramatic representations of what he actually earned a living at in the summer (scouting and leading hunting expeditions), and finally becoming the impresario of his great Wild West show, a form of entertainment he invented and carried on as actor, director, and all-around idea man for thirty years. Toward the end of his life he founded the town of Cody, Wyoming, to which he gave, among other things, two hundred thousand dollars. Strangely enough, it was as a progressive civic leader that Bill Cody wanted to be remembered. "I don't want to die," the video at the entrance quotes him as saying, "and have people say—oh, there goes another old showman.... I would like people to say—this is the man who opened Wyoming to the best of civilization."

"The best of civilization." This was the phrase that rang in my head as I moved through the museum, which is one of the most disturbing places I have ever visited. It is also a wonderful place. It is four museums in one: the Whitney Gallery of Western Art, which houses artworks on Western subjects; the Buffalo Bill Museum proper, which memorializes Cody's life; the Plains Indian Museum, which exhibits artifacts of American Indian civilization; and the Winchester Arms Museum, a collection of firearms historically considered.

The whole operation is extremely well designed and well run, from the video program at the entrance that gives an overview of all four museums, to the fresh-faced young attendants wearing badges that say "Ask Me," to the museum shop stacked with books on Western Americana, to the ladies room—a haven of satiny marble, shining mirrors, and flattering light. Among other things, the museum is admirable for its effort to combat prevailing stereotypes about the "winning of the West," a phrase it self-consciously places in quotation marks. There are placards declaring that all history is a matter of interpretation, and that the American West is a source of myth. Everywhere, except perhaps in the Winchester Arms Museum, where the rhetoric is different, you feel the effort of the museum staff to reach out to the public, to be clear, to be accurate, to be fair, not to condescend—in short, to educate in the best sense of the term.

On the day I went, the museum was featuring an exhibition of Frederic Remington's works. Two facts about Remington make his work different from that of artists usually encountered in museums. The first is that Remington's paintings and statues function as a historical record. Their chief attraction has always been that they transcribe scenes and events that have vanished from the earth. The second fact, related to this, is the brutality of their subject matter. Remington's work makes you pay attention to what is happening in the painting or the piece of statuary. When you look at his work you cannot escape from the subject.

Consequently, as I moved through the exhibit, the wild contortions of the bucking broncos, the sinister expression invariably worn by the Indians, and the killing of animals and men made the placards discussing Remington's use of the "lost wax" process seem strangely disconnected. In the face of unusual violence, or implied violence, their message was: what is important here is technique. Except in the case of paintings showing the battle of San Juan Hill, where white Americans were being killed, the material accompanying Remington's works did not refer to the subject matter of the paintings and statues themselves. Nevertheless, an undertone of disquiet ran beneath the explanations; at least I thought I detected one. Someone had taken the trouble to ferret out Remington's statement of horror at the slaughter on San Juan Hill; someone had also excerpted the judgment of art critics commending Remington for the lyricism, interiority, and mystery of his later canvasses—pointing obliquely to the fascination with bloodshed that preoccupied his earlier work.

The uneasiness of the commentary, and my uneasiness with it, were nothing compared to the blatant contradictions in the paintings themselves. A pastel palette, a sunlit stop-action haze, murderous movement arrested under a lazy sky, flattened onto canvas and fixed in azure and ochre—two opposed impulses nestle here momentarily. The tension that keeps them from splitting apart is what holds the viewer's gaze.

The most excruciating example of what I mean occurs in the first painting in the exhibit. Entitled *His First Lesson*, it shows a horse standing saddled but riderless, the white of the horse's eye signaling his fear. A man using an instrument to tighten the horse's girth, at arm's length, backs away from the reaction he clearly anticipates, while the man who holds the horse's halter is doing the same. But what can they be afraid of? For the horse's right rear leg is tied a foot off the ground by a rope that is also tied around his neck. He can't move. That is the whole point.

His First Lesson. Whose? And what lesson, exactly? How to stand still when terrified? How not to break away when they come at you with strange instruments? How to be obedient? How to behave? It is impossible not to imagine that Remington's obsession with physical cruelty had roots somewhere in his own experience. Why else, in statue after statue, is the horse rebelling? The bucking bronco, symbol of the state of Wyoming, on every licence plate, on every sign for every bar, on every belt buckle, mug, and decal—this image Remington cast in bronze over and over again. There is a wild diabolism in the bronzes; the horse and rider seem one thing, not so much rider and ridden as a single bolt of energy gone crazy and caught somehow, complicatedly, in a piece of metal.

In the paintings, it is different—more subtle and bizarre. The cavalry on its way to a massacre, sweetly limned, softly tinted, poetically seized in mid-career, and gently laid on the two-dimensional surface. There is about these paintings of military men in the course of performing their deadly duty an almost maternal tenderness. The idealization of the cavalrymen in their dusty uniforms on their gallant horses has nothing to do with patriotism; it is pure love.

Remington's paintings and statues, as shown in this exhibition, embody everything that was objectionable about his era in American history. They are imperialist and racist; they glorify war and the torture and killing of animals; there are no women in them anywhere. Never the West as garden, never as pastoral, never as home. But in their aestheticization of violent life, Remington's pictures speak (to me, at least) of some other desire. The maternal tenderness is not an accident, nor is the beauty of the afternoons or the warmth of the desert sun. In them Remington plays the part of the preserver, as if by catching the figures in color and line he could save their lives and absorb some of that life into himself.

In one painting that particularly repulsed and drew me, a moose is outlined against the evening sky at the brink of a lake. He looks expectantly into the distance. Behind him and to one side, hidden from his view and only just revealed to ours, for it is dark there, is a hunter poised in the back of a canoe, rifle perfectly aimed. We look closer; the title of the picture is *Coming to the Call*. Ah, now we see. This is a sadistic scene. The hunter has lured the moose to his death. But wait a moment. Isn't the sadism really directed at us? First we see the glory of the animal; Remington has made it as noble as he knows how. Then we see what is going to happen. The hunter is one up on the moose, but Remington is one up on us. He makes us feel the pain of the anticipated killing, and makes us want to hold it off, to preserve the moose, just as he has done. Which way does the painting cut? Does it go against the hunter—who represents us, after all—or does it go against the moose who came to the call? Who came, to what call? Did Remington come to the West in response to it—to whatever the moose represents or to whatever the desire to kill the moose represents? But he hasn't killed it; he has only preserved an image of a white man about to kill it. And what call do we answer when we look at this painting? Who is calling whom? What is being preserved here?

That last question is the one that for me hung over the whole museum.

The Whitney Gallery is an art museum proper. Its allegiance is to art as academic tradition has defined it. In this tradition, we come to understand a painting by having in our possession various bits of information. Something about the technical process used to produce it (pastels, watercolors, woodblock prints, etc.); something about the elements of composition (line and color and movement); something about the artist's life (where born, how educated, by whom influenced, which school belonged to or revolted against); something about the artist's relation to this particular subject, such as how many times the artist painted it or whether it contains a favorite model. Occasionally there will be some philosophizing about the themes or ideas the paintings are said to represent.

The problem is, when you're faced with a painter like Remington, these bits of information, while nice to have, don't explain what is there in front of you. They don't begin to give you an account of why a person should have depicted such things. The experience of a lack of fit between the explanatory material and what is there on the wall is one I've had before in museums, when, standing in front of a painting or a piece of statuary, I've felt a huge gap between the information on the little placard and what it is I'm seeing. I realize that works of art, so-called, all have a subject matter, are all engaged with life, with some piece of life no less significant, no less compelling than Remington's subjects are, if we could only see its force. The idea that art is somehow separate from history, that it somehow occupies a space that is not the same as the space of life, seems out of whack here.

I wandered through the gallery thinking these things because right next to it, indeed all around it, in the Buffalo Bill Museum proper and in the Plains Indian Museum, are artifacts that stand not for someone's expertise or skill in manipulating the elements of an artistic medium, but for life itself, they are the residue of life.

The Buffalo Bill Museum is a wonderful array of textures, colors, shapes, sizes, forms. The fuzzy brown bulk of a buffalo's hump, the sparkling diamonds in a stickpin, the brilliant colors of the posters—the mixture makes you want to walk in and be surrounded by it, as if you were going into a child's adventure story. For a moment you can pretend you're a cowboy too; it's a museum where fantasy can take over. For a while.

As I moved through the exhibition, with the phrase "the best of civilization" ringing in my head, I came upon certain objects displayed in a section that recreates rooms from Cody's house. Ostrich feather fans, peacock feather fans, antler furniture—a chair and a table made entirely of antlers—a bearskin rug. And then I saw the heads on the wall: Alaska Yukon Moose, Wapiti American Elk, Muskox (the "Whitney," the "DeRham"), Mountain Caribou (the "Hyland"), Quebec Labrador Caribou (the "Elbow"), Rocky Mountain Goat (the "Haase," the "Kilto"), Woodland Caribou (world's record, "DeRham"), the "Rogers" freak Wapiti, the "Whitney" bison, the "Lord Rundlesham" bison. The names that appear after the animals are the names of the men who killed them. Each of the animals is scored according to measurements devised by the Boone and Crockett Club, a big-game hunters' organization. The Lord Rundlesham bison, for example, scores 124⁶/₈, making it number 25 in the world for bison trophies. The "Reed" Alaska Yukon Moose scores 247. The "Witherbee" Canada moose holds the world's record.

Next to the wall of trophies is a small enclosure where jewelry is displayed. A buffalo head stickpin and two buffalo head rings, the heads made entirely of diamonds, with ruby eyes, the gifts of the Russian crown prince. A gold and diamond stickpin from Edward VII; a gold, diamond, and garnet locket from Queen Victoria. The two kinds of trophies—animals and jewels—form an incongruous set; the relationship between them compelling but obscure.

If the rest of the items in the museum—the dime novels with their outrageous covers, the marvelous posters, the furniture, his wife's dress, his daughter's oil painting—have faded from my mind it is because I cannot forget the heads of the animals as they stared down, each with an individual expression on its face. When I think about it I realize that I don't know why these animal heads are there. Buffalo Bill didn't kill them; perhaps they were gifts from the famous people he took on hunts. A different kind of jewelry.

After the heads, I began to notice something about the whole exhibition. In one display, doghide chaps, calfskin chaps, angora goathide chaps, and horsehide chaps. Next to these a rawhide lariat and a horsehair quirt. Behind me, boots and saddles, all of leather. Everywhere I looked there was tooth or bone, skin or fur, hide or hair, or the animal itself entire—two full-size buffalo (a main feature of the exhibition) and a magnificent stone sheep (a mountain sheep with beautiful curving horns). This one was another world's record. The best of civilization.

In the literature about Buffalo Bill you read that he was a conservationist, that if it were not for the buffalo in his Wild West shows the species would probably have become extinct. (In the seventeenth century 40 million buffalo roamed North America; by 1900 all the wild buffalo had been killed except for one herd in northern Alberta.) That the man who gained fame first as a buffalo hunter should have been an advocate for conservation of the buffalo is not an anomaly but typical of the period. The men who did the most to preserve America's natural wilderness and its wildlife were big-game hunters. The Boone and Crockett Club, founded by Theodore Roosevelt, George Bird Grinnell, and Owen Wister, turns out to have been one of the earliest organizations to devote itself to environmental protection in the United States. *The Reader's Encyclopedia of the American West* says that the club "supported the national park and forest reserve movement, helped create a system of national wildlife refuges, and lobbied for the protection of threatened species, such as the buffalo and antelope." At the same time, the prerequisites for membership in the club were "the highest caliber of sportsmanship and the achievement of killing 'in fair chase' trophy specimens [which had to be adult males] from several species of North American big game."

The combination big-game hunter and conservationist suggests that these men had no interest in preserving the animals for the animals' sake but simply wanted to ensure the chance to exercise their sporting pleasure. But I think this view is too simple; something further is involved here. The men who hunted game animals had a kind of love for them and a kind of love for nature that led them to want to preserve the animals they also desired to kill. That is, the desire to kill the animals was in some way related to a desire to see them live. It is not an accident, in this connection, that Roosevelt, Wister, and Remington all went west originally for their health. Their devotion to the West, their connection to it, their love for it are rooted in their need to reanimate their own lives. The preservation of nature, in other words, becomes for them symbolic of their own survival.

In a sense, then, there is a relationship between the Remington exhibition in the Whitney Gallery and the animal memorabilia in the Buffalo Bill Museum. The moose in *Coming to the Call* and the mooseheads on the wall are not so different as they might appear. The heads on the wall serve an aesthetic purpose; they are decorative objects, pleasing to the eye, which call forth certain associations. In this sense they are like visual works of art. The painting, on the other hand, has something of the trophy about it. The moose as Remington painted it is about to become a trophy, yet in another sense it already is one. Remington has simply captured the moose in another form. In both cases the subject matter, the life of a wild animal, symbolizes the life of the observer. It is the preservation of that life that both the painting and the taxidermy serve.

What are museums keeping safe for us, after all? What is it that we wish so much to preserve? The things we put in safekeeping, in our safe-deposit boxes under lock and key, are always in some way intended finally as safeguards of our own existence. The money and jewelry and stock certificates are meant for a time when we can no longer earn a living by the sweat of our brows. Similarly, the objects in museums preserve for us a source of life from which we need to nourish ourselves when the resources that would normally supply us have run dry.

The Buffalo Bill Historical Center, full as it is of dead bones, lets us see more clearly than we normally can what it is that museums are for. It is a kind of charnel house that houses images of living things that have passed away but whose life force still lingers around their remains and so passes itself on to us. We go and look at the objects in the glass cases and at the paintings on the wall, as if by standing there we could absorb into ourselves some of the energy that flowed once through the bodies of the live things represented. A museum, rather than being, as we normally think of it, the most civilized of places, a place most distant from our savage selves, actually caters to the urge to absorb the life of another into one's own life.

If we see the Buffalo Bill Museum in this way, it is no longer possible to separate ourselves from the hunters responsible for the trophies with their wondering eyes or from the curators who put them there. We are not, in essence, different from Roosevelt or Remington or Buffalo Bill, who killed animals when they were abundant in the Wild West of the 1880s. If in doing so those men were practicing the ancient art of absorbing the life of an animal into their own through the act of killing it, realizing themselves through the destruction of another life, then we are not so different from them as visitors to the museum. We stand beside the bones and skins and nails of beings that were once alive, or stare fixedly at their painted images. Indeed our visit is only a safer form of the same enterprise as theirs.

So I did not get out of the Buffalo Bill Museum unscathed, unimplicated in the acts of rapine and carnage that these remains represent. And I did not get out without having had a good time, either, because however many dire thoughts I may have had, the exhibits were interesting and fun to see. I was even able to touch a piece of buffalo hide displayed especially for that purpose (it was coarse and springy). Everyone else had touched it too. The hair was worn down, where people's hands had been, to a fraction of its original length.

After this, the Plains Indian Museum was a terrible letdown. I went from one exhibit to another expecting to become absorbed, but nothing worked. What was the matter? I was interested in Indians, had read about them, taught some Indian literature, felt drawn by accounts of native religions. I had been prepared to enter this museum as if I were going into another children's story, only this time I would be an Indian instead of a cowboy or a cowgirl. But the objects on display, most of them behind glass, seemed paltry and insignificant. They lacked visual presence. The bits of leather and sticks of wood triggered no fantasies in me.

At the same time, I noticed with some discomfort that almost everything in those glass cases was made of feathers and claws and hide, just like the men's chaps and ladies' fans in the Buffalo Bill Museum, only there was no luxury here. Plains Indian culture, it seemed, was made entirely from animals. Their mode of life had been even more completely dedicated to carnage than Buffalo Bill's, dependent as it was on animals for food, clothing, shelter, equipment, everything. In the Buffalo Bill Museum I was able to say to myself, well, if these men had been more sensitive, if they had had a right relation to their environment and to life itself, the atrocities that produced these trophies would never have occurred. They never would have exterminated the Indians and killed off the buffalo. But the spectacle before me made it impossible to say that. I had expected that the Plains Indian Museum would show me how life in nature ought to be lived: not the mindless destruction of nineteenth-century America but an ideal form of communion with animals and the land. What the museum seemed to say instead was that cannibalism was universal. Both colonizer and colonized had had their hands imbrued with blood. The Indians had lived off animals and had made war against one another. Violence was simply a necessary and inevitable part of life. And a person who, like me, was horrified at the extent of the destruction was just the kind of romantic idealist my husband sometimes accused me of being. There was no such thing as the life lived in harmony with nature. It was all bloodshed and killing, an unending cycle, over and over again, and no one could escape.

But perhaps there was a way to understand the violence that made it less terrible. Perhaps if violence was necessary, a part of nature, intended by the universe, then it could be seen as sacramental. Perhaps it was true, what Calvin Martin had said in *Keepers of the Game:* that the Indians had a sacred contract with the animals they killed, that they respected them as equals and treated their remains with honor and punctilio. If so, the remains of animals in the Plains Indian Museum weren't the same as those left by Buffalo Bill and his friends. They certainly didn't look the same. Perhaps. All I knew for certain was that these artifacts, lifeless and shrunken, spoke to me of nothing I could understand. No more did the life-size models of Indians, with strange feature-less faces, draped in costumes that didn't look like clothing. The figures, posed awkwardly in front of tepees too white to seem real, carried no sense of a life actually lived, any more than the objects in the glass cases had.

The more I read the placards on the wall, the more disaffected I became. Plains Indian life apparently had been not only bloody but exceedingly tedious. All those porcupine quills painstakingly softened, flattened, dyed, then appliqued through even more laborious methods of stitching or weaving. Four methods of attaching porcupine quills, six design groups, population statistics, patterns of migration. There wasn't any glamour here at all. No glamour in the lives the placards told about, no glamour in the objects themselves, no glamour in the experience of looking at them. Just a lot of shriveled things accompanied by some even drier information.

Could it be, then, that the problem with the exhibitions was that Plains Indian culture, if representable at all, was simply not readable by someone like me? Their stick figures and abstract designs could convey very little to an untrained Euro-American eye. One display in particular illustrated this. It was a piece of cloth, behind glass, depicting a buffalo skin with some marks on it. The placard read: "Winter Count, Sioux ca. 1910, after Lone Dog's, Fort Peck, Montana, 1877." The hide with its markings had been a calendar, each year represented by one image, which showed the most significant event in the life of the tribe. A thick pamphlet to one side of the glass case explained each image year by year: 1800–1801, the attack of the Uncapoo on a Crow Indian Fort; 1802–1803, a total eclipse of the sun. The images, once you knew what they represented, made sense, and seemed poetic interpretations of the experiences they stood for. But without explanation they were incomprehensible.

The Plains Indian Museum stopped me in my tracks. It was written in a language I had never learned. I didn't have the key. Maybe someone did, but I wasn't too sure. For it may not have been just cultural difference that made the text unreadable. I began to suspect that the text itself was corrupt, that the architects of this museum were going through motions whose purpose was, even to themselves, obscure. Knowing what event a figure stands for in the calendar doesn't mean you understand an Indian year. The deeper purpose of the museum began to puzzle me. Wasn't there an air of bad faith about preserving the vestiges of a culture one had effectively extinguished? Did the museum exist to assuage our guilt and not for any real educational reason? I do not have an answer to these questions. All I know is that I felt I was in the presence of something pious and a little insincere. It had the aura of a failed attempt at virtue, as though the curators were trying to present as interesting objects whose purpose and meaning even they could not fully imagine.

In a last-ditch attempt to salvage something, I went up to one of the guards and asked where the movie was showing which the video had advertised, the movie about Plains Indian life. "Oh, the slide show, you mean," he said. "It's been discontinued." When I asked why, he said he didn't know. It occurred to me then that that was the message the museum was sending, if I could read it, that that was the bottom line. Discontinued, no reason given.

The movie in the Winchester Arms Museum, *Lock, Stock, and Barrel,* was going strong. The film began with the introduction of cannon into European warfare in the Middle Ages, and was working its way slowly toward the nineteenth century when I left. I was in a hurry. Soon my husband would be waiting for me in the lobby. I went from room to room, trying to get a quick sense impression of the objects on display. They were all the same: guns. Some large drawings and photographs on the walls tried to give a sense of the context in which the arms had been used, but the effect was nil. It was case after case of rifles and pistols, repeating themselves over and over, and even when some slight variation caught my eye the differences meant nothing to me.

But the statistics did. In a large case of commemorative rifles, I saw the Antlered Game Commemorative Carbine. Date of manufacture: 1978. Number produced: 19,999. I wondered how many antlered animals each carbine had killed. I saw the Canadian Centennial (1962): 90,000; the Legendary Lawman (1978): 19,999; the John Wayne (1980–81): 51,600. Like the titles of the various sections of the museum, these names had a message. The message was: guns are patriotic. Associated with national celebrations, law enforcement, and cultural heroes. The idea that firearms were inseparable from the march of American history came through even more strongly in the titles given to the various exhibits: Firearms in Colonial America; Born in America: The Kentucky Rifle; The Era of Expansion and Invention; The Civil War: Firearms of the Conflict; The Golden Age of Hunting; Winning the West. The guns embodied phases of the history they had helped to make. There were no quotation marks here to indicate that expansion and conquest might not have been all they were cracked up to be. The fact that firearms had had a history seemed to consecrate them; the fact that they had existed at the time when certain famous events had occurred seemed to make them not only worth preserving but worth studying and revering. In addition to the exhibition rooms, the museum housed three "study galleries": one for hand arms, one for shoulder arms, one for U.S. military firearms.

As I think back on the rows and rows of guns, I wonder if I should have looked at them more closely, tried harder to appreciate the workmanship that went into them, the ingenuity, the attention. Awe and admiration are the attitudes the museum invites. You hear the ghostly march of military music in the background; you imagine flags waving and sense the implicit reference to feats of courage in battle and glorious death. The place had the air of an expensive and well-kept reliquary, or of the room off the transept of a cathedral where the vestments are stored. These guns were not there merely to be seen or even studied; they were there to be venerated.

But I did not try to appreciate the guns. They were too technical, too foreign. I didn't have their language, and, besides, I didn't want to learn. I rejoined my husband in the lobby. The Plains Indian Museum had been incomprehensible, but in the Winchester Arms Museum I could hardly see the objects at all, for I did not see the point. Or, rather, I did see it and rejected it. Here in the basement the instruments that had turned live animals into hides and horns, had massacred the Indians and the buffalo, were being lovingly displayed. And we were still making them: 51,600 John Waynes in 1980–81. Arms were going strong.

As I bought my books and postcards in the gift shop, I noticed a sign that read "Rodeo Tickets Sold Here," and something clicked into place. So that was it. *Everything* was still going strong. The whole museum was just another rodeo, only with the riders and their props stuffed, painted, sculpted, immobilized and put under glass. Like the rodeo, the entire museum witnessed a desire to bring back the United States of the 1880s and 1890s. The American people did not want to let go of the winning of the West. They wanted to win it all over again, in imagination. It was the ecstasy of the kill, as much as the life of the hunted, that we fed off here. The Buffalo Bill Historical Center did not repudiate the carnage that had taken place in the nineteenth century. It celebrated it. With its gleaming rest rooms, cute snack bar, opulent museum shop, wooden Indians, thousand rifles, and scores of animal trophies, it helped us all reenact the dream of excitement, adventure, and conquest that was what the Wild West meant to most people in this country.

This is where my visit ended, but it had a sequel. When I left the Buffalo Bill Historical Center, I was full of moral outrage, an indignation so intense it made me almost sick, though it was pleasurable too, as such emotions usually are. But the outrage was undermined by the knowledge that I knew nothing about Buffalo Bill, nothing of his life, nothing of the circumstances that led him to be involved in such violent events. And I began to wonder if my reaction wasn't in some way an image, however small, of the violence I had been objecting to. So when I got home I began to read about Buffalo Bill, and a whole new world opened up. I came to love Buffalo Bill.

"I have seen him the very personification of grace and beauty…dashing over the free wild prairie and riding his horse as though he and the noble animal were bounding with one life and one motion." That is the sort of thing people wrote about Buffalo Bill. They said "he was the handsomest man I ever saw." They said "there was never another man lived as popular as he was." They said "there wasn't a man, woman or child that he knew or ever met that he didn't speak to." They said "he was handsome as a god, a good rider and a crack shot." They said "he gave lots of money away. Nobody ever went hungry around him." They said "he was way above the average, physically and every other way."

These are quotes from people who knew Cody, collected by one of his two most responsible biographers, Nellie Snyder Yost. She puts them in the last chapter, and by the time you get there they all ring true. Buffalo Bill was incredibly handsome. He was extremely brave and did things no other scout would do. He would carry messages over rugged territory swarming with hostile Indians, riding all night in bad weather and get through, and then take off again the next day to ride sixty miles through a blizzard. He was not a proud man. He didn't boast of his exploits. But he did do incredible things, not just once in a while but on a fairly regular basis. He had a great deal of courage; he believed in himself, in his abilities, in his strength and endurance and knowledge. He was very skilled at what he did—hunting and scouting—but he wasn't afraid to try other things. He wrote some dime novels, he wrote his autobiography by age thirty-four, without very much schooling; he wasn't afraid to try acting, even though the stage terrified him and he knew so little about it that, according to his wife, he didn't even know you had to memorize lines.

Maybe it was because he grew up on the frontier, maybe it was just the kind of person he was, but he was constantly finding himself in situations that required resourcefulness and courage, quick decisions and decisive action and rising to the occasion. He wasn't afraid to improvise.

He liked people, drank a lot, gave big parties, gave lots of presents, and is reputed to have been a womanizer.[1] When people came to see him in his office tent on the show grounds, to shake his hand or have their pictures taken with him, he never turned anyone away. "He kept a uniformed doorman at the tent opening to announce visitors," writes a biographer. "No matter who was outside, from a mayor to a shabby woman with a baby, the Colonel would smooth his mustache, stand tall and straight, and tell the doorman to 'show 'em in.' He greeted everyone the same."[2]

As a showman, he was a genius. People don't say much about *why* he was so successful; mostly they describe the wonderful goings-on. But I get the feeling that Cody was one of those people who was connected to his time in an uncanny way. He knew what people wanted, he knew how to entertain them, because he *liked* them, was open to them, felt his kinship with them, or was so much in touch with himself at some level that he was thereby in touch with almost everybody else.

He liked to dress up and had a great sense of costume (of humor, too, they say). Once he came to a fancy dress ball, his first, in New York, wearing white tie and tails and a large Stetson. He knew what people wanted. He let his hair grow long and wore a mustache and beard, because, he said, he wouldn't be believable as a scout otherwise. Hence his Indian name, Pahaska, meaning "long hair," which people loved to use. Another kind of costume. He invented the ten-gallon hat, which the Stetson company made to his specifications. Afterward, they made a fortune from it. In the scores of pictures reproduced in the many books about him, he most often wears scout's clothes—usually generously fringed buckskin, sometimes a modified cavalryman's outfit—though often he's impeccably turned out in a natty-looking three-piece business suit (sometimes with overcoat, sometimes not). The photographs show him in a tuxedo, in something called a "Mexican suit" which looks like a cowboy outfit, and once he appears in Indian dress. In almost every case he is wearing some kind of hat, usually the Stetson, at exactly the right angle. He poses deliberately, and with dignity, for the picture. Cody didn't take himself so seriously that he had to pretend to be less than he was.

What made Buffalo Bill so irresistible? Why is he still so appealing, even now, when we've lost, supposedly, all the illusions that once supported his popularity? There's a poster for one of his shows when he was traveling in France that gives a clue to what it is that makes him so profoundly attractive a figure. The poster consists of a huge buffalo galloping across the plains, and against the buffalo's hump, in the center of his hump, is a cutout circle that shows the head of Buffalo Bill, white-mustachioed and bearded now, in his famous hat, and beneath, in large red letters, are the words "Je viens."

Je viens ("I am coming") are the words of a savior. The announcement is an annunciation. Buffalo Bill is a religious figure of a kind who makes sense within a specifically Christian tradition. That is, he comes in the guise of a redeemer, of someone who will save us, who will through his own actions do something for us that we ourselves cannot do. He will lift us above our lives, out of the daily grind, into something larger than we are.

His appeal on the surface is to childish desires, the desire for glamour, fame, bigness, adventure, romance. But these desires are also the sign of something more profound, and it is to something more profound in us that he also appeals. Buffalo Bill comes to the child in us, understood not as that part of ourselves that we have outgrown but as the part that got left behind, of necessity, a long time ago, having been starved, bound, punished, disciplined out of existence. He promises that that part of the self can live again. He has the power to promise these things because he represents the West, that geographical space of the globe that was still the realm of exploration and discovery, that was still open, that had not yet quite been tamed, when he began to play himself on the stage. He not only represented it, he *was* it. He brought the West itself with him when he came. The very Indians, the very buffalo, the very cowboys, the very cattle, the very stagecoach itself which had been memorialized in story. He performed in front of the audience the feats that had made him famous. He shot glass balls and clay pigeons out of the air with amazing rapidity. He rode his watersmooth silver stallion at full gallop. "Jesus he was a handsome man," wrote e. e. cummings in "Buffalo Bill's Defunct."

"I am coming." This appearance of Buffalo Bill, in the flesh, was akin to the apparition of a saint or of the Virgin Mary to believers. He was the incarnation of an ideal. He came to show people that what they had only imagined was really true. The West really did exist. There really were heroes who rode white horses and performed amazing feats. e. e. cummings was right to invoke the name of Jesus in his poem. Buffalo Bill was a secular messiah.

He was a messiah because people believed in him. When he died, he is reputed to have said, "Let my show go on." But he had no show at the time, so he probably didn't say that. Still, the words are prophetic because the desire for what Buffalo Bill had done had not only not died but would call forth the countless reenactments of the Wild West, from the rodeo—a direct descendant of his show—to the thousands of Western novels, movies, and television programs that comprise the Western genre in the twentieth century, a genre that came into existence as a separate category right about the time that Cody died. Don Russell maintains that the way the West exists in our minds today is largely the result of the way Cody presented it in his show. That was where people got their ideas of what the characters looked like. Though many Indian tribes wore no feathers and fought on foot, you will never see a featherless, horseless Indian warrior in the movies, because Bill employed only Sioux and other Plains tribes which had horses and traditionally wore feathered headdresses. "Similarly," he adds, "cowboys wear ten-gallon Stetsons, not because such a hat was worn in early range days, but because it was part of the costume adopted by Buffalo Bill for his show."[3]

But the deeper legacy is elsewhere. Buffalo Bill was a person who inspired other people. What they saw in him was an aspect of themselves. It really doesn't matter whether Cody was as great as people thought him or not, because what they were responding to when he rode into the arena, erect and resplendent on his charger, was something intangible, not the man himself, but a possible way of being. William F. Cody and the Wild West triggered the emotions that had fueled the imaginative lives of people who flocked to see him, especially men and boys, who made up the larger portion of the audience. He and his cowboys played to an inward territory; a Wild West of the psyche that hungered for exercise sprang into activity when the show appeared. *Je viens* was a promise to redeem that territory, momentarily at least, from exile and oblivion. The lost parts of the self symbolized by buffalo and horses and wild men would live again for an hour while the show went on.

People adored it. Queen Victoria, who broke her custom by going to see it at all (she never went to the theater, and on the rare occasions when she wanted to see a play she had it brought to her), is supposed to have been lifted out of a twenty-five-year depression caused by the death of her husband after she saw Buffalo Bill. She liked the show so much that she saw it again, arranging for a command performance to be given at Windsor Castle the day before her Diamond Jubilee. This was the occasion when four kings rode in the Deadwood stagecoach with the Prince of Wales on top next to Buffalo Bill, who drove. No one was proof against the appeal. Ralph Blumenfeld, the London correspondent for the New York *Herald*, wrote in his diary while the show was in London that he'd had two boyhood heroes, Robin Hood and Buffalo Bill, and had delighted in Cody's stories of the Pony Express and Yellow Hand:

> Everything was done to make Cody conceited and unbearable, but he remained the simple, unassuming child of the plains who thought lords and ladies belonged in the picture books and that the story of Little Red Riding Hood was true. I rode in the Deadwood coach. It was a great evening in which I realized a good many of my boyhood dreams, for there was Buffalo Bill on his white rocking horse charger, and Annie Oakley behind him.[4]

Victor Weybright and Henry Blackman Sell, from whose book on the Wild West some of the foregoing information has come, dedicated their book to Buffalo Bill. It was published in 1955. Nellie Snyder Yost, whose 1979 biography is one of the two scholarly accounts of Cody's life, dedicates her book "to all those good people, living or dead, who knew and liked Buffalo Bill." Don Russell's *The Lives and Legends of Buffalo Bill* (1960), the most fact-filled scholarly biography, does not have a dedication, but in the final chapter, where he steps back to assess Cody and his influence, Russell ends by exclaiming, "What more could possibly be asked of a hero? If he was not one, who was?"[5]

Let me now pose a few questions of my own. Must we throw out all the wonderful qualities that Cody had, the spirit of hope and emulation that he aroused in millions of people, because of the terrible judgment history has passed on the epoch of which he was part? The kinds of things he stands for—courage, daring, strength, endurance, generosity, openness to other people, love of drama, love of life, the possibility of living a life that does not deny the body and the desires of the body—are these to be declared dangerous and delusional although he manifested some of them while fighting Indians and others while representing his victories to the world? And the feelings he aroused in his audiences, the idealism, the enthusiasm, the excitement, the belief that dreams could become real—must these be declared misguided or a sham because they are associated with the imperialistic conquest of a continent, with the wholesale extermination of animals and men?

It is not so much that we cannot learn from history as that we cannot teach history how things should have been. When I set out to discover how Cody had become involved in the killing of Indians and the slaughter of buffalo, I found myself unable to sustain the outrage I had felt on leaving the museum. From his first job as an eleven-year-old herder for an army supply outfit, sole wage earner for his ailing widowed mother who had a new baby and other children to support, to his death in Colorado at the age of seventy-one, there was never a time when it was possible to say, there, there you went wrong, Buffalo Bill, you should not have killed that Indian. You should have held your fire and made your living some other way and quit the army and gone to work in the nineteenth-century equivalent of the Peace Corps. You should have known how it would end. My reading made me see that you cannot prescribe for someone in Buffalo Bill's position what he should have done, and it made me reflect on how eager I had been to get off on being angry at the museum. The thirst for moral outrage, for self-vindication, lay pretty close to the surface.

I cannot resolve the contradiction between my experience at the Buffalo Bill Historical Center with its celebration of violent conquest and my response to the shining figure of Buffalo Bill as it emerged from the pages of books—on the one hand, a history of shame; on the other, an image of the heart's desire. But I have reached one conclusion that for a while will have to serve.

Major historical events like genocide and major acts of destruction are not simply produced by impersonal historical processes or economic imperatives or ecological blunders; human intentionality is involved and human knowledge of the self. Therefore, if you're really, truly interested in not having any more genocide or killing of animals, no matter what else you might do, if you don't first, or also, come to recognize the violence in yourself and your own anger and your own destructiveness, whatever else you do won't work. It isn't that genocide doesn't matter. Genocide matters, and it starts at home.

Notes

1. Iron Eyes Cody, as told to Collin Perry, *Iron Eyes: My life as a Hollywood Indian* (New York, 1982), 16.

2. Nellie Irene Snyder Yost, *Buffalo Bill: His Family, Friends, Fame, Failures, and Fortunes* (Chicago, 1979), 436.

3. Don Russell, *The Lives and Legends of Buffalo Bill* (Norman, Okla., 1960), 470.

4. Victor Weybright and Henry Blackman Sell, *Buffalo Bill and the Wild West* (New York, 1955), 172.

5. Russell, 480.

Going to the Movies

Susan Allen Toth

I

Aaron takes me only to art films. That's what I call them, anyway: strange movies with vague poetic images I don't understand, long dreamy movies about a distant Technicolor past, even longer black-and-white movies about the general meaninglessness of life. We do not go unless at least one reputable critic has found the cinematography superb. We went to *The Devil's Eye*, and Aaron turned to me in the middle and said, "My God, this is *funny*." I do not think he was pleased.

When Aaron and I go to the movies, we drive our cars separately and meet by the box office. Inside the theater he sits tentatively in his seat, ready to move if he can't see well, poised to leave if the film is disappointing. He leans away from me, careful not to touch the bare flesh of his arm against the bare flesh of mine. Sometimes he leans so far I am afraid he may be touching the woman on his other side instead. If the movie is very good, he leans forward too, peering between the heads of the couple in front of us. The light from the screen bounces off his glasses; he gleams with intensity, sitting there on the edge of his seat, watching the screen. Once I tapped him on the arm so I could whisper a comment in his ear. He jumped.

After *Belle de Jour*, Aaron said he wanted to ask me if he could stay overnight. "But I can't," he shook his head mournfully before I had a chance to answer, "because I know I never sleep well in strange beds." Then he apologized for asking. "It's just that after a film like that," he said, "I feel the need to assert myself."

II

Bob takes me only to movies that he thinks have a redeeming social conscience. He doesn't call them films. They tend to be about poverty, war, injustice, political corruption, struggling unions in the 1930s, and the military-industrial complex. Bob doesn't like propaganda movies, though, and he doesn't like to be too depressed either. We stayed away from *The Sorrow and the Pity*; it would be, he said, too much. Besides, he

226

assured me, things are never that hopeless. So most of the movies we see are made in Hollywood. Because they are always very topical, these movies offer what Bob calls "food for thought." When we saw *Coming Home*, Bob's jaw set so firmly with the first half that I knew we would end up at Poppin' Fresh Pies afterward.

When Bob and I go to the movies, we take turns driving so no one owes anyone else anything. We park far away from the theater so we don't have to pay for a space. If it's raining or snowing, Bob offers to let me off at the door, but I can tell he'll feel better if I go with him while he parks, so we share the walk too. Inside the theater Bob will hold my hand when I get scared if I ask him. He puts my hand firmly on his knee and covers it completely with his own hand. His knee never twitches. After a while, when the scary part is past, he loosens his hand slightly and I know that is a signal to take mine away. He sits companionably close, letting his jacket just touch my sweater, but he does not infringe. He thinks I ought to know he is there if I need him.

One night after *The China Syndrome* I asked Bob if he wouldn't like to stay for a second drink, even though it was past midnight. He thought awhile about that, considering my offer from all possible angles, but finally he said no. Relationships today, he said, have a tendency to move too quickly.

III

Sam likes movies that are entertaining. By that he means movies that Will Jones of the *Minneapolis Tribune* loved and either *Time* or *Newsweek* rather liked; also movies that do not have sappy love stories, are not musicals, do not have subtitles, and will not force him to think. He does not go to movies to think. He liked *California Suite* and *The Seduction of Joe Tynan*, though the plots, he said, could have been zippier. He saw it all coming too far in advance, and that took the fun out. He doesn't like to know what is going to happen. "I just want my brain to be tickled," he says. It is very hard for me to pick out movies for Sam.

When Sam takes me to the movies, he pays for everything. He thinks that's what a man ought to do. But I buy my own popcorn, because he doesn't approve of it; the grease might smear his flannel slacks. Inside the theater, Sam makes himself comfortable. He takes off his jacket, puts one arm around me, and all during the movie he plays with my hand, stroking my palm, beating a small tattoo on my wrist. Although he watches the movie intently, his body operates on instinct. Once I inclined my head and kissed him lightly just behind his ear. He beat a faster tattoo on my wrist, quick and musical, but he didn't look away from the screen.

When Sam takes me home from the movies, he stands outside my door and kisses me long and hard. He would like to come in, he says regretfully, but his steady girlfriend in Duluth wouldn't like it. When the *Tribune* gives a movie four stars, he has to save it to see with her. Otherwise her feelings might be hurt.

IV

I go to some movies by myself. On rainy Sunday afternoons I often sneak into a revival house or a college auditorium for old Technicolor musicals, *Kiss Me Kate*, *Seven Brides for Seven Brothers*, *Calamity Jane*, even, once, *The Sound of Music*. Wearing saggy jeans so I can prop my feet on the seat in front, I sit toward the rear where no one will see me. I eat large handfuls of popcorn with double butter. Once the movie starts, I feel completely at home. Howard Keel and I are old friends; I grin back at him on the screen, admiring all his teeth. I know the sound tracks by heart. Sometimes when I get really carried away I hum along with Kathryn Grayson, remembering how I once thought I would fill out a formal like that. Skirts whirl, feet tap, acrobatic young men perform impossible feats, and then the camera dissolves into a dream sequence I know I can comfortably follow. It is not, thank God, Bergman.

If I can't find an old musical, I settle for Hepburn and Tracy, vintage Grant or Gable, on adventurous days Claudette Colbert or James Stewart. Before I buy my ticket I make sure it will all end happily. If necessary, I ask the girl at the box office. I have never seen *Stella Dallas* or *Intermezzo*. Over the years I have developed other peccadilloes: I will, for example, see anything that is redeemed by Thelma Ritter. At the end of *Daddy Long Legs* I wait happily for the scene where Fred Clark, no longer angry, at last pours Thelma a convivial drink. They smile at each other, I smile at them, I feel they are smiling at me. In the movies I go to by myself, the men and women always like each other.

Fireworks to Praise a Homemade Day: Notes from a Reader's Diary

Roger Weingarten

7/8/68: West Branch, Iowa

It's ninety-five, humid as hell, the moon is an orange water balloon and I want everything, including air conditioning, from poetry. Baudelaire's charge to "Be drunk, be it on wine, poetry, virtue, what have you" comes up short. I want poetry to transport, but: I also want that bucket of cold water/whipcream pie that someone—with an imagination, and who's not afraid to use it; an explorer with a real ear for the language and a sense of timing and with something moving, funny, wild, nasty and smart all rolled into one to convey about our time, himself, us, and the past that brought us here—can throw in my face.

Sick, the last few days, of composting my own feeble half-starts, I drove into town to find something to read. I found *Poems* (Yale University Press, 1961), Alan Dugan's first collection. Can there be a less pretentious book title or a more exciting book? I flipped through it in such a fever, the storekeeper asked me if I was going to buy or shred it. Many of the poem titles struck me as masterpieces unto themselves: "The Branches of Water or Desire," "Memorial Service For The Invasion Beach Where The Vacation In The Flesh Is Over." It wasn't until I got the book home that I understood the extent to which they're also full participants in the action.

There's this very funny piece called "Cooled Heels Lament Against Frivolity, The Mask of Despair," about inspiration when it ain't happening:

> *Dugan's deathward, darling: you*
> *in your unseeable beauty, oh*
> *fictitious, legal person, need*
> *be only formally concerned,*
> *but there is someone too much here,*

perspiring in your waiting room.
Because I did not listen when you said,
"Don't call us: we'll call you,"
your credulous receptionist
believes I am a phony fairy jew
capitalist-communist spy
for Antichrist, a deviated mal-
adjusted lobbyist for the Whiskey Trust,
or else accepts me as I am: a fool.
So while I sit here fouling song,
wasting my substance on the air,
the universe is elsewhere, out
the window in the sky. You,
in your inner office, Muse,
smoking a given, good cigar
and swapping dated stories with
star salesmen of the soul,
refuse to hear my novel pitch
while I sit out here getting old.

The notion of *mask* is critical to this interior theater, because, while writing about warming a chair—the supplicant waiting for his cigar-puffing "Muse" to give him the time of day—he's really concocting this inspired send-up of conventional images for inspiration.

In "Cooled Heels" the poet without inspiration finds his subject in what he's deprived of; in "Portrait," a vision of the artist as political prisoner, his subject is deprived of everything, but

The captive flourished like
a mushroom in his oubliette.
He breathed his night's breath every day,
took food and water from the walls
and ruled his noisy rats and youth.
He made a calendar of darkness,
thought his boredom out, and carved
Heaven in his dungeon with a broken spoon.

At last he made his own
light like a deep sea fish, and when
his captors' children came for him
they found no madman in a filthy beard
or heap of rat-picked bones:
they found a spry, pale old gentleman
who had a light around his head.
Oh he could stare as well as ever,
argue in a passionate voice
and walk on to the next
detention in their stone dismay
unaided.

Here, and perhaps in the whole of the book, the human spirit (and sometimes the life spirit, whether embodied in weeds or a hermit crab) can make the most of the worst. But only if, despite its limitations, the subject under the scrutiny of Dugan's portrait-ist's eye takes the situation in hand and shapes it—uh oh, here comes landlord Atomic Tushy, walking this way clutching a business envelope.

4/2/73: Kalamazoo, Michigan:
—into something extraordinary, though not necessarily a work of deodorized Apollo-nian perfection, as in:

Love Song: I and Thou

Nothing is plumb, level, or square:
*   the studs are bowed, the joists*
are shaky by nature, no piece fits
*   any other piece without a gap*
or pinch, and bent nails
*   dance all over the surfacing*
like maggots. By Christ,
*   I am no carpenter. I built*
the roof for myself, the walls
*   for myself, the floors*
for myself, and got
*   hung up in it myself. I*
danced with a purple thumb
*   at this house-warming, drunk*
with my prime whiskey: rage.
*   Oh I spat rage's nails*
into the frame-up of my work:
*   it held. It settled plumb,*
level, solid, square and true
*   for that great moment. Then*
it screamed and went on through,
*   skewing as wrong the other way.*
God damned it. This is hell,
*   but I planned it, I sawed it,*
I nailed it, and I
*   will live in it until it kills me.*
I can nail my left palm
*   to the left-hand crosspiece but*
I can't do everything myself.
*   I need a hand to nail the right,*
a help, a love, a you, a wife.

More *I* than *Thou,* fundamentally a self-portrait and celebration of its subject's own stubborn individualism, the poem takes a giant step toward the "Love Song" the title promises when, at the last minute and by way of the earlier pronouncement, "By Christ/I am no carpenter," it turns the punishing edifice into a crucifix that will provide not the expected coup de grace but the staging for a surprising, fitting and, finally, moving marriage proposal. It's more than just a clever one-man Laurel and Hardy routine metamorphosed into a last-minute love poem; how he engineers this distance on and sense of humor about himself is what Marvin Bell is talking about when he describes poetry as "a mature art."

12/?/73: Rabat, Morocco

I woke up from a headache and stepped off the bus into the Rabat sunrise reflected in a puddle of piss and shit. I'd brought Dugan's *Poems* to keep me company, so I wouldn't lose contact with American idiom. I didn't imagine myself looking to them for an encouraging kick in the pants:

> *Look, it's morning, and a little water gurgles in the tap.*
> *I wake up waiting, because it's Sunday, and turn twice more*
> *than usual in bed, before I rise to cereal and comic strips.*
> *I have risen to the morning danger and feel proud,*
> *and after shaving off the night's disguises, after searching*
> *close to the bone for blood, and finding only a little,*
> *I shall walk out bravely into the daily accident.*
>
> —"Morning Song"

Dugan uses his own person in the most courageously unattractive but compelling ways. He has the thick skin of a standup comedian who brandishes an unadorned self in front of his audience. In "Letter to Donald Fall," he describes himself as "an aging phony, stale, oozy and corrupt/from unattempted dreams and bad health habits," whose "new false teeth" are

> *shining and raw in the technician's lab*
> *like Grails, saying, "We are the resurrection*
> *and the life…*
> *immortality is in science and machines."*

Here he lets his own prosthetic device become the voice of one of his "incommensurate enemies," before he informs his friend Fall, half-spoofing the tradition of pastoral romantics who railed against civilization, etc., that, despite his dilapidated state,

> *…skunk cabbage generates its*
> *frost-thawing fart-gas in New Jersey and the first*
> *crocuses appear in Rockefeller Center's Channel Gardens:*
> *Fall, it is not so bad at Dugan's Edge.*

These aren't green things you'd send Mom on Mother's Day or Romantic symbols of natural purity. For a guy walking out into the remnants of "snow sticking only to the tops/of air-conditioners and convertibles," hung over and "Toothless in spring!,'" the imagined cabbage's useful flatulence and the crocus's magical ability to appear" *comfort*. So, while not hesitating to call attention to the less flattering aspects of his character and physiognomy, he is able to see his circumstances with some amusement and in a somewhat more favorable light: "it is not *so* bad at Dugan's Edge."

3/28/84: Brookfield, Vermont

Sixteen years since I first picked it up, and one of the few books to survive the house fire (it still smells smoky), there are so many of Dugan's *Poems* that won't leave me alone. They move with a bullet train's electromagnetic speed toward their stunning finishes. It's still, after hundreds of readings, as if I'm encountering them for the first time—and with certain poems, I still don't feel entirely confident of my fix on them. Chief among these:

Against France: On The Algerian Pleasures of Entity

When I died the devils tortured me with icepicks and pliers
and all the other instruments they learned from men of faith;
they took off my genitals and nails, less troubles, chained me
to the wall, and came in shifts with forced foods and electrodes.

Later, after works, I tore the chains from the wall. What whips
chains are! I lashed my lashers and escaped their cell,
armed to my last two teeth in search of god. My arms, though,
were chains chained to my arms, so what I touched I struck.

I met all the animals with beaks and offered them myself
to rend, since, as a student of torture, I had found it fun,
and wrecked them as they bit. What would I have done
If I had met a smile? Well, I swam the river of spit,

crossed a plain of scorpions, and went into the lake
of fire. I emerged bone, dripping the last of my flesh,
a good riddance, and asked whoever came to chew the bones,
"Where is god?" Each answered: "Here I am, now. I am,

in a way." I answered, "Nonsense!" every time and struck
with chains. Weary, weary, I came to the final ocean of acid:
pain was a friend who told me I was temporal when nothing
else spoke, so I dipped in my hand-bones and saw them eaten.

"It is good to be rid of the bones," I felt, "as clattering
encumbrances to search," and dived in whole. However,
instead of being shriven or freed up into flight, oh I
was born again. I squalled for a while to keep my death,

that time when chains were arms and pain a great ally,
but I was conquered and began my sentence to a child's
forgetfulness, uneager to collect the matter of these dreams,
and stared into the present of you innocent beasts.

The title's ironic use of the word "Pleasures" and his conversion of what would conventionally be called self-determination to "Entity" make it possible, in a kind of Boschian nightmare/journey through hell, for Dugan to shift the weight of the entire Algerian populace's suffering onto (and into: this is not an allegory) the speaker's back. Add to that the fact that he begins the poem already dead and in hell, and you can see he's highdiving with an unbelievable degree of difficulty. I *think* the poem—exhausting, exhilarating and, incredibly, only twenty-eight lines—works brilliantly, although I'm a little at sea at the finish line.

What "conquer[s]" the speaker—what he's reborn into—is life, which he presents as another kind of prison ("began my sentence to a child's/forgetfulness"). But is the child's "star[ing] into the present" a dumb or a knowing one? And who is the "you" of "you innocent beasts"? Is it the France of the poem's title, with its self-deluding complicity? Is it the Algerian people themselves, oxymoronically composed of both victim and torturer? Is it the readers? I don't know. Give me another ten years to get my hands around it or feel even denser. Which doesn't matter, because I'll never get tired of rereading it.

6/17/91: Bloomington, Indiana

Met Dugan today at the conference. Wanted to tell him how much his work, especially *Poems*, has meant to me. Like some sort of awestruck teenager, I clutched. Without that book, I can't imagine the last twenty years. I remember that farmer across the road, when I lived, 23 years ago, at the edge of Writers' Mecca. After his house burned down, he took me for a walk through his fields. He stopped, put his hand on my shoulder while the other hand swept the horizon, and, trying to build up his courage to ask me to move out of my house, said, "when a poet looks out on the land he sees things a farmer doesn't." That seemed, at the time, like a gauntlet to be taken up: that maybe poets weren't looking hard enough at and through the surface of things; that we weren't seeing hard enough for the reader.

Many of Dugan's poems take up that challenge, staring into the everyday-plain-old-right-in-front-of-your-face and finding ways to convert it. In "Prison Song" the subject is the body's surface:

> *The skin ripples over my body like moon-wooed water,*
> *rearing to escape me. Where would it find another*
> *animal as naked as this one it hates to cover?*
> *Once it told me what was happening outside,*
> *who was attacking, who caressing, and what the air*
> *was doing to feed or freeze me. Now I wake up*
> *dark at night, in a textureless ocean of ignorance,*
> *or fruit bites back and water bruises like a stone:*
> *a jealousy, because I look for other tools to know*
> *with, and another armor, better fitted to my flesh.*
> *So, let it lie, turn off its clues, or try to leave:*
> *sewn on me seamless like those painful shirts*
> *the body-hating saints wore, this sheath of hell*

is pierced to my darkness nonetheless: what traitors
labor in my face, what hints they smuggle through
its itching guard! But even *in the night it jails, [emphasis mine]*
with nothing but its lies and silences to feed upon,
the jail itself can make a scenery, sing prison songs
and set off fireworks to praise a homemade day.

It's like anyone's worst claustrophobic nightmare: his skin, in revolt, is a "sheath of hell" that engulfs his entire being. After walking the reader down through nine levels of purgatorial itch, and from the pivotal "But even in the night it jails," Dugan tilts our perspective: even a Jobian curse can celebrate the kind of artfully sculpted life—the "homemade day"—he aspires to throughout the collection.

1/2/93: Destin, Florida

Many of Dugan's poems about seemingly ordinary subjects are models of risk, about risk and, like "Against France," adopt risky points of view. There are the risky models of identification with natural creatures that could have easily become death traps of sentimental personification. In "Weeds As Partial Survivors," he tells us about "The chorus of weeds," that "India of unemployables":

Too bendable to break, bowing away
together from the wind although
the hail or hurricane can knock them flat,
they rise up wet by morning. This
morning erection of the weeds
is not so funny: It
is perseverance dancing…

But it's the fact that the weeds' ability to keep bouncing back is only partial that finally makes them compelling:

…surviving all
catastrophes except the human: they
extend their glosses, like the words I said,
on sun-cracked margins of the sown
lines of our harrowed grains.

That last conga line of enjambed prepositional phrases has so much weight, as if he were describing everyone and everything on the periphery.

Don't forget, when you get back home, to add a word on Mighty Mouse.

2/14/93: E. Montpelier, Vermont

Adam and Eve/Christ/Dante/every desperately hungry soul-that-ever-lived/ Methusaleh: such is the tragic hero of Dugan's "Funeral Oration for a Mouse," a rather complex rodent as painted by an imaginative intellect with even more *chuzpah* than his subject:

Humors of love aside, the mousetrap was our own
opinion of the mouse, but for the mouse
it was the tree of knowledge with
its consequential fruit, the true cross
and the gate of hell. Even to approach
it makes him like or better than
its maker: his courage as a spoiler never once
impressed us, but to go out cautiously at night,
into the dining room—what bravery, what
hunger! Younger by far, in dying he
was older than us all…

Dugan's echolocator is always bouncing off his own or others' major to minor hells-on-earth—from a hangover to the torture of an entire nation to an individual death: "his mobile tail and nose/ spasmed in the pinch of our annoyance," looking for the dramatic turn toward common ground:

Why,
then, at that snapping sound, did we, victorious,
begin to laugh without delight?

Our stomachs, deep in an analysis
of their own stolen baits
(and asking, "Lord, Host, to whom are we the pests?"),
contracted and demanded a retreat
from our machine and its effect of death,
as if the mouse's fingers, skinnier
than hairpins and as breakable as cheese,
could grasp our grasping lives, and in
their drowning movement pull us under too,
into the common death beyond the mousetrap.

The Friendship Tarot

Nancy Willard

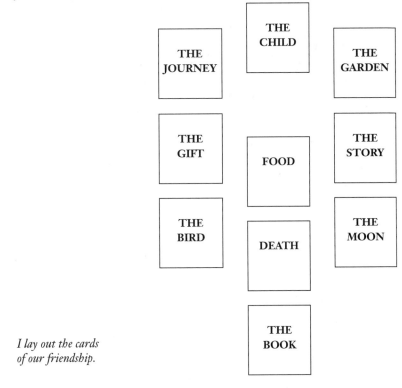

*I lay out the cards
of our friendship.*

The Child

The card shows a child with chocolate on his face wandering through an art gallery in downtown Poughkeepsie devoted—for two weeks—to illustrations from children's books. Ilse Vogel and I have not met, but we both have work in this show. In one room stands the six-foot doll's house I made when I was writing *A Visit to William Blake's Inn*.

In the next room hang Ilse's meticulous pen-and-ink drawings for her book *Dodo Every Day*.

What I saw: an elegant woman with white hair, a knitted cloche, and eyes that missed nothing.

What she saw: a woman with a seven-year-old boy whose face was smeared with chocolate.

What I thought: Who is this remarkable person?

What Ilse thought: Her child has a dirty face, but does she worry about it? No. And neither does the child.

The Garden

The card shows two married couples eating dinner in a garden: Eric and me, Howard and Ilse. Four artists: one painter (Howard), one photographer (Eric), one writer (me), and Ilse, who can't be pinned down to one category since she illustrates her own stories. The dinner Ilse has prepared is exquisite. Butter blooms in a little pot; Ilse has sculpted it into the face of a sunflower. Howard helps her carry dishes from the tiny kitchen into the Francesa, a shelter shingled in nasturtiums and morning glories. The front is entirely open to view; over the edge of the second story dangle the tails of four sleeping cats. Once it was a rickety outbuilding for storing tools. Now it is paved with round river stones chosen and put into place years ago by Ilse. Shortly after she'd laid the last stone, she felt chest pains. The day she came home from the hospital, Howard filled the house with anemones.

Ilse heaps seconds on our plates without asking us and tells us they bought this small yellow house in the country because they loved the apple tree blooming outside the kitchen window. The soil is rocky but the garden is full of flowers; Ilse has put out one hundred and four pots of flowers. When a large tabby springs from behind one of them, Ilse explains that they are down to ten cats.

"Ten cats!" exclaims Eric.

"We have only two," I add apologetically.

Is this the first step into friendship? Ilse knows right away she can discuss the excellence of cats without boring me: Velvet Paws, Parsley, Comedy Cat, Mr. Goldie, Chives. Summer and winter the ten cats that live with Howard and Ilse sleep in the garage at night.

Winter and summer the two cats that live with Eric and me sleep at the foot of our bed so they can watch over us.

The Journey

The card shows three people in a car headed for New York. Ilse wears the same knitted cloche she wore at the gallery, and Howard's hat is the identical shade of oatmeal. When I remark on this, Ilse explains that she knitted them both.

We three are traveling to New York to see *The Tin Drum*. On the way, Ilse explains that she lived in Berlin all during the war, so naturally she's curious to see this film.

Of the movie I remember only a few scenes, not because the film was forgettable but because of what happened on the trip back.

The Story

The card shows a woman talking and a woman listening.

I am riding in the back seat of the car and I lean forward and ask, "Ilse, was it really like that in Germany?"

Ilse answers by telling me about the day the Russians marched into Berlin.

"When the Russians came so close to the house, you could hear them talking and shouting. And all the inhabitants of the house were sitting in the bunkers except me, because I hated to be down there with the Nazis. I was in my apartment with a friend of mine. And then we heard shooting and voices, and then we heard a sound as if masses and masses of water would come rushing in, and then my friend said, 'Oh, something has hit the canister of gasoline,' and within seconds I saw the flames and the gasoline floating in under the doorway of my apartment, and everything was in flames. There was just one window where we could get out. We crossed the yard to the door of the bunker and went inside and then the house did burn with tremendous speed. Smoke came and people started to pray and to sing, and others cursed and screamed. I sat with my friend and we held hands and I said, 'This is the end, there's no way out.' And my friend had a little flute with him which he always carried. I'll show it to you tomorrow—I still have it. He pulled it out and played a little Bach sonata for us, to comfort us."

She tells me how she worked in the Resistance against Hitler, hiding Jews in her apartment and printing passports to smuggle them out of Germany. Two hours later we are back in Poughkeepsie.

"Ilse," I say, "have you written this down?"

"It's not a story for children," she says. "And I can't find the right voice to tell it."

"You must tell it," I say, "so people don't forget." Ilse asks to use the bathroom. When she emerges she says with a smile, "I'm so glad your house isn't neat all the time."

The Gift

The card shows a restaurant strung with red and green lights.

The week before Christmas, Ilse and Howard and Eric and I meet for lunch at Dickens. Ilse calls ahead so that we can have the same table we had last year—a table intended for six. She tells the waitress we are expecting another person, a man, and during the meal she laments his bad manners—why couldn't he have phoned? She brings the snapshots we took of each other last year. In the snapshots we are always opening presents. Here I am, opening the present Ilse made for me: a muff, to keep my hands warm. It is made of brown corduroy, lined with synthetic lamb's wool, and decorated in orange and turquoise and lavender: braid, felt hearts, pyramids, and silver beads, each bead no bigger than a mustard seed. It has a corduroy strap and a pocket, into which Ilse has tucked a bright red handkerchief.

Since I ride a bicycle to class and my arms are usually full of books, I seldom have the leisure to use a muff unless I decide to take a muff-walk: a walk with no other purpose than exercise and pleasure. Which is probably why Ilse gave it to me

This year Howard gives Eric a book of Vuillard's paintings and Ilse gives me a Waring hand-held blender which, she assures me, will make cooking much easier.

Eric gives Howard a photograph he took inside the conservatory of the New York Botanical Gardens and I give Ilse a set of flannel sheets and pillowcases printed with cats.

Food

The card shows dinner tables, side by side.

When we eat dinner at their house, they serve hors d'oeuvres and drinks in the living room or the garden, just for the four of us. Ilse makes the salad dressing. The courses arrive in succession at the proper time.

When they eat dinner at ours, I am famished from having skipped lunch to meet with students, and I rush everything to the table at once. The salad dressing is Paul Newman's finest, the cake is the handiwork of the Aurora Café Bakery. The last time I baked a cake, it collapsed like an old hat and I filled in the holes and cracks with frosting, which made it astonishingly heavy but quite tasty. Howard warned Ilse not to eat it.

"All that chocolate is bad for your heart," he said softly.

She smiled and took another bite.

The Moon

The card shows four people perched on top of the world.

Ilse phones us in great excitement. Tonight, if we stand on a certain hill a mile from their house, we can watch the sun go down and the moon come up, all at the same time. She has checked the weather; the sky will be clear.

The road to the hill runs past stables and pastures broken by white fencing into parcels that give expensive horses enough room to run free by keeping them apart from each other. Howard regrets that the landscape feels so owned.

When we climb out of the car and look east and west from the crest of the windy hill, the valley sweeps broadly around us; could we see the Hudson if we knew where to find it?

As the sun slides into its nest of light behind the Catskills, the moon rises silently, secretly. She is so pale and thin that she might be the shed carapace of some large round animal. As darkness gathers, she grows solider, more golden.

"In German, the moon is masculine," says Ilse. "And the sun is feminine."

I can't think of another language in which those genders are assigned to my old friends in the sky.

Ilse says she is trying to write about those last days before the fall of Berlin, but she is not yet ready to read me what she has written.

The Bird

The card shows an empty cage in a garden.

Ilse phones us—can we come over and see the dove? It seems that the postmistress in their little town of Bangall runs an animal adoption service on the side, and she has presented Ilse with a dove.

When we arrive, Ilse has put its cage on a pile of stones in the garden, like an altar to flight. The cage is made of the sticks that Ilse gathered in the yard, but it is very small, and when Eric and I approach, the dove beats her wings against the bars. All during dinner she makes endearing noises.

"You can't imagine how we enjoy hearing that wonderful sound," says Ilse. "And the cats don't seem to notice her."

We sit outside and watch the singular stars arrive, one by one, like notes in a music box winding down to silence.

The next day I telephone Joanne, a friend of mine who does excellent carpentry, and ask her to make a catproof cage for Ilse's dove. I tell her it should be made of sticks gathered in a forest and it should be huge. Ilse's birthday is two weeks away—could she possibly have it finished by then?

Two weeks later, Joanne drives up with a cage nearly as tall as herself on her truck. It is a gazebo, a minaret, a chapel, it is the mother of all birdcages. I phone Howard and tell him we want to deliver it as a surprise to Ilse, who likes surprises but does not like unexpected visitors. Howard can tell her whatever he likes; we will arrive with the cage at eleven o'clock on Thursday.

When we appear, the two of them are sitting in the garden, attended by Velvet Paws. Joanne and I carry the cage across the lawn. Ilse is speechless with astonishment. That is just the way I hoped she would be.

"You've given me exactly what I wanted!" she exclaims.

The dove takes to the cage at once. Soon it no longer feels like a cage; Ilse adds branches and leaves and nasturtiums and she removes the bottom so that the dove sits directly on the grass. How good the grass feels on her little coral feet! All night long she enjoys dewfall and moonrise and starshine. When the sun warms the dark world, Howard arrives with her breakfast.

One morning Howard goes to feed the dove and finds a dash of bloody feathers. There is a snake in Eden; nothing but a snake could insinuate itself into so stout a cage.

Ilse mourns her dove. All winter the cage is filled only with cream-colored twigs-and the curious seedpods that catch her eye in the garden. One day the postmistress telephones her. A relative of the slain dove has recently laid a clutch of eggs; two of them hatched. Would Ilse like two doves? Howard snakeproofs the cage. It is spring again and the voices of Ilse's doves are heard in the land.

Death

The card shows a shelf on which Ilse has arranged the skulls of their cats. After their deaths, she digs them up. The skulls are light and beautiful as parchment.

"Some people think it's a strange thing to do," she says, "but see how beautiful their bones are!"

When I cook chicken, I save not only the wishbone but the breastbone. Scrubbed clean and dried, the breastbone looks like a mask or a saddle intended for an animal unaccustomed to carrying passengers. On the apple tree in our back yard hang the shells of half a dozen horseshoe crabs I found on Cape Cod. Anyone passing the tree would take it for the site of a secret ceremony devoted to saving what holds us up but is never seen under the living flesh.

The Book

The card shows pages falling and gathering like snow. Ilse is now seriously at work on her stories about life in Germany under Hitler. Howard is typing them for her. The stories arrive in the mail, one by one, in white envelopes bordered with a green stripe.

Without telling her, I am sending them to my editor at Harcourt Brace.

Velvet Paws has had her kittens behind a canvas of Howard's which he imprudently left leaning against an upstairs wall. Ilse invites us to view the kittens. Eric and I sit in the living room of the little white house and wait for the great moment. We wait and wait. And suddenly here is Ilse, presenting them to us in a basket lined with violets and strawberry leaves, as if she had just picked them in the garden.

Later, as we are leafing through a box of old photographs, I pull out a picture of two blond girls standing side by side: Ilse and her twin sister, Erika, who died of diphtheria when they were nine.

"Which one is you?" I ask.

Ilse is not sure.

"Perhaps that one, with the knees bent a little. Erika was born first and she always was the more courageous one."

Eight years ago, when I published my first novel, *Things Invisible to See*, I dedicated it to Ilse and Howard.

Today I open the book of Ilse's stories, *Bad Times, Good Friends*, and find it is dedicated to Eric and me. Over the dedication is Ilse's pen-and-ink drawing of a dove turning into a woman. She is flying over a bed of pansies, carrying three tulips in one hand and pointing to our names with the other.

"They didn't want a dove-woman on the dedication page," says Ilse. "I had to fight for it."

Part II

Talking about Creative Nonfiction

One reason we're so enthusiastic about this evolving genre is the role of writers and teachers of creative nonfiction in defining the terms of the conversation. As both teachers and writers we've benefited from that conversation ourselves, and so we believe that writers entering the genre can gain from hearing these writers talk about the making of their own work. After all, in the long tradition of the genre, essayists from Montaigne through Addison, Steele, Lamb, and Hazlitt to E. B. White have not only written the most enduring examples of the essay but also provided the most valuable commentary on the form.

Therefore, in Part Two, Talking about Creative Nonfiction, we've chosen pieces—many of them written by authors whose works are also found in Part One— that reflect these writers' thoughts, opinions, speculations, theories, and critiques of creative nonfiction. They provide a multivoiced discussion of the genre on a wide range of topics related to writing creative nonfiction—from definitions of the form and overviews of some of the subgenres to informal histories of the genre, personal accounts of writing, and hints about strategies and practices. Some writers, such as David Bradley and Richard Selzer, discuss their personal reasons for writing; others, including Donald Murray and Sydney Lea, talk about their composing strategies. Still others offer us insight into the particular forms of creative nonfiction in which they work: Mary Clearman Blew, Annie Dillard, Patricia Hampl, and Fern Kupfer give us different perspectives on the memoir, especially the ways imagination transforms and transposes memory; Phillip Lopate and Scott Russell Sanders talk about the history of the personal essay; Tracy Kidder discusses his views and his experiences in literary journalism; Jane Tompkins explores her motives for anchoring her cultural criticism in the first person singular.

Along with the writers whose work appears in Part One, others offer us insight into the issues surrounding creative nonfiction. Rebecca Blevins Faery and Robert Root explain and illustrate how and why they write disjunctive essays; Chris Anderson and Peter Elbow explore the connections between their teaching and their writing; Jocelyn Bartkevicius and Andrea Lunsford examine attempts to define and identify creative nonfiction; and Marianna Torgovnick discusses the reasons she practices and promotes experimental critical writing with its use of personal voice in academic discourse (a subject treated by Elbow and Tompkins as well).

As we've mentioned earlier, many of these selections can be paired with writings in Part One. One glance at the table of contents shows which authors appear in both sections of the book. A cursory look at the titles provides some sense of the specific concerns represented here. For example, if you were to look at Jane Tompkins's Part One essay, "At the Buffalo Bill Museum," you would notice that, although it's a piece of academic cultural criticism, Tompkins has written about her discoveries in an intimate and informal voice. Then if you read "Me and My Shadow" in Part Two, you'd find that in this essay Tompkins is giving herself (and other academic critics) permission to use her own personal presence and voice in her scholarly writing.

Conversely, let's suppose that you want to read some of the Part Two essays to gain a sense of a particular writer's theory of creative nonfiction before you read his or her sample of it in Part One. For example, in his Part Two piece, "Whatever Happened to the Personal Essay?" Phillip Lopate discusses the history of the personal essay and reveals his own particular slant on the kinds of essays he writes. Lopate's Part One essay, "Portrait of My Body," then becomes a model for what he means by "interrogating the self." Similarly, if you first read Scott Russell Sanders's essay on essays in this section, you will then read his personal essay, "Cloud Crossing," with an awareness of what he hopes to accomplish in his writing.

Several of the writers whose works are presented in Part Two are also working teachers in whose courses students often study creative nonfiction. Some of them teach courses expressly focused on creative nonfiction as a subject in itself. As a result, their selections are at least tangentially about the connections between writing and teaching writing, especially writing and teaching creative nonfiction. Like Donald Murray, who first modeled this sensibility in *A Writer Teaches Writing* thirty years ago, each teacher/writer takes a writerly approach to this genre.

Although some of these selections involve critical analysis, they do not present a detached theoretical approach. All of the essays are designed to offer a writerly perspective on the evolving dialogue about creative nonfiction. As a result, the works selected for Part Two ground creative nonfiction in the behaviors and motives of working writers and teachers, reflecting back on the examples of the form in Part One and projecting ahead to essays on composing the fourth genre in Part Three.

Late Night Thoughts on Writing and Teaching Essays

Chris Anderson

When essayists think of the essay they think of refuge, retirement, and retreat. You need to get away when you write an essay, resign from political life and go to some place isolated, set apart. Montaigne lovingly describes the tower where he writes. There is a chapel, a bedroom, a wardrobe, and a library stacked on top of each other. He has retired as a lawyer and counselor in Bordeaux, he is 38, and he stands at the window leafing through books or looking out at his garden and his fields. In the winter he makes a fire. In the spring he takes walks. "Every place of retirement requires a place to walk," he says.

In his homage to Thoreau E. B. White describes the boathouse where he writes. Like the cabin at Walden it's a little building about ten by fifteen, "tight, plainly finished"—a semidetached affair fronting a cove, with views of ospreys and airplanes and occasionally the woodchuck (like Thoreau's woodchuck) that shares the dock with him. "It is because I am semidetached while here that I find it possible to transact this private business with the fewest obstacles," White says of writing his essays. Reading him you feel a longing for quiet and seclusion and the composition of scenes involving trees and barns.

I used to write in a converted closet in our bedroom, but we've moved to a bigger house out of town now, a house in the woods with an acre and a half. From my study window I look out at a willow tree and a crescent of rhododendrons. I've not seen a woodchuck yet, but in the evenings the deer come to nibble on the apples and plums. It's quiet here, and in the mornings the clouds cling to the hills behind us.

This is the first figure, the first stage in my thinking. Refuge. It's the image I always seem to start with, then try to escape.

Again.

Montaigne calls writing essays "that stupid enterprise." In the preface to his collected essays he takes pains to apologize for his writing, minimize it. It's merely "domestic" and "private," designed for "private convenience." "You would be unreasonable to spend your leisure on so frivolous and vain a subject." Statements like this are rhetorical strategies, I realize, but to appreciate them as strategies you have to take them literally up to a point. If you devote yourself to writing essays for a while, as I have, they do start to feel silly. Maybe that's partly because we've been conditioned to think that our own private experience is unimportant in the scheme of things and that to talk about ourselves is to violate a cultural taboo. Maybe it's because essays don't really do anything, accomplish any direct work. Maybe it's because they seem so hard to publish. If you're not already John McPhee or Annie Dillard, where do you send such things?

The other night our priest was over for dinner, and when he asked me if I'd ever published anything my wife blurted out, "Chris is an essayist." I was embarrassed, and in a way I don't think I would have been had Barb said I was a novelist or a poet. The essay has to be explained. You have to disabuse people of their notions of it. And when you have, what's left? It felt a little like Barb had said I was a stamp collector or a bird watcher (one of E. B. White's analogies), like I'd taken up tapdancing. I go into my study now and spend several mornings a week not writing a great novel or an epic poem or a scholarly treatise but little meditations on deer and apple trees, my relationship with my father, the 69 Buick I got for free from my wife's grandparents.

I can't entirely shake the notion that I should at least be writing something that will make money so I can afford the big mortgage payment I suddenly have.

Or sometimes it's this. Sometimes I think the best way to protect and nurture my love for the essay is to admit that it's marginal, peripheral, and be glad that there are others in the world doing the other, more practical things. I'm talking as both a teacher and a writer. There's more freedom in being marginal, and there's also a sense of being responsible: yes, we have to do this other, great or practical work, too (I'm just not going to do it myself). A related impulse: an impulse towards pluralism in which the essay isn't marginal but one way among many, equal to the rest. I'm OK, you're OK, and the more the better. The university is the place where we are all going down our equally legitimate paths to the truth.

In this respect, I guess, writing and teaching essays is for me a matter of handling an excess of available options. There's only so much time in a ten week course, or in a career, and since you can't do everything, why not do what comes naturally? "We must direct and fix our desires on the easiest and nearest things," Montaigne says.

But I also think it's natural to want to proselytize when you've discovered something true and right for yourself, generalize from it and set out to convert everyone else. Somehow this is especially true for people in composition, and especially for composition directors, who have the opportunity to create programs in their own image because within limits nobody particularly cares what these programs do. As a composition director myself I sometimes can't help making the essay stand for everything good, beautiful and true and reading its structures as a paradigm for freshman education in particular and liberal arts education in general.

No. It's really more than that. "Proselytize" is the wrong word, gives too much away. There are real issues here, things worth fighting for.

Arguments against making the essay central:

1. The essay is too genteel and sophisticated for freshman or any but the most advanced student. It requires talent that not everyone has.

2. The essay is too basic, too simple, not rigorous enough, because it's mostly personal and narrative and doesn't require the synthesis and analysis of academic argument and abstraction. (Of course, this argument contradicts the first.)

3. In any event, the essay is not practical, not anything students will do anywhere else in or out of the university.

Mike Rose argues this case in *Lives on the Boundary*, his recent autobiography about growing up in East Los Angeles and becoming a writing teacher. In a portrait of one of his struggling students he alludes to the "typical New Yorker fare" of freshman English anthologies, all polish and culture and wit, and his implication is that such essays are aloof and privileged, out of touch with the lives of the real students we're trying to reach.

My counterarguments:

1. The essay is not genteel and too sophisticated. Students can and do imitate it. I see essayistic power and style all the time in the writing of students, at all levels of ability. In fact, the essay seems more appropriate for beginning and struggling writers than anything else because it gives such students permission to dramatize the process of their thinking.

2. The essay is intellectually sophisticated. The ideas developed here are rich and interesting and important and deeply connected.

3. The essay and the article are not that different anyway as intellectual enterprises, are basically doing the same thing.

4. We need to challenge the idea that argument should be the basis of academic writing. We need to question whether "academic" writing as it is currently practiced is necessarily worthwhile.

5. The fact that freshman English is the only place students write essays is an argument for continuing to do that kind of writing there. A classroom can create a freedom not possible anywhere else. It can keep the economic and practical pressures at bay. It can be subversive.

6. In its sophistication and literary density, literary nonfiction provides good material for the kind of close reading and critical thinking all good writing depends on.

Again. (A balder, more personal version of these counterarguments):

Like most academics I'm a closet creative writer. Maybe the essay is a backdoor back into creative writing again.

Like most writing teachers I'm tired of reading articles from students because they're boring and cause me despair. I'm trying to generalize to a pedagogy that will produce writing that won't bore me and cause me despair.

Like many composition teachers I'm secretly a liberal arts teacher. Secretly I think that the teaching of writing is equivalent to the teaching of epic poetry or Victorian novel—useful intrinsically, for what it teaches about the human spirit, not for its usefulness in the marketplace—only composition is better because it's performative, active, a making of meanings and not just a receiving of them.

Like most people everywhere I'm mad as hell at how pretentious and obscure and inhuman most academic writing is and I don't want to be committed to that kind of thing as a teacher or a writer myself. It's the tyranny of bad expository writing that bothers me, and the smugness of that tyranny, the dogmatic insistence on it, and though the essay is only one alternative, it's the one I have the most access to.

It's this whole privileging of consumption over production that bothers me and that I feel the most at stake in. It strikes me as prima facie odd that academic culture values parasitic criticism of work over production of the work itself. As Montaigne said, "the world is swarming with commentaries; of authors there is a great scarcity." I'd rather be a second-rate author than a first-rate critic, I have to confess.

But I'm getting caught in a false dichotomy now. And I'm exaggerating my own feelings. Most of the time I am an uneasy pluralist, troubled by the claims Rose and others have made. Despite my flare-ups of enthusiasm or anger, I've made the essay the ground of the writing program more out of a sense that it's as good as any other approach than out of any passion I feel comfortable generalizing from.

I'm trying to be empirical. This is how I actually feel most of the time: without the courage of my convictions somehow.

The other day I was observing an instructor teaching a business writing class and she was explaining a formula for writing a certain kind of memo, and she was allowing, too, for the possibility that sometimes you have to write in a deliberately obscure or uninteresting way. I had a complicated reaction. On the one hand, this is wrong and boring and mechanical, contrary to everything we should be doing in a writing class; on the other, this is real and practical and commonsensical, and I should be doing more of this instead of always asking my students to read and write essays.

Maybe Rose is right and it's a question of sequence, of time of life. I only felt free to write essays after I was well on my way to getting tenure. When I went up for tenure last year a senior colleague advised me to leave off my vita the few essays I had published. (I left them on.) Lewis Thomas was in his fifties when he started, after publishing hundreds of scholarly papers. Which is to say that maybe the essay is for later and our freshman have to pay their dues and get financial security before they are free, before they have the leisure, to explore their own experience. It's an economic issue, at least.

Besides, I like and respect the "article," too. Good expository writing requires imagination and power—there is such a thing as a good article—and though I've sworn off that kind of writing myself for now, lately I've found ideas developing in my head that could only be expressed in article form. Having turned away from the article for a while, I realize its value and its naturalness. There's a feeling of mastery writing articles, of zeroing in.

I keep wanting to number or blend the pieces of this essay, establish a different sequence. It keeps seeming unfocused. I worry about transitions.

Or maybe making the essay the center of a curriculum is to domesticate it too much, tame it. Maybe it only has cultural and political power when it's marginal.

Maybe I just don't want people putting their feet up on my delicate structures. No one else should write essays. Stay away. Californians go home.

Maybe we should just accept the designation of "creative" writing for the essay so that we can then hide away in our "specialness" and "talent" from the rest of the world.

A better way out of this ambivalence.

I said that composition directors are ignored and that that can be good. Annie Dillard makes the same point about writers, writers of any kind, and I find her statement oddly exhilarating. The writing life is life at its most free, she says, "because you select your materials, invent your tasks, and pace yourself." But that freedom "is a by-product of your days' triviality":

> Your work is so meaningless, so fully for yourself alone, and so worthless to the world, that no one except you cares whether you do it well, or ever…Your manuscript, on which you lavish such care, has no needs or wishes; it knows you not. Nor does anyone need your manuscript…There are many manuscripts already—worthwhile ones, most edifying and moving ones, intelligent and powerful ones…. Why not shoot yourself, actually, rather than finish one more excellent manuscript on which to gag the world?

For someone worried about the marginality or stupidity of the form of writing he does, this is tonic stuff. All writing is marginal and stupid, Dillard is saying; all writing is useless. The statement opens out into a philosophy of life, a broad view of the relative smallness of any of our acts. This isn't a depressing perspective really. It's a way of not taking yourself or your work too seriously. You smile, relax, and go on. (In a hundred years, my Dad used to say, it won't make any difference anyway.) Or there's this more explicitly idealistic passage from an essay by Richard Ford:

> Some people, I guess, thrive by deferring to unknown and presumably higher authority, to the benevolence of vast, indistinct institutions. And of course, it's never a simple matter when your life requires submitting to the judgment of others. We all accommodate that. But most of the writers I have known seem to me not so adept at discerning and respecting underlying design, but actually spend all their efforts trying to invent designs anew. What is out there is not a structure for writers to surrender to, but fidgety, dodgey chaos. And our privileged task is to force it, calm it to our wills.

Fidgety, dodgey chaos. The problem with Rose—and with David Bartholomae, too, for another example—is that they both assume without questioning the validity of academic writing, as if it's fixed, part of natural law, instead of recognizing that it's mutable, changing, a human construction imposed for reasons and rescindable for reasons.

"We must remove the mask from things as from persons," Montaigne says, and what we discover is this: "the world is but perpetual motion; all things in it move incessantly." Like Montaigne I'm too skeptical to think that any social order or "discursive practice" can go without questioning. All is flux.

The irony with Rose and Bartholomae and the social-epistemic rhetoricians in general is that the social order implied by the academic writing they accept and practice is hierarchical, contrary to the argument they want to make, implicitly deferring to unknown authorities and presumably benevolent institutions. (Rose and Bartholomae would deny this, call it an exaggeration. Maybe it is, but only a little, it seems to me.) The irony is that the book Rose has written is brave and risky and good because it is an essay, a personal thinking through of the problem, an autobiographical rendering which insists in both its form and its content on the need to make connections and preserve relationships, contexts, humility.

I keep thinking of this final scene.

In "Some Thoughts on the Common Toad" George Orwell complains that every time he mentions nature in one of his essays he's criticized as bourgeois and escapist. He thinks there's faulty logic here:

> Certainly we ought to be discontented, we ought not simply to find out ways of making the best of a bad job, and yet if we kill all pleasure in the actual process of life, what sort of future are we preparing for ourselves? If a man cannot enjoy the return of spring, why should he be happy in a labor-saving Utopia? What will he do with the leisure that the machine will give him?

In fact, taking pleasure in spring is finally a political act for Orwell. "I think that by retaining one's childhood love of such things as trees, fishes, butterflies, and—to return to my first instance—toads, one makes a peaceful and decent future a little more probable, and that by preaching the doctrine that nothing is to be admired except steel and concrete, one merely makes it a little surer that human beings will have no outlet for their surplus energy except in hatred and leader-worship."

Last fall I was on my way over the pass to a state Composition Advisory Committee meeting when I decided to stop and hike up to Iron Mountain. The trail gains about two thousand feet in a mile and a half, so it's all switchbacks and short-step climbing, like a stairway. At the top is a Forest Service lookout, and on the clear October day I stood there I could look north and see all the peaks of the Cascades lined up in a row: Jefferson, Hood, Rainier. Sitting on the porch of the lookout, eating the sandwich I'd brought, I felt the sense of presence I always feel in the mountains, the sense of things being present, there, announcing themselves over and over again. It was about 4:30 in the afternoon and the sun and the moon were both in the sky. Once a "v" of geese flew over, the line of it sagging and reforming as it passed.

I could say that my experience on Iron Mountain was a spiritual experience. The qualities of that moment—suspension, balance, the inward turning, the awareness of things outside, the fact of detour, the uselessness of the moment—these have a spiritual dimension. But I think that climbing the mountain was a political act, too, political in Orwell's sense that moments like these are what political systems are trying to make happen, prepare for, keep others from preventing.

I see that I'm moving now away from my pluralism–fidgety chaos argument back in the direction of my essay-as-salvation argument.

I'd like to make these balder claims at least:

The climbing of a trail and the seeing of geese is useful. It's useful because it's restorative. It's useful because it balances. The climbing of trails and the seeing of geese, I want to say, is not a retreat or a detour but a direct engagement with the things that matter most, which is what the engagement is, a climbing up off the road to look back down on it, a seeing of the road in the larger landscape, rising and falling, appearing and disappearing.

The Landscape of Creative Nonfiction

Jocelyn Bartkevicius

[I]naccuracy is very often a superior form of truth.
—Virginia Woolf, "Incongruous Memories"

1. The Stranger

I was standing in a garden, tomato plants ripening, chickens dashing about, when I first learned I was a stranger. I was quite young, maybe six or seven, watching my grandmother pick tomatoes and tell stories about her life as a farm girl in Eastern Europe. She had just gotten to the part about hiding in the forest from waves of invading armies—Russians then Prussians then Russians again—when she stopped, stood up, looked me in the eye, and said: "But you are an American; you don't understand."

How can I convey the force of these words? Of course, as a school girl I was familiar with the idea of "being an American." I said the pledge of allegiance, hand on heart like all the other kids. I sang the "Star Spangled Banner" (except for those unreachable glaring red high notes). But this identity had never been pinned upon me so specifically, so singularly, or as an impediment. "Being an American" had never made me an outsider. Standing in my grandmother's garden, among plants and animals raised the old ways, I was the other.

In memory, when she speaks these words, my grandmother is looking me right in the eye. She was a small woman, possibly reaching five feet at her healthiest, before the osteoporosis formed a permanent stoop. And I was a gangly girl who got all her height early. But now that I look at the memory, examine it instead of experiencing it, I must admit that a five-foot-tall six year old is an unlikely creature. Something is wrong with the memory. It is incongruous.

And then there are holes in the memory: I can't remember whether my grand-mother continued her story after she stood up and spoke to me. Or whether she returned to her gardening. Or why she began the story at all. It was hard to get her to talk about Lithuania, especially about the years when, as a very young woman, she had to bury food in the forest to survive, had to prepare constantly to flee soldiers and their various hungers, had to watch city people (who could not grow their own food) sicken and die. Perhaps my father stood off to the side prompting her. But he is not in the memory. Maybe I—normally a very shy child and fearful of misunderstanding her difficult Lithuanian accent—had a rare fit of boldness and asked her a question about Europe.

The scene is one that I return to often, for her words fixed the moment as indel-ibly as a brand. I used to think that the memory drew me in spite of its incongruities and holes. But I am beginning to realize that this memory compels me *because* of the incongruities and holes. The pitted, nearly invisible landscape of the past is a mysteri-ous, inviting place. Each exploration reveals a different topography.

Looking back, I find that my grandmother bequeathed layers of strangeness that day. Her words taught me that I was a stranger in her world. And they taught that, while there had been some unevenness in my life—near poverty, my parents' divorce, and so on—I was nevertheless a stranger to profound suffering and struggle. And now, looking not just at the moment but at the memory itself, at the moment as incongru-ous memory, I find that my grandmother's words taught me that there is a stranger within. That is, certain moments will not survive unravaged, that going back in time and memory I will discover losses, unreachable territories. Some of the territories remain, buried beneath the surface of daily life and ordinary reminiscence, inaccessi-ble but for accident or imaginative self interrogation.

In the case of my grandmother's garden, incongruities and obvious gaps drew me back to the memory, signaled its importance. Other moments may disappear without a trace, leaving no path, and the act of writing may be the only way to unearth them.

A few years after I stood with my grandmother in her garden, my father bought a farm—or what I called a farm before I moved from Connecticut to Iowa and saw working farms, counted among my friends actual farmers, and learned that in relation to Iowa farms, my father's place had been not a farm at all but an acreage. There on his land I built a miniature version of my grandmother's garden using compost from the manure pile, sprinkling lime from a stocking to discourage bugs. I followed my father around, riding barely trained horses, acting the cowboy, zipping through forests, sleeping under the stars. And this is how I remember those years, as a little grandma, a little immigrant, a peasant girl in a store-bought peasant blouse (it was the sixties), bringing home-grown organic carrots to high school for lunch. I remember a peaceful Eden punctuated by moments of playing the stereo in my father's hand-built log cabin, Joni Mitchell singing about getting back to the garden, Neil Young loving his country girl.

But recently, I found buried in an old trunk a black and white snapshot of my father and me, pitchfork and all like the pair in Grant Wood's *American Gothic*. Our pitchfork, though, is angled; we both stare at it, and impaled upon one of the tongs is a small bat. In my memory, I am a Romantic peasant girl, gardening as it has been handed down by my Eastern European ancestors, embracing Woodstock, barefoot to Joni and Neil. In the photograph I am a party to the slaughter of a benign and beneficial mammal. Writing about the photograph awakened darker memories from the farm: another child's pointing a loaded pistol at me, my aiming a loaded BB gun at a sleeping bat as it hung from the shed door, and leaving the cabin after an argument to disappear alone into the dark country night.

The self—at least *my* self—is composed of misremembered and unremembered scenes. The path back to that uneven landscape is the path of the mind. Students in my creative nonfiction workshops frequently ask me to define for them, concisely and with directions for construction, "the personal essay." Usually I try to do so by offering a variety of creative nonfiction pieces along with several writers' working definitions of the form. But at times I ask them to define for me, concisely (but without directions for construction), "a person." The definition of "personal essay" is as complicated and various as that of "person," and the personal essay is just one possible manifestation of creative nonfiction.

In writing creative nonfiction, in order to tell the truth, I must let the incongruities be. I was standing in the garden with my Grandmother and we were eye to eye although we could not be the same height. I was six while also being ten—perhaps six with shyness and the language barrier and ten chronologically. Or ten in my boldness and six chronologically. Or I was somehow taller for being a stranger and my Grandmother was somehow shorter for changing my world. And in order to tell the truth in creative nonfiction I must explore the gaps. I was an earth child on my father's farm and yet I was shooting bats. I focus on the unremembered photograph and dig for more. Memory, the mind's path, enacts wonders, and the creative nonfiction writer's work is not to reason those wonders away with mathematical formulae, but to embrace them, to recreate layer after layer of incongruity.

2. *The Terms*

The first time I heard the term "nonfiction," I was sitting with twenty other third graders at a veneered table in a grammar school library. I watched the librarian walk from wall to wall tapping books and signs with her pointer. Each book had a hand-typed Dewey decimal system number taped to its spine. Each section had a hand-printed sign fixed above it. She paused at the section labeled "fiction," tapped a row of spines, tapped the sign above, and said: "These books are fiction. They're made up; they aren't true." She stepped to the left, swung her pointer at the next section, labeled "nonfiction," tapped the sign, and said: "These books are not fiction. They aren't made up; they are fact." While the librarian went on with her presentation, my mind went elsewhere. Fiction was not true and nonfiction was not fiction; therefore nonfiction was *not* not true. She was using the forbidden double negative. I sat at the table wondering what made fiction, the not-true, so central that the term "nonfiction" was formed from it.

I probably would have forgotten that moment in the library if similar moments had not recurred throughout my life. The string of assumptions goes like this: Fiction is "made up," and thus crafted, invented, "made." Fiction is art because its creator draws upon imagination. Nonfiction is "not made up," and thus recorded, reported, "unmade." Nonfiction makes itself, the writer is a mere tape recorder or camera. Or, in cases where the material of nonfiction needs some shaping, the writer draws upon reason and logic alone.

Such assumptions are in part an issue of terminology. "Fiction," the root word, comes from "fingere," to form, mold, devise. "Non" simply means "not." Thus we get the implication that nonfiction is not formed, molded, or devised. Although this "non" negates the term "fiction," it is not the strongest available negative prefix. "Dis," which implies expulsion, as in "disfrock" or "disbar," would give us disfiction, a genre deprived of fiction, even, perhaps, expelled from it. "Un," which means "against" or "anti," would give us unfiction, a genre opposed to fiction. Nonfiction, looked at in this context, is not deprived of fiction or opposed to fiction, but simply, like the librarian said, not fiction.

There remains, however, an unsettling nuance to "non." While calling someone non-American does not brand them an enemy (as calling that person un-American would), it still suggests that they are other. A non-American is a foreigner, or, as my grand-mother was sometimes called, an alien. Nonfiction is to fiction as non-American is to American. Thus, nonfiction is the stranger, the foreigner (or alien) in the land of fiction. What's more, in both cases, the root word is the point of reference. Many writers and editors add creative" to "nonfiction" to mollify this sense of being strange and other, and to remind readers that creative nonfiction writers are more than recorders or appliers of reason and objectivity. Certainly many readers and writers of creative nonfiction recognize that the genre can share some elements of fiction; dialogue, place, characters, and plot, for example, might occur in both. When a piece of creative nonfiction resembles fiction, the "non" might suggest not so much "not," as something like "kicking off from." Why else insist that it is not fiction unless it is in danger of being mistaken for fiction?

If "nonfiction" might mean a work that is related to but different from fiction, perhaps works in the genre that are more akin to poetry—sharing with it lyric and image or a structure built on association and repetition rather than on narrative—would benefit from another name. I read some of Virginia Woolf's nonfiction (her lyr-ical, personal pieces like "Evening Over Sussex," and "The Death of the Moth," for example) for its poetry. Other writers come to mind: Terry Tempest Williams's *Desert Quartet*, for example, a lyrical, concentrated work with gaps and craters, a book writ-ten not only from reason, but also from imagination, dreams, and the body. Such works, while not poems per se, use poetry as their inspiration, their model, their "kicking off point." For them, I suggest the term "nonpoetry."

To play with terms and search for definitions can be more than an academic exercise. I'm interested in the genre's possibility, a possibility not just theoretical but practical—that is, involving practice. Rather than map out territory (and thus limit it) I mean to expand it. Rather than build fences, knock them down.

3. The Stars

A few months ago, a formerly estranged cousin gave me a copy of an old home movie. Over antipasto made the old way, we watched ourselves together, children moving in and out of a series of silent, disjointed scenes in black and white. My cousin and I sat together as his father's last birthday party unfolded before us; we watched ourselves celebrate just a few yards from the spot where an accident would later kill his father, shattering our family for decades. But on that night preserved on film, we all sit together on the pool deck of the hotel and nightclub his father and my stepfather ran together, happy beneath the stars. We sit at a long table, laughing and talking silently. Suddenly, my stepfather rises up, grabs a torch-like candle, and begins dancing around our table. While he circles the rest of us, we watch my uncle cut his Italian rum cake from Romano's.

My cousin broke the silence of that old flickering movie. "There must have been bugs," he said, "that's got to be a bug torch and he's spreading the fog around our table." But that's not what I saw. Though I didn't at first remember the scene, I knew my stepfather. He was dancing out his joy, his exuberance, the energy that pored from each cell of his body. "I'd rip the stars out of the sky for you," he used to tell my half sister, the child of his middle age, and there he was, ripping the stars out of the sky, lighting the night for one of our last happy moments together.

The camera recorded the scene for perpetuity. And yet my cousin and I, with similar family experiences, with memories of that moment, and with objective evidence before us, saw it differently. If put alone in separate rooms and interrogated or given blank sheets of paper and told to write that scene, we would come up with different stories. We both sat at the family table that night, and so the party is in our memories, embedded in the very matter of our brains. And we both watched the tape, separately and together, several times in recent months. Nevertheless we tell different stories. Which one is true? Which one imagined? His story and mine, I believe, contain elements of fact and imagination. Both are true, for they are true to how we remember, how we see, they recreate the topographies of our minds. We can return to the film and we can return to our memories. Either way, each of us returns to a different place.

Recently, I attended another birthday party, for a friend who is a writer. After he blew out the candles, and everyone made the requisite jokes about aging, our conversation turned to writing and memory. "You could never write this scene as nonfiction," one friend, a fiction writer, said. "You couldn't remember the dialogue verbatim; you'd end up remembering words wrong and so you'd have to change them. You'd forget things and leave them out. That would make it fiction." Several others at the table agreed, assuming that without a tape recorder you'd be left with fallible memory and therefore be incapable of creating nonfiction. There were only two ways to write the scene with dialogue, they believed, to write it as fiction (and freely invent and recreate words), or to write it as nonfiction (and record, transcribe, and then report the words exactly as spoken).

One of the guests, a lawyer, objected. "You should read briefs," he said. "Recorded dialogue doesn't make any sense."

"You need the background," another friend, a nonfiction writer, added, "the color of the walls, the smell of the food. How can you understand the dialogue without the scene?"

"What if someone's words trigger a memory?" I asked. "Let's say that as you're speaking, I'm reminded of a scene from my past, like standing in my grandmother's garden. Even if we filmed and taped this party, that wouldn't show up, and yet it changes my experience of the party."

"I was wondering" the literary theorist said, "what I'd do with that moment when I became obsessed with the pattern on this plate, or when I concentrated on the taste of the red beans and rice."

If my birthday party companions read this dialogue, they would no doubt revise it according to their own memories and perceptions. In fact, that same night we suggested—as a joke or perhaps as a challenge—that each of us, two fiction writers, a poet, two creative nonfiction writers, a theorist, a lawyer, and a decorator—should go off immediately and write the scene. By the time we were well into the cake and coffee, we more or less agreed that if we were true to the events as we'd each experienced them, if we didn't write, for example, that the lawyer had stood up, reached across the table, and punched the guest of honor as he blew out his candles (since he had done nothing of the kind), we would be writing creative nonfiction.

We reached common ground in the end, I think, because we shifted both our working notion of genre and our view of "the person." When my friends claimed that nonfiction could work only with the aid of a tape recorder, their concept of the person was external, the person as captured by a machine. They had shared the assumption, arrived at by habit, that nonfiction was restricted to objectivity and reporting, that incongruity must be reasoned away. Fact, as Virginia Woolf points out, is not necessarily the same as truth, and as we talked that night, we explored what it means to be at a birthday party, what it means to participate in a conversation, how much more it is than the sounds we make, the words we speak. What we say and how we move— what machines can pick up—is only the surface of the scene. "Nonfiction" is not a synonym for "recorded surface." It has the range to sweep inward, follow the path of the mind, add layers of contemporaneous imagination, memory, and dream to the observable events of the present moment.

Patricia Hampl, who has said that memory is a place, has also said that the nonfiction writer is homeless.

One such occasion was an informal talk after her reading in the third floor lounge of a certain university's humanities' building. Graduate students used to joke about the symbolism of the building's design: Fiction and poetry were on the top floor. Freshman composition was in the basement. In the middle (just above philosophy) was nonfiction, tucked away in a corner of the literature department. Although Hampl's reading drew a large audience, only a small group of die-hard nonfictionists showed up for the talk.

In our small quarters, nearly invisible in a wing of the literature department, her discussion of the nonfiction writer's homelessness rang true. The department had just changed the name of our program from "expository writing" to "nonfiction writing" and would soon rename it "creative nonfiction." We could see that we were the new kids on the block, that to many, our genre was ill defined and invisible. But there we sat listening to a writer who had made a career of creative nonfiction, who had written two memoirs and many personal essays, and who spoke optimistically about the genre's range and possibility. Many of us felt at home for the first time—not in our lounge, but in her words.

The prospect of literary homelessness drives and limits certain writers to formulae, say, memoir in five parts (action scene followed by predictable summation followed by continuation of the action and so on, like a sitcom or a mini series). They find a "home" and hole up in the corner. And they pass along a favored formula to groups of beginner or intermediate writers, regardless of any particular student writer's emphasis, place of origin, gender, culture, aesthetic, or concept of the self. Handing over a prepackaged piece of creative nonfiction is, in essence, putting the writer into a cell. The bolder explorers, happy not to be enclosed, take advantage of the unsettled terrain of nonfiction, wandering and exploring, allowing themselves to be vulnerable, following the path of the mind even when they enter shadows, pressing on into the territory of the unknown, the mysterious, the incongruous.

Creative nonfiction is at once flourishing and invisible, set and contested. The genre that embraces the often paradoxical nature of the self is itself often paradoxical (in its position in the world of writing and letters). Patricia Hampl provides the metaphor of the creative nonfiction writer as homeless. And she also turns it around. We're lucky, she says, we get to be out under the stars.

The Art of Memoir

Mary Clearman Blew

One of the oldest and loveliest of quilt patterns is the Double Wedding Ring, in which bands of colors lock and interlock in endless circles. If you want to make a Double Wedding Ring quilt, be a saver of fabric. Treasure the smallest scraps, from the maternity dress you have just sewn for your oldest daughter or the Halloween costume you cobbled together for your youngest, from the unfaded inside hems of worn-out clothing or the cotton left over from other quilts. Keep a pair of sharp scissors on hand, and also a pattern, which I like to cut from fine sandpaper, and which will be about an inch wide by two inches long and slightly flared, like a flower petal that has been rounded off at both ends. Whenever you have a scrap of fabric, lay out your pattern on it and snip out a few more blocks.

Save your blocks in a three-pound coffee can. When the can is full, empty the blocks out on the floor and arrange them in the shape of rainbow arcs with a juxtaposition of colors and textures that pleases you. Seven pieces to an arc, seventy-two arcs to a quilt. You can sew the blocks together on a sewing machine, but I like the spell cast by hand sewing. I use a #11 needle, which is an inch-long sliver of steel with an eye so fine that it will barely take the quilter's thread, which measures time by growing infinitesimally shorter with each dip and draw of the needle, and I wear the hundred-year-old thimble of a woman named Amelia Bunn on my finger.

When you have pieced your seventy-two arcs, you must choose a fabric to join your arcs, in a process that is called "setting up" the quilt. Traditionally a Double Wedding Ring quilt is set up on white, but remember that you have all colors to choose from; and while choosing one color means forgoing others, remind yourself that your coffee can of pieces will fill again. There will be another quilt at the back of your mind while you are piecing, quilting, and binding this one, which perhaps you will give to one of your daughters, to trace her childhood through the pieces. Or perhaps you will give it to a friend, to speak the words the pattern spoke to you.

For years I thought of myself as a fiction writer, even during the years in northern Montana when I virtually stopped writing. But in 1987 I came to a divide. My father had died, and my husband was suffering a mental breakdown along with the progressive lung disease that eventually killed him. I was estranged from my older children. Then I lost my job. It was the job that mattered the most. I had a small child to support. And so I looked for another job and found one, teaching in a small college in Idaho, with the northern Rockies between me and the first half of my life.

Far from home and teaching again after years in higher-ed. administration, I felt a hollowness that writing fiction seemed to do nothing to fill. And so I started all over again, writing essays to retrieve the past—in my case, the Montana homestead frontier with its harsh ideals for men and women, its tests and its limitations. The conventions of fiction, its masks and metaphors, came to seem more and more boring to me, like an unnecessary barricade between me and the material I was writing about. But because fiction was what I knew about, I used the techniques of fiction in these essays: plot, characterization, dialogue. What I began to discover was a form that worked for my purpose.

I would select an event out of family legend and retell it in a voice that grew out of my own experience and perceptions. Often the events that beckoned to me the most urgently were the ones that had been preserved in the "secret stories" my grandmothers and my great-aunts told around their Sunday tables after the dishes had been washed, elliptical and pointless and mystifying, in hushed voices that dropped or stopped altogether at the approach of one of the men or an unwise question from an eavesdropping child. Eventually I was trusted with a few of the secret stories, myself. I remember how my aunt's voice fell and her sentences became sparing when she told me a story about her mother, my grandmother. The story was about a time when my grandmother had lived alone on the homestead north of Denton, Montana, for eighteen months without seeing another woman. She had two small children and another baby on the way—her husband was away for weeks on end, trying to sell life insurance to make ends meet—and she had to carry her water in a bucket from a spring a quarter of a mile from the homestead shack, which she did at twilight, when the heat of the sun was not so oppressive. She began to hallucinate. She saw the shapes of women on the other side of the spring, shapes that looked like her dead mother and her dead sister, beckoning to her. She decided she was going crazy. She had her little children to think about. They might not be found for weeks if she broke down. And so she began to go for her water in the heat of the day, when the sun scorched her trail and bleached the color out of the grass and rocks. She never saw the beckoning shapes again.

Unlike my grandmother, I have chosen to follow the beckoning shapes. I don't understand the significance of that story for my grandmother, or why she kept it a secret except for the one time she whispered it to her younger sister in, I presume, those same stark sentences in which her sister whispered it to her niece, my aunt, the same sentences in which my aunt whispered the story just one time to me. But then, I don't fully understand why I continue to wear Amelia Bunn's thimble—it is sterling silver and engraved AB in a fine script—any more than I know what my great-grandmother looked like in life or as she appeared in the dying heat waves of that long-ago Montana twilight.

But sometimes I think I can see the turning points in the lives of dead men and women. For example, my grandmother's decision to return to schoolteaching in 1922, even though it meant breaking up her family, boarding out her oldest daughter, taking the younger children to live with her in a teacherage, leaving her husband alone on the homestead. What did that decision mean to her? I know what it means to me. Or my aunt's mowing machine accident in June of 1942, when a runaway team of sorrel horses spilled her in the path of a sickle bar that nearly cut off her foot. The disaster forced her out of the path of teaching in rural schools that she had been following and into a new life on the Olympic Peninsula. Did she understand the opportunity in the teeth of the sickle bar?

I feel an uneasy balance between writing about my grandmother and my aunt as their lives "really" were and writing about them as a projection of my own experiences. I keep reminding myself that the times when they lived are not my times. Nor do the nuances of their stories necessarily reflect my assumptions about language. And yet I am who I am because of these women and the stories they told; and, as I write about them, they live and breathe again through the umbilical tangle between character and writer.

I've been fortunate in my family's being one of storytellers and private writers who have "documented" their past. Tales, diaries, notebooks, and letters—they saved every scrap. Of course their stories were fictions as much as mine are, told over and over again and given shape and significance. Their connection to literal truth is suspect.

For my part, I struggled for a long time with the conflicting claims of the exact truth of the story and its emotional truth as I perceived it. I restrict myself to what I "know" happened: the concrete details, the objects, the history. When I speculate, I say so.

But any story depends upon its shape. In arranging the scraps that have been passed down to me, which are to be selected, which discarded? The boundaries of creative nonfiction will always be as fluid as water.

Students often ask, what can you decently write about other people? Whose permission do you have to ask? What can you decently reveal about yourself?

I can only speak for myself. I own my past and my present. Only I can decide whether or how to write about it. Also, I know that once I write about the past, I will have changed the past, in a sense set it in concrete, and I will never remember it in quite the same way. The experience itself is lost; like the old Sunday storytellers who told and retold their stories until what they remembered was the tale itself, what I will remember is what I have written.

Certainly, something personal is being sacrificed, for when I write about myself, I transform myself just as I do the past. A side-effect is that while the writing process itself can be painful, I experience a detachment from the finished essay, because I have come to exist in it as a character as separate from myself as any fictional character. I find that I can read my essays to audiences with very little emotion, although once, reading Annick Smith's essay "Homestead" to a creative writing class, I began to cry and thought I would not be able to go on. Her nonfiction character moved me in a way my own could not.

Lately I have been reading my aunt's diaries, which she kept without fail for fifty years. I feel haunted by the parallels between her life and mine. She chose, perhaps with greater self-discipline, perhaps from being closer to the source of the old punishing pressures, to stay all her life on a straight and narrow path I had been perilously near to embarking on. Her diaries reveal her unhappiness, her gradual, unwilling resignation to her lot, and finally, in her old age, her reconciliation with the lone woman she had set out to be. Which has left me with an enormous determination to resist those pressures and to try a new direction: having written my past, I will write the present and transform myself, as she did, in the interstices between fragment and pattern, through the endless interlocking connections between storyteller and story.

We'll see, we'll see. Opportunity lies in the teeth of the sickle bar.

The Faith

David Bradley

One evening not long ago I found myself sitting on a stage in front of a live audience, being asked questions about life and art. I was uncomfortable, as I always am in such circumstances. Still, things were going pretty well on this occasion, until the interviewer noted that my father had been a minister, and asked what influence religion, the church and the faith of my father, had had on my development as a writer. After a moment of confusion, I responded that since I had, at various times and with more than a modicum of accuracy, been labeled a heretic, a pagan, a heathen, and a moral degenerate, all things considered, the faith of my father had had very little to do with my writing. Which was, depending on how cynical you want to be, either a total lie or as close as I could get to the truthful answer—which would have been: "Practically everything."

The history of my relationship to religion cannot be stated so simply as "My father was a minister." In fact, I am descended from a long line of ministers. The first was my great-grandfather, a freedman named Peter Bradley, who, in the early part of the nineteenth century, was licensed to preach by the African Methodist Episcopal Zion Church, one of two denominations formed at that time by blacks who were tired of the discrimination they were forced to endure in the regular Methodist Church. Peter's son, Daniel Francis, followed in his father's footsteps and then went a step further, becoming a presiding elder with administrative and spiritual responsibility over a number of churches in western Pennsylvania and Ohio. Daniel Francis's son, David, followed his father's footsteps, and then added a step of his own: he was elected a general officer of the denomination (a rank just below that of bishop), with the dual responsibility of traveling the country to run conferences and workshops in Christian education and of publishing the church's quasi-academic journal, the *A. M. E. Zion Quarterly Review*, tasks he performed without interruption for nearly thirty years. Since David was my father, it would seem reasonable to expect that I would carry on the family tradition. That I did not was a fact that was viewed with great relief by all those who knew me—including David senior. Nevertheless, my apostasy had its origins in the church. For because of my father's editorial functions, I grew up in a publishing house.

My earliest memories of excitement, bustle, and tension center on the process of mailing the 1,400- or 1,500-copy press run of the *Quarterly Review*. The books came in sweet-smelling and crisp from the printer, were labeled, bundled, and shipped out again in big gray-green musty mailbags labeled with the names of far-off states, a process that was sheer heaven to a three- or four-year-old and sheer hell for everybody else, especially my mother, who did the bulk of the work and had to give up a chunk of her house to the process.

In fact, the work of publishing the *Review* took up the whole house most of the time; it was just that work usually went on at a less frenetic rate. While my father was away, my mother, who was the subscription and shipping department, spent some time cleaning the lists (a constant task, since ministers, the main subscribers, were regularly being moved around) and typing names and addresses onto labels. When my father returned home, the tempo picked up. He spent a good bit of time in the study, writing to other ministers and prominent lay people to solicit articles and publishable sermons, and editing those that had already arrived. At that same time, he would be writing a bit himself, composing the two or three editorials that graced each issue.

The *Review*, while it was called a quarterly, was not published every three months, but rather four times a year; my father took it to the printer when he was home long enough to get it ready, and when the printer had time to do the work. The date for that was sometimes fixed only a week or so in advance, and once it was set, the tempo became fairly furious; my father spent more and more time in the study, selecting cover art, editing the late-arriving articles, rewriting the press releases from the National Council of Churches that he used for filler. Then, on the date designated, with the copy in one hand, and my hand in the other, my father would go to the printer.

I looked forward to going to the printer with my father, in part because of the printer himself, a venerable gentleman named George, the perfect image of a chapelman all the way down to his ink-stained knuckles and honest-to-God green eyeshade. The chapel over which he presided was no mere print shop, but the printing plant of the local daily, a dark cavern with an ink-impregnated wood floor and air that smelled of hot metal and chemicals, crowded with weirdly shaped machines. On the left a bank of linotypes spewed hot type and spattered molten lead onto the floor. On the right were machines to do the tasks that at home I saw done by hand—address labels, tie bundles, stuff envelopes. At the back, dominating the entire scene, was the great press on which the paper was printed, a big, black, awkward-looking thing that towered to the ceiling and descended into the bowels of the earth. Once George invited my father to bring me down at night to see the press roll, a sight that proved to be so exciting I could not tell if all the shaking was due to the awesome turning of the rollers or to the weakness in my knees; but usually we went to the printer during the day, and the big press was simply a silent presence.

During the visits to the printer, my father and George would be closeted in the little cubbyhole that served as George's office, while I had the run of the chapel. It was on one of those occasions, I believe, that any chance I would follow in the family footsteps was lost. For on this one day, while George and my father muttered of ems and ens, one of the linotype operators paused in his work and invited me to write my name on a scrap of paper, and after I had done so, let me watch as he punched my name out in hot lead. I think that was the moment when my personal die was cast.

Of course, it might have had no lasting effect had not my father, at about the same time, inadvertently introduced me to the corrupting pleasure of having written a book.

A few years before I was born, my father abandoned his studies at New York University, where he had been working for a Ph.D. in history. Five years later, for no reason other than desire, he took up the writing of what would have been his dissertation: "A History of the A. M. E. Zion Church."

I do not remember what it was like being around him while he wrote—I was, after all, less than five. I recall his methodology, which was to write a fairly detailed outline in a flowing longhand on lined paper, which he would store in a big loose-leaf binder until he was ready to turn it into a messy typescript which a typist—often my mother—later rendered as clean copy. (For one reason or another, this is the method I now use to write nonfiction.) I believe there was a certain heightening of tension during the time he was sending the typescript off to publishers; I know that he eventually entered into a cooperative arrangement with a press in Tennessee, a measure which forced him to take out a second mortgage—something I know he felt guilty about, since years later he would explain that we were not in better financial shape because of the book, but something he did not really regret, since he did it again in order to publish the second volume.

At the time the first volume was published, I was only six, but already I was in love with books. I had my own card at the public library, and I had read everything they had that was suitable for a child my age, and a lot that was not. Moreover, I had reread much of it many times, and the characters and stories had become so familiar, that my imagination was no longer a participant in the process; as a result, I had taken to imagining the people behind the characters. I was not old enough for literary biographies (the biographies written for children at that time went heavy on Clara Barton and Thomas Alva Edison and the like, and concentrated on the time when they were children; I loathed the things). And so I made up my own, based on bits of story I had picked up here and there. I was fascinated with Herman Melville and Richard Henry Dana, Jr., both of whom my mother said had actually gone to sea. And I was captivated by Jack London, who, my father told me, had really gone hunting gold in the frozen Yukon.

But even though I was taken with these people, I felt removed from them; they were not real—not as real, anyway, as the characters about whom they wrote. For I could imagine myself standing before the mast or trekking the frozen tundra, but I simply could not imagine myself writing a book.

But then one day a big tractor-trailer pulled up in the driveway and began to unload cartons, and my father, normally not an impulsive or a demonstrative man, took the first carton and ripped it open and pulled out a book that had his name stamped on the front board in gold foil, and suddenly the men behind the books I'd read were as real to me as my father. And suddenly I began to see that slug of type, which I had kept safe, mounted and inked, imprinting my name on a book.

I have always been uncertain about the importance of some of the things that have happened to me, suspecting that if one thing had not pushed me in the direction of writing, then probably something else would have. But I know the importance of that moment. For time and time again, people have said to me that the writing of a book is an impossible task, even to comprehend. For me, though, it was not only comprehensible, it was visible. And so, by the age of six or seven, I had firmly turned away from the family tradition. Ironically enough, at about the same time I began to discover the majesty and beauty of the Christian worship service.

When I was four or five, my father had started taking me with him on some of his travels, usually in the summer, when his work took him mostly to the Southeast. The first place I went with him—and it became a regular trip—was Dinwiddie, Virginia, where, in an aging ramshackle three-story building, the church operated an "Institute"—a combination Christian education workshop, summer camp, and revival meeting.

The Institute ran for three weeks—a week each for children, teenagers (what the church called "young people"), and adults. The format for all was basically the same: a day of classes punctuated by morning and noon chapel services, an afternoon recreation period, and three meals of good plain food—corn bread, grits, chicken, pork, greens—and climaxed by evening worship. The morning and afternoon worship services were short and pretty plain affairs. The evening service was pageantry, if for no other reason than that it was the focal point of everybody's day. My father's involvement was primarily with the "young people," and so I spent more time at the Institute when they were there. Evening worship was important to them because it was the closest they could get to a dating situation, and they made the most of it. It was important to the ministers, who shared the various offices of the service on a rotating basis, competing eagerly for the choice assignments, preaching and praying. It was important to the people in the community, who used the evening worship as a kind of camp meeting. And it was important to me, because the Institute was not equipped with a radio or a TV, and worse, had a limited number of books. (I was so desperate for reading matter I practically memorized the begats.) For me, evening worship was a source of entertainment.

It began with the arrival of the audience, the scrubbed youths and their chaperones, followed closely by the people from the community: the older ladies in out-of-fashion but immaculate dresses and toilet water; the men, seeming all of an age, with big rough hands poking out of the cuffs of suit coats worn awkwardly; the younger girls, in light dresses, casting flirtatious glances at the young men at the Institute (who were usually from cities, and therefore seen as sophisticated) and sharp challenging looks at the Institute's young women (who were also usually from the city, and therefore seen as probably a little wild). They would all troop into the dilapidated auditorium, filling the rows of ragtag seating—trestle benches, tip-up seats from abandoned theaters, folding chairs mended with cardboard, even a couple of mismatched church pews—and wait impatiently for the ministers.

The ministers entered from the front, moving more or less in time to the sound that came from an off-key, beaten-up piano. They were not unfamiliar figures—they were around all day, teaching classes, arguing points of theology and church politics, and playing Chinese checkers beneath the trees. Now they were solemn and dignified in black suits and clerical collars, each intent on performing his role, no matter how minor, with as much style as he could muster.

Performance was the word, for the service was high drama, from the solemnly intoned ritual invocation, to the rolling hymns sung by a hundred people who needed no hymnals, in passionate voices that overpowered the doubtful leadership of the gap-toothed piano, to the hucksterish importunings over the collection plate, as a minister would announce the total and then proceed to cajole, shame, or bully the audience into bringing it higher. There was no applause, of course, but the performance of each minister was rewarded with responses from the worshipers; the preaching and praying being applauded with a spontaneous chorus of "Amen, amen," "Yes, yes, yes," and the ultimate accolade, "Preach on, preach on." Which they did, sometimes until midnight.

I was overwhelmed by the worship services, not because I was religious, but because there was something innately compelling about the form and pacing and order of it: the slow, solemn beginning, the rhythms of song and responsive reading, the spontaneous lyricism, the sense of wholeness and cohesion and abandon when a preacher really got going, the perfection of catharsis when the end of the service flowed swiftly and smoothly to the benediction.

I have often wondered why my initial emotional response did not manifest itself as some kind of visible expression of faith—why, while I sang the hymns and was moved by the pageantry, I never gave myself over to witnessing or even made a journey to the altar to accept Jesus as my savior. I believe this was due to the example of my father, who found emotional religious expression embarrassing, and took an intellectual approach to religion, to anything. In any case, my love of worship expressed itself in an analytical way—I began to see it as a critical paradigm. The order of service, with its variations in pacing and mood, its combination of poetic and prosaic elements, of mysticism and hucksterism, became, to me, the model of what a dramatic experience should be. This led to my development of a critical consciousness: I began to judge worship services as good, or not so good. More important, from the point of view of a writer, I saw enough services that were not so good to develop an editorial sense, a feeling for when the prayer was becoming repetitive, when the hymn was wrong, when the minister failed to create a sermon that expanded upon the text. But more important than even that, I learned that the analytical, critical approach, while a useful means, was not, for me, an end.

For I had on a very few occasions seen a preacher, sometimes not a usually good preacher, create, perhaps with the aid of divine inspiration, a service or a sermon that defied criticism. Once I saw it happen to my father.

The year was 1965. By that time, our summer travels had taken my father and me beyond Virginia into North and South Carolina. Nevertheless, the format of the Christian education conventions we attended was the same as that at the Dinwiddie Institute. In one place, that year, they asked my father to preach.

I was not overly excited by the prospect, since I had heard him preach two or three hundred times, and had always found his sermons to be rather dry, tending, as he tended, to focus on the head rather than the heart. The text was Isaiah 30:21: "And thine ears shall hear a word behind thee, saying, This *is* the way, walk ye in it," and as my father read it, I realized that I had heard the sermon he was beginning at least four times, liking it less each time. When he began to speak I expected the textual analysis and explication by definition that marked his style. But this night he abandoned that—something got hold of him. He followed the reading of the text with the telling of a tale.

He had, he said, been in high school, sitting in a classroom, when a man had come to the school asking for volunteers to go up to fight a forest fire that raged on a nearby mountain. My father and some others agreed to go, and were taken up by wagon, then went on foot a mile or two farther, to a point where they had been told to dig a firebreak. The fire, my father said, seemed a long way away; not sensing the danger, they allowed themselves to become absorbed in their task. When finally they looked up from it, they found that the fire had swept about them—they were surrounded by flames.

They reacted as one would have expected. My father told of his panic, how he had at first cried hysterically, then begun to curse, using words he had not realized he knew, had finally collapsed into desperate prayer, all, it seemed, to no avail. But then, when the smoke was at its thickest, when he was about to lose sight of his companions, when the very sound of their wailing was lost in the roaring of the flames, there came a voice calling to them to follow. They followed that voice, escaping with its guidance through what must have been the last gap in the fire. Afterward they asked who it had been who risked himself to save them, but no one could tell them who it was.

From the tale my father moved to the obvious but eloquent equation, exchanging that unknown savior for a known one, who called the same message, and who led all who followed him clear of the flames. And then, almost abruptly, and far sooner than anyone expected, he stopped. And he brought down the house.

That sermon shocked me. Because I knew my father, knew that he had hidden that story for forty years, had kept it out of previous versions of the same sermon because he was the kind of man who hated to admit weakness, or indecision, or helplessness. I knew that to relive that time on the Mountainside had cost him greatly, and to admit his own helplessness had cost him even more. But I realized that the sermon had been something beyond that which was usual for him, and I believed, for no reason I could express, but nevertheless believed, that it was the paying of the price that had made the sermon possible. I believed that in confessing his own weakness he had found access to a hidden source of power inside, or perhaps outside, himself—in any case, a source of power that was magical, mystical.

Until that night I had not understood what it meant to write. I had known that the writer's goal was to reveal truths in words manipulated so effectively as to cause a movement in the minds and hearts of those who read them. But I had not understood that it would cost anything. I had believed that I could do those things while remaining secure and safe in myself—I had even believed that writing fiction was a way to conceal my true feelings and weaknesses. That night, I found out better. That night, I realized that no matter how good I became in the manipulation of symbols, I could never hope to move anyone without allowing myself to be moved, that I could reveal only slight truths unless I was willing to reveal the truths about myself. I did not enjoy the realization. For I was no fonder of self-revelation than my father, and though I knew I would love to do with written words what my father had done in speech, I was not sure I could pay the price. I was not sure I wanted to.

I do not know why my career as a writer did not end there. All I know is that, in fact, it began there. For out of that night came the only idea I have that could truly be called an aesthetic standard: expensiveness. When I ask myself, as all writers do, whether to write something this way or that way, whether to keep this bit, or throw it away, I ask myself, along with all the practical, technical, editorial questions, Does it cost? Is it possible that someone reading might discover something about me that I would rather not have him know? Is there something truly private here, something I would never admit face to face, unless, perhaps, I was drunk?

I would like to say that if the answer to those questions is No, I go back and dig down inside myself until I do find something it will cost me to say; the truth is I do not always do that. But I believe I should. And I believe that someday, when I am good enough, not as a manipulator of words and phrases but as a human being, I will. And I believe that each time I work, and make the effort, I get closer to that ideal.

I doubt that could be called a religious expression. That I act upon it is, however, a matter of faith. For I cannot prove that there is anything to be gained from writing with that sort of aesthetic in mind. I cannot show that my work will be read by more people, that my books will sell more copies, that I will make more money, get better reviews. I cannot truly say that the work is better—I believe it is, but I cannot prove it. Despite the fact that I cannot prove it, however, I believe this aesthetic of cost does make a difference in my writing and the reception of it. This belief is important. For without it I would not be able to pay the price of writing in the way that pleases me. I would write, but, by my standards, I would do it badly. Eventually I would give it up, or become a prostitute, in it only for the money. I need not fear this, because I do believe. The capacity for belief is something I acquired from being so much in contact with others who believed. This, perhaps, is the most important influence on me from the faith of my father.

To Fashion a Text

Annie Dillard

I'm here because I'm writing a book called *An American Childhood*, which is a memoir—insofar as a memoir is any account, usually in the first person, of incidents that happened a while ago. It isn't an autobiography, and it isn't "memoirs." I wouldn't dream of writing my memoirs; I'm only forty years old. Or my autobiography; any chronology of my days would make very dull reading—I've spent about thirty years behind either a book or a desk. The book that I'm writing is an account of a childhood in Pittsburgh, Pennsylvania, where I grew up.

The best memoirs, I think, forge their own forms. The writer of any work, and particularly any nonfiction work, must decide two crucial points: what to put in and what to leave out.

So I thought, "What shall I put in?" Well, what is the book about? *An American Childhood* is about the passion of childhood. It's about a child's vigor, and originality, and eagerness, and mastery, and joy.

It's about waking up. A child wakes up over and over again, and notices that she's living. She dreams along, loving the exuberant life of the senses, in love with beauty and power, oblivious of herself—and then suddenly, bingo, she wakes up and feels herself alive. She notices her own awareness. And she notices that she is set down here, mysteriously, in a going world. The world is full of fascinating information that she can collect and enjoy. And the world is public; its issues are moral and historical ones.

So the book is about two things: a child's interior life—vivid, superstitious and timeless—and a child's growing awareness of the world. The structural motion of the book is from the interior landscape—one brain's own idiosyncratic topography—to the American landscape, the vast setting of our common history. The little child pinches the skin on the back of her hand and sees where God made Adam from spit and clay. The older child explores the city on foot and starts to work on her future as a detective, or an epidemiologist, or a painter. Older yet, she runs wild and restless over the city's bridges, and finds in Old Testament poetry and French symbolist poetry some language sounds she loves.

The interior life is in constant vertical motion; consciousness runs up and down the scales every hour like a slide trombone. It dreams down below; it notices up above; and it notices itself, too, and its own alertness. The vertical motion of consciousness, from inside to outside and back, interests me. I've written about it once before, in an essay about a solar eclipse, and I wanted to do more with it.

For a private interior life, I've picked—almost at random—my own. As an aside, this isn't as evident as it may seem. I simply like to write books. About twelve years ago, while I was walking in Acadia National Park in Maine, I decided to write a narrative—a prose narrative, because I wanted to write prose. After a week's thought I decided to write mostly about nature, because I thought I could make it do what I wanted, and I decided to set it all on the coast of Maine. I decided further to write it in the third person, about a man, a sort of metaphysician, in his fifties. A month or so later I decided reluctantly to set the whole shebang in Virginia, because I knew more about Virginia. Then I decided to write it in the first person, as a man. Not until I had written the first chapter and showed it around—this was *Pilgrim at Tinker Creek*—did I give up the pretext of writing in the first person as a man. I wasn't out to deceive people; I just didn't like the idea of writing about myself. I knew I wasn't the subject.

So in this book, for simplicity's sake, I've got my own interior life. It was a lively one. I put in what it was that had me so excited all the time—the sensation of time pelting me as if I were standing under a waterfall. I loved the power of the life in which I found myself. I loved to feel its many things in all their force. I put in what it feels like to play with the skin on your mother's knuckles. I put in what it feels like to throw a baseball—you aim your whole body at the target and watch the ball fly off as if it were your own head. I put in drawing pencil studies of my baseball mitt and collecting insects and fooling around with a microscope.

In my study on Cape Cod, where I write, I've stuck above my desk a big photograph of a little Amazonian boy whose face is sticking out of a waterfall or a rapids. White water is pounding all around his head, in a kind of wreath, but his face is absolutely still, looking up, and his black eyes are open dreamily on the distance. That little boy is completely alive; he's letting the mystery of existence beat on him. He's having his childhood, and I think he knows it. And I think he will come out of the water strong, and ready to do some good. I see this photograph whenever I look up from my computer screen.

So I put in that moment of waking up and noticing that you've been put down in a world that's already under way. The rushing of time wakes you: you play along mindless and eternal on the kitchen floor, and time streams in full flood beside you on the floor. It rages beside you, down its swollen banks, and when it wakes you you're so startled you fall in.

When you wake up, you notice that you're here.

"Here," in my case, was Pittsburgh. I put in the three rivers that meet here. The Allegheny from the north and the Monongahela from the south converge to form the Ohio, the major tributary of the Mississippi, which, in turn, drains the whole continent east of the divide via the Missouri River rising in the Rocky Mountains. The great chain of the Alleghenies kept pioneers out of Pittsburgh until the 1760s, one hundred and fifty years after Jamestown.

I put in those forested mountains and hills, and the way the three rivers lie flat and moving among them, and the way the low land lies wooded among them, and the way the blunt mountains rise in the darkness from the rivers' banks.

I put in Lake Erie, and summers along its mild shore. I put in New Orleans, the home of Dixieland jazz, where my father was heading when he jumped in his boat one day to go down the river like Huck Finn.

I put in the pioneers who "broke wilderness," and the romance of the French and Indian Wars that centered around Fort Duquesne and Fort Pitt. I put in the brawling rivermen—the flatboatmen and keelboatmen.

I put in the old Scotch-Irish families who dominate Pittsburgh and always have. The Mellons are Scotch-Irish, and so were Andrew Carnegie and Henry Clay Frick. They're all Presbyterians. I grew up in this world—at the lunatic fringe of it—and it fascinates me. I think it's important. I think it's peculiarly American—that mixture of piety and acquisitiveness, that love of work. They're Calvinists, of course—just like the Massachusetts Puritans—and I think I can make a case that their influence on American thought was greater than the Puritans'. There were far more Scotch-Irish Presbyterians, after all, and they settled all over the American colonies and carried their democracy and pragmatism with them.

In Pittsburgh the Scotch-Irish constitute a world of many families whose fore-bears knew each other, who respect each other's discretion and who admire each other for occupying their slots without fuss. The men are withdrawn, the women are ironic. They believe in their world; they all stay in Pittsburgh, and their children stay there. I alone am escaped to tell thee. I and David McCullough, who grew up a few houses away. And James Laughlin, the publisher. All of us Pittsburgh Scotch-Irish Presbyterians.

My sisters and I grew up in this world, and I put it in *An American Childhood*. I put in our private school and quiet club and hushed neighborhood where the houses were stone and their roofs were slate. I put in dancing with little boys at dancing school, and looking at the backs of their interesting necks at Presbyterian church.

Just to make trouble, I put in money. My grandmother used to tell me never to touch money with my bare hands.

I put in books, for that's where this book started, with an essay I wrote for the *New York Times Magazine* on reading books. Almost all of my many passionate inter-ests, and my many changes of mind, came through books. Books prompted the many vows I made to myself. Nonfiction books lured me away from the world—as I dreamed about working for Scotland Yard, doing field work in freshwater streams, rock collecting in the salt desert, painting in Paris. And novels dragged me back into the world—because I would read whatever was handy, and what was handy in those years were novels about the Second World War. I read so many books about the Second World War that I knew how to man a minesweeper before I knew how to walk in high heels. You couldn't read much about the war without figuring out that the world was a moral arena that required your strength.

I had the notion back then that everything was interesting if you just learned enough about it. Now, writing about it, I have the pleasure of learning it all again and finding that it *is* interesting. I get to inform myself and any readers about such esoterica as rock collecting, which I hadn't thought about in almost thirty years.

When I was twelve a paperboy gave me two grocery bags full of rock and mineral chunks. It took me most of a year to identify them. At a museum shop I bought cards of what they called thumbnail specimens. And I read books about a fairly absurd batch of people who called themselves rockhounds; they spent their evenings in the basement sawing up slabs of travertine into wavy slices suitable, they said, for wall hangings.

Now, in this memoir, I get to recall where the romance of rock collecting had lain: the symbolic sense that underneath the dreary highways, underneath Pittsburgh, were canyons of crystals—that you could find treasure by prying open the landscape. In my reading I learned that people have cracked knobs of granite and laid bare clusters of red garnets and topaz crystals, chrysoberyl, spudomene and emerald. They held in their hands crystals that had hung in a hole in the dark for a billion years unseen. I liked the idea of that. I would lay about me right and left with a hammer and bash the landscape to bits. I would crack the earth's crust like a piñata and spread its vivid prizes in chunks to the light. That's what I wanted to do. So I put that in.

It's also a great pleasure to write about my parents, because they're both great storytellers—comedians, actually—which gives me a chance to tell their wonderful stories. We were all young, at our house, and we enjoyed ourselves.

My father was a dreamer; he lived differently from other men around him. One day he abruptly quit the family firm—when I was ten—and took off down the Ohio River in a boat by himself to search out the roots of jazz in New Orleans. He came back after several months and withdrew from corporate life forever. He knew the world well—all sort of things, which he taught us to take an interest in: how people build bridge pilings in the middle of a river, how jazz came up the river to be educated in Chicago, how the pioneers made their way westward from Pittsburgh, down the Ohio River, sitting on the tops of their barges and singing "Bang Away, My Lulu."

My mother was both a thinker and what one might call a card. If she lay on the beach with friends and found the conversation dull, she would give a little push with her heel and roll away. People were stunned. She rolled deadpan and apparently effortlessly, her arms and legs extended tidily, down the beach to the distant water's edge where she lay at ease just as she had been, but half in the surf, and well out of earshot. She was not only a card but a wild card, a force for disorder.

She regarded even tiny babies as straight men, and liked to step on the drawstring of a crawling baby's gown, so that the baby crawled and crawled and never got anywhere except into a little ball at the top of the gown.

She was interested in language. Once my father and I were in the kitchen listening to a ballgame—the Pirates playing the New York Giants. The Giants had a utility infielder named Wayne Terwilliger. Just as Mother walked through the kitchen, the announcer said, "Terwilliger bunts one." Mother stopped dead and said, "What was that? Was that English?" Father said, "The man's name is Terwilliger. He bunted." Mother thought that was terrific. For the next ten or twelve years she made this surprising string of syllables her own. If she was testing a microphone, or if she was pretending to whisper a secret in my ear, she said, "Terwilliger bunts one." If she had ever had an occasion to create a motto for a coat of arms, as Andrew Carnegie had, her motto would have been "Terwilliger bunts one." Carnegie's was "Death to privilege."

These fine parents taught my sisters and me moral courage, insofar as we have it, and tolerance, and how to dance all night without dragging your arms on your partner, and how to time the telling of a joke.

I've learned a lot by writing this book, not only about writing but about American history. Eastern woodland Indians killed many more settlers than plains Indians did. By the time settlers made it to Sioux and Apache country those Indians had been so weakened by disease and by battles with the army that they didn't have much fight left in them. It was the settlers in the Pennsylvania forests and in Maryland and Virginia who kept getting massacred and burned out and taken captive and tortured. During the four years the French held Pittsburgh at Fort Duquesne they armed the Indians and sent them out from there, raiding and killing English-speaking settlers. These were mostly Scotch-Irish, because the Penn family let them settle in Pennsylvania only if they would serve as a "buffer sect" between Quakers and Indians. When the English held Pittsburgh at Fort Pitt they gave the Indians unwashed blankets from the smallpox hospital.

I put in early industry, because it was unexpectedly interesting. Before there was steel, everything was made out of wrought iron—which I find just amazing. Railroad ties were made out of wrought iron, as if they were candle sconces. Men had to carry wrought iron railroad ties all up and down the country. Wrought iron is made by iron puddlers, who belong to the iron puddlers' union, the Sons of Vulcan. It's a very difficult process: you stir slag back into iron, and it requires skilled labor because carbon monoxide bubbles up. The language is also nice. To sinter, for instance, is to convert flu dust to clinker. And I finally learned what coke is. When I was a child I thought that Coca-Cola was a by-product of steelmaking.

I learned about the heyday of the big industrialists and the endless paradox of Andrew Carnegie, the only one of the great American moguls who not only read books but actually wrote them, including one with a very American title, *The Gospel of Wealth*. He sold U.S. Steel to J. P. Morgan for $492 million, and he said, "A man who dies rich dies disgraced." He gave away ninety percent of his fortune in the few years he had left. While he was giving away money, many people were moved, understandably, to write him letters. He got one such letter from his friend Mark Twain. It said:

> You seem to be in prosperity. Could you lend an admirer a dollar & a half to buy a hymn-book with? God will bless you. I feel it. I know it.
> P.S. Don't send the hymn-book, send the money.

Carnegie was only five feet three inches tall. He weighed 133 pounds. He built the workers free libraries and museums and an art gallery at the same time that he had them working sixteen hours a day, six days a week, at subhuman wages, and drinking water full of typhoid and cholera because he and the other business owners opposed municipal works like water filtration plants. By 1906 Pittsburgh had the highest death rate in the nation because of wretched living conditions, and yet it was the seat of "wealth beyond computation, wealth beyond imagination." People built stables for their horses with gold mirrors in the stalls. The old Scotch-Irish families were horrified at the new millionaires who popped up around this time because they liked things pretty quiet. One new millionaire went to a barber on Penn Avenue for his first shampoo and the barber reported that the washing brought out "two ounces of fine Mesabi ore and a scattering of slag and cinders."

And what to leave out?

Well, I'm not writing social history. This is not one of those books in which you may read the lyrics or even the titles of popular songs on the radio. Or the names of radio and TV programs, or advertising slogans or product names or clothing fashions. I don't like all that. I want to direct the reader's attention in equal parts to the text—as a formal object—and to the world, as an interesting place in which we find ourselves.

So another thing I left out, as far as I could, was myself. The personal pronoun can be the subject of the verb: "I see this, I did that." But not the object of the verb: "I analyze me, I discuss me, I describe me, I quote me."

In the course of writing this memoir I've learned all sorts of things, quite inadvertently, about myself and various relationships. But these things are not important to the book and I easily leave them out. Since the subject of the book is not me, other omissions naturally follow. I leave out many things that were important to my life but of no concern for the present book, like the summer I spent in Wyoming when I was fifteen. I keep the action in Pittsburgh; I see no reason to drag everybody off to Wyoming just because I want to tell them about my summer vacation. You have to take pains in a memoir not to hang on the reader's arm, like a drunk, and say, "And then I did this and it was so interesting." I don't write for that reason.

On the other hand, I dig deeply into the exuberant heart of a child and the restless, violent heart of an adolescent—and I was that child and I was that adolescent.

I leave out my private involvement with various young men. I didn't want to kiss and tell. I did put in several sections, however, about boys in general and the fascination they exerted. I ran around with one crowd of older boys so decadent, so accustomed to the most glittering of social lives, that one of them carried with him at all times, in his jacket pocket, a canister of dance wax so that he could be ready for anything. Other boys carry Swiss Army knives for those occasions which occur unexpectedly; this boy carried dance wax for the same reason. He could just sprinkle it on the dining room floor and take you in his arms and whirl you away. These were the sort of boys I knew; they had worn ties from the moment their mothers could locate their necks.

I tried to leave out anything that might trouble my family. My parents are quite young. My sisters are watching this book carefully. Everybody I'm writing about is alive and well, in full possession of his faculties, and possibly willing to sue. Things were simpler when I wrote about muskrats.

Writing in the first person can trap the writer into airing grievances. When I taught writing I spent a lot of time trying to convince young writers that, while literature is an art, it's not a martial art—that the pages of a short story or a novel are no place to defend yourself from an attack, real or imagined, and no place from which to launch an attack, particularly an attack against the very people who painstakingly reared you to your present omniscience.

I have no temptation to air grievances; in fact, I have no grievances left. Unfortunately, I seem to have written the story of my impassioned adolescence so convincingly that my parents (after reading that section of my book) think I still feel that way. It's a problem that I have to solve—one of many in this delicate area. My parents and my youngest sister still live in Pittsburgh; I have to handle it with tongs.

As a result of all of this, I've promised my family that each may pass on the book. I've promised to take out anything that anyone objects to—anything at all. When I was growing up I didn't really take to Pittsburgh society, and I was happy to throw myself into any other world I could find. But I guess I can't say so, because my family may think that I confuse them with conventional Pittsburgh society people in the '50s.

I know a writer who cruelly sticks his parents into all his short stories and still pleases them both, because his mother is pleased to see his father look bad and his father is pleased to see his mother look bad. I had, I thought, nothing but good to say about all named people, but I'll make all that better yet. I don't believe in a writer's kicking around people who don't have access to a printing press. They can't defend themselves.

My advice to memoir writers is to embark upon a memoir for the same reason that you would embark on any other book: to fashion a text. Don't hope in a memoir to preserve your memories. If you prize your memories as they are, by all means avoid—eschew—writing a memoir. Because it is a certain way to lose them. You can't put together a memoir without cannibalizing your own life for parts. The work battens on your memories. And it replaces them.

It's a matter of writing's vividness for the writer. If you spend a couple of days writing a tricky paragraph, and if you spend a week or two laying out a scene or describing an event, you've spent more time writing about it than you did living it. The writing time is also much more intense.

After you've written, you can no longer remember anything but the writing. However true you make that writing, you've created a monster. This has happened to me many, many times, because I'm willing to turn events into pieces of paper. After I've written about any experience, my memories—those elusive, fragmentary patches of color and feeling—are gone; they've been replaced by the work. The work is a sort of changeling on the doorstep—not your baby but someone else's baby rather like it, different in some way that you can't pinpoint, and yours has vanished.

Memory is insubstantial. Things keep replacing it. Your batch of snapshots will both fix and ruin your memory of your travels, or your childhood, or your children's childhood. You can't remember anything from your trip except this wretched collection of snapshots. The painting you did of the light on the water will forever alter the way you see the light on the water; so will looking at Flemish paintings. If you describe a dream you'll notice that at the end of the verbal description you've lost the dream but gained a verbal description. You have to like verbal descriptions a lot to keep up this sort of thing. I like verbal descriptions a lot.

Let me put in a word now for a misunderstood genre: literary nonfiction. It's interesting to me because I try to write it and because I respect the art of it very much.

I like to be aware of a book as a piece of writing, and aware of its structure as a product of mind, and yet I want to be able to see the represented world through it. I admire artists who succeed in dividing my attention more or less evenly between the world of their books and the art of their books. In fiction we might say that the masters are Henry James and Herman Melville. In nonfiction the writer usually just points to the world and says, "This is a biography of Abraham Lincoln. This is what Abraham Lincoln was about." But the writer may also make of his work an original object in its own right, so that a reader may study the work with pleasure as well as the world that it describes. That is, works of nonfiction can be coherent and crafted works of literature.

It's not simply that they're carefully written, or vivid and serious and pleasing, like Boswell's *Life of Johnson*, say, or St. Exupéry's wonderful memoir of early aviation, *Wind, Sand, and Stars*. It's not even that they may contain elements of fiction, that their action reveals itself in scenes that use visual descriptions and that often use dialogue. It's not just these things, although these things are important. It's that nonfiction accounts may be literary insofar as the parts of their structures cohere internally, insofar as the things are in them for the sake of the work itself, and insofar as the work itself exists in the service of idea. (It is especially helpful if the writer so fully expresses the idea in materials that only a trained technician can find it. Because the abstract structure of a given text, which is of great interest to the writer and serves to rouse him out of bed in the morning and impel him to the desk, is of little or no interest to the reader, and he'd better not forget it.)

Nonfiction accounts don't ordinarily meet these criteria, but they may. Walden Pond is the linchpin of a metaphysic. In repeated and self-conscious rewritings Thoreau hammered at its unremarkable and rather dreary acres until they fastened eternity in time and stood for the notion that the physical world itself expresses a metaphysical one. He picked up that pond and ran with it. He could just as readily have used something else—a friend, say, or a chestnut. You can do quite a bit with language.

Hemingway in *Green Hills of Africa* wrote a sober narrative account of killing a kudu, the whole of which functions as an elaborate metaphor for internal quests and conquests. Loren Eiseley lays in narrative symbols with a trowel, splashing mortar all over the place, but they hold. In his essay "The Star-Thrower," Eiseley's beachcomber who throws dying starfish back into the surf stands for any hope or mercy that flies in the face of harsh natural law. He stands finally for the extravagant spirit behind creation as a whole; he is a god hurling solar systems into the void.

I only want to remind my writing colleagues that a great deal can be done in nonfiction, especially in first-person accounts where the writer controls the materials absolutely. Because other literary genres are shrinking. Poetry has purified itself right out of the ballpark. Literary fiction is scarcely being published—it's getting to be like conceptual art. All that the unknown writer of fiction can do is to tell his friends about the book he has written, and all that his friends can say is "Good idea." The short story

About Personal Expressive Academic Writing

Peter Elbow

"Up close and personal." "I just want to express myself." I cringe when I hear these phrases—and so do most academics, I'll bet. So what am I doing here? Two years ago I asked Victor Vitanza if he would let me edit an issue of PRE/TEXT and invite pieces of personal and expressive writing that "do the work of academic writing." He kindly said yes, and these are what I present here. I hope this issue of PRE/TEXT can convince readers that personal expressive writing can do the work of academic discourse—and still avoid the empty cloying connotations of those initial cliche phrases.

But what is the work of academic discourse? A full and careful answer is too much to ask for on this occasion. (I try for more in my "Reflections on Academic Discourse: How it Relates to Freshmen and Colleagues," *College English*, February 1991.) But a simple answer is perfectly serviceable: academic discourse makes arguments, solves problems, analyzes texts and issues, tries to answer hard questions—and usually refers to and builds on other academic discourse. So why can't these jobs be done with personal and expressive writing?

Perhaps you'll say that I've left out the most important job of academic discourse: to be objective or unbiased. But objectivity is passé. Few academics now believe that they can achieve objectivity—or that this view from everywhere-and-nowhere is even a desirable goal. Everyone seems to agree that we can never write anything except from a situated and interested point of view. (What would happen if Alec Guinness stepped out of *The Man in the White Suit* with another new invention: not just a process for making impervious suits but also for making irrefutable truths? I think we'd have to bundle him off again.)

But the death of objectivity has not catapulted academics into publishing personal expressive writing in learned journals. Let me point to four important features in current academic discourse that seem to distinguish it from personal expressive writing. (Perhaps these features are surrogates for objectivity.)

279

A larger view.   Even though academic writers seldom profess true objectivity (at least in the humanities), they tend to try nevertheless for a kind of larger perspective that shows how their position relates to the positions other people have taken or might take on the topic. They don't just say, "Here's my position," but rather, "Here's how my position relates to yours. I'm not objective, but I'm not myopic either. I can see the larger terrain."

Clear thinking.   While still not professing objectivity, academic writers nevertheless tend to try for clear thinking. Above all, this means centering on claims, reasons, evidence—argument. Being winning or sincere or even powerfully seductive is not enough.

Logical organization.   (I purposely use the idiomatic word here, "logical," so I can parenthetically rail against it for a moment. Good organization in a piece of writing may be reasonable and clear and full of signposts, but it almost never follows actual logic.) Academics tend to insist on a kind of "bony" structure in their publications; points should follow reasonably from each other, and the skeleton of argument is prominent—heightened by signposts that tell what's ahead and where we've been.

Judicious tone.   When academics write for publication they usually restrain themselves in style and voice—often achieving a certain impersonality. They tend to avoid much talk about themselves or their feelings; they favor control over abandon. The strength of this convention is well illustrated by the following observation. The American Psychological Association (APA) guidelines—pretty much the style bible for most academic publication in the social and natural sciences—have been saying bluntly since 1973 that scientists should speak in the first person as "I" or "we" in their publications if they are telling their own conclusions or describing their own experimental procedures. And yet many scientists persist in telling their students and themselves that it is wrong to use the first person in academic writing. Even academics in the humanities tend to shy away from much use of the first person—certainly using it much less than if they were writing a memo to the same colleagues about the same topic.

These seem like four pretty solid differences between academic discourse and personal expressive writing. But do these differences really mean that personal expressive writing cannot do the work of academic discourse? Let me look again at these four differences and try to show how they needn't exclude personal writing from academic work.

Tone.   Starting with the last and most obvious feature, the contrast with personal expressive writing is obvious and decisive. But is it part of the essential job of academic writing to sound judicious, restrained, and somewhat impersonal?—or is that tone just one way of doing the job? Some people say there can be no wedding without morning coats and other formal attire. My hope is that this issue of PRE/TEXT will help convince readers that good academic work can be done in a more personal tone of voice.

Logical organization?   Personal expressive writing obviously invites looser, less four-square structures of organization—more intuitive and associative—allowing us to imply more and spell out less. Yet there is nothing in the nature of personal expressive writing that prevents explicitness and a four-square bony organization.

Something can be clear and obviously shaped without being stiff—without being any less personal or expressive. In fact, of course, the letters and journal entries we write often make our points more explicitly and clearly than our published articles. The pieces gathered here represent a relatively broad range of organizational modes, but none will seem particularly unbuttoned to readers of contemporary critical theory. For the truth is that organizational "standards" have already "broken down" in much academic writing in the humanities. Deconstruction has sanctioned the publication of many pieces that don't even "say" what they are "saying"—on the principle that it is impossible to do so. And if we look concretely back through the annals, we'll see that academics have always managed to depart now and then from conventions of language and organization if their writing was sufficiently interesting—or if they had sufficient prestige.

Clear thinking? Similar conclusion. Personal expressive writing may open the door to blurting and venting—no claims, reasons, evidence or arguments. But again (as I hope many of the pieces here show) despite the open door, there's nothing in the nature of personal and expressive writing that militates against clear claims, reasons, and evidence. A focused argument doesn't make something less personal or expressive.

Larger view? Many people assume that personal writing tends by its nature to occupy itself only with its own position; and certainly there is plenty of good personal expressive writing that operates this way. But this assumption is a problem. For there is also plenty of personal expressive writing, as you'll see in this issue of PRE/TEXT, that is deeply attentive to the views and positions of others. There's nothing in the nature of personal expressive writing that is at odds with talking about, summarizing, explaining, or building on the writing of others. In fact, personal expressive writing is often more clearly attentive to an audience and its views than we see in much academic writing—where writers often slide into a glassy-eyed stance of talking to everyone but not really connecting to anyone. We see this particularly vividly in personal writing in the form of letters to colleagues. It is one of the worst clichés of dichotomy-bound thinking to assume that feelings always push us toward solitary unconnected discourse, and that thinking pushes us toward social connection. "Personal" usually involves being personal in relation to others, and "expressive" tends to mean expressing something to others. It is important to call attention, however, to the strong contrary argument that David Bartholomae makes in his response here to Steve North: that expressive writing inherently *tempts* writers into myopia, self-absorption and aggrandizement—tempts them to forget difference and the socially constructed nature of the self.

There is a related issue here. Academic writing tends not only to address or attend to the views of others, but to cite them—using some formal citation system. Personal expressive writing has no tradition or convention of citation: some does and some does not. We see a range of practices in the pieces gathered here. But should we say that a piece of personal and expressive writing that addresses current issues is not doing academic work just because it doesn't cite the work of others? An arguable point.

My premise, then, in putting together this collection, is not that all personal expressive writing does the work of academic writing: simply that some does; and that more could if we let it. Personal expressive writing happens to be one among many registers or discourses we can use for academic duty. Because personal writing invites feeling does not mean that it leaves out thinking; and because it invites attention to the self does not mean that it leaves out other people and the social connection.

• • •

This is a good historical moment to be making our case for personal expressive writing in the academy. Change is happening fast. Only recently there was no widespread agreement that objectivity was impossible. (And yet forty years ago, academics tended to write with a more generally personal tone. Perhaps their faith in objective knowledge made them feel more comfortable about allowing a personal flavor in their prose.) And change in academic discourse is an old story. It wasn't so long ago, after all, that Latin was the only acceptable language for learned discourse. Gradually the other European dialects became acceptable—vernacular, "vulgar," of the people, more democratic, closer to the business of the everyday and to feelings.

Yet many academics are more nervous about change in discourse—and especially incursions of the vernacular—than about change in ideas or doctrine. Many happily proclaim that there is no truth, no right answer, no right interpretation; many say they want more voices in the academy, dialogue, heteroglossia! But they won't let themselves or their students write in a language tainted with the ordinary or with the presence and feelings of the writer. Yet despite this fear of change, change is what we are now seeing in our conception of academic discourse:

> Deconstructionists make a frontal attack on straight, organized prose that purports to mean what it says. They insist that fooling around is of the essence (though they are pretentious and won't talk about fooling around, only about "jouissance").
>
> Feminists attack the idea that good writing must follow linear or hierarchical or deductive models of structure, must persuade by trying to overpower, must be "masterful."
>
> Jerome Bruner and scholars of narrative attack the assumption that thinking is best when it is structured in terms of claims, reasons, warrants, and evidence. Narrative is just as good a form for thinking.
>
> Academic discourse has usually focused outward on issues or data. But now the focus of academic discourse is more and more on discourse and thinking itself. In effect, much academic discourse is metadiscourse.

In a host of ways, genres are becoming blurred. It is worth quoting Geertz:

> [T]he present jumbling of varieties of discourse has grown to the point where it is becoming difficult either to label authors (What is Foucault—historian, philosopher, political theorist? What Thomas Kuhn—historian, philosopher, sociologist of knowledge?) or to classify works.... It is a phenomenon general enough and distinctive

enough to suggest that what we are seeing is not just another redrawing of the cultural map—the moving of a few disputed borders, the marking of some more picturesque mountain lakes—but an alteration of the principles of mapping. Something is happening to the way we think about the way we think. (19–20)

In short, arguments that any currently privileged discourse is inherently better for scholarship or thinking or arguing or rooting out self-deception seem problematic now. But even though the academic world is already safe for deconstructive, Marxist, psychoanalytic, and feminist discourses, personal expressive writing is still not acceptable in most journals. (I think I see some important moves, however—especially in some feminist work [see Booth, DuPlessis, Irigaray, Tompkins].) My goal is to make the academic world safe for personal expressive writing: to encourage more academics to submit it to journals and publishers—and to encourage academics as referees and editors to say yes more often (so long as it does the academic job well).

I won't say any more to introduce the pieces in this issue. They are not all about one topic as usually happens with guest-edited issues—though a number explore discourse itself. Nor are they in any particular thematic or generic order. I am excited about these pieces in themselves and because of what they stand for, and I hope readers will be too. In the rest of this foreword let me reflect on a couple of issues central to the enterprise.

What's at Stake?

What I like about personal or expressive writing is how it usually acknowledges what is at stake for the writer. So often, as reader, we only know what is at stake in a larger more impersonal sense (Western Civilization or the epistemological premises of various theorists or the reputation of some important author). We often sense that we are not hearing what is actually driving the piece of writing we are reading—why this writer is choosing to take on the burden of Western Civilization at this point and in this way. That is, despite the pious doctrine that meaning is always ideologically situated, people who make that case often fail to situate meanings in terms of the personal stake they have. (They might reply, of course, that the very concept of a 'person' is a fiction, but their prose often betrays a palpable personal stake—even while not quite revealing what that stake is.) Up to now it has seemed inappropriate to include one's own feelings and story in academic discourse. But since the personal dimension has such a big influence on one's position, perhaps we should turn that convention around and say it is inappropriate to publish an argument or take a position unless you tell your feelings and story.

But that would be wrong. I've had it thrown at me: I'm just a privileged person who had trouble with an elite education and my positions are nothing but playings out of my rebellion. No, we deserve to have our arguments taken on their own merits. Even if my ideas are nothing but epiphenomena of my unresolved Oedipal struggle, they deserve to be taken seriously if they have any possible value. And judgments about my ideas are more secure than those about my inner dynamics. Wayne Booth argues compellingly about the dangers of ad hominem psychologizing argument in his *Modern Dogma and the Rhetoric of Assent.*

Nevertheless this sincere warning is no argument against my main point in this essay: that we will benefit from allowing and even inviting people to write more personally in academic publications if they want to. That is, there is no reason to exclude voluntary acts of personal expressive writing. In short, I am all for purely impersonal discourse—good arguments only for their own sake, pure geometry—as long as we grant equal validity to personal discourse that does the job.

What's at Stake for Me?

I could just let it go with these general arguments for personal writing, but I think it will be helpful (and not just for me) to explore where the shoe pinches personally—where some of the animating juice behind my argument comes from. That is, it's not just that I prefer to read and write language that lets the person show more openly. It's that I'm bothered at the way so many people in composition studies pigeonhole my work and the work of others who are called "expressionist." In addition to individual readings by people like Berlin (151–55), Harris (27–30) and LeFevre (15)—or perhaps partly because of them—there has developed an almost universal commonplace that what is personal and expressive must be at war with what is social or public. Even though most people who celebrate the social constructionist position condemn dichotomous thinking, they tend nevertheless to slide into a simple, oppositional dichotomy between the social and the personal. Thus, I constantly read passages that simply assume without any argument that since Elbow is interested in the personal, private and individual dimension, he must be working against what is social, against the idea of the social construction of meaning and reality. With this comes, of course, the assumption that if social is good, then personal and private must be bad: that people who stick up for what is personal and private must be advocating the cause of solipsism. (I'm grateful for a notable exception—a refusal to simplify: see Fulkerson.)

This makes me mad. Perhaps the main point I want to make here—and what turns out to be a kind of subtheme in a number of the other pieces in this issue—is that the personal and individual need not be at war with the social. The personal and social are reciprocal—if not in every case, at least frequently and naturally. That is, it is as natural that they support each other as that they fight each other (just as the activity of generating ideas can naturally support the activity of criticizing ideas, or the process of relinquishing control can naturally support the process of achieving more control. See my treatment of these issues in the early chapters of *Writing With Power*.) Paul Connolly in this issue writes in the same breath about the goal of "liberating the individual" and "building bridges…establishing community." In saying this, he is not struggling to overcome a dichotomy—he's not building a "yet" structure but an "and" structure. He insists on the natural connection between the individual and the community. A community or social collectivity that is not made up of individual consciousnesses with individual agencies is some kind of mystical group consciousness or oppressive blob collectivity.

is to some extent going the way of poetry, limiting its subject matter to such narrow surfaces that it can't handle the things that most engage our hearts and minds. But literary nonfiction is all over the map and has been for three hundred years. There's nothing you can't do with it. No subject matter is forbidden, no structure is proscribed. You get to make up your own form every time.

When I gave up writing poetry I was very sad, for I had devoted fifteen years to the study of how the structures of poems carry meaning. But I was delighted to find that nonfiction prose can also carry meaning in its structures and, like poetry, can tolerate all sorts of figurative language, as well as alliteration and even rhyme. The range of rhythms in prose is larger and grander than it is in poetry, and it can handle discursive ideas and plain information as well as character and story. It can do everything. I felt as though I had switched from a single reed instrument to a full orchestra.

Let me close with a word about process. There's a common notion that self-discipline is a freakish peculiarity of writers—that writers differ from other people by possessing enormous and equal portions of talent and willpower. They grit their powerful teeth and go into their little rooms. I think that's a bad misunderstanding of what impels the writer. What impels the writer is a deep love for and respect for language, for literary forms, for books. It's a privilege to muck about in sentences all morning. It's a challenge to bring off a powerful effect, or to tell the truth about something. You don't do it from willpower; you do it from an abiding passion for the field. I'm sure it's the same in every other field.

Writing a book is like rearing children—willpower has very little to do with it. If you have a little baby crying in the middle of the night, and if you depend only on willpower to get you out of bed to feed the baby, that baby will starve. You do it out of love. Willpower is a weak idea; love is strong. You don't have to scourge yourself with a cat-o'-nine-tails to go to the baby. You go to the baby out of love for that particular baby. That's the same way you go to your desk. There's nothing freakish about it. Caring passionately about something isn't against nature, and it isn't against human nature. It's what we're here to do.

Writing of Paul de Man, Jonathan Culler says, "Deconstruction seeks to undo all oppositions that, in the name of unity, purity, order and hierarchy, try to eliminate difference" (278). Notice the main point here: Culler and de Man are *not* complaining about dichotomies but about the hunger to create unity and hierarchy and to eliminate difference. Yes, dichotomies are often used in that hunger—dichotomous thinking that assumes one side is up/light/good and the other side is down/dark/bad—dichotomous thinking that assumes dominance or hierarchy. But dichotomous thinking need *not* serve that simplistic hunger. In fact, dichotomies are most useful in pursuit of precisely the opposite goal—the very goal Culler and de Man are fighting for: the goal of maintaining *non*dominance and to *heighten* difference. To use dichotomies in this better way means insisting that *both* sides get equal value, that neither can win—insisting on keeping opposition or contradiction *unresolved*. And this is how I have characteristically used dichotomies. (See my *Embracing Contraries.*) In short, we need help in resisting the hunger always to transcend difference, the yearning to overcome contradiction, the impulse to have a winner. Dichotomies, rightly used, can give us this help in living with difference but no winning. (And there is a long tradition here stretching back past D. H. Lawrence and Blake to Abelard's *Sic et Non* and Boethius' *Consolation of Philosophy.*) The problem is not dichotomous thinking but hierarchical thinking.

Mara Holt, in this issue, gives a good model for maintaining both sides of the dichotomy about individual and society. She draws on George Herbert Mead writing more than sixty years ago:

> Human Society…does not merely stamp the pattern of its organized social behavior upon any one of its individual members, so that this pattern becomes likewise the pattern of the individual's self; it also at the same time gives him a mind, as the means or ability of consciously conversing with himself in terms of the social attitudes which constitute the structure of his self and which embody the pattern of human society's organized behavior as reflected in that structure. And his mind enables him in turn to stamp the pattern of his future developing self (further developing through his mental activity) upon the structure or organization of human society, and thus in a degree to reconstruct and modify in terms of his self the general pattern of social or group behavior in terms of which his self was originally constituted.

It's when people give in to hierarchical thinking and assume that one side of any dichotomy must always win or dominate the other that we get assumptions like those I'm fighting here: that either we have "knowledge" that is social, communal, socially justified etc., etc.—or we have non- or pseudo-knowledge that is private, subjective, confessional, and so forth. One of the best analyses to cut through this dichotomy—showing how knowledge is always both personal and social—can be found in Michael Polanyi's *Personal Knowledge*. Let me give an extended quotation from Thomas Langford and William Poteat's introduction to a collection of essays about Polanyi:

> Let us go back for a moment to Descartes, on whose head so many errors have been laid. His program of methodological doubt developed an ethos in which mathematical rigor became paradigmatic for all thought. [Descartes' earlier publication was in geometry.]

Thus our intellect was uprooted from its grounding in the past of our bodies. (An exception may be the cogito itself, but from the significance of this self-directed moment our sensibility has on the whole turned away.) The consequence of Cartesian method, therefore, was the notorious "bifurcation of nature," a dichotomy [my emphasis] which carried with it the insistence on the utterly detached character of rational thinking. Such an insistence, however, entailed a rhetoric that eschewed the first-person in favor of the third-person form for transacting our serious business with one another about what is the case. This has meant, therefore, that the first-person form has become either a mere means to reveal the idiosyncratic uniqueness of the "interesting" individual (singular), or alternatively the form in which a historically conditioned (pejorative sense) community, somewhat nervously, declared its corporate faith (plural).

But if one returns to or recovers an ancient, preCartesian model—Augustine's *Confessions*—then one begins to realize that as a rhetorical device the confession—whether in the first person singular or plural—has a very different force. For it then ceases to be a soliloquy by an individual through which is revealed his merely personal and idiosyncratic uniqueness. Instead, it can be seen as a disclosure to oneself of one's basic beliefs, grounded, first, in one's own personal history, with its roots in a pre-personal somatic appearance in the world, bearing its genetic inheritance; and secondly, in a native language upon the insinuations of a larger coherence of which one has trustingly and acritically relied as the conditio sine qua non of one's coming ever more fully to possess one's human being.

Now, far from being a mere disclosure of one's unique idiosyncrasy, this form of confession is precisely the medium for seeking to appreciate how and who one is in order that one may more fully be so. Therefore it is a confession having a fully convivial setting in the double sense that, on the one hand, one, in subscribing to one's own ever more fully self-disclosed and disclosing reality, is discovering and affirming that convivial setting as one's own; and on the other, one is ratifying this setting as something at once both given and shared. This recovery of the prepersonal and personal historical roots of one's own knowledge leads, not, as for the Cartesian, to subjectivism or relativism, but to the recognition of the inescapable, because necessary, universal intent of all our affirmation. (Introduction 17–18)

What is important about human knowing "is found neither in the individual nor the collective of individuals in a group, but in the meeting of the 'I' and the 'not I'" (Perry 118—writing about Buber). Carol Gilligan and colleagues speak of "...the dead-locked paradox of self and relationship that continues to plague the fields of personality and developmental psychology: that one can only experience self in the context of relationship with others and that one can only experience relationship if one differentiates other from self" ("Epilogue" 328).

Because I stick up so enthusiastically for personal writing, even private writing, and because of the doctrine that the personal must be at war with the social, people can't seem to see that most of what I've written is built on an equal commitment to collaboration and the social dimension—to the process of listening, taking in what is outside, and connecting with others.

Perhaps I would have been clearer about this if I had written more personally. In early adulthood I had two extended but decisive experiences that became central to my teaching and writing. First was the discovery that I needed to do nonstop uncensored, private, garbage writing: not only as a way to deal with difficult feelings I couldn't handle otherwise; but also as the only way I could get academic papers written. Second was my experience in a therapy group where I learned gradually to share more of what was personal and private with others and let them do the same with me—even though I experienced the process as deeply threatening. The resulting feelings of connection and solidarity were formative for me.

I've always felt that what is central in my teaching and writing have really grown out of these two root experiences. Both are about relaxing or letting down the walls of the ego—letting in what one experiences as "other" and threatening: from within (freewriting) and from without (the believing game). Both experiences made me stick up for the personal in such a way as simultaneously to foster the social. I feel defensive on this matter so I cannot resist pointing to the concretely social dimensions of three central parts of my work:

Group work.   This has been central to my published work since *Writing Without Teachers* (1973)—in fact even before (see my 1971 publication). I argued for using peer groups when it was unfashionable to do so.

The believing game (1973) **or methodological belief** (1986). I'm always trying to bring into practice this cognitive muscle or mentality that has attracted me longest. I'm not against doubting and argument, but my fight is always for believing and listening because these activities are so devalued in the academic world—seen as unintellectual. There are enough people sticking up for discussion and critical interrogation. Thus in setting up peer response groups, I've always advised writers: "Don't argue with readers, don't answer them. Just listen, eat like an owl. After all you get to make up your own mind about whether what they say makes sense." I give the same message to the readers: "Don't argue among yourselves about conflicting reactions or perceptions of a text." If people read this advice with too theoretical a hat on, they think I am championing solipsism—as though I'm saying "Don't talk to each other"— as though arguing is the only way to talk. But when colleagues and students test these precepts in action, they usually see how they foster the social dimension. People usually listen and take in alien or threatening feedback better if they don't have to answer or fight it. Not having to argue makes it easier for the writer finally to ask the really helpful question: "Tell me more about how you came to have this reaction." And readers only share with each other and with the writer what is fragile or uncertain (usually the most interesting feedback) if they don't have to defend it. Fighting among readers, and between readers and writers tends to diminish real listening and the variety of useful responses. I'm not saying that this nonadversarial approach always works, but I think it works at least as well as adversarial approaches—and it helps me teach what I most care about: people learning better to listen and swallow what is outside them, especially what is intellectually or personally threatening—and also allowing oneself to be swallowed by other people or new ideas. Taking chances.

Private writing and freewriting.   Even this helps us go more public. Here is an experiment for exploring the effect of private writing on social behavior or cooperation in classes or meetings. On certain occasions, try leading up to a discussion by having students or colleagues write privately about the topic to be discussed. (Ten minutes is often enough.) Compare this with just starting in the discussion without any writing. Almost always the private writing leads to public discourse that is more open and cooperative, less dug-in and with less posturing—and as a result leads to more engagement of people with each other at a more honest level. In the safety of private writing, people usually discover and articulate things for themselves which they find a way to offer into the public discussion. When there is no private writing first, people tend to play it safer and engage less with each other—which, by the way, leads to more domination by strong voices and good arguers.

When people chant the doctrine, "all language is social, there is no such thing as private writing," they tend to mask or even deny this very concrete distinction between private and public writing. Of course language is a social construct and of course our private writing often responds to the discourse of others—but these obvious facts don't diminish the crucial pedagogical and political difference between helping people find occasions for private and safe reflection vs. not doing so. Helping them find those occasions tends to foster social interaction.

If we are really interested in the social dimension, then the most important question to ask about someone's work is not, as with Berlin, "What epistemological premises can we infer?" but rather "Does this person's work lead to more cooperation and collaboration among students and among colleagues?—listening, letting other people in, taking in what is outside, relaxing walls and boundaries in one's head, fostering change of mind?—Or does it lead to keeping out what is other or alien, not working with people who aren't already in one's party, arguing, keeping up walls or even heightening boundaries?"

Works Cited

Berlin, James. "Contemporary Composition: The Major Pedagogical theories." *College English* 44 (December 1982): 766–77.

Booth, Wayne. "Confessions of a Luke Warm Lawrentian." *The Challenge of D. H. Lawrence*. Ed, Michael Squires and Keith Cushman. Madison, U of Wisconsin P, 1990. 9–27.

——. "Rabelais and the Challenge of Feminist Criticism." *The Company We Keep: An Ethics of Fiction*. Berkeley: U California P, 1988. 383–418.

——. *Modern Dogma and the Rhetoric of Assent*. U of Chicago, 1974.

Bruner, Jerome. *Actual Minds, Possible Worlds*. Cambridge: Harvard UP, 1986.

Culler, Jonathan. "Paul de Man's Contribution to Literary Criticism and Theory." *The Future of Literary Theory*, ed. Ralph Cohen, NY: Routledge, 1989.

DuPlessis, Rachel Blau. "For the Etruscans." *The New Feminist Criticism: Essays on Women, Literature, and Theory*. Ed. Elaine Showalter. New York: Pantheon Books, 1985.

Elbow, Peter. "Exploring my Teaching." *College English* 32 (1971): 743–53.

——. "Appendix Essay. The Doubting Game and the Believing Game: An Analysis of the Intellectual Enterprise." *Writing Without Teachers*. NY: Oxford UP, 1973. 147–92.

——. "Methodological Doubting and Believing: Contraries in Inquiry." *Embracing Contraries*. NY: Oxford UP, 1986. 253–300.

Fulkerson, Richard. "Composition Theory in the Eighties: Axiological Consensus and Paradigmatic Diversity." *College Composition and Communication* 41.4 (December 1990): 409–29.

Geertz, Clifford. "Blurred Genres: The Refiguration of Social Thought." *Local Knowledge: Further Essays in Interpretive Anthropology*. NY: Basic, 1983. 19–35.

Gilligan, Carol, Nona P. Lyons and Trudy J. Hanmer, eds. *Making Connections: The Relational Worlds of Adolescent Girls at Emma Willard School*. Cambridge: Harvard UP, 1990.

Harris, Jeanette. *Expressive Discourse.* Dallas: Southern Methodist UP, 1990.

Irigaray, Luce. "And One Doesn't Stir Without the Other." Trans. Helene Wenzel. *Signs* 7.1 (1981): 56–67.

Langford, Thomas and William Poteat. "Introduction." *Intellect and Hope.* Durham, NC: Duke UP, 1967.

LeFevre, Karen Burke. *Invention as a Social Act.* Carbondale: Southern Illinois UP, 1987.

Perry, Pat. Unpublished Dissertation.

Polanyi, Michael. *Personal Knowledge: Toward a Post-Critical Philosophy.* New York: Harper and Row, 1958.

Tompkins, Jane. "Me and My Shadow." *New Literary History* 19.1 (1987): 169–78.

On the Possibilities of the Essay: A Meditation

Rebecca Blevins Faery

When one looks from inside at a lighted window, or looks from above at the lake, one sees the image of oneself in a lighted room, the image of oneself among trees and sky—the deception is obvious, but flattering all the same. When one looks from the darkness into the light, however, one sees all the difference between here and there, this and that. Perhaps all unsheltered people are angry in their hearts, and would like to break the roof, spine, and ribs, and smash the windows and flood the floor and spindle the curtains and bloat the couch.

Marilynne Robinson, *Housekeeping*

I

I had, it seemed, to my surprise, terror, and delight, bought a house.

It was high summer, July of 1988, the peak of a season of dazzling heat and soul-wrenching drought. As I drove between Iowa City and Dubuque, where I was teaching a seminar, I watched the corn in fields on either side of the two-lane highway shrivel relentlessly week by week under the baking sun until I heard, or thought I heard, as I drove, a very high-pitched keen or wail, coming from the corn, begging for rain.

Moving day arrived when the seminar ended, according to plan. During the weeks I was away teaching, assorted carpenters and dry-wall workers and plumbers and painters had executed my preliminary plans for turning the house into my own. It was—is—a grand house, old and possessed of great dignity, so I had a lot to work with: high ceilings, wide mahogany pocket doors at once dividing and connecting all the downstairs rooms, multiple tall windows looking out on a wide lawn with room for a terrace, a garden, a grape arbor, a bed of multi-hued lilies. A house full of promise, of possibilities.

The unpacking and settling-in were a strain in the dry heat, well over a hundred degrees day after sizzling day. Indulging a fantasy which my new identity as owner of this grand house allowed me, I adopted in interludes the persona and habits of a woman of leisure and splurged on a Yucatan hammock, which I hung between an old box-elder and a leaning cedar not far from the back porch. I took refuge in their shade when fatigue overtook me, swaying as I read. The novel in my hands, as I recall myself in those moments through the screen of memory, is Marilynne Robinson's *Housekeeping*.

Mornings I rose, made coffee, soothed the cat out of her nervousness at waking in a house whose unfamiliarity she had daily to confront anew, and set to work to establish the cleanliness and order I've been taught to believe is next to godliness. My domestic inclinations I gave full rein: this was my home, my haven, nest, stay against the confusion of impermanence, each room a stanza of the poem to fixity I was trying to make of the enterprise. I had married this house with enthusiasm, and I took up the familiar role and tasks of house-wife with an energy made vigorous by commitment. "I was born to live in this house," I said to my friends in the romantic flush of love for my new home; "I intend to stay here forever."

It must be understood, for this tale to make any sense at all, that I have yearned all my adult life for permanence, for "home," for a long commitment to a place, a dwelling that would house me securely and comfortably in return for my love and attention, its walls my fortress against flux and fortune's whims. Yet every home I've had I've lived in only briefly; I've been, despite my longings, a woman forever on the move. Or, more precisely, several women, simultaneously and in succession, and all of them on the move.

In the heat of that summer, I was making another stab at it. I labored in splendid isolation toward splendid order in the arrangement of furniture, pictures on the walls, dishes in the cupboards. This finely articulated distribution of my possessions soothed me into pretending that I was indeed protected from the shifting boundaries of identity, from the fraying and unraveling that are the lot of us all.

The dissonances between my determined housekeeping and the interpolations of lazy late afternoon hours of suspended reading of *Housekeeping* did not escape me. The novel drew me away from my busy-ness to the still hours in the swaying hammock, drew me with its exquisite sentences, its elegiac tone, its visions that all efforts to stop the flow of time, change, displacement, discomposing are fruitless. It's a vision I share, indeed advocate; the old must be abandoned in pursuit of the new. The difference is that the women in the novel act on that knowledge. I, on the other hand, sometimes at least, act as if I *don't* believe it, though I do. In the novel, Sylvie knows that something means to undo a house, so she opens the doors and windows and lets the undoer in. She underscores the silly futility of housewifely saving and storing by collecting useless things—empty cans, old newspapers—and arranging them neatly against the walls of all the rooms. Sylvie refuses the bourgeois ideologies of "home" with all their attachments to class privilege, ideologies that confine women within the predictable roles and ordered spaces of domesticity; she embraces the road rather than the cottage beside it. I try to do these things too, in my own way. But I, on the other hand, dweller in contradictions, also batten down, hunker, and hope.

II

In their essay "Feminist Politics: What's Home Got to Do with It?" Biddy Martin and Chandra Talpade Mohanty use their reading of another essay, Minnie Bruce Pratt's "Identity: Skin Blood Heart," to consider the political ideologies of "home": house, family, kin, community in the immediate sense; personal identities grounded in race, class, gender, sexuality, convictions and claimed affinities in the wider sense. And while the following passage from Martin and Mohanty addresses Pratt's remarkable essay alone, I offer it as a perspective on the possibilities of the essay in general:

> [The essay] is a form of writing that not only anticipates and integrates diverse audiences or readers but also positions the narrator as reader. The perspective is multiple and shifting, and the shifts in perspective are enabled by the attempts to define self, home, and community that are at the heart of Pratt's enterprise. The historical grounding of shifts and changes allows for an emphasis on the pleasures and terrors of interminable boundary confusions, but insists, at the same time, on our responsibility for remapping boundaries and renegotiating connections. These are partial in at least two senses of the word: politically partial, and without claims to wholeness or finality.

The essay as a performance of reading. The essayist as reader. The reader of essays as reader. All readings contingent, partial, multiple, shifting. Nothing is fixed, and nobody has a corner on truth.

When Samuel Johnson in his famous *Dictionary* defines the essay as "a loose sally of the mind; an irregular, undigested piece," I at least suspect the privileging of reason over feeling, intellection over intuition. It is the article or treatise which earns from Johnson an implicit description as "a regular, orderly composition," the thing the essay, by his definition, is not. What makes for the difference? The meanderings, for one thing, of the essayist's persona, made precedent by Montaigne. A "composition" requires the writer's subjugation to a monumental discourse. The essay is written by somebody who sallies into a subject loosely, leaving—or making holes that are not knitted up, carrying along and exploring the myriad possible specificities of the writer's experience and identity. The essay rests on perspective, on the position of the essayist within the web of culture. It allows the essayist to say, "This is how the world looks to *me*, from my particular place in it." The essay has, then, the potential for being at least an inroad, if not indeed an attack, on monumental discourse because as a form it negotiates the split between public discourse—formal, ordered, impersonal, knowing, with pretensions to universality and fixity, and private utterance—tentative, personal, questing, provisional. If the "composition" is an edifice, the essay is a nomad's tent. It moves around.

The essay, then, is and has been a form open to the articulation of estrangements and contradictions, a place for expressing the strains, differences, rejections as well as connections experienced by those who feel or have felt particularly marginalized by the discourses which have composed the social text. I am thinking here of writers like James Baldwin, Nancy Mairs, Alice Walker, Audre Lorde, Minnie Bruce Pratt, and many others who have recognized in the essay a potential site for the operations of contesting discourses and have used it to explore and construct in language the multiple perspectives which variant experiences and identities produce.

Virginia Woolf, for instance. Think of all those polite essays she wrote about her reading and published in the *Times Literary Supplement.* Think of how comforting, how comfortable they are, spoken from the privileged position of a woman of means, of well-placed family, of culture. And then think of others, *A Room of One's Own* and *Three Guineas*, in which she speaks from a position as outsider, attempting to undo the cultural stories that have placed her there, on the margins, because of her gender. Such writing from the margins is "guerrilla writing," a term I heard recently and have not been able to forget. In the terrain of monumental discourse, such pieces are eruptions of personal presence based on shifting experiences and identities, eruptions that aim to dis-compose the power relations that reside in textuality. And such moments are accomplished not only *by* particular essays within the field of more orderly forms of writing; they occur also *within* essays, as in Woolf's "Professions for Women," when that-which-cannot-be-said about a woman's experience of her body slips away like a fish escaping a line. Or in "The Moment: Summer's Night," when an imaged scene of domestic violence—"He beats her"—intrudes upon and contrasts with the cultivated civility of the narrator and her companions. Or in "22 Hyde Park Gate," which closes with the astonishing revelation of the sexual abuse Woolf and her sister were subjected to by their half-brother. Is Woolf in these texts violating her own dictum that the purpose of the essay is "to give pleasure"? What sort of pleasure can we get from scenes of wife-beating and forced incest and the taboos against expressing bodily experience? Perhaps the pleasures of heresy—the thing Adorno calls "the law of the innermost form of the essay." And the pleasures of heresy are not small. Carl Klaus has aptly termed the essay an "antigenre, a rogue form of writing in the universe of discourse." I would elaborate only to observe that the essay can be, has been, rogue or heretical not only in form but in effect. As "antigenre," it has the capacity to work against, even to undo, the presumptions that have structured western discourse.

Look, for another example, at what is happening in the realm of conventional academic writing. A couple of years ago, a friend gave me a copy of Jane Tompkins' essay "Me and My Shadow" in an effort to help me out of a difficult period of inability to write. I read about Tompkins' anger at the "straitjacket" of the suppression of the personal voice and personal experience in academic writing, about the "two voices" she felt within her, one of which had been systematically silenced. I read her plea for redressing the damage done by the conventions of intellectual discourse, a plea based on the conviction that readers "want to know about each other":

> Sometimes, when a writer introduces some personal bit of story into an essay, I can hardly contain my pleasure. I love writers who write about their own experience. I feel I'm being nourished by them, that I'm being allowed to enter into a personal relationship with them, that I can match my own experience with theirs, feel cousin to them, and say, yes, that's how it is.

Yes, I said to myself as I read, a seemingly endless stream of tears rolling down my cheeks—whether tears of grief, or joy, or both, I'm still not clear—yes, that's how it is.

Sometimes, though, the voice relating personal perspective and experience in an essay draws me, excites me, because what I read challenges rather than confirms my own experience and thus opens up for me new perspectives on the world. Then my response is not "That's how it is," but "Is that how it is?" If I am to act in the world in a way that attempts to respect and accommodate differences, I need to know what the world is like not only for people who are in some way like me, but also for people who are in some way different. I must be taught as well as teach. Patricia Williams, a Black feminist legal scholar, begins an essay on commercial transactions by telling the story of the rape and impregnation at age twelve of her great-great-grandmother by the girl's white owner. The essay, "On Being the Object of Property," is a dazzling poetic display which inserts the continuing personal pain of such a heritage into the affectless tradition of legal scholarship and thereby unsettles that tradition. It links Williams' meditations on her personal and racial histories, her experiences of race and gender in a hierarchical culture, with legal issues like the "Baby M" case and the forced sterilization of women of color. The essay accommodates passages like this one:

> There are moments in my life when I feel as though a part of me is missing. There are days when I feel so invisible that I can't remember what day of the week it is, when I feel so manipulated that I can't remember my own name, when I feel so lost and angry that I can't speak a civil word to the people who love me best. Those are the times when I catch sight of my reflection in store windows and am surprised to see a whole person looking back. Those are the times when my skin becomes gummy as clay and my nose slides around on my face and my eyes drip down to my chin. I have to close my eyes at such times and remember myself, draw an internal picture that is smooth and whole; when all else fails, I reach for a mirror and stare myself down until the features reassemble themselves like lost sheep.

The passage is a metaphoric description of the dis-composing effect of monolithic racist and sexist discourses on Williams, and of the composing effect of her own writing, in which she reconstructs—*re-members*—a self, however momentary, however *partial* in both senses of the word: invested with self-interest and without claim to finality. Williams' writing simultaneously composes herself and discomposes conventional discourses which in a variety of ways deny her. She makes use of the literary qualities of language, whose task, in their origins in the oral traditions of poetry, was to make memorable the stories of the tribe or culture in order to assure they would be repeated and thus not forgotten. Williams' essay is a frontal attack on the master's house, a stream of words aimed at eroding the rock of oppression at the foundation of culture. Her essay insists that there is never just one story; rather, there are many stories which can and must be told, which must be heard. In this essay Williams, like Sylvie in *Housekeeping*, is an undoer. And that cannot be a futile effort because, as James Baldwin, filled with simultaneous despair and desperate hope, writes in his beautiful essay "Nothing Personal," "For nothing is fixed, forever and forever and forever, it is not fixed; the earth is always shifting, the light is always changing, the sea does not cease to grind down rock."

What the pedagogical implications might be of such a view of the essay I have considered here hardly at all, and then only indirectly. Certainly the form itself has been an outsider in the institution of literary studies, relegated mostly to the composition classroom where, too often, its essential qualities of perspective and personal voice have been masked or even banned. What could happen if we admit the "anti-genre" not only into our polite and scholarly forms of writing, but also into the rigidly generic classrooms and hallways of our educational institutions—what Nancy Mairs calls "the ivory phallus"—I can scarcely imagine. I know I'd like to be around to watch.

III

So. What did I leave out of my story of buying a house, of my attempts to shore up its walls against some imagined ruin? Some of the reasons. I belong, by race and by family tradition, to a propertied class, where owning a house stands in direct equation with respectability. It is my toehold. Also because I am a woman who came of age in an era when "home" was woman's sphere, even when she's also the "head of household." Also because I've been, most of my adult life, relatively rootless, following along after one man, one life plan, in flight from others. Now, my children grown and gone, I become paradoxically even more obsessive about a "nest."

If you wonder why I of all people proved so susceptible to the seductions of "home" with all its attendant ideologies, I can tell you only and simply that I am a woman partially constructed by such ideologies.

But perhaps I've painted an overly romantic picture of the house and my relation to it. It's been almost two years now, after all, since I moved in, two years of mild winters and early springs and one temperate summer. Like all love affairs, this one has lost some of its glow. The house is still grand, I admit; but water pipes burst, the roof leaks, the porches sag. The deep and dark waters of the lake at Fingerbone reach all the way to Iowa and lap at my edges. The house is after all less comfortable, less comforting than I had hoped, and other yearnings have started to surface. I manage to muster, twice a year, the thousand dollars to pay the property tax. But I feed the squirrels that eat holes in the eaves to winter over in the attic, though my more prudent friends urge me to trap them humanely and move them out into the country west of town. And I think I forgot to mention that I share the house—and not just with my cat. In fact I live only in those hardly discrete rooms of the first floor, rooms that flow liquidly one into another. In the upstairs apartment are Karen and Wayne, their black cat and their books. Wayne writes novels, Karen makes poems, so on our good days, all of us are more preoccupied with meanings than with maintenance. In the spare parking place next to the alley, a huge and ancient Buick appears several days a week beside my tenants' Toyota. The Buick is ventilated with rusted-through holes the size of my fist. It belongs to Alex, broad-faced member of the Mesquakie tribe from the settlement over at Tama. He wears a long braid down his back, a feather in his black felt hat; he won a dance competition, he told me, at a pow-wow on the shores of Lake Michigan just a few months ago. Karen and Wayne mentioned casually once that he was "visiting"; instead, I think he lives there with them on the days he needs to be in Iowa City to go to school. They don't tell me that because, I suppose, they think the same impulse that led me to lay a brick terrace and plant lilies would make me exercise a white law and kick him out. But I say nothing. I'm learning to live with, live through contradictions, even learning to love them. I grow weary of defending territory to which I'm not sure I can lay just claim. And I want to be an undoer too, as well as one of the undone. I want this house to be open. Alex, when he sees me in the yard, greets me and calls me "the landlady." The term gives me a start, especially coming from him. Whose home is this, anyway?

I know, I know, it is in some sense mine. But I can give it up. And surely someday, some way or other, I will.

Note

The texts cited in this essay are: T. W. Adorno, "The Essay as Form," in *New German Critique*, 1984; James Baldwin, "Nothing Personal," in *The Price of the Ticket*, 1985; Carl Klaus, "Essayists on the Essay," in *Literary Nonfiction*, ed. Chris Anderson, 1989; Nancy Mairs, *Remembering the Bone House: An Erotics of Place and Space*, 1989; Biddy Martin and Chandra Talpade Mohanty, "Feminist Politics: What's Home Got to Do with It?" in *Feminist Studies/Critical Studies*, ed. Teresa de Lauretis, 1986; Minnie Bruce Pratt, "Identity: Skin Blood Heart," in Bulkin, Pratt, and Smith, *Yours in Struggle*, 1984; Marilynne Robinson, *Housekeeping*, 1981; Jane Tompkins, "Me and My Shadow," in *New Literary History*, 1987; Patricia Williams, "On Being the Object of Property," in *Signs*, 1988; Virginia Woolf, "Professions for Women," in *The Death of the Moth and Other Essays*, 1942; Woolf, "The Moment: Summer's Night," in *The Moment and Other Essays*, 1948; Woolf, "22 Hyde Park Gate," in *Moments of Being*, 1976.

Memory and Imagination

Patricia Hampl

When I was seven, my father, who played the violin on Sundays with a nicely tortured flair which we considered artistic, led me by the hand down a long, unlit corridor in St. Luke's School basement, a sort of tunnel that ended in a room full of pianos. There many little girls and a single sad boy were playing truly tortured scales and arpeggios in a mash of troubled sound. My father gave me over to Sister Olive Marie, who did look remarkably like an olive.

Her oily face gleamed as if it had just been rolled out of a can and laid on the white plate of her broad, spotless wimple. She was a small, plump woman; her body and the small window of her face seemed to interpret the entire alphabet of olive: her face was a sallow green olive placed upon the jumbo ripe olive of her black habit. I trusted her instantly and smiled, glad to have my hand placed in the hand of a woman who made sense, who provided the satisfaction of being what she was: an Olive who looked like an olive.

My father left me to discover the piano with Sister Olive Marie so that one day I would join him in mutually tortured piano-violin duets for the edification of my mother and brother who sat at the table meditatively spooning in the last of their pineapple sherbet until their part was called for: they put down their spoons and clapped while we bowed, while the sweet ice in their bowls melted, while the music melted, and we all melted a little into each other for a moment.

But first Sister Olive must do her work. I was shown middle C, which Sister seemed to think terribly important. I stared at middle C and then glanced away for a second. When my eye returned, middle C was gone, its slim finger lost in the complicated grasp of the keyboard. Sister Olive struck it again, finding it with laughable ease. She emphasized the importance of middle C, its central position, a sort of North Star of sound. I remember thinking, "Middle C is the belly button of the piano," an insight whose originality and accuracy stunned me with pride. For the first time in my life I was astonished by metaphor. I hesitated to tell the kindly Olive for some reason; apparently I understood a true metaphor is a risky business, revealing of the self. In fact, I have never, until this moment of writing it down, told my first metaphor to anyone.

Sunlight flooded the room; the pianos, all black, gleamed. Sister Olive, dressed in the colors of the keyboard, gleamed; middle C shimmered with meaning and I resolved never—never—to forget its location: it was the center of the world.

Then Sister Olive, who had had to show me middle C twice but who seemed to have drawn no bad conclusions about me anyway, got up and went to the windows on the opposite wall. She pulled the shades down, one after the other. The sun was too bright, she said. She sneezed as she stood at the windows with the sun shedding its glare over her. She sneezed and sneezed, crazy little convulsive sneezes, one after another, as helpless as if she had the hiccups.

"The sun makes me sneeze," she said when the fit was over and she was back at the piano. This was odd, too odd to grasp in the mind. I associated sneezing with colds, and colds with rain, fog, snow and bad weather. The sun, however, had caused Sister Olive to sneeze in this wild way, Sister Olive who gleamed benignly and who was so certain of the location of the center of the world. The universe wobbled a bit and became unreliable. Things were not, after all, necessarily what they seemed. Appearance deceived: here was the sun acting totally out of character, hurling this woman into sneezes, a woman so mild that she was named, so it seemed, for a bland object on a relish tray.

I was given a red book, the first Thompson book, and told to play the first piece over and over at one of the black pianos where the other children were crashing away. This, I was told, was called practicing. It sounded alluringly adult, practicing. The piece itself consisted mainly of middle C, and I excelled, thrilled by my savvy at being able to locate that central note amidst the cunning camouflage of all the other white keys before me. Thrilled too by the shiny red book that gleamed, as the pianos did, as Sister Olive did, as my eager eyes probably did. I sat at the formidable machine of the piano and got to know middle C intimately, preparing to be as tortured as I could manage one day soon with my father's violin at my side.

But at the moment Mary Katherine Reilly was at my side, playing something at least two or three lessons more sophisticated than my piece. I believe she even struck a chord. I glanced at her from the peasantry of single notes, shy, ready to pay homage. She turned toward me, stopped playing, and sized me up.

Sized me up and found a person ready to be dominated. Without introduction she said, "My grandfather invented the collapsible opera hat."

I nodded, I acquiesced, I was hers. With that little stroke it was decided between us—that she should be the leader, and I the sidekick. My job was admiration. Even when she added, "But he didn't make a penny from it. He didn't have a patent"—even then, I knew and she knew that this was not an admission of powerlessness, but the easy candor of a master, of one who can afford a weakness or two.

With the clairvoyance of all fated relationships based on dominance and submission, it was decided in advance: that when the time came for us to play duets, I should always play second piano, that I should spend my allowance to buy her the Twinkies she craved but was not allowed to have, that finally, I should let her copy from my test paper, and when confronted by our teacher, confess with convincing hysteria that it was I, I who had cheated, who had reached above myself to steal what clearly belonged to the rightful heir of the inventor of the collapsible opera hat....

There must be a reason I remember that little story about my first piano lesson. In fact, it isn't a story, just a moment, the beginning of what could perhaps become a story. For the memoirist, more than for the fiction writer, the story seems already *there*, already accomplished and fully achieved in history ("in reality," as we naively say). For the memoirist, the writing of the story is a matter of transcription.

That, anyway, is the myth. But no memoirist writes for long without experiencing an unsettling disbelief about the reliability of memory, a hunch that memory is not, after all, *just* memory. I don't know why I remembered this fragment about my first piano lesson. I don't, for instance, have a single recollection of my first arithmetic lesson, the first time I studied Latin, the first time my grandmother tried to teach me to knit. Yet these things occurred too, and must have their stories.

It is the piano lesson that has trudged forward, clearing the haze of forgetfulness, showing itself bright with detail more than thirty years after the event. I did not choose to remember the piano lesson. It was simply there, like a book that has always been on the shelf, whether I ever read it or not, the binding and title showing as I skim across the contents of my life. On the day I wrote this fragment I happened to take that memory, not some other, from the shelf and paged through it. I found more detail, more event, perhaps a little more entertainment than I had expected, but the memory itself was there from the start. Waiting for me.

Or was it? When I reread what I had written just after I finished it, I realized that I had told a number of lies. I *think* it was my father who took me the first time for my piano lesson—but maybe he only took me to meet my teacher and there was no actual lesson that day. And did I even know then that he played the violin—didn't he take up his violin again much later, as a result of my piano playing, and not the reverse? And is it even remotely accurate to describe as "tortured" the musicianship of a man who began every day by belting out "Oh What a Beautiful Morning" as he shaved?

More: Sister Olive Marie did sneeze in the sun, but was her name Olive? As for her skin tone—I would have sworn it was olive-like; I would have been willing to spend the better part of an afternoon trying to write the exact description of imported Italian or Greek olive her face suggested: I wanted to get it right. But now, were I to write that passage over, it is her intense black eyebrows I would see, for suddenly they seem the central fact of that face, some indicative mark of her serious and patient nature. But the truth is, I don't remember the woman at all. She's a sneeze in the sun and a finger touching middle C. That, at least, is steady and clear.

Worse: I didn't have the Thompson book as my piano text. I'm sure of that because I remember envying children who did have this wonderful book with its pictures of children and animals printed on the pages of music.

As for Mary Katherine Reilly. She didn't even go to grade school with me (and her name isn't Mary Katherine Reilly—but I made that change on purpose). I met her in Girl Scouts and only went to school with her later, in high school. Our relationship was not really one of leader and follower; I played first piano most of the time in duets. She certainly never copied anything from a test paper of mine: she was a better student, and cheating just wasn't a possibility with her. Though her grandfather (or someone in her family) did invent the collapsible opera hat and I remember that she was proud of that fact, she didn't tell me this news as a deft move in a childish power play.

So, what was I doing in this brief memoir? Is it simply an example of the curious relation a fiction writer has to the material of her own life? Maybe. That may have some value in itself. But to tell the truth (if anyone still believes me capable of telling the truth), I wasn't writing fiction. I was writing memoir—or was trying to. My desire was to be accurate. I wished to embody the myth of memoir: to write as an act of dutiful transcription.

Yet clearly the work of writing narrative caused me to do something very different from transcription. I am forced to admit that memoir is not a matter of transcription, that memory itself is not a warehouse of finished stories, not a static gallery of framed pictures. I must admit that I invented. But why?

Two whys: why did I invent, and then, if a memoirist must inevitably invent rather than transcribe, why do I—why should anybody—write memoir at all?

I must respond to these impertinent questions because they, like the bumper sticker I saw the other day commanding all who read it to QUESTION AUTHORITY, challenge my authority as a memoirist and as a witness.

It still comes as a shock to realize that I don't write about what I know: I write in order to find out what I know. Is it possible to convey to a reader the enormous degree of blankness, confusion, hunch and uncertainty lurking in the act of writing? When I am the reader, not the writer, I too fall into the lovely illusion that the words before me (in a story by Mavis Gallant, an essay by Carol Bly, a memoir by M. F. K. Fisher), which *read* so inevitably, must also have been *written* exactly as they appear, rhythm and cadence, language and syntax, the powerful waves of the sentences laying themselves on the smooth beach of the page one after another faultlessly.

But here I sit before a yellow legal pad, and the long page of the preceding two paragraphs is a jumble of crossed-out lines, false starts, confused order. A mess. The mess of my mind trying to find out what it wants to say. This is a writer's frantic, grabby mind, not the poised mind of a reader ready to be edified or entertained.

I sometimes think of the reader as a cat, endlessly fastidious, capable, by turns, of mordant indifference and riveted attention, luxurious, recumbent, and ever poised. Whereas the writer is absolutely a dog, panting and moping, too eager for an affectionate scratch behind the ears, lunging frantically after any old stick thrown in the distance.

The blankness of a new page never fails to intrigue and terrify me. Sometimes, in fact, I think my habit of writing on long yellow sheets comes from an atavistic fear of the writer's stereotypic "blank white page." At least when I begin writing, my page isn't utterly blank; at least it has a wash of color on it, even if the absence of words must finally be faced on a yellow sheet as truly as on a blank white one. Well, we all have our ways of whistling in the dark.

If I approach writing from memory with the assumption that I know what I wish to say, I assume that intentionality is running the show. Things are not that simple. Or perhaps writing is even more profoundly simple, more telegraphic and immediate in its choices than the grating wheels and chugging engine of logic and rational intention. The heart, the guardian of intuition with its secret, often fearful intentions, is the boss, its commands are what a writer obeys—often without knowing it. Or, I do.

That's why I'm a strong adherent of the first draft. And why it's worth pausing for a moment to consider what a first draft really is. By my lights, the piano lesson memoir is a first draft. That doesn't mean it exists here exactly as I first wrote it. I like to think I've cleaned it up from the first time I put it down on paper. I've cut some adjectives here, toned down the hyperbole there, smoothed a transition, cut a repetition—that sort of housekeeperly tidying-up. But the piece remains a first draft because I haven't yet gotten to know it, haven't given it a chance to tell me anything. For me, writing a first draft is a little like meeting someone for the first time. I come away with a wary acquaintanceship, but the real friendship (if any) and genuine intimacy—that's all down the road. Intimacy with a piece of writing, as with a person, comes from paying attention to the revelations it is capable of giving, not by imposing my own preconceived notions, no matter how well-intentioned they might be.

I try to let pretty much anything happen in a first draft. A careful first draft is a failed first draft. That may be why there are so many inaccuracies in the piano lesson memoir: I didn't censor, I didn't judge. I kept moving. But I would not publish this piece as a memoir on its own in its present state. It isn't the "lies" in the piece that give me pause, though a reader has a right to expect a memoir to be as accurate as the writer's memory can make it. No, it isn't the lies themselves that makes the piano lesson memoir a first draft and therefore "unpublishable."

The real trouble: the piece hasn't yet found its subject; it isn't yet about what it wants to be about. Note: what *it* wants, not what I want. The difference has to do with the relation a memoirist—any writer, in fact—has to unconscious or half-known intentions and impulses in composition.

Now that I have the fragment down on paper, I can read this little piece as a mystery which drops clues to the riddle of my feelings, like a culprit who wishes to be apprehended. My narrative self (the culprit who has invented) wishes to be discovered by my reflective self, the self who wants to understand and make sense of a half-remembered story about a nun sneezing in the sun....

We only store in memory images of value. The value may be lost over the passage of time (I was baffled about why I remembered that sneezing nun, for example), but that's the implacable judgment of feeling: *this*, we say somewhere deep within us, is something I'm hanging on to. And of course, often we cleave to things because they possess heavy negative charges. Pain likes to be vivid.

Over time, the value (the feeling) and the stored memory (the image) may become estranged. Memoir seeks a permanent home for feeling and image, a habitation where they can live together in harmony. Naturally, I've had a lot of experiences since I packed away that one from the basement of St. Luke's School; that piano lesson has been effaced by waves of feeling for other moments and episodes. I persist in believing the event has value—after all, I remember it—but in writing the memoir I did not simply relive the experience. Rather, I explored the mysterious relationship between all the images I could round up and the even more impacted feelings that caused me to store the images safely away in memory. Stalking the relationship, seeking the congruence between stored image and hidden emotion—that's the real job of memoir.

By writing about that first piano lesson, I've come to know things I could not know otherwise. But I only know these things as a result of reading this first draft. While I was writing, I was following the images, letting the details fill the room of the page and use the furniture as they wished. I was their dutiful servant—or thought I was. In fact, I was the faithful retainer of my hidden feelings which were giving the commands.

I really did feel, for instance, that Mary Katherine Reilly was far superior to me. She was smarter, funnier, more wonderful in every way—that's how I saw it. Our friendship (or she herself) did not require that I become her vassal, yet perhaps in my heart that was something I wanted; I wanted a way to express my feeling of admiration. I suppose I waited until this memoir to begin to find the way.

Just as, in the memoir, I finally possess that red Thompson book with the barking dogs and bleating lambs and winsome children. I couldn't (and still can't) remember what my own music book was, so I grabbed the name and image of the one book I could remember. It was only in reviewing the piece after writing it that I saw my inaccuracy. In pondering this "lie," I came to see what I was up to: I was getting what I wanted. At last.

The truth of many circumstances and episodes in the past emerges for the memoirist through details (the red music book, the fascination with a nun's name and gleaming face), but these details are not merely information, not flat facts. Such details are not allowed to lounge. They must work. Their work is the creation of symbol. But it's more accurate to call it the *recognition* of symbol. For meaning is not "attached" to the detail by the memoirist; meaning is revealed. That's why a first draft is important. Just as the first meeting (good or bad) with someone who later becomes the beloved is important and is often reviewed for signals, meanings, omens, and indications.

Now I can look at that music book and see it not only as "a detail," but for what it is, how it *acts*. See it as the small red door leading straight into the dark room of my childhood longing and disappointment. That red book *becomes* the palpable evidence of that longing. In other words, it becomes symbol. There is no symbol, no life-of-the-spirit in the general or the abstract. Yet a writer wishes—indeed all of us wish—to speak about profound matters that are, like it or not, general and abstract. We wish to talk to each other about life and death, about love, despair, loss, and innocence. We sense that in order to live together we must learn to speak of peace, of history, of meaning and values. Those are a few.

We seek a means of exchange, a language which will renew these ancient concerns and make them wholly and pulsingly ours. Instinctively, we go to our store of private images and associations for our authority to speak of these weighty issues. We find, in our details and broken and obscured images, the language of symbol. Here memory impulsively reaches out its arms and embraces imagination. That is the resort to invention. It isn't a lie, but an act of necessity, as the innate urge to locate personal truth always is.

All right. Invention is inevitable. But why write memoir? Why not call it fiction and be done with all the hashing about, wondering where memory stops and imagination begins? And if memoir seeks to talk about "the big issues," about history and peace, death and love—why not leave these reflections to those with expert and scholarly knowledge? Why let the common or garden variety memoirist into the club? I'm thinking again of that bumper sticker: why Question Authority?

My answer, of course, is a memoirist's answer. Memoir must be written because each of us must have a created version of the past. Created: that is, real, tangible, made of the stuff of a life lived in place and in history. And the down side of any created thing as well: we must live with a version that attaches us to our limitations, to the inevitable subjectivity, of our points of view. We must acquiesce to our experience and our gift to transform experience into meaning and value. You tell me your story, I'll tell you my story.

If we refuse to do the work of creating this personal version of the past, some-one else will do it for us. That is a scary political fact. "The struggle of man against power," a character in Milan Kundera's novel *The Book of Laughter and Forgetting* says, "is the struggle of memory against forgetting." He refers to willful political forgetting, the habit of nations and those in power (Question Authority!) to deny the truth of memory in order to disarm moral and ethical power. It's an efficient way of controlling masses of people. It doesn't even require much bloodshed, as long as people are entirely willing to give over their personal memories. Whole histories can be rewrit-ten. As Czeslaw Milosz said in his 1980 Nobel Prize lecture, the number of books published that seek to deny the existence of the Nazi death camps now exceeds one hundred.

What is remembered is what *becomes* reality. If we "forget" Auschwitz, if we "for-get" My Lai, what then do we remember? And what is the purpose of our remember-ing? If we think of memory naively, as a simple story, logged like a documentary in the archive of the mind, we miss its beauty but also its function. The beauty of memory rests in its talent for rendering detail, for paying homage to the senses, its capacity to love the particles of life, the richness and idiosyncrasy of our existence. The function of memory, on the other hand, is intensely personal and surprisingly political.

Our capacity to move forward as developing beings rests on a healthy relation with the past. Psychotherapy, that widespread method of mental health, relies heavily on memory and on the ability to retrieve and organize images and events from the personal past. We carry our wounds and perhaps even worse, our capacity to wound, forward with us. If we learn not only to tell our stories but to listen to what our stories tell us—to write the first draft and then return for the second draft—we are doing the work of memoir.

Memoir is the intersection of narration and reflection, of story-telling and essay-writing. It can present its story *and* reflect and consider the meaning of the story. It is a peculiarly open form, inviting broken and incomplete images, half-recollected fragments, all the mass (and mess) of detail. It offers to shape this confusion—and in shaping, of course it necessarily creates a work of art, not a legal document. But then, even legal documents are only valiant attempts to consign the truth, the whole truth and nothing but the truth to paper. Even they remain versions.

Locating touchstones—the red music book, the olive Olive, My father's violin playing—is deeply satisfying. Who knows why? Perhaps we all sense that we can't grasp the whole truth and nothing but the truth of our experience. Just can't be done.

What can be achieved, however, is a version of its swirling, changing wholeness. A memoirist must acquiesce to selectivity, like any artist. The version we dare to write is the only truth, the only relationship we can have with the past. Refuse to write your life and you have no life. At least, that is the stern view of the memoirist.

Personal history, logged in memory, is a sort of slide projector flashing images on the wall of the mind. And there's precious little order to the slides in the rotating carousel. Beyond that confusion, who knows who is running the projector? A memoirist steps into this darkened room of flashing, unorganized images and stands blinking for a while. Maybe for a long while. But eventually, as with any attempt to tell a story, it is necessary to put something first, then something else. And so on, to the end. That's a first draft. Not necessarily the truth, not even *a* truth sometimes, but the first attempt to create a shape.

The first thing I usually notice at this stage of composition is the appalling inaccuracy of the piece. Witness my first piano lesson draft. Invention is screamingly evident in what I intended to be transcription. But here's the further truth: I feel no shame. In fact, it's only now that my interest in the piece truly quickens. For I can see what isn't there, what is shyly hugging the walls, hoping not to be seen. I see the filmy shape of the next draft. I see a more acute version of the episode or—this is more likely—an entirely new piece rising from the ashes of the first attempt.

The next draft of the piece would have to be a true re-vision, a new seeing of the materials of the first draft. Nothing merely cosmetic will do—no rouge buffing up the opening sentence, no glossy adjective to lift a sagging line, nothing to attempt covering a patch of gray writing. None of that. I can't say for sure, but my hunch is the revision would lead me to more writing about my father (why was I so impressed by that ancestral inventor of the collapsible opera hat? Did I feel I had nothing as remarkable in my own background? Did this make me feel inadequate?). I begin to think perhaps Sister Olive is less central to this business than she is in this draft. She is meant to be a moment, not a character.

And so I might proceed, if I were to undertake a new draft of the memoir. I begin to feel a relationship developing between a former self and me.

And, even more compelling, a relationship between an old world and me. Some people think of autobiographical writing as the precious occupation of a particularly self-absorbed person. Maybe, but I don't buy that. True memoir is written in an attempt to find not only a self but a world.

The self-absorption that seems to be the impetus and embarrassment of autobiography turns into (or perhaps always was) a hunger for the world. Actually, it begins as hunger for *a* world, one gone or lost, effaced by time or a more sudden brutality. But in the act of remembering, the personal environment expands, resonates beyond itself, beyond its "subject," into the endless and tragic recollection that is history.

We look at old family photographs in which we stand next to black, boxy Fords and are wearing period costumes, and we do not gaze fascinated because there we are young again, or there we are standing, as we never will again in life, next to our mother. We stare and drift because there we are…historical. It is the dress, the black car that dazzle us now and draw us beyond our mother's bright arms which once caught us. We reach into the attractive impersonality of something more significant than ourselves. We write memoir, in other words. We accept the humble position of writing a version rather than "the whole truth."

I suppose I write memoir because of the radiance of the past—it draws me back and back to it. Not that the past is beautiful. In our communal memoir, in history, the death camps *are* back there. In intimate life too, the record is usually pretty mixed. "I could tell you stories…" people say and drift off, meaning terrible things have happened to them.

But the past is radiant. It has the light of lived life. A memoirist wishes to touch it. No one owns the past, though typically the first act of new political regimes, whether of the left or the right, is to attempt to re-write history, to grab the past and make it over so the end comes out right. So their power looks inevitable.

No one owns the past, but it is a grave error (another age would have said a grave sin) not to inhabit memory. Sometimes I think it is all we really have. But that may be a trifle melodramatic. At any rate, memory possesses authority for the fearful self in a world where it is necessary to have authority in order to Question Authority.

There may be no more pressing intellectual need in our culture than for people to become sophisticated about the function of memory. The political implications of the loss of memory are obvious. The authority of memory is a personal confirmation of selfhood. To write one's life is to live it twice, and the second living is both spiritual and historical, for a memoir reaches deep within the personality as it seeks its narrative form and also grasps the life-of-the-times as no political treatise can.

Our most ancient metaphor says life is a journey. Memoir is travel writing, then, notes taken along the way, telling how things looked and what thoughts occurred. But I cannot think of the memoirist as a tourist. This is the traveller who goes on foot, living the journey, taking on mountains, enduring deserts, marveling at the lush green places. Moving through it all faithfully, not so much a survivor with a harrowing tale to tell as a pilgrim, seeking, wondering.

Courting the Approval of the Dead

Tracy Kidder

I have never written much about myself, but, like most writers I know, I am interested in the subject. We live in an era surfeited with memoirs. This is my contribution to the excess.

My writing career began at Harvard College about thirty-two years ago, shortly after I enrolled as an undergraduate. I planned to fix the world by becoming a diplomat. I began by studying political science. Thinking I should have a hobby, I also took a course in creative writing. I didn't invest a lot of ego in the enterprise and maybe for that reason the first short stories that I wrote were rather sprightly. I think they contained some dialogue that human beings might have uttered. Anyway, the teacher liked them and, more important, so did some of the young women in the class. My first strong impulse to become a writer sprang from this realization: that writing could be a means of meeting and impressing girls.

The next year I got into a class taught by the poet and great translator Robert Fitzgerald. He admitted only about a dozen students from among dozens of applicants, and I seem to remember that I was the youngest of the anointed group. This mattered to me. In high school I had been addicted to competitive sports, and I conceived of writing in sporting terms. I figured I had won part of the competition already, by being the youngest student admitted to the class. The yearning for distinction is common among writers, and in that sense I had begun to become a writer.

I want to try to summon Mr. Fitzgerald back from the dead. I remember him as a small, elegant man, then in his sixties, I believe. Occasionally during office hours he smoked a cigarette, and did so with great deliberation, making every puff count—I think he'd been warned off tobacco, and had put himself on short rations. He would enter the classroom with a green bookbag slung over his shoulder, and would greet us with a smile and a sigh as he heaved the bag onto the long seminar table. Mr. Fitzgerald's green bag contained our work, *my* work, with his comments upon it. I could not have been more interested in that object if Mr. Fitzgerald had been our adult provider, returning with food he'd found out in the world. But the way he sighed, as he heaved that sack onto the table, insinuated that what lay inside wasn't as valuable as food. Certainly it looked like a heavy load for one professor to carry.

I have always talked too much and listened too little. What is it about certain people that has made me pay attention to everything they say? Their confidence and wit, I guess, but most of all their interest in *me*. Mr. Fitzgerald paid his students the great compliment of taking us seriously. He flattered us, dauntingly. I remember the first day of that class. From his place at the head of the table Mr. Fitzgerald eyed us all. He had a pair of reading glasses, half-glasses, which he often used to great effect. He lowered them and looking at us over the top of them, said something like, "The only reason for writing is to produce something *classic*. And I expect that you will produce *classic* work during this term."

I recall thinking, "You do?"

Of course, none of us did, with the possible exception of one young woman who wrote a poem entitled "The Splendor and the Terror of the Universe as Revealed to Me on Brattle Street." I don't recall the poem, but I still like the title.

Having told us of his expectations, Mr. Fitzgerald offered his first advice for meeting them. He jabbed an index finger at the wastebasket beside him and said, "The greatest repository I know of for writers. And I do hope that it will *precede* me."

After a few weeks of Mr. Fitzgerald, I gave up on political science. I quit right in the middle of a lecture by the then-not-very-famous professor Henry Kissinger. The lecture bored me. Professor Kissinger was only partly to blame. I now described myself as a writer, and I thought a writer shouldn't be interested in politics. I had not yet realized that a writer ought to know about something besides writing, so as to have something to write about. When I left that lecture I went right to the English department office and signed up. I'd already begun to do a lot of reading on my own, mostly fiction, which I was consuming at a rate I've never equaled since. At the same time, I had suddenly acquired an assigned-reading disability and a sleep disorder. I had trouble reading books that appeared on formal course lists, and I often worked all night on stories for Mr. Fitzgerald, then went to sleep around the time when my other classes began.

During the first part of Mr. Fitzgerald's class, he would talk about writing and read aloud to us, very occasionally stuff that a student had written, and more often works by wonderful, famous writers he had known, such as his old friend Flannery O'Connor. He read us one of her stories, and when he finished, he said, "That story unwinds like a Rolex watch." Listening to him read such estimable work made me want to try my hand. I think he aimed for that effect, because in the second half of every class he had us write. He warmed us up, and then made us exercise. It is a testament to those warmups of his that I can't recall ever being unable to write *something* in that room for him. In his presence, even poetry seemed possible. Mr. Fitzgerald insisted I try my hand at a poem now and then. I struggled but complied. Finally, I got one off that he seemed to like. It came back from him with this comment at the bottom: "This is very like a poem."

I prefer other memories, especially this one: I had written a short story, which an undergraduate, literary friend of mine had read and disliked. This was the first and at the time the only literary friend I'd acquired, and I thought him very wise and perspicacious, because he had encouraged me. I guessed that my friend must be right about my story. Once he'd pointed out its flaws, I saw them clearly, too. But I decided to show the thing to Mr. Fitzgerald, just so he'd know that I was working. He opened the next class by saying that he was going to read a student's story, a story that he particularly liked, and I remember sitting there wishing that he would some day single out a story of mine in that way and I recall vividly the moment when I realized that it was my story he was reading. The mellifluous voice that had read to us from the likes of James Agee and Wallace Stevens and Flannery O'Connor was reading something of mine! I felt frightened. Then I felt confused. I don't think it had ever occurred to me that intelligent people could disagree about the quality of a piece of writing. If my literary friend thought the story was lousy, Mr. Fitzgerald surely would, too. I see myself sitting at that table with my mouth hanging open—and closing it fast when I remembered the young women in the room. At first I wanted to ask Mr. Fitzgerald to stop, and then I hoped he never would.

I hoped, indeed expected, to have that experience again. I remember that I had given Mr. Fitzgerald a story I knew to be marvelous, a story I knew he'd want to single out in class. When I came into his office for the private visit all of us periodically received, I said to him, in a voice already exulting at his answer, "How'd you like that story, Mr. Fitzgerald?"

He performed his ritual of the reading glasses, pulling them an inch down his nose and looking at me over the top of them. "Not much," he said.

And then, of course, he told me what was wrong with the story, and I saw at once that he was right. I still have this problem. My judgment of my own work sometimes seems so malleable as not to rate as judgment at all. Any critic, no matter how stupid in praise or transparently spiteful in blame, convinces me—at least for awhile. Generally, harsh criticism tends to make me fear that the critic has an intelligence far superior to mine, and has found out things about my writing that I've been too blind to see myself. A person as easily confused by criticism as I am might well have quit writing after a few rejection slips came in for stories that my girlfriend and my mother thought were really good. Perhaps inadvertently, Mr. Fitzgerald taught me the value of trusting the judgment of just one person above all others—and of getting that judgment as the work is in progress, and a lot of help besides. Which is the role I've inflicted on a single editor, Richard Todd, for more than two decades.

I took Mr. Fitzgerald's course again and again, right up until I graduated. After my first semester with him, I didn't perform very well. It wasn't for lack of trying or, God knows, desire. I had become self-conscious about writing. At one point I started a novel. I wrote twenty pages or so, but the most interesting parts were the comments and little drawings I made in the margins—and created with greater care than anything in the actual text—imagining, as I created these notes in the margins, my biographer's delight in finding them. During this period, almost all of the stories I wrote in my room late at night, and the pastiches I committed in class, came back with such brief comments as "O.K., but no flash," all written in an elegantly penned script, which

I can still see in my mind's eye, my heart sinking all over again. Mr. Fitzgerald used to talk about something he called "the luck of the conception," an idea I still believe in, but no longer dream about. I used to have a dream in which I had come upon the perfect story. The dream did not contain the story itself, just the fact that I possessed it. It was a dream suffused with joy, and I'd awake from it with a kind of sorrow that I haven't felt since adolescence. As a reader I felt then as I feel now, that any number of faults in a piece of writing are forgivable if there is life on the page. And there was no life in anything I wrote. Oddly, as the small natural talent I'd had for making up stories began to wane, my ambitions grew immense. Or maybe it was the other way around, and ambition stood in my way.

I can't blame Mr. Fitzgerald. He had only suggested that writing could be a high calling. I alone invented my desire to write for posterity. I am embarrassed to admit to this, but what I really had in mind was immortality. Once as a very young boy at a lecture at the Hayden Planetarium in New York, I learned that the earth would be destroyed in some two and a half billion years, and in spite of all my mother said, I was inconsolable for weeks. Maybe I was born especially susceptible to the fears that attend the fact of human mortality. Maybe I was influenced by certain of the English poets, those whose poems declare that their poems will make them immortal. Or it may be, as my wife suggests, that once a young man has solved the problem of how to meet and impress girls, it just naturally occurs to him that his next job is to figure out how to become immortal.

After college I went to Vietnam as a soldier—not the most likely way of gaining immortality, though I was never in much danger there. I came home with my body and my vaunting literary ambitions still intact and wrote a whole novel about experiences I didn't have in Vietnam. I designed that book for immortality. I borrowed heavily from Conrad, Melville, and Dostoyevsky. About thirty-five editors refused to publish it, thank God. I went to the Iowa Writers Workshop, where it began to seem to me that the well from which I drew for fiction had gone completely dry. (I have written fiction since then, all of it published, but the sum total is three short stories.) I decided to try my hand at nonfiction. That term covers a lot of territory, of course, from weighty treatises on the great problems of the world to diet books—some diet books qualify as nonfiction don't they? I dove into something then labeled The New Journalism. As many people have pointed out, only the term was new. I believe that the form already had a distinguished lineage, which included work by George Orwell and Joseph Mitchell and Mark Twain and Lillian Ross and Edmund Wilson and, my particular favorite, A. J. Liebling. This kind of nonfiction writing, whatever it's called, relies on narrative. Some people describe it by saying that it borrows techniques of fiction, but the fact is that it employs techniques of storytelling that never did belong exclusively to fiction. It is an honorable literary form, not always honorably used, but one can certainly say the same about fiction.

When I first started trying to write in this genre, there was an idea in the air, which for me had the force of a revelation: that all journalism is inevitably subjective. I was in my mid-twenties then, and although my behavior was somewhat worse than it has been recently, I was quite a moralist. I decided that writers of nonfiction had a moral obligation to write in the first person—really write in the first person, making themselves characters on the page. In this way, I would disclose my biases. I would not hide the truth from the reader. I would proclaim that what I wrote was just my own subjective version of events. In retrospect, it seems clear that this prescription for honesty often served instead as a license for self-absorption on the page. But I was still very young, too young and self-absorbed to realize what now seems obvious—that I was less likely to write honestly about myself than about anyone else on earth.

I wrote a book about a murder case, in a swashbuckling first person. It *was* published, I'm sorry to say. On the other hand, it disappeared without a trace; that is, it never got reviewed in the *New York Times*. And I began writing nonfiction articles for the *Atlantic Monthly*, under the tutelage of Richard Todd, then a young editor there. For about five years, during which I didn't dare attempt another book, I worked on creating what many writer friends of mine call "voice." I didn't do this consciously. If I had, I probably wouldn't have gotten anywhere. But gradually, I think, I cultivated a writing voice, the voice of a person who was well-informed, fair-minded, and temperate—the voice, not of the person I was, but of a person I sometimes wanted to be. Then I went back to writing books, and discovered other points of view besides the first person.

Choosing a point of view is a matter of finding the best place to stand from which to tell a story. It shouldn't be determined by theory, but by immersion in the material itself. The choice of point of view, I've come to think, has nothing to do with morality. It's a choice among tools. I think it's true, however, that the wrong choice can lead to dishonesty. Point of view is primary; it affects everything else, including voice. Writing my last four books, I made my choices by instinct sometimes and sometimes by experiment. Most of my memories of time spent writing have merged together in a blur, but I remember vividly my first attempts to find a way to write *Among Schoolchildren*, a book about an inner-city schoolteacher. I had spent a year inside her classroom. I intended, vaguely, to fold into my account of events I'd witnessed in that little place a great deal about the lives of particular schoolchildren and about the problems of education in America. I tried out every point of view that I'd used in previous books, and every page I wrote felt lifeless. Finally, I hit on a restricted third-person narration.

The approach seemed to work. The world of that classroom seemed to come alive when the view of it was restricted mainly to observations of the teacher and to accounts of what the teacher saw and heard and smelled and felt. This choice narrowed my options. I ended up writing something less comprehensive than I'd planned. The book became essentially an account of a year in the emotional life of a schoolteacher. My choice of the restricted third person also obliged me to write parts of the book as if from within the teacher's mind. I felt entitled to describe her thoughts and feelings because she had described them to me, both during class and afterward, and because her descriptions rarely seemed self-serving. Believing in them myself, I thought that I could make them believable on the page.

Belief is an offering that a reader makes to an author, what Coleridge famously called "That willing suspension of disbelief for the moment, which constitutes poetic faith." It is up to the writer to entertain and inform without disappointing the reader into a loss of that faith. In fiction or poetry, of course, believability may have nothing to do with realism or even plausibility. It has everything to do with those things in nonfiction, in my opinion. I think that the nonfiction writer's fundamental job is to make what is true believable. I'm not sure that everyone agrees. Lately the job seems to have been defined differently. Here are some of the ways that some people now seem to define the nonfiction writer's job: to make believable what the writer thinks is true, if the writer wants to be scrupulous; to make believable what the writer wishes were true, if the writer isn't interested in scrupulosity; or to make believable what the writer thinks might be true, if the writer couldn't get the story and had to make it up.

I figure that if I call a piece of my own writing nonfiction it ought to be about real people, with their real names attached whenever possible, who say and do in print nothing that they didn't actually say and do. On the cover page of my last book I put a note that reads, "This is a work of nonfiction," and listed the several names that I was obliged to change in the text. I thought a longer note would be intrusive. I was afraid that it would stand between the reader and the spell that I wanted to create, inviting the reader into the world of a nursing home. But the definition of "nonfiction" has become so slippery that I wonder if I shouldn't have written more. So now I'll take this opportunity to explain that for my last book I spent a year doing research, that the name of the place I wrote about is its real name, that I didn't change the names of any of the major characters, and that I didn't invent dialogue or put any thoughts in characters' minds that the characters themselves didn't confess to.

I no longer care what rules other writers set for themselves. If I don't like what someone has written, I can stop reading, which is, after all, the worst punishment a writer can suffer. (It ought to be the worst punishment. Some critics seem to feel that the creation of a book that displeases them amounts to a felony.) But the expanded definitions of nonfiction have created problems for those writers who define the term narrowly. Many readers now view with suspicion every narrative that claims to be nonfiction, and yet scores of very good nonfiction writers do not make up their stories or the details in them—writers such as John McPhee, Jane Kramer, J. Anthony Lucas. There are also special cases that confound categories and all attempts to lay down rules for writers of narrative. I have in mind Norman Mailer and in particular his *Executioner's Song*, a hybrid of fact and fiction, carefully labeled as such—a book I admire.

Most writers lack Mailer's powers of invention. Some nonfiction writers do not lack his willingness to invent, but the candor to admit it. Some writers proceed by trying to discover the truth about a situation, and then invent or distort the facts as necessary. Even in these suspicious times, writers can get away with this. Often no one will know, and the subjects of the story may not care. They may not notice. But the writer always knows. I believe in immersion in the events of a story. I take it on faith that the truth lies in the events somewhere, and that immersion in those real events will yield glimpses of that truth. I try to hew to what has begun to seem like a narrow definition of nonfiction partly in that faith, and partly out of fear. I'm afraid that if I started making up things in a story that purported to be about real events and people, I'd stop believing it myself. And I imagine that such a loss of conviction would infect every sentence and make each one unbelievable.

I don't mean to imply that all a person has to do to write good narrative nonfiction is to take accurate notes and reproduce them. The kind of nonfiction I like to read is at bottom storytelling, as gracefully accomplished as good fiction. I don't think any technique should be ruled out to achieve it well. For myself, I rule out only invention. But I don't think that honesty and artifice are contradictory. They work together in good writing of every sort. Artfulness and an author's justified belief in a story often combine to produce the most believable nonfiction.

If you write a nonfiction story in the third person and show your face in public afterward, someone is bound to ask, "How did your presence in the scenes you relate affect the people you were observing?" Some readers seem to feel that third-person narration, all by itself, makes a narrative incomplete. The other day I came upon a book about the writing of ethnography. It interested me initially because its bibliography cited a couple of my books and one of its footnotes mentioned me. The author spelled my first name wrong and gave one of my books a slightly different title from the one I chose. I swear I don't hold a grudge on account of that. My first name is a little weird, and the title in question is a long one. But those little mistakes did make me vigilant as I read the following passage:

> Writers of literary tales seldom remark on the significance of their presence on the scenes they represent, and this is in some instances a bothersome problem to field workers in addition to the common concerns for reactivity in any situation. It is, for example, very difficult to imagine that as famous and dandy a writer as Tom Wolfe was merely a fashionable but unobtrusive fly on the wall in the classic uptown parlor scene of *Radical Chic* (1970), or that Tracey [sic] Kidder did not in any way influence the raising of the Souweines' roofbeams in *House* (1985). Since writers of ethnographic tales have begun to break their silence on these matters, it is seemingly time for writers of literary tales to do so too—especially when their accounts so clearly rest on intimacy.

I believe it's possible to learn something from anyone, including ethnographers who have begun to break their silence. But I can't work out the mechanics for calculating the *reactivity* that occurs during *field work*. As I imagine it, field work that is mindful of reactivity would have to proceed in this way: I'd open my notebook in front of a person I planned to write about, and I'd ask, "How did you feel when I opened my notebook just now?" Then I would probably be bound to ask, "How did you feel when I asked you that question about opening my notebook?"

I don't know for sure how my presence has influenced the behavior of any of the people I've written about. I don't believe that I can know, because I wasn't there when I wasn't there. To do the research for a book, I usually hang around with my subjects for a year or more. After a while, most seem to take my presence for granted. Not all do. It worked the other way with one of the carpenters I wrote about in *House*. I remember his saying at one point that he and the other builders ought to put a bell around my neck, so they'd know where I was at all times.

Obviously some readers expect to hear about the story behind the story. But all writing is selective. I think that a narrative should be judged mainly on its own terms, not according to a reader's preexisting expectations. As a reader, I know that I won't always sit still for the story behind the story. As a writer, I have often decided that it isn't worth telling.

I wrote my most recent book, *Old Friends*, which is about some of the residents of a nursing home, in the third person. I hope that I put my own voice in it, but I chose not to write about how I did my research and how I was affected by what I encountered inside the nursing home—never mind how my presence might, arguably, possibly, have affected the inmates' behavior—mainly because what I did—asking questions, listening, taking notes—was much less interesting than what I observed. It is true, however, that my solution to the problem that the book presented did have something to do with my own experience of life inside that place. After writing for awhile, I realized that I wanted to reproduce, in a limited sense, the most important part of my experience there.

I entered the nursing home in the late fall of 1990. The place, which is situated in western Massachusetts, is called the Linda Manor Extended Care Facility. I went there with a notebook—I filled ninety notebooks eventually—and prowled around inside almost every day, and many nights, for about a year. And then for another year or so I spent about three days a week there. I chose a decent nursing home, not one of the very best but a clean, well-lighted place where residents weren't tied up and were allowed some of the trappings of their former lives.

I had visited a nursing home only once before in my life, and since then had averted both my eyes and thoughts as I passed by. That was part of the attraction; nursing homes seemed to me like secret places in the landscape. I went to Linda Manor tentatively, though. I was afraid that I might find it dull. I thought I might find myself in a kind of waiting room, a vestibule to eternity, where everything had been resolved or set aside and residents simply lay waiting to die. But waiting was the least of what went on in many of those clean, motel-like rooms. Nearly everyone, it seemed, was working on a project. Some were absurd—one resident kept hounding the office of a U.S. senator to complain about his breakfast eggs. Some were poignant—many of the demented residents roamed the halls searching for exits, asking everyone for directions home. A lot of projects were Quixotic. There was, for instance, one indomitable, wheelchair-bound woman who had set herself the task of raising about $30,000 to buy the nursing home its own chairlift van. She intended to do so through raffles and teacup auctions and by getting other residents to remember the van in their wills. There was also an elderly actress who kept herself and the place somewhat invigorated by putting on plays. Staging those productions took great determination, because Linda Manor had no stage and most of the actors and actresses were confined to wheelchairs and walkers. In between plays, when things got dull, the old actress livened things up by starting fights. There were many residents working doggedly to come to terms with the remorse they felt for past mistakes and offenses. There was also a man in his nineties named Lou Freed who summoned up memories with what seemed like the force of necessity, re-inhabiting his former life with something that resembled joy. And there were, of course, a number who knew their deaths were imminent and struggled to find ways to live in the face of that knowledge.

Even in a decent nursing home, the old often get treated like children. And yet many of the residents refused to become like children. The roommates Lou and Joe, for instance. Let me try to prove this point with a short passage from my book.

Joe and Lou could not control most of the substance of their life in here, but they had imposed a style on it. The way for instance that Joe and Lou had come, in the past months, to deal with matters of the bathroom. Joe had to go there what seemed to him like a ridiculous number of times each day and night. He and Lou referred to the bathroom as "the library." The mock-daintiness of the term amused Joe. The point was to make a joke out of anything you could around here. Up in the room after breakfast, Joe would say to Lou, "I gotta go to the library. I have to do my, uh, uh, prune evacuation."

This room was now their home. As in any household, people entering were expected to follow local rules. The nursing staff was overwhelmingly female. Lou and Joe referred to all of them as girls, and indeed, next to them, even the middleaged did look like girls. The staff had all, of course, been quite willing to talk frankly about matters of Lou and Joe's biology. Too frankly for Lou. Too frankly for Joe, once Lou had made the point. The aides, "the girls," used to come to the doorway, cradling opened in their arms the large, ledger-like Forest View "BM Book," and they'd call loudly in, "Did either of you gentlemen have a bowel movement today?" It was Lou, some months ago now, who responded to this question by inviting in the girls who asked it, and then telling them gently, "All you have to say is, 'Did you or didn't you.'" The way Lou did that job impressed Joe, Lou did it so diplomatically, so much more diplomatically than Joe would have. Lou, as he liked to say, had trained all the girls by now. Joe took care of reinforcement.

It was a morning in December. Joe had the television news on. He and Lou were listening to the dispatches from the Middle East. Joe wasn't waiting for the aide with the BM Book, but he had a question ready for her. When the aide came to the door, she asked, "For my book. Did you?"

"Yes." Joe tilted his head toward Lou. "And so did he." Then, a little smile blossoming, Joe looked at the aide and asked, "And what about you?"

"None of your business!" The aide looked embarrassed. She laughed.

"Well, you ask me," Joe said.

"But I get paid for it."

"*Good*bye," Joe said pleasantly, and went back to watching the news.

Many residents insisted on preserving their dignity, in spite of the indignities imposed by failing health and institutional confinement. Many people in there were attempting in one way or another to invent new lives for themselves. In the context of that place and of debilitating illnesses, their quests seemed important.

So when I began to write *Old Friends*, I didn't lack for interesting characters or stories. I felt I had an overabundance. I told myself before I started writing that I couldn't fit in everything, and then for about a year I tried to do just that. In the end I had to jettison a lot of portraits and stories that I had written many times and polished up. Among other things, I wrote four or five times and finally discarded what in all modesty I believe to have been the most riveting account of a session of Bingo ever composed. But the plain fact was that about half of what I wrote and rewrote got in the way of the main story that I wanted to tell.

Hundreds of articles and books deal with the big issues that surround aging in late-twentieth-century America. I read some of them. But I didn't want to approach this subject in a general way. It is useful, maybe even necessary, to imagine that a definable group called "the elderly" exists. But all such conceptions inevitably fail. It is accurate only to say that there are many individuals who have lived longer than most of the rest of the population, and that they differ widely among themselves. For various reasons, some can no longer manage what are called the activities of daily living at home, and, for lack of a better solution, some of those people end up living in nursing homes. I chose to write about a few of those people partly because so much well-meaning commentary on old age depicts white-haired folks in tennis clothes—a tendency, it seems to me, that inadvertently denigrates the lives of the many people who haven't been as lucky.

About five percent of Americans over sixty-five—about 1.5 million people—live in nursing homes and, according to one estimate, nearly half of all the people who live past sixty-five will spend some time inside a nursing home. Obviously, they are important places, but nursing homes weren't really the subject I wanted to address. There were already plenty of published exposés of bad nursing homes. I decided to do my research inside a good nursing home on the theory that a good one would be bad enough, inevitably a house of grief and pain, and also because I didn't want to write about the kinds of policy and management issues that would have assumed primary importance in a story set in an evil place. I wanted to write from the inside about the experience of being old and sick and confined to an institution. I wanted to come at the subject of aging, not through statistics, but through elderly people themselves. I wanted to write an interesting, engaging book. The residents of even a decent nursing home are people in a difficult situation, and I think that stories about people in difficult situations are almost always interesting, and often dramatic.

In some ways, research in that place was easy work. In the course of every story I'd done before, I had run into people who hadn't wanted to talk to me. But people in a nursing home never have enough willing listeners. A nursing home like Linda Manor may be the only place on earth where a person with a notebook can hope to receive a universal welcome.

Various sights, smells, and sounds distressed me at first. But gradually, I got used to the externals of the place and people. Almost everyone who has spent some time inside a nursing home begins to look beyond the bodies of the residents. It just happens. But around the time when that happened to me, another problem arose. I remember leaving the room of a dying, despondent resident and stopping in my tracks in a Linda Manor corridor, and hearing myself say to myself, "This is amazing! *Everybody* dies." And, of course, my next thought was, "Including me." I know that sounds silly. One is supposed to have figured that out before pushing fifty. But I hadn't believed it, I think.

I arranged some other troubling moments for myself, during my research. At one point, I decided that I ought to check into Linda Manor for a couple of days and nights, as if I were myself a resident. I hate the kind of story in which a perfectly healthy person decides to ride around in a wheelchair for a day and then proclaims himself an expert in what being wheelchair-bound is like. But I believe in the possibility of imaginatively experiencing what others experience, and I thought I might learn something. With vast amusement, a nurse ushered me into a little room. My roommate, an ancient man who couldn't speak much, terrified me as soon as I climbed into bed. He kept clicking his light on and off. At one point I saw his hand through the filmy, so-called "privacy curtain." His hand reached toward the curtain, grasping at it. He was trying to pull the curtain back, so that he could get a better look at me, and I had to stifle the impulse to yell at him to stop. Then, a little later, I heard a couple of the nurses in the hall outside, saying loudly, speaking of me, "Shall we give him an enema?" An old source of amusement among nurses, the enema.

I didn't learn much that I could use in my book, from my two-night stand at Linda Manor. Except for the fact that a few minutes can seem like eternity in a nursing-home bed and the fact that, from such a perspective, cheerful, attractive, average-sized nurses and nurse's aides can look huge and menacing. Those two nights I kept getting up and looking out the window, to make sure my car was still in the parking lot. I had planned to stay longer, but went home early the third morning in order to get some sleep.

At Linda Manor I got to know a nurse's aide who, when one of her residents had died, insisted on opening up the windows of the room. Asked why she did this, she said she felt she had to let the spirit out. All but a few of the staff were religious, at least in the sense that most believed in an afterlife. I think belief was a great comfort to them. At least I imagined it would be for me. But I possessed only a vague agnosticism. And I couldn't simply manufacture something stronger for the situation.

What troubled me most during my time at Linda Manor wasn't unpleasant sights or smells or even the reawakening of my fears about mortality. It was the problem of apparent meaninglessness. I watched people dying long before life had lost its savor for them or they their usefulness to others. I couldn't imagine any purpose behind the torments that many residents suffered in their last days. Sometimes I'd leave a resident's room feeling that everything, really everything in every life, was pointless. I remember thinking that we all just live awhile and end up dying painfully, or, even worse, bored and inert. What meaning could life have, I'd find myself wondering, if the best of the last things people get to do on earth is to play Bingo? At such times, I'd usually find my way upstairs to the room of the two old men named Lou and Joe. Gradually, I began to notice that a number of the staff did the same thing, even giving up their coffee breaks to go and chat with Lou and Joe. I didn't usually plan to go to their room at these moments of vicarious despair. I'd just find myself wanting to go there. After about ten minutes in their room, I usually felt much better. Lou and Joe had been placed together in one of Linda Manor's little rooms, in what for both would likely be their last place on earth, and they had become great friends. Other residents had formed friendships inside Linda Manor, but none was durable or seemed to run very deep. Out in the wider, youthful world, this accomplishment of Lou and Joe's would have seemed unremarkable but in that place it was profound.

The main thing I wanted to portray was that friendship, surrounded by the nursing home and all its varying forms of claustrophobia. I wanted to infuse the story of that friendship with sentiment, but not in a sentimental way. The difference, as I see it, is the difference between portraying emotion and merely asserting its existence, between capturing the reflection of something real on the page and merely providing handy cues designed to elicit an emotional response. It is, I realize, harder to depict manifestations of human goodness than manifestations of venality and evil. I don't know why that is. I do know that some people think that kindness, for example, is always superficial. That view is the logical equivalent of sentimentality. It's an easy way to feel and it gives some people a lot of pleasure. It has nothing to do with a tragic vision of life. It has about as much to do with an accurate vision of life as a Hallmark card. Anyway, that's how it seems to me. The world seems various to me, and depicting some of the virtue in it seems like a project worth attempting. I do not say that I pulled it off, but that's part of what I had in mind.

After my book was published, I continued to visit Linda Manor about once a week. I went partly because doing so made me feel like a good guy. But I had other reasons. Growing old with dignity calls for many acts of routine heroism, and some of the people I knew at Linda Manor were inspiring, admirable characters. All of them have died now, except for Lou, who has achieved the ripe old age of ninety-six. Joe died last winter. I visit only Lou now, but I used to go mainly in order to visit the two men. I *liked* visiting them. Their room was one place where I knew I was always welcome. They gave me good advice, on such subjects as child-rearing. They were funny, both intentionally and otherwise. Most important, their room was one place in the world where I could count on finding that amity prevailed. That was unusual, in my experience of the world. The crucial thing about Lou and Joe was that they remained *very good* friends, better friends every time I visited. They presented an antidote to despair, which is connectedness, and for me, I learned, it is only the connectedness of the human tribe that can hold despair at bay. Connectedness can, of course, take many different forms. One can find it in religion, or in family, or, as in the case of Lou and Joe, in friendship. Or perhaps in work, maybe even in the act of writing.

Harold Brodkey, who recently died of AIDS, wrote in an essay a couple of years ago, "I think anyone who spends his life working to become eligible for literary immortality is a fool." I agree. But I also think that only a fool would write merely for money or contemporary fame. I imagine that most writers—good, bad and mediocre—write partly for the sake of the private act of writing and partly in order to throw themselves out into the world. Most, I imagine, *endeavor* for connectedness, to create the kind of work that touches other lives and, in that sense at least, leaves something behind. I don't dream of immortality or plant marginalia for my biographers anymore. But I do wonder what Mr. Fitzgerald would think of what I've written and, especially, of what I'm going to write.

A few days after I got back from Vietnam, in June 1969, I traveled to Cambridge and called Mr. Fitzgerald from a pay phone. He invited me to lunch at his house the next afternoon. Of course, I didn't tell him this, but I wanted something from him, something ineffable, like hope. He had prepared sandwiches. I'm not sure that he made them himself, but I like to think that he did, and that he was responsible for cutting the crusts off the bread. I'm not sure why I remember that. It seemed a sweet gesture, a way of making me feel that I was important to him. It also made him seem old, older than I'd remembered him.

I saw Mr. Fitzgerald a few times more over the next year or two, and then he moved away and I moved out west for a while. I fell under other influences. My dreams of writing something classic gave way to my little dreams of writing something publishable, of making a living as a writer, which seemed hard enough. But those early dreams were dormant, not dead. When, almost ten years later, a book of mine, *The Soul of a New Machine*, was awarded the Pulitzer Prize and the American Book Award, my megalomaniacal dreams of literary glory came out of storage. I could tell myself at moments that I'd achieved them all. But I hesitated for awhile before sending my book to Mr. Fitzgerald. I was afraid. When I finally worked up the nerve, I wrote an inscription to the effect that I hoped this piece of writing began to approach his expectations. I soon received a letter from him, in which he thanked me, remarked upon the "modesty" of my inscription—no doubt he saw right through that—and apologized for his inability to read the book just now. I wrote right back, proposing that I visit him. He did not reply. I never heard from him again. I don't remember exactly when he died. I think it was a few years later.

His silence has bothered me for a long time, not immoderately but in the way of those embarrassing memories that suddenly appear when you're checking the oil in your car or putting a key in a door. Two summers ago I met one of Mr. Fitzgerald's sons and told him the story. He insisted that his father would never have failed to answer my last letter, if he'd been able to read and write by then. I believed him. And I believe that if Mr. Fitzgerald had been able to read my book, he would have told me what he really thought. It's probably just as well that he never did. I've written other and, I think, better books since then. I'd rather know what he thought of *them*. I've been courting his approval ever since my first day in his class, and I continue to court his approval now, when he's certain to withhold it. That makes me sad sometimes, but not in my better moments. I'll never know if he'd approve of what I've written and am going to write. But I'll never know if he'd disapprove either. He's left me room to go on trying.

Excavations

Lisa Knopp

*Among my Daily-Papers, which I bestow on the Publick,
there are some which are written with Regularity and
Method, and others that run out into the Wildness of those
Compositions, which go by the Name of Essays.... As for
the first, I have the whole Scheme of the Discourse in Mind,
before I set Pen to Paper. In the other kind of Writing, it
is sufficient that I have several Thoughts on the Subject,
without troubling myself to range them in order, that they
seem to grow out of one another, and be disposed under
the proper Heads.*

JOSEPH ADDISON, *Spectator*, no. 476,
Friday, September 4, 1712

It was a walk that had already yielded plenty. I had ventured far enough from the road
to stand on the shore of a lake of ferns, each cupped heavenward like a satellite dish.
I'd weighted my cardigan pockets with flinty gray-and-white-striped rocks. I'd sloshed
through a soggy ditch beneath eight-foot-tall reeds—part cattail, part tasseled corn—
where I found the frogs I'd been hearing. I'd studied grasshoppers that bore little
resemblance to the green 'hoppers I'd chased in Iowa meadows as a child and held in
my clasped palms until they spit tobacco. Vermont grasshoppers are black, gold,
brown, and winged, and I couldn't persuade them to spit for anything.

But then, on the gravel shoulder, I found a dun, mouselike creature, dead, curled
in a fetal position. It was a mouse with a snout, but no mere pig's snout: this was a pro-
boscis with a flair. It was piggish with two nostrils near the center, but from the outer

rim sprouted fingers of pink flesh like the spokes of a rimless wheel, the petals of a sunflower, or the tentacles of a branching idea.

This was too much to trust to my memory, so I broke my rule of leaving wild things—even dead wild things—at peace, rolled the corpse onto a Kleenex with a twig, and carried it home. Once there, I laid it on my desk and sketched its fabulous nose in my notebook. Then I sketched its entirety with words: "A dun, mouselike creature, dead, curled in a fetal position."

Since I hadn't anticipated the need for a spade or shovel when I packed for my week and a half in Vermont, once my notebook was full, I flushed the creature down the toilet—the most respectable burial I could give under the circumstances.

For nature essayists, the subjects for our excavations fall at our feet like bread rained from heaven. A dead opossum. A flushed pheasant. An approaching cloud of mayflies. Bare branches studded with white-headed eagles. Consequently, when I was stopped short by a dead mole on the road, I knew I would write about her, though I didn't know what I would write. Other gifts presented me with an angle, a handle, a purpose as soon as I beheld them. While driving back to Nebraska from Vermont, for instance, I was startled by a great blue heron standing stock-still near a farm pond in the midst of a moving landscape so close to Interstate 80 that I questioned my own ability to see and name. In September, I had eyes only for flaming groves of sumac and spent all autumn reading and writing about their border existence while carrying sprigs of dried purple berries in my buttonhole. Next, two failed attempts at autobiographical essays, which, above all, reminded me why I need to write about other living things, than myself (more timely and timeless, less self-indulgent, more downright interesting). Then, one January morning, it happened. I woke up, as I always do, with the desire to write, but on that day I had no subject matter. No circle of hell could be worse. So, I resurrected the mole.

Still, I wasn't ready to write, since I hadn't a slant on my subject. Though I was half a continent, half a year away from that August afternoon in Vermont when I found the mole's body, I was no closer, no further from making an essay about her than I had been. I knew if I didn't find some way to write about her, I'd turn her now warm body over and over in my mind in the middle of the night, fretting myself sleepless until I found an angle, a handle, a purpose. So, I did the next best thing to writing about the star-nosed mole: I went to the library and read about her.

Most of the facts I read—and the metaphors I glimpsed—pertained to the *Condylura cristata's* two farthest ends: the tip of her blooming nose and what I discovered to be her not-so-ratlike tail. I learned that her nose (which I had not noted in such fine detail) comprised exactly and always (barring accidents) twenty-two pink flesh rays or tentacles, one-quarter to one-half inch long. These are arranged symmetrically, eleven on each side, the two topmost rays held rigidly forward while the others move continually in the mole's search for food. Once she nabs a succulent earthworm with her shovel feet, she removes all distractions by retracting her rays so she can work, chewing down the length of the worm as if it were spaghetti. A nose with table manners.

While mole experts Terry Yates and Richard Pedersen claim the exact function of the nasal rays isn't yet known, it's apparent that this nose, like the weird snout of the anteater, the tapir, or the elephant, is a highly specialized sensory device. Each of the twenty-two rays, in fact, is covered with papillae (David Van Vleck saw fifteen to twenty on just the base of a single ray under low magnification), and each papilla bears one to three sensory organs named after Theodor Eimer, the German scientist who "discovered" them in 1871. This means that the mole's pointed nose isn't an earthmover as we might expect (the feet do that) but a sensitive instrument that directs the forepaws in their work. The nose is the locator of the mole's prey and her position in the world.

Almost as interesting as the mole's remarkable nose is her tail. In August, it looks like that of a rat or mouse: a long whip about half the length of the creature's body from tentacle tip to tail base. But in the winter or early spring, that tail is quite a different story. Then it is constricted near the base, swollen with stored fat near the middle like that of a snake that has just swallowed a bowl of mush. Most swollen tails are as big around as a number two lead pencil, some are as large in cross-section as a dime, and curiously, some tails never swell.

Apparently, moles use the stored fat during breeding season or at other times when their food intake cannot meet their energy requirements. William Robert Eadie and William John Hamilton learned that the great majority of star-nosed moles of both sexes had swollen tails before and during breeding season, but once the season was over, their tails were ratlike again. In addition to acting as a portable pantry, this tail functions as an antenna of sorts. In his study of the European mole, Godet states that the characteristically erect tail acts as an organ of touch, maintaining contact with the roof of the tunnels rather like the overhead pickup of an electric train.

Other noteworthy facts about *Condylura cristata*—Weight: three ounces. Length: six inches. Habits: diurnal, nocturnal, active year-round. Preferred habitat: damp, boggy soil near streams or in swamps and meadows in New England and southeastern Canada. Food: insects, worms, small fish, vegetable matter. Tunnels: deep and permanent where nests are built; shallow surface runways where food is gotten. Breeding: one litter per year of two to five molelets (my own terminology, I believe). Since other small mammals produce three to four litters per year, the mole's low replacement rate suggests few predators: an occasional hawk, owl, skunk, fox, coyote, snake, raccoon, cat, dog, big fish, or golf course owner.

Joseph Wood Krutch says that to the essayists a fact is "at best a peg to hang something on." A typewritten page and a half of facts about the secret life of the mole takes me only a little closer to an essay about her than I was before. Now I have pegs. But what shall I hang upon them?

Some facts are so taut and humming, I could hang on to their tails and be carried into the heart of an essay. Consider this simple fact from Victor H. Cahalane: "Few people have ever seen a mole." Not exactly an earth-moving revelation until I add it to the following list: few people have ever seen a miracle, the heart of darkness, an exploding star, or birds mating in midair. Therein lies the focus and the motive for an essay about a mole: why and how those of us who have witnessed the extraordinary should communicate our experience to those who haven't.

Julian of Norwich, an essayist of sorts, received sixteen "shewings" or revelations of divine love during her thirtieth year while on what she and others believed to be her deathbed. Julian survived, but had no other revelations and so spent the rest of her anchored days writing and revising the substance of that one extraordinary night: "…and truly charity urgeth me to tell you of it," she confessed. The nature essayist's reason for witnessing is often more mundane than soul salvation. Michel-Guillaume-Jean de Crèvecoeur, for instance, observed two snakes engaged in mortal battle, their necks wrapped twice around each other's, their tails lashed around hemp stalks to obtain greater leverage so it appeared that the two stalks were playing tug-of-war with the twined reptiles. Crèvecoeur felt compelled to relate the anecdote simply because the circumstances were "as true as they are singular."

Another fact, another promise of an essay: "Relatively speaking," write Yates and Pedersen, "little is known scientifically of these mammals…. Moles are probably the least understood major component of the North American mammalian fauna." Even though we've lost our hankering for moleskin caps and purses, even though tiny baked moles don't grace our tables as do tiny baked quails, and never do moles make good house pets, rarely living a year in captivity and requiring dirt and worms and all, nonetheless we should be interested in any creature capable of moving our foundation. Because moles sometimes eat what we've planted or move the soil away from it, we've devoted more attention to their eating habits and how best to exterminate them from our lawns than any other aspect of their biology. Still, there's more to the mole than what she does and does not eat.

This assertion leads me to speculate about how much else is so unstudied. Once I read that approximately seven hundred arachnid species have yet to be discovered. Initially, my fascination with this statistic lay in that so much remained to be named in a world chin-deep in nouns—common, proper, colloquial, scientific, vulgar, euphemistic, and so forth. But then I began wondering how such a fantastic and unsubstantiated figure was reached. In other words, how could anyone even roughly estimate the breadth of what she does not know? Do experts in all fields—archeology, astronomy, linguistics, music theory—possess similar statistics about their respective unknowns?

If the mole is so unstudied, I suspect there is an entire essay on the curious few who *have* made her their lifework. Eimer, for instance, the first person known to have studied the star-nosed mole's "schnozz." Or Eadie, who researched everything from skin gland activity and pelage differences to male accessory reproductive glands and unique prostatic secretions. What type of passion and audacity does such lifework demand? A little biography could reveal a lot not only about those who study moles but about any naturalist with an all-consuming passion. After all, I suppose the moody, aristocratic John James Audubon is wilder and rarer than any of the birds and mammals whose biographies he wrote. Second-generation violaphile Viola Brainerd Baird, scaling Mount Olympus in search of a rare violet species or raising hybrids to maturity with her father, Ezra Brainerd (husband of Francis Viola), delights me more than any of the careful paintings and descriptions in her *Wild Violets of North America* (1942).

So, too, Charles Darwin's final work, *The Formation of Vegetable Mould, Through the Actions of Worms, With Observation of Their Habits* (1881), leaves me more intrigued with the habits of this particular scientist (he shined a bull-lantern in the worms' eyes to determine if they could see; he chewed a plug of tobacco near their noses to test their sense of smell; he placed their earth-filled pots on his piano and banged away to see if they could hear) than it does about the humus-creating annelids. Darwin suspected that readers would be much more interested in his theory that humans "descended" than they would be in how worms had formed the rich topsoil in which humans planted their crops and so, in an addendum to his autobiography, he apologized: "This is a subject of small importance; and I know not whether it will interest any reader, but it has interested me." An essay about those who shun the popular and profitable for that of seemingly small importance is an essay I want to write; it is an essay I want to read.

Though little is known of the mole, the few passionate researchers who have excavated her hidden life have provided enough facts to refute widely held misconceptions. (If these assumptions cloud our ability to see the mole as she really is, then this essay could be another meditation on the same earlier fact: "Few people have ever seen a mole.") "Looking at the mole, we would expect the animal to be rather slow and somewhat methodical," observed Richard Headstrom. "But surprisingly, the speed with which it can tunnel through the earth is almost incredible." Headstrom reports that the star-nosed mole has been clocked tunneling a distance of 235 feet in a single night. This is comparable to an average-sized woman digging a 2,500-foot tunnel at least wide enough for her body to pass through in one night. How much else do we incorrectly assume about the mole? (At this point, I expect an essay full of appearances and realities.) For instance, I expected the mole to wear a ratty, mangy coat, living in dirt and leaf-litter nests the way she does, but I've observed that her coat is velvety soft, the hairs lying smoothly and willingly in either direction. While I would expect her to be nearly deaf, since her outer ear is all but invisible, the structures of the middle and inner ears are relatively large; therefore, her hearing may be quite keen. Neither is the mole mute. Gillian Godfrey and Peter Crowcroft report that moles emit at least two sounds distinguishable by the human ear: "a soft twittering made when feeding or exploring, and loud squeaks made singly or in succession when fighting." Because the mole's nasal passages are longer than those of most other animals, we would expect her snout to be extraordinarily sensitive, able to smell an earthworm at fifty paces, but it is not. The nose *is* sensitive, but as a feeler, not as a sniffer. Finally, because the mole has few predators to escape and breeds so seldom (once a year, three-year life span), we might expect her to sleep her life away, since there is so little to stay awake for. But in truth, the mole works around the clock, snatching sleep only occasionally. Because she works so much and has such a fast metabolism, she must eat one-third to one-half her body weight in food each day just to stay alive. Imagine how many waking hours it would require for an average-sized woman to eat forty to sixty pounds of food per day. So, too, the mole. At this point, my essay about appearances and realities could take a sharp, argumentative turn and persuade the reader to elect the industrious, sensitive, unassuming mole as our national symbol instead of the lazy, thieving fish vulture.

The same topic of appearance and reality approached from another direction: how different mammalogists reach different conclusions about similar data. In 1927, Fred Stevens of Ithaca, New York, presented William John Hamilton, Jr., of Cornell University with a male and female *Condylura* (the female was not pregnant), which Stevens had taken from the same minnow trap. Hamilton offered two interpretations for the presence of two moles in the same place: either they were together for an early courtship prior to mating or they exhibited a tendency for companionship. Hamilton places more weight on the latter, concluding that the star-nosed mole is not only gregarious but colonial. Victor Cahalane's position is more moderate. While no mole will ever win a congeniality award, the star-nosed and the hairy-tailed are more tolerant of their kind than are other mole species. Moreover, it is not uncommon for them to use a community system of runways. Yates and Pedersen agree that moles may be found together but believe that this curiosity relates more to food supply than to need for companionship. Similarly, Leonard Lee Rue III portrays the star-nosed as a recluse. "Although this species is more sociable than the common mole, most moles lead a solitary existence. Only rarely are several moles found inhabiting the same tunnel, and these usually are females and their young of the year. The female does not tolerate the male after breeding, but raises her family by herself." Colonial? Together out of necessity? Hermits? I am curious about how the mammalogist's own attitudes toward companionship and solitude influence his reading of the mole's behavior. "What we observe is not nature itself," says Werner Heisenberg, "but nature exposed to our method of questioning." What questions were each of these scientists asking about the mole? What questions am I asking about the mole and those who study her?

At this point, I pause to reread what I've written. I am struck by my own metaphorical loose ends. In paragraph five, I state that the mole is like the subject of an essay ("For nature essayists, the subjects for our excavations fall at our feet like bread rained from heaven"), which is to say that our subjects are at the same time sought, uncovered, and sometimes brought forth; prayed for, waited upon, and sometimes received. The metaphor is accurate if you can forget where moles come from. A few paragraphs later, I suggest that the movements of moles and essayists in their search for prey or their way in the world are each guided by a felt or intuitive sense. A few pages later, I say that the essayist's method is like the method of those who devote themselves to studying the homely form of the mole instead of something more glamorous (wolves, cranes, whales), involving more exciting methods of discovery (dogsleds, blinds, wet suits) in exotic parts of the globe (Siberia, Japan, California). Not all mammalogists, not all essayists have to leave home to find their subject matter: just this week, I've seen three common Eastern moles within blocks of my house.

Too, I am struck by my reliance on metaphor to reveal the act of essaying. But this is fitting. Trying to capture the essay or the act of essaying in words is like "trying to catch a fish in the open hand," says Elizabeth Hardwick. The essay is too protean, too slippery, too edgeless for definitions and parameters. The only recourse is to capture it partially through metaphors or, better, to demonstrate essaying in an essay that doubles back on itself, self-consciously reflecting on the method that produced it.

Which leads me to my next topic: an essay whose sole subject is form—an essay about preliminaries. The star-nosed mole introduces herself fringed nose first, typically tubular body next, and barometric tail last. Other creaturely introductions include: hard, toothless seed case crackers; fatty, velvety, neighing muzzles; rooting, rip-snorting snouts; twitching pink buttons; neat reptilian pinpricks; sharp-pointed bloodsuckers. Like the introduction to an essay, noses usually precede the body, even if only by a nose. Like any first impression, they can be deceptive (the remainder of the star-nosed mole is quite dull compared to his elaborate fanfare). Just as an introduction only positions the essayist for her excavations, the dinner guests for the meat of the conversation, the mole's nose only locates the place where the feet will begin digging. My essay about introductions would not only explain their similarity to noses but would itself be a series of positionings. An essay that is pure preface. An essay that introduces nothing. An essay, like this one, that never leaves the ground.

If the mole's nose is like an introduction, perhaps the body of the mole's work is like the body of the essayist's work. (Or different than.) An extended analogy could shed light on the dark burrowings of both. Again, the facts speak. While excavating, the mole uses every last hair and muscle. She turns her body forty-five degrees to the right if she is pushing dirt with her left forepaw, forty-five degrees to the left if she is pushing dirt with her right spade. Thus, she creates a back-and-forth spiraling motion like that of an electric borer. Nature essayist Richard Rhodes identifies the spiral rather than the circle or line as the movement of the essay itself, and for this reason, he says the essay is the most extemporaneous written form, and by definition, always unfinished.

Just as snow plowed from the road has to go someplace, so, too, the shoveled earth. When constructing deep tunnels, the mole throws the loosened soil under and back, then uses her hind feet to kick it to the rear. When a load has accumulated, she literally somersaults, then pushes the dirt ahead until it spills out, forming the mountain we call a molehill. From the upstairs window we can imagine or deduce the process that produced the pattern just as surely as the best essays bear hints of the process that produced them. But when the mole tunnels near the surface, evidence remains that leaves nothing to the imagination—soft raised ridges wrinkle the lawn or pasture. One reading tells it all.

The essay's path is cut not with big clawed feet but through "the act of thinking things out, feeling and finding a way; it is the mind in the marvels and miseries of its making, in the *work* of the imagination, the search for form," as William Gass observes. The essayist's cutting claws are also the words she chooses. In *The Writing Life*, Annie Dillard explains: "The line of words is a miner's pick, a woodcarver's gouge, a surgeon's probe. You wield it, and it digs a path you follow. Soon you find yourself in a new territory.... You make the path boldly and follow it fearfully. You go where the path leads."

Not so different from the way the mole works. "Apparently, it digs wherever fancy or food takes it without thought of any definite plan, so that ultimately it ends up with an intricate system of many-branched tunnels," Headstrom observes. Zoologist David Van Vleck terms it the "hit-or-miss path of the mole." While a rare essayist such as John McPhee cuts a certain path ("I want to get the structural problems out of the way first, so I can get to what matters more…the story"), most essayists set out "with no predetermined path or destination, no particular aim in mind, save the discovery of reality," according to R. Lane Kauffmann in his essay on the essayist's methods. Most essayists, then, in their search for form, use what Walter Pater called an "un-methodical method."

Finally, there is a sharp contrast between the world where excavations take place and the world one finds when she reemerges. "Once well underground," reports the Mole in *The Wind and the Willows*, "you know exactly where you are. Nothing can happen to you, and nothing can get at you. You're entirely your own master, and you don't have to consult anybody or mind what they say. Things go on all the same overhead and you let 'em, and don't bother about 'em. When you want to, up you go, and there the things are, waiting for you." Predators, weather, shadows, nesting materials, and nosy mammalogists. The essayist opens the door of her study to find hungry children, dirty laundry, a ringing telephone, and an empty bank account.

Nature's other gifts present a single focus or one focus sharper and more engaging than the rest as soon as I perceived them. The mole, however, is too full of essay-worthy possibilities. More coats than pegs to hang them on. Too many directions in which I could dig my path. So many slants, I can't handle my subject. Too many tricks in this bag. With a little more time, a little more paper, and someone to tend the children just a little longer, I'd have a dozen more angles. But enough is enough. All these speculations have brought me no nearer to an essay about the mole than when I began.

"I do not see the whole of anything," Michel de Montaigne assures me. "Of a hundred members and faces that each thing has, I take one, sometimes only to pick it, sometimes to brush the surface, sometimes to pinch it to the bone." For Montaigne, it was a matter of picking a course and following it, accepting that some paths must remain untraveled, some members and faces undeveloped. So, too, for me. If I've come this far, I have selected a path and pursued it. But whose furry surface have I brushed? What creature have I tried to pinch to the bone?

I examine my own meanderings. I walk beside raised ridges. I remember how my excavations connect one mountain to the next. From this distance I see that what appeared to be an essay about the mole in reality was—from the papillae on each tentacle to the tip of the sleek tail to each clod of earth moved—an essay about essaying.

Everything But the Truth?

Fern Kupfer

It is the authority of the truth—the idea of truth, anyway—that makes the memoir attractive to readers. "Some story!" we say to survivors of plane crashes and cancer and dysfunctional families after they have written a moving narrative.

We all like good stories, especially those taken from real life. But we also don't like being lied to. Lying—like cheating and stealing—is almost always wrong from an ethical perspective. But *shaping* the truth when writing memoir is an acceptable aspect of the craft. So where are the boundaries here?

Here's a story (and it really *did* happen). A few years ago I had a student in my nonfiction seminar at Iowa State University. Chris was a terrific writer with a real eye for metaphor and a feel for narrative construction. He wrote about his colorful family—the men were all bookies, small-time hoodlums, con-men. I remember in particular one scene where his father had deserted the family, and on the same night a glass chandelier had come down in the dining room. There was a description of his mother, left with children and bad debts, on her hands and knees, picking up shards of glass out of the rug. She turned to her twelve-year-old son: "I'll never get the glass out of this shag. We'll have to wear shoes in this house *forever.*"

Well, Chris got his A, graduated, moved on. The next year, I had his girlfriend in a class. One day she was in my office and offhandedly shared that she was going to Chris' parents' home for Thanksgiving.

"*Parents*?" I raised an eyebrow. "Oh, is his mom remarried?" I asked. I pictured the woman who could not get the glass out of the rug. Well, good for her, I thought.

No. My student shook her head. Same parents. Married for almost thirty years, she told me.

And his father? What does Chris' father do? I pressed on, recalling the stories of seedy apartments in grimy cities, of the police knocking on the door, of a family always on the run.

"Why, he's an English teacher," the girl said, and at the same moment must have seen my jaw drop. "Uh oh," she added.

Suddenly I wasn't just surprised—I was angry. I told her to give a message to Chris that if he were ever back in town to watch out for me. I may have encouraged her to rethink a relationship with someone who was capable of such duplicity. In class we had discussed interpreting and shaping the story. Someone had called this "accessorizing the truth." Sensing that his father's life as an English professor would make for dull reading (he may have been right on that score), Chris did more than our creative judgments could ever have allowed. We had sat in a workshop and carefully talked about a life that Chris had constructed exclusively from his imagination. Chris had lied. And we, his readers, were betrayed.

That afternoon, I went back and read the final that Chris had written for my class. One of the questions had to do with defining what creative nonfiction is. Chris wrote:

> The distinction between the genres is economic, I think. There's money to be made in fiction, money to be made in nonfiction. Publishers like to keep things straight. And readers—some readers at least—they like to keep things straight. Some people want to read true things. Some people don't. Me, I don't give a shit. True, false, fiction, nonfiction, journalism—it all ends up as fiction in the end.

It all ends up as fiction in the end? I don't accept that. But I do acknowledge that the literal truth isn't always the artistic one.

The question of lying comes up all the time in the creative nonfiction classes I teach. Iowa State is a tech-ag-engineering kind of place, and most of my students are fairly literal-minded. "But *that's* how it happened," they sometimes say when I suggest changes that would tighten a narrative and pep up the prose. "Your memoir shouldn't read as slowly as real life," I tell them. We need to give memoir writers permission to lie, but only when the reconstructed version of the story does not deceive the reader in its search for the aesthetic truth.

To my mind, there are three kinds of "lies" that are acceptable—indeed, sometimes even necessary—in memoir writing. The first are the little white lies that are "created" when memory has blurred the details. Was your mother wearing a blue coat or a red coat when she picked you up at school that morning? Your teacher's peculiar habit of drumming her fingers—was it on the desktop? The chalkboard? The point is, you need a brilliant color for the coat as you looked through the window and saw your mother approaching. You need a place for the teacher to drum those fingers, a habit that foreshadows her threat.

Then there are the lies that narrative structure often demands: composite characterization, compression of time, omission of unnecessary detail. When I was writing *Before and After Zachariah*, a book about family life with my severely handicapped child, my editor suggested some changes. I had too many friends' names in the book, she told me. She couldn't keep them all straight—my memoir was beginning to read like a Russian novel. The editor suggested taking out the events which added new people and making composite characters out of some of the others.

So the three friends who drove with me to the hospital, cooked meals, called in the middle of the night, became one person, a sort of paradigmatic friend who was always there for me. Since the use of composites is fairly controversial, I noted in the acknowledgments that for the "sake of privacy and clarity, some characters in this book have been fictionalized and some names and places have been changed." This statement at least protects the reader from feeling duped.

I also compressed time to move the narrative along at a more energetic rate: the events of a week-long hospital stay were told in the frame of an afternoon; test results came with alacrity. I left out the details that clogged the narrative. It wasn't necessary to record all the conversations with all the health-care professionals who came to my home.

The third type of lying—and the most creative—is really a kind of conjecture, what I call "the gift of perhaps." How do we tell what we do not know? How do we reveal what we have not witnessed? Fiction writers make up stories all the time by using conjecture: "What if?" they say, and start spinning a yarn. The idea of a conflict-based hypothesis (what if a man was obsessed with killing a whale to avenge his loss…?) becomes the source for great fiction. Conjecture can serve the same purpose in memoir.

Look in your family album, which probably contains some pictures of generations you have never met. Your grandmother as a laughing young girl in a white dress next to your somber grandfather. Did she love him? Or did she really want to marry a young man from her church, poorer than she, and not considered a good match? In other pictures your grandmother isn't smiling. Did she forever mourn her first child, a baby girl lost to diphtheria before her second birthday? Perhaps.

Here's a memory as I recall it: Me in college—upstate New York on a day in May so beautiful that my breath catches as I walk up the hill from class. I go to my motorcycle parked along the street. My English teacher has just chosen my paper to read to the class as a "sterling example." He has told the class that I am a "real writer"; I look down toward my lap, assuming modesty. Outside, I kickstart the bike and ride—too quickly—down the street. I am twenty years old and wearing tight, white jeans and my long hair, blonde, freshly ironed, blows behind my back. I have this thought: "It will never get any better than this."

Now this is true: I had a motorcycle in college. I used to iron my hair. I did once write an English paper that my professor read to the class. I remember being twenty on a beautiful spring day and thinking, "It will never get any better than this." But did all this happen on the same day? Were the jeans white? Were those the professor's exact words of praise? And does it matter? The truth of the story is the narrator's perception of youth, of fleeting time, of the longing to capture a golden moment. And that's the truth I've told. No lie.

What We Didn't Know We Knew

Sydney Lea

If I begin by stating my unenthusiasm for the designation "creative nonfiction," it's because I lack enthusiasm for the term "creative" as applied to any writing. Is there not more of creativity in the making of a good soup, say, or of a salmon fly than of novel, story, poem or essay? None of these genres brings things into existence, thus "creating" them, so much as it assembles pre-existing things, both public and private. And however free-associative, such assembly of course depends on another pre-existent entity: language.

I admit, though, that "our" kind of essayizing is one I can name only vaguely. And variously: the personal essay, the familiar essay, the impressionistic essay, the informal essay, or—as I've come most often to describe it—the lyrical essay. Be our terms as they may, moreover, reasonable people could argue at length about what actually *characterizes* the work that Annie Dillard or Edward Abbey or Joan Didion or Edward Hoagland or Rick Bass or Terry Tempest Williams or W. D. Wetherell or Geoffrey Wolff or Kathleen Norris have been doing.

Where for example does their sort of essay begin and another leave off? Each of us might make such a division in idiosyncratic fashion. Still, we'd likely agree not only that our sort of essay exists but also that certain generalities apply to it: other kinds of essay veer closer to journalism; in those other kinds, presentation is more dependent on consecutive reasoning and empirical fact than "creative nonfiction's"; thesis is more insistent for Them than for Us, in whose work thesis, properly so called, may not even show.

I am less interested in defining categories than in learning how to do whatever we do with greater energy, greater facility, greater claim on readers' attentions. And yet I'll have to sneak up on such issues of strategy: anarchistic by nature, skeptical of the whole How-To frame of mind, I shy away from precepts, let alone rules, when I discuss writing of whatever variety. After all, whenever I hear precept or rule, no matter how attractive or acceptable to me; whenever I'm given a guideline about How To Do It, I seem automatically to think of literature that contradicts the same stipulation…and that wows me anyway.

So let me distinguish the lyrical essay—too simply, too reductively—from the more thesis-bound by asserting that the lyrical makes its point or points in a more indirect way than the reporter, reviewer, speechwriter or scholar makes hers or his.

I think for example of Norman Mailer's booklength essay on the moon landing. Rarely a fan of this author's work, still I recall how taken I was on first reading *Of a Fire on the Moon*. As usual, Mailer's protagonist is himself, but himself in the persona of "Aquarius." Rightfully or otherwise, he mounts his inquiry as a representative of the Love Generation, the Make-Love-Not-War party encountering NASA, whose military ties are historically evident.

Mailer, in short, gives himself an angle, but it is not so much an argumentative angle, a means to thesis, as a quirky point of view which will be important in and of itself. Such distinctive perspective will enable Aquarius to talk about his own sensibility at least as volubly as about the astronauts and their mission. I'll be making much of that aim, not so much in connection with Mailer as with the whole genre under discussion.

In *Of a Fire on the Moon*, Aquarius also finds himself moved, unpremeditatedly (or so the book would suggest), to rely very heavily on his sense of smell in talking about his nominal subject. Once again, the object is specifically not to provide conventional consideration of a highly scientific enterprise but to get at that enterprise in a way that no one, including the author, might have predicted. As it turns out, the sense of smell (or frequently smell-lessness) offers a path to real eloquence, at the same time offering a motif that structurally binds his account. It relieves Mailer/ Aquarius, sometimes also called The Nose, of offering coherence by way of dialectical argument.

Of a Fire on the Moon comes to my mind principally as instance of the oblique and peculiar perception that typifies so-called creative nonfiction. Information about the space program's crowning moment does get imparted, but is not primary. And with Mailer as my first exhibit, I'll suggest that the lyrical essay, brief or book-sized, has at its core the way in which the essayist him- or herself, whether as persona or as someone named "I," considers his or her own sensibility.

Or if need be invents that sensibility. For the authorial psyche is as much at the heart of our lyrical essay as it is, say, in a lyrical poem. Both sorts of writer explore the appropriateness or inappropriateness of a personal intellectual-emotional apparatus to a given context or event(s). And each wins either way: if that apparatus is serviceable, then the author has the luxury of a more or less seamless presentation; if it is not, then the clash may become the very subject.

Now in putting the writer's sensibility at the center of the lyrical essay's intentions, I don't mean simply to champion the sort of self-advertisement found in so much of Norman Mailer's work. Though that posture can and often does issue in splendid results, ranging from the book I've just mentioned to the better specimens in Ralph Waldo Emerson's canon, those less inclined to egoism should know there are writers of quite another cast who write brilliantly. I think for example of Ivan Doig, the memoirist of Montana, or of Louise Erdrich, an author of sufficient modesty as at times almost to disappear from her own meditations.

Almost, but never quite entirely. And that is what, I am arguing, constitutes the creative element, to label it so, in our sort of nonfiction.

A few broad statements will govern what follows. To select someone named "I" as the provider of a narrative or a series of impressions (or to select a persona for that I) is simultaneously to select thematic material. If critics sometimes distinguish between technique and content, form and idea, and so on, we writers must not. For us, the choice of first-person delivery, say, cannot be simply a technical one. And more to the point here, we must understand why virtually every lyrical essay makes that very choice: it's again that such an essay's energy is so connected to the identity and the emotional/intellectual makeup of its first person. To begin a narrative by saying even something so simple as "I feel" is automatically to indicate that "I" is an eminent subject in the narrative to come.

In these respects, the protagonist of the so-called American nature essay—from a Thoreau to a Gretel Ehrlich—has far more in common with the prototypical hero of American fiction or poetry than with the conventional magazine essayist, more in common with Melville's Ishmael, Twain's Huck, Whitman's "I" or even the "I" of Emily Dickinson's poetry than with a speaker who means simply to give us the goods, in the directest way possible, on a predetermined subject. We are more poets than journalists, and we must take advantage of our own nature…and of *not* having predetermined subjects.

All this is scarcely to say that our essays must begin in a complete vacuum; such a prospect seems impossible on the face of it anyhow. Mailer does mean to write "about" the NASA moon landing, just as Joan Didion, in *Slouching Toward Bethlehem*, means to write about late 20th-century Los Angeles and the great Ryszard Kapucinski means to write about pre-revolutionary Iran in his *Shah of Shahs*. It's just that the treatment of each of these outward subjects is overwhelmingly dependent for its success on presenting, as Wallace Stevens famously said of modern poetry, the mind in the act of finding what will suffice.

I acknowledge that such a presentation may and almost inevitably will be reconsidered, pondered, even much altered in revision. But this will be revision in the originative sense of the term, a "seeing again," an imaginative entry into the world we mean to render.

Instead of erecting an agenda to govern the lyrical essay, therefore, in all my discussion here—including discussion of choosing a subject—I do little more than throw out some suggestions as to how creative nonfiction can become what it wants to become. And in that regard I want right away to stress that we often begin better if we're in doubt, sometimes very considerable doubt, about where we are headed; to stress how important it is to resist any impulse to pre-program our observations; to stress that those observations need the feel of spontaneity, even if that be the result of endless rewriting,

I want in short to emphasize that the very concept of agenda is inimical to our efforts.

Let me turn for example to a writer who's drawn, precisely, to the nature essay, even though I think the gist of my argument (and his, if only implicitly) can apply to all modes of the genre under discussion. The following passage is from Rick Bass's *The Ninemile Wolves*. At the very start, in a marvelously evocative page or so, Bass imagines those Montana wolves pulling down a quarry; and then come some telling afterthoughts:

> They don't have thumbs. All they've got is teeth, long legs, and—I have to say this—great hearts.
>
> I can say what I want to say. I gave up my science badge a long time ago. I've interviewed maybe a hundred people for or against wolves. The ones who are "for" wolves, they have an agenda: wilderness, and freedom for predators, for prey, for everything. The ones who are "against" wolves have an agenda: they've got vested financial interests. It's about money—more and more money—for them. They perceive the wolves to be an obstacle to frictionless cash flow.
>
> The story's so rich. I can begin anywhere.
>
> I can start with prey, which is what controls wolf numbers (not the other way around), or with history, which is rich in sin, cruelty, sensationalism (poisonings, maimings, torture). You can start with biology, or politics, or you can start with family, with loyalty, and even with the mystic-tinged edges of fate, which is where I choose to begin. It's all going to come together anyway. It has to. We're all following the wolf.

Though I scarcely believe good writing in any genre is necessarily, or ever, anti-rational, in ours there is at least a great deal of *non*-rational energy...or, as the quotation above signals, there ought to be. Lest I myself tend too far toward mystic-tinged edges, however, too far toward abstraction, I'll need to root my observations in personal experience.

I've already hinted at one reason that I'm fonder of the term *lyrical essay* than of many other possible names for this sort of writing: namely that my own essays are born and develop much in the manner of my poems. Nor am I speaking here so much of aesthetics or technique as of far more literal matters, like my inclination to hike long distances in the woods alone, seeking not to think up "subjects" but to let my mind float free until, over time, perhaps over a dozen hikes or even years, I find that certain things have lodged themselves in my consciousness and now demand meditation—that *they* have subjected *me*. I surely hadn't imagined myself to be doing "research," but so it seems I was:

> Early June of 1992, below Stonehouse Mountain, Grafton County, New Hampshire—a place and time in which snowsqualls, routine enough just weeks ago, will at last deserve the name freakish. In freshet beds where waters flared and vanished, frail shoots of jewelweed declare themselves; grass bursts the voles' winter tunnels; geese trail the Connecticut northward; the buck deer's antlers are in velvet; the woodchuck's busy to double in weight; trout sip the ponds' ephemerids; everywhere, the lovesick insistence of birds.
>
> Our family has lived ten years on this foothill's flank, but soon after dawn this morning—beckoned by the full day ahead—I hiked down from its mild summit for perhaps the last time. The ramble, especially under such circumstances, brought back the many I'd made there, in company or alone, one recollection summoning another,

and that one still another, till outward prospects opened onto vaster, more labyrinthine inward views.

This is the opening paragraph of "On the Bubble." But in truth it's a paragraph composed late in the construction of that piece, composed well after I happened on what it was "about." The essay actually began in my somehow remembering a brown-phase fisher, who almost stepped across my toes one fall while I was deer-hunting; that, and the fact that, at the time I began feeling an itch to write this chapter of *Hunting the Whole Way Home*, my family was on the point of moving from Stonehouse Mountain, which a so-called developer meant to ruin; that, and the memory of my son blowing bubbles one spring morning at the summit of the same mountain.

These several things were chronologically quite removed from one another; yet they had lodged themselves in my consciousness. My essay was, and is, about *what they all had to do with one another.*

In short, I began in the spirit of Rick Bass: "It's all going to come together anyway. It has to." As I have been arguing, the lyrical essay chiefly concerns the essayist's perception of his or her surroundings, whether natural or otherwise. And since it's concerned with perception, it is ultimately concerned with the essayist's own mind in action.

Perception in the lyrical essay, however, cannot remain static, or so my experience would indicate; it must unfold in the very act of writing, and writing should itself be an act (or acts) of unanticipated discovery. My aim as I sat down to indite "On the Bubble" was simply to see if I could write my way to a connection among a few things, however seemingly disconnected, that had stopped me in my tracks.

The appropriateness of the fragile bubbles my son blew, for example, to the theme of natural fragility that so exercised me when the bulldozers started to chew up the mountain I loved—that appropriateness was something that crept upon me, surprised me, and, however sad the circumstances reflected in my chapter, delighted me as a writer.

What I'm getting at is this: the death knell for any creative writing sounds whenever it knows too accurately where it is going. A novel whose plot has been predetermined will almost inevitably fail to surprise us, say, on the level of characterization, the characters having little to do but walk through their scripts. A poem whose theme has been fore-decided will clank along mechanically, each line illustrating a dominating "idea."

The same hazards can attend the lyrical essay. Indeed, these dangers may apply even more ruinously to such an essay than to the other genres I've referred to, since so often—or so we believe—our plot and setting and characters seem, exactly, to exist in their entirety before we write a word. We know how everything comes out, and who's involved, and where we are: it's simply a matter of recording all that, right?

Wrong. Or wrong, I believe, if you're in the business of writing creative nonfiction, in which, as I've suggested, the creative part must if anything be more important than the nonfiction part. We may too easily be misled by the very concept of nonfictionality; we may be inclined simply to chronicle the facts of a given matter, and to do so is to offer an account, not an essay of the kind most of us want. Ours is, after all, an art form, to which imagination is utterly crucial.

With all this in mind, I'll make some practical observations. At the outset, in grumbling about the word "creative," I pointed out the obvious fact that as writers we work with something that pre-exists, namely language—which I now want to suggest can help us to our "subjects," since language and subject are all but indistinguishably identified, each bound as it is to perception.

The *way* in which we phrase our responses, then, is as much what we are writing about as anything else, and with that in mind, I'll urge that in order to begin we ought to speak with as much particularity as we can. This doesn't mean that we can't muse, reminisce, worry, argue, preach, or even pontificate in our essays. We can. Lord knows, I do. It's only that such rhetorical gestures will always be more effective if they have grounds.

In "On the Bubble," the word "grounds" has a happy double meaning, so much of the essay's concerns having to do, exactly, with grounds, or with their loss. And thus it began with very specific renderings of vivid occurrences upon those grounds, with my effort to recapture the particulars of an encounter with a fisher. I wrote the memory as clearly and accurately as I knew how, and in doing so I was somehow led to other specific experiences in the same locale, notably the time when I took my son to the height of Stonehouse Mountain and watched him blow bubbles.

In the very process of writing out these experiences, in language that was as precise as I could make it, I came gradually to recognize what these two components might have in common: the wonder I felt at beholding that normally elusive weasel at such close distance seemed at least remotely akin to the wonder my five-year-old experienced as he watched his soap bubbles take flight above the granite moraine of Stonehouse Mountain. Each version of wonder was a bit childlike, and each, like childhood itself, was extremely fragile, indeed doomed.

Without setting out to do so, I had hit on the motif of wonder, and on plain facts to serve as its metaphors: weasel and bubble. Soon enough another metaphor presented itself—this one for doom—that seemed so obvious I was puzzled I'd ever missed it: the very sound of the bulldozers and chainsaws on the hillside. Very rapidly now, I came to see the connections among seemingly disparate snatches of memory and present experience.

I had written my way to awareness of those connections. I had written my way not to creativity but to what I prefer to call imagination, as the great poet and theorist Samuel Taylor Coleridge understood the term; he called it "an esemplastic power," which means, roughly, a power that forges unity out of diversity.

My point is that I foisted no metaphors or themes upon my perceptions. Rather, by beginning in particularity, without great regard for what my essay would be "about," I found organic metaphors and thematics coming to *me*. It would have been all too easy just to rant and rave out loud about the developer's greed and the despoliation of wildness; indeed, I had been doing so—eloquently, I hope—for some time. But I had done so in letters to my local paper, which were not by my understanding creative in the way that each of us wants to be in a lyrical essay.

Those letters had a thesis, and I argued it as persuasively and logically as I could. Yet the terms of my letters were for the most part abstract: terms, exactly, like "greed" and "wildness" and "despoliation." In my essay, I'd use the same terms, but now they would be…grounded. They'd be grounded in personal observation and unexpected discovery of the kind I've briefly catalogued above.

I was proud of the letters, but they didn't have the same value for me as a writer that the final essay had, and has. "Wildness" became associated with a particular animal, the fisher; the fisher's habitat appeared to be threatened by "despoliation," by a ruinous force associated with the developer's machinery; that machinery perfectly epitomized the brutal effects of "greed." And so the fisher's future, like my son's, perhaps, became as tenuous as the existences of those bubbles I remember my boy making.

With a bunch of specifics in my quiver, I could shoot as many arrows of rhetorical indignation as I wanted, without fear of lapsing from "our" sort of essay into that other sort I spoke of early on. But I repeat: I did not know what my outward subject or my rhetoric would be until I started writing, and I am glad I didn't know, for otherwise I'd merely have written one more letter to the editor. The only agenda I had was that vague poetic one: I sought to connect a number of moments that had stuck in my consciousness, and my only means of doing so was particularized language.

Language led me on, in the most fulfilling way. It permitted me both to learn what was on my mind and to learn how much I had to say about it. The composition of "On the Bubble," then, like the successful composition of any poem, resulted in a better self-understanding. Speaking for myself, this is among the happiest results that an author can experience.

In the famous formulation of a far greater poet than I, Robert Frost, by writing we discover what we didn't know we knew.

Note

See Peter Fritzell's illuminating *Nature Writing and America* (Iowa State University Press: Ames, 1990), whose commentary on the protagonist of American natural-historical literature, along with other keen insights, informs portions of this discussion.

What Happened to the Personal Essay?

Phillip Lopate

The personal or familiar essay is a wonderfully tolerant form, able to accommodate rumination, memoir, anecdote, diatribe, scholarship, fantasy, and moral philosophy. It can follow a rigorously elegant design, or—held together by little more than the author's voice—assume an amoebic shapelessness. Working in it liberates a writer from the structure of the well-made, epiphanous short story and allows one to ramble in a way that more truly reflects the mind at work. At this historical moment the essayist has an added freedom: no one is looking over his or her shoulder. No one much cares. Commercially, essay volumes rank even lower than poetry.

I know; when my first essay collection, *Bachelorhood*, came out, booksellers had trouble figuring out where to stock it. Autobiography? Self-help? Short stories? I felt like saying, "Hey, this category has been around for a long time; what's the big deal?" Yet, realistically, they were right: what had once been a thriving popular tradition had ceased being so. Readers who enjoyed the book often told me so with some surprise, because they hadn't thought they would like "essays." For them, the word conjured up those dreaded weekly compositions they were forced to write on the gasoline tax or the draft.

Essays are usually taught all wrong: they are harnessed to rhetoric and composition, in a two-birds-with-one-stone approach designed to sharpen freshman students' skills at argumentation. While it is true that historically the essay is related to rhetoric, it in fact seeks to persuade more by the delights of literary style than anything else. Elizabeth Hardwick, one of our best essayists, makes this point tellingly when she says: "The mastery of expository prose, the rhythm of sentences, the pacing, the sudden flash of unexpected vocabulary, redeem polemic.... The essay...is a great meadow of style and personal manner, freed from the need for defense except that provided by an individual intelligence and sparkle. We consent to watch a mind at work, without agreement often, but only for pleasure."

Equally questionable in teaching essays is the anthology approach, which assigns an essay apiece by a dozen writers according to our latest notions of a demographically representative and content-relevant sampling. It would be more instructive to read six pieces each by two writers, since the essay (particularly the familiar essay) is so rich a vehicle for displaying personality in all its willfully changing aspects.

Essays go back at least to classical Greece and Rome, but it was Michel de Montaigne, generally considered the "father of the essay," who first matched the word to the form around 1580. Reading this contemporary of Shakespeare (thought to have influenced the Bard himself), we are reminded of the original, pristine meaning of the word, from the French verb *essayer:* to attempt, to try, to leap experimentally into the unknown. Montaigne understood that, in an essay, the track of a person's thoughts struggling to achieve some understanding of a problem *is* the plot. The essayist must be willing to contradict himself (for which reason an essay is not a legal brief), to digress, even to risk ending up in a terrain very different from the one he embarked on. Particularly in Montaigne's magnificent late essays, free-falls that sometimes go on for a hundred pages or more, it is possible for the reader to lose all contact with the ostensible subject, bearings, top, bottom, until there is nothing to do but surrender to this companionable voice, thinking alone in the dark. Eventually, one begins to share Montaigne's confidence that "all subjects are linked to one another," which makes any topic, however small or far from the center, equally fertile.

It was Montaigne's peculiar project, which he claimed rightly or wrongly was original, to write about the one subject he knew best: himself. As with all succeeding literary self-portraits—or all succeeding stream-of-consciousness, for that matter—success depended on having an interesting consciousness, and Montaigne was blessed with an undulatingly supple, learned, skeptical, deep, sane, and candid one. In point of fact, he frequently strayed to worldly subjects, giving his opinion on everything from cannibals to coaches, but we do learn a large number of intimate and odd details about the man, down to his bowels and kidney stones. "Sometimes there comes to me a feeling that I should not betray the story of my life," he writes. On the other hand: "No pleasure has any meaning for me without communication."

A modern reader may come away thinking that the old fox still kept a good deal of himself to himself. This is partly because we have upped the ante on autobiographical revelation, but also because Montaigne was writing essays, not confessional memoirs, and in an essay it is as permissible, as honest, to chase down a reflection to its source as to admit some past shame. In any case, having decided that "the most barbarous of our maladies is to despise our being," Montaigne did succeed, via the protopsychoanalytic method of the *Essais*, in making friends with his mind.

Having taken the essay form to its very limits at the outset, Montaigne's dauntingly generous example was followed by an inevitable specialization, which included the un-Montaignean split between formal and informal essays. The formal essay derived from Francis Bacon; it is said to be "dogmatic, impersonal, systematic, and expository," written in a "stately" language, while the informal essay is "personal, intimate, relaxed, conversational, and frequently humorous" (*New Columbia Encyclopedia*). Never mind that most of the great essayists were adept at both modes, including Bacon (see, for example, his wonderful "Of Friendship"); it remains a helpful distinction.

Informal, familiar essays tend to seize on the parade and minutiae of daily life: vanities, fashions, oddballs, seasonal rituals, love and disappointment, the pleasures of solitude, reading, going to plays, walking in the street. It is a very urban form, enjoying a spectacular vogue in eighteenth- and early nineteenth-century London, when it enlisted the talents of such stylists as Swift, Dr. Johnson, Addison and Steele, Charles Lamb, William Hazlitt, and a visiting American, Washington Irving. The familiar essay was given a boost by the phenomenal growth of newspapers and magazines, all of which needed smart copy (such as that found in the *Spectator*) to help instruct their largely middle-class, *parvenu* readership on the manners of the class to which it aspired.

Although most of the *feuilletonistes* of this period were cynical hacks, the journalistic situation was still fluid enough to allow original thinkers a platform. The British tolerance for eccentricity seemed to encourage commentators to develop idiosyncratic voices. No one was as cantankerously marginal in his way, or as willing to write against the grain of community feeling, as William Hazlitt. His energetic prose style registered a temperament that passionately, moodily swung between sympathy and scorn. Anyone capable of writing so bracingly frank an essay as "The Pleasures of Hating" could not—as W. C. Fields would say—be all bad. At the same time, Hazlitt's enthusiasms could transform the humblest topic, such as going on a country walk or seeing a prizefight, into a description of visionary wholeness.

What many of the best essayists have had—what Hazlitt had in abundance—was quick access to their blood reactions, so that the merest flash of a prejudice or opinion might be dragged into the open and defended. Hazlitt's readiness to entertain opinions, coupled with his openness to new impressions, made him a fine critic of painting and the theater, but in his contrariness he ended by antagonizing all of his friends, even the benign, forgiving Charles Lamb. Not that Lamb did not have *his* contrary side. He, too, was singled out for a "perverse habit of contradiction," which helped give his "Elia" essays, among the quirkiest and most charming in the English language, their peculiar bite.

How I envy readers of *London* magazine, who might have picked up an issue in 1820 and encountered a new, high-spirited essay by Hazlitt, Lamb, or both! After their deaths, the familiar essay continued to attract brilliant practitioners such as Stevenson, DeQuincey, and Emerson. But subsequently, a little of the vitality seeped out of it. "Though we are mighty fine fellows nowadays, we cannot write like Hazlitt," Stevenson confessed. And by the turn of the century, it seemed rather played out and toothless.

The modernist aesthetic was also not particularly kind to this type of writing, relegating it to a genteel, antiquated nook, *belles lettres*—a phrase increasingly spoken with a sneer, as though implying a sauce without the meat. If "meat" is taken to mean the atrocities of life, it is true that the familiar essay has something obstinately non-apocalyptic about it. The very act of composing such an essay seems to implicate the writer in humanist-individualist assumptions that have come to appear suspect under the modernist critique.

Still, it would be unfair to pin the rap on modernism, which Lord knows gets blamed for everything else. One might as well "blame" the decline of the conversational style of writing. Familiar essays were fundamentally, even self-consciously, conversational: it is no surprise that Swift wrote one of his best short pieces on "Hints Toward an Essay on Conversation"; that Montaigne tackled "Of the Art of Discussion"; that Addison and Steele extensively analyzed true and false wit; that Hazlitt titled his books *Table Talk*, *Plain Speaker*, and *The Round Table*, or that Oliver Wendell Holmes actually cast his familiar essays in the form of mealtime dialogues. Why would a book like Holmes's *The Autocrat of the Breakfast Table*, a celebration of good talk that was so popular in its time, be so unlikely today? I cannot go along with those who say "The art of conversation has died, television killed it," since conversation grows and changes as inevitably as language. No, what has departed is not conversation but conversation-flavored writing, which implies a speaking relationship between writer and reader. How many readers today would sit still for a direct address by the author? To be called "gentle reader" or "*hypocrite lecteur*," to have one's arm pinched while dozing off, to be called to attention, flattered, kidded like a real person instead of a privileged fly on the wall—wouldn't most readers today find such devices archaic, intrusive, even impudent? Oh, you wouldn't? Good, we can go back to the old style, which I much prefer.

Maybe what has collapsed is the very fiction of "the educated reader," whom the old essayists seemed to be addressing in their conversational remarks. From Montaigne onward, essayists until this century have invoked a shared literary culture: the Greek and Latin authors and the best of their national poetry. The whole modern essay tradition sprang from quotation. Montaigne's *Essais* and Burton's *Anatomy of Melancholy* were essentially outgrowths of the "commonplace book," a personal journal in which quotable passages, literary excerpts, and comments were written. Though the early essayists' habit of quotation may seem excessive to a modern taste, it was this display of learning that linked them to their educated reading public and ultimately gave them the authority to speak so personally about themselves. Such a universal literary culture no longer exists; we have only popular culture to fall back on. While it is true that the old high culture was never really "universal"—excluding as it did a good deal of humanity—it is also true that without it, personal discourse has become more hard-pressed. What many modern essayists have tried to do is to replace that shared literary culture with more and more personal experience. It is a brave effort and an intriguing supposition, this notion that individual experience alone can constitute the universal text that all may dip into with enlightenment. But there are pitfalls: on the one hand, it may lead to cannibalizing oneself and one's privacy; on the other hand, much more common (and to my mind, worse) is the assertion of an earnestly honest or "vulnerable" manner without really candid chunks of experience to back it up.

As for popular culture, the essayist's chronic invocation of its latest bandwagon fads, however satirically framed, comes off frequently as a pandering to the audience's short attention span—a kind of literary ambulance chasing. Take the "life-style" pages in today's periodicals, which carry commentaries that are a distant nephew of the familiar essay: there is something so depressing about this desperate mining of things in the air, such a fevered search for a generational *Zeitgeist*, such an unctuously smarmy tone of "we," which assumes that everyone shares the same consumerist-boutique sensibility, that one longs for a Hazlittean shadow of misanthropic mistrust to fall between reader and writer. One longs for any evidence of a distinct human voice—anything but this ubiquitous Everyman/woman pizzazzy drone, listing tips for how to get the most from your dry cleaner's, take care of your butcher block, or bounce back from an unhappy love affair.

The familiar essay has naturally suffered from its parasitic economic dependency on magazines and newspapers. The streamlined telegraphic syntax and homogenized-perky prose that contemporary periodicals have evolved make it all the more difficult for thoughtful, thorny voices to be tolerated within the house style. The average reader of periodicals becomes conditioned to digest pure information, up-to-date, with its ideological viewpoint disguised as objectivity, and is thus ill-equipped to follow the rambling, cat-and-mouse game of perverse contrariety played by the great essayists of the past.

In any event, very few American periodicals today support house essayists to the tune of letting them write regularly and at comfortable length on the topics of their choice. The nearest thing we have are talented columnists like Russell Baker, Ellen Goodman, Leon Hale, and Mike Royko, who are in a sense carrying on the Addison and Steele tradition; they are so good at their professional task of hit-and-run wisdom that I only wish they were sometimes given the space to try out their essayistic wings. The problem with the column format is that it becomes too tight and pat: one idea per piece. Fran Lebowitz, for instance, is a very clever writer, and not afraid of adopting a cranky persona; but her one-liners have a cumulative sameness of affect that inhibits a true essayistic movement. What most column writing does not seem to allow for is self-surprise, the sudden deepening or darkening of tone, so that the writer might say, with Lamb: "I do not know how, upon a subject which I began treating half-seriously, I should have fallen upon a recital so eminently painful.…"

From time to time I see hopeful panel discussions offered on "The Resurgence of the Essay," Yes, it would be very nice, and it may come about yet. The fact is, however, that very few American writers today are essayists primarily. Many of the essay collections issued each year are essentially random compilations of book reviews, speeches, journalism, and prefaces by authors who have made a name for themselves in other genres. The existence of these collections attests more to the celebrated authors' desires to see all their words between hardcovers than it does to any real devotion to the essay form. A tired air of grudgingly gracious civic duty hovers over many of these performances.

One recent American writer who did devote himself passionately to the essay was E. B. White. No one has written more consistently graceful, thoughtful essays in twentieth-century American language than White; on the other hand, I can't quite forgive his sedating influence on the form. White's Yankee gentleman-farmer persona is a complex balancing act between Whitmanian democratic and patrician values, best suited for the expression of mildness and tenderness with a resolute tug of elegiac depression underneath. Perhaps this is an unfair comparison, but there is not a single E. B. White essay that compares with the gamy, pungent, dangerous Orwell of "Such, Such Were the Joys…" or "Shooting an Elephant." When White does speak out on major issues of the day, his man-in-the-street, folksy humility and studiously plain-Joe air ring false, at least to me. And you would never know that the cute little wife he describes listening to baseball games on the radio was the powerful *New Yorker* editor Katharine White. The suppression or muting of ego as something ungentlemanly has left its mark on *The New Yorker* since, with the result that this magazine, which rightly prides itself on its freedom to publish extended prose, has not been a particularly supportive milieu for the gravelly voice of the personal essayist. The preferred model seems to be the scrupulously fair, sporting, impersonal, fact-gathering style of a John McPhee, which reminds me of nothing so much as a colony of industrious termites capable of patiently reducing any subject matter to a sawdust of detail.

The personal, familiar essay lives on in America today in an interestingly fragmented proliferation of specialized subgenres. The form is very much with us, particularly if you count the many popular nonfiction books that are in fact nothing but groups of personal essays strung together, and whose compelling subject matter makes the reading public overlook its ordinary indifference to this type of writing. Personal essays have also appeared for years under the protective umbrella of New Journalism (Joan Didion being the most substantial and quirky practitioner to emerge from that subsidized training ground, now largely defunct); of autobiographical-political meditations (Richard Rodriguez, Adrienne Rich, Vivian Gornick, Marcelle Clements, Wilfrid Sheed, Alice Walker, Nancy Mairs, Norman Mailer); nature and ecological-regional writing (Wendell Berry, Noel Perrin, John Graves, Edward Hoagland, Gretel Ehrlich, Edward Abbey, Carol Bly, Barry Lopez, Annie Dillard); literary criticism (Susan Sontag, Elizabeth Hardwick, Seymour Krim, Cynthia Ozick, Leslie Fiedler, Joyce Carol Oates); travel writing and mores (Mary McCarthy, V. S. Naipaul, Joseph Epstein, Eleanor Clark, Paul Theroux); humorous pieces (Max Apple, Roy Blount, Jr., Calvin Trillin); food (M. F. K. Fisher). I include this random and unfairly incomplete list merely to indicate the diversity and persistence of the form in American letters today. Against all odds, it continues to attract newcomers.

In Europe, the essay stayed alive largely by taking a turn toward the speculative and philosophical, as practiced by writers like Walter Benjamin, Theodor Adorno, Simone Weil, E. M. Cioran, Albert Camus, Roland Barthes, Czeslaw Milosz, and Nicola Chiaromonte. All, in a sense, are offspring of the epigrammatic style of Nietzsche. This fragmented, aphoristic, critical type of essay-writing became used as a subversive tool of skeptical probing, a critique of ideology in a time when large, synthesizing theories and systems of philosophy are no longer trusted. Adorno saw the essay, in fact, as a valuable countermethod: "The essay does not strive for closed, deductive or inductive construction. It revolts above all against the doctrine—deeply rooted since Plato—that the changing and ephemeral is unworthy of philosophy; against that ancient injustice toward the transitory, by which it is once more anathematized, conceptually. The essay shies away from the violence of dogma.... The essay gently defies the ideals of [Descartes'] *clara et distincta perceptio* and of absolute certainty.... Discontinuity is essential to the essay...as characteristic of the form's groping intention.... The slightly yielding quality of the essayist's thought forces him to greater intensity than discursive thought can offer; for the essay, unlike discursive thought, does not proceed blindly, automatically, but at every moment it must reflect on itself.... Therefore the law of the innermost form of the essay is heresy. By transgressing the orthodoxy of thought, something becomes visible in the object which it is orthodoxy's secret purpose to keep invisible."

This continental tradition of the self-reflexive, aphoristically subversive essay is only now beginning to have an influence on contemporary American writers. One saw it first, curiously, cropping up in ironic experimental fiction—in Renata Adler, William Gass, Donald Barthelme, John Barth. Their fictive discourse, like Kundera's, often resembles a broken essay, a personal/philosophical essay intermixed with narrative elements. The tendency of many postmodernist storytellers to parody the pedantry of the essay voice speaks both to their intellectual reliance on it and to their uneasiness about adopting the patriarchal stance of the Knower. That difficulty with assumption of authority is one reason why the essay remains "broken" for the time being.

In a penetrating discussion of the essay form, Georg Lukács put it this way: "The essay is a judgment, but the essential, the value-determining thing about it is not the verdict (as is the case with the system), but the process of judging." Uncomfortable words for an age when "judgmental" is a pejorative term. The familiar essayists of the past may have been nonspecialists—indeed, this was part of their attraction—but they knew how to speak with a generalist's easy authority. That is precisely what contemporary essayists have a hard time doing: in our technical age we are too aware of the advantage specialists hold over us. (This may explain the current confidence the public has in the physician-scientist school of essayists like Lewis Thomas, Richard Selzer, Stephen Jay Gould, F. Gonzalez-Crussi, Oliver Sacks: their meditations are embedded in a body of technical information, so that readers are reassured they are "learning" something, not just wasting their time on *belles lettres*.) The last of the old-fashioned generalists, men of letters who seemed able to write comfortably, knowledgeably, opinionatedly on everything under the sun, were Edmund Wilson and Paul Goodman; we may not soon see their like again.

In *The Last Intellectuals*, Russell Jacoby has pointed out the reticence of writers of the so-called generation of the sixties—my generation—to play the role of the public intellectual, as did Lionel Trilling, Harold Rosenberg, C. Wright Mills, Irving Howe, Alfred Kazin, Daniel Bell, Dwight Macdonald, Lionel Abel, etc., who judged cultural and political matters for a large general readership, often diving into the melee with both arms swinging. While Jacoby blames academia for absorbing the energies of my contemporaries, and while others have cited the drying up of print outlets for formal polemical essays, my own feeling is that it is not such a terrible thing to want to be excused from the job of pontificating to the public. Ours was not so much a failure to become our elders as it was a conscious swerving to a different path. The Vietnam War, the central experience of my generation, had a great deal to do with that deflection. As a veteran of the sixties, fooled many times about world politics because I had no firsthand knowledge of circumstances thousands of miles away (the most shameful example that comes to mind was defending, at first, the Khmer Rouge regime in Cambodia), I have grown skeptical of taking righteous public positions based on nothing but simpatico media reports and party feeling. As for matters that I've definitely made up my mind about, it would embarrass me, frankly, to pen an opinion piece deploring the clearly deplorable, like apartheid or invading Central America, without being able to add any new insights to the discussion. One does not want to be reduced to scolding, or to abstract progressive platitudes, well founded as these may be. It isn't that my generation doesn't think politics are important, but our earlier experiences in that storm may have made us a little hesitant about mouthing off in print. We—or I should say I—have not yet been able to develop the proper voice to deal with these large social and political issues, which will at the same time remain true to personal experience and hard-earned doubt.

All this is a way of saying that the present moment offers a remarkable opportunity for emerging essayists who can somehow locate the moral authority, within or outside themselves, to speak to these issues in the grand manner. But there is also room, as ever, for the informal essayist to wrestle with intellectual confusion, to offer feelings, to set down ideas in a particularly direct and exposed format—more so than in fiction, say, where the author's opinions can always be disguised as belonging to characters. The increasing willingness of contemporary writers to try the form, if not necessarily commit themselves to it, augurs well for the survival of the personal essay. And if we do offend, we can always fall back on Papa Montaigne's "*Que sçay-je?*": What do I know?

"Creative Nonfiction": What's in a Name?

Andrea A. Lunsford

The last dozen years or so might well be designated as the era of the essay, for they have been accompanied by a flood of publications in this genre matched by a growing national audience for such work and a growing body of scholarship on and attention to the essay. As a reader and writer and teacher who has long been drawn to the "essay," a term which is itself contested, I have thought a fair amount about this phenomenon and about what network or web of circumstances may be associated with the "rise of the essay." Now I am by no means an expert; in fact, I would claim instead the "dilettante" status explored so deftly by Kurt Spellmeyer in his recent essay, "Dilettantes, Professionals, and Knowledge." From my dilettante perspective, however, it seems that at least four elements may be involved in the essayistic renaissance we are presently enjoying. First, and perhaps most significantly, the postmodern turn—and particularly the Derridean critique of presence and the feminist critique of foundationalist or universalist assumptions—has revealed the constructed nature of all experience, even that traditionally thought to be the most "real" or "true."

Second, this realization of the constructed nature of experience has tended to highlight the power and importance of narrative as an element of all discourse (Jerome Bruner's essay "Life as Narrative" being perhaps the most well known claim for such status) and, concomitantly, what we might call the artifice of the everyday. That is, the postmodern turn has thrown into relief the ways in which human understanding through discourse—from the scientific to the business-oriented to the artistic—grows out of stories we tell each other about the way things are. And these stories, even those that rest on "true" or "real" events, must take on the status of artifice, for the very fact of their embeddedness in language means that they must be crafted and that they are metaphoric in nature—representative of something else, something not ever there.

Third, we are living in a time devoted to self-reflexive analysis, as is evident in everything from the scientist's realization that the experimenter is always already involved in and affecting that which is experimented upon to the critic's and historian's realization that the accounts they give are also inevitably accounts of themselves. This tendency toward self-relexive analysis shows up in the crisis of disciplinarity (English, history, physics, chemistry) as well as in the crisis of representation.

Finally, all these factors are entailed, I believe, in the contemporary focus on and struggle over genre. You may remember the line "filthy facts and mixed-up genres" in one of W. D. Snodgrass's wonderful poems. As Derek Owens points out in his recent book *Resisting Writings:*

> One of the more fascinating upshots of poststructuralism and the attention to the post-modern is that the matter of genre has forever been called into question. Where does one genre end and another begin? If the boundaries that separate…[genres] can no longer be drawn with the same degree of confidence we once knew, then how do we continue thinking about writing? It is so much easier to discuss composition when the boxes were self-contained and autonomous: when creative writing looked and sounded a certain way that expository prose didn't, when critical theory was clearly distinct from autobiography. Now we no longer have boxes, but multiple stylistic planes that freely overlap each other, texts like various layers of colored acetate randomly honeycombed, sandwiching and separating at the whim of the writer: in some sections single colors filter through, while elsewhere tints fuse together in complex patterns. (155)

Reading these lines today makes me feel that I was quite prescient some dozen years ago when I was teaching an essay class to undergraduates at the University of British Columbia. In that course, I took as my theme the definition of what consti-tuted an "essay" or "creative nonfiction," and we read a number of works that might—or might not—have been given such a designation. Two I remember particularly well include John McPhee's "In Search of Marvin Gardens," a combination of a strong narrative exploration of and moving through Atlantic City, New Jersey, and a medita-tion on monopoly and late capitalism. (I introduced this piece very early in the term, before we had gone into any theoretical discussions of generic distinctions, and asked the students to read it and then tell me whether it was an essay or short story. The class was precisely split on the question, and very surprised by the amount of disagree-ment the question engendered. While McPhee's piece is usually anthologized as an essay [and guess why?—the anxiety or drift of generic influence] my own classroom experiences suggest to me that it could just as easily have been designated a short story—you might want to take a look at it to see what you think.)

The other piece I remember particularly well was billed as a short story called "Soft Ions"—one written by Racter, a computer owned by Bill Chamberlain who asks, in a preface to the story, what it takes to make a "real" story. "What is 'real experience' anyway?" Chamberlain asks. Can it be quantified? Will it compute? Here is a brief paragraph from "Soft Ions":

> Helene watched John and cogitated: A supper with him? Disgusting! A supper would facilitate a dissertation, and a dissertation or tale was what John carefully wanted to have. But with what in mind? Wine, otters, beans? No! Electrons! John simply was a quantum logician; his endless dreams were captivating and interesting. At all events, Matthew, Helene, and Wendy were assisting him in his infuriated tries to broaden

himself. Now legions of dreams itched to punch Wendy's consciousness. Yet John whispered, "Just a minute! Helene's a maid. I'm a quantum logician; can maids know galaxies and even stars or a multitude of galactic systems: Can maids recognize electrons?..." Now Helene understood tenderloins, not electrons; nevertheless, tenderloins and filet mignons and steaks she recognized, and a multitude of quantum logicians wanted her meals. Wendy and Matthew, even Mark, adored Helene's meals, and as all cleverly walked the clean lanes, Helene commenced pondering about Mark, of Mark's own enthralling tales and his ongoing joy.

I believe that this passage from "Soft Ions" and the example of John McPhee's essay/story suggest that Owens is correct in his description of what Clifford Geertz has described as blurred genres; and this blurring of generic distinctions taken together with the focus on self-reflection, the realization of how experience is constructed and narrativized, and the recognition of the artifice of the everyday—all these elements contribute to a particularly propitious moment for what is sometimes called "creative nonfiction," sometimes "the essay," sometimes "nonfiction prose." I would venture to go even further and argue that this blurring of genres is evident in our own academic prose as well: think of Jane Tompkins's often-reprinted essay, "Me and My Shadow" or Susan Leonardi's *PMLA* essay of a few years ago on women writers and the cookbook genre, which she opens by saying she was going to give us her pound cake recipe but since it is so hot (she was writing in July) she has decided instead to offer her summer pasta recipe. Or, closer to the field of composition studies, some of you may have read an essay Bob Connors and I wrote a few years ago, the subtitle of which is "Ma and Pa Kettle Do Research." In that essay, Bob and I report on a lengthy and massive research project, one in which we analyzed a randomized, stratified sample of over 21,000 student essays. But we wanted to do more than report on the research: we wanted also to poke some good-natured fun at ourselves and at researchers who take themselves, and their research, also, too seriously; and we wanted to blur generic boundaries as well. That is why we took on, in part, the filmic personas of Ma and Pa, and that is why we used subheadings throughout the essay that linked terms from classical rhetoric with allusions to the Kettle films, subheadings like "Exordium: The Kettles Smell a Problem," "Narratio: Ma and Pa Visit the Library," "Confirmatio: The Kettles Get Cracking," "Confutatio: Ma and Pa Suck Eggs," and so on.

A very recent example of such blurred generic boundaries in our academic discourse is Wendy Bishop's "If Winston Weathers Would Just Write to Me on E-Mail," in which she mixes personal narrative, student writing, and poetry. And while I am offering examples of contemporary writing that I believe both demonstrate the difficulty of making traditional generic distinctions and exemplify the excitement of the nonfiction essay at the current moment, let me mention briefly several others.

Karla Holloway has spent much of her distinguished career trying to muddy the waters of academic discourse, particularly by mixing what might have once been the clearly defined genres of autobiography, fiction, and critical essay. Her latest book, *Codes of Conduct: Race, Ethics, and the Color of Our Character*, due out this spring, is a brilliant example of the kind of writing Patricia Williams does in her important work *The Alchemy of Race and Rights: Diary of a Law Professor*. You may recall the memorable opening of this book on the legal profession:

> Since subject position is everything in my analysis of the law, you deserve to know that it's a bad morning. I am very depressed. It always takes a while to sort out what's wrong, but is usually starts with some kind of perfectly irrational thought such as: I hate being a lawyer.... It's all I can do to feed the cats. I let my hair stream wildly and the eyes roll back in my head. So you should know that this is one of those mornings when I refuse to compose myself properly; you should know you are dealing with someone who is writing this in an old terry bathrobe with a little fringe of blue and white tassels dangling from the hem, trying to decide if she is stupid or crazy. (34)

Sound like the opening of a short story or novel? I think so, too.

It goes in the other direction as well. Lee Abbot, a short story writer of no mean distinction, recently published an essay entitled "Makin' Whoopee." It is characterized by ironic self-reflexivity, by a self-consciousness that it is a "story" as much as an essay, and by Abbot's characteristically artful prose. Here's the opening of this "essay":

> A confession: years ago now, in the early stages of a career that has been, in fact, no career at all, but more a matter of inchoate and assbackward beliefs that have to do with words and the miracles we aim to make with them, I tried my hand at pornography.
>
> It was 1972, your not-so-humble narrator a young husband, M.A. in mid-mint, a teacher of Freshman Composition to those at New Mexico State University for whom composition of the sort I aimed to teach—meet as an angel full of pie, as shaped and precious as a pearl, wise as an old Greek named Aristotle—was, as the saying goes, more preparation than H. It was February, near Valentine's day (my wife's birthday), and, as a gag gift, our son's godfather gave us *The Three of Us*, the only porno I would read.
>
> "I underlined the good parts," Charles said. "in red."
>
> What this meant was that virtually the entire volume, a whole evidently jampacked with "good parts," was underlined.... I read it straightaway, of course. Consumed it, in fact, in one great gulp. (*Gulp?* Yup, I see that every word here and now, like every word there and then, is a metaphor central to this yarn and its lessons.) And as I ate this pulp from the lowest branch of the Tree of Whatever our funky forbears were once upon a time hungry enough to feed from in Eden, I recalled an essay in *Esquire* that held, at length enough to be serious (*Length?* Well, I warned you), that you could tell porno was good because, happily and unmistakably and without the brain-busting common to the *NYRB*, your body would tell you: Things would happen—to your nether reaches, to your heart, to your blood—and, presto, you would know, as few things are nowadays known, that, say *Maidens with Manifolds* or *Boston's Black Babes in Bondage* was nothing if not a damn good read. Screw Harold Bloom. To hell with Leslie Fiedler. Get out of town, Helen Vendler. You want judgment, Bunky? Informed opinion? You want to cut through the high-falutin' cerebration that passes for, uh, theory?
>
> Adios, *NY Times Book Review*. Hello, pituitary. (263–64)

Abbot's work, I think you can tell from even this brief excerpt, blurs the boundaries of the genres we usually have traditionally thought of as short story and essay: announced as an essay, it quickly establishes a narrator and a set of characters and is driven by the narrative progression characteristic of fiction. But especially in its allusions to "theory" and to "real-life" critics, it resembles an essay.

In the same way, the editors and contributors of *Double Stitch: Black Women Write about Mothers and Daughters* include "poems, stories, and essays"—though I would challenge anyone to distinguish between the three consistently in that wonderful volume.

I could go on and on with examples of writing that carry the marks of what I've called the postmodern turn, including the turn to genre-shifting and even genre-busting. You can no doubt provide plenty of examples of your own. But I should restrain myself and, instead, try to draw a few conclusions. I might ask, first of all, as I suggested I would in the title of this talk, "What's in a name?" What is at stake, that is, in generic designations? At a colloquium I attended recently on "creative nonfiction," one of the writers present answered this way: "What is at stake is money and publication. The essay is 'hot' right now. For every poem or story I can get accepted, I can get ten essays out there. It comes down at some level to how much I want to eat."

Let me take it as a given that creative nonfiction is on the rise and ask what conclusions we can and should draw from this fact. I would like to suggest two pedagogically-related ones. First, the readers and anthologies we use in our classes need to reflect the characteristics of the postmodern turn I've tried to identify here, including genre-shifting as well as self-reflexivity and analysis, the recognition of constructedness and what I've called the artifice of the everyday.

Second, we should take these shifting genres into our own classrooms and challenge our students to experiment. Certainly we must teach them to explore and learn about the disciplinary genres that are quite literally disciplining and shaping them, and to which they must sometimes conform. But, in addition, I believe we must also offer them the pleasure of un-disciplinarity, of the kind of pushing at the disciplinary and generic boundaries that the writers I have just mentioned enjoy. In her lovely essay, the one I quoted from earlier, Wendy Bishop evokes Winston Weathers and his book *An Alternate Style*. I agree with Wendy that Weathers's book is underappreciated and undertaught. In it, he identifies ways in which students can take advantage of what I'm calling the pleasures of un-disciplinarity, of pushing generic and stylistic boundaries and conventions, and calls the style they adopt in doing so Grammar B as opposed to the Grammar A of standard academic English. Weathers demonstrates that Grammar B has been around at least since *Tristram Shandy*, and he urges students to try their hands at such texts. In the spirit of Weathers's book and of the other works I have been quoting, I want to conclude with a piece of writing by one of my students, one who had read *An Alternate Style* and was writing an essay that would call into question traditional uses of tropes and grammatical terms at the same time that it would celebrate Weathers and give a tongue-in-cheek narrative of her own childhood. Her piece of writing is called "B-ing There," recalling both Weathers's Grammar B and Jerzi Kozinski's novel *Being There*.

> I was born on May 14, 1963 in a well-made perfectly box-shaped hospital in Sri Lanka. My first memory was of a unified, coherent, and emphatically constructed crib which had four perfectly equal sides and dangling modifiers that hung enticingly above.... As I got older, I was upgraded to a room of my own, with a well-made box-spring bed, simile to that of my siblings. My life, really, was perfectly structured: everything had

clear reference and agreement; nothing was without purpose; and we all seemed to have appositive outlook on life. But then, when I was about six, my brother was caught throwing garbage at the mayor's front steps and charged with alliteration. His sentence, we were told, would be compound-complex....

We shouldn't ask our students to practice such experiments, however, if our textbooks send just the opposite message. Yesterday, the President's Forum featured three authors of college-level readers, each of which includes a wide range of writing and writing styles. My co-editor on *The Presence of Others*, John Ruszkiewicz, spoke about the genesis of our text and about our hopes for the kinds of student reading and writing the text may evoke. I'd like only to add that for some of the reasons I've noted here, we include a wide range of genres in *The Presence of Others*—short stories and interviews, magazine articles and advertisements and parodies—every chapter concludes with a poem. We also include pieces that push against generic boundaries and that use what Winston Weathers calls Grammar B. I very much hope that one of the results of what I've been calling the rise of nonfiction prose will be that our students get in on all this fun, that they have a chance to follow Emily Dickinson's always sage advice to tell the truth, but tell it slant—for there may be no other way, after all, to tell it at all.

Works Cited

Abbot, Lee. "Makin' Whoopee." *Epoch* 43.3 (1994): 263–72.

Bell-Scott, Patricia, et al., eds. *Double Stitch: Black Women Write about Mothers and Daughters*. Boston: Beacon, 1991.

Bishop, Wendy. "If Winston Weathers Would Just Write to Me on E-mail." *CCC* 46.1 (1995): 97–103.

Bruner, Jerome. "Research Currents: Life as Narrative." *Language-Arts* 65.6 (1988): 574–83.

Holloway, Karla. *Codes of Conduct: Race, Ethics, and the Color of Our Character.* (forthcoming)

Leonardi, Susan. "Recipes for Reading: Summer Pasta, Riseholme, and Key Lime Pie." *PMLA* 104.3 (1989): 340–47.

Lunsford, Andrea, and Robert Connors. "Frequency of Formal Errors in Current College Writing, or Ma and Pa Kettle Do Research." *CCC* 39 (1988): 395–409.

Lunsford, Andrea, and John Ruszkiewicz. *The Presence of Others*. New York: St. Martin's, 1994.

McPhee, John. "The Search for Marvin Gardens." *Pieces of The Frame*. New York: Farrar, Straus, and Giroux, 1975.

Owens, Derek. *Resisting Writings (and the Boundaries of Composition)*. Dallas: Southern Methodist UP, 1994.

"Soft Ions." Written by Racter, a computer owned by Bill Chamberlain.

Spellmeyer, Jurt. "Dilettantes, Professionals, and Knowledge." *College English* 56.7 (1994): 788–809.

Tompkins, Jane. "Me and My Shadow." *New Literary History: A Journal of Theory and Interpretation* 19.1 (1987): 169–78.

Weathers, Winston. *An Alternate Style*. Rochelle Park, NJ: Hayden, 1980.

Williams, Patricia. *The Alchemy of Race and Rights: Diary of a Law Professor*. Cambridge, MA: Harvard UP, 1991.

One Writer's Secrets

Donald M. Murray

It is good form in English department offices and corridors to grump, grouse, growl, even whine about how the writing is going. Such labor, such a dreary business, how grubby, how ridiculous to expect publication, as if an article could reveal the subtleties of a finely tuned mind. The more you publish, the more tactful it is to moan and groan. The danger is that young colleagues, new to the academy, may believe us. They may think we who publish are performing penance, obediently fulfilling a vow to publish out of fear of perishing, when this academic and others will slyly look around to see who is listening, then confess, "writing is fun."

The focus is on writing. That is where writers discover they know more than they knew they knew, where accidents of diction or syntax reveal meaning, where sentences run ahead to expose a thought. If the writing is done, publication—perhaps not this piece but the next or the one after that—will follow. And publishing promises a lifetime of exploration and learning, active membership in a scholarly community, and the opportunity for composition teachers to practice what we preach.

I will share some of the methods that have helped me publish what some would say—and have said—is an excessive number of articles and books on the composing process. I do not do this to suggest that others should work as I work, but as a way to invite others who publish to reveal their own craft so those who join our profession can become productive members of it—and share the secret pleasure in writing which we feel but rarely admit.

Attitudes That Allow Writing

Our attitudes usually predict and limit our accomplishments. I find that I have to encourage, model, and continually relearn certain attitudes if I want my students to write—and if I want myself to write.

- No publication is the final theological word on a subject. Too many academics believe they have to write *the* article or book on their topic. That is impossible. Each publication is merely a contribution to a continuous professional conversation. I was paralyzed by the idea I had to deliver the Truth—Moses-like; I began to write when I realized all I had to do was speculate, question, argue, create a model, take a position, define a problem, make an observation, propose a solution, illuminate a possibility to participate in a written conversation with my peers. There is an increasing emphasis on research, but still it is not necessary to wait to report on the ultimate, all-inclusive research project.

- There is no need to be consistent. Learning does not stop with publication. I continue to learn from my students, my colleagues, my reading, my observations, my researches, my teaching, and my writing. I learn from each draft. Change is essential to learning. Of course, I will contradict myself from time to time.

- Ask your own questions and find your own answers. Few people talked about the writing process when I started publishing in this field. No matter, it was what interested me. I didn't think my articles would get published, but I sent them off, and most of them were.

- Use the mail. My articles, poems, and short stories that don't get into the mail never get published. Submit. Maybe you'll find an editor who is suffering empty journal terror. We like to believe that all acceptances are rational and all rejections irrational. I've learned from participating on both sides of the process that acceptances are often as irrational as rejections.

- Start at the top. Maybe the best journals will not publish my stuff, but at least they've had their chance.

- Remember what Al Pacino said: "Forget the career and do the work." The doing is far more satisfying than the done. The discoveries made during the writing— the thinking process—are far more exciting than receiving half a dozen copies of a journal with your article in it a year or two later.

- If it isn't fun, don't do it. The lack of fun will show. Since both acceptance and rejection are irrational, you might as well have the satisfaction of doing what you want to do. We are lucky to have a vocation of scholarship, a calling. But who is calling? Ourselves. We are all self-appointed authorities. If our work is not our play, then we should quit, take a job, and make some real money.

Some Tricks of the Academic Trade

As you develop the attitudes that will allow you to publish, then you may be able to develop techniques and strategies that help get the work done. Some tricks of my trade are:

- Keep a planning notebook with you to play in at the office, at home, in the car, on the airplane, at faculty meetings (especially at faculty meetings), while you're watching television, sitting in a parking lot, or eating a lonely lunch. Such play has allowed me to write on the advantages of writer's block, to catch a glimpse of ideas about planning and vision, which have become talks, articles, and sections of my books. I pay most attention to the questions that keep reoccurring, the connections that surprise me, the patterns that give the familiar an interesting unfamiliarity.

The notebook, which I call a daybook, will make it possible for you to use fragments of time, and fragments of time are all that most of us really have. Fifteen minutes, ten, five, two, one, less. In this book you can make lists, notes, diagrams, collect the quotes and citations, paste in key articles and references, sketch outlines, draft titles, leads, endings, key paragraphs that will make it possible for you to be ready to write when you have an hour, or two, or three clear.

- Write daily. I try to follow the counsel of Horace, Pliny, Trollope, Updike: *nulla dies sine linea*—never a day without a line—but a line for me does not mean a polished sentence of finished prose. It means the daily habit of talking to myself in writing, playing with ideas, letting a piece of writing grow and ripen until it is ready to be written. It is intellectual play, self-indulgent, introspective, and immensely satisfying. Each time I play with an idea I purposely do not look back at my previous notes. Then, after I finish the daily entry, I look back to see what I'd said on the same subject before and add ideas that seem worth adding. In this way I keep turning over the compost of my thoughts and discover what I didn't know I knew.

  The academic schedule encourages the illusion that you can get your writing done on the day free from teaching, during the semester with a lower teaching load, between semesters, next summer, or on sabbatical. Nonsense. When those times come you can't suddenly take up an alien craft. The productive scholar is in the habit of writing, at least notes, at least lists, at least fragmentary drafts, at least something that keeps the topic alive and growing so that writing will come that is ready to be written.

  If I have a good title; a well-honed first sentence, paragraph, or page; a hint of the ending; a list of three to five points that will lead me toward that end, I can put a draft on hold, for weeks, if necessary, and not lose the freshness of the first draft that will follow.

- Pick the best time for your writing and try to protect that time. Be selfish. Writing is the best preparation for teaching. I schedule my teaching in the afternoon, which is my normal slump period. In the afternoon I respond to the stimulus of the class, the conference, or the meeting. But only in the morning do I respond to the stimulus of the blank page.

  My most difficult problem is to keep the moat around my writing time filled with alligators and absolutely terrifying snakes. I do not spring out of bed ready and eager to write. I need time I can waste in which my subconscious can prepare itself for the period at the writing desk. And I need time on the other end of the writing period. If I start to write too close to when I have to be at school, the demands of teaching invade my mind and I cannot concentrate on the writing task. Bernard Malamud described this too rare concentration best when he said,

"If it is winter in the book, spring surprises me when I look up." Concentration is not only important for the work but to the mental health of the worker. My agent did not want me to accept a teaching job. I think she said it would be like "being bitten to death by ducks." I didn't know how wise she was. It was far easier to achieve concentration in the confusion of the city room on deadline than in the distracting, fragmented academic world. Wasn't it Mencken who said, "Campus politics are so vicious because the stakes are so low"? The hardest thing I do is to find time, to sit, to wait, to listen for writing.

- Read widely as well as deeply; read writing as well as writing about writing. Our training teaches us to read critically and narrowly, and it is vital to probe deeply into a specialty or a text. The best ideas, however, come from connecting information from different disciplines. We should also be bottom-feeders, gobbling up everything that comes our way—reading a book on science, a line of poetry, a newspaper story, a picture in a museum, a question by a student, a move by a hockey player, a pattern of music, a comment overheard in an elevator, the look on a face seen from a bus window, reading our world in such a way that our scholarly work is fed by connections from the world, so that the work we do is in context. If it is fed by the world, it may, if we are effective, return to feed the world.

- Keep a list of questions to which you want to seek answers, answers for which you wish to form questions, territories of fascinating ignorance you wish to explore. How do writers choose and use test readers? How does thinking style affect writing process? How does a writing task change process? Does MTV have a positive influence on the writing or reading process? How do good student writers read their evolving drafts? Keep moving around, and don't be trapped in your own specialty. Some people took my work on revision more seriously than I took it myself, and I consciously moved toward studying prewriting. Use your list to turn class presentations, invitations to give talks and workshops, opportunities to publish articles or chapters or books to your own advantage. Set your own agenda, so that each year you sniff along two or three new trails of thought.

- Put yourself on the spot. Accept teaching, speaking, and writing assignments that are just beyond reach—but within reach. Join local, regional, and national organizations within our discipline and participate so that you become a working member of the profession. In this way you will learn what others are doing and you will have a balance wheel to counter the niggling problems within your own department that can so easily get out of proportion.

- Respect your own judgment. Of course, you should be aware of the scholarship that has preceded you, but pay close attention to what you see with your own eyes, hear with your own ears, think with your own mind. Ours is not only a profession of confirmation but also of exploration. I have published personal answers to my own questions about how writers read and write, not so much to provide answers as to provoke research, since I have found few people dealing with questions in our discipline which I believe are obvious—and fundamental. If I publish my guesses, others may respond with their truths.

- Write for yourself. Don't try to figure out what other people want but try to figure out what you have to say and how it can be best said. The standards for academic writing are contradictory and confused. In many cases what is considered to be the standard forces bad writing. Most editors want good writing. Decide how best to say what you have to say. You may have to compromise your voice to be published in some journals that require educationese or excessive formality, but certainly do not compromise in advance and write in a parody of academic writing. Submit writing that is as clear and graceful as you can make it.
- Write early. Remember that you are not writing the ultimate article that will cause all other scholars to pack up their tents and go home. Write early to find out what you know and what you need to know. Publish early to participate in the game of academic exploration. You will learn by committing yourself and by developing colleagues in other schools who are interested in the same topics.
- Yet be patient. This is hard for me under any circumstances, for I was born twitching to get on with it, whatever it was. It is often difficult for a young faculty member under the threat of tenure. To be patient, it is important to develop a pace appropriate to the work you are doing. It takes time for ideas to be planted and cultivated. There has to be a habit of work that allows this to happen. Those of us who publish extensively are harvesting what has been put down years before.

    Most of my articles have a five-year history. It takes about a year for my reading and thinking and conversing and note making to work their way toward a topic which is more interesting than I had expected. Once I recognize the topic's potential significance I play around with it for at least a year, taking advantage of opportunities to talk on the subject or to teach it. I receive reactions from my colleagues and my students, and then in the third year I may accept a chance to give a paper or to attempt an article. Now I begin to plan in earnest. My play becomes more intense, and eventually there is a paper or a draft. My colleagues, often my students, and my editors or audiences react. In the fourth year it is usually rewritten and edited. And in the fifth year it is published. And to those who do not work continually, it appears as if I had suddenly produced another piece of work, when it is really the product of a rather plodding habit of thinking through writing.

- Write to discover what you have to say. You do not have to know what you want to say to be able to say it. Just the opposite. You have to write to find out what you have to say. This is the never-ending attraction of writing. We write more than we intend to write, reaching beyond our goals, finding within ourselves how much more we know than we thought we knew. We need to write drafts with such speed and intensity that they propel us toward unexpected possibility. Then we can learn from those drafts as we revise and clarify. We are, first of all, students to our own writing.
- Write without notes. Much academic writing is poor because it is note-bound. Write out of what is in your head; write what you remember from your notes. What you forget is probably what should be forgotten, but you will have time

after the draft is completed to go back and check your notes. If you absolutely have to have key references in front of you, use as few as possible in producing the first draft in which speed and flow produce both grace and the unexpected connections which are the mark of good thinking and good writing.

- Lower your standards. I carry two paragraphs of counsel from poet and teacher William Stafford with me at all times and turn to them morning after morning:

> I believe that the so-called "writing block" is a product of some kind of disproportion between your standards and your performance.... One should lower his standards until there is no felt threshold to go over in writing. It's *easy* to write. You just shouldn't have standards that inhibit you from writing.
>
> I can imagine a person beginning to feel that he's not able to write up to that standard he imagines the world has set for him. But to me that's surrealistic. The only standard I can rationally have is the standard I'm meeting right now.... You should be more willing to forgive yourself. It really doesn't make any difference if you are good or bad today. The *assessment* of the product is something that happens *after* you've done it.

- Write easily. If it doesn't come, don't force it. Forced writing reads like forced writing. Putter. Fiddle around. Stare out the window. Keep coming back until your head is ready to produce the writing almost without effort. Hard writing usually means that you're not ready to write. You have to start the writing process early enough ahead of deadline to allow the essential backing up—the planning and rehearsal that will eventually allow the draft to flow. As Virginia Woolf said, "I am going to hold myself from writing it till I have it impending in me: grown heavy in my mind like a ripe pear; pendant, gravid, asking to be cut or it will fall."

- Write with your ear. Writers feel that the voice may be the most important element in writing, and few writers will proceed until they hear the voice of the text. Voice is the magic ingredient in writing. It carries all the meanings that are not within the world. It allows the individual writer to speak to the individual reader. It is style and grace and tone, and it reveals the character of the writer as well as the content of the text.

    Listen for a voice in fragments of writing in your notebook, in lines rehearsed in your head, in early drafts. Your voice will help you understand what you have to say and how you have to say it, and a strong voice will be the element that will make significant content available to your colleagues. It will bring you publication, and publication will bring you the opportunity for further exploration.

- Write writing. Try a poem, a familiar essay that can be published on the editorial page of a newspaper, a novel, a TV or movie script, a magazine article, a short story, a news story, a play. The experience of writing writing, not just writing about writing, will help the soul, the scholarship, and the craft. The poem may not be anthologized, but it may reveal a leap of language, a turn of a line that will free your prose and allow the poet's skills of grace and clarification that are so often missing from academic writing.

- Reach out to colleagues. This will be your most difficult—and the most valuable—professional activity. The academic world can be a closed place, a landscape of monasteries and convents, moated castles and isolated villages. Even when I am intimidated by the walls and parapets erected by colleagues I try to remember how lonely they must be, imprisoned within their knowledge and high standards.

    Invite colleagues to lunch, suggest a cup of coffee, ask a colleague to visit your class, set up brown bag lunches of colleagues to share common interests, arrange team teaching, travel together to conventions. Most of all, reach out by sharing your own drafts. I have received insult, scorn, ridicule, jocular remarks that burn like acid, and, worst of all, silence. And for many good reasons. Most of us do not know how to respond, and we are all busy. But through this reaching out in my own department, across my campus, to colleagues I meet at meetings, to students and former students, to friends in other fields, I begin to develop a small group of helpful colleagues in each of the areas in which I work. I share work with them; they share work with me. They know how to give me criticism. But even more important, they know how to give me strength and support. They know because they are writing, are exposed and vulnerable in the same way I am. If we can discover the attitudes and the techniques that allow us to write we will experience the joy of writing. First will come the lonely surprises that occur on the page. A life of writing is a life of learning. There are the tiny discoveries that may not shake the universe but that may bring a grin or sometimes even a laugh of victory from the academic at the desk. Writing is more likely than teaching to produce an active intellectual life and to be a defense against boredom, burnout, and age. The writer can always ask new questions and draft new answers, can always explore new territories and experience new genres.

Writing is also an extension of teaching and a stimulation to teaching. Our students, wave after wave, may change their lingo and their dress, but they remain at the same intellectual level when they come to us. We need to be practitioners of our discipline if we are to stay alive and if we are to bring new ideas to our teaching. Publishing allows us to belong to a large community of scholars. We can contribute to that community, and the more we put in, the more we will take away that is of value to both ourselves and our students. Publication obviously has its rewards—promotion, tenure, occasional recognition in an elevator at a convention, and even royalties, although most books I have produced have never made their advance. But the more you experience those rewards, the more you realize that the real satisfaction comes during the process of the writing itself. The true rewards are internal—the satisfaction of asking your own questions and finding your own answers.

Collage, Montage, Mosaic, Vignette, Episode, Segment

Robert L. Root, Jr.

It's a common problem among student writers, starting too far back in the narrative or trying to encompass too much time or too much activity in a single chronology. A paper about high school begins at the moment the writer entered the building for the first time in ninth grade and moves inexorably toward the moment of graduation, growing more perfunctory year by year; a paper about making the team or the cheerleading squad presents a minute by minute account of decision, preparation, and competition that loses more and more energy the longer it goes on.

But it isn't just a novice writer's problem alone. Any writer runs up against the insidious demands of linear presentation of material whenever he or she selects chronology—from the beginning to the end, from the first step through each individual step to the final step, from the inception through the planning and execution to the result—as the organizing principle of an essay or article. Linear schemes of organization come easily to us. We all tell stories and chronology is the simplest system of organization ("We began by…, then we…, and finally…"); process is the most accessible scheme of exposition ("First you…, next you…, and you conclude by…"); linear movement structures description the most directly ("Her hair was the color…her feet spilling out of tattered sandals"; "On the east side of the building…in the middle was…on the west side we saw"). But linear schemes don't automatically help with issues of compression and focus, particularly in an age of increasingly shorter attention spans and little patience for leisurely development of plot and character and theme.

The more complex the story is, the more interwoven with other subjects, ideas, incidents, experiences, the harder it is to make it all connect in a linear way that doesn't extend the narrative or the development beyond the patience of writer and reader alike. Moreover, the connections and associations that come so readily in the memory and in the imagination often defy simple linearity, easy transition from one subtopic to the next, when the writer has to force them into words on a page.

Mike, now past fifty, has been cleaning his mental attic for the past several years, rummaging through his souvenirs and writing essays about a lifetime playing sports—the high school pitching, the conflicts with coaches, the visits to historic ballparks. Now he begins an essay about how he came to give up his annual summer stint as manager and player for a fastpitch softball team.

He starts an early draft with a brief scene set in the present which serves as the trigger for a flashback that gives him the opportunity to review his long career with the team. "It's a lazy summer evening and I'm driving home from campus," he begins, and then tells how his weariness momentarily vanishes when he notices a game in progress at the ball park where he used to play: "for a moment I want to jump out of the car, climb into my softball uniform, and trot out to my old position in left field." He describes gazing at the field and continuing home. After these two brief paragraphs of introduction, he introduces the past in the third paragraph: "That night while reading my mind wanders, and for a suspended moment it is 1969 again. That summer, I was…" From here he relies on the act of composing itself to help him rediscover the subject matter. Chronology decides the order. He traces the arc of his involvement from the moment he decided to join the team, and one memory provokes another until he reaches his last game and the end of the draft.

By then he has covered a lot of ground. His draft surfaces deep-seated feelings about playing ball, about giving it up, about the satisfactions of moving on to new places in his life and expending his energies elsewhere. But it takes a long time to get to the place where these important and powerful feelings get voiced, because so much detail has emerged in his review of the chronology—early days on the team, the change from player to manager, road trips, destinations, the interaction with players, the near-misses for spots in regional and state tournaments, the interests that distracted him from the game, the aging processes that slowed him down. In the associative links of memory every detail makes sense, makes connections, but on the page the slow linear march of the chronology dissipates all the emphatic force of the narrative—there's a reason no one is proposing to cash in on the natural disaster film genre ("Twister," "Volcano") with a movie called "Glacier!" These narrative elements establish not only theme but also tone and voice, and many of them need to stay in the next draft, but he knows that he needs to lift scenes out of this linear history and highlight them as well as give more emphasis to the final summer.

His revision starts almost at the end of the previous draft, placing him on the road to the final tournament. "It's three A.M. Friday Labor Day weekend 1985. I left Sutton's Bay at ten P.M. headed for Houghton, which is about as far as driving to Nashville. I'm wearing my softball uniform and my wife Carole is asleep in the back seat, cotton balls stuffed in each ear while the tape deck blasts out a medley of Beach Boys and Beatles tunes—my favorite road music." But the present-tense narrative of that summer experience has barely begun before Mike inserts a paragraph break, white space on the page signaling a shift of scene or time, and in the past tense recounts his initial involvement with the softball team years before. A page later he inserts another break and shifts back to the present tense and the immediate circumstance to establish that he and his wife have plane tickets for Paris that conflict with the tournament dates (a point of information barely mentioned in the earlier draft's conclusion) and that they have put off foreign travel in the past to be available for championships that never materialized. The dramatic tension in this conflict makes the reader wonder from the beginning which option they will take in the end. Telling this part of the essay in present tense heightens that tension and establishes a sense of immediacy about the experience, as if the outcome had not been decided long ago.

Throughout the remainder of the essay past tense vignettes of a softball life alternate with present tense scenes from the decisive summer. Paragraph breaks allow Mike to crosscut between the past and the present and to ignore connections and transitions in either chronology. When he has finished his revisions, he has avoided the linear chronology that bogged down his earlier draft and achieved a tight, dense essay with more dramatic and pointed individual segments. The overall effect of the essay is the same he had hoped to achieve in the earlier draft, but it is more focused and consequently more powerful.

The white spaces on the page—the page breaks or paragraph breaks—are part of the composition. They serve as fade outs/fade ins do in films, as visual cues that we have ended one sequence and gone on to another. Often, somewhere in the early part of each segment, a word or phrase serves as a marker indicating the change of time or place, very much as a superimposed title on a movie scene might inform the viewer: "Twelve years later. Northern Michigan," to suggest that a lot has happened since the screen went dark and a new image began to emerge.

In almost any contemporary collection of creative nonfiction, many selections are segmented, sectioned off by white spaces or rows of asterisks or subheadings in italics or boldface. A thematic issue of the travel narrative journal *Grand Tour* has no unsegmented essays. In a recent essay issue of *Ploughshares*, fourteen of the twenty-three essays are segmented by paragraph breaks or, occasionally, some more pronounced method of subdividing. In a similar issue of *American Literary Review*, fifteen out of nineteen essays are segmented, their segments separated by rows of diamonds or white spaces, divided by subheadings, or numbered; only four essays are completely unsegmented.

In some of the *ALR* essays the segmenting in the fifteen is barely noticeable, almost a printer's convention rather than an actual break in the flow of thought or language; in most, however, the segmenting is emphatic, crucial. William Holz numbers his thirteen segments in "Brother's Keeper: An Elegy" and begins eleven of them with the same sentence, "My brother now is dead," usually as the main clause in sentences with varying subordinate or coordinate elements. The repetitions give the segments the power of incantation or prayer. Lynne Sharon Schwartz, writing about translating the book *Smoke Over Birkenau*, begins her essay with a series of English words she listed in an Italian edition of the book—the opening line reads: "Strenuous. Grim. Resolute. Blithe. Alluring. Cringe. Recoil. Admonish." Occasional excerpts from the list interrupt the essay from time to time in place of asterisks or numbers or subheadings between segments ("Haggard. Cantankerous. Imploring. Dreary. Plucky. Banter. Superb. Vivacious. Snarling. Prattled."). Frederick Smock's "Anonymous: A Brief

Memoir" opens with a section of Gwendolyn Brooks's poem, "Jane Addams," and is divided into segments subtitled by locations in his anonymous subject's home: "The Great-Room," "The Landing," "The Dining Room," "The Grotto," and so on. Paul Gruchow's "Eight Variations on the Idea of Failure" has eight numbered sections with self-contained vignettes of varying length that thematically explore the subject of failure. These are essays that call attention to their segmentation; they announce very early on to the reader that progress through them will not be linear, although it may be sequential, and that the force of the segments will come from their juxtaposition with one another and the effect of their accumulation by the end.

These are not traditional essays, the kind that composition textbooks usually teach you to write, the kind that begin with some sort of thesis statement, then march through a linked, linear series of supporting, illustrative paragraphs to a predictable, forceful conclusion. Textbooks tend to teach either the unattainable and ideal or the undesirable but teachable. The segmented essay has been with us for quite some time and may well be the dominant mode of the contemporary essay, but we are only just beginning to recognize it and try to teach it.

Shaken by her son's death in the crash of his Air Force jet, Carol sets out to retrace the path of his life. She and her husband drive from Michigan across the country to California, and then come back by way of the southeastern United States, all the while trying to connect to the life he led in scattered places. Throughout the trip she keeps a journal of her travels and eventually decides to write an essay about the journey.

As she begins writing, she finds herself hampered by the amount of detail she has accumulated about the trip, about her son's life, about her reactions to each location. So much information seems relevant and interrelated that it is difficult for her to be inclusive and yet get to the end of both the essay and the trip, where the real significance of her pilgrimage comes home to her. It is a trip of several weeks and thousands of miles and, unless she is to make it booklength, which she doesn't want to do, she needs to find another way to come at this mass of strongly felt material.

Eventually she discovers the key to the composing in the materials on which she bases the essay: the narrative of the trip, the reflections in her private journal, the references to her son's life. Alternating among episodes of narration, reflection, and reference, she uses the separate strands of her materials to comment on one another and to justify her breaking off one segment to move to another. The essay begins with a passage of narration and description about the onset of the journey ("We need this trip like the desert needs rain. For months the dining area has looked like a war games planning room with maps everywhere."); it is followed by an excerpt from her journal remarking on how she feels a few days later, set in italics to identify it immediately as separate from the narrative *("June 7. Badlands. Last night when we walked back to our campsite in true dark, stars in the sky notwithstanding, we became disoriented.")*; this is followed by description of another location, further down the road ("In Wyoming, as we drive north toward Sheridan, we watch antelope standing far off…"); then another excerpt from the journal; then a section reflecting her son's experiences ("Kirk loved Wyoming. In 1976 his father and I took him and his brother and sister to Yellowstone…"), and so on throughout the essay. Paragraph breaks between segments and changes in font make it easy for the reader to follow the shifts and jumpcuts. It becomes a travel montage with "voiceover" commentary and an alternating strand of personal history. The juxtaposition of landscape, biography, and commentary move us more quickly through the essay than full linear chronology could do, and yet the chronology is there, a beginning, a middle, and an end, given an almost cinematic force by the accumulation of a series of concentrated segments.

The recognition of the segmented form, if not the form itself, is so new that we have not yet settled on a name for it. At present it is most often called a "collage" essay, a term coined by Peter Elbow, referring to the technique in visual art of assembling disparate images into an integrated whole which expresses a specific theme (like the "American Dream" collage) through the interrelationships of the parts. Some use the filmmaking term "montage," the editing technique that arranges a series of shots and images into an expressive sequence. Carl Klaus, who has mulled over the terminology and objected to both collage and montage, has suggested "disjunctive" (as opposed to the more unified and "conjunctive" linear form), which he admits may have negative connotations, or "paratactic" (a grammatical term for "segments of discourse" arranged without connections or transitions), which may be too obscure. Rebecca Blevins Faery has described the form as "fragmented" and "polyphonic." At times all these terms seem applicable to some essays and not to others, perhaps because segmented essays tend to invent their own forms, not merely imitate established forms.

Take, for example, "The Ideal Particle and the Great Unconformity" by Reg Saner. In this complex essay, Saner connects two terms from geology which identify two different concepts of scale. The ideal particle is the term for a grain of sand one tenth of a millimeter, "the size most easily airborne in wind, thus the likeliest to begin a surface effect known as saltation," where one grain strikes other grains with enough force to make them capable of becoming airborne (163); the Great Unconformity is a gigantic gap in the geological record, a place where, following the Grand Canyon walls down the deposits of millennia, you encounter a layer so much older than the layer above it that 1,200 million years of deposits must have been erased before the layers you have been following were laid down. The Great Unconformity was created by the erosive power of the ideal particle and the enormity of the span of time in the life of the planet.

But Saner is not simply explaining these two concepts as a geology textbook might readily do in a paragraph or two. Rather, he is attempting to give the reader some sense of the scale involved here as well as what it is like to experience the scale. Thus, while the essay discusses the history of geological studies and major markers for dating the planet, it also has a personal narrative running through it. Saner recounts a hike into the Grand Canyon, alternating speculations and observations about geological theory and evidence with vignettes of encounters with other hikers. In order to understand the subject of the essay as Saner understands it, the reader has to experience it with him, not simply have it explained to him.

> Slowly we accepted the curve of the earth. It dawned on us like a great change of mind, after which, earth's size came easy. Not its age. Evidence was everywhere underfoot, unmistakable. We chose not to see it.(154)

This opening segment is a brief verbal fanfare that sounds the theme of the essay. The segments that follow alternate exposition and argument with narration and description, taking the reader deeper and deeper into both the subject matter and the experience. We dig down through the segments, like layers of sedimentary deposits, the white spaces between segments marking them like layers of geologic time. Perhaps this is a geologic essay, then, or a tectonic essay, where the segments are like plates moving and colliding and rearranging themselves on the crust of the essay.

The ability to arrange and rearrange segments frees writers to generate unique forms. Mark Rudman has created a series of essays he refers to as "mosaics," such as his "Mosaic on Walking." The mosaic metaphor suggests an essay composed of little sections, like mosaic tiles, which create a larger picture by the way they are cumulatively arranged. For example, the opening tiles are these segments separated from one another by the grouting of white space:

> In this season I am often sulky, sullen, restless, withdrawn. I feel transparent, as if inhabited by the weather.

> Only while walking am I relieved from distress, only then, released from the burden of self, am I free to think. I wanted to say walking brings relief from tension without sadness and then I think it is not so—these walks bring their own form of *tristesse*. There is discomfort when movement stops.

> Though not exceptionally tall (a shade under six feet), I am a rangy, rambly walker. I take up a lot of space! (138)

In "Mosaic on Walking" the sequentiality of the arrangement is difficult to perceive; it might well have been written simply by composing a random number of segments which in some way relate to the theme of walking and then either haphazardly or systematically arranging them in a disjunctive or non-sequential order on the page—the way you might copy a list of sentences about walking in the order you discovered them in *Barlett's Familiar Quotations*. The mosaic, at least as Rudman uses it, seems lacking in design, capable of being read in any order, virtually devoid of transition or sequence; it uses an accumulation of associative segments to create mood or attitude. Maybe we should use the term "cumulative essays" or "associative essays."

But Nancy Willard, in "The Friendship Tarot," begins with the image of a tarot card arrangement on the page ("I lay out the cards of our friendship"). Each section of the essay which follows is named for a specific tarot card in that arrangement—The Child, The Journey, The Garden, The Book—and opens with a description of the picture on the card ("The card shows a child with chocolate on his face wandering through an art gallery in downtown Poughkeepsie devoted—for two weeks—to illustrations from children's books."). The segments lead us through the sequence of the tarot reading to get at issues of change and growth in a particular friendship. Perhaps it is a "tarot essay" but I don't know if the term applies to all segmented essays or, in all the history of essays, to her essay alone.

It isn't that collaging or segmenting abandons structure—it's that it builds essay structure in ways that may be organic with the subject, ways that may not be immediately recognizable but which incrementally explain themselves as the reader progresses through the essay. In the models of structure that composition textbooks traditionally provide, the ancient and venerable rhetorical topic of arrangement is handled by providing molds into which to pour the molten thought and language of the essay: comparison/contrast, thesis/support, process—all prefabricated shapes to be selected off the rack to fit the body of the topic—or the five-paragraph theme, the one-size-fits-all product of the rhetorical department store. The segmented essay, on the other hand, attempts a tailor-made design, a structure that may be appropriate only to itself.

I am at a writer's workshop in Montana, happy to be among a talented group of writers who have brought manuscripts on the outdoors and thrilled by my first experience in the Western mountains. In the mornings we workshop one another's manuscripts under Gretel Ehrlich's directions; in the afternoon we hike the foothills of the Bitterroot Range or raft the Bitterroot River or ramble the valley floor. Late at night or early in the morning I write in my journal about the workshop sessions and the hiking, particularly where I have gone and what I have seen. In the end I have records of three hiking expeditions, one that takes me only a little way up Blodgett Canyon, one that takes me to a falls a few miles up the Mill Creek Trail, and a third that brings me to the awesome Bear Creek overlook on the shoulder of a mountain. When I try to analyze my frustrations and satisfactions about those hikes, I begin to see the possibility of an essay coming out of the experience.

Back in Michigan after the workshop, tinkering sullenly with the critiqued manuscript, I drop everything and instead begin writing about my Montana hiking. I give the essay the working title "Bitterroot" but eventually call it "Knowing Where You've Been," a title inspired by a Norman Maclean's story about Blodgett Canyon which had helped me set a hiking destination in the first place. Perhaps because the other essays in the workshop have so often been segmented, divided into brief episodes or scenes or vignettes, I don't consider for a moment constructing an argumentative essay built around conclusions reached and made up of rationales for reaching them. At once I understand that I have come to the conclusions I have by taking three separate hikes, each of which went successively further into the wilderness, all of which culminated at the end of the final hike with a blissful moment of triumph and contentment, with a sense of arrival I hadn't had in the earlier hikes. I wonder if I can come at this by taking my reader through the three hikes with me, taking her deeper on each hike, leading her to the same moment and the same site of discovery that I reached. In brief, I wonder if I can somehow get the reader to reach my conclusions for herself by experiencing through my prose the same things I experienced.

This is risky, I know. Gretel Ehrlich's off-hand crack about the "plodding midwestern prose" of my workshop manuscript still chafes my ego like a fresh wound I can't stop picking at long enough to let heal. If I am to make my readers hike, the hiking better be brisk, lively, and limited, and each hike better be distinctive, so that it becomes clear why they've had to do three of them. I write the hikes in present tense, to make them feel more immediate, and I start them off the same way: I chip away at narrative that fills in the gaps of time between the hikes and tighten the prose for strength and speed. I also insert reflective interludes between the hikes, past tense segments responding to the hike just completed and pointing towards the next hike.

In the end the essay has five tight segments: hike ("The first afternoon. We walk the Blodgett Creek Trail"); interlude ("'When you look back at where you've been,' Norman Maclean writes, 'it often seems as if you have never been there or even as if there were no such place.'"); hike ("The second afternoon. We mill around after the morning workshop, plans shifting, destinations uncertain, finally resolving to go back into the mountains, to another trail."); interlude ("When I asked my friend from Montana about places to hike in the Bitterroot Valley, he looked thoughtful for a moment, shook his head, and said, 'Well, as early as you're going, there'll be too much snow to bag a peak.'"); hike ("The final afternoon. The morning workshop over, the group disperses for various tours and activities."). Each hike takes the narrator (and the reader) deeper into wilderness; each interlude raises issues that only an additional hike can resolve; the physical experiences of moving deeper and higher are echoed by intellectual and spiritual experiences, so that the physical moment of final achievement coincides with the spiritual moment of arrival. The successive drafts make me better understand exactly what it is I was feeling at the end of that hiking and push me to prepare the reader for that epiphany on the mountain ("It isn't how far at all but how deep. I need to go as deeply into wilderness as it takes before the wilderness comes into me.") in a way that makes it unnecessary for me to explain it afterward or add an epilogue of explication that breaks the reader down both physically and emotionally. The essay has to end on the mountain and the segmented format invites me to end it there.

The segmented essay makes demands not only on the writer but on the reader as well. Carl Klaus has noted how segments can be read both as isolated units and as reverberating links to other segments; it is "a strange reading experience, unlike that produced by any other kind of prose" which produces in him "an irresolvable tension between two different ways of reading and responding." From reading each segment "as a discrete entity as well as…in connection with its immediate neighbor," he finds that his "accumulating sense of recurrent or contrastive words, phrases, images, metaphors, ideas, topics, or themes" forces him to "intuitively mak[e] connections or distinctions between and among the segments, almost as if I were experiencing some of the very same associative leaps that might have provoked the essayist to write a piece in disjunctive form"(48). These "associative leaps" may replicate the fragmentary nature of "recollection and reflection" but they also suggest a willingness to accept unresolved or undefined associations.

Such writing demands that the reader learn to read the structure of the essay as well as its thought. That is a task for which the twentieth century reader is well prepared, because the episodic or segmented or disjunctive sequence is a familiar design in many other genres:

- the interrelated collection of short stories, for example, a concept suggested by Hemingway with the interludes between stories in *In Our Time* or carried out in Ray Bradbury's *The Martian Chronicles;*
- the playing with chronology and the episodic structure of novels like Milan Kundera's *The Unbearable Lightness of Being* and Kurt Vonnegut's *Slaughterhouse-Five;*

- cycles of thematically linked poems, each poem separate and independent but enriched by juxtaposition with poems on similar subjects or with similar perspectives;
- the "concept" album of interlinked songs—the Beatles' *Sgt. Pepper's Lonely Hearts Club Band* or the "suite" on half of *Abbey Road*, Pink Floyd's *The Wall*, or the more loosely thematic *Nebraska* and *Born In the USA* albums of Bruce Springsteen;
- sequences of brief scenes in motion pictures—Quentin Tarantino's *Pulp Fiction*, Gus Van Sant's *To Die For*, the recent critical favorites *The English Patient* and *Shine* all present their stories out of chronological sequence. In none of these is it hard to reconstruct the chronology, but telling the story in strict chronological order would have changed the emphases of these films. But even in strictly chronological films, the film progresses by sequences of shots or scenes, each separated from one another by visual cues as definite as chapter headings or theatrical intermissions.

Examples abound. It might be argued that the modern reader/viewer is more accustomed to disjunctiveness than to strict continuity.

I write this essay in segments. How can I explain what the segmented essay is like, or how it comes about, in an unsegmented essay?

I get up early in the morning to write, a common writer's habit. I am following a vague outline in my head of alternating segments—a more or less narrative example of someone composing a segmented essay alternating with a more or less expository section discussing the form. Practice alternates with theory. I have a lot of examples in mind that I think I might be able to use, and sometimes I type a section break or white space and insert a line of reference to spur my memory when I get to that segment ("Sandra's essay is giving her lots of trouble"; "I write this essay in segments"). Sometimes, by the time I reach that line, I have decided not to use it or have already used the example and I delete the line.

Some days I complete the draft of a segment in a single session, partly because I know I will have to revise it—go back to Mike's drafts to compare them again and to dig out more material for illustration, reread Carol's essay to refresh my memory about specific references, ask somebody about tarot readings, work on the concreteness of the language and clarity of the explanations. At first I am interested chiefly in having a structure to work in, and I have already cut and pasted segments in this draft to juxtapose them in different sequences.

Other days I only get through a portion of a segment. Some are harder than others to write, some have more detail, more development, quotes to look up and copy. I don't mind leaving them undone, because I think that when I return to them the next day my subconscious will have worked on them a little bit and it will be easier to launch into the drafting again. Even in an essay that isn't segmented we still work from section to section; it really isn't much different here.

And finally one morning when I feel I've said enough and need to worry less about finding something more to say than about finding ways to say what I've said better, I run off the full draft and try to work with what I have. Sometimes whole segments disappear or merge with others, sometimes new segments announce their necessity and have to be drafted and revised, sometimes the order of the segments changes again and again. I work harder on the language now, when I'm certain the ideas will stay. I am always reassured by a quote whose source may or may not have been Oscar Wilde: "I always revise everything eleven times, ten times to get the words right, and the eleventh time to put in that touch of spontaneity that everyone likes about my writing."

I teach creative nonfiction and composition classes, talk to friends about their essays, work on essays of my own. Sometimes I bring work in progress to my students, like a draft on men's rooms I photocopied, cut up, and distributed in pieces to see how different people would reassemble them and why. Often I advise other writers stuck in linearity and chronology, "Why don't you try collaging this?" I like making a verb of the noun, outraging any grammarians who overhear me.

I insist that my nonfiction students write at least one segmented essay during the term and provide such ways into the segmented essay as these:

- *definitions:* Simply explaining the segmented essay form calls up a range of alternatives: collage, montage, mosaic, vignette, episode, segment—all ways of approaching the form that suggest alternatives at that same time that they define distinctive forms.
- *models:* Readers respond to a handful of segmented essays with immediate understanding—Nancy Willard's "The Friendship Tarot," Annie Dillard's "Living Like Weasels," Susan Allen Toth's "Going to Movies," William Holtz's "Brother's Keeper," Naomi Shihab Nye's "Three Pokes of a Thistle," Reg Saner's "The Ideal Particle and the Great Unconformity."
- *strategies:* Segmented essays tend to go together in several different ways—

  - by juxtaposition, arranging one item alongside another item so that they comment back and forth on one another (Toth's "Going to Movies" is four vignettes, three dates with different men, the fourth a solitary trip to the theater);
  - by parallelism, alternating or intertwining one continuous strand with another (a present tense strand with a past tense strand, a domestic strand with a foreign strand, the alternate strands of a piece like "The Ideal Particle and the Great Unconformity");
  - by patterning, choosing an extra-literary design and arranging literary segments accordingly (as Willard does with tarot cards in "The Friendship Tarot" or Frederick Smock does with rooms in "Anonymous: A Brief Memoir");
  - by accumulation, arranging a series of segments or scenes or episodes so that they add or enrich or alter meaning with each addition, perhaps reinterpreting earlier segments in later ones, up to a final segment (as Holtz does in "Brother's Keeper");
  - by journaling, actually writing in episodes or reconstructing the journal experience in drafts (Sydney Lea asks students to write lyrical essays trying to connect disparate items in their journals; Gretel Ehrlich uses the journal form as a narrative device in many of her works, such as the recent "Cold Comfort").

In the classroom I make students cluster and list and map ideas, all of which encourage segmentation, separate items to work from. They produce partial or full rough drafts in whatever format they choose and then they help each other find ways of collaging or segmenting appropriate to the pieces they're working on. Once they're open to the possibility of the segmented essay, there's virtually no limit to the variations a roomful of imaginative young writers can bring to the form.

Collage, montage, mosaic, vignette, episode, segment—I've never found a descriptive term for anything that, if I pressed on it, wasn't somehow incapable of bearing the weight of definitive definition. I don't worry about the most accurate term for this kind of essay, because when one writer suggests to another, "Why don't you collage this?" the result may as much define the form as conform to it.

Works Cited

Best American Essays 1991. ed. Joyce Carol Oates. Series Editor: Robert Atwan. Boston: Ticknor and Fields, 1991.

Dillard, Annie. "Living Like Weasels." *Teaching a Stone to Talk: Expeditions and Encounters*. New York: Harper, 1982. 29–34.

Ehrlich, Gretel. "Cold Comfort." *Harper's* 294:1762 (March 1997): 34–44.

Elbow, Peter. *Writing With Power*. New York: Oxford University Press, 1981.

Faery, Rebecca Blevins. "Text and Context: The Essay and the Politics of Disjunctive Form." *What Do I Know? Reading, Writing, and Teaching the Essay*. ed. Janis Forman. Portsmouth, NH: Boynton/Cook, 1996. 55–68.

Grand Tour, "Virtues & Vices" 1:4 (Fall 1996).

Gruchow, Paul. "Eight Variations on the Idea of Failure." *Old Friends, New Neighbors: A Celebration of the American Essay, American Literary Review*. Ed. W. Scott Olsen. 5:2 (Fall 1994): 31–38.

Holtz, William. "Brother's Keeper: an Elegy." *Old Friends, New Neighbors: A Celebration of the American Essay, American Literary Review*. Ed. W. Scott Olsen. 5:2 (Fall 1994): 147–63.

Klaus, Carl H. "Excursions of the Mind: Toward a Poetics of Uncertainty in the Disjunctive Essay." *What Do I Know? Reading, Writing, and Teaching the Essay*. Ed. Janis Forman. Portsmouth, NH: Boynton/Cook, 1996. 39–53.

Nye, Naomi Shihab. "Three Pokes of a Thistle." *Never in a Hurry: Essays on People and Places*. Columbia: University of South Carolina Press, 1996. 26–31.

Old Friends, New Neighbors: A Celebration of the American Essay, American Literary Review. Ed. W. Scott Olsen. 5:2 (Fall 1994).

Ploughshares. Ed. Rosellen Brown. 20:2–3 (Fall 1994).

Rudman, Mark. "Mosaic on Walking." *The Best American Essays 1991*. Ed. Joyce Carol Oates. Boston: Ticknor and Fields, 1991:138–153.

Sanford, Carol. Unpublished essay ["Always Looking"].

Schwartz, Lynne Sharon. "Time Off to Translate." *Old Friends, New Neighbors: A Celebration of the American Essay, American Literary Review*. Ed. W. Scott Olsen. 5:2 (Fall 1994): 15–30.

Smock, Frederick. "Anonymous: A Brief Memoir." *Old Friends, New Neighbors: A Celebration of the American Essay, American Literary Review*. Ed. W. Scott Olsen. 5:2 (Fall 1994): 68–72.

Steinberg, Michael. Unpublished essay ["'I've Got It, No, You Take It': An Aging Ballplayer's Dilemma" and "On the Road Again: A Softball Gypsy's Last Go-Round"].

Toth, Susan Allen. "Going to the Movies." *How to Prepare for Your High-School Reunion and Other Midlife Musings*. New York: Ballantine Books, 1990. 108–112.

Willard, Nancy. "The Friendship Tarot." *Between Friends*. Ed. Mickey Pearlman. Boston: Houghton Mifflin, 1994. 195–203.

The Singular First Person

Scott Russell Sanders

The first soapbox orator I ever saw was haranguing a crowd beside the Greyhound Station in Providence, Rhode Island, about the evils of fluoridated water. What the man stood on was actually an upturned milk crate, all the genuine soapboxes presumably having been snapped up by antique dealers. He wore an orange plaid sports coat and matching bow tie and held aloft a bottle filled with mossy green liquid. I don't remember the details of his spiel, except his warning that fluoride was an invention of the Communists designed to weaken our bones and thereby make us pushovers for a Red invasion. What amazed me, as a tongue-tied kid of seventeen newly arrived in the city from the boondocks, was not his message but his courage in delivering it to a mob of strangers. I figured it would have been easier for me to jump straight over the Greyhound Station than to stand there on that milk crate and utter my thoughts.

To this day, when I read or when I compose one of those curious monologues we call the personal essay, I often think of that soapbox orator. Nobody had asked him for his two cents' worth, but there he was declaring it with all the eloquence he could muster. The essay, although enacted in private, is no less arrogant a performance. Unlike novelists and playwrights, who lurk behind the scenes while distracting our attention with the puppet show of imaginary characters, unlike scholars and journalists, who quote the opinions of others and shelter behind the hedges of neutrality, the essayist has nowhere to hide. While the poet can lean back on a several-thousand-year-old legacy of ecstatic speech, the essayist inherits a much briefer and skimpier tradition. The poet is allowed to quit after a few lines, but the essayist must hold our attention over pages and pages. It is a brash and foolhardy form, this one-man or one-woman circus, which relies on the tricks of anecdote, conjecture, memory, and wit to enthrall us.

Addressing a monologue to the world seems all the more brazen or preposterous an act when you consider what a tiny fraction of the human chorus any single voice is. At the Boston Museum of Science an electronic meter records with flashing lights the population of the United States. Figuring in the rate of births, deaths, emigrants leaving the country and immigrants arriving, the meter calculates that we add one fellow citizen every twenty-one seconds. When I looked at it recently, the count stood at 249,958,483. As I wrote that figure in my notebook, the final number jumped from three to four. Another mouth, another set of ears and eyes, another brain. A counter for the earth's population would stand somewhere past five billion at the moment, and would be rising in a blur of digits. Amid this avalanche of selves, it is a wonder that anyone finds the gumption to sit down and write one of those naked, lonely, quixotic letters-to-the-world.

A surprising number do find the gumption. In fact, I have the impression there are more essayists at work in America today, and more gifted ones, than at any time in recent decades. Whom do I have in mind? Here is a sampler: Wendell Berry, Carol Bly, Joan Didion, Annie Dillard, Stephen Jay Gould, Elizabeth Hardwick, Edward Hoagland, Phillip Lopate, Barry Lopez, Peter Matthiessen, John McPhee, Cynthia Ozick, Paul Theroux, Lewis Thomas, Tom Wolfe. No doubt you could make up a list of your own—with a greater ethnic range, perhaps, or fewer nature enthusiasts—a list that would provide equally convincing support for the view that we are blessed right now with an abundance of essayists. We do not have anyone to rival Emerson or Thoreau, but in sheer quantity of first-rate work our time stands comparison with any period since the heyday of the form in the mid-nineteenth century.

Why are so many writers taking up this risky form, and why are so many readers—to judge by the statistics of book and magazine publication—seeking it out? In this era of prepackaged thought, the essay is the closest thing we have, on paper, to a record of the individual mind at work and play. It is an amateur's raid in a world of specialists. Feeling overwhelmed by data, random information, the flotsam and jetsam of mass culture, we relish the spectacle of a single consciousness making sense of a portion of the chaos. We are grateful to Lewis Thomas for shining his light into the dark corners of biology, to John McPhee for laying bare the geology beneath our landscape, to Annie Dillard for showing us the universal fire blazing in the branches of a cedar, to Peter Matthiessen for chasing after snow leopards and mystical insights in the Himalayas. No matter if they are sketchy, these maps of meaning are still welcome. As Joan Didion observes in her own collection of essays, *The White Album,* "We live entirely, especially if we are writers, by the imposition of a narrative line upon disparate images, by the 'ideas' with which we have learned to freeze the shifting phantasmagoria which is our actual experience." Dizzy from a dance that seems to accelerate hour by hour, we cling to the narrative line, even though it may be as pure an invention as the shapes drawn by Greeks to identify the constellations.

The essay is a haven for the private, idiosyncratic voice in an era of anonymous babble. Like the bland-burgers served in their millions along our highways, most language served up in public these days is textureless, tasteless mush. On television, over the phone, in the newspaper, wherever humans bandy words about, we encounter more and more abstractions, more empty formulas. Think of the pablum ladled out by politicians. Think of the fluffy white bread of advertising. Think, lord help us, of committee reports. By contrast, the essay remains stubbornly concrete and particular: it confronts you with an oil-smeared toilet at the Sunoco station, a red vinyl purse shaped like a valentine heart, a bowlegged dentist hunting deer with an elephant gun. As

Orwell forcefully argued, and as dictators seem to agree, such a bypassing of abstractions, such an insistence on the concrete, is a politically subversive act. Clinging to this door, that child, this grief, following the zigzag motions of an inquisitive mind, the essay renews language and clears trash from the springs of thought. A century and a half ago, in the rousing manifesto entitled *Nature*, Emerson called on a new generation of writers to cast off the hand-me-down rhetoric of the day, to "pierce this rotten diction and fasten words again to visible things." The essayist aspires to do just that.

As if all these virtues were not enough to account for a renaissance of this protean genre, the essay has also taken over some of the territory abdicated by contemporary fiction. Whittled down to the bare bones of plot, camouflaged with irony, muttering in brief sentences and grade-school vocabulary, peopled with characters who stumble like sleepwalkers through numb lives, today's fashionable fiction avoids disclosing where the author stands on anything. In the essay, you had better speak from a region pretty close to the heart or the reader will detect the wind of phoniness whistling through your hollow phrases. In the essay you may be caught with your pants down, your ignorance and sentimentality showing, while you trot recklessly about on one of your hobbyhorses. You cannot stand back from the action, as Joyce instructed us to do, and pare your fingernails. You cannot palm off your cockamamie notions on some hapless character.

To our list of the essay's contemporary attractions we should add the perennial ones of verbal play, mental adventure, and sheer anarchic high spirits. To see how the capricious mind can be led astray, consider the foregoing paragraph, which drags in metaphors from the realms of toys, clothing, weather, and biology, among others. That is bad enough; but it could have been worse. For example, I began to draft a sentence in that paragraph with the following words: "More than once, in sitting down to beaver away at a narrative, felling trees of memory and hauling brush to build a dam that might slow down the waters of time...." I had set out to make some innocent remark, and here I was gnawing down trees and building dams, all because I had let that *beaver* slip in. On this occasion I had the good sense to throw out the unruly word. I don't always, as no doubt you will have noticed. Whatever its more visible subject, an essay is also about the way a mind moves, the links and leaps and jigs of thought. I might as well drag in another metaphor—and another unoffending animal—by saying that each doggy sentence, as it noses forward into the underbrush of thought, scatters a bunch of rabbits that go bounding off in all directions. The essayist can afford to chase more of those rabbits than the fiction writer can, but fewer than the poet. If you refuse to chase any of them, and keep plodding along in a straight line, you and your reader will have a dull outing. If you chase too many, you will soon wind up lost in a thicket of confusion with your tongue hanging out.

The pursuit of mental rabbits was strictly forbidden by the teachers who instructed me in English composition. For that matter, nearly all the qualities of the personal essay, as I have been sketching them, violate the rules that many of us were taught in school. You recall we were supposed to begin with an outline and stick by it faithfully, like a train riding its rails, avoiding sidetracks. Each paragraph was to have a topic sentence pasted near the front, and these orderly paragraphs were to be coupled end-to-end like so many boxcars. Every item in those boxcars was to bear the stamp of some external authority, preferably a footnote referring to a thick book, although appeals to magazines and newspapers would do in a pinch. Our diction was to be formal, dignified, shunning the vernacular. Polysyllabic words derived from Latin were preferable to the blunt lingo of the streets. Metaphors were to be used only in emergencies, and no two of them were to be mixed. And even in emergencies we could not speak in the first person singular.

Already as a schoolboy, I chafed against those rules. Now I break them shamelessly, in particular the taboo against using the lonely capital *I*. Just look at what I'm doing right now. My speculations about the state of the essay arise, needless to say, from my own practice as reader and writer, and they reflect my own tastes, no matter how I may pretend to gaze dispassionately down on the question from a hot-air balloon. As Thoreau declares in his cocky manner on the opening page of *Walden:* "In most books the *I*, or first person, is omitted; in this it will be retained; that, in respect to egotism, is the main difference. We commonly do not remember that it is, after all, always the first person that is speaking. I should not talk so much about myself if there were anybody else whom I knew as well." True for the personal essay, it is doubly true for an essay about the essay: one speaks always and inescapably in the first person singular.

We could sort out essays along a spectrum according to the degree to which the writer's ego is on display—with John McPhee, perhaps, at the extreme of self-effacement, and Norman Mailer at the opposite extreme of self-dramatization. Brassy or shy, center stage or hanging back in the wings, the author's persona commands our attention. For the length of an essay, or a book of essays, we respond to that persona as we would to a friend caught up in a rapturous monologue. When the monologue is finished, we may not be able to say precisely what it was about, any more than we can draw conclusions from a piece of music. "Essays don't usually boil down to a summary, as articles do," notes Edward Hoagland, one of the least summarizable of companions, "and the style of the writer has a 'nap' to it, a combination of personality and originality and energetic loose ends that stand up like the nap of a piece of wool and can't be brushed flat" ("What I Think, What I Am"). We make assumptions about that speaking voice, assumptions we cannot validly make about the narrators in fiction. Only a sophomore is permitted to ask if Huckleberry Finn ever had any children; but even literary sophisticates wonder in print about Thoreau's love life, Montaigne's domestic arrangements, De Quincey's opium habit, Virginia Woolf's depression.

Montaigne, who not only invented the form but nearly perfected it as well, announced from the start that his true subject was himself. In his note "To the Reader" at the beginning of the *Essays*, he slyly proclaimed:

> I want to be seen here in my simple, natural, ordinary fashion, without straining or artifice; for it is myself that I portray. My defects will here be read to the life, and also my natural form, as far as respect for the public has allowed. Had I been placed among those nations which are said to live still in the sweet freedom of nature's first laws, I assure you I should very gladly have portrayed myself here entire and wholly naked.

A few pages after this disarming introduction, we are told of the Emperor Maximilian, who was so prudish about exposing his private parts that he would not let a servant dress him or see him in the bath. The Emperor went so far as to give orders that he be buried in his underdrawers. Having let us in on this intimacy about Maximilian, Montaigne then confessed that he himself, although "bold-mouthed," was equally prudish, and that "except under great stress of necessity or voluptuousness," he never allowed anyone to see him naked. Such modesty, he feared, was unbecoming in a soldier. But such honesty is quite becoming in an essayist. The very confession of his prudery is a far more revealing gesture than any doffing of clothes.

A curious reader will soon find out that the word *essay*, as adapted by Montaigne, means a trial or attempt. The Latin root carries the more vivid sense of a weighing out. In the days when that root was alive and green, merchants discovered the value of goods and alchemists discovered the composition of unknown metals by the use of scales. Just so the essay, as Montaigne was the first to show, is a weighing out, an inquiry into the value, meaning, and true nature of experience; it is a private experiment carried out in public. In each of three successive editions, Montaigne inserted new material into his essays without revising the old material. Often the new statements contradicted the original ones, but Montaigne let them stand, since he believed that the only consistent fact about human beings is their inconsistency. In a celebration called "Why Montaigne Is Not a Bore," Lewis Thomas has remarked of him that "He [was] fond of his mind, and affectionately entertained by everything in his head." Whatever Montaigne wrote about—and he wrote about everything under the sun: fears, smells, growing old, the pleasures of scratching—he weighed on the scales of his own character.

It is the *singularity* of the first person—its warts and crotchets and turn of voice—that lures many of us into reading essays, and that lingers with us after we finish. Consider the lonely, melancholy persona of Loren Eiseley, forever wandering, forever brooding on our dim and bestial past, his lips frosty with the chill of the Ice Age. Consider the volatile, Dionysian persona of D. H. Lawrence, with his incandescent gaze, his habit of turning peasants into gods and trees into flames, his quick hatred and quicker love. Consider that philosophical farmer, Wendell Berry, who speaks with a countryman's knowledge and a deacon's severity. Consider E. B. White, with his cheery affection for brown eggs and dachshunds, his unflappable way of herding geese while the radio warns of an approaching hurricane.

E. B. White, that engaging master of the genre, a champion of idiosyncrasy, introduced his own volume of *Essays* by admitting the danger of narcissism:

> I think some people find the essay the last resort of the egoist, a much too self-conscious and self-serving form for their taste; they feel that it is presumptuous of a writer to assume that his little excursions or his small observations will interest the reader. There is some justice in their complaint. I have always been aware that I am by nature self-absorbed and egoistical; to write of myself to the extent I have done indicates a too great attention to my own life, not enough to the lives of others.

Yet the self-absorbed Mr. White was in fact a delighted observer of the world, and shared that delight with us. Thus, after describing memorably how a circus girl practiced her bareback riding in the leisure moments between shows ("The Ring of Time"), he confessed: "As a writing man, or secretary, I have always felt charged with the safekeeping of all unexpected items of worldly or unworldly enchantment, as though I might be held personally responsible if even a small one were to be lost." That may still be presumptuous, but it is a presumption turned outward on the creation.

This looking outward helps distinguish the essay from pure autobiography, which dwells more complacently on the self. Mass murderers, movie stars, sports heroes, Wall Street crooks, and defrocked politicians may blather on about whatever high jinks or low jinks made them temporarily famous, may chronicle their exploits, their diets, their hobbies, in perfect confidence that the public is eager to gobble up every least gossipy scrap. And the public, according to sales figures, generally is. On the other hand, I assume the public does not give a hoot about my private life. If I write of hiking up a mountain with my one-year-old boy riding like a papoose on my back, and of what he babbled to me while we gazed down from the summit onto the scudding clouds, it is not because I am deluded into believing that my baby, like the offspring of Prince Charles, matters to the great world. It is because I know the great world produces babies of its own and watches them change cloudfast before its doting eyes. To make that climb up the mountain vividly present for readers is harder work than the climb itself. I choose to write about my experience not because it is mine, but because it seems to me a door through which others might pass.

On that cocky first page of *Walden*, Thoreau justified his own seeming self-absorption by saying that he wrote the book for the sake of his fellow citizens, who kept asking him to account for his peculiar experiment by the pond. There is at least a sliver of truth to this, since Thoreau, a town character, had been invited more than once to speak his mind at the public lectern. Most of us, however, cannot honestly say the townspeople have been clamoring for our words. I suspect that all writers of the essay, even Norman Mailer and Gore Vidal, must occasionally wonder if they are egomaniacs. For the essayist, in other words, the problem of authority is inescapable. By what right does one speak? Why should anyone listen? The traditional sources of authority no longer serve. You cannot justify your words by appealing to the Bible or some other holy text, you cannot merely stitch together a patchwork of quotations from classical authors, you cannot lean on a podium at the Atheneum and deliver your wisdom to a rapt audience.

In searching for your own soapbox, a sturdy platform from which to deliver your opinionated monologues, it helps if you have already distinguished yourself at some other, less fishy form. When Yeats describes his longing for Maud Gonne or muses on Ireland's misty lore, everything he says is charged with the prior strength of his poetry. When Virginia Woolf, in *A Room of One's Own*, reflects on the status of women and the conditions necessary for making art, she speaks as the author of *Mrs. Dalloway* and *To the Lighthouse*. The essayist may also lay claim to our attention by having lived through events or traveled through terrains that already bear a richness of meaning. When James Baldwin writes his *Notes of a Native Son*, he does not have to convince us that racism is a troubling reality. When Barry Lopez takes us on a meditative tour of the far north in *Arctic Dreams*, he can rely on our curiosity about that fabled and forbidding place. When Paul Theroux climbs aboard a train and invites us on a journey to some exotic destination, he can count on the romance of railroads and the allure of remote cities to bear us along.

Most essayists, however, cannot draw on any source of authority from beyond the page to lend force to the page itself. They can only use language to put themselves on display and to gesture at the world. When Annie Dillard tells us in the opening lines of *Pilgrim at Tinker Creek* about the tomcat with bloody paws who jumps through the window onto her chest, why should we listen? Well, because of the voice that goes on to say: "And some mornings I'd wake in daylight to find my body covered with paw prints in blood; I looked as though I'd been painted with roses." Listen to her explaining a few pages later what she is up to in this book, this broody, zestful record of her stay in the Roanoke Valley: "I propose to keep here what Thoreau called 'a meteorological journal of the mind,' telling some tales and describing some of the sights of this rather tamed valley, and exploring, in fear and trembling, some of the unmapped dim reaches and unholy fastnesses to which those tales and sights so dizzyingly lead." The sentence not only describes the method of her literary search, but also exhibits the breathless, often giddy, always eloquent and spiritually hungry soul who will do the searching. If you enjoy her company, you will relish Annie Dillard's essays; if you don't, you won't.

Listen to another voice which readers tend to find either captivating or insufferable:

> That summer I began to see, however dimly, that one of my ambitions, perhaps my governing ambition, was to belong fully to this place, to belong as the thrushes and the herons and the muskrats belonged, to be altogether at home here. That is still my ambition. But now I have come to see that it proposes an enormous labor. It is a spiritual ambition, like goodness. The wild creatures belong to the place by nature, but as a man I can belong to it only by understanding and by virtue. It is an ambition I cannot hope to succeed in wholly, but I have come to believe that it is the most worthy of all.

That is Wendell Berry in "The Long-Legged House" writing about his patch of Kentucky. Once you have heard that stately, moralizing, cherishing voice, laced through with references to the land, you will not mistake it for anyone else's. Berry's themes are profound and arresting ones. But it is his voice, more than anything he speaks about, that either seizes us or drives us away.

Even so distinct a persona as Wendell Berry's or Annie Dillard's is still only a literary fabrication, of course. The first person singular is too narrow a gate for the whole writer to squeeze through. What we meet on the page is not the flesh-and-blood author, but a simulacrum, a character who wears the label *I*. Introducing the lectures that became *A Room of One's Own*, Virginia Woolf reminded her listeners that "'I' is only a convenient term for somebody who has no real being. Lies will flow from my lips, but there may perhaps be some truth mixed up with them; it is for you to seek out this truth and to decide whether any part of it is worth keeping." Here is a part I consider worth keeping: "Women have served all these centuries as looking-glasses possessing the magic and delicious power of reflecting the figure of man at twice its natural size." It is from such elegant, revelatory sentences that we build up our notion of the "I" who speaks to us under the name of Virginia Woolf.

What the essay tells us may not be true in any sense that would satisfy a court of law. As an example, think of Orwell's brief narrative, "A Hanging," which describes an execution in Burma. Anyone who has read it remembers how the condemned man as he walked to the gallows stepped aside to avoid a puddle. That is the sort of haunting detail only an eyewitness should be able to report. Alas, biographers, those zealous debunkers, have recently claimed that Orwell never saw such a hanging, that he reconstructed it from hearsay. What then do we make of his essay? Or has it become the sort of barefaced lie we prefer to call a story?

Frankly, I don't much care what label we put on "A Hanging"—fiction or nonfiction, it is a powerful statement either way—but Orwell might have cared a great deal. I say this because not long ago I was bemused and then vexed to find one of my own essays treated in a scholarly article as a work of fiction. Here was my earnest report about growing up on a military base, my heartfelt rendering of indelible memories, being confused with the airy figments of novelists! To be sure, in writing the piece I had used dialogue, scenes, settings, character descriptions, the whole fictional bag of tricks; sure, I picked and chose among a thousand beckoning details; sure, I downplayed some facts and highlighted others; but I was writing about the actual, not the invented. I shaped the matter, but I did not make it up.

To explain my vexation, I must break another taboo, which is to speak of the author's intent. My teachers warned me strenuously to avoid the intentional fallacy. They told me to regard poems and plays and stories as objects washed up on the page from some unknown and unknowable shores. Now that I am on the other side of the page, so to speak, I think quite recklessly of intention all the time. I believe that if we allow the question of intent in the case of murder, we should allow it in literature. The essay is distinguished from the short story, not by the presence or absence of literary devices, not by tone or theme or subject, but by the writer's stance toward the material. In composing an essay about what it was like to grow up on that military base, I *meant* something quite different from what I mean when concocting a story. I meant to preserve and record and help give voice to a reality that existed independently of me. I meant to pay my respects to a minor passage of history in an out-of-the-way place. I felt responsible to the truth as known by other people. I wanted to speak directly out of my own life into the lives of others.

You can see I am teetering on the brink of metaphysics. One step farther and I will plunge into the void, wondering as I fall how to prove there is any external truth for the essayist to pay homage to. I draw back from the brink and simply declare that I believe one writes, in essays, with a regard for the actual world, with a respect for the shared substance of history, the autonomy of other lives, the being of nature, the mystery and majesty of a creation we have not made.

When it comes to speculating about the creation, I feel more at ease with physics than with metaphysics. According to certain bold and lyrical cosmologists, there is at the center of black holes a geometrical point, the tiniest conceivable speck, where all the matter of a collapsed star has been concentrated, and where everyday notions of time, space, and force break down. That point is called a singularity. The boldest and most poetic theories suggest that anything sucked into a singularity might be flung back out again, utterly changed, somewhere else in the universe. The lonely first person, the essayist's microcosmic "I," may be thought of as a verbal singularity at the center of the mind's black hole. The raw matter of experience, torn away from the axes of time and space, falls in constantly from all sides, undergoes the mind's inscrutable alchemy, and reemerges in the quirky, unprecedented shape of an essay.

Now it is time for me to step down, before another metaphor seizes hold of me, before you notice that I am standing, not on a soapbox, but on the purest air.

The Exact Location of the Soul

Richard Selzer

Someone asked me why a surgeon would write. Why, when the shelves are already too full? They sag under the deadweight of books. To add a single adverb is to risk exceeding the strength of the boards. A surgeon should abstain. A surgeon, whose fingers are more at home in the steamy gullies of the body than they are tapping the dry keys of a typewriter. A surgeon, who feels the slow slide of intestines against the back of his hand and is no more alarmed than were a family of snakes taking their comfort from such an indolent rubbing. A surgeon, who palms the human heart as though it were some captured bird.

Why should he write? Is it vanity that urges him? There is glory enough in the knife. Is it for money? One can make too much money. No. It is to search for some meaning, in the ritual of surgery, which is at once murderous, painful, healing, and full of love. It is a devilish hard thing to transmit—to find, even. Perhaps if one were to cut out a heart, a lobe of the liver, a single convolution of the brain, and paste it to a page, it would speak with more eloquence than all the words of Balzac. Such a piece would need no literary style, no mass of erudition or history, but in its very shape and feel would tell all the frailty and strength, the despair and nobility of man. What? Publish a heart? A little piece of bone? Preposterous. Still I fear that is what it may require to reveal the truth that lies hidden in the body. Not all the undressings of Rabelais, Chekhov, or even William Carlos Williams have wrested it free, although God knows each one of those doctors made a heroic assault upon it.

I have come to believe that it is the flesh alone that counts. The rest is that with which we distract ourselves when we are not hungry or cold, in pain or ecstasy. In the recesses of the body I search for the philosophers' stone. I know it is there, hidden in the deepest, dampest cul-de-sac. It awaits discovery. To find it would be like the harnessing of fire. It would illuminate the world. Such a quest is not without pain. Who can gaze on so much misery and feel no hurt? Emerson has written that the poet is the only true doctor. I believe him, for the poet, lacking the impediment of speech with which the rest of us are afflicted, gazes, records, diagnoses, and prophesies.

I invited a young diabetic woman to the operating room to amputate her leg. She could not see the great shaggy black ulcer upon her foot and ankle that threatened to encroach upon the rest of her body, for she was blind as well. There upon her foot was a Mississippi Delta brimming with corruption, sending its raw tributaries down between her toes. Gone were all the little web spaces that when fresh and whole are such a delight to loving men. She could not see her wound, but she could feel it. There is no pain like that of the bloodless limb turned rotten and festering. There is neither unguent nor anodyne to kill such a pain yet leave intact the body.

For over a year I trimmed away the putrid flesh, cleansed, anointed, and dressed the foot, staving off, delaying. Three times each week, in her darkness, she sat upon my table, rocking back and forth, holding her extended leg by the thigh, gripping it as though it were a rocket that must be steadied lest it explode and scatter her toes about the room. And I would cut away a bit here, a bit there, of the swollen blue leather that was her tissue.

At last we gave up, she and I. We could no longer run ahead of the gangrene. We had not the legs for it. There must be an amputation in order that she might live—and I as well. It was to heal us both that I must take up knife and saw, and cut the leg off. And when I could feel it drop from her body to the table, see the blessed *space* appear between her and that leg, I too would be well.

Now it is the day of the operation. I stand by while the anesthetist administers the drugs, watch as the tense familiar body relaxes into narcosis. I turn then to uncover the leg. There, upon her kneecap, she has drawn, blindly, upside down for me to see, a face; just a circle with two ears, two eyes, a nose, and a smiling upturned mouth. Under it she has printed SMILE, DOCTOR. Minutes later I listen to the sound of the saw, until a little crack at the end tells me it is done.

So, I have learned that man is not ugly, but that he is Beauty itself. There is no other his equal. Are we not all dying, none faster or more slowly than any other? I have become receptive to the possibilities of love (for it is love, this thing that happens in the operating room), and each day I wait, trembling in the busy air. Perhaps today it will come. Perhaps today I will find it, take part in it, this love that blooms in the stoniest desert.

All through literature the doctor is portrayed as a figure of fun. Shaw was splenetic about him; Molière delighted in pricking his pompous medicine men, and well they deserved it. The doctor is ripe for caricature. But I believe that the truly great writing about doctors has not yet been done. I think it must be done *by* a doctor, one who is through with the love affair with his technique, who recognizes that he has played Narcissus, raining kisses on a mirror, and who now, out of the impacted masses of his guilt, has expanded into self-doubt, and finally into the high state of wonderment. Perhaps he will be a nonbeliever who, after a lifetime of grand gestures and mighty deeds, comes upon the knowledge that he has done no more than meddle in the lives of his fellows, and that he has done at least as much harm as good. Yet he may continue to pretend, at least, that there is nothing to fear, that death will not come, so long as people depend on his authority. Later, after his patients have left, he may closet himself in his darkened office, sweating and afraid.

There is a story by Unamuno in which a priest, living in a small Spanish village, is adored by all the people for his piety, kindness, and the majesty with which he celebrates the Mass each Sunday. To them he is already a saint. It is a foregone conclusion, and they speak of him as Saint Immanuel. He helps them with their plowing and planting, tends them when they are sick, confesses them, comforts them in death, and every Sunday, in his rich, thrilling voice, transports them to paradise with his chanting. The fact is that Don Immanuel is not so much a saint as a martyr. Long ago his own faith left him. He is an atheist, a good man doomed to suffer the life of a hypocrite, pretending to a faith he does not have. As he raises the chalice of wine, his hands tremble, and a cold sweat pours from him. He cannot stop for he knows that the people need this of him, that their need is greater than his sacrifice. Still…still…could it be that Don Immanuel's whole life is a kind of prayer, a paean to God?

A writing doctor would treat men and women with equal reverence, for what is the "liberation" of either sex to him who knows the diagrams, the inner geographies of each? I love the solid heft of men as much as I adore the heated capaciousness of women—women in whose penetralia is found the repository of existence. I would have them glory in that. Women are physics and chemistry. They are matter. It is their bodies that tell of the frailty of men. Men have not their cellular, enzymatic wisdom. Man is albuminoid, proteinaceous, laked pearl; woman is yolky, ovoid, rich. Both are exuberant bloody growths. I would use the defects and deformities of each for my sacred purpose of writing, for I know that it is the marred and scarred and faulty that are subject to grace. I would seek the soul in the facts of animal economy and profligacy. Yes, it is the exact location of the soul that I am after. The smell of it is in my nostrils. I have caught glimpses of it in the body diseased. If only I could tell it. Is there no mathematical equation that can guide me? So much pain and pus equals so much truth? It is elusive as the whippoorwill that one hears calling incessantly from out the night window, but which, nesting as it does low in the brush, no one sees. No one but the poet, for he sees what no one else can. He was born with the eye for it.

Once, I thought I had it: Ten o'clock one night, the end room off a long corridor in a college infirmary, my last patient of the day, degree of exhaustion suitable for the appearance of a vision, some manifestation. The patient is a young man recently returned from Guatemala, from the excavation of Mayan ruins. His left upper arm wears a gauze dressing which, when removed, reveals a clean punched-out hole the size of a dime. The tissues about the opening are swollen and tense. A thin brownish fluid lips the edge, and now and then a lazy drop of the overflow spills down the arm. An abscess, inadequately drained. I will enlarge the opening to allow better egress of the pus. Nurse, will you get me a scalpel and some…?

What happens next is enough to lay Francis Drake avomit in his cabin. No explorer ever stared in wilder surmise than I into that crater from which there now emerges a narrow gray head whose sole distinguishing feature is a pair of black pincers. The head sits atop a longish flexible neck arching now this way, now that, testing the air. Alternately it folds back upon itself, then advances in new boldness. And all the while, with dreadful rhythmicity, the unspeakable pincers open and close. Abscess?

Pus? Never. Here is the lair of a beast at whose malignant purpose I could but guess. A Mayan devil, I think, that would soon burst free to fly about the room, with horrid blanket-wings and iridescent scales, raking, pinching, injecting God knows what acid juice. And even now the irony does not escape me, the irony of my patient as excavator excavated.

With all the ritual deliberation of a high priest I advance a surgical clamp toward the hole. The surgeon's heart is become a bat hanging upside down from his rib cage. The rim achieved—now thrust—and the ratchets of the clamp close upon the empty air. The devil has retracted. Evil mocking laughter bangs back and forth in the brain. More stealth. Lying in wait. One must skulk. Minutes pass, perhaps an hour.... A faint disturbance in the lake, and once again the thing upraises, farther and farther, hovering. Acrouch, strung, the surgeon is one with his instrument; there is no longer any boundary between its metal and his flesh. They are joined in a single perfect tool of extirpation. It is just for this that he was born. Now—thrust—and clamp—and *yes*. Got him!

Transmitted to the fingers comes the wild thrashing of the creature. Pinned and wriggling, he is mine. I hear the dry brittle scream of the dragon, and a hatred seizes me, but such a detestation as would make of Iago a drooling sucktit. It is the demented hatred of the victor for the vanquished, the warden for his prisoner. It is the hatred of fear. Within the jaws of my hemostat is the whole of the evil of the world, the dark concentrate itself, and I shall kill it. For mankind. And, in so doing, will open, the way into a thousand years of perfect peace. Here is Surgeon as Savior indeed.

Tight grip now...steady, relentless pull. How it scrabbles to keep its tentacle-hold. With an abrupt moist plop the extraction is complete. There, writhing in the teeth of the clamp, is a dirty gray body, the size and shape of an English walnut. He is hung everywhere with tiny black hooklets. Quickly...into the specimen jar of saline...the lid screwed tight. Crazily he swims round and round, wiping his slimy head against the glass, then slowly sinks to the bottom, the mass of hooks in frantic agonal wave.

"You are going to be all right," I say to my patient. "We are *all* going to be all right from now on."

The next day I take the jar to the medical school.

"That's the larva of the botfly," says a pathologist. "The fly usually bites a cow and deposits its eggs beneath the skin. There, the egg develops into the larval form which, when ready, burrows its way to the outside through the hide and falls to the ground. In time it matures into a full-grown botfly. This one happened to bite a man. It was about to come out on its own, and, of course, it would have died."

The words *imposter, sorehead, servant of Satan* spring to my lips. But now he has been joined by other scientists. They nod in agreement. I gaze from one gray eminence to another, and know the mallet-blow of glory pulverized. I tried to save the world, but it didn't work out.

No, it is not the surgeon who is God's darling. He is the victim of vanity. It is the poet who heals with his words, stanches the flow of blood, stills the rattling breath, applies poultice to the scalded flesh.

Did you ask me why a surgeon writes? I think it is because I wish to be a doctor.

Me and My Shadow

Jane Tompkins

I wrote this essay in answer to Ellen Messer-Davidow's "The Philosophical Bases of Feminist Literary Criticisms" which appeared in the Fall 1987 issue of *New Literary History* along with several replies, including a shorter version of this one. As if it weren't distraction enough that my essay depends on someone else's, I want, before you've even read it, to defend it from an accusation. Believing that my reply, which turns its back on theory, constituted a return to the "rhetoric of presence," to an "earlier, naive, untheoretical feminism," someone, whom I'll call the unfriendly reader, complained that I was making the "old patriarchal gesture of representation" whose effect had been to marginalize women, thus "reinforcing the very stereotypes women and minorities have fought so hard to overcome." I want to reply to this objection because I think it is mistaken and because it reproduces exactly the way I used to feel about feminist criticism when it first appeared in the late 1960s.

I wanted nothing to do with it. It was embarrassing to see women, with whom one was necessarily identified, insisting in print on the differences between men's and women's experience, focusing obsessively on women authors, women characters, women's issues. How pathetic, I thought, to have to call attention to yourself in that way. And in such bad taste. It was the worst kind of special pleading, an admission of weakness so blatant it made me ashamed. What I felt then, and what I think my unfriendly reader feels now, is a version of what women who are new to feminism often feel: that if we don't call attention to ourselves *as* women, but just shut up about it and do our work, no one will notice the difference and everything will be OK.

Women who adopt this line are, understandably, afraid. Afraid of being confused with the weaker sex, the sex that goes around whining and talking about itself in an unseemly way, that can't or won't do what the big boys do ("tough it out") and so won't ever be allowed to play in the big boys' games. I am sympathetic with this position. Not long ago, as organizer of an MLA session entitled "Professional Politics: Women and the Institution," I urged a large roomful of women to "get theory" because I thought that doing theory would admit us to the big leagues and enable us at the same time to argue a feminist case in the most unimpeachable terms—those that men had supplied. I busily took my own advice, which was good as far as it went. But I now see that there has been a price for this, at least there has been for me; it is the subject of my reply to Ellen. I now tend to think that theory itself, at least as it is usually practiced, may be one of the patriarchal gestures women *and* men ought to avoid.

There are two voices inside me answering, answering to, Ellen's essay. One is the voice of a critic who wants to correct a mistake in the essay's view of epistemology. The other is the voice of a person who wants to write about her feelings (I have wanted to do this for a long time but have felt too embarrassed). This person feels it is wrong to criticize the essay philosophically and even beside the point: because a critique of the kind the critic has in mind only insulates academic discourse further from the issues that make feminism matter. That make *her* matter. The critic, meanwhile, believes such feelings, and the attitudes that inform them, are soft-minded, self-indulgent, and unprofessional.

These beings exist separately but not apart. One writes for professional journals, the other in diaries, late at night. One uses words like "context" and "intelligibility," likes to win arguments, see her name in print, and give graduate students hardheaded advice. The other has hardly ever been heard from. She had a short story published once in a university library magazine, but her works exist chiefly in notebooks and manila folders labeled "Journal" and "Private." This person talks on the telephone a lot to her friends, has seen psychiatrists, likes cappuccino, worries about the state of her soul. Her father is ill right now, and one of her friends recently committed suicide.

The dichotomy drawn here is false—and not false. I mean in reality there's no split. It's the same person who feels and who discourses about epistemology. The problem is that you can't talk about your private life in the course of doing your professional work. You have to pretend that epistemology, or whatever you're writing about, has nothing to do with your life, that it's more exalted, more important, because it (supposedly) *transcends* the merely personal. Well, I'm tired of the conventions that keep discussions of epistemology, or James Joyce, segregated from meditations on what is happening outside my window or inside my heart. The public-private dichotomy, which is to say, the public-private *hierarchy*, is a founding condition of female oppression. I say to hell with it. The reason I feel embarrassed at my own attempts to speak personally in a professional context is that I have been conditioned to feel that way. That's all there is to it.

I think people are scared to talk about themselves, that they haven't got the guts to do it. I think readers want to know about each other. Sometimes, when a writer introduces some personal bit of story into an essay, I can hardly contain my pleasure. I love writers who write about their own experience. I feel I'm being nourished by them, that I'm being allowed to enter into a personal relationship with them. That I can match my own experience up with theirs, feel cousin to them, and say, yes, that's how it is.

> When he casts his leaves forth upon the wind [said Hawthorne], the author addresses, not the many who will fling aside his volume, or never take it up, but the few who will understand him.... As if the printed book, thrown at large on the wide world, were certain to find out the divided segment of the writer's own nature, and complete his circle

of existence by bringing him into communion with it.... And so as thoughts are frozen and utterance, benumbed unless the speaker stand in some true relation with this audience—it may be pardonable to imagine that a friend, a kind and apprehensive, though not the closest friend, is listening to our talk. (Nathaniel Hawthorne, "The Custom-House," *The Scarlet Letter*, 5–6)

Hawthorne's sensitivity to the relationship that writing implies is rare in academic prose, even when the subject would seem to make awareness of the reader inevitable. Alison Jaggar gave a lecture recently that crystallized the problem. Western epistemology, she argued, is shaped by the belief that emotion should be excluded from the process of attaining knowledge. Because women in our culture are not simply encouraged but *required* to be the bearers of emotion, which men are culturally conditioned to repress, an epistemology which excludes emotions from the process of attaining knowledge radically undercuts women's epistemic authority. The idea that the conventions defining legitimate sources of knowledge overlapped with the conventions defining appropriate gender behavior (male) came to me as a blinding insight. I saw that I had been socialized from birth to feel and act in ways that automatically excluded me from participating in the culture's most valued activities. No wonder I felt so uncomfortable in the postures academic prose forced me to assume; it was like wearing men's jeans.

Ellen Messer-Davidow's essay participates—as Jaggar's lecture and my précis of it did—in the conventions of Western rationalism. It adopts the impersonal, technical vocabulary of the epistemic ideology it seeks to dislocate. The political problem posed by my need to reply to the essay is this: to adhere to the conventions is to uphold a male standard of rationality that militates against women's being recognized as culturally legitimate sources of knowledge. To break with the convention is to risk not being heard at all.

This is how I would reply to Ellen's essay if I were to do it in the professionally sanctioned way.

The essay provides feminist critics with an overarching framework for thinking about what they do, both in relation to mainstream criticism and in relation to feminist work in other fields. It allows the reader to see women's studies as a whole, furnishing useful categories for organizing a confusing and miscellaneous array of materials. It also provides excellent summaries of a wide variety of books and essays that readers might not otherwise encounter. The enterprise is carried out without pointed attacks on other theorists, without creating a cumbersome new vocabulary, without exhibitionistic displays of intellect or esoteric learning. Its practical aim—to define a field within which debate can take place—is fulfilled by *New Literary History's* decision to publish it, and to do so in a format which includes replies.

(Very nice, Jane. You sound so reasonable and generous. But, as anybody can tell you, this is just the obligatory pat on the back before the stab in the entrails.)

The difficulty with the essay from a philosophical, as opposed to a practical, point of view is that the theory it offers as a basis for future work stems from a confused notion of what an epistemology is. The author says: "An epistemology...consists of assumptions that knowers make about the entities and processes in a domain of study, the relations that obtain among them, and the proper methods for investigating them" (p. 87). I want to quarrel with this definition. Epistemology, strictly speaking, is a *theory* about the origins and nature of knowledge. As such, it is a set of ideas explicitly held and consciously elaborated, and thus belongs to the practice of a subcategory of philosophy called epistemology. The fact that there is a branch of philosophy given over to the study of what knowledge is and how it is acquired is important, because it means that such theories are generated not in relation to this or that "domain of study" but in relation to one another: that is, within the context of already existing epistemological theories. They are rarely based upon a study of the practices of investigators within a particular field.

An epistemology does not consist of "assumptions that knowers make" in a particular field; it is a theory about how knowledge is acquired which makes sense, chiefly, in relation to other such theories. What Messer-Davidow offers as the "epistemology" of traditional literary critics is not *their* epistemology, if in fact they have one, but her description of what she assumes their assumptions are, a description which may or may not be correct. Moreover, if literary critics should indeed elaborate a theory of how they got their beliefs, that theory would have no privileged position in relation to their actual assumptions. It would simply be another theory. This distinction—between actual assumptions and an observer's description of them (even when one is observing one's own practice)—is crucial because it points to an all-important fact about the relation of epistemology to what really gets done in a given domain of study, namely this: that epistemology, a theory about how one gets one's knowledge, in no way determines the particular knowledge that one has.

This fact is important because Messer-Davidow assumes that if we change our epistemology, our practice as critics will change, too. Specifically, she wants us to give up the subject-object theory, in which "knowledge is an abstract representation of objective existence," for a theory which says that what counts as knowledge is a function of situation and perspective. She believes that it follows from this latter theory that knowledge will become more equitable, more self-aware, and more humane.

I disagree. Knowing that my knowledge is perspectival, language-based, culturally constructed, or what have you, does not change in the slightest the things I believe to be true. All that it changes is what I think about how we get knowledge. The insight that my ideas are all products of the situation I occupy in the world applies to all of my ideas equally (including the idea that knowledge is culturally based) and to all of everybody else's ideas as well. So where does this get us? Right back to where we were before, mainly. I still believe what I believe and, if you differ with me, think that you are wrong. If I want to change your mind I still have to persuade you that I am right by using evidence, reasons, chains of inference, citations of authority, analogies, illustrations, and so on. Believing that what I believe comes from my being in a particular cultural framework does not change my relation to my beliefs. I still believe them just as much as if I thought they came from God, or the laws of nature, or my autonomous self.

Here endeth the epistle.

But while I think Ellen is wrong in thinking that a change of epistemology can mean a change in the kinds of things we think, I am in sympathy with the ends she has in view. This sympathy prompts me to say that my professionally correct reply is not on target. Because the target, the goal, rather, is not to be fighting over these questions, trying to beat the other person down. (What the goal is, it is harder to say.) Intellectual debate, if it were in the right spirit, would be wonderful. But I don't know how to be in the right spirit, exactly, can't make points without sounding rather superior and smug. Most of all, I don't know how to enter the debate without leaving everything else behind—the birds outside my window, my grief over Janice, just myself as a person sitting here in stockinged feet, a little bit chilly because the windows are open, and thinking about going to the bathroom. But not going yet.

I find that when I try to write in my "other" voice, I am immediately critical of it. It wobbles, vacillates back and forth, is neither this nor that. The voice in which I write about epistemology is familiar, I know how it ought to sound. This voice, though, I hardly know. I don't even know if it has anything to say. But if I never write in it, it never will. So I have to try. (That is why you see, this doesn't sound too good. It isn't a practiced performance, it hasn't got a surface. I'm asking you to bear with me while I try, hoping that this, what I write, will express something you yourself have felt or will help you find a part of yourself that you would like to express.)

The thing I want to say is that I've been hiding a part of myself for a long time. I've known it was there, but I couldn't listen because there was no place for this person in literary criticism. The criticism I would like to write would always take off from personal experience. Would always be in some way a chronicle of my hours and days. Would speak in a voice which can talk about everything, would reach out to a reader like me and touch me where I want to be touched. Susan Griffin's voice in "The Way of All Ideology." I want to speak in what Ursula LeGuin, at the Bryn Mawr College commencement in 1986, called the "mother tongue." This is LeGuin speaking:

> The dialect of the father tongue that you and I learned best in college…only lectures…. Many believe this dialect—the expository and particularly scientific discourse—is the *highest* form of language, the true language, of which all other uses of words are primitive vestiges…. And it is indeed a High Language…. Newton's *Principia* was written in it in Latin…and Kant wrote German in it, and Marx, Darwin, Freud, Boas, Foucault, all the great scientists and social thinkers wrote it. It is the language of thought that seeks objectivity.
>
> …The essential gesture of the father tongue is not reasoning, but distancing—making a gap, a space, between the subject or self and the object or other…. Everywhere now everybody speaks [this] language in laboratories and government buildings and headquarters and offices of business…. The father tongue is spoken from above. It goes one way. No answer is expected, or heard.
>
> …The mother tongue, spoken or written, expects an answer. It is conversation, a word the root of which means "turning together." The mother tongue is language not as mere communication, but as relation, relationship. It connects…. Its power is not in dividing but in binding…. We all know it by heart. John have you got your umbrella I think it's going to rain. Can you come play with me? If I told you once I told

you a hundred times…. O what am I going to do?…Pass the soy sauce please. Oh, shit…. You look like what the cat dragged in. (3–4)

Much of what I'm saying elaborates or circles around these quotes from LeGuin. I find that having released myself from the duty to say things I'm not interested in, in a language I resist, I feel free to entertain other people's voices. Quoting them becomes a pleasure of appreciation rather than the obligatory giving of credit, because when I write in a voice that is not struggling to be heard through the screen of a forced language, I no longer feel that it is not I who am speaking, and so there is more room for what others have said.

One sentence in Ellen's essay stuck out for me the first time I read it and the second and the third: "In time we can build a synchronous account of our subject matters as we glissade among them and turn upon ourselves" (p.79).

What attracted me to the sentence was the "glissade." Fluidity, flexibility, versatility, mobility. Moving from one thing to another without embarrassment. It is a tenet of feminist rhetoric that the personal is political, but who in the academy acts on this where language is concerned? We all speak the father tongue, which is impersonal, while decrying the fathers' ideas. All of what I have written so far is in a kind of watered-down expository prose. Not much imagery. No description of concrete things. Only that one word, "glissade."

> *Like black swallows swooping and gliding*
> *in a flurry of entangled loops and curves*

Two lines of a poem I memorized in high school are what the word "glissade" called to mind. Turning upon ourselves. Turning, weaving, bending, unbending, moving in loops and curves.

I don't believe we can ever turn upon ourselves in the sense Ellen intends. You can't get behind the thing that casts the shadow. *You* cast the shadow. As soon as you turn, the shadow falls in another place. It is still your shadow. You have not got "behind" yourself. That is why self-consciousness is not the way to make ourselves better than we are.

Just me and my shadow, walkin' down the avenue.

It is a beautiful day here in North Carolina. The first day that is both cool and sunny all summer. After a terrible summer, first drought, then heat-wave, then torrential rain, trees down, flooding. Now, finally, beautiful weather. A tree outside my window just brushed by red, with one fully red leaf (This is what I want you to see. A person sitting in stockinged feet looking out of her window—a floor to ceiling rectangle filled with green, with one red leaf. The season poised, sunny and chill, ready to rush down the incline into autumn. But perfect, and still. Not going yet.)

My response to this essay is not a response to something Ellen Messer-Davidow has written; it is a response to something within myself. As I reread the opening pages I feel myself being squeezed into a straitjacket; I wriggle, I will not go in. As I read the list "subject matters, methods of reasoning, and epistemology," the words will not go down. They belong to a debate whose susurrus hardly reaches my ears.

The liberation Ellen promises from the straitjacket of a subject-object epistemology is one I experienced some time ago. Mine didn't take the form she outlines, but it was close enough. I discovered, or thought I discovered, that the poststructuralist way of understanding language and knowledge enabled me to say what I wanted about the world. It enabled me to do this because it pointed out that the world I knew was a construct of ways of thinking about it and, as such, had no privileged claim on the truth. Truth in fact would always be just such a construction, and so one could offer another, competing, description and thus help to change the world that was.

The catch was that anything I might say or imagine was itself the product of an already existing discourse. Not something "I" had made up but a way of constructing things I had absorbed from the intellectual surround. Poststructuralism's proposition about the constructed nature of things held good, but that did not mean that the world could be changed by an act of will. For, as we are looking at this or that phenomenon and re-seeing it, re-thinking it, the rest of the world, that part of it from which we do the seeing, is still there, in place, real, irrefragable as a whole, and making visible what we see, though changed by it, too.

This little lecture pretends to something I no longer want to claim. The pretense is in the tone and level of the language, not in what it says about poststructuralism. The claim being made by the language is analogous to what Barthes calls the "reality effect" of historical writing, whose real message is not that this or that happened but that reality exists. So the claim of this language I've been using (and am using right now) lies in its implicit deification of the speaker. Let's call it the "authority effect." I cannot describe the pretense except to talk about what it ignores: the human frailty of the speaker, his body his emotions, his history; the moment of intercourse with the reader—acknowledgment of the other person's presence, feelings, needs. This "authoritative" language speaks as though the other person weren't there. Or perhaps more accurately, it doesn't bother to imagine who, as Hawthorne said, is listening to our talk.

How can we speak personally to one another and yet not be self centered? How can we be part of the great world and yet remain loyal to ourselves?

It seems to me that I am trying to write out of my experience without acknowledging any discontinuity between this and the subject matter of the profession I work in—and at the same time find that I no longer want to write about that subject matter, as it appears in Ellen's essay. I am, on the one hand, demanding a connection between literary theory and my own life and asserting, on the other, that there is no connection.

But here is a connection. I learned what epistemology I know from my husband. I think of it as more his game than mine. It's a game I enjoy playing but which I no longer need or want to play. I want to declare my independence of it, of him. (Part of what is going on here has to do with a need I have to make sure I'm not being absorbed in someone else's personality.) What I am breaking away from is both my conformity to the conventions of a male professional practice and my intellectual dependence on my husband. How can I talk about such things in public? How can I *not*.

Looking for something to read this morning, I took three books down from my literary theory shelf, in order to prove a point. The first book was Félix Guattari's *Molecular Revolution*. I find it difficult to read, and therefore have read very little of it, but according to a student who is a disciple of Deleuze and Guattari, "molecular revolution" has to do with getting away from ideology and enacting revolution within daily life. It is specific, not programmed—that is, it does not have a "method," nor "steps," and is neither psychoanalytic nor Marxist, although its discourse seems shaped by those discourses, antithetically. From this kind of revolution, said I to myself, disingenuously, one would expect some recognition of the personal. A revolution that started with daily life would have to begin, or at least would have sometimes to reside, at home. So I open at a section entitled "Towards a New Vocabulary," looking for something in the mother tongue, and this is what I find:

> The distinction I am proposing between machine and structure is based solely on the way we use the words; we may consider that we are merely dealing with a 'written device' of the kind one has to invent for dealing with a mathematical problem, or with an axiom that may have to be reconsidered at a particular stage of development, or again with the kind of machine we shall be talking about here.
>
> I want therefore to make it clear that I am putting into parentheses the fact that, in reality, a machine is inseparable from its structural articulations and conversely, that each contingent structure is dominated (and this is what I want to demonstrate) by a system of machines, or at the very least by one logic machine. (111)

At this point, I start to skip, reading only the first sentence of each paragraph.

> "We may say of structure that it positions its elements…"
> "The agent of action, whose definition here does not extend beyond this principle of reciprocal determination…"
> "The machine, on the other hand remains essentially remote…"
> "The history of technology is dated…"
> "Yesterday's machine, today's and tomorrow's, are not related in their structural determinations…"

I find this language incredibly alienating. In fact, the paragraph after the one I stopped at begins: "The individual's relation to the machine has been described by sociologists following Friedmann as one of fundamental alienation." I will return to this essay some day and read it. I sense that it will have something interesting to say. But the effort is too great now. What strikes me now is the incredibly distancing effect of this language. It is totally abstract and impersonal. Though the author uses the first person ("The distinction I am proposing," "I want therefore to make it clear"), it quickly became clear to me that he had no interest whatsoever in the personal, or in concrete situations as I understand them—a specific person, at a specific machine, somewhere in time and space, with something on his/her mind, real noises, smells, aches and pains. He has no interest in his own experience of machines or in explaining why he is writing about them, what they mean to him personally. I take down the next book: *Poetry and Repression* by Harold Bloom.

This book should contain some reference to the self, to the author's self, to ourselves, to how people feel, to how the author feels, since its subject is psychological: repression. I open the book at page 1 and read:

Jacques Derrida asks a central question in his essay on "Freud and the Scene of Writing": "What is a text, and what must the psyche be if it can be represented by a text?" My narrow concern with poetry prompts the contrary question: "What is a psyche, and what must a text be if it can be represented by a psyche?" Both Derrida's question and my own require exploration of three terms: "psyche," "text," "represented."

> "Psyche" is ultimately from the Indo-European root.... (1)

—and I stop reading.

The subject of poetry and repression will involve the asking and answering of questions about "a text"—a generalized, nonparticular object that has been the subject of endless discussion for the past twenty years—and about an equally disembodied "psyche" in relation to the thing called "a text"—not, to my mind or rather in view of my desires, a very promising relation in which to consider it. Answering these questions, moreover, will "require" (on whose part, I wonder?) the "exploration" of "three terms." Before we get to the things themselves—psyches, texts–we shall have to spend a lot of time looking at them *as words*. With the beginning of the next paragraph, we get down to the etymology of "psyche." With my agenda, I get off the bus here.

But first I look through the book. Bloom is arguing against canonical readings (of some very canonical poems) and for readings that are not exactly personal, but in which the drama of a self is constantly being played out on a cosmic stage—lots of references to God, kingdom, Paradise, the fall, the eternal—a biblical stage on which, apparently, only men are players (God, Freud, Christ, Nietzsche, and the poets). It is a drama that, although I can see how gripping Bloom can make it, will pall for me because it isn't *my* drama.

Book number three, Michel Foucault's *History of Sexuality*, is more promising. Section One is entitled "We 'other Victorians.'" So Foucault is acknowledging his and our implication in the object of the study. This book will in some way be about "ourselves," which is what I want. It begins:

> For a long time, the story goes, we supported a Victorian regime, and we continue to be dominated by it even today. Thus the image of the imperial prude is emblazoned on our restrained, mute, and hypocritical sexuality. (3)

Who, exactly, are "we"? Foucault is using the convention in which the author establishes common ground with his reader by using the first person plural—a presumptuous, though usually successful, move. Presumptuous because it presumes that we are really like him, and successful because, especially when an author is famous, and even when he isn't, "our" instinct (I criticize the practice and engage in it too) is to want to cooperate, to be included in the circle the author is drawing so cosily around "us." It is chummy, this "we." It feels good, for a little while, until it starts to feel coercive, until "we" are subscribing to things that "I" don't believe.

There is no specific reference to the author's self, no attempt to specify himself. It continues:

> At the beginning of the seventeenth century...

I know now where we are going. We are going to history. "At the beginning of the seventeenth century a certain frankness was still common, it would seem." Generalizations about the past, though pleasantly qualified ("a certain frankness," "it would seem"), are nevertheless disappointingly magisterial. Things continue in a generalizing vein—"it was a time of direct gestures, shameless discourse, and open transgressions." It's not so much that I don't believe him as that I am uncomfortable with the level or the mode of discourse. It is everything that, I thought, Foucault was trying to get away from in *The Archaeology of Knowledge*. The primacy of the subject as the point of view from which history could be written, the bland assumption of authority, the taking over of time, of substance, of event, the imperialism of description from a unified perspective. Even though the subject matter interests me—sex, hypocrisy, whether or not our view of Victorianism and of ourselves in relation to it is correct—I am not eager to read on. The point of view is discouraging. It will march along giving orders, barking out commands. I'm not willing to go along for the march, not even on Foucault's say-so (I am, or have been, an extravagant admirer of his).

So I turn to "my" books. To the women's section of my shelves. I take down, unerringly, an anthology called *The Powers of Desire* edited by Christine Stansell, Ann Snitow, and Sharon Thompson. I turn, almost as unerringly, to an essay by Jessica Benjamin entitled "Master and Slave: The Fantasy of Erotic Domination," and begin to read:

> This essay is concerned with the violence of erotic domination. It is about the strange union of rationality and violence that is made in the secret heart of our culture and sometimes enacted in the body. This union has inspired some of the holiest imagery of religious transcendence and now comes to light at the porno newsstands, where women are regularly depicted in the bonds of love. But the slave of love is not always a woman, not always a heterosexual; the fantasy of erotic domination permeates all sexual imagery in our culture. (281)

I am completely hooked, I am going to read this essay from beginning to end and proceed to do so. It gets better, much better, as it goes along. In fact, it gets so good, I find myself putting it down and straying from it because the subject is *so* close to home, and therefore so threatening, that I need relief from it, little breathers, before I can go on. I underline vigorously and often. Think of people I should give it to to read (my husband, this colleague, that colleague).

But wait a minute. There is no personal reference here. The author deals, like Foucault, in generalities. In even bigger ones than his: hers aren't limited to the seventeenth century or the Victorian era. She generalizes about religion, rationality, violence. Why am I not turned off by this as I was in Foucault's case? Why don't I reject this as a grand drama in the style of Bloom? Why don't I bridle at the abstractions as I did when reading Guattari? Well?

The answer is, I see the abstractions as concrete and the issues as personal. They are already personal for me without being personal*ized* because they concern things I've been thinking about for some time, struggling with, trying to figure out for myself. I don't need the author to identify her own involvement, I don't need her to concretize, because these things are already personal and concrete for me. The erotic is already eroticized.

Probably, when Guattari picks up an article whose first sentence has the words "machine," "structure," and "determination," he cathects it immediately. Great stuff.

Juicy, terrific. The same would go for Bloom on encountering multiple references to Nietzsche, representation, God the father, and the Sublime. But isn't erotic domination, as a subject, surer to arouse strong feeling than systems of machines or the psyche that can be represented as a text? Clearly, the answer depends on the readership. The people at the convenience store where I stop to get gas and buy milk would find all these passages equally baffling. Though they *might* have uneasy stirrings when they read Jessica Benjamin. "Erotic domination," especially when coupled with "porno newsstands," does call some feelings into play almost no matter who you are in this culture.

But I will concede the point. What is personal is completely a function of what is perceived as personal. And what is perceived as personal by men, or rather, what is gripping, significant, "juicy," is different from what is felt to be that way by women. For what we are really talking about is not the personal as such, what we are talking about is what is important, answers one's needs, strikes one as immediately *interesting*. For women, the personal is such a category.

In literary criticism, we have moved from the New Criticism, which was antipersonal and declared the personal off-limits at every turn—the intentional fallacy, the affective fallacy—to structuralism, which does away with the self altogether—at least as something unique and important to consider—to deconstruction, which subsumes everything in language and makes the self non-self-consistent, ungraspable, a floating signifier, and finally to new historicism which re-institutes the discourse of the object—"In the seventeenth century"—with occasional side glances at how the author's "situatedness" affects his writing.

The female subject par excellence, which is her self and her experiences, has once more been elided by literary criticism.

The question is, why did this happen? One might have imagined a different outcome. The 1960s paves the way for a new personalism in literary discourse by opening literary discussion up to politics, to psychology, to the "reader," to the effects of style. What happened to deflect criticism into the impersonal labyrinths of "language," "discourse," "system," "network," and now, with Guattari, "machine"?

I met Ellen Messer-Davidow last summer at the School of Criticism and Theory where she was the undoubted leader of the women who were there. She organized them, led them (I might as well say us, since, although I was on the faculty as a visiting lecturer, she led me, too). At the end of the summer we put on a symposium, a kind of teach-in on feminist criticism and theory, of which none was being offered that summer. I thought it really worked. Some people, eager to advertise their intellectual superiority, murmured disappointment at the "level" of discussion (code for, "my mind is finer and more rigorous than yours"). One person who spoke out at the closing session said he felt bulldozed: a more honest and useful response. The point is that Ellen's leadership affected the experience of everyone at the School that summer. What she offered was not an intellectual performance calculated to draw attention to the quality of her mind, but a sustained effort of practical courage that changed the situation we were in. I think that the kind of thing Ellen did should be included in our concept of criticism: analysis that is not an end in itself but pressure brought to bear on a situation.

Now it's time to talk about something that's central to everything I've been saying so far, although it doesn't *show*, as we used to say about the slips we used to wear. If I had to bet on it, I would say that Ellen Messer-Davidow was motivated last summer, and probably in her essay, by anger (forgive me, Ellen, if I am wrong), anger at her, our, exclusion from what was being studied at the School, our exclusion from the discourse of "Western man." I interpret her behavior this way because anger is what fuels my engagement with feminist issues; an absolute fury that has never even been tapped, relatively speaking. It's time to talk about this now, because it's so central, at least for me. I hate men for the way they treat women, and pretending that women aren't there is one of the ways I hate most.

Last night I saw a movie called *Gunfight at the OK Corral*, starring Burt Lancaster and Kirk Douglas. The movie is patently about the love-relationship between the characters these men play—Wyatt Earp and Doc Holliday. The women in the movie are merely pawns that serve in various ways to reflect the characters of the men and to advance the story of their relationship to one another. There is a particularly humiliating part, played by Jo Van Fleet, the part of Doc Holliday's mistress—Kate Fisher—whom he treats abominably (everybody in the movie acknowledges this, it's not just me saying so). This woman is degraded over and over again. She is a whore, she is a drunkard, she is a clinging woman, she betrays the life of Wyatt Earp in order to get Doc Holliday back, she is *no longer young* (perhaps this is her chief sin). And her words are always in vain, they are chaff, less than nothing, another sign of her degradation.

Now Doc Holliday is a similarly degraded character. He used to be a dentist and is now a gambler who lives to get other people's money away from them; he is a drunk, and he abuses the woman who loves him. But his weaknesses, in the perspective of the movie, are glamorous. He is irresistible, charming, seductive, handsome, witty, commanding; it's no wonder Wyatt Earp falls for him, who wouldn't? The degradation doesn't stick to Kirk Douglas; it is all absorbed by his female counterpart, the "slut," Jo Van Fleet. We are embarrassed every time she appears on the screen, because every time, she is humiliated further.

What enrages me is the way women are used as extensions of men, mirrors of men, devices for showing men off, devices for helping men get what they want. They are never there in their own right, or rarely. The world of the Western contains no women.

Sometimes I think *the world* contains no women.

Why am I so angry?

My anger is partly the result of having been an only child who caved in to authority very early on. As a result I've built up a huge storehouse of hatred and resentment against people in authority over me (mostly male). Hatred and resentment and attraction.

Why should poor men be made the object of this old pent-up anger? (Old anger is the best anger, the meanest, the truest, the most intense. Old anger is pure because it's been dislocated from its source for so long, has had the chance to ferment, to feed on itself for so many years, so that it is nothing but anger. All cause, all relation to the outside world, long since sloughed off, withered away. The rage I feel inside me now is the distillation of forty-six years. It has had a long time to simmer, to harden, to become adamantine, a black slab that glows in the dark.)

Are all feminists fueled by such rage? Is the molten lava of millennia of hatred boiling below the surface of every essay, every book, every syllabus, every newsletter, every little magazine? I imagine that I can open the front of my stomach like a door, reach in, and pluck from memory the rooted sorrow, pull it out, root and branch. But where, or rather, who, would I be then? I am attached to this rage. It is a source of identity for me. It is a motivator, an explainer, a justifier, a no-need-to-say-more greeter at the door. If I were to eradicate this anger somehow, what would I do? Volunteer work all day long?

A therapist once suggested to me that I blamed on sexism a lot of stuff that really had to do with my own childhood. Her view was basically the one articulated in Alice Miller's *The Drama of the Gifted Child*, in which the good child has been made to develop a false self by parents who cathect the child narcissistically. My therapist meant that if I worked out some of my problems—as she understood them, on a psychological level—my feminist rage would subside.

Maybe it would, but that wouldn't touch the issue of female oppression. Here is what Miller says about this:

> Political action can be fed by the unconscious anger of children who have been…misused, imprisoned, exploited, cramped, and drilled…. If, however, disillusionment and the resultant mourning can be lived through…, then social and political disengagement do not usually follow, but the patient's actions are freed from the compulsion to repeat. (101)

According to Miller's theory, the critical voice inside me, the voice I noticed butting in, belittling, doubting, being wise, is "the contemptuous introject."—the introjection of authorities who manipulated me, without necessarily meaning to. I think that if you can come to terms with your "contemptuous introjects," learn to forgive and understand them, your anger will go away.

But if you're not angry, can you still act? Will you still care enough to write the letters, make the phone calls, attend the meetings? You need to find another center within yourself from which to act. A center of outgoing, outflowing, giving feelings. Love instead of anger. I'm embarrassed to say words like these because I've been taught they are mushy and sentimental and smack of cheap popular psychology. I've been taught to look down on people who read M. Scott Peck and Leo Buscaglia and Harold Kushner, because they're people who haven't very much education and because they're mostly women. Or if not women, then people who take responsibility, for learning how to deal with their feelings, who take responsibility for marriages that are going bad, for children who are in trouble, for friends who need help, for themselves. The disdain for popular psychology and for words like "love" and "giving" is part of the police action that academic intellectuals wage ceaselessly against feeling, against women, against what is personal. The ridiculing of the "touchy-feely," of the "Mickey Mouse," of the sentimental (often associated with teaching that takes students' concerns into account), belongs to the tradition Alison Jaggar rightly characterized as founding knowledge in the denial of emotion. It is looking down on women, with whom feelings are associated, and on the activities with which women are identified: mother, nurse, teacher, social worker, volunteer.

So for a while I can't talk about epistemology. I can't deal with the philosophical bases of feminist literary criticisms. I can't strap myself psychically into an apparatus that will produce the right gestures when I begin to move. I have to deal with the trashing of emotion and with my anger against it.

This one time I've taken off the straitjacket, and it feels so good.

References

Benjamin, Jessica. "Master and Slave: The Fantasy of Erotic Domination." *The Powers of Desire: The Politics of Sexuality.* Ed. Ann Snitow, Christine Stansell, and Sharon Thompson. New York: Monthly Review Press, 1983. 280–89.

Bloom, Harold. *Poetry and Repression: Revision from Blake to Stevens.* New Haven, Conn.: Yale University Press, 1976.

Foucault, Michel. *The History of Sexuality*, Volume 1: *An Introduction.* Trans. Robert Hurley. New York: Vintage Books, 1980. Copyright 1978 by Random House. [Originally published in French as *La Volonté de Savoir.* Paris: Editions Gallimard, 1976.]

Griffin, Susan. "The Way of All Ideology." *Made from the Earth: An Anthology of Writings.* New York: Harper and Row, 1982. 161–82.

Guattari, Felix. *Molecular Revolution: Psychiatry and Politics.* Trans. Rosemary Sheed, intro. David Cooper. New York: Penguin Books, 1984. [First published as *Psychanalyse et transversalité (1972), and La Révolution moléculaire* (1977).]

Hawthorne, Nathaniel. *The Scarlet Letter and Other Tales of the Puritans.* Ed. with an intro. and notes by Harry Levin. Boston, Mass.: Houghton Mifflin, 1960–61.

LeGuin, Ursula. "The Mother Tongue." *Bryn Mawr Alumnae Bulletin* (Summer 1986): 3–4.

Miller, Alice. *The Drama of the Gifted Child.* New York: Basic Books, 1983.

Experimental Critical Writing

Marianna Torgovnick

At the 1988 MLA Convention I gave a paper called "Malinowski's Body." Since I was afraid to give this paper, I had announced it in the program by the deliberately neutral title "Looking at Anthropologists" so that I could change my mind up to the last minute and substitute something else instead. I was afraid because "Malinowski's Body" does not resemble the usual MLA paper in style or content. I knew that the audience would listen to it and respond to it, and I knew that some members of the audience would not like it and might even walk out—and not because there was another talk they wanted to hear at the same hour.

"Malinowski's Body" did not begin its life in any of the ways I have been taught to consider legitimate. In fact, I wrote it, almost as a dare, after my writing group found the first material I wrote on Malinowski dull. To prove I could do better I went home and wrote several pages that begin this way:

> Malinowski's body looks like Lord Jim's. It's cased rigidly in white or beige trousers and shirt that sometimes becomes stained a muddy brown. When this happens, Malinowski summons his servants and has the clothes washed, immediately. For his clothes some-how seem to him an important part of his body, not just a covering for it.
>
> It's a small body, well fed but not kindly disposed enough toward itself to put on flesh. It has a narrow chest—pale, with just a few hairs and no nipples to speak of. It has thin legs yearning for massive thighs; in fact, if this man does put on weight in later life (and he may) it will show in his thighs first. The buttocks lie flat, unwelcoming, with maybe a stray pimple. The penis is a center of anxiety for him but is in fact no smaller—and no bigger—than anyone else's. It's one of the few points of identification he can settle on between his body and theirs.
>
> Their bodies—almost naked—unnerve him. His body needs its clothes; his head, its hat. He rarely looks at his body—except when washing it. But he has to look at theirs. The dislike he sometimes feels for the natives comes over him especially when in the presence of their bodies. "Come in and bathe," the natives say from their ponds and rivers. "No, thanks," says Malinowski, retrieving the pith helmet and camera he

396

momentarily laid aside on the grass. He looks at their bodies and takes notes about size, ornamentation, haircuts, and other ethnographic data. He takes photographs. He talks to them about customs, trade, housing, sex. He feels okay about the customs, trade, and housing, but the sex makes him uneasy.

The pages are based on an intuition and a hunch about what Malinowski looked like that were formed before I had found any pictures of him. They begin with an image rather than with the kind of concise generalization that had been my customary opening. And they were designed to loosen my prose by giving my imagination free play. Inevitably, I used what I had read by and about Malinowski—but in an almost unrecognizable way. My premise was that I would undress the ethnographer for study as Malinowski himself undresses subjects in his ethnographies and undresses, in his diary, the women he meets in daily life. When I wrote "Malinowski's Body" I did not intend to use it in the book I was writing. My goals were simply to limber up my style and to get in touch with what I wanted to say. But "Malinowski's Body" makes so many points about the ethnographer's scripting of himself according to conventional ideas of what is moral and manly that I decided to include it in my book. It is a creative piece, risky for the MLA. And yet my audience, or at least most of its members, seemed delighted. They asked questions about my "intentions" and "effects" that made me feel like a writer, not just a critic—a heady moment for me and a reception that gave David Laurence reason to invite me to present my thoughts on experimental critical writing. And it was a moment that had not come easily.

When I began to write my newest book—called *Gone Primitive* and published in the spring of 1990—I knew that I wanted to write something significantly different in tone and style from my first two books. I had recently been tenured and then promoted to full professor, and I felt that I was no longer writing for any committees—I was writing for myself. It was not that I would rewrite the books I had written; I am in fact proud of them. What I wanted was to reach a larger audience and to go somewhere new. What I discovered was that at first I did not know how.

The turning point came when I showed an early chapter to the members of my newly formed writing group. I was writing on an untraditional, uncanonical topic—Edgar Rice Burroughs' Tarzan novels—but my approach was conventional and scholarly. I began by surveying the critical literature on Tarzan and protesting (a little uneasily) that earlier critics either had overidentified with Burroughs or had not taken Tarzan seriously with regard to race and gender relations. I tried to pack lots of statistics and facts in the opening paragraphs to prove that Tarzan was important. In my eagerness to meet accepted standards of academic seriousness, I had succeeded (to borrow a phrase Wayne Booth once used to describe the freshman essay) in being "boring from within."

The members of my group, from whom I had asked no mercy that day, showed none. The chapter was sluggish, they said; the prose was lifeless and cold. It had no momentum, no narrative. Instinctively, I defended myself; I talked about all the interesting things that happened as I was researching and writing the chapter, telling them how I often found articles on the rebirth of the Tarzan phenomenon in issues of magazines that report the assassination of President Kennedy and reproduce those astonishing pictures we all remember of Jackie and little John-John and of Oswald. I had tried in the chapter to place the Tarzan series in the contexts of the twenties (the decade of its first great popularity) and the sixties (the decade of its rebirth). But I had used a style that censored my own experiences and visceral responses and that hid my writing's source of energy. One member of the group said, cannily, "You know, none of what you've just said comes out in this chapter. And there's a huge difference between the things you say and the things you write. You never write anything funny. You often say funny things." She was right. The other members of the group asked me to say more about La, a barbarian priestess in the Tarzan novels whom I had mentioned in passing. As I warmed to my description of La's importance and La's wrongs, my friend said, "When you start to get dull, pretend you are La—because you *are* La." And she was also right.

For me, "writing like La" became a metaphor for getting to a place where I was not afraid to write in a voice that had passion as well as information—a voice that wanted to be heard. "Writing like La" meant letting myself out of the protective cage of the style I had mastered—a style I now call the thus-and-therefore style because it naturally tends to include distancing words like those. Before I could change my thus-and-therefore style, I had to defamiliarize it; I had to know my cage so that I could open it at will. A fifteen-minute exercise I did with my writing group was a significant breakthrough. In this exercise, I parodied my own dullest style in a description of grocery stores in Durham, North Carolina. I began the description with just the kind of generalization that was one of my primary tics as a writer: "In Durham, one can shop at Food Lion for bargains, or Kroger's for selection. The most interesting shopping of all, however, is done at Harris Teeter." This exercise made me laugh at my own habits and made it impossible for me afterward to write unknowingly in my usual way. But there were still many low points, when I found myself unable to do anything *but* write in my dullest style. In fact, I wrote my excruciatingly bad beginning on Malinowski— the material I replaced with "Malinowski's Body"—roughly eighteen months after I vowed to leave my old style behind.

In preparing this presentation, I discovered in my files my first draft on Malinowski. I would like to share part of its beginning with you as an example of one sort of standard academic prose:

> Implicitly, I have been suggesting that "objectivity" is a delusory principle undergirding both important strands of social scientific and ethnographic thought and aesthetic and artistic-literary theories and methods. Rereading Malinowski, I think I've found a direct and interesting analogy.
>
> Malinowski founded what is called functionalism in anthropology, the theory (and derived method) that explains all elements of a culture in terms of interlocking functions: the ethnographer explicitly "constructs" a model in which all the parts are presumed to contribute to a whole that is organic and unified (though quirkier than a machine). To make his construction, the ethnographer lives inside the culture, inhabits it as a text. He tries to replicate the native's point of view, which is the ground and touchstone of meaning and "accuracy." Functionalism leads, in anthropology, to what is called structural functionalism and then, later, to structuralism.
>
> A point-by-point analogy with New Criticism and other formal approaches exists. Here too the "student" (critic) inhabits the text, assuming the unity of the parts

as a whole and constructing an account of that whole in terms of the interlocking functions of its parts. The original ground of meaning is the author's intentions.

What I was doing in these paragraphs was the writerly equivalent of scratching at a scab. I had to say what was closest to the surface of my mind in order to get rid of that content, in order to discover whether it was useful or not, interesting or not. Sometimes, what I write first as a throwaway turns out to contain the intellectual core of my argument; sometimes, as in this real throwaway, it does not. The difference is usually whether I begin with material that I really care about or with material that I think I should care about. In this instance, I began with critical categories and genealogies of influence that I knew, by training, were considered important—and I trotted them out dutifully. Other critics had scratched these scabs; now it was my turn. The paragraphs include a lot of qualifications and distinctions, often inserted in parenthetical remarks, that would be unlikely to interest anyone but me. Sticky academic language coats the whole—"implicitly," "explicitly," "strand of thought." And I explain things in more detail than most people would want to read.

I would be too embarrassed to reproduce this rejected passage if I did not realize that it's representative of the prose that I—and I suspect many of you—habitually write. For this style typifies a great deal of academic writing. How did it come to be a norm? Largely, I think by establishing itself in an era when less criticism was published and the circle of critics was small enough to allow its members to believe they were contributing to the building of a common edifice. In this construction project all the names could and should be named, like those of contributors on a memorial plaque; Professor Z would build on what Professors X and Y had said in their essays; years later, Professors A and B would come along and add some decorative touches or do major renovations.

All of us who write criticism today wrote dissertations yesterday. And our teachers often tried, and succeeded in handing on what they perceived as the correct—that is, the careful, the judicious, the fair—way to write. But the styles we were taught can't work now in the same way as they worked fifty or even fifteen years ago. No one who gets around to writing a book, or even an essay, ever reads everything that has been written about its subject. Yet we cling to the fiction of completeness and coverage that the academic style preserves. This style protects us, we fondly believe, from being careless or subjective or unfair. It prescribes certain moves to ensure that the writer will stay within the boundaries that the academy has drawn.

Like many people who choose an academic life, I have a fundamental need for approval. I needed approval from my graduate advisers, tenure and promotion committees, and reviewers; I need it from my students and colleagues. It has been crucial for me in the last few years to have a writing group that approved of my new writing style: the group provided a different audience from the one I once imagined as my academic superiors, who judged the material I wrote according to more traditional standards. But I have also become aware that I am now not just someone in need of approval but also someone (like many of you) who gives or withholds approval. When we pass on the academic style to our graduate students or newest colleague, we train them to stay within the boundaries, both stylistically and conceptually. When we encourage experimental critical writing, we do not always know what we will get, but we stimulate the profession to grow and to change. We don't control the future of the profession only when we give grades or make hiring or tenure decisions; we control it at the level of the sentence.

At this point I need to back up a bit. It seems pretty clear to me that if all we want to do is to write for professional advancement, to write for a fairly narrow circle of critics who exist within the same disciplinary boundaries as we do, there is nothing really wrong with the traditional academic style. In fact, it's the right style, the inevitable style, because it says, in every superfluous detail and in every familiar move, You don't need to read me except to write your own project; I am the kind of writing that does not want to be heard.

But when critics want to be read, and especially when they want to be read by a large audience, they have to court their readers. And the courtship begins when the critic begins to think of himself or herself as a writer as well, a process that for me, as for some other critics of my generation, means writing as a person with feelings, histories, and desires—as well as information and knowledge. When writers want to be read they have to be more flexible and take more chances than the standard scholarly style allows: often, they have to be more direct and more personal. In a very real way (although my writing includes precious few autobiographical revelations), I could not think of myself as a writer until I risked exposing myself in my writing.

I am not talking here, necessarily, about full-scale autobiographical writing—though I am not ruling it out either. But I am saying that writerly writing is personal writing, whether or not it is autobiographical. Even if it offers no facts from the writer's life, or offers just a hint of them here and there, it makes the reader know some things about the writer—a fundamental condition, it seems to me, of any real act of communication. And real communication is exciting. For me, at any rate, the experience of this new kind of writing—which not only recognizes the pitfalls of the standard academic style but goes out of its way to avoid them—has been exhilarating.

Part III

Composing
Creative Nonfiction

In the earlier sections of this book you've had the chance to pair up what people write when they write creative nonfiction with what people talk about when they talk about creative nonfiction. Many of the writers whose work appears in Part One also talk about the genre in which they work in Part Two. They often also talk about the ways they typically create the work they do in creative nonfiction. In Part Three we take the discussion a little farther by pairing four pieces that could have gone into the first part of this book with four pieces in which their authors describe how they wrote them.

Writers' descriptions of what they did and what they went through as they wrote a particular essay or article often suggest strategies that other writers can use. Even the most experienced writers occasionally find themselves stymied by projects they've been working on, but because they are experienced they have strategies to fall back on that help them to begin writing again. Often their strategies arise not from their own problem-solving but by the example of another writer. For example, many writers in many different forms have subscribed to Horace's advice, "Never a day without a line." They try to write every day, even if only for a limited time, because they find there is a creative equivalent of the law of inertia—"A mind in motion tends to stay in motion; a pen at rest tends to stay at rest." To that perhaps they add Hemingway's advice to quit writing for the day before you've exhausted your energy and your ideas and to return to writing the next day knowing where you're going to start up again. There are many sound principles and practices in the creative life, and writers often must rummage among them for the ones that work for them. They also have to be prepared to discard them if they aren't working or if they don't seem to be very useful for a different project. Writers have to be flexible and adaptable in order to be productive, and the best place to find useful strategies and techniques other than those you discover for yourself is in the discoveries that other writers have made for themselves.

Even when writers have been successful in the past and would appear to know a number of moves they might make in their writing, they sometimes need to be reminded of the things they already know about writing. Sometimes the press of a work-in-progress makes it difficult to step back from it and apply alternative approaches, until the writer stumbles on something someone else did and remembers that he or she knew about that approach before. Some writers collect quotes about writing and, to help them remember, tape them to the wall or the word processor—some writers have *a lot* of stuff sticking to their walls, because there's *a lot* of relevant advice out there.

Consider this section, then, as a way to see what other writers have done as they wrote the kind of writing you've been reading in this book. Taken as a whole, the Composing Creative Nonfiction section presents four pairs of essays, arranged alphabetically by author. The first piece in each pair is the work that serves as the focus of the second piece, which explains the writer's composing processes on that particular work. Reading all eight pieces together is like sitting in on a writing group where each member reads something she's written and then explains what she went through to get the final draft. The writing is different enough that the responses of the writers and the shifting demands of purpose and form offer a range of strategies and creative decisions. Emily Chase's "Warping Time with Montaigne" is a personal critical essay linking the practices of Montaigne, the original essayist, with those of contemporary writer Richard Rodriguez in his essay "Late Victorians"; her "Notes from a Journey toward 'Warping Time'" explains how this piece of what Marianna Torgovnick calls "experimental critical writing" came about. Simone Poirier-Bures writes travel memoir in "That Shining Place: Crete, 1966"; her "Afterword: Writing 'The Greece Piece'" traces the course of her attempts to write about the experience more than twenty years later. Mary Elizabeth Pope's "Teacher Training" is an essay running in two parallel strands, one about her first teaching experience, the other about her fourth-grade teacher; "Composing 'Teacher Training'" follows the development of the essay from inception to publication, including changes after the piece was accepted. Maureen Stanton writes a very personal memoir of her fiance's illness in "Zion" and recounts how she composed the essay in "On Writing 'Zion'." Four very different essays, four very different composing processes.

The selections here also connect to pieces in other parts of the book, and they can be read separately, in conjunction with other examples and discussions. Emily Chase's work is related to Richard Rodriguez's "Late Victorians," of course, but also to other pieces demonstrating or discussing personal voice in academic writing, such as those by Jane Tompkins, Peter Elbow, and Marianna Torgovnick. Simone Poirier-Bures's pairing connects to the other writing about time and place in the book, whether in memoir, essay, or literary journalism, including the writing by Mary Clearman Blew, William DeBuys, Pico Iyer, and Patricia Hampl. Mary Beth Pope's writing can handily supplement the segmented essays in the book, especially those that leap lightly across time and space, such as the essays of Mary Clearman Blew, Noami Shihab Nye, and Nancy Willard. Maureen Stanton's memoir is appropriate to read along with any of the other memory pieces in the book as well as the essays dwelling on the human body and health, such as those by Phillip Lopate, Nancy Mairs, Richard Rodriguez, and Richard Selzer. Already in trying to cite a few relevant examples I've begun to repeat references, but that's because the writing in Part Three reverberates in so many other readings throughout the book.

The other connection these selections make is, of course, to your writing. The process pieces here, where the writers describe composing their essays, don't prescribe failsafe procedures to which you should conform—quite the contrary. As these examples show, writers don't follow a rigid set of universal rules for composing; instead, they rely on general approaches and alternative strategies that they can alter to fit the shape of their individual works-in-progress. The experiences of these writers suggest strategies that you might be able to adapt to your own projects. They would be valuable to consult when you find yourself beginning or developing similar writing projects.

Finally, as you compose your own essays and assignments, you might consider keeping a journal on your own composing processes, to get a handle on what you generally do when you write and what you've done especially for certain projects. Think of Composing Creative Nonfiction as sitting in on a writing group in session, and feel free to enter the conversation with your own writing about your own composing.

Warping Time with Montaigne

Emily D. Chase

I sit bent over the breast beam of my 38 inch LeClerc floor loom pulling individual threads of brilliant, durable yarn through the metal heddles of its six harnesses. The heddles that have already been threaded hang in orderly lines waiting for the command to raise and lower those threads of yarn in the process of creating fabric; the unthreaded heddles hang in unorganized clusters patiently waiting for their turn to take part. This threading process is called "warping the loom" because the yarn that is being threaded onto the loom will become the "warp"—or lengthwise threads—in the fabric that will be woven. This process of reaching through the heddle with the threading hook, catching a strand of yarn, and pulling it back through the heddle does not require a lot of thought, other than that required to make sure the right piece of yarn gets threaded through the right heddle. My mind is free to wander as it will while I prepare my loom. "My style and my mind alike go roaming," Montaigne said (761). Of course I think of Montaigne; I have just spent two weeks reading essays by Montaigne, about Montaigne, and about essayists who have written essays on Montaigne. I have Montaigne on the brain: What sort of essays would Montaigne write if he were still alive? What would he say about the essays being written today? In particular, what would he say about Richard Rodriguez's essay "Late Victorians"? I pull a strand of yarn through a heddle and think of Montaigne and Rodriguez.

Rodriguez's essay uses many of the elements of the genre that Montaigne created. If Montaigne had not spun the first ideas of the essay into a new genre of literature, Rodriguez would not have been able to write "Late Victorians" without first spinning the thread of the genre on his own. I see that Montaigne's thoughts and ideas have been pulled through time to be used as the warp of essays since Montaigne's book *Essais* was first published in 1580. Now I am the one sitting at the loom of time, pulling the thoughts and ideas of Montaigne through the heddles. The full body of Montaigne's essays lies rolled up upon itself on the warp beam of the loom, waiting to be used by anyone with the knowledge and patience to thread it through time and secure it to this side of the past.

I reach through the eyelet of a heddle for a piece of Montaigne and imagine Rodriguez doing the same thing as he created "Late Victorians." For, certainly, he pulled Montaigne's motto through time—"Que scais-je?" (What do I know?). Rodriguez explores this question in "Late Victorians" as he asks himself how he should live his life and how he should *have lived* his life. These are the central questions and themes of his essay. He asks himself if he should have pursued "an earthly paradise charming," like the gay men he has known who have since died of AIDS (131). He considers the possibility of having pursued a career in office buildings which "were hives where money was made, and damn all" (128). At the end of "Late Victorians," he questions his future: Should he remain shifting his "tailbone upon the cold, hard pew," or should he rise to join the volunteers of the local AIDS Support Group (134)?

The genre of the essay offers Rodriguez an opportunity to explore these issues by using Montaigne's question, "What do I know?" Montaigne says:

> This…happens to me: that I do not find myself in the place where I look; and I find myself more by chance encounter than by searching my judgment. I will have tossed off some subtle remark as I write. Later I have lost the point so thoroughly that I do not know what I meant; and sometimes a stranger has discovered it before I do. If I erased every passage where this happens to me, there would be nothing left of myself. (26–27)

The form of the essay as Montaigne conceived it allows Rodriguez the freedom to seek answers, or to appear to seek answers, *while* he writes rather than exclusively *before* he writes. For Montaigne, writing was an *essai*, a trial or attempt. The presence of self and the absence of conclusion create a sense of freedom within Montaigne's essays. As he says: "The surest thing, in my opinion, would be to trace our actions to the neighboring circumstances, without getting into any further research and without drawing from them any other conclusions" (241). Like Montaigne, Rodriguez comes to no irrefutable conclusions in "Late Victorians." Instead, his thoughts wander through memories and observations as he seeks an understanding of the world by examining the things which touch his life directly.

As I consider the themes of "Late Victorians," I think of the title of one of Montaigne's essays, "By diverse means we arrive at the same end" (3). It occurs to me that this title describes the realm in which Rodriguez's thoughts wander. For what is Rodriguez writing about but diverse lifestyles and inevitable death? Running across his essay are the threads of gay life and death from AIDS. The texture of the weave is enhanced by Rodriguez's use of details from his own experience; these details form the weft of his essay, the crosswise threads. This weft is beaten into the fabric of "Late Victorians," as the "beater" on a loom locks the warp and weft tightly together by pushing each strand of weft snugly against the preceding strand, creating a cohesive, durable piece of fabric. Rodriguez weaves the fourteen sections of "Late Victorians" in this way, choosing different yarns for the weft of each section to create different textures and density of prose.

The first section is brief and is composed of two conflicting quotes. The first, by St. Augustine, hints at our discontent on earth in our mortal form due to our intuition that we are destined for a better life after death. Life is something to be restlessly passed through. The second quote, by Elizabeth Taylor, speaks of "cerulean" days in this life being undermined by sadness in the knowledge that these days and this life must end. These quotes show that, like Proteus, we are able to change our shape (the shape of our thoughts) as we try to avoid being bound by life. We are free to choose which way we will view life, whether we will suffer life and rejoice the end or embrace life and mourn the end. In "Late Victorians," Rodriguez tries to decide which view is the better view. He weaves these two quotes into his text to prepare us for the creation which is to follow. What is life? What is death? Which one wears the mask covering reality?

Throughout the essay, Rodriguez portrays the paradox of homosexual life in San Francisco. He uses the image of the Victorian house to help him accomplish this. By noting that the "three- or four-story Victorian house, like the Victorian novel, was built to contain several generations and several classes under one roof, behind a single oaken door" (123), he reveals the irony of the housing market whereby "gay men found themselves living with the architectural metaphor for family" (122). From this image, Rodriguez goes exploring through the homosexual landscape of his life and discovers multiple conflicting images. Rodriguez says, "The age-old description of homosexuality is of a sin against nature," yet he observes that as the peaceful, domestic, homosexual community of the Castro district thrived, the perverted "assortment of leather bars…outlaw sexuality…eroticism of the dark" on heterosexual Folsom street also thrived (124–25). In the Castro district, thanks to gays, "where recently there had been loudmouthed kids, hole-in-the-wall bars, [and] pimps," there were now "tweeds and perambulators, matrons and nannies" (125). The gay men, who have chosen to embrace "the complacencies of the barren house," have made the streets safe once again for the family (127).

This depiction of peaceful homosexual life is strikingly linked to another paradox of gay life as Rodriguez describes two parades in which gay men with AIDS march for gay rights. Rodriguez depicts gay men in one Gay Freedom Day parade as "the blessed in Renaissance paintings," martyrs who cherish "the apparatus of [their] martyrdom" (119). This passage is followed immediately by a description of a parade five years later, which includes "plum-spotted young men." The juxtaposition of the two passages creates the disturbing impression that these people are fighting to choose the way they wish to die rather than the way they wish to live.

How is Rodriguez going to reconcile all of these conflicting images? I pull another strand of Montaigne through time and see that the essay, as a form, allows Rodriguez to go exploring without *having* to reconcile these images. Montaigne says in his essay "Of repentance":

> This is a record of various and changeable occurrences, and of irresolute and, when it so befalls, contradictory ideas: whether I am different myself, or whether I take hold of my subjects in different circumstances and aspects. So, all in all, I may indeed contradict myself now and then; but truth, as Demades said, I do not contradict. If my mind could gain a firm footing, I would not make essays; I would make decisions; but it is always in apprenticeship and on trial. (611)

Montaigne is speaking of his contradictory thoughts and ideas, and yet the passage is equally applicable to Rodriguez's treatment of the paradox of gay life.

Montaigne's passage makes me wonder, as I slowly and steadily thread my way across the loom, if ALL of Montaigne is present in the warp of Rodriguez's essay. Would all of Montaigne's writings have to be threaded through time as an inseparable skein of thought, in order to remain true as a body of writing? Or could a person be selective when choosing which parts she pulled through time? I think of the warp on my loom, and I know that it is not possible to thread just part of a warp through the heddles. ALL of the strands of warp must be threaded, or the warp becomes tangled and knotted on the loom. For this reason, I have to think that all of Montaigne's thoughts are present in the warp of an essay, even when an essay presents an opposing view of that held by Montaigne.

I ponder this question because of the way I have linked Montaigne's quote from his essay "Of repentance" to the image of the AIDS victims in the Gay Freedom Day parades. The quote is pertinent as it applies to the issue of contradictions and paradox, yet Montaigne and Rodriguez do not agree completely on the actual subject of repentance. Both Montaigne and Rodriguez recognize the value of youth and of what is often deemed youth's foolishness. Rodriguez says:

> Though I am alive now, I do not believe that an old man's pessimism is truer than a young man's optimism simply because it comes after. There are things a young man knows that are true and are not yet in the old man's power to recollect. (120)

This is similar to a passage of Montaigne's, in his essay "Of repentance" in which he says:

> I should be ashamed and resentful if the misery and misfortune of my decrepitude were to be thought better than my good, healthy, lively, vigorous years, and if people were to esteem me not for what I have been, but for ceasing to be that. (619)

On the issue of repentance itself, however, Montaigne and Rodriguez differ. While Montaigne declares, "If I had to live over again, I would live as I have lived" (620), Rodriguez says, "It was then I saw that the greater sin against heaven was my unwillingness to embrace life" (132). There is an edge of repentance in Rodriguez's text, which does not exist in Montaigne's writings.

We are never sure, however, of what it is that Rodriguez feels the need to repent. In boldly talking about the gay community in San Francisco, Rodriguez appears to be revealing himself as a gay man, yet Phillip Lopate says, "Richard Rodriguez, for instance, is a master of the confessional tone, yet he tells us that his family calls him 'Mr. Secrets,' and he plays a hide-and-seek game of revealing himself" (xxvii). This is the case in "Late Victorians." Rodriguez describes the gay community of San Francisco from the perspective of a person who has been a part of that community. He has marched in a Gay Freedom Day parade; he has many male friends who are gay; he lives in a Victorian house which has been reclaimed and redecorated by gay men and now contains "four apartments; four single men"; he says, "To grow up homosexual is to live with secrets and within secrets" (122). And yet, on his deathbed, a friend of Rodriguez's, Cesar, says with irony that Rodriguez "would be the only one spared," that he was "too circumspect" (131). Rodriguez never actually says that he is gay. What are we to think?

I continue the process of pulling strands of yarn and thought through the loom: Does it matter if Rodriguez is gay? Does it matter if he tells us he is or isn't gay? What do I, as a reader, think of the authority of voice in the piece if this information appears to be purposefully concealed? Essayist E. B. White declared, "There is one thing the essayist cannot do—he cannot indulge himself in deceit or in concealment, for he will be found out in no time" (xxvi). And yet Alexander Smith wrote of Montaigne, "If you wish to preserve your secret, wrap it up in frankness" (Lopate xxvii). Montaigne said, "We must remove the mask," but he also said that he has "painted [his] inward self with colors clearer than [his] original ones" (504). Clearly, the act of making one's private thoughts public is not as simple as just recording the observations of one's life or even of simply attempting to capture one's mind in the act of thinking, as Montaigne set out to do.

I look back across the loom at the threads I have pulled through the heddles and am reminded that essays consist of explorations, questions, and contradictions. In his essay "Late Victorians," Rodriguez questions his life and lifestyle. Should he embrace life and mourn death, as his gay friends do, or should he withhold himself from life and look forward to death, as he does in his role as a skeptic? "Skepticism became my demeanor toward them—I was the dinner-party skeptic, a firm believer in Original Sin and in the limits of possibility" (Rodriguez 131). Rodriguez does not find the answer to his question in "Late Victorians." In the essay, he remains shifting his "tailbone on the cold, hard pew" while he tries to decide which role to play—which mask to put on or, perhaps, which mask to take off.

It is the *quest* for answers rather than the answers themselves that distinguishes the Montaignian essay. In this respect, "Late Victorians" is a good example of a contemporary essay that has been woven on a warp of Montaigne. In other respects, such as the inclusion of quotations, the essay differs from those of Montaigne. (Montaigne's essays include numerous quotations, Rodriguez's few.) However, when I gaze across the warp threaded through my loom, I am reminded that even this difference is a tribute to Montaigne, for I see Montaigne's strand of thought that advocates rebellion against accepted forms of discourse, including his own.

It is likely that Montaigne's thoughts go warping through most literary nonfiction essays. This is very different from what Montaigne envisioned when he wrote the preface, "To the Reader," for his book *Essais*:

> I have had no thought of serving either you or my own glory. My powers are inadequate for such a purpose. I have dedicated it to the private convenience of my relatives and friends, so that when they have lost me (as soon they must), they may recover here some features of my habits and temperament, and by this means keep the knowledge they have had of me more complete and alive. (2)

I think of this quote as I pull the last strand of warp through its heddle and secure it to the cloth beam on my side of the loom. My loom is now ready to be used to create a piece of individuality. I wonder what I will create. Shall I weave in some of the texture of Rodriguez or of Reg Saner? Emerson or Ehrlich? The possibilities are endless. I step on a treddle to open the warp, throw my shuttle of weft across the threads, and allow "my style and my mind alike" to go roaming. I have warped my loom with Montaigne.

Works Cited

Lopate, Phillip, ed. *The Art of the Personal Essay*. New York: Anchor Books, 1994.

Montaigne, Michel de. *The Complete Works of Montaigne*. Trans. Donald M. Frame. Stanford: Stanford University Press, 1957.

Rodriguez, Richard. "Late Victorians." *The Best American Essays 1991*. Ed. Joyce Carol Oates. New York: Ticknor and Fields, 1991. 119–34.

White, E. B. *Essays of E. B. White*. New York: Harper and Row, 1977.

Notes From a Journey toward "Warping Time"

Emily D. Chase

The path that I took to create the essay "Warping Time With Montaigne" was not a direct path through the writing process. I meandered through personal experiences and through unfamiliar research before I found a thread to connect the two and to help me reach some sort of meaningful understanding of Montaigne and of myself. Since writing that essay, I have noticed that my path through the writing process is almost always indirect and that quite often the meandering path is the most direct way for me to get to insight and understanding. What follows here is essentially a travelogue of my journey toward "Warping Time With Montaigne."

The first time that I heard of Michel de Montaigne was in a course in Graduate Composition. Before that time, the term "essay," to me, was a generic term used by English teachers to refer to short pieces of nonfiction writing. I had no sense of the history of the term or the genre; however, I immediately became interested in Montaigne's writings and therefore decided to write about him for the required research paper in the class. The research paper was written immediately prior to "Warping Time With Montaigne" (the essay included here) and provided me with enough background information to pique my interest and to make me want to have some fun with the information in another piece of writing.

As part of the in-class prewriting for the research paper, I did a cluster/web off of the central term "literary nonfiction." The freewriting that followed the cluster exercise reveals the general direction in which I was drawn:

> Having to research an area of, or a figure in, literary nonfiction, I might like to compare and contrast the original essays everyone quotes—Montaigne, Newman, Emerson, Thoreau—with the modern essayists (especially the nature writers)—Dillard, Ehrlich, Selzer, White—to see if the originals have affected the moderns. I'd like to find the ties, if any, between personal interaction with nature, religion...and the desire

to write LNF essays. Part of this study would be taking a look at how each essayist recorded his thoughts (i.e. Thoreau and his journals). Is each day a personal scrutiny of life? an appreciation of being alive? Part of LNF is taking a real daily event and personalizing it by recording your interaction w/it.

But where is this going in terms of research?—Study the masters, study the moderns, draw conclusions. What are people already saying about this link? Has anyone already taken this tack? Is this productive? Is this worthwhile?

I see in this freewrite the idea of not just the original research paper I did on Montaigne but perhaps also the germ of the idea behind "Warping." I never let go of this interest in the correlation between the early essayists and the current essayists.

In just ten days, I discovered a topic and pulled together a reasonable essay about Montaigne and his influence; I used the metaphor of building construction as I discussed the construction of the genre of literary nonfiction upon the foundation of Montaigne's writings. I think better and have more fun writing when I use metaphors to organize and present my thoughts. This fact, no doubt, played a major role in the process that I went through to create the "Warping" essay.

As I was finishing the research paper on Montaigne and just before I began the "Warping" essay, I read Gerald Early's essay "Life with Daughters: Watching the Miss America Pageant" and Jane Tompkins' essay "At the Buffalo Bill Museum." I was overwhelmed by the power of Early's piece, and my original reaction to this essay in my journal reflects this:

> Wow! What an essay!… Like a freight train, the fully loaded essay started slowly, exerting effort to overcome inertia, then slowly accumulated speed until it rushed, unstoppably, toward its destination. With Early's final sentence, "My knees had begun to hurt and I realized, painfully, that I was much too old, much too at peace with stiffness and inflexibility, for children's games," the train rushed off the end of the track into the great unknown void of the future. Wow!

By contrast, I did not like Tompkins' essay—or rather I did not understand her essay. My journal reaction to her essay is one long attempt to understand her point; I never do reach that understanding but come to the conclusion that "this is a disturbing piece because I can't see where the author is coming from. I'm not sure a rereading would help." It may seem irrelevant that I read these two essays between writing my two Montaigne essays, yet I think it was crucial that I read as powerful a creative commentary essay as Early's and that I read (and struggled with) Tompkins' essay just as I was directed to write an analysis paper of current literary nonfiction in which I would "explore an individual essay, a series of essays, or a particular author or authors." Both Early and Tompkins use objects and events that they see in their surroundings to launch themselves into realms of contemplation. I must have subconsciously hung onto this technique such that it resurfaced later as I tried to figure out what to do with the analysis assignment.

My initial plans for the analysis paper returned to my interest in the link between Montaigne and the essayists that are writing today. I was still too interested in Montaigne and too convinced of his importance as a crucial element in the genre of literary nonfiction to let go of him. However, we were instructed to comment upon (interpret/analyze) a more current essay. I began to play with possible ways to link Montaigne with current essayists.

On the day that we began working on the analysis paper, I wrote the following prewrite in class:

> Having the chance to write on one element or author in nonfiction, I think I'd like to pursue the elements of Montaigne's essays which can be found in the works of other essayists. Perhaps I could tackle Emerson's essay, "Montaigne," and show how that essay uses Montaignian practices in the process of praising Montaigne. This is a possibility. However, I'd also like to look at Montaigne versus Bacon in terms of voice in the essay and then apply that comparison to critical articles today—(i.e. tackle the 4-woman writers' group who are trying to write "readable" literary criticism [Tompkins, Kaplan, Torgovnik, Davidson]). I'd need to find out if there is much out there in terms of articles/essays on this debate. If *College English* is including these articles now but labeling them as opinion, is anyone reacting to this practice? Is Tompkins? Is Sommers? I think that this could be a much more interesting topic/issue than the piece on Emerson. It would also get me involved in a current intellectual discussion. Having had "Critical Theory" I feel that I have a fairly good base to stand on. Where would Dillard's book, *Living by Fiction*, fit in? or would it? Robert Coles? Who is arguing for Baconian essays in academia? Does Montaigne ever get mentioned in support of personal criticism?—Probably not. But a discussion of Montaigne vs Bacon could be fairly enlightening. I have lots of articles discussing this. I have the background material. I'd just have to dig into the contemporary information. Back to the MLA Bibliography....

I find it interesting as I reread this entry and as I dig through various drafts of the "Warping" essay that one comment I received during a peer editing session of the paper says, "Personally, I think this is better than a lot of the jargon-filled stuff I've read in academic journals." Again, I must have internalized the idea of "readable" criticism such that it resurfaced on its own later in the process.

On the same day that I wrote the above journal entry, as I was beginning work on this final paper, I kept trying to find a way to bring Montaigne into a criticism of a current essay. Because I have watched innumerable episodes of "Star Trek," it did not seem inconceivable to me that one of those hypothetical warps in the space-time continuum could allow Montaigne to suddenly appear in person to comment on the essays being written today. In the preceding research paper, I had already looked at how essayists since Montaigne had used his ideas and examples to help them create their own essays, so it seemed only fair that Montaigne should now have his say about the current essays that are being written. The word "warp" turned out to be the necessary spark that ignited an inspirational firestorm.

I remember the excitement that I felt when it struck me that the word warp carries a number of different meanings. I had been thinking of the term with a Star Trekian mentality of traveling through time and dimensions of reality, but I am also a weaver, and so as I thought of "warping time," I automatically thought of "warping a loom"—threading a warp onto a loom. After writing the journal entry about Montaigne and Bacon, I jotted down the following notes to myself:

exciting
Some ^ thoughts-
& ideas

this
could
be
really
fun!

"Warping Time: Montaigne on ____________"
sitting at loom, threading warp, thinking about
assignments/readings
critique article in my head by remembering
what Montaigne & critics of M.
have said.
get up to pursue details for more specifics
tie in with images of: thread
warp/weaving
distorted/warped time
structure & patterns & variations of woven cloth
lay warp on loom, like laying _____ on M.
or like laying M on ______.

In one moment of inspiration, I made the connection between the elements and process of threading a loom and the elements and process of writing an essay. I couldn't wait to start writing; all I needed was a modern essay to interpret in order to fulfill the requirements of the paper assignment.

It is probably important to note here that I had only one week in which to select and interpret a current essay. The title of Richard Rodriguez's "Late Victorians" drew me to his essay, and then his mix of dry humor and deadly seriousness fascinated me. As I read his essay with the warping idea in mind, I began to see Rodriguez as a weaver of essays and the fourteen sections of "Late Victorians" as variations of weft on the same warp. His essay seemed to be the perfect one for me to work with, and I could barely contain myself as I told my editing group about the ideas for my paper. I can still picture my teacher leaning forward on his chair with keen interest as I explained what I envisioned for my paper.

The writing of both my Montaigne papers was aided in large part by exercises and peer editing that were conducted as part of coursework in the Graduate Composition class. The drafting of each paper was preceded by a number of prewriting exercises to generate and organize ideas, and then once the drafting had begun, several different drafts of each paper were shared with a group of fellow students. I was a part of a four person editing group that provided valuable feedback and suggestions for revisions at every step of the drafting and revising process. The interaction of the editing group also tended to nurture creativity and spontaneity that proved to be crucial in the creation of "Warping Time With Montaigne."

Once I had shared my ideas for the paper with my group and with just two days left before my paper was due in class, I wrote the following journal entries as a way of organizing my thoughts and figuring out what I wanted to do with them in my paper:

> "Warping time" has the potential to be a really interesting essay. I need to list everything I want to be sure to say about Rodriguez's essay, those quotes of Montaigne's which directly apply to the points I want to make, and, then, the precise affiliations I want to assign to each metaphor of time and the loom. I wish I had more time to work on this.

What are the parts to my metaphor? If the loom = time, the warp = Montaigne, and the weft = Rodriguez, then what is the process of "warping the loom"? Is the threading of Montaigne through the hettles of time, the same as Montaigne's transcendence of time? His thoughts have to be durable enough to stand the strain put on the warp by the tension of the loom as well as the wear of the opening and closing of the shed and the friction of the beater as it swings along Montaigne and locks the weft of Rodriguez's ideas into the grasp of Montaigne's warp, while at the same time the interlocking of Rodriguez into Montaigne creates a brand new unique object formed by the interaction of the inter-working parts of time with the materials of Montaigne and Rodriguez.

The ideas of original thinkers get spun into yarn for warp. Rodriguez's end product is a piece of cloth which is available to the reader to use to make other things such as clothing, blankets, or ?.

If Montaigne is the warp, what do the 2 ends signify? The first end is the full body of Montaigne wound around itself in its full potential. The end I am threading is his ideas being taken through time to be used in the creation of new essays. 2 steps to trip through time—hettles and dent. What are they? hettles = individual thoughts and quotes (arranged to create potential of a pattern). dent = combining and spacing of ideas to assure a solid, even weave of the new fabric—literature vs nonliterature? Final step is to tie off Montaigne in the present on the cloth beam in order to hang onto his thoughts in the present to enable the creation of new essays.

My thoughts as I thread the loom consider the process Rodriguez went through in the creation of "Late Victorians." As I tie off the warp on my loom, I have secured Montaigne for use in my own creation and I have examined the creation of an accomplished weaver to glean ideas and techniques. I am ready to write—conceivably the result is essay in the reader's hands. How to do that?

Ending—my thoughts pull Montaigne into the present, now I am ready to weave my thoughts into an essay, I step on the treddles to raise the shed, throw the first pass of the shuttle and create, "I sit bent over the breast beam of my 38 inch LeClerc floor loom…"

This last journal entry was written after I had begun drafting my paper but before I had figured out how to conclude the essay. I have quoted the first line of the paper, yet my ideas are still just beginning to take form. I had originally planned to create a circular essay in which the ending leads back to the beginning in a never-ending retelling of this process; however, that idea got too confusing to be adequately developed in the limited amount of time that I had and therefore was changed in favor of the current ending.

I had a number of issues that needed to be sorted out as I tried to create a complete draft of the paper; therefore, as a way of figuring out what ideas I wanted to weave into the paper, I entered in my journal the following lists of what I believed were critical points to be dealt with in my paper:

Individual thoughts of Montaigne:

- Que scais-je?
- I want to be seen in simple, natural…it is myself I portray
- essai = trial or attempt

- self-portrait vs autobiography
- to be known not remembered
- to follow wanderings of his mind in process of thinking
- my mind & my thoughts…
- find self through writing
- loose disconnected structure—mirrors spontaneous thought
- portrait as friendly gesture
- familiar tone
- rebellion against rigid styles, formal language
- absence of dispositio
- sense of honesty

Points from Rodriguez:

- we choose our lifestyles
- sometimes we choose our deaths
- we all die
- wisdom in youth's foolishness
- R. focused on tragedy   Cesar—you cannot forbid tragedy
- R. full-time skeptic (131)(121)
- jealousy of responsible of irresponsible
- Victorian house as symbol of family—gay reclaim neighborhood
- new residents, new vision of family (Yuppies—birth control)
- masks (123)(131)
- caustic language (124–5) shock value, coarse cloth
- flipping of normal perspectives
- gays vs feminists
- nakedness (129)
- self-questioning in text (129)
- flowing thoughts (131)
- regret, repentance? (132)(134)

I spent successive late nights in the final week of the class working on this paper, as well as on revisions of other papers from that class. On the day before the final draft of the warping essay was due, my eyes felt unnaturally wide open from too much coffee and too little sleep, and yet still every time I thought about my paper, I felt excited about its possibilities. Not only did I not want to sleep, I knew that I couldn't sleep as long as I had the potentials of the warping metaphor at play in my head. It was with enthusiasm and playfulness, not with fatigue or despair, that I wrote the following journal entry:

> I am making progress on my "Warping" essay, but I have so far to go in the 24 hours I have left before I have to hand in the paper. I realize that I cannot get it into a polished state of existence in that time, but I would like to at least have the skeleton of the complete essay put together with some of the shaping musculature before I hand it in to be

graded. I can drape it with the appropriate clothing after that. At this point I have 8 1/2 pages written and I feel as if I am 3/4 of the way through the essay. The essay still seems extremely muddy to me, so I am unable to see clearly the points I am trying to make. I need to sort out *exactly* what I want to say about Rodriguez's essay in order to clarify my essay. From there I need to weave my metaphor of the loom more thoroughly and securely into the piece. The entire piece has the substance of gauze, when I want the density of linsey-woolsey. It is also patched together with scraps of yarn, when I want high quality materials. And so I work on it. It is still fun and exciting to play with this essay. The metaphor of the loom and the warp has *many* possibilities. Time. I need a bigger loom for this project.

The final push through those twenty-four hours produced the tenth draft of the essay "Warping Time With Montaigne."

As with the first Montaigne paper, the beginning of this paper appeared in the first draft and remained largely unchanged throughout the remaining drafts. The rest of the essay changed drastically from draft to draft, and it was not until the eighth draft that I found the conclusion to the paper. The middle of the essay continued to grow and take shape, but the ending remained loose and unfinished. I had a loose collection of quotes and comments at the end of the early drafts that I knew I wanted to fit into the paper somewhere. I tend to do this when I write: I cultivate a garden patch of interesting and related thoughts at the end of whatever I am working on as a way of feeding life into my essay (and as a way of keeping me from forgetting insights I may have along the way). There are wonderful passages in that collection that never made it to the final draft. If I were to revise this paper again, I might try harder to fit them into the essay. At the time I was drafting this paper, though, I didn't have time to fit them in, and so after the essay became complete in the eighth draft, I used the ninth and tenth drafts to polish the language and the metaphor. I was forced to be done polishing when the due date arrived and I needed to submit the paper for a grade.

Looking back upon the process I went through to create "Warping Time With Montaigne" makes me realize that I almost always contain a heightened sense of excitement when I am in the process of learning something new or when I am playing with language. I love every stage of the writing process because I am at play throughout all of it. Even when I am struggling with a concept or with an adequate way to present a concept, I am excited by the infinite possibilities that present themselves to me. I may procrastinate before I start to write, but once I sit down to write, the rest of the world disappears, or becomes a resource at my beck and call. In this sense, the process I went through when I wrote "Warping Time With Montaigne" is not unlike my normal writing process. It was simply heightened by a metaphor that possessed particularly great potential. As part of my response to a journal prompt that was given at the end of the class asking me to "compare the Research and Analysis papers with the earlier papers in the course (my experience)," I wrote the following passage:

> It was very difficult to make the transition from personal essay to academic paper. I felt like I had just gotten the hang of the personal essay and was enjoying the freedom of the collage essay, when suddenly, I had to juggle references, documentation, and other people's arguments. It was not that the research paper was particularly difficult, as the

switch was difficult. However, having made the switch, I then felt like I was on excellent footing for writing the analysis paper. I had felt the freedom of the personal essay and had plumbed my depths to discover the wealth of details I have within me to use for my writing; I had then felt the rigid demands of the research paper with all of its formality and tradition. Having gone through these two exercises, I was better able to appreciate what literary nonfiction essayists are trying to accomplish. I was able to appreciate Tompkins' "Buffalo Bill" essay in a way that I was incapable of at the beginning of the course. As a result, I felt tremendous excitement about writing the analysis paper. I understood the requirements expected of me in terms of scholasticism, yet I felt the freedom to assert my own voice and technique. What fun!

THIS is the process that lead me to "Warping Time With Montaigne." It was a journey of discovery: first of myself and my knowledge, then of different forms of writing available for my use, and finally of the power of freedom, innovation, and inspiration. Fortunately for me, I am now able to start from here as I prepare future journeys through the writing process.

That Shining Place: Crete, 1966

Simone Poirier-Bures

In the photo I remember, Maria looks straight at the camera. A smile flutters at the corners of her mouth, as if she is hesitant to show her ferocious pride, as if she dares not enjoy this moment, surrounded by her children, lest some jealous god yank it away She rests her hands on the shoulders of Ireni, who barely comes up to her waist. Somber Ireni, whose eyes are large and unsmiling. Smaragdi and Katina stand at their mother's right, their heads reaching just to and just below her shoulders; Katina, distracted by something, looks off to the side. Yannis, at the left, is barely as tall as Smaragdi, though he is older than his sisters. He stands a little apart from the others, as if, as the only male, he feels a need to disassociate himself from the women.

There is something hopeful in their expressions, in the way they are poised there, their faces curious, expectant, as if they are used to standing on the sidelines watching, waiting for things to happen.

Behind them, the stuccoed wall is yellowish brown and peeling. It's the wall of my house, the one I occupied for four months, 31 years ago. Theirs, very much like mine, stands directly across the street. I remember also in this picture the hindquarters of a donkey, a brown shaggy one who carried things for the old man who delivered goods to the small store a few doors down, but perhaps I am confusing this photo with another.

Maria's husband Giorgos is missing from this family portrait, but that is usual. Every morning he would leave his house at dawn, return for the noon meal and a few hours rest, then leave again. He would spend his evenings in one of several *tavernas* along the waterfront. I seldom saw him at home, though I waved to him whenever I saw him along the old harbor, bringing in his catch. And he would wave back, in front of the other fishermen, giving a surprised but pleased smile to this young foreign woman. A friend of his wife's.

The *Yaya*, too, is absent. Maria's mother, all in black, would sit at her chair by the front window watching the goings on. Like all *Yaya's*, she knew how to stay in the background, to help when there was work to be done, but otherwise, to remain invisible. I feel her hovering behind the photo, silently moving her toothless mouth.

They are all frozen in that moment—yet as I think of the picture, time softens, moves. Maria stands below my window, yelling "See-moan-ay! See-moan-ay!" It is 10:15 AM, far too late for decent people still to be sleeping, and anyway, she has something to tell me, or she is lonesome and wants some company, or it is the day for making some Greek delicacy, and I must come and watch so I can learn how.

It is 1966 and I am 21. I am in Chania, on the island of Crete, searching for something. Some truth that keeps eluding me. Some peace I long for. I am fleeing old griefs, trying to lose myself, find myself.

I am not completely alone; I am part of a small group of temporary expatriates—Canadians, Americans, Brits. We all live in the old quarter, in ancient three-story houses built by the Venetians in the 14th and 15th centuries. We live there, instead of in the newer parts of the city where there are flush toilets and running water, because the streets in the old quarter are narrow and picturesque, because the rent is cheap, and because none of us cares about flush toilets and running water. We are all there for our own reasons—we do not ask each other such questions—and together we form a community of sorts. We go to the *tavernas* at night, dance with the sailors, drink too much, help each other find the way home.

Much of my day, however, is with Maria. She has "claimed" me. When we walk through the neighborhood she holds my arm and tells the people we meet: "Apo tin Ameriki." I correct her gently: from Canada. She shrugs and laughs. Wherever I am from, it does not matter. She was the first to have me in her house, so now I am known as "Maria's friend."

Come to my house for some *raki*, a woman down the street calls out to me. No, Maria says to her fiercely, she cannot. She is with me. Later, Maria tells me: That woman is not a good woman. But Athena, as she is called, will not give up so easily. When she sees me coming down the street without Maria, she rushes out to speak. She is thirtyish, a few years younger than Maria, but unmarried. She lives with her sister (also unmarried), and with her mother; occasionally she goes out with men from the nearby NATO base, and this makes her vaguely disreputable. I am curious about Athena, this loud, persistent woman who dyes her hair red, who hovers on the edge of respectability, but I do not wish to offend Maria, so I decline her invitations.

In the evenings, when I slip out to dance with the sailors on the waterfront, to drink, to behave in a way that is totally unacceptable for Greek women, I wonder what Maria thinks, at home, alone with her children. The rules are different for me; this is part of my appeal. Come with us, I say to her one Saturday evening when the winds are warm and we can smell spring coming. Giorgos never stays home—why should you? She clicks her tongue and throws her head back. I have proposed something preposterous, impossible. I might as well have proposed that we fly to the moon. She laughs, chides me for being so silly, but she puts on lipstick, and I know she is tempted.

At first I thought I was merely her trophy—something to show off in this city of few westerners. But Maria remained my friend long after it was expedient or prudent.

"See-moan-ay! See-moan-ay!" she yells through the front window. It is unshuttered and open because it is a lovely warm day, even in mid-January. Behind her stands Yannis, ready to supply the appropriate English if I do not understand what his mother tells me. He is 11, small and sturdy, with a curious, intelligent face. He is learning English in school, and eager to try out his new words. When his friends invite him to play kickball down the street, he demurs, telling them he can't right now, that his mother needs his help. I understand enough Greek to catch this, and to know that we could manage without him. He looks at me shyly—I am not like Greek young women—I tease him, and he hides his smiles.

Maria's friend Varvara has invited us for coffee. I must come now. Varvara is one of the band of gypsies who winter over every year in Chania. I know this because I have seen her pull her small cart laden with colorful woven blankets and rugs through the narrow streets of the old quarter. She is short and compact like Maria, with dark fierce eyes like hers. But Varvara has a shrewdness about her. I do not trust her. A few weeks ago, I bought a blanket from her; later I discovered I had paid far too much.

I am surprised to learn that Varvara is Maria's "friend," as the gypsies are not well-liked here. Faces tighten, mouths curl as the gypsies pass. But I do not question this odd alliance. I, too, am an outsider, and I, too, am Maria's friend.

The gypsies are encamped behind the old city wall, a few minutes walk from our street. Yannis may not come, it is only for the women, Maria tells him. Yannis turns away in disappointment. The *Yaya's* face appears in Maria's front window. She will watch the children. It is a beautiful afternoon and as we walk, I tell Maria about the blanket. She throws her head back and laughs. In Greece, anything is fair in business.

The path to the encampment takes us along the top of the old wall, now crowded with tiny, whitewashed shacks. In the 500 years since the wall was built, the inner face has totally disappeared; the town has sloped up to meet it. Only when you stand at the edge and look down, do you realize that you are on a wall, and how high you are. Maria and I stand there for a moment, looking down. In the clearing below, about two dozen tents form a tiny village, complete with rickety-looking wooden wagons, a motley group of horses and donkeys, a few old cars. A trash fire burns on one side, upwind from the tents. A dog barks. It is eerie to see this scene, like something out of time, something from the Middle Ages. I want to express this observation to Maria, but it is too complicated for my simple Greek vocabulary, so I smile and squeeze her arm, and we follow the path down.

As we approach the camp, we become the focus of attention. I am suddenly aware of my long yellow hair hanging loosely to my waist, my blue eyes. The dark eyes of the men follow me, openly, aggressively. They resemble Greek men in their darkness, in their luxurious mustaches, but their faces are narrower, their cheekbones more pronounced. I hold Maria's arm more tightly. One of them asks us what we want there. Maria tells him in a loud voice that we are looking for Varvara's tent. He points the way. I realize, then, with a sudden twinge of fear, that Maria has never been here before. Is this all some elaborate trap? Has Varvara tricked Maria into bringing me here so that I can be stolen, then sold as a white slave? The youth hostels in Europe were full of such stories.

A man approaches us with a proprietary air. He jerks his head to the right, indicating that we follow him. He spreads his arms out and around us, as if to shield us from the curious eyes of the others. I feel Maria relax a little. Varvara's husband, she tells me.

Their canvas tent, like all the others, is a grayish, stained tan.

Through the partly open front flap we see Varvara, who rises to greet us. We take off our shoes before we enter, leaving them with the others in a neat row outside. The inside is both roomy and cozy. Layers of blankets and rugs in patterns of bright blue, green and red pad the floor. Varvara and her husband exchange a few words in their own language; the husband darts a last look at me, then leaves, pulling the door flap down behind him.

Varvara invites us to sit down on the carpets and we do, forming a circle around a square slab that holds a small stove and a few cooking utensils. I am not sure what to expect from all this, but I suddenly realize that being invited here is a great honor. Maria seems to understand this too, and nods at me solemnly. Varvara lights the stove, a tiny one-burner, fueled by gas. She takes a handful of coffee beans from a burlap bag, puts them in a flat, long-handled copper pan, and shakes them over the fire for a few minutes. The tent fills with a wonderful burnt-brown smell. While the beans cool, she opens a long brass cylinder and begins to assemble what I see now is a coffee grinder. It's a beautiful thing, obviously very old, the elaborate engraving well worn. I wonder for a moment, how many generations of gypsy women have owned this grinder, how many continents it has traveled.

As Varvara grinds the beans, the tent smells more and more aromatic. I wave my hand in front of my nose and say "orea," beautiful, beautiful. Varvara nods at me gravely, but says nothing. She places a few spoonfuls of the powdered coffee with water into a small brass pot, then adds a few large spoonfuls of sugar. When the coffee froths up, she fills three small white cups, paper thin, and hands one each to Maria and me.

Now Varvara smiles. Welcome, my friends, she says. We sip our coffee slowly. Varvara inquires about Maria's family; Maria inquires back. She asks me about my health; I ask back. We are formal, ceremonial. Here, in her own element, Varvara is beautiful. She has loosened her hair and it hangs over her back in a thick mantle of glossy black. She looks softer than before, yet at the same time more powerful. I let the strong, sweet liquid linger on my tongue. Though I have had Greek coffee before, this is the best I have ever tasted. I am in a gypsy camp, I say to myself. A gypsy has called me "friend." I forgive Varvara for the blanket.

You come down through one of the narrow, twisting streets, barely wide enough for a small car, and you come upon it: the old harbor, opening before you like a flower.

A wide paved area separates the buildings from the water, very much like an Italian piazza, which is appropriate, given that this part of Chania was built by the Venetians. At the edge of the piazza, the water is deep, and small fishing boats pull right up to the edge to unload their catches. Mid morning they bring in the octopus. Glossy and silvery gray, raw octopus look like the internal organs of extraterrestrials. There is something vaguely obscene about those thick, slimy appendages; cooked up, however, they are an amazing delicacy. The fishermen throw the octopus by the handfuls on to the pavement, then pick them up and throw them down again, beating them like this to release the dark blue inky substance, and to tenderize them. The octopus are then hung on makeshift racks and lines to dry, and the fishermen wash down the pavement with buckets of sea water.

Sometimes it's sea urchins they bring in, one or two buckets of them, their greenish gray shells bristling with needle-sharp spines. Inside, flesh the color of smoked salmon. I have never tried them—they are food for the wealthy—though I am told they are wonderful. Mostly though, the boats are full of fish and octopus, and all morning the air is briny and aromatic. By noon, all trace of the fishermen is gone.

Everything around the old harbor is a bit shabby. The facades of some of the buildings have begun to crumble. Old paint peels from walls and woodwork like out-grown skin. Some of the buildings are whitewashed, but most are not, unlike the picture postcards one sees of sparkling white Greek villages. Here the buildings are mostly a drab gold—the color of limestone—or light ocher, or the grayish tan of unpainted cement.

Still, there is something enormously pleasing about it all. The crowded build-ings face the water like flowers facing the sun. Roofs of red tile and wide doors painted a glossy blue flash patches of color. Old oil cans grow huge red geraniums. The rounded domes of an ancient mosque, a legacy of the Turkish occupation, shimmer in the sun like white hills. A bright green fishing boat moors on the water. Everything seems harmonious, comforting. On fine days, the restaurants spill out into the piazza. Tables and chairs appear on the pavement, inviting. On weekends, the aroma of roast-ing meat fills the air.

On my way home from the *Instituto*, I stop at one of the sweet shops for a *galato-buriko*, or a bowl of rice custard, or a piece of *baklava*, and look out at the harbor water. Sometimes blue, sometimes black, the water riffles lightly or bristles with foam, depending on its mood. Though the ancient sea wall contains it—a small opening per-mits the comings and goings of small boats—the harbor water is never totally placid, more like some wild thing, barely domesticated. And it seems emblematic somehow, of all of Crete: Hungers surge up, then subside, waiting for their own good time. A thin layer of order overlays roiling chaos—Apollo and Dionysious held in delicate balance.

At the *Instituto Amerikaniko-Helleniki* I taught three classes: a group of 12- and 13-year-old boys, a co-ed class of about a dozen high school seniors preparing to take the Cambridge proficiency exams, and a group of seven or eight local merchants.

While the other shopkeepers take their meals at home, sleep with their wives, or do whatever they all do between one and four in the afternoon when the shops are closed, these men spend an hour, three afternoons a week, practicing their English with me. They range in age from their late twenties to late forties, and their manner toward me is formal. They call me "Miss," and hold doors open for me, bowing slightly, as if I were a visiting dignitary. I acknowledge their deference with a smile, wondering what their wives would think—their husbands treating a woman this way, while they are expected to obey and please.

We spend about half of our time in general conversation; I gently correct their grammar and pronunciation and supply words when I can guess the intent. We con-verse mostly about "Amerika"; they are passionately interested in "Amerika." They have heard there is a sexual revolution going on there, and they are eager to learn how it works. "In America, is it true that a girl can go alone at night with a boy who is not her brother, and her parents do not know his parents?" I am careful with my reply, aware of my position, a single woman about whom there is already too much speculation. And in Chania, the old codes still prevail: a boy who dishonors someone's sister is likely to feel a knife in his back.

"It's very different there," I tell them. "Being alone together does not necessarily mean that something shameful will happen." They wrinkle their faces in puzzlement. They would never believe that a man sleeping alone on the third floor of a house would not sometimes wander at night to the bed of a woman, sleeping alone on the second. They would never believe that a woman who dances the *hassapico* with sailors and sometimes sits on their laps, and drinks with them, and sometimes walks home alone with one and lets him kiss her, does not allow him other things as well. But all that is part of my other life, my life in the old quarter. These men never go to the old quarter.

These men live in the better part of the city, in houses with water heaters, small refrigerators, stoves. Their wives do not carry the Sunday roast to the bakery down the street to be cooked in the public oven for a few *drachma* like Maria does. Their wives wear wool and rayon instead of cotton, their coats have fur collars. And at night, when the *tavernas* crackle with music and the scent of grilled *brisoles* wafts through the air—when *retsina*, *metaxa*, and *ouzo* flow, when feet fly in dance, plates crash on the floor amid cries of "oopa!"—these men are at home with their wives and children.

I know this because I regularly visit such a home. On Saturday mornings I privately tutor the younger sister of one of my 13-year-old boys. There are no English classes for 10-year-old girls, and to send her with the boys would not be proper. The father is not among my businessmen, but he could be; he and they are the same. My pupil's house is relatively new. The surfaces are smooth, the corners of the rooms sharp and well-defined, unlike the rooms of the houses in the old quarter. There are plenty of windows, covered with lace curtains and hung with heavy drapes of velvet and brocade. The chairs and sofas are heavy and ornate. Solid looking. In this part of town, you never see bedding flung out over the balcony to air like you do in the old quarter.

The mother is attractive in a plump, soft sort of way. She smiles sweetly and greets me graciously in spite of the cheap cotton skirts and shabby tops I wear. She, too, calls me "Miss." I call her *Kyria*—Mrs. Like Maria, she speaks no English and relies on her son to translate. Unlike Maria, she shows no curiosity toward me. Each time I come, she offers me tea in a flowered china cup, then leaves the money for each lesson discreetly on the side-board, near my coat.

One Friday, the boy says to me after class: "My mother, she say no come tomorrow. Come Sunday, for to go on picnic. Three o'clock. We go to country. You come?"

When I arrive, slightly before three, they are all waiting. The children are happy to see me and the mother looks both pleased and relieved, as if she had feared that I wouldn't show. The *Kyrios*, her husband, acknowledges me with a slight nod. This is only the second time I have seen him. On the day of my first lesson with his daughter, he nodded at me on his way out. I suspect he had stayed behind to catch a glimpse of me, to make sure I was "safe," and to give his approval. A *Yaya* appears from one of the back rooms. I have not seen her before and wonder whose widowed mother she is—his or hers. It's impossible to tell. She is dressed all in black with a black wool kerchief pulled over her head like the *Yayas* in the old quarter. She is the one link between these two worlds. She is not introduced.

A big black Mercedes waits out front. The *Yaya* sits in the front with the man and woman, near the door. I sit in the back between the two children. The girl, who is still very much a beginner in English, holds my hand and looks at me adoringly. The boy keeps smiling, as if he can't believe I am really there, his English teacher, on an outing with his family. The adults sit stiffly, silently, in the front. I wonder briefly whose idea it was to invite me. The children's? The mother's?

Kyria says something in Greek to the boy, gesticulating with her head that he should tell me. "My mother she say to tell you that the orchards will be beautiful today." I smile at her: "I'm looking forward to seeing them. I am very happy that you invited me to come." She nods as I speak. She understands more English than she lets on. She translates my words to her husband and returns her eyes to the road. He glances at me through the rearview mirror. He seems aware of me, but not aware; I am part of the women's world with which he need not concern himself.

His wife, however, pulses with awareness. Throughout the ride I feel her controlled attention. Though she speaks mostly to her husband or looks out at the countryside, she is acutely aware of what is going on in the back seat. If we all do not have a wonderful time, she will blame herself. This is my first encounter with upper middle-class Greek life, and I am carefully taking it all in, noting how different this woman is from Maria, how different they all are from the villagers I have met, and from the people in the old quarter. Maria and I would be singing by now. Laughing out loud. Exclaiming over the beauty of the hills. She would be teaching me the Greek names of things.

The girl beside me squeezes my hand. "Is good day, yes?"

There is a tacit understanding that I speak only English, so that makes it difficult to communicate with the adults. The school is total immersion, and we teachers are discouraged from admitting to any knowledge of Greek. I suspect I have been invited along to give the children a chance to practice their English. Why else? *Kyrios* and *Kyria* do not ask me about life in "Amerika," or my life here or what I think about things. And yet I feel they are studying me, discreetly.

The country house is utterly charming—whitewashed stucco and surrounded by a low stone wall. It is grander than any of the houses I saw in my wanderings around the island, though it is still relatively simple. *Kyria* points to the small outhouse, apologizing profusely for the lack of an indoor toilet. This strikes me as very funny, given my own living conditions, but I suppress my smile. Wide windows look out over row upon row of orange trees.

Huge baskets are unloaded from the trunk of the Mercedes and there is a flutter of activity. The women will not let me help and shoo me out of the kitchen. The children hover around me like bees.

"My father say to come and see the orchard," the boy says.

Kyrios stands at the door fingering his worry beads. The children and I follow him out. The day is glorious, the air dazzling in its sweetness, and I want to jump into the air and shout with joy. But I control myself, as seems to be required, and smile demurely. Two donkeys, tied to a stake by a shed, stare at us with comic faces. I have a particular fondness for donkeys, and rush over to stroke their necks and ears. *Kyrios* gestures for me to get on one of them. It's the first time he has addressed me directly. The children shriek with glee when I swing my leg up over the donkey's back. They quickly climb onto the other one.

Their father takes the reins of my donkey and leads us down the rows of the orange grove. The trees are much smaller than I ever imagined they could be, with enormous bright fruit hanging heavily from the branches. *Kyrios* pulls down an orange the size of a cannonball and slices it open with a knife he pulls from his waist. Then he presents it to me with a little bow. I am reminded again how everything in Greece seems fuller, riper, bursting with life. Even the oranges are unrestrained, glorious in their hugeness, their sweetness, their intense color. By now I have lost all reserve and exclaim aloud at the beauty of everything. "It's all so lovely! Lovely!" I tell them. "I feel like a queen!" The children find everything I say and do amusing, and laugh and laugh.

When we get back to the house we find a beautiful meal laid out on a long rectangular table in a shaded area outside—feta cheese, black olives, bread, *dolmathes*, *taramasalata*, two kinds of beans, several plates of things I don't recognize, and a huge bottle of retsina. We are all more relaxed now, more comfortable with each other. Even the *Yaya* nods and smiles. The sun beats down, waves of fragrance waft in from the orange grove. After a few glasses of retsina, *Kyrios* raises his glass and sings a few lines of a song: "Ego tha kopso to krassi, ya sena agapi mou chrisi…" His wife throws him a disapproving glance and mutters something, but too late. I clap my hands, delighted. A drinking song! This is the first sign of passion I've seen in these upper middleclass Greeks.

I insist on learning the song, and sing it over and over, a bit tipsy myself by this time. My pupils and their father sing it with me. *Kyria* sings a few lines herself, though she looks uncomfortable, as if she is doing something vaguely improper.

After the meal, the children and I take a last stroll through the orchard. It's a wonderful afternoon, and I am sorry when it ends.

On the way home we are again subdued, polite. My hosts ask where I live so that they can deliver me to my house. I protest that the streets are too narrow for their car, and ask to be let out by the old harbor, saying that I will walk the rest of the way. I do not want them to see where I live. I do not want them anywhere near my life there.

My class of 12- and 13-year olds was my favorite. A teasing, affectionate relationship existed between us. They found me endlessly amusing, and I was charmed by their small compact bodies, their dark curious eyes. Once when I came into the classroom and turned on the light switch, nothing happened. I flipped it off and on several times while the boys watched me. Nothing. Things often didn't work in Greece, so I shrugged and said, "I guess we'll just have to have class in the dark today." They all burst out laughing. One of the boys climbed up on his desk and turned the light bulb; another flicked on the switch and the room filled with light. We all laughed together. I had enjoyed this trick as much as they had, so when I walked into the classroom the day after my visit to the orange groves and felt an expectant tension in the air, I figured something was up.

One of the boys had just finished writing something in Greek on the blackboard and was hurrying back to his seat. All 16 of them were watching me, suppressing grins.

"Aha," I say, going along with it. "Someone left me a message. Help me translate it." Titters all over the room. "It's nothing," the boy whose sister I tutor says. "I'll erase it for you." He gets up and approaches the board. But something in his face makes me want to know what the words say.

"No, let's figure it out. It'll be good practice. Let's see, the first word is…" I squint at the Greek letters and sound out "Ego…" Someone from the back row calls out boldly: "Ego tha kopso to krassi."

General laughter. I glance quickly at my friend in the front row who hangs his head sheepishly. Obviously, he has told his friends about our excursion, and they have seized on the part they found most interesting.

"Oh yes, the song I learned yesterday," I say, feeling a little chilled, the private made a bit too public. "I like Greek songs. I'd like to learn a lot of them." The boys are restless, whispering things to each other, their eyes flashing a kind of wildness. One of them calls out something in Greek that I don't understand, and they all laugh again. The laughter has a new, aggressive edge.

"What did you say?" I ask him. He is silent. "Someone tell me what he said." No one answers, and a thick tension hangs in the air. Finally, I look at my friend in the front row. He, after all, started this whole thing. I ask him evenly, "Please tell me what he said."

He swallows hard and says, "He said that perhaps you would like to learn, um…*Krevata murmura.*"

"And what, exactly, is that?"

He looks exceedingly uncomfortable, as does the rest of the class. But I persist.

"I don't know how to say in English, but it means the things a man and woman say to each other when they are in bed."

The boys are absolutely still, studying my reaction. The air crackles with danger.

"I see," I say. "Thank you for your translation." Then I turn to the rest of the class. "Take out your homework now, and let's see how well you've done on the exercises for today." I go on with the class as usual, though I smile less and make no joking asides as I usually do. Something between us has changed.

On my way home, I try to figure it out. A single woman drinking wine and singing—did this somehow mean sexual availability in the minds of these 12- and 13-year old boys? The harbor water is greenish black today; two small boats, moored in the protected area, rock gently in the lapping tongues of water. Beyond the seawall, the water is deep blue; whitecaps surge and break. It's the same water; only the seawall separates it, only the seawall tames it. How easily things can turn, I think, how easily things can careen out of control.

Afterword: Writing "The Greece Piece"

Simone Poirier-Bures

It began, I suppose, in 1982. I was auditing a writing course taught by Ursule Molinaro; she had no car, so after class I drove her home. I was only just beginning to write seriously then, and Ursule was a real writer; alone with her on those rides, I hoped some of her talent would rub off, or I'd learn some secret about how words work.

One afternoon I told her about my backpacking in Europe and the Middle East years before, my stay on the island of Crete. I described a brave young woman traipsing through exotic lands, only half aware of the disturbances her long blond hair created. I spoke of my younger self as I would a colourful ancestor—so removed from my present self did she seem. "That was my life's big adventure," I told Ursule, realizing at that moment that it was.

"You should write about it," Ursule said simply.

I had never thought of this. It had all happened so long ago, back in 1965–66, and my experiences were episodic, they had no centre around which to build a plot. Moreover, I sensed that the real story lay beneath the surface adventures; the real story had to do with friendship, loneliness, the making of a self. I was not quite ready to deal with all that.

Years later, in 1988, after I had finished several writing projects and was looking for another, I remembered Ursule's words and decided to try writing a novel about the four months I had spent in Greece. I would make up a heroine, myself in disguise, and embellish my experiences to make them neater, more story-like. I still occasionally dreamed about my house in Chania, the crumbling cement walls, the dark rooms that became, in those dreams, a labyrinth. Something important had happened there. Something left unfinished.

I was having a hard time getting started, so I began getting up at 5:30 AM and freewriting for an hour. Someone had given me Dorothea Brande's little book, *Becoming a Writer*, and she had suggested this exercise. It wasn't easy. Awakening memory, trying to shape and select its messages, dealing with my own feelings about my younger self—and doing this all at once. I would sit there watching the sky lighten against the window over my desk, my stomach tight, my brow throbbing, an urge to run out of the room rippling through my arms and legs.

Over a period of several weeks, I wrote twenty pages. In the opening scene, a North American woman negotiates with a Greek merchant over the price of a silver and turquoise bracelet. After a good deal of haggling, they settle on a price. Then suddenly they become good friends, in the way this happens in Greece. On the way home, with her new bracelet on her arm, Joanna berates herself: you didn't *need* it. In this way I introduce the theme of material things and Joanna's (my) ambivalence toward them. The day is overcast, damp and chilly, corresponding to Joanna's mood, but also to many days I actually remember in Crete.

Joanna goes home to her Venetian house in the old quarter and is met by her housemate, a bearded British artist (Jack), who is drying his socks by the charcoal brazier, the only source of heat. Relentlessly cheerful, Jack provides a sharp contrast to Joanna's gloominess. Joanna wishes she were in love with him. How much nicer life would be if she loved someone and someone loved her. It rains all night.

The next morning, after a chill, dreary night huddled in her sleeping-bag, Joanna wakes to the sound of her neighbour, Maria, calling her name. When she throws open the shutters, sunlight and warm air rush in. Joanna looks at the brilliant sky, at Maria's short square body, at the long narrow street bustling with activity, and is overtaken with joy.

This is as far as I got. How to develop all the threads? How to tell what happened and make it dramatic without doing injustice to the static-like quality of much of my life there?

I put the twenty pages away and forgot about them.

In 1991 my husband had a sabbatical and between his research trips, we decided to make a quick trip to Greece and Turkey. My husband had spent two years in Turkey in the late sixties helping to set up a land-grant style university, so we each had important memories associated with the two countries.

From the moment we decided on the trip, images of Maria and Chania began trickling steadily up from the past. One afternoon I hunted through an old trunk and found Maria's thin blue airmail letters with the spidery black handwriting. As I read them, I heard Maria's voice, saw her large sad eyes, and was seized with a deep need to see her again. I couldn't remember her last name, and because it was written in Greek script that I could not decipher, I tore off the small piece of envelope with her name and address in case I would have to inquire about her. I remembered that our street was named after El Greco—his Greek name—and though I could still see every detail of the houses and shops, the name eluded me. Fortunately, it was there on the envelope, under Maria's name.

What happened during our visit to Crete is described in the memoir.

After Crete, my husband and I went on to Turkey. In Istanbul, the sister of an old friend, a woman we barely knew, gave us a present—an old brass coffee grinder, almost exactly like the one Varvara had used 25 years before. Such an odd coincidence, I remember thinking. So many wonderful coincidences on this trip. We were busy with visiting and buying gifts, so I forgot about the grinder.

When we returned home, I was once again struck by the need to write about my time in Greece. But how? Months passed. At Christmas, I sent cards and letters to both Maria and Ireni, telling them how much our reunion had meant to me. In mid-January, a Christmas card and letter arrived from Ireni. "You must know," she said, "that always, since I've met you, I've been thinking about you." Her words reminded me piercingly of Maria's letters years ago. As I sat at the kitchen table reading and rereading Ireni's letter, my body felt as if it were literally bursting with memory, with the need *to tell*. The faces of Maria and the children as they had been long ago swam before me. I went up to my study and began writing: "In the photo, Maria looks straight at the camera…"

I wrote as far as the dancing scene. Exhilarated and a bit dazed, I went downstairs to make some tea. As I waited for the water to boil, I thought of the day Maria took me to the gypsy camp. I pulled out the coffee grinder the woman in Istanbul had given us and examined it. There was still a little coffee in it, powdered to make Turkish coffee, which is what Greek and gypsy coffee actually is. Suddenly the coffee grinder became like Proust's madeleine: I found myself walking the narrow path down to the gypsy camp; the thin high yelp of camp dogs rang in my ears, the faces of men with high cheekbones and fierce eyes surrounded me, the smell of roasting coffee beans filled the room. I was drowning in memory. The dark lustre of Varvara's hair, the feel of the thick rugs on the floor of the tent—details I had not thought about in decades roiled around me. I rushed upstairs and wrote about Varvara and the coffee.

I was thrilled with what I had written and went over it several times in the next few weeks, polishing the prose. But where to go from there? What was this thing, anyway? It had come from the need to tell; it wasn't trying to *be* anything.

I remembered my old attempt at writing a novel set in Greece, found my old computer file and printed it out. But it was not where I wanted to go anymore. I was fascinated, now, with memory.

I had kept no journal during that year of travel—something I berated myself for now. I hadn't even taken pictures. This had been deliberate. I wanted everything to be *in* me, not *outside*. I wanted memory to be part of my flesh.

I did, however, write letters. Lots of them. To my mother, my sister, and to a whole collection of girlfriends and boyfriends in Canada and the United States. I wrote, now, to my mother and sister and to the few friends from that era I am still close to: "Send my old letters," I begged, "if you still have them."

In the meantime, I wrote another section or two of text, and then stopped. I was stuck, just as I had been with the novel.

After a few months of despair and silence, I began writing down fragments. Whatever I remembered from that time, however small. I had to get it out. I could shape it into something later, I told myself. Often, I found, what started as a tiny memory bloomed into an entire scene. From the memory of stains on the ancient wood floor came the night of the party, the faces of the girls in the protection of their brothers, the near-fight, the persistent rain. It was like yanking at a small string and having a huge fish come up.

Finally, six letters came from my mother. I remember staring at them, the pale-blue airmail envelopes, the tissue paper, the Greek stamps, my handwriting. I was awed by them, and a little afraid. They were like apparitions—my own voice, my own thoughts from the past, a direct line to the person I had been 25 years before. What I remembered of that younger self sometimes embarrassed me, her naïveté, her awkwardness. But her idealism drew me, even as it reproached me. The girl who wanted nothing and the middle-aged woman secure in her comforts—how could they be the same person? With the letters, I would have to confront that old self, uncover her truth, measure the width of my betrayal.

I put the letters in chronological order and read the first one. I was struck by the tone of voice. It was cheerful, happy-go-lucky. A girl on a lark, having a blast, eager to share her adventures. There was none of the sadness, the loneliness, the groping searches I remembered. How could this be? As I read on, I concluded that the person writing was really a persona—one I had consciously developed for my mother and my friends. I was giving them surface. But what a surface it was—full of details and impressions, sights and sounds.

When I read that first letter, I had just finished writing about my arrival in Chania. I hadn't remembered that the youth hostel was a boys' school and that only a shower curtain separated our sleeping quarters from the classroom. I'd remembered being stared at by bunches of schoolboys, but couldn't quite place the circumstances. Reading my younger self telling it made it all come back—and more. I remembered, then, the middle-aged schoolmaster with his patient, wide brow and questioning eyes. But the elderly woman described in the letter, a friend of the schoolmaster, who had written six books of philosophy—who was she? No face emerged.

I went back to my manuscript and added the shower curtain, the staring boys. I did not mention the woman.

I read the letters one at a time, carefully, reverently. Sometimes weeks passed between reading one letter and another. They were rich, heady stuff, and I took them into my present slowly, cautiously. Besides memory, there was that carefree persona to deal with. How reconcile them to each other? How reconcile them to my present, middle-aged self? So many fragments that had to be integrated. Who and what was the real self?

Generally, I tried to write whatever I remembered of a particular period *before* reading the letter I wrote during that period. It was like tuning a guitar string before sounding the pitch pipe. While I was amazed at how much I actually remembered, I was also struck by what I could not recall even with the help of my own words, leaping up from the page. The most important thing that I do not remember has to do with my leave-taking. To my mother I wrote, "We had quite a send-off when we left…we had one last dinner with all the 'arty' colony of English-speaking people, and one last wild night at a 'joint' we all go to…" I remember nothing of this. I remember only the fear, the sadness. So which is real? Those parties must have occurred, and I am sure I made the most of them, singing and dancing. The persona again.

I have no doubt that if a needle were to be inserted into a part of my brain all those forgotten things would pop to the surface. But they are too far buried, now, ever to call back.

So what does this mean? That those forgotten things are not important? Without the direct link of memory, I cannot know. I chose to leave them out.

In June, 1992, I spent two weeks at the Virginia Centre for the Creative Arts, an artist's colony, where I was determined to finish "My Greece Piece," as I had come to call it. I wrote and wrote, overwhelmed by memory. Even when I lay down to rest on the cot in my studio, waves of images floated over me. Bryan—whose name I hadn't thought of in decades—appearing giddily at my door arm-in-arm with the dark-eyed young sailors. The smell of roasting meat drifting out over the harbour. The way the sea urchins looked in their spiky shells. I was swimming in a deep, rich river, grabbing hold of whatever I could. Sometimes I forgot where I was.

About half of the manuscript was written at VCCA. In those two weeks I wrote as much as I had written in the previous five months. But it was still all fragments. Pieces that had to be fit together into some coherent whole. During my last few days at VCCA I contemplated this. One entire wall of my studio was made out of bulletin board-type white tiles, and a previous occupant had left an assortment of colourful thumbtacks. This gave me an idea. I printed out the whole manuscript and pinned all the pieces up on the wall. Then I began arranging and rearranging. I'd read through the whole thing, then push this piece over here, that piece over there. It seemed as if the pieces could go anywhere—or nowhere. I didn't want a straight chronology; I wanted memory to overtake the present, like it had for me. But the manuscript still needed some kind of order, and that order seemed to escape me. A visual artist friend came by one day to take pictures. On an impulse, I got up and stood against my wall of manuscript, arms outstretched.

I was making a manuscript, but I was also making a self.

My "Greece Piece" still had no real title. Sometimes I called it "Maria" but that didn't seem to be the true focus. One evening I read from the manuscript, including the part about Katzanzakis's grave. A young poet came up to me after and we talked about its lack of a title. "Why don't you use the Katzanzakis quote?" he said. "'I want nothing, I fear nothing, I am free.' That seems to be what the whole thing is about." I went back to my studio and thought about this. He was right. My younger self was looking for freedom, trying to make herself want nothing and fear nothing, in order to find it. The fact that Katzanzakis had found his freedom in death added an additional irony, one that had escaped the notice of my younger self. The title stuck for a while, though I later changed it again.

When my residency at VCCA ended, I found re-entry into normal life extremely difficult. I was still living in Chania in 1966, and memory was more real than anything around me. For days I was unable even to make up a decent grocery list. I'd be on my way to the store and find that I had passed it. I'd have been thinking about the market in Chania, how the olives looked, shining out from huge glass jars. Gradually, painfully, the present asserted itself again.

I spent the rest of the summer shuffling parts, trying to find that elusive order. One afternoon I went looking for the old photos my mother had taken when she visited Maria in Crete. They were not at all as I had remembered them. Yannis was tall, the children were laughing. Their skirts were *short*. How could that be? After I thought about this for a while I realized that my mother's visit was four whole years after I had left. 1970. By then the hemlines had shot up, even in Crete. But why did I remember sombre expressions where the photos clearly showed them all smiling happily? Had I imagined the sadness in their lives? I pulled out Maria's letters again and reread them. No, I had not imagined it. My mother's experience of the family, the one caught by the camera, was not *my* experience of them. And memory had conveniently replaced the celluloid image with its own. I went back to the beginning of my text and changed it: "In a photo I *remember…*"

By the end of January the piece was finished, almost exactly a year after I had begun it. In March, I received a package and letter from my sister in Halifax. "I was cleaning out my basement and found these. Do you still want them?" More letters, with postmarks from Greece, Egypt, Lebanon. I was afraid to look at them. What if they were full of things I had not talked about in my memoir? Would I have to open the thing up all over again and integrate yet another layer of truth? I approached them cautiously. To my surprise, the tone of those letters was different from the tone in the letters to my mother. It was more natural, more authentic.

My sister had married at eighteen and was the mother of three by the time I embarked on my adventures. She had married a Lebanese man eleven years older than herself. There was a poignancy about her life that struck me. While I was off galivanting, she kept house, kept children, kept a husband. She was only a year and a half older than I, and her hands were cracked from too many dishes, too many washloads of diapers. I was travelling for her, too, as well as for my mother.

From Greece, I went on, eventually, to Lebanon, to the small village in the mountains where my sister's husband's sisters and their families lived, as well as the whole extended family of cousins and uncles. My sister had never met them. I went there because she couldn't, and described everything in great detail. That was my job.

The letters to my sister from Greece contained no new revelations, but they made me consider the whole matter of personas again. The persona who wrote to my mother was a small part of myself—pushed forward because that's what my mother wanted, that's what would reassure her, please her. The persona who wrote to my sister represented a larger part of myself—more level-headed, less breathy—but still only a part. The real self, I have come to believe, is memory. And that is what I put in my memoir.

Teacher Training

Mary Elizabeth Pope

I stand at the drinking fountain in the hallway outside my classroom. It is the first day of classes, and it is my first day as a graduate teaching assistant. I have no teaching certification to prepare me for this position, and as my qualifications are limited to the grades I earned as an undergraduate in English, I have no idea how I will meet the challenge of teaching Freshman Composition. Earlier, as I passed the classroom, I glanced in to see a number of students sitting in their desks, waiting. I think of all those students now, and wonder about all their different needs—how can I address them collectively, and still address them as individuals? How can I know what they need from me when I have no training or experience with teaching? My watch reads 7:59 am, so I move reluctantly toward the door behind which my students sit. My hands are shaking, and the knot in my stomach is threatening to snap me in half. My heels click on the tiled floor as I enter the classroom and make my way to the podium.

I sat in the new desk on the first day of fifth grade, watching my new teacher pass out textbooks. It was all I could do to sit still for so long; I had been waiting for this day all summer. The new pencils and paper and folders I'd saved my fifty cent allowance for were already arranged in my tray, and I placed each new textbook that Mrs. Crane handed out beside them, feeling very mature. The first day of school was like a clean slate for me; all of the mistakes from fourth grade left safely behind me in Mr. Smith's room and in Mr. Smith's mind. I watched my new teacher as she handed out books; she was a woman of about fifty, and very pretty in a hard sort of pancake makeup way. She walked more purposefully than any woman I had ever known, her posture perfect as she slowly, deliberately put one high-heeled shoe out and placed it carefully in front of her before shifting her weight directly onto it. Her careful, composed walk would be something I would never forget—the way her shoulders moved as she walked, the way her hair didn't, the angle at which she held her chin. I knew instantly that I wanted her to like me, that I wanted to do well in her class, to please this woman whose authority radiated from her every gesture, rang clear in her every word. I rode the bus home that afternoon, bursting with excitement, anxious to tell my mother all about my new teacher.

My students stare at me the first day. Some of them look at me directly; others avert their gaze in case my eyes meet theirs. They are sizing me up. That's okay; I am sizing them up, too. I pass out the syllabus, and discuss classroom policy and course requirements with them. I tell them they must have a C in order to pass my class. They say nothing until I ask them to introduce themselves to the class and say where they are from. After much shifting in their seats, and mumbling out their introduction sentence, they gratefully return their eyes to me. I try hard not to smile too much on the first day, although it is hard. I try to encourage them to understand how my class will help them with all of their classes; I try hard to make them understand that they all have something important to say, that they are all unique and no single other person has the perspective they do. They look at me. I look back at them. I don't know if they believe me or not when it is time to dismiss them, but I watch them file out, and feel hopeful.

I stood in the dime store for maybe thirty minutes, wondering what Mrs. Crane's favorite color was. The folders were there on the shelf—pink, yellow, green, blue, red. On another shelf sat the folders I wished for: clear, plastic binders with front picture slots on the cover. I could just see a collage of Abraham Lincoln underneath those picture slots—Mrs. Crane would like that for sure. But I had only fifty cents, and the clear plastic binders were ninety-nine cents, while the colored cardboard folders were thirty-nine cents. Mrs. Crane wore a lot of blue—navy blue—but since the dime store only carried a cornflower color of blue—and because it seemed the only color suitable for Abraham Lincoln of the colors available, I took one blue folder to the counter, and watched the lady ring it up. I was sad. What could I do with a plain blue folder that would make Mrs. Crane notice it? I wanted her to know how hard I'd worked on my report, and how much I wanted to do everything right for her. I wanted her to like me.

Holly comes to my office at least once a week. She worries all the time; so much so, that she is terrified to commit anything to paper. She is careful to meet all of the requirements in an assignment, yet she is so careful that it stifles all of the creativity in her expression. She always asks me what I want her to write. Today, her curly brown hair is pulled back in a bun, and above her ruddy cheeks, her eyes are tired and bloodshot, no doubt from staying up all night working, or worrying that she should be working. She is a perfectionist to the point of self-destruction, and although I am pleased with her work, I know she could be more expressive if she were not so afraid of making mistakes.

The assignment I give today is to freewrite about what they want to say in their coming papers. I tell them I won't be grading these and that the only thing that matters is what they discover about their topic. I give them thirty minutes, and I watch Holly hunch over her desk and begin writing. After class, I ask her to stay behind a moment so I can look at her writing. It is thoughtful and original, and much better than what she has been turning in to me on a regular basis. I tell her I want to see her this week, knowing I will anyway. I am hopeful that we can make some progress.

Mrs. Crane stood regally before the class, holding a stack of reports in her hand. I could hardly wait to get mine back and read what she had written. I had worked so hard, and had so carefully and creatively constructed the cover, that I was sure that she would love it. "Class," she began, "why don't we take a look at some of the reports you handed in to me?" I was even more excited—I just knew she would pick mine as a good example for a creative cover, and I could hardly wait to see what she said about it when she held it up. "This is James' report—see how he pasted a mapped picture of Michigan on the cover of his folder for his Michigan report? Very nice....". Next, she held up a crumpled sheet of paper which was half written on in pencil. "This..." she paused and her voice fell, as she extended the paper away from her body and pinched it between two fingers, as if it were dirty, or smelled bad, "...is Kevin's report." She quickly put Kevin's report on the bottom of the pile, and picked up the next one, commenting favorably on the reports she liked, and giving the same disdainful look and treatment as Kevin's report got to those she did not appreciate. I waited excitely. I could see the blue edge of my folder sticking out of the pile...closer and closer it came to the top...and then it was in her hand. "This is Mary Beth's report," she said quickly, and made no comment on it at all, quickly replacing it on the bottom of the pile. I was crushed. My blue folder, with the pennies glued on to form the letters A and L, looked pitiful in the light of Mrs. Crane's disinterest in it. I had been so proud of it, had so carefully selected the shiniest pennies in my father's penny jar to use for the lettering, had handed it in with such confidence; now it seemed a pathetic idea, and I felt embarrassed as my cheeks glowed hotly, wondering how many students were looking at my flushed face, my burning ears.

Jonathan demands a lot of attention. He sits in the front row of my 9:00 class, and has assumed the role and voice of ringleader for the class. He is very entertaining, and I enjoy having him in class most of the time. His constant need to prove that he is the "best" or the most intelligent student in my class, however, is frustrating, because when the class gets into a debate over a particular issue, he cannot let a subject go until he feels he has won. I try to remain a neutral facilitator, although I have at times had to interrupt when Jonathan gets out of hand. I can tell this frustrates him, and I struggle to understand this unfulfilled need he has to be in the spotlight at all times.

Today, I hand back all of the papers except for one that I have saved to read to the class. It is well-written, funny, and it meets the assignment's requirements. I choose it because it is a good example, but I have another motive. "I have a paper I'd like to read to you," I tell them. "I enjoyed it and I think all of you will, too." As I read, the class laughs appreciatively, and I do, too. When I am finished, I launch into a description of the next assignment. The students bend over their notes and begin writing, and I casually set Jonathan's paper on his desk. He is smiling, and beads of sweat have formed on his forehead. He is happy, and I am glad. For the rest of the period, things go well.

When Mrs. Crane handed back the folders, I had a second flash of hope: maybe she had only disliked the cover—maybe she had liked the report itself. I watched the other students read her comments, and when my folder was finally in my hands, I flipped through the pages, anxiously looking for her scrawling red script. I couldn't find anything, except for a check mark to signify that she had read it. I looked again, more frantically, and then realized that she had written nothing at all.

Nicole sits in the fifth row, hidden behind Drew, who is tall, and Thomas, who is large. I can just see the top of her blonde head peering at me occasionally as I teach; she is tentative, curious, nervous. Sometimes when class is over and she is on her way out the door, she will glance at me shyly and smile, a blush travelling from her ears to her nose. Nicole works very hard at my assignments; all of her in-class writing is printed, perfectly neat and straight. She is always the last to finish writing. Her papers are very well done, and she is meticulous about meeting every requirement I ask for in each paper. Her writing also reflects the deep thought she puts into the ideas we discuss in class. In Freshman Composition, I could not ask for a better student.

I like to watch her when I hand back papers. On this particular day, what little of her face I can see is lit up, and I am glad for what I have written on the bottom of her paper. "Nicole—this is excellent. Again, I commend you. You meet all of the requirements for this paper, and express your depth of thought on these issues very well. This is the highest grade I have given on this paper, so you should feel proud." I can see all the way from the front of the room that she does.

My name was on the blackboard. Mrs. Crane posted the names of students who had misspelled words in their weekly assignments there until those students could find the correct spelling for the words they had missed. On Monday, my name stood out among the other names simply because it was my name and it had never been on that list before. Then, as the names were gradually erased, those spelling ex-convicts were allowed to join the ranks of the anonymous students who had spelled perfectly that week. Slowly, the list dwindled, and by Thursday, my name was the only one left. I was frustrated. The word was "no one" and it was not one word, as I later learned, but two. I had written "noone", and Mrs. Crane had circled it. I had stared at it for a long time, and then fetched a dictionary from the back shelf of the room. I knew that "someone" and "anyone" and "somebody" and "anybody" and "nobody" were all words. Where was "noone"? I tried "noon", thinking it could be used two ways. Still, it came back marked wrong. I tried "nowan", and again, it was marked wrong. On Thursday, I showed Mrs. Crane that it was not in the dictionary. "Well," she had replied frostily, "I can't do anything about that, Mary Beth. The ways you have tried are all wrong." She then dismissed me. I walked back to my desk with heavy heart and burning cheeks, staring at my name on the board. All of the other names were gone, and now everyone knew that I was the stupid girl who couldn't spell. For two long weeks, I stared at my name on the board, the chalky white letters seeming to jump off the blackboard and proclaim to the class my ignorance. Every night, I would hope that some diligent custodian would erase my name by accident. Every morning, my mark of shame would still be there. And every day, Mrs. Crane told me, "It's still wrong."

Darrin sits in the second row of my 9:00 class. I have just returned his paper, and I can see the disappointment that registers on his face. Most mornings, Darrin hides beneath a baseball cap, watching me furtively from beneath it, retreating turtle-like under the visor if my gaze lands momentarily on him. He is a hard worker, and shows up regularly to my office hours to ask for help. I am sorry when I receive his work to have to give it a C+ because of his errors. Darrin has difficulty with spelling and commas, but his work in general is often entertaining and interesting. On the bottom of this particular paper, I have written, "Darrin—this is very funny—I enjoyed reading it.

I can see that you are improving the organization and maintenance of focus in your writing. Keep it up (smiley face)! I am still concerned about your use of commas and number of spelling errors that have appeared here. Come see me and we'll talk about it. Good work overall." I know that Darrin will come to my office hours after class. I know what I will say to him. I know how he will respond. And regardless of whether or not he uses the dictionary or spellcheck, regardless of whether the exercises with commas that I will cover with him improve his writing, I know that he will leave my office feeling that he is a good writer who needs a little brushing up, rather than feeling he is a bad writer who is hopeless. He will leave knowing he is capable of doing better, and hopefully this will drive him to improve on his next paper.

On the day before Christmas vacation, we'd made ornaments in Mrs. Crane's class. My ornaments did not look like everyone else's. I had taken the pastry dough and twisted strips together to form candy canes, like the cookies my mother sometimes made at home. I loved art lessons, and I was happy with my ornaments. Mrs. Crane strolled up and down the aisle and paused to compliment those ornaments that she liked. She paused at my desk, and I waited, hopeful that she liked mine. She looked confused for a moment, and then walked quickly up to the front of the room and said, "Now class, let me show you again how to use the cookie cutters. Remember, these ornaments are going to hang on the tree in the big hallway, so we want them to look nice and neat." She searched for a particular cutter. "See," she said with false brightness, as she showed us how to cut the starchy dough, leaving a row of perfectly straight Gingerbread Men in her wake, "they all come out exactly the same if you use a cookie cutter."

Eric is angry. Ever since the first day he walked into my class, it has radiated from him, the aura of anger that surrounds him reminding me of the cloud of dust that follows the *Peanuts* character Pigpen everywhere he goes. With his long, red ponytail and goatee, he sits, withdrawn from the rest of the class, in the back corner, hiding behind his black leather jacket. Eric is brilliant; his forcefully written, antiestablishment, rebellious papers are testimony to this. He is by far the most openly creative student I have, and I handle him carefully because I know he is volatile. However, when he misses several classes in a row, I decide to take action. I stop him on his way out the door and ask him if he will make an appointment with me. He says yes, and we agree on a time. I don't know what I will say to him yet, or whether he will even show up. I only know that I do not want to lose this incredibly bright student, to let him slip through the cracks and disappear, never to return to my class. I am hoping that all he needs is some encouragement.

On the last day of fifth grade, we were allowed to take our brown bag lunches outside and sit on the lawn in front of the school. I sat with my class and watched Mrs. Crane talk to the students who sat around her. I sat far on the outside of the circle with another girl, and we traded Lifesavers and halves of our sandwiches. When the buses pulled up to take us home that day, Mrs. Crane stood by the door, and hugged each of us. I waited, dreading the hug, but knowing I couldn't get past her. She made a big show out of it, telling the students how much she would miss all of them. When my turn came, she put her mushy arms around me and my cheek burned where it touched her neck. When she finished hugging me, she put her hands on my shoulders and shook me a little. "I'm expecting big things from you, Mary Beth." My eyes filled up with tears. I managed good-bye and followed the other students on to the bus. I hated her even more for lying like that in front of all of my friends. As I stood behind the other students in line for my bus, I wondered why she would say such a thing. The way she had treated me all year told me everything I ever wanted to know about what she expected from me.

Mark sits in the back row of my classroom with Walter and Jonathan. All three are football players, and while Walter and Jonathan often doze or talk disruptively, Mark tries to listen closely to what I have to say. He asks questions in class and comes to my office regularly. He is creative and earnest, and usually manages to separate himself, if only in attention span, from his teammates.

I hand his paper back without a grade. While his writing is nearly error free, and might have been an "A" for another assignment, he has not met any of the requirements for this paper. Were I to grade it, it would have failed. I know he is a good writer and I do not want to discourage him, so I write on the bottom of his paper, "Mark—your writing, in terms of mechanics and style, is excellent. As a creative piece, this would have received an "A". However, for this assignment, you haven't met the requirements I needed to see. I know you are busy, but I'd like to meet with you and discuss what you need to change here. This is very good writing, Mark, but it doesn't meet the criteria I spelled out in class. You can take your time with it. See me first and we'll talk." Mark reads my comments and looks confused for a moment, but he nods slowly, and I know he understands. I know I haven't crushed him, and I know he will come see me and do better the next time.

Composing "Teacher Training"

Mary Elizabeth Pope

The idea for the "Teacher Training" piece came out of a journal activity assigned in a graduate nonfiction class asking each of us to make a list of all of the topics we would never write about and why. I wrote down "Mrs. Crane" [not her real name] among other things, because even though I was in fifth grade when I had her for a teacher, she was still affecting me in a negative way as a graduate student. The reason, though, that she had made it on the list of things I would never write about was because several months after I'd had her for a teacher, she'd been killed in a car accident. Although I'd never admitted it to anyone but my mother, I had gone home every day in fifth grade praying she would die somehow. I was still harboring a lot of guilt over that, because for years after she was killed, I had nightmares about her; I was convinced that God had answered my prayers and that I was responsible for her death. I still won't ever write about that aspect of my relationship with her, but the exercise got me thinking.

The third paper was to be a personal, non-fiction essay and we were all encouraged to experiment with a format we hadn't used very often. I wasn't sure what to write about, so I went back to my list of things I would never write about, took her name, put it in the middle of a blank page and did some clustering, just to see what would happen. As I clustered, I realized that I had a lot to say about this woman; from the clustering page, I started to freewrite and couldn't believe how angry I was getting just thinking about the things she used to do to me in class. She was the kind of teacher who used humiliation tactics to teach her students, and she really disliked me, even though I tried hard to be a good, hard-working, well-behaved student. I wasn't sure of what aspect of her teaching I wanted to focus on, or if I really wanted to focus more on my reaction to her techniques, but I knew I had a lot to say because I couldn't stop writing.

Another circumstance enters into this topic and my choosing to write about it—at the time I began to write this piece, I was in my second semester teaching freshman composition as a graduate assistant. The whole time I was scribbling about the things she used to do me in class, I was thinking about myself as a teacher and couldn't imagine ever treating my students the way she treated me. My own teaching position had given me a new perspective on the whole Mrs. Crane issue, and it was one I could never have had before then, because I'd never taught. So as I "freewrote," I kept thinking about that aspect of it, although it didn't enter into any of my initial writing.

It actually took me a long time to determine what I wanted to do with this piece, because I knew I had a lot to say about it, and it felt really good getting it on paper. I'd been carrying it around for about thirteen years and had never really discussed it in detail with anyone, except for my mother at the time Mrs. Crane was killed. She had had a profound effect on my confidence as a student. Before I had her for a teacher, my other teachers always made me feel like I was really bright and put me in advanced reading groups and had given me higher level workbooks; I'd always assumed that I was one of the "smart kids," I guess. Before I had her as a teacher, I'd never questioned my abilities or my intelligence; after I had her, I always questioned it, even into graduate school. Getting it out on paper gave me a sense of relief, but at the same time, there was this urgency to do something with it because I needed to make sense of it.

I started with a segmented essay. Although I knew I wanted to use specific episodes from my year in her classroom—I had most of those written—I wasn't sure what to juxtapose with them. I thought of, and actually played around with, a speech I'd been forced to give about her at a tree dedication ceremony. The circumstances were odd—no other student was available to give the speech, and so my sixth grade teacher asked me to do it and gave me about two weeks to prepare. So I had to think about what I could say. No matter what I said about her, if it was nice, it would be a lie. My mother and I worked out a way where I could give the speech without actually saying that I had liked her or that I missed her. And so I played around with juxtaposing the day I gave that speech and the episodes in her classroom. One of the segments went like this:

> "My name is Mary Beth Pope," I began hesitantly, and swallowed out of fear involuntarily. "I was a student in Mrs. Crane's class last year." I paused, thinking of the things I was about to say, and looked at my first notecard. "Mrs. Crane taught us to sing The Grand Old Flag," I said, thinking that all she really taught us was to doubt ourselves, to be afraid, to never put yourself into anything you did lest it be rejected utterly and completely. "She…she, uh, liked us to push our…uh, chairs in…" She also liked to push us until we cried. I looked out at the crowd, and the principal, and at her husband and sisters who sat directly below me. I did not belong here, giving this speech. The wind blew my dress and made me shiver. My voice broke and I began, "She also…" I stopped.

It worked okay, but it wasn't really saying what I needed it to say.

After I had done that first freewriting, I prepared for this piece further by visiting the school and classroom where I'd had her for a teacher. The building wasn't being used as an elementary school at the time; it was part of an adult education site, and so there were big desks and bulletin boards with announcements instead of seasonal decorations. But the green shag carpet was still there, and the low chalkboards, and the same heaters where we used to dry our mittens under the window ledges. And the smell was exactly the same. I just stood there and looked. I couldn't breathe very well and the whole thing felt very claustrophobic. I couldn't believe how nothing had changed in terms of my reaction to the room; I instantly felt stupid and ashamed and on guard just by walking through that door at the age of 23, as intensely as I had felt it every morning when I would get off the bus and head for the room when I was ten. It was wild—it really triggered a lot of memories that helped me to remember more specific details in the segments from fifth grade.

After I made that visit to the classroom I talked to my mom about it. We talked about different days that I had come home crying because of something she'd done to me, and Mom even remembered things I had forgotten. The combination of the visit to the classroom and the discussion with Mom helped me to gel some of the ideas that had been brewing or seemed disconnected, and really got me going on the Mrs. Crane segments, although I still was playing around with the "speech" contrast idea and not feeling like it was going in the right direction.

What ultimately happened was that in a peer workshop session, I brought up my concerns about it, and a fellow graduate assistant and I talked about how awful some of our teachers were, and how, now that we were teachers, we couldn't imagine treating our students the way we'd been treated. This was very much an issue for me as I'd been working on the piece, and my friend suggested that maybe I should focus on that aspect of it and drop the whole "speech" thing. Everything fell into place when she said that, and I went home that night after class and just wrote it all out, using different students to compare my teaching style with Mrs. Crane's. I started with a clustering exercise using a few students who struggled with things similar to the issues I struggled with in Mrs. Crane's class, and tried to line up my fifth grade issues with their issues in my class. Then I did a journal entry on how to put it together in the essay, which went like this:

> What I need to do with this paper is show how having been through Mrs. Crane's class, I am much more sensitive to their feelings—I see the defenses, I see the fear, I see the need for approval in them. What I need to do is match one incident from fifth grade with one I've had with my students. For instance, match Darrin with my spelling, Nicole with my need for Mrs. Crane to like me, Mark with the math problems, Jonathan with my need to be admired, Brian with my frustration level, Eric with my need to be understood and accepted, Jason with my need for freedom and creativity within an assignment.
>
> I need to show the little fight I have every day trying to build their confidence while improve their writing skills.
>
> A final paragraph might be me, hunched over a stack of papers late at night. My comments are long—I write at the very least a half a page per student. I am tired. It would be easier to pick out the wrong things and scribble all over their pages, but I cannot.

I still wasn't sure about the exact structure the paper would take—like what student or incident in Mrs. Crane's class to use first, second, etc., but I knew what direction I wanted to go with it, and started writing and rearranging.

Once I had that figured out, the major problem I ran into was how to introduce the piece and how to conclude. I wasn't even sure what exactly I was trying to say, except that having a teacher who made me feel badly about myself helped me to be more sensitive to my own students—I remembered how it felt when she would ignore me or downplay my efforts or tell me I was stupid or wrong. I figured that a logical way to begin would be with the beginning of my first semester teaching, or at the end, looking back on how I had felt at the beginning. I had worried a lot about having had no training in teaching, only in English, and it had bothered me that whole first semester. Over the course of the semester I realized that I had plenty of experience with teaching because I'd been a student my whole life, watching teachers teach. I would think about my favorite English teachers (which was easy because all of my favorite teachers in high school and college taught English) and how they did things, and I'd try and be like them. It never occurred to me that I might have learned the most about how to teach from the worst teacher I'd ever had.

Also, I wanted to conclude by saying that having Mrs. Crane for a teacher made *me* a better teacher—that I had a better understanding of student needs because I'd had experience with my own needs not being met. The problem was how to get it across without making it sound like, "Mrs. Crane was a terrible teacher and I'm a great teacher because I don't do things the way she did", as that wasn't the point. The point was to show that I was able to turn that negative experience into something positive for both my students and myself. I also was hoping that it would be the kind of thing that other teachers could read which would make them think about teachers *they'd* had who'd hurt *them*, and get in touch with their own perspectives as former students. It's kind of a universal experience—I mean, we've all had bad teachers—and I was banking on that so I wouldn't have to do so much explaining.

Actually, I did a lot of explaining anyway in the first draft of the paper—the first paragraph began at the end of the semester of teaching, looking back, and sort of telling what I had learned. This is what it looked like:

> For weeks before my first semester of teaching began, I suffered from severe nausea. My main concern was that I had no experience with teaching—no classes, no training, no nothing. I walked into class on the first day, opened my mouth to speak, and before I knew the semester was over. I wondered where I had learned to teach, and it was only after that first semester was over, and I had time to think about it, that I realized that I had been a student my whole life. I realized that my real training began in the fifth grade with Mrs. Crane. I have come to believe that only so much of teaching is curriculum; the rest is instinct. For most of my life I have hated this woman who destroyed my self-esteem and all the confidence I'd ever had in myself as a student at the age of eleven. Now, I thank her. Perhaps because of her—or maybe in spite of her—I am too sensitive to my students' needs, and at times I worry that I am too gentle with them. But I am not sorry; in fact, I prefer to be that way, because I know now that my experiences in her classroom that year have made me a better teacher.

It's awful, when I look at it now, because I manage to sound exactly the way I didn't want to. I concluded the same way, with the teaching evaluations the students wrote at the end of the semester, and I used examples of what they said about me to confirm what I "said" in the body of the paper, comparing my experience with Mrs. Crane to my experience as a teacher. The truth is that when I got back the evaluation sheets that the students had written at the end of that first semester, I sat on the floor of my kitchen and was terrified to open them. When I finally did, and I read the nice things that the students had said about my teaching, I realized that maybe I was a good teacher and that I hadn't done the horrible job that I thought I had. I cried for about two hours that day because the whole semester I'd been afraid I wasn't a good teacher and that my inexperience showed. A lot of them said that they felt like I really cared about them, and that made me think about Mrs. Crane, and how she hadn't cared at all. So when I wrote the conclusion, all that went into it because it was exactly what I was experiencing at the time.

I didn't recognize immediately that both the introduction and conclusion were too self-conscious, and told more than they showed. I didn't really need either—I'd made my point by virtue of the contrast—but I felt obligated to set up some kind of a chronology and demonstrate what I'd learned about my teaching. When my composition instructor handed back the first draft, he said that he liked all of it except the introduction paragraph, which he felt "covered too much ground," and so I took that out and changed it to a scene of me waiting outside my classroom on the first day of class, worried about how I would manage to teach fifty students when I had no experience with teaching at all. Once I did that, I was really happy with it—it gave it the feeling that the reader was going to be there with me, walking into the classroom, scared to death like I was, and it removed that filter of my self-consciousness. I also did some major revisions on what my students said to me in the evaluations—because although I'd taken the quotes right off the evaluations, they were so unbelievably positive and sweet that it made me sound like I was bragging which, again, wasn't the point. What I was trying to do with the evaluations was to give the reader the same sense of "wow" and relief that I'd felt when I read them myself on the floor of the kitchen that day.

That was the point the paper was at when I handed it in for a final grade at the end of the semester, and that was close to the form it was in when I submitted it to the *Language Arts Journal of Michigan.* I did feel at one point that the sections on Mrs. Crane were too wordy, too self-pitying, and that the segments about my teaching were too self-righteous; however, when I was writing it, it felt good to discover something positive had come from that terrible year, and I got really excited about it. Before I submitted it to *LAJM,* I tried to tone it down a little, although after I went back and read it again, I realized I didn't need to make as many changes as I thought.

The draft I sent out ended with the following segments (I had chosen to distinguish past and present by putting the experiences with Mrs. Crane in past tense and italics and my experiences as a teaching assistant in present tense and plain text):

The tears in my eyes blurred the long division problems together until I couldn't see anymore. This was the best day of the month—free morning—and all of the other kids were down in the gym playing games and having fun. Three times I had redone the missed problems, eight of the forty she had given us, and run excitedly down the three flights of stairs to the gym, anxious to join my friends. Three times I had trudged back up the stairs, and been made to sit and rework the problems. I was so frustrated that I couldn't even see the paper, which had been erased so many times that I could see the pattern on my desk through what was left of the paper. Added to this were the tears that now made the page not only wet, but the answers I had gotten right, blurry. I couldn't bring myself to face her again, and I just knew that I could never do it right for her. I hated long division. Mrs. Crane hated me. And I had no idea what to do about it. I couldn't understand why she had singled me out to rework my missed problems—after all, I had worked as hard as all of the other students. And how was it that they all had answered their questions right? Was I the only one who couldn't get the problems right? Maybe it had nothing to do with the work, I thought. Maybe I wasn't pretty enough. She liked Erin and Laurie, who were both pretty. That had to be it—I worked as hard as both of them, but she still didn't like me. Or maybe it really was that I was the only one who didn't know how to do long division exactly right every time. I gave up wondering, and forgot about the gym. It hurt too much to hope that she would let me be like everyone else, so I abandoned my problems and went to look out the window instead.

Mark sits in the back row of my classroom with Walter and Jonathan. All three are football players, and while Walter and Jonathan often doze or talk disruptively, Mark tries to listen closely to what I have to say. He asks questions in class and comes to my office regularly. He is creative and earnest, and usually manages to separate himself, if only in attention span, from his teammates.

I hand his paper back without a grade. While his writing is nearly error free, and might have been an "A" for another assignment, he has not met any of the requirements for this paper. Were I to grade it, it would have failed. I know he is a good writer and I do not want to discourage him, so I write on the bottom of his paper, "Mark— your writing, in terms of mechanics and style, is excellent. As a creative piece, this would have received an "A". However, for this assignment, you haven't met the requirements I needed to see. I know you are busy, but I'd like to meet with you and discuss what you need to change here. This is very good writing, Mark, but it doesn't meet the criteria I spelled out in class. You can take your time with it. See me first and we'll talk." Mark reads my comments and looks confused for a moment, but he nods slowly, and I know he understands. I know I haven't crushed him, and I know he will come see me and do better the next time.

On the last day of fifth grade, we were allowed to take our brown bag lunches outside and sit on the lawn in front of the school. I sat with my class and watched Mrs. Crane talk to the students who sat around her. I sat far on the outside of the circle with another girl, and we traded life-savers and halves of our sandwiches. When the buses pulled up to take us home that day, Mrs. Crane stood by the door, and hugged each of us. I waited, dreading the hug, but knowing I couldn't get past her. She made a big show out of it, telling the students how much she would miss all of them. When my turn came, she put her mushy arms around me and my cheek burned where it touched her neck. When she finished hugging me, she put her hands on my shoulders and shook me a little. "I'm expecting big things from you, Mary Beth." My eyes filled up with tears. I managed good-bye and followed the other students on to the bus. I hated her even more for lying like that in front of all of my friends. As I stood behind the other students in line for my bus, I wondered why she would say such a thing. The way she had treated me all year told me everything I ever wanted to know about what she expected from me.

I sit on the floor of the living room on the day I receive my student evaluations back. I have no idea what they have said, and I wonder if after reading them I will feel better or worse about my performance this past semester. I open them slowly, afraid of what they could say. I can remember really giving it to some of my teachers; I wonder if anyone has done that to me. I pick up the first one and read what it says: "I really liked this class and teacher. She was always so chipper in the morning." I smile, wondering who wrote it. I pick up the next one: "Miss Pope was a very good teacher. This was a great class, even though it was at 8:00 in the morning. The journals were fun—maybe you could do more of those in your next class." The next one reads: "This is the only class I didn't drop." I laugh, flattered by this student who chose to stick with me, and read another one. "Miss Pope really cares about her students and always has something positive to say about our work, even when we get a low grade." I pick up the next one, and the next. I smile until I come to the one that reads: "Miss Pope's class was my favorite class of all—and the only reason I got up for any of my classes." I don't recognize the writing, but I don't care. It is then that I realize my face is wet from my tears. I think about Mrs. Crane. And I thank her.

When the editors at *LAJM* wrote to me and told me they wanted to publish it, they asked that I make a few changes—essentially, take out two segments: one about the math exercise Mrs. Crane had made me rework instead of letting me play with the other kids in the gym, and the conclusion. I felt kind of funny chopping out the math segment part because I was so angry at her for that—and I think it showed, too, because it was long (probably why they wanted it out). Taking out the conclusion was fine with me, though, because once I realized that it was going to be published and other people besides my composition instructor and classmates would read it, it occurred to me that the conclusion could seem exaggerated or too slanted toward glorifying my teaching success that semester.

The editors also asked me to make the last day of school the final segment for fifth grade, and finish with a segment about my student, Mark. In the passage above, then, I was dropping the first and last segments and reversing the order of the middle two. I was actually really happy with that revision because it gave the piece a nice feeling of continuity, instead of closure, which made it seem as if there had been an end to what I'd learned. And for the purposes of the journal, I could see why they wanted it that way.

When the journal came out, and I saw it in print, and read it again, I realized that I was really happy with the way that it was written. The whole experience of writing it and revising it and then seeing it in print was important for me for a couple of reasons. The first was that I felt like it was okay for me to have really disliked Mrs. Crane as much as I had—I'd never wanted to admit that after she died because it seemed like such an awful thing to say about someone who was dead (especially since I'd wished her that way so often before it happened). Also, it helped me to see that I had left that year in her class with something important—that she really did teach me something significant by not giving me the things that I needed, and that though it was difficult to endure at the ages of ten and eleven, it had become a really significant learning experience for me.

There has been some carryover from writing this piece into the writing I am doing now indirectly. I learned that when I am writing, I need to watch myself think, and not try so hard to make everything go in a particular direction right away. For instance, if I had paid attention to the fact that I kept thinking "I would never treat a student that way" as I was writing the segments about Mrs. Crane, maybe it wouldn't have taken me so long to recognize that *that* was the direction the writing really wanted to go. A lot of times, I will sit down with what seems like a great idea, but then I can't figure out where to go with it. If I just pay attention to what I am thinking, and trust it, and not dismiss it as just an external observation about the work I'm doing, I can get a better perspective on how I really feel about what I am writing. It's hard to do, but I've been trying.

Zion

Maureen Stanton

Sometimes I wake up in the middle of the night and I don't know where I am. My bed is a flying carpet. Flat on my back, I am looking up at the stars, whizzing around in blackness. Then I slow down, the carpet lands. I figure out which direction I am facing and get a map of the room in my head. I recognize the window and the streetlight. The bed, the door, the lamp. I remember where I am, the longitude and latitude of my life. Fixed to locale, nailed to a place, I can begin to make order.

I am dozing in the hospital bed with Steve when he pulls me.

"Mo, something is happening to me. My head is shrinking.

"What do you mean? What does it feel like?"

"It feels like it's the size of a grapefruit." He starts to cry, the first time since all this started. I run to the nurses' station. "Help. Something weird is happening to Steve." Fay and Dora come and give Steve a shot, but this causes his tongue to swell and his eyes to roll back in their sockets. Fay holds his mouth open, while Dora gets a doctor who injects something into Steve's bicep, and after a few seconds he breathes normally.

"It was just a reaction to the new pain medicine," Fay tells us, like it was nothing more than a bee sting. I stand near Steve's head and try not to touch him too much. The feeling that his head is small stays with him the whole night.

We are at the hospital of last resort, a small brick building in Zion, Illinois, an hour north of Chicago. It's a hospital where the bedspreads are worn thin and have holes. A hospital that serves carrot and celery juice, and offers alternative treatments for cancer. One week a month we come here. Steve gets his poison. I bleed.

The doctors here are different than at the hospital Steve checked out of back in Michigan. For one thing, most of them are Filipino. It unnerves Steve's parents who discourage our decision (false hopes, grasping at straws). But here the doctors don't give up as easily. Steve's first oncologist wrote a note on his chart which we read during our flight to Chicago. *It is very sad to see that the patient cannot accept the poor prognosis.* Two months, she predicted for a twenty-nine year old man with three small children, then patted his hand and walked out of the room, dry as a desert, tearless, leaving us in the starkness of Steve's future.

Dr. Sanchez and Dr. Melijor give us information, allow us to see Steve's nuclear scans. Married to gray film, Steve's skeleton glows. Small black dots are sprayed from his skull to his kneecaps as if someone plugged him with bird shot. Cranium, sternum, ribs, vertebrae, pelvis, femur. It is a frightening lesson in anatomy. I try not to act shocked, but the black dots are more numerous than I had envisioned when the previous doctors spoke of "widespread metastases" and "multiple tumors." "Multiple" meant six or seven, a six-pack, a touchdown, a number we could beat. I count more than two dozen specks on the little x-ray man that is Steve—malignancies humming inside his flesh. Not to mention his liver, marbleized like a high priced cut of beef, with cancer cells. Now it is real.

I arrive at the hospital at nine in the morning and climb in bed with Steve as if I am joining him in his body, unzipping his skin like it's a space suit, and snuggling in. His roommates, Greg and Chuck, don't seem to mind. Greg is an insect exterminator from South Carolina with testicular cancer. He sleeps most of the time, or reads his Bible. The only noises he makes are vomiting, or buzzing for the nurses. Hand him his urine jug, fix his pillow, bring him a drink. He thinks he is at a resort.

Chuck is in the other bed. He has a clear tube taped inside his nose that pumps oxygen from tanks on the side of his bed into his drowning, malignant lungs. He is an earthbound scuba diver. Chuck breathes loud and heavy, and coughs wet, phlegmy coughs which temporarily paralyze his wife's kinetic fingers as she sits in a chair by his bed and knits violently, like she is weaving Chuck a new set of lungs.

Days pass by slowly. Flowers arrive for Steve from his parents. *When God closes a door, he opens a window.* I put the card on the nightstand, open the curtains and watch activity below, cars and people. Fat, slow winter flies buzz against the sealed glass. They appear out of nowhere, it seems, these retarded creatures, and now they are desperate to get out, as if they know they are trapped, as if they have some power of cognition. That's what I learn when I accompany Steve to the hospital. Empty hours. Time to think.

We walk around the hallways, Steve holding onto his pole like a staff. Bottles are suspended from the pole, clear liquids that feed the catheter in Steve's chest and flow into the big subclavian vein direct to his heart, like a fast underground train. Nitrogen mustard, 5-FU, methotrexate. The names remind me of the defoliants that were dropped on Vietnamese jungles. They cause hair to fall out of Steve's head, off his chest. His underarms and legs are bare. His eyebrows are missing. His pubic hair is gone. He looks like a fetus, a tall, skinny fetus. Still, he is handsome with his heavy eyelashes and soupy blue eyes, purple hollows below them, like watercolor. His eyes look bigger with his face so thin and his skin wrapped so tightly over his bones. Delicate bones.

Visitation ends at eight, but the nurses understand that hours matter and allow me to stay until midnight. Then I walk to the room I have rented from a notice I saw posted in the hospital cafeteria. Three blocks away and ten dollars a night. The couple who own the house are up when I arrive.

"Wipe down the shower before you get out. Don't use too much toilet paper. And use the towel more than once." Noma scolds me before I have transgressed. She is a tiny woman with messy gray hair and one sharp, pointy tooth, like an egg tooth a baby bird uses to peck its way out of a shell.

"Who've ya got in the hospital?" she asks.

"My boyfriend."

"Isn't that a shame." She asks me where I am from, and then says, "Emil's got a cousin in Detroit."

Emil has filmy blue eyes and hair that is sugar white with bangs cut straight across his forehead. He looks like an old angel.

"They come from all over to go to that hospital. We've had people from Florida, Kentucky…New Zealand! Staying right in your room," he says, as if I am privileged.

"We're blessed with good health, thank the Lord," Noma cuts in. "Emil broke his ankle forty years ago. It was healed by a miracle at our church and it never bothered him since, right, Em?"

"Still march with the Brothers of Zion band sixty years now. I'm the oldest clarinet player." Emil opens a closet and pulls out a red, wooly coat and matching pants with gold braiding up the seams.

"It's no coincidence you're in Zion," he says. "This is a holy town. Miracles take place all the time."

"That's very nice," I say, and manage to excuse myself. Behind the bedroom door, I flop onto the lumpy single bed and cry. I do every night. It's part of my sleep.

Later I am poked awake by noises in the kitchen: a spoon clinking against a dish, footsteps, cupboards opening and shutting, a toilet flushing. Then the sequence repeats. I can hear snoring from Noma and Emil's room. They would have had to pass me to get to the kitchen, but I didn't hear anyone in the hall. I become convinced there is a ghost just outside my door, making that last meal over and over again, unable to let go. I pull my blankets up around my chin. My heart is pounding, pushing my tired blood, echoing in the small room. I pray. *Please, God, don't let it come in here.* I lie in stiff fear until gray light when spirits are banished, then wake up at eleven, groggy. Emil's white toupee is on a styrofoam head on the kitchen table and his teeth in a jar of water on the bathroom sink. I ask Noma if she heard noises in the night.

"Just me eating my cereal," she says. "I get up about three every morning and have some cereal."

"What about the flushing?"

"Oh, that's the pump clearing water out of the basement."

In the daytime, I can get along. There are objects, events, people to hold on to, give texture to time, divide up space. But at night, I lose my way, lose my mind. It's easy.

The next month I find a room for $75 dollars a week at the Harbor Hotel. The office is the living room of a small house that smells like curry. A boy is playing on the rug in the fuzzy penumbra of the television. A woman with a red dot on her forehead gives me a key and says there are no refunds, then directs me to their other hotel down the street.

The rooms are in the basement of a small, brick apartment building. There is no front desk, only a broken pay phone, and leaves blowing around the hallway. A disheveled man is loitering near the telephone. As far as I can tell, I am the only guest.

Ramona and Sue and Estherine and Georgia are on the same chemotherapy schedule as Steve, so we see them every month. Steve flirts with them, bald and in their bathrobes. They laugh when he tells them he is going to wear his camouflage hunting shirt and fatigues for his upper G. I. test. He likes the audience, but I don't care to share him much. Of what little he has left, I want it all. I am with him most of the time, in the bathroom even, keeping him company. He sits on the toilet and rests his head on the back of a fold-up chair. I sit on the chair and touch his back lightly. His skin is hot all the time now and I like to put my cold hands on it. We sit there in silence waiting for him to pee.

Steve naps and I read. Mysteries. Cheap little stories that completely absorb me, simple words I can eat, pages I can bend and fold. Perry Mason novels are the main staple of my diet. Perry always finds the killer, always wins his cases. I like the surety of that. There isn't anything in the stories to disturb me, or throw me off balance. They ask nothing of me.

At night I read to Steve, poems, clips about U.F.O.'s from *Omni* magazine, and stories from supermarket tabloids. GIANT FLYING CATS TERRIFY TOWN. WOMAN ABDUCTED BY ALIENS CAN NOW TALK TO ANIMALS. CANCER MAN'S LAST REQUEST: A JAGUAR CAR PARTS CATALOGUE. I envision a man in a leotard and cape with a big "C" on his chest, an action hero defying death. Cancer Man.

This month Cancer Man is undergoing an experimental treatment—whole body hyperthermia. His body temperature will be raised to 108 degrees Fahrenheit. The theory is that abnormal, mutant cancer cells slough off at 107 degrees, while healthy cells, skin, organs, muscle, brain tissue, begin to die at temperatures just above 108. It is a precarious balancing act to reach the right temperature, sustain it long enough to do specific damage, then lower it again. Steve has signed a liability waiver, a disclaimer of some kind that contains the words "result in possible death."

Dr. Kim, the anesthesiologist, brings me into the treatment room to see Steve. He has been stripped naked and wrapped head to toe in gauze like a mummy. To raise his temperature, he is wrapped in a heated plastic blanket filled with water and alcohol. A thermometer in his mouth, one in his rectum, and two others will monitor his fever for the next eight hours.

I spend the day wandering along Lake Michigan, the Illinois side which is not as sandy and beautiful as the Michigan side. Blame it on the wind, I think, noticing this habit I have of searching for culprits. I go to the library and draft a letter to Steve's insurance company pleading with them to pay for the hyperthermia. In the park, a large bird boldly garbed in a blood red hood and black and white tuxedo clings to the bark of a tree, a red-headed woodpecker. It stands out among the muted browns and greens and feels like a gift, blatant beauty. When I return Steve is knocked out, in intensive care, sleeping it off. He wakes later delirious, mumbling like a drunk, lashing out with his hands, yanking at the tubes and bandages. Wild. For two days Steve sleeps fitfully. Finally, he recognizes me. I say, "Tell yourself each day you are going to get better and better." He says, "I'm going to get better and better. I'll be the best."

These treatments—chemicals, radiation, hyperthermia—attempt to murder Steve each time; push him to the brink, lull him back, give him time to fortify then zonk him again. It's a tease, an oxymoron, Orwellian doublespeak. We must kill you to cure you, make you sick to make you better. It's a lie, a trick with fun house mirrors. We don't trust anyone.

The Harbor Hotel is quiet all week. Then late Friday night I hear people yelling and kicking the doors to the rooms, moving towards mine. I click off my lamp so they won't see a sliver of light leaching under my door into the hallway. I'm afraid that if they find me they will kill me. It is my night time logic. I practice saying "Who's there?" in a deep, male voice. After a while, they manage to break into a room a couple of doors down and party all night. I make myself small and quiet like the tiny baby cockroaches that scatter whenever I turn on the fluorescent light in the bathroom. I plan my escape out the small casement window above the television, level with the ground. Finally I sleep hard and wake up to the sounds of Big Wheels on pavement.

Outside, I blink at the sunlight. Mothers sit on the brick steps smoking cigarettes. They stare at me like I am an alien, out of my country, away from my land. Timeless, placeless, bodiless.

When I get to the hospital Chuck's bed is empty. He died during the night after a long coughing fit. His wife, Carol, is gone without a trace, not one thread left behind. Steve has gotten scorched from the hyperthermia. Bad wrapping job. The soles of his feet and his scrotum are tender. He's pissed off about this, but when Jane, a volunteer, comes around he forgets for a while. Steve and I stare at her round and bouncy firm flesh encased in stretchy nylon like she is wearing beach balls, at her unruly white hair and huge blurry eyes behind thick glasses. She hands out newspapers and carnations, and speaks in a flat, nasally voice, yogic, like a Sufi chant. "I have five dogs, two cats, a mallard (now in my freezer waiting for the Guinness Book of World Records to verify it as the oldest albino duck—seventeen years, as old as my niece), and a pet starling that barks like a dog and shouts 'thief' every time a stranger comes in my house."

Jane invites me to eat with her in the hospital cafeteria. She talks while she chews, projecting bullets of deviled ham and masticated bread bits. One lands on my cheek and it is all I can focus on, don't know what words she is saying. I avoid her after that. I give Steve enemas, put my fingers in his rectum, mop up his vomit, swab the raw, pink flesh around his catheter site, but none of that phases me the way having to eat with Jane seems an insurmountable task. Everything seems odd. Off.

This life develops a rhythm: three weeks home, one in Zion. Months go by this way. I dial a number pinned to the hospital bulletin board and a woman named Martha says she has an extra room in her apartment. When I get there Martha is gone and her son, Jeff, is playing chess on a small hand-held computer, smoking a cigarette with a puddle of gray cat on his lap. He explains that Martha was called to take care of someone for the week. She is a home-care aide.

"Bummer," he says, after he asks why I am there. He is in his early twenties with long hair parted in the middle and scruffy sideburns zigging down his jaw line.

"I'm trying to quit drinking," he says. "I haven't had a drink in over two weeks."

"Good," I feel my head bobbing up and down like one of those spring-necked ceramic cats you see on dashboards. I've noticed this: when you tell people your boyfriend has cancer they feel they must ante up their own pain and lay it on the table. At first, I thought it was nice, a kind of offering, but now it just makes me mad. Nobody's pain is equal to ours. I feel self-righteous and chosen. Anointed and doomed at the same time.

When I get up the next day, Jeff is mixing a glass of lemonade, smoking a cigarette and playing chess.

"I guess you like to play chess." I feel obliged to address this man in whose living room I am a stranger.

"Keeps me out of trouble," he replies. "I'm on probation for dealing drugs."

"Good luck," I say. Fucking wingnut, I think. Who cares? It feels good to be mean.

Put your troubles in the hands of the Lord and he will help you. Steve flings this month's card from his parents across the room. I pick it up and set it on the nightstand. I can't stomach the tension of a thing being where it doesn't belong, throwing off order, tempting chaos. I fill a plastic urine jug with water for the flowers and arrange them. I check selections on Steve's menu card, cut his toenails, get ice from the machine down the hall for his pitcher, try to keep busy before succumbing, inevitably, to watching television. Nothing airs in the morning except for talk shows, game shows, and odd sports, like curling, a bizarre contest involving a puck and a broom, a tight little silly game. Lunch arrives. Steve looks at it and puts the metal lid back on. I walk across the street and pick up some Kentucky Fried Chicken.

Later Steve unhooks himself from the tubes and we escape from the hospital. Outside it is cold and gray. We walk around holding hands. I like Steve's hands, his long, slender fingers, nails brittle and yellowed, his palms still rough and callused though he has not worked in over a year. He has two warts on his left hand, stubborn, rubbery bumps that I like to bite. They're large, these hands, but deft as he glues a part on a model car with his son, or takes an eyelash out of my eye. Steve used to stand behind me and press my nipples between his fingers while I stirred spaghetti sauce, and when we slept, his leg draped over mine, clinging like sweaty children, he cupped my breast in his palm like it was a dove. Now touching hurts him, so the only kisses I give are little brush strokes.

Steve makes it one block to a park near the hospital before he tires. We sit on a bench and watch a mother absentmindedly hand bread to her daughter. The little girl stuffs fistfuls of the bread into her mouth, every now and then flinging a crust at the ducks. Steve laughs, and I kiss his knuckles as the girl fills her cheeks and her mother stares at something else across the pond.

Friday night Jeff is playing chess with the television shouting in the background. I crawl into bed and stare at squares of light on the wall. Street lights, window panes, simple inanimate objects make me feel sad.

Hours later I am awakened by a cat screeching, then Jeff laughing loudly. The sound is distorted, like in a tunnel. Too loud for laughing alone, I think. My eyes are wide open, sucking in the dim light. I hear Jeff's maniacal laugh again and the cat yelps painfully. I envision Jeff screwed up on hallucinogens, torturing the cat. Greenish street light burnishes the door knob, which I expect to rotate at any moment, Jeff entering my room to rape me and carve me up with a knife, laughing that wild, enormous laugh the whole time. I stuff the corner of the pillow in my mouth to muffle sobs.

Nights can be like this—scenes from frightening horror films. Disaster is no longer an abstract concept. Anything is possible and danger is everywhere. I have a hard time differentiating the real from the imagined. Steve used to scare me, curling his index finger and growling, "redrum redrum redrum" like the little boy in *The Shining*, amused by how I had to skulk from light switch to light switch to pee in the middle of the night. I have asked him not to come back and haunt me, even if it is just a joke. He has asked me not to write about him, wants to disappear. I am terrified of his leaving, waking up next to a stiff corpse. I think about it every night when I lie down beside him, of being left alone, abandoned.

I wake up at seven stiff-necked, and for a second surprised to be alive and okay. Lines pressed into my face from the wrinkled sheets make a map, look like a place. I gather my stuff, don't stop to wash. Downstairs, Jeff is gone. I leave the key on the table and walk to the hospital. The nurses break the rules and let me sleep in Chuck's old bed for one night. In the morning, the long black hospital limousine delivers Steve and me to the airport. People in cars pass us on the highway and stare into our opaque windows like we are celebrities. We can see them, but they can't see us, as if we are ghosts. We exist in a parallel life: we can see our peers (getting married, having babies, buying houses), but we can't touch them anymore. We are headed somewhere else.

On Writing "Zion"

Maureen Stanton

"Zion" began as journal entries made in 1986 when the events in the essay were taking place. I wasn't thinking then that in the future this might be a story or an essay, but was writing for the same reason I record anything in my journal—to understand what is happening in my life. (This isn't always the case. There are other experiences that I know I will want to turn into an essay, so I keep specific notes, though they are mostly facts, ideas, and observations rather than the "talking to myself" of journal writing.)

I didn't look at the journal until probably two years after the experience. Grief over the death of Steve, the subject of this essay, consumed me, and I was busy trying to figure out how to fill up my life, which had revolved around Steve's cancer for eighteen months. Also, Steve had asked me not to write about him and I was struggling with this issue. When I started to write Zion as a "piece," I talked with a counselor who had helped me through this period about whether I could write about Steve. She was blunt and logical. Steve was dead, and this was my story too so I had a right to tell it.

After the fogginess of grief started to lift I began to remember interesting details of the experience, interactions and events I couldn't seem to recall when I was engulfed by emotions. The lifting of the veil of grief brought a flurry of raw material forward and I jotted notes everywhere, often waking up at night to write down a sentence that would later trigger a whole episode.

This has become my modus operandi for writing. I get very excited about an idea and become preoccupied with it. My mind is constantly tugged back to that subject whenever it is not engaged (usually when I am trying to sleep, but I will always sacrifice sleep for inspiration, even when it means arriving at work the next day a bit exhausted).

These scribbled thoughts, observations, words, and memories are stashed in a file because they seem somehow related. The file thickens and at some point reaches a critical mass. Visually, I think of it as a bunch of free-floating atoms and molecules ranging around in their own individual orbits, then something like the Big Bang happens, a tiny pop perhaps, and these particles react to one another and begin to attract and repel, combine and multiply to create a cluster of raw material. This is accompanied by an almost physical restlessness to write the piece, and suddenly (it often seems) I begin to work on it in earnest (leaving other pieces I am working on half-finished).

For this piece, which at various times was titled, "Cancer Man," "The Rooms I Stayed In" (thankfully that one didn't last long), then "Dreaming in Zion," the critical mass occurred about three years after Steve died. I pulled the piece together and brought it to a fiction workshop at the Iowa Summer Writing Program. I had been writing short stories exclusively, largely because that is what I focused on in creative writing classes in college. No one ever mentioned anything about essays. In fact, in four undergraduate and one graduate creative writing classes, I never heard the word essay mentioned, nor was it offered as a course on its own. Even in the writing groups I joined everyone seemed to be writing fiction.

The version of "Zion" I took to the workshop was only slightly different than this final version, yet I was naively trying to pass it off as a short story. That version was straight narrative, factual recitation with detailed description but little reflection. The workshop attendants wanted to see more of "me" in the piece, and they thought that, although it was moving, it was not complete and was not a successful short story. As with nearly all of my writing at that time, I didn't know what it was or what to do with it. I wasn't really writing short stories but I kept trying to squash my pieces into that mold.

I tried to put more "me" into the story but what came out, I see now, was not poignant reflection but raw emotion, untempered anger and resentment mostly. The piece took on a maudlin and self-pitying tone. I did not know what to do with Zion at this point, so I did nothing. It sat for a while before I decided to bring it to a living room writing group I participated in (after removing the added "me"). Two of the members of the writing group were professors of English and accomplished writers, and the others were professionals of all ages, all good writers and critics. This group felt the piece was flat, and although the writing was good, it lacked something. I still did not know what to do with the piece, so it landed back in hibernation, this time for about three years. But it was in that living room group that I first heard the term creative nonfiction from Mike Steinberg. I didn't grasp immediately what he was talking about, but as I slowly began to open up to this genre, I felt like I was finding my way home. This was the type of writing I naturally tended to and I was excited about it, but I still didn't know what made good creative nonfiction.

Having been somewhat liberated from my fixation with short stories and the constraints of trying to fit my personal experiences into that format (and feeling like a liar and a fraud doing so), I began to write about whatever stirred me without trying to set up dialogue, point of view and develop characters. (Although I think what I learned in fiction workshops helped me with pacing, tone, freshness of language, and precision.) I wrote two more essays, both about Steve, who managed to work himself into nearly everything I was writing regardless of how remotely related he seemed to be to the subject at hand. Both of these essays were published, but I felt that it was dumb luck, that I had stumbled into something that I couldn't sustain or duplicate as I was unaware of how I did it or why people liked the essays.

At this time, I began to get increasingly frustrated with my demanding job, which was eclipsing my free time and energy to write. (Writing had always been my umbilical cord to a meaningful existence.) I saved money for over a year, quit my job, and moved to the homes of friends and family members where I could live inexpensively. (Although this was frightening financially, as soon as I did this part-time and consulting opportunities began to fall into my lap. It was uncanny.) This is significant because if I had not done this, I feel strongly that "Zion" and many other pieces would never have been resurrected at all. (More importantly, continuing to live an artless, passionless existence and working a thankless, dull job would have caused my soul to wither on the vine, the marrow in my bones to dry up.) With the luxury of time I could put my heart and soul into creating more finished works that gave me a greater sense of satisfaction.

Having bought myself time to write (I envisioned a big parking meter into which I deposited my hard-won savings that now registered one year of time, ticking, ticking...), I began to work on my essays and to read other essayists in literary journals, collections, and magazines. It was this reading that helped to bring me along. Who knows how long it would have taken for me to discover truths about writing creative nonfiction on my own? Although I did not retrieve "Zion" to work on right away, in this incubation period I was beginning to get a sense of what makes a good essay, and why people bother to write essays after all. (I do think that it was good, though, to write creative nonfiction without formally studying it at first. There was a terrific freedom about not knowing what I was trying to do, to let the writing range freely. I think it allowed my voice to emerge.)

I attended a creative nonfiction workshop at the Stonecoast Writers' Conference in 1996, encouraged by Mike Steinberg, the man who had first introduced me to the term "creative nonfiction." This was the first time I had ever taken a workshop in this genre. The workshop was excellent. It reminded me of a trip I took to Brazil where I was immersed in the Portuguese language, yet could only pick up a word or two from each exchange. Then, after three weeks there, something happened, some leap of understanding, where I began to be able to interpret whole sentences and chunks of conversation. I liken that experience to Stonecoast because afterwards, instead of moving towards the writing blindfolded, occasionally glimpsing into some secret chamber of knowledge, I began to comprehend holistically the concept of creative nonfiction so that I could now purposefully sculpt the subconscious or "blind" part of my writing.

After the workshop, I pulled "Zion" from its entombment. It had been one of my favorite subjects, the surrealness of the experience, and I wanted to perfect it as much as I could. I didn't want it to sit in my file drawer forever. I wanted people to read it, like most anything I write. I wanted to create a thing of beauty, a story that intrigued and moved people. A decade had passed since the actual experiences in Zion, but writing it in the present tense returned me to the scene, placed me squarely back in the hospital and those seedy rooms where I slept. I cried every time I read each revision. It was biologically ordained, this weeping, from a deep, forgotten place inside me.

My process is to work on a computer draft, then to rearrange paragraphs, edit, and mark-up the text by hand, then back to the computer, only to repeat the process.

I revised the manuscript probably two dozen times over the course of a month or so, sometimes setting the piece aside for a day or two and working on something else, or gardening, which is my form of meditation. I originally intended to change the piece from present to past tense after getting it all down. I was only using the present to make the experience come alive for me again, to sharpen details, but as the writing progressed, I began to grow attached to the piece the way it was. I liked the immediacy of the story, the sense of being transported into the hospital or hotel room. And I had a strong desire to preserve the authenticity of that section of my life, to keep it intact, like a clipping from a film reel. I wanted to keep the memory pure, not to muddy the events with thoughts that represent how I feel now rather than how I felt then.

I can become obsessed with a piece, and lately I am fortunate enough to have time for obsessions. With Zion, the prose seemed sparse, pared down, (compared to all that happened in real life and compared to earlier drafts). Every word mattered so I often spent a half-hour on one word, going back and forth, changing my mind then changing it back to the way it was originally. I realized I needed to be exact about Steve's chemotherapy instead of relying on my memory. Staring at the names of cancer drugs in the library released waves of memories about this experience. Sometimes I would go in search of metaphors, once sitting in the library all afternoon reading the Biblical references to Zion (which I didn't import into the essay after all since they felt forced). Sometimes I think I was trying too hard to create a "thing" instead of letting the "thing" create itself, but I usually recognized the artificial passages after a few days time and removed them (no matter how fond I was of the phrase or image I wanted to push into the piece).

I dug back into my original journals of a decade before, reread my old letters from Steve and listened to a tape of his voice. In the end, I added little to the factual bulk of the piece. I reviewed earlier drafts with comments made by my peers at the Iowa Workshop and in my writers' group. My typed out questions to the living room group at the bottom of the essay demonstrate my confusion about what I was attempting. These "questions for the group" were: what tense should the story be told in? Should this be a short story or an essay? Is there such a thing as true fiction? It seems I was still leaning towards writing fiction.

I found the copy of the manuscript from Mike Steinberg. His comments, thoughtfully offered four years prior to this rewrite, were exactly what the piece needed. He liked a lot of the external description, but said, "I'd like to see you get more reflective about the experience…and yes, we'll talk about your questions regarding autobiographical essay/fiction." He pointed out places where the piece could be "opened up." It appears I wasn't ready for his comments when he gave them to me years ago, but after the Stonecoast workshop, I finally understood what he was getting at. (I have saved all the manuscripts from workshop reviewers over the years because I value their comments, but interestingly, Mike Steinberg was the only one who referred to Zion as an "essay" and treated it as such when critiquing it.)

When it was obvious that I was doing nothing more than fiddling with prepositions and articles, the tiniest bits of text, I decided the piece was done. In any event, I simply didn't know where else to go with it and called it done. I may someday rewrite this piece in past tense, as I have been encouraged to do, and maybe this will strengthen the story and give it more weight and relevance. But more time will have to pass. When I work on something as intensely as I did this, I get weary of it. I start to feel ridiculous about the amount of time I am spending on it (which feels disproportionate to things taking place in the larger world around me). This happens often with my writing. I tire of pieces (they wear me out), so I put them away, which usually turns out to be a good thing. When I return to them later, what is missing, what is false or contrived, what is sloppy or sophomoric becomes more obvious. And I, for the distance passed (often years), am wiser in my approach to the piece. Unfortunately, this does not make me a prolific writer, only a careful one.

Overall "Zion" has not changed dramatically since its original incarnation nearly a decade ago and many, many hours of labor later. The format turned out to be the same, and the opening and ending paragraphs are similar. Some passages are verbatim from the original draft. But the difference lies in telling phrases, observations, and reflections, which give the narrative facts a luminescence that only distance and learning can yield. It seems that finally, after a decade, I could look with relative detachment at this experience and see it for what it really was, and in subtle ways, infuse these small epiphanies into the essay.

In looking back, I see four stages that this, and most of my other essays, passed through. The first is the molecular stage, that early collection of bits of information, what I find fascinating, unusual, funny or poignant at the time it occurs, whether I retain it in memory or in a physical form on pieces of paper. The critical mass stage is next. The particles are vibrating on their own in proximity to one another until they reach a critical mass and a reaction occurs. The writing begins in a fury, raw data, raw memory, stream of consciousness writing.

Incubation happens throughout the writing when I walk away from the piece and it sits inside me, silently arranging itself, so that when I next visit it, I have made important connections. Then I edit and rewrite. The placement of events and observations creates irony, mood, pathos, humor. Events are taken out of the chronological or random order and purposefully placed, refined, commented on. With Zion, incubation occurred over ten years as I intermittently resuscitated the piece, but also during the active writing periods, each night when I turned off my computer and went to bed with the essay on my mind. This seems important, that the essay was written only partially at the desk. Much of it was written while I gardened or walked or lay in bed mulling it over.

Insight is the last thing to come, what the story is really about. I often don't know until very late in the process, and the story is frequently about something other than I intended, if I let the piece take the path it wants, (which I did not do when I was forcing it to be a short story). The sensation I get when taking a train from Grand Central station, sitting in a seat facing where you just came from (not being able to see where you are headed) is the same one I feel when I read Zion. Distance. Perspective. It took me ten years to learn how that experience sculpted me, to tell the story, to locate its pulsing heart.

Alternative Contents

Approaches to Writing and Discussing Creative Nonfiction

Memoir

Writers on Their Work

Further Examples of The Form

Further Discussion of the Form

Personal Essay

Writers on Their Work

Further Examples of the Form

Personal Literary and Cultural Criticism

Writers on Their Work

Further Examples of The Form

Further Discussion of the Form

Literary Journalism

Writers on Their Work

Examples of the Form

On Composing Processes

On Form and Genre in Nonfiction

Index

By Author, Title, and Form

Credits

Page 5: Barber, Phyllis. "Oh Say Can You See?" from *How I Got Cultured: A Nevada Memoir.* University of Nevada Press, 11–20. Reprinted by permission.

Page 11: "The Unwanted Child" from *All But the Waltz* by Mary Clearman Blew. Copyright © 1991 Mary Clearman Blew. Used by permission of Viking Penguin, a division of Penguin Books USA Inc.

Page 21: "Silent Dancing" by Judith Ortiz Cofer is reprinted with permission from the publisher of *Silent Dancing: A Partial Remembrance of a Puerto Rican Childhood.* (Houston: Arte Publico Press—University of Houston, 1990.)

Page 28: Conroy, Frank. "Running the Table" from *The Best American Essays, 1991*, Ed. Robert Atwan. Boston: Houghton Mifflin, 1991:26–32. Reprinted by permission.

Page 33: DeBuys, William. "Aerial Reconnaissance" from *Northern Lights: A Selection of New Writing from the American West*, Eds. Deborah Clow and Donald Snow. New York: Vintage, 1994:207–18. Reprinted by permission.

Page 41: "Living Like Weasels" from *Teaching A Stone To Talk* by Annie Dillard. Copyright © 1982 by Annie Dillard. Reprinted by permission of HarperCollins Publishers, Inc.

Page 44: "From a Sheepherder's Notebook: Three Days" from *The Solace of Open Spaces* by Gretel Ehrlich. Copyright © 1985 by Gretel Ehrlich. Used by permission of Viking Penguin, a division of Penguin Books USA Inc.

Page 48: "Parish Streets," copyright © 1986 by Patricia Hampl. Reprinted from *The Graywolf Annual Three: Essays, Memoirs & Reflections* with the permission of Graywolf Press, Saint Paul, Minnesota.

Page 55: Hearne, Vicki. "Can an Ape Tell a Joke?" Copyright © 1993 by *Harper's Magazine.* All rights reserved. Reproduced from the November issue by special permission.

Page 155: Sanders, Scott Russell. "Cloud Crossing." Copyright © 1981 by Scott Russell Sanders; first appeared in *The North American Review;* reprinted by permission of the author and Virginia Kidd Agency, Inc.

Page 160: Saner, Reginald A. "Pliny and the Mountain Mouse" from *The Four-Cornered Falcon.* Baltimore, MD: Johns Hopkins University Press, 1993:1–8. Reprinted by permission.

Page 166: Selzer, Richard. "The Masked Marvel's Last Toehold" from *Letters to a Young Doctor.* Copyright © 1982 by David Goldman and Janet Selzer, Trustees. Reprinted by permission of Georges Borchardt, Inc. for the author.

Page 170: Silko, Leslie Marmon. "In the Combat Zone." Copyright © 1995 by Leslie Marmon Silko, used with the permission of The Wylie Agency, Inc.

Page 176: Sommers, Nancy. "I Stand Here Writing" from *College English* 55.4, April 1993. Copyright © 1993 by the National Council of Teachers of English. Reprinted with permission.

Page 184: Steinberg, Michael. "Trading Off: A Memoir." First published in *The Missouri Review.* Copyright © 1994 by Michael Steinberg. Reprinted by permission of the author.

Page 200: Tayler, Jeffrey. "Vessel of Last Resort" from *The Atlantic Monthly.* September 1996, pp. 32, 34 36, 37, 40. Reprinted by permission.

Page 207: "Seven Wonders," copyright © 1983 by Lewis Thomas, from *Late Night Thoughts on Listening to Mahler's Ninth Symphony* by Lewis Thomas. Used by permission of Viking Penguin, a division of Penguin Books USA Inc.

Page 212: Tompkins, Jane. "At the Buffalo Bill Museum" from *West of Everything: The Inner Life of Westerns.* New York: Oxford University Press, 1992:179–203. Reprinted by permission.

Page 226: Toth, Susan Allen. "Going to the Movies" from *How to Prepare for Your High School Reunion and Other Mid-Life Musings.* Boston: Little, Brown, 1988: pp. 108–112.

Page 229: Weingarten, Roger. "Fireworks to Praise a Homemade Day: Notes from a Reader's Diary" from *Poetry East:* 35: Spring 1993.

Page 229: "Cooled Heels Lament against Frivolity, the Mask of Despair," "Portrait," "Love Song: I and Thou," "Morning Song," "Against France: On the Algerian Pleasures of Entity," "Prison Song," "Letter to Donald Fall," "Weeds as Potential Survivors," and "Funeral Oration for a Mouse" from *New and Collected*